Praise for
THE WAR BELOW

"This is the most absorbing narrative of submarine warfare that I've read in years. The research is so deep, and the writing so vivid, I could practically feel the vast ocean closing over me as these three boats ranged the Pacific looking for the kill."

—James D. Hornfischer, author of *Neptune's Inferno: The U.S. Navy at Guadalcanal* and *The Last Stand of the Tin Can Sailors*

"Scott has a gift for dramatic narrative that illuminates the human dimension of this drama beneath the seas. . . . This is a riveting tale for World War II buffs."

—Hank H. Cox, *The Washington Post*

"Beautifully researched and masterfully told, James Scott's book is an enthralling and important addition to the story of undersea warfare."

—Alex Kershaw, *New York Times* bestselling author of *Escape from the Deep* and *The Liberator*

"Meticulously researched and vividly written. Scott transports us convincingly to the wardroom of the *Silversides,* the bridge of the *Tang,* the torpedo room of the *Drum.* If you want to know what it was like to fight in a U.S. submarine during World War II, this is your book."

—Jonathan Parshall, co-author of *Shattered Sword: The Untold Story of the Battle of Midway*

"Award-winning journalist James Scott provides an excellent narrative of three of World War II's best-performing American submarines. . . . A well-written and meticulously researched book, of interest to any audience and applicable to sailors of any rank."

—Col. John Abbatiello, USAF (Ret.), *Naval History*

"James Scott brilliantly captures the intensity of submarine combat with his pulse-racing narrative about three famous boats of the Pacific Fleet. You'll need a towel to wipe the perspiration from your brow."

—Bruce Gamble, author of *Fortress Rabaul* and *Black Sheep One*

"A must-read. . . . A spell-binding narrative that transcends the simple historical genre and makes present and accessible the personalities and perils of submarine warfare during wartime."

—Commander Beth E. Coye, USN (Ret.), *Naval War College Review*

"James Scott has crafted a superb tale about a group of young Americans who went unflinchingly to war with the odds very much against them—a tale that won't (and shouldn't) be forgotten."

—Flint Whitlock, author of *The Depths of Courage: American Submariners at War with Japan, 1941–1945*

"*The War Below* is a cut above. . . . This fast-paced book will be a welcomed addition to the personal libraries of even the most well-read students of submarine warfare."

—Stephen L. Moore, author of *Battle Surface!* and *Presumed Lost*

"In the seven decades since WW II, U.S. Navy submarines' primary mission has been passive, as a nuclear deterrent. But within living memory 'the silent service' waged a genuine war against a formidable enemy in the world's greatest ocean. *The War Below* provides an intensely personal look inside the pressure hulls of three Pacific Fleet submarines that established historic records against the Japanese Empire. The epic war patrols of USS *Silversides, Drum,* and *Tang* provide gripping reading and serve as a memorial to the lost boats and crews 'still on patrol.'"

—Barrett Tillman, author of *Whirlwind* and *Enterprise*

"Scott places the reader inside the boats for an understanding of the humor, the self-control, the ingenuity, the tenacity and self-sacrifice of submarine sailors at war. . . . The world of vignettes that he sprinkles throughout *The War Below* makes his book hard to put down. It's a gripping tale that spans half the globe."

—Carl LaVO, author of *Back from the Deep* and *The Galloping Ghost*

"Gripping. . . . Readers may find it difficult to resist the tension, drama, and fireworks of this underappreciated but dazzlingly destructive American weapon of WWII."

—*Kirkus Reviews*

"Beautifully crafted and carefully researched. . . . to read this book is to recognize that these brave submariners, toiling underwater in extremely cramped quarters, did more than their share to achieve victory."

—Al Hutchison, *The Tampa Tribune*

"Scott doesn't exaggerate when he says that the impact of U.S. submarines on the war far outweighed their numbers. . . . Their story is remarkable, and the author tells it remarkably well."

—Terry Plumb, *The News & Observer* (Raleigh, North Carolina)

"This is exciting naval history and a fitting tribute to the sailors of the 'silent service.'"

—William D. Bushnell, *Military Officer*

ALSO BY JAMES SCOTT

The Attack on the Liberty:
The Untold Story of Israel's Deadly 1967 Assault on a U.S. Spy Ship

THE WAR BELOW

The Story of Three Submarines
That Battled Japan

JAMES SCOTT

SIMON & SCHUSTER PAPERBACKS

New York   London   Toronto   Sydney   New Delhi

For the officers and crew of
Silversides, Drum, *and* Tang

Simon & Schuster Paperbacks
A Division of Simon & Schuster, Inc.
1230 Avenue of the Americas
New York, NY 10020

First Simon & Schuster paperback edition May 2014

SIMON & SCHUSTER PAPERBACKS and colophon are registered trademarks
of Simon & Schuster, Inc.

For information about special discounts for bulk purchases,
please contact Simon & Schuster Special Sales at
1-866-506-1949 or business@simonandschuster.com.

The Simon & Schuster Speakers Bureau can bring authors
to your live event. For more information or to book an event,
contact the Simon & Schuster Speakers Bureau at
1-866-248-3049 or visit our website at www.simonspeakers.com.

Designed by Ruth Lee-Mui
Maps by Paul Pugliese
Submarine cutaway illustration by Fred Freeman, U.S. Naval Institute

Manufactured in the United States of America

10 9 8 7 6 5

Library of Congress Cataloging-in-Publication Data is available.

ISBN 978-1-4391-7683-2
ISBN 978-1-4391-7684-9 (pbk)
ISBN 978-1-4391-7685-6 (ebook)

CONTENTS

THE SKIPPERS

SILVERSIDES

- Creed Burlingame—patrols 1–5 (December 1941–July 1943)
- John Coye—patrols 6–11 (July 1943–November 1944)

DRUM

- Robert Rice—patrols 1–3 (November 1941–November 1942)
- Bernard McMahon—patrols 4–7 (November 1942–October 1943)
- Delbert Williamson—patrols 8–9 (October 1943–June 1944)
- Maurice Rindskopf—patrols 10–11 (June 1944–November 1944)

TANG

- Richard O'Kane—patrols 1–5 (October 1943–October 1944)

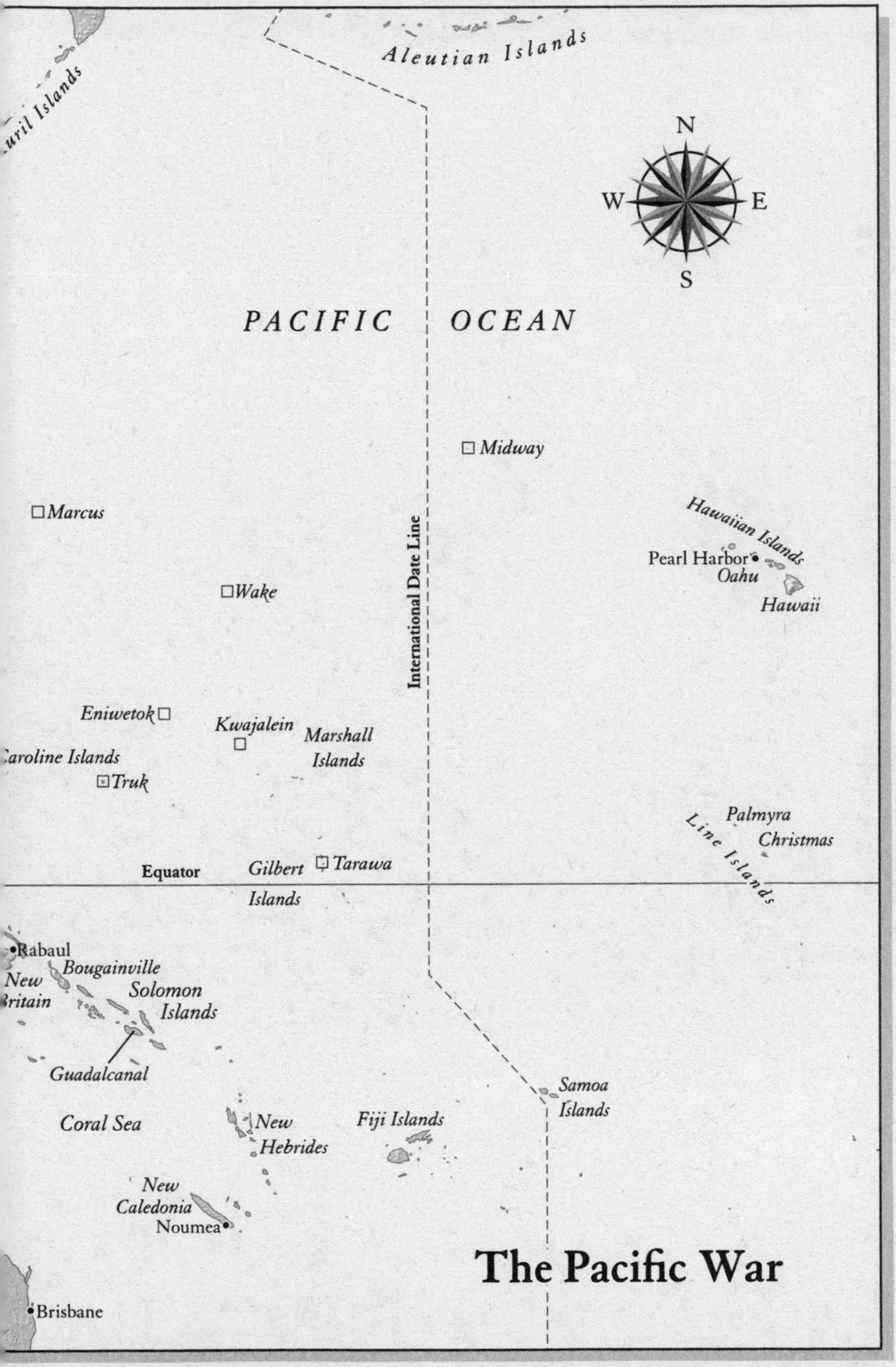

Kuril Islands

Aleutian Islands

N
W   E
S

PACIFIC   OCEAN

□ Midway

□ Marcus

Hawaiian Islands

Pearl Harbor •
Oahu

□ Wake

Hawaii

International Date Line

Eniwetok □

Kwajalein
□   Marshall
Islands

Caroline Islands

□ Truk

Palmyra
Christmas

Equator   Gilbert   □ Tarawa
Islands

Line Islands

• Rabaul
New   Bougainville
Britain   Solomon
Islands

Guadalcanal

Coral Sea   New
Hebrides

Fiji Islands

Samoa
Islands

New
Caledonia
Noumea •

The Pacific War

• Brisbane

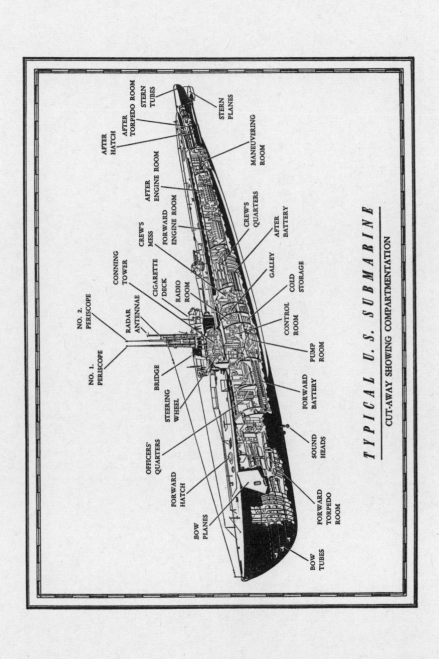

TYPICAL U.S. SUBMARINE

CUT-AWAY SHOWING COMPARTMENTATION

"In the cankerous mind of the devil
    There festered a fiendish scheme;
He called his cohorts around him
    And designed the submarine."

—"The Submarine," by Walter Bishop,
radioman killed aboard *S-4*

THE WAR
BELOW

1

SILVERSIDES

"No one knows how long this will last, but long enough to make everyone very tired of it."

—Slade Cutter,
February 9, 1942, letter

Lieutenant Commander Creed Cardwell Burlingame paced the bridge of the USS *Silversides* as it departed the submarine base at Pearl Harbor at 9:51 a.m. on April 30, 1942. The thirty-seven-year-old skipper, nicknamed "Burly," felt anxious this warm Thursday morning. The last fourteen years, ten months, and twenty-eight days of his career had led to this moment. A Kentucky native with a thirst for bourbon, Burlingame had served on six submarines, the last three as the skipper. He had run countless drills, ordered crash dives, and fired practice torpedoes on maneuvers in waters from Connecticut to China. He had even survived a collision with a destroyer in an exercise off Corregidor that had sheared off the top of his periscope barrel, the jagged remnant now an ashtray in which he tapped out the burnt tobacco from his corncob pipe. But today was different. Much different.

Today he went to war.

The *Silversides* buzzed with anticipation. Lookouts perched atop the periscope shears, scanning the horizon with binoculars. Down in the maneuvering room, sailors tugged levers to control the submarine's various speeds. Cooks in the galley and stewards in the wardroom brewed coffee by the gallon for the seventy officers and crewmembers. More than 3,500 miles of open ocean stood between Burlingame and his destination—the empire of

Japan. Armed with twenty-four torpedoes and enough frozen meat, canned vegetables, and coffee to last three months, *Silversides* would take almost two weeks to cover that distance at an average speed of thirteen knots or about fifteen miles per hour. Burlingame planned to use that time to drill his men: a deep dive for trim and tightness, daily surprise dives, and a battle surface drill to test the gun crew. The skipper knew every action mattered.

Newspaper headlines captured America's new reality 144 days into the war. The Army belatedly ordered coastal homes, businesses, and high-rises from Maine to Miami to kill nighttime lights that silhouetted offshore supply ships, easy prey for enemy submarines. Two days earlier, the garish billboards and marquees around Times Square advertising such films as Rita Hayworth's *My Gal Sal*, and a rerelease of Charlie Chaplin's famous *The Gold Rush* went dark for the first time since a 1917 coal shortage. Draft registration and volunteering now soared—more than 1,000 people a minute enrolled at one point—as millions queued up outside fire stations, post offices, and schools. The press predicted that some canned goods, coffee, and gasoline would soon be rationed as the war's price tag swelled to a staggering $100 million a day, a figure President Franklin Roosevelt estimated that week in a fireside radio chat would double by year's end.

The wreckage of Japan's December 7 surprise attack still littered the cool waters of Pearl Harbor. The burned-out battleship *Arizona* rested on the muddy bottom with 1,100 sailors entombed inside. The Hawaiian sun reflected off the rusty keels of the capsized battleship *Oklahoma* and former battleship-turned-target-ship *Utah*, Burlingame's first ship after he graduated from the Naval Academy. Thousands of divers, welders, and engineers now risked poisonous gas and unexploded ordnance to untangle the destruction. Grim reminders of the tragedy still surfaced. Workers salvaged thousands of waterlogged and rust-stained Christmas cards from one vessel, while marked-out dates on a calendar discovered in a storeroom of the sunken battleship *West Virginia* revealed that three men had survived until December 23 before oxygen ran out.

Japan steamrolled across Asia and the Pacific as America struggled to rebound. The opening lines of Burlingame's secret orders read like a depressing scorecard with the United States and its Allies the clear loser: "Japanese forces now control the Philippines, French Indo China, Malaya, part of Burma, Dutch East Indies, part of New Guinea, New Britain, Guam and Wake, in addition to former Japanese territory." But the enemy had made what would prove a fatal misstep in its infamous attack on Pearl Harbor. The bombers and fighters that Sunday morning, in the chaotic fury to destroy America's battle-wagons, had failed to target the submarine base, a compound that housed 2,500 officers and crew along with a torpedo plant, machine shops, and repair installations to service the twenty-two Hawaii-based boats, as the subs were often called by those in the service. Likewise, nearby surface tanks filled with 4.5 million barrels of precious fuel oil had miraculously escaped destruction, more than enough fuel to power *Silversides* and the other submarines that now set off for the empire's waters.

Burlingame's mission demanded that he not only target Japan's aircraft carriers, battleships, and cruisers, but that he also hunt down and destroy all tankers, freighters, and transports that made up the enemy's merchant fleet. The submarine war that American strategists envisioned boiled down to simple economics. Japan's merchant ships—many now under the control of its army and navy—served as the lifeblood of an empire that stretched across more than twenty million square miles and seven time zones. Merchant ships not only hauled the precious oil, iron ore, and rubber that fed the nation's ravenous war machine but also the soybeans, beef, and sugar that nourished the Japanese people. The outbreak of war had only increased those demands. Merchant ships and transports now ferried troops to the far reaches of the empire along with the bullets, toilet paper, and tooth powder needed to sustain them. If American submarines could destroy Japan's merchant fleet, strategists theorized, the island nation that so hungered for raw materials would starve.

The success of this strategy depended on skippers like Burlingame, a man who on first inspection did not appear the most formidable figure. The son of a receiver for the Jefferson County Circuit Court, he stood barely five-feet, eight-inches tall and topped out in college at just 156 pounds. But Burlingame's short stature disguised a rugged toughness that came with being the oldest—and smallest—of three boys in a home dominated by a stern father who ruled with his hand in the wake of his wife's death in October 1917. The survival instinct and dogged perseverance he honed as the family's "runt" would prove to be a vital trait, one the future skipper needed just to get into the Navy.

The Naval Academy rejected Burlingame in 1922 after his 83.9 percent grade point average from Louisville Male High School fell short of the 85 percent required. Rather than give up, Burlingame applied again, appointed by home state Republican senator Richard Ernst. He took classes at the University of Louisville that fall and crammed for several months with a tutor before he sat for the academy's entrance exam on February 7, 1923—and passed. Burlingame's struggle to become a sailor continued after he arrived at Annapolis. This time the issue wasn't grades, but vision after a routine physical his senior year found him colorblind, a critical deficiency in a job that required him to read flags and signals. The Navy debated whether to bounce him from the service or send him into the Supply Corps.

Burlingame again rose to battle, petitioning for a retest, which was granted. The Navy issued its report three days later. "Upon examination," concluded the report, "it is considered that this man has sufficiently acute color perception to warrant his retention in the service."

Despite his mediocre academics—he graduated 243 out of 580—Burlingame would prove a gifted leader. His dislike of the Navy's rigidity made him a natural fit for submarines where starched uniforms gave way at sea to shorts, T-shirts, and sandals. Burlingame spurned the traditional class system that divided officers and enlisted men, preferring his coffee to come from the crew's mess and inviting young sailors to his cabin to share concerns. The only formality required was that enlisted men call officers "Mister." Otherwise Burlingame preached that every sailor, from the skipper down to the galley potato peeler, be treated the same. "You are not going to start pulling rank," he once commented. "You have to live with him. You can't mistreat him, because he might be the guy that turns the right nut or bolt—or whatever it is—that saves the ship." Burlingame's sense of fair play earned him fierce loyalty from his crew, as evidenced by the observation of one of his pharmacist's mates: "There were people on that vessel who would have cut their arm off for that old boy."

But Burlingame wasn't without his quirks and flaws. He shared a prejudice common among his generation toward blacks and Jews, though he never discriminated on board ship. A healthy dose of superstition would prompt the skipper and his crew to install a miniature Buddha statue in the *Silversides'* conning tower and in each torpedo room. A rub of the belly, he boasted, promised good luck during depth charge attacks or when firing torpedoes. Burlingame's greatest weakness was his taste for booze, which on one occasion prompted him to down a bottle of Chanel #5 perfume that he mistook for jitter juice; he joked afterward that he had a hard time keeping the boys at bay. But the skipper never touched liquor at sea other than the so-called medicinal alcohol the Navy provided to calm the nerves after depth charge attacks. To satisfy his craving, Burlingame instead nibbled chocolate. He likewise demanded his men forgo alcohol on board. "I drink more than any of you on this ship," Burlingame lectured at the start of each patrol. "When I put to sea, I don't drink and when I put to sea with you, you don't drink."

Years of hard living had marked the skipper with deep lines etched on his forehead, crow's-feet stamped around his blue eyes, and the gray that peppered the beard he often grew at sea. He looked a decade older than his actual age. Though he had often won past battles, Burlingame privately doubted he would survive the war, a pessimism shared by many and reflected in a letter Lieutenant j.g. Robert Worthington wrote to his mother before departure. "Lord knows when we'll see each other again," the *Silversides'* gunnery officer wrote. "Maybe never."

The Navy Burlingame had fought so hard to join expected him to pursue the enemy with ruthless determination. "Press home all attacks. Do not be shaken off," his orders demanded. "Make sure that torpedoed vessel sinks." Burlingame and other American submarine skippers over the course of the war would battle enemy destroyers armed with deck guns and depth charges, dodge aerial bomb attacks from the skies, and navigate waters filled with mines. These dangers coupled with torpedo malfunctions, groundings, and operational mishaps would ultimately claim one out of every five American submarines. But Burlingame's anger at the Japanese—and a desire to exact revenge—overshadowed thoughts of his own death. His anger was common among many servicemen in the wake of Pearl Harbor. "We hate those yellow rats something fierce," one of Burlingame's colleagues wrote in a letter to his mother four days after the attack. "They will pay plenty."

Burlingame planned to make sure.

The weapon Burlingame skippered through the waves off Pearl Harbor represented decades of evolution in submarine policy and construction. German U-boats surrendered after the Great War had revealed the serious weakness in American submarine designs. The U-boats boasted superb diesel engines that gave them greater cruising ranges along with double hulls that could

better withstand depth charges. The German boats sported superior ventilation systems, air compressors, gyroscopes, and enhanced periscope optics and
narrow penciled tops that cut down on wakes and made the subs difficult for
lookouts to spot. More important to combat submarines, U-boats could dive
in just thirty seconds, much faster than American subs and critical for escape.

Engineers wrestled with how to overcome the inferiority of American
submarine design against the backdrop of numerous peacetime tragedies,
ranging from groundings and sinkings to hydrogen explosions and chlorine
gas poisonings that by 1927 had claimed the lives of 146 sailors. The loss that
December of the submarine *S-4* following a collision off Cape Cod galva-
nized public demands for improved submarine safety. The Navy developed
the McCann Submarine Rescue Chamber, a device that could be lowered to
a stricken boat and used to ferry sailors to the surface. But experts realized
submariners could not always wait on rescue—sailors needed to learn to save
themselves. The Navy developed rubber rebreathers—dubbed the Momsen
lung after its inventor, Charles Momsen—and constructed escape towers at
the submarine school in Connecticut and the Pearl Harbor sub base. Filled
with 280,000 gallons of water—and with mermaids painted on the walls—
the towers allowed submariners to practice escape from a stricken submarine
at depths of eighteen, fifty, and 100 feet of water, a skill that would prove
crucial for a few fortunate sailors during the war with Japan.

This safety push coincided with a debate over the strategic role of submarines that would further influence design. Veterans challenged the traditional
view that submarines operated best as coastal defenders or as part of larger
fleet operations. Relegating submarines to defense failed to maximize the
weapon's stealth offensive potential. What other vessel could penetrate enemy
harbors and sink ships? Geographic and strategic realities factored into the
debate as Americans saw the rise of Japan as a military power and the potential for conflict in the far Pacific. To take the fight to foreign shores, submarines had to be self-sufficient, capable of cruising up to 12,000 miles, and
must carry enough food, fuel, and torpedoes to patrol for ninety days. Longer
missions demanded better quarters, ventilation, and air-conditioning to keep
crews rested and efficient. Through this debate modern fleet boats, like the
Silversides, were born.

Silversides represented the latest in American submarine technology.
Workers at Mare Island Navy Yard near San Francisco had laid the keel of

the $6 million Gato class submarine on November 4, 1940. Shipfitters, welders, and electricians labored under the warm California sun for the next 473 days. Eight watertight compartments ran from bow to stern, encapsulated inside a steel hull that could withstand the pressure of depths up to 300 feet, though skippers knew in a pinch the boats could go deeper. More than a dozen fuel and ballast tanks hugged the outside of the pressure hull protected by a second steel skin. A conning tower perched atop with a hatch that led to an exterior bridge, deck, and mounted guns. Once completed, *Silversides* stretched 312 feet—almost the length of a football field—but only twenty-seven feet wide.

Each compartment played a vital role, beginning at the bow with the forward torpedo room. Six bronze torpedo tubes lined the forward bulkhead while racks along either side held up to eight spares, cinched down with straps of braided steel cable wrapped in leather. Two additional spares were stored beneath the deck plates. A rear watertight door led to officers' country, which housed the wardroom, several staterooms, and the chief petty officer's quarters. Even the skipper's cabin proved just large enough for a single bed, fold-down desk, and sink. Next came the control room, the brain of the submarine's central nervous system. Crewmen there operated the pumps and planes to dive and maneuver the boat underwater, plotted the ship's course on the chart table, and decoded top secret messages in the radio room. A ladder in the control room's center led to the conning tower above. The cramped compartment served as Burlingame's battle station and housed the radar and sonar displays, periscopes, and the torpedo data computer used by the fire control party to make attacks.

The next compartment contained the crew galley and mess, where as many as twenty-four men dined family-style around four green rectangular tables bolted to the deck to weather rough seas. A mess room door opened into the crew's berth that offered precious shut-eye for up to three dozen sailors while the bulkheads held shoebox-sized lockers for men to stash wallets, toothbrushes, and packs of cigarettes. Sailors laid out uniforms under their mattresses, which doubled not just as storage but also as a way to keep them pressed. The crew's head and showers were wedged in the rear of the compartment near the door that led to the first of the submarine's two engine rooms. Following the engine rooms came the maneuvering room, where sailors regulated the submarine's power and speed while the stern housed the after torpedo room with four additional tubes along with racks loaded with up to four spares.

The heart of the submarine's propulsion system was four Fairbanks Morse diesel engines that each produced 1,600 horsepower to drive the generators and power the motors. Two bronze screws that spun in opposite directions propelled *Silversides* on the surface at a maximum surface speed of 20.25 knots or about twenty-three miles per hour. When the klaxon sounded and the submarine dove, enginemen shut down the diesels and switched to battery power. Two battery wells—one located under officers' country, the other beneath the crew's space—each held 126 cells. *Silversides* could submerge for up to forty-eight hours at a two-knot crawl before it needed to surface, fire up the engines, and recharge its batteries, an operation skippers preferred to perform at night under the cover of darkness. If the submarine ran at its maximum submerged speed of 8.75 knots, the batteries would die in just an hour.

Despite the advanced technology, submarines remained a dangerous workplace. Sailors not only risked dying in depth charge and aerial bomb attacks, but also faced threats of injury and death from accidents. World War II would see more than 1,200 such injuries as submariners suffered electrical burns, broke ribs clearing the bridge, and shattered teeth when tossed about topside. One sailor hit so hard that two broken teeth lodged in the roof of his mouth. Accidents would claim the lives of another sixty-two men. One such tragedy occurred when a rogue wave struck *Tullibee*, hurling a lookout against the platform railing with such force that he died less than eighteen hours later from massive internal injuries. An accidental discharge during an inspection of *Blueback*'s twin .50 caliber machine gun ripped two holes through the gunnery officer's chest. Every torpedoman's worst fear played out on *Pollack* when a reload skid slipped, crushing a sailor's head between two 3,000-pound torpedoes. Seventeen submariners would drown throughout the war. Typhoons and hurricanes washed some overboard while others vanished when a submarine dove or battle-surfaced. Many of those lost were performing repair work topside when unexpected rough seas hit.

Beyond the dangers, submarine life proved austere. Men lived on top of one another in bunks stacked three high and just eighteen inches apart. Others slept on cots tucked between the one-and-a-half-ton torpedoes. Sailors jokingly labeled the two bunks that dangled side by side from the forward torpedo room overhead the "bridal suite," the close quarters usually occupied by the submarine's black, Filipino, or Guamanian mess attendants. The ship's desalination plant purified 1,500 gallons of seawater a day, but much of that fed the batteries and the galley. Sailors often bathed with condensation collected from the ship's air-conditioning system, though showers rarely consisted of little more than a wipe-down with a wet washcloth or a refreshing rainsquall while on lookout. A bucket of soapy water served as the ship's washing machine while men draped clothes atop the engines to dry. Off-duty sailors played games of Acey Deucey and cribbage, checked out paperback detective novels from the ship's library, or listened to phonograph records of Bing Crosby, Glenn Miller, and Billie Holiday.

Meals proved the highlight of the day and like everything else had to be designed around tight space and mission longevity. Fresh fruits and vegetables vanished within a few weeks, forcing cooks to resort to canned and frozen foods. *Silversides* boasted a freezer beneath the crew's mess—accessible by hatch in the deck and a small ladder—that kept hams, turkeys, and chicken at an icy fifteen degrees while a neighboring forty-degree refrigerator allowed cooks to store fruits, vegetables, and thaw meats. The rest of the boat served as a makeshift pantry. Men stashed crates of potatoes, cabbages, and carrots in the cool space beneath the deck in the forward torpedo room while others lined cans of sugar, flour, and coffee along the narrow path that ran between the engines and bulkhead. A plank laid across the cans allowed engineers to walk atop if needed. Sailors crammed food in unused double hatches, the escape chamber, and even filled one of the ship's two showers with canned milk.

The Navy depended on such creativity. Rather than clutter the galley with cumbersome bottles of soda, the *Silversides* carried 100 gallons of Coca-Cola syrup that could be mixed with fresh water and carbonated with miniature CO_2 canisters. The same rationale applied to frozen meats; only boneless was allowed. Cooks knew cabbage remained fresh longer than other vegetables while preserved fruits helped spark appetites, improve hydration, and battle constipation. Veterans learned to mix powdered milk with creamy Avoset to make the drink more palatable. The real pros even left a few eggshells out on the galley counters when serving powdered eggs—a subliminal message designed to trick the crew. When weevils invariably infested a boat's flour, some bakers removed them with a sifter. The craftier ones would simply toss in caraway seeds to disguise the bugs and bake rye bread.

• • •

Burlingame's cramped and well-engineered submarine closed to within 600 miles of the Japanese coast on the morning of May 10. Other than a three-hour-and-ten-minute stop at Midway—long enough to unload a chronically seasick sailor and top off with 14,000 gallons of diesel—the voyage had proved uneventful, giving the skipper time to hone his men for war. He ordered two officers on watch at all times, alternating between the periscope and diving controls when submerged. On the surface, Burlingame demanded one officer stationed forward, the other aft, while on days he patrolled submerged he planned to dive about an hour before dawn and surface again just after sunset. The pharmacist's mate passed out vitamins and fired up the sun lamp for sailors who seldom ventured topside. Cooks set a mealtime schedule of 7:30 a.m., 11:30 a.m., and 7:30 p.m.—with an open icebox policy that allowed the hungry to snack.

The skipper had yet to fire a single torpedo at the enemy but already had suffered his share of wartime tragedy. Burlingame's youngest brother, Paul—his junior by almost four years—had opted to follow his brother into the military, though he chose the Army over the Navy, enrolling at the United States Military Academy at West Point. With chiseled features and curly dark hair, the junior sibling—known as "B'Game" to his friends—was a gifted basketball and football player, his gridiron success often highlighted in the *New York Times*. Even after he graduated and earned his wings, the married father of two young girls returned each fall to his alma mater to help coach his beloved leatherheads.

At 8:15 a.m. on the sunny morning of June 17, 1940, Lieutenant Burlingame lifted off from New York's Mitchel Field in his B-18 bomber on a training mission to teach reserve pilots to fly in formation. Half an hour later, Burlingame's twin-engine bomber and three others roared over Queens at about 2,500 feet in a diamond formation. On the ground below, children played in yards behind white picket fences as fathers hustled out the door to work. The thirty-one-year-old Burlingame, who served as the mission's flight leader, radioed the other pilots to rotate positions. His bomber suddenly collided and locked wings with another. Both planes spiraled down to the crowded Bellerose neighborhood below. One crashed in the front lawn of a single-story house on 239th Street, setting two homes ablaze. The other slammed into the grassy median in middle of Eighty-seventh Avenue.

One of the worst disasters in the history of the Army Air Corps killed all eleven men on board both planes and turned a quiet New York neighborhood into an inferno. One airman, somehow dislodged from his bomber as it plummeted, smashed through the roof of a home and landed in the kitchen where his body rolled out the back door and stopped at the feet of a housewife hanging the wash on the line. The violent impact tossed the burning bodies of three other airmen into the driveway of one home, where a frantic neighbor used a garden hose to extinguish the flames. Repelled by the intense heat of the blaze, neighbors could only watch in horror as the bodies of several other airmen roasted inside what one newspaper called "funeral pyres of flaming, melting metal."

Paul Burlingame's tragic death weighed upon his older brother, who was now responsible for the safety of *Silversides* and its crew as the submarine closed in on the Japanese island of Honshu, its designated patrol area. The time for training and drills had passed. The next engagement would be real—and could come at any time. Men needed to remain alert against the threat of patrol planes, warships, and enemy submarines. Foul weather seemed to forecast *Silversides'* arrival in hostile waters. Gray skies pressed down on the empty ocean as heavy waves pounded the bow, sending sea spray over the bridge. The lookouts perched above on the periscope shears in foul weather gear suddenly spotted a Japanese trawler in the distance at 8:05 a.m., *Silversides'* first enemy contact of the war.

The officer of the deck summoned Burlingame, who arrived on the bridge in seconds. The skipper pressed the binoculars to his eyes and studied the 131-ton *Ebisu Maru No. 5*, which tossed on the angry waves some three miles away. The wooden boat proved a far cry from the enemy aircraft carrier, battleship, or tanker Burlingame had hoped he would find. Though *Ebisu Maru* appeared to be just a fishing trawler, Burlingame knew such boats often doubled as patrol and picket boats, gathering far more than tuna, cod, and salmon. These trawlers and ocean sampans bobbed hundreds of miles offshore and served as a defensive perimeter, radioing any sightings of enemy ships or submarines. Burlingame recognized that the tiny boat didn't warrant an expensive $10,000 torpedo, but he decided *Silversides* could sink it with its deck gun. He ordered his men to battle stations at 8:06 a.m.

Officers and crew throughout the submarine, many of whom had just finished breakfast, hustled to prepare for *Silversides'* first battle. Submarines are best suited to attack from a distance with torpedoes, firing either on the surface at night when protected by darkness or underwater during the day. Daytime gun battles on the surface were risky. *Silversides* would lose the element of surprise, one of its best tactical advantages. Such an attack also would expose the gun crew to return fire and risk damaging blows to the submarine's thin steel skin, a serious danger since it needed to operate at great depths and pressures. But Burlingame judged *Ebisu Maru* a worthy target, an opportunity to rob the enemy of an intelligence collector. The gun crew reported to the conning tower, strapping on steel helmets. Other sailors climbed down into the magazine below the crew's mess and handed the thirty-four-pound rounds up the ladder, forming an ammunition train that ran from the mess deck through the control room and up the ladder to the conning tower.

Petty Officer 3rd Class Patrick Carswell, a sight setter for the deck gun, crouched in the conning tower. The skinny eighteen-year-old South Carolinian had enlisted as a signalman. Down the ladder from him in the control room stood Petty Officer 3rd Class Mike Harbin, a loader for the deck gun. Five years older than his friend Carswell, the burly torpedoman had traded life in rural Oklahoma for that of a sailor in the fall of 1940.

Silversides cut through the rough waves at fifteen knots. The gun and ammunition crews waited largely in silence as the submarine closed the distance to about 1,200 yards. Carswell felt little fear as he anticipated his first battle. The target after all was only a small fishing boat, not an armed warship such as a destroyer or cruiser. Burlingame ordered the crew to man the deck gun at 8:25 a.m. The conning tower door popped open and the gun crew darted one after the other across the wet deck as waves crashed over the bow. Bolted on a pedestal on the submarine's after deck, the three-inch fifty-caliber gun packed a punch, firing thirteen-pound projectiles a half mile per second at targets up to eight miles away. The massive gun required a team to operate. A pointer and a trainer sat on opposite sides, using hand wheels to swivel the gun and move the barrel up and down. A sight setter stood on a platform on the back of the gun and adjusted the scope's accuracy while a team of loaders fed rounds one after the other.

Carswell hopped up on the sight setter's platform. Sea spray drenched him and the other members of the gun crew. Gunnery officer Lieutenant j.g. Robert Worthington studied *Ebisu Maru* through binoculars, shouting range and bearing changes to Carswell. A loader slid a projectile into the gun's breech and rammed it into place. The trainer sighted the enemy boat through a scope, and the pointer seconds later mashed the firing pedal. The gun roared. The spent shell clanged to the deck. Water splashed off the target's bow. A miss. A loader rammed in another round. The gun roared again. Then again. Errant projectiles peppered the waves around *Ebisu Maru*. Executive officer Lieutenant Roy Davenport and Worthington both barked changes to Carswell. The sight setter struggled to hear as violent waves hammered the submarine, soaking the gun crew and making it difficult for the men to sight the target.

Suddenly the Japanese boat returned fire. Machine gun bullets whizzed past the sailors. One missed Burlingame's head by just a few centimeters, singeing the hair on the skipper's right ear. Others pinged off the conning tower. Burlingame's instincts were right: this was not just a fishing boat. What had begun as a simple task of sinking an apparent trawler now evolved into a furious gun battle. One of the loaders, caught under the barrel when the gun first fired, felt blood run down his beard; the thunder had broken both of his eardrums. The loader now tasted a salty mix of sea spray and blood. Sailors in the magazine below ripped open ammunition boxes with bloodied fingers and fed shells to the hungry ammo train that passed them one after the other up through the submarine. *Ebisu Maru* now struggled to escape as *Silversides*' gun roared almost every twenty seconds. With each shot, the gunners' aim improved. The men could see that the projectiles now blasted the wooden boat. Carswell noted that the powerful projectiles, best suited to shred the metal skin of an airplane or warship, seemed to blow right through *Ebisu Maru*.

Rollicking waves thrashed *Silversides*, making it difficult to load and fire the gun. A wave hit Carswell from behind and knocked him off the sight setter's platform. He landed on his back and slid toward the edge of the deck before he stopped himself. The soaked sight setter climbed back up on the gun only to have another wave knock him off again moments later. He struggled again to stop his slide as he plummeted toward the side of the deck. If he went overboard in the middle of the battle, he knew *Silversides* wouldn't stop to pluck him from the churning seas. He would drown in minutes without a life preserver in the cold and turbulent ocean. Carswell's heart pounded. He fought to stop himself as he slid from the wooden to the metal deck where his speed accelerated. He banged into the hatch over the after torpedo room before his leg snagged a second later on the wire extension that ran along the edge of the deck and stopped him.

Ebisu Maru caught fire and billowed smoke. Still, its crew peppered *Silver-sides* with machine gun rounds. Burlingame watched from the bridge as the picket boat, which throughout the attack had tried to escape, now turned on his submarine. The wounded trawler planned to fight it out. "Suddenly he realized his case was hopeless," the skipper later recalled of the *Ebisu Maru*. "He turned around and came toward us with his machine guns going full blast." The sailors on deck tried to take cover as the bullets zipped past. A projectile struck the underside of the foot-firing pedal on the three-inch deck gun and sprained the pointer's ankle. Machine gun fire knocked the steel helmets off of two loaders, but did not injure them. A bullet hit Seaman 2nd Class Hal Schwartz's helmet as he passed shells to Harbin next to him. The eighteen-year-old loader dropped to the deck. "It broke the strap and knocked me out," Schwartz later recalled. "It was like getting hit in the head with a sledge-hammer."

Harbin handed a shell to the next loader in line just as a bullet hit him. His red blood splattered on the shell, which the ammunition crew reflexively loaded and fired as Harbin collapsed facedown on the wooden deck. The gun and ammunition crew stopped and stared. Blood seeped out from beneath him. Less than an hour into the first sea battle and *Silversides* already suffered a man down. No one had expected this. Carswell and the others jumped down from the gun to pick up Harbin even as the *Ebisu Maru* still charged toward them. Worthington unholstered his pistol and lowered it by his side so the men could see it. "Get back on that damn gun or I'll shoot everyone," he shouted. "We'll take care of Mike." Petty Officer 1st Class Albert Stegall and another sailor grabbed Harbin and struggled to pull him inside the conning tower. Harbin's head rested against Stegall's shoulder. "His mouth was working. I thought his helmet was causing him to choke. I got his helmet off. I found out it wasn't his helmet that was causing it. He had been hit in the head," recalled Stegall, who looked at Harbin's wound and knew immediately the loader was dead. "It pretty much went through his head."

An hour to the minute after the sailors had vaulted onto the deck, Burlingame ordered the gun crew to stop firing. Flames engulfed *Ebisu Maru*, its guns now silent. The skipper watched his victim burn. The wooden boat would not sink, but Burlingame suspected—albeit incorrectly—that the fire eventually would consume it; the submarine *Scorpion* would, in fact, later sink *Ebisu Maru*, in April 1943. Regardless, the skipper knew the torched guard boat would serve as a beacon to other enemy ships that might patrol the area, its black clouds alerting them of the submarine's passing and foreshadowing more destruction to come. No other ships would venture near. Burlingame recorded the battle's outcome in his patrol report. "He was on fire but did not sink," the skipper wrote. "Since he could not reach land in his condition and further expenditure of ammunition was futile, resumed course."

Carswell climbed down into the control room, the roar of the deck gun still ringing in his ears. The cold Pacific had soaked the terrified young signal-man. Twice the thrashing waves had nearly washed him overboard. He had watched one of his friends take a bullet to the head. One minute Harbin loaded shells, the next he lay on the wooden deck, the seawater washing his dark blood overboard. Carswell's couldn't stop shivering. He recognized the signs of shock and knew he had to get warm. He stumbled through the control room, crew's mess and berth, and into the forward engine room. There he climbed down in the narrow crevasse between the engine and port bulkhead. The 1,600-horsepower diesels had powered the submarine all morning. Heat radiated from them. Carswell drew his knees up against his chest, closed his eyes, and felt the warmth of the engines wash over him. "Harbin's dead," he could hear men cry out. "He's gone."

Shock permeated the crew. Ten days into the first patrol and already the submarine suffered its first casualty. The battle with the trawler, which Burlingame had expected to last a few minutes, had dragged on for an hour. The gun crew's tally showed that *Silversides* had fired 164 rounds on the three-inch-50 caliber and recorded only about a dozen hits. The thunder of the deck gun broke three eardrums, including one on the pointer. The pharmacist's mate tended to the injured men and bandaged Burlingame's bullet-singed right ear.

Sailors carried Harbin down from the conning tower and placed him in a middle bunk in the crew's berth by the entrance to the mess deck and right next to where Carswell slept. The blond torpedoman, who just an hour earlier had charged out onto the submarine's deck, lay silent. *Silversides'* freezer, packed with hams, turkeys, and roasts, had no room for a man's remains. Likewise, the submarine could not turn back to Midway or Pearl Harbor because of the loss of one sailor. The mission had to continue; Japan awaited. The men would bury Mike Harbin at sea. The pharmacist's mate, aided by the chief of the boat and a couple of torpedomen, wrapped Harbin's body inside a piece of white canvas and stitched it shut with heavy white line, one loop at a time. The men tied a gun shell around Harbin's legs, which guaranteed that his body would sink. One of the torpedomen cried as the men worked.

The chaotic morning evolved into a quiet afternoon as *Silversides* zigzagged west on the surface at fourteen knots, each turn of the screws taking the submarine closer to Japan. Burlingame triggered the loudspeaker microphone at 7 p.m. to announce Harbin's funeral. The skipper clutched a prayer book, the conning tower now his pulpit. "We therefore commit his body to the deep," he read, "looking for the general Resurrection in the last day, and the life of the world to come, through our Lord Jesus Christ; at whose second coming in glorious majesty to judge the world, the sea shall give up her dead." Burlingame ended his brief service with the Lord's Prayer, his Kentucky drawl crackling over the loudspeakers below in the control room, crew's mess, and the forward and after torpedo rooms, where sailors stood, heads bowed.

Torpedomen who had worked alongside Harbin carried his flag-draped remains through the mess deck and into the control room. The pallbearers hoisted the torpedoman's body up through the narrow hatch to the conning tower above and then out onto the submarine's wooden deck, the same path Harbin had taken that morning as he raced to load the submarine's deck gun. The gray skies and heavy waves that had pounded *Silversides* as it battled *Ebisu Maru* had vanished. The afternoon sun set and the cold blue Pacific was calm. The evening stars shone above as the submarine idled alone in the empty ocean. Burlingame executive officer Davenport, the chief of the boat, and a few officers and crewmembers gathered on deck around Harbin. The rest of the men stood alert throughout the submarine, ready to dive if an enemy plane appeared overhead.

Burlingame had deemed *Ebisu Maru* not worth an expensive torpedo, but in the end the Japanese boat had cost far more, the life of a twenty-three-year-old sailor from Oklahoma, one of the first submariners of the war killed in a gun battle. The skipper, who still grieved over the loss of his own brother, felt crushed. He knew that a chaplain would soon call on the Harbin family 6,000 miles away, a knock on the door that would forever change their lives. Was this one boat worth Mike Harbin's life? The hard-charging Burlingame would regret his decision to attack for decades. "It was a stupid thing to do," he later confessed. "We were all pretty damn dumb in the early part of the war."

The sun faded as the men slipped Harbin's body in its canvas cocoon into the ocean, watching as it disappeared in the dark waters. The quartermaster recorded Harbin's final resting place in the ship's log; two coordinates on a map, Latitude 33°13'30" North, Longitude 151°57'30" East. Burlingame sensed the crew's sorrow. "It was quite a problem as to morale," he recalled. "He was a very fine man, very well thought of by the entire crew, and at the very start of our first patrol to suffer a casualty like that wasn't quite the way we had hoped to start the war." The skipper gathered his men in the crew's mess after dinner. He needed to rally them. "The first fish we fire," he ordered, using a nickname common for torpedoes, "will have Harbin's name on it." The sailors stared at him for a while in silence. Finally one of the chief petty officers spoke. "Wherever you lead, captain," he said, "we'll follow." Whether the others all shared his enthusiasm wasn't clear, but the final entry in the log that night reflected Burlingame's commitment: "Underway as before."

2

DRUM

"We have every type of man aboard—all races and creeds—but there's something about this fight we're in that proves that theory—about all men being created equal."

—Dudley "Mush" Morton,
July 13, 1943, radio interview

Lieutenant Commander Robert Henry Rice stretched out on the bridge of the USS *Drum* as the submarine inched north toward the Japanese coast on the evening of May 1, 1942. The thirty-eight-year-old Rice, who hoped to grab a few hours of rest before his submarine reached the waters off Nagoya at daybreak, had ordered Portsmouth shipfitters to weld a steel bunk on the bridge. The unorthodox addition allowed the ambitious skipper to drag a spare mattress up from below each night and stretch out at the feet of the officer of the deck, ready for anything. The move reflected the great pressure Rice felt to succeed. He still clung to the congratulatory letter former chief of naval operations Admiral Harold Stark sent on the eve of *Drum*'s commissioning the previous fall. "It is now your privilege to be the first to inject into this vessel the life, spirit and character of a fighting ship," Stark wrote. "May the USS *Drum* always maintain the splendid tradition of the submarine service."

But Rice faced more than just professional pressure. He sat down to holiday dinners across the table from Rear Admiral Russell Willson, his father-in-law. The two-star admiral had played a critical role in World War I in developing the Navy Code Box, a device used to encrypt messages that the Germans never cracked. That ingenuity earned him the Navy Cross when the war ended. Congress even paid him $15,000 in 1935 for use of the device. Willson later commanded a division of battleships and served as superintendent of the Naval Academy before the new chief of naval operations, Admiral Ernest King, picked him as his chief of staff. As the son-in-law of a legendary admiral, Rice knew the Navy's top officers would monitor his performance closely. The skipper warned his men what to expect: "We'll either get so many Navy Crosses," he told them, "or we won't come back."

Rice appeared an unlikely warrior. Unlike *Silversides'* rowdy skipper—a fellow 1927 Naval Academy alumnus—Rice favored academics over sports. The five-foot, eleven-inch midshipman never chased golf balls down the fairway or swung a tennis racket and only rarely rode horses or swam. Much to the frustration of his future wife, Rice even disliked dancing. The blue-eyed son of a local furniture store owner—Rice & Kelly in downtown Pittsfield, Massachusetts—preferred more cerebral pursuits. He excelled at bridge, won fencing awards, and built a personal library of classical literature in his room that proved the envy of his classmates. His hard work showed when he graduated eighty out of a class of 580. "Bob is quiet, reserved, and knows a lot more than he lets on. His witticisms and cynicisms are as amusing as his sarcasms are cutting," Rice's roommate wrote in the *Lucky Bag* yearbook. "Bob's intelligence, quickness of action and coolness will make him a success in any field of endeavor."

But Rice's academic success had failed to translate into a prized assignment upon graduation. The new ensign had requested duty on a small ship where he joked that as soon as an officer knew which end of the gun to load, the skipper promoted him to gunnery officer. Officers on large ships with crowded wardrooms in contrast struggled to earn real responsibility. Rice believed the most dreaded assignment, however, would be a battleship that doubled as an admiral's flagship. Flagship crews suffered close scrutiny that kept officers edgy, feeling at all times as though on parade. Rather than base assignments on class standing, academy graduates drew lottery numbers. Rice picked the second-to-last number and landed on the battleship *Texas*—flagship of the Atlantic Fleet. Despite his disappointment, Rice enjoyed the assignment. He tangled with an inebriated Ernest Hemingway in a Key West bar and later transported President Calvin Coolidge and Secretary of State Frank Kellogg to Havana and New Orleans.

Two years after he climbed the *Texas* gangway, Rice reported aboard the old armored cruiser *Pittsburgh*, flagship of the Asiatic Fleet that roamed the China Sea from Manila to Manchuria. Rice found the *Pittsburgh*'s atmosphere far more relaxed though still crowded with junior officers vying for responsibility, including ten fellow 1927 classmates. He soon transferred to a Yangtze River gunboat where he served on the shallow-draft *Luzon* that helped patrol some 1,300 miles of river, protecting American property. Rice thrived on the adventure, even escorting famed pilot Charles Lindbergh on a visit to the region. When Rice's time in China ended in the spring of 1932, the ambitious officer still hungered for action. After he completed submarine school in May 1933, Rice reported aboard *S-12*, a World War I–era boat based in Coco Solo in the Panama Canal Zone. But the Navy had bigger plans for Rice. The skipper arrived in Portsmouth in June 1941 with orders to command one of America's newest and soon to be completed fleet boats: the *Drum*.

The half dozen officers aboard his 1,500-ton submarine—now slicing through the dark night toward the east coast of Japan—reflected America's ethnic diversity. That is, within certain limits: there were no African American sailors on board submarines in anything more than menial jobs such as mess attendants. *Drum*'s executive officer, Lieutenant Nicholas Nicholas, grew up the son of Greek parents who had settled in New Hampshire. Engineering and diving officer Lieutenant j.g. Manning Kimmel, the son of Admiral Husband Kimmel, who was relieved as the commander of the Pacific Fleet after the Pearl Harbor attack, was of German ancestry. Lieutenant j.g. Maurice Rindskopf, *Drum*'s torpedo officer, grew up in Brooklyn, the son of Jewish parents whose families left Germany a century earlier. Communications officer Ensign John Harper sported "rangy red-hair" that reflected his Scottish heritage while commissary officer Ensign Verner Utke-Ramsing, Jr., suffered endless taunts over his double name, courtesy of his Danish parents. But Ensign Eugene Pridonoff had traveled the farthest: born in Russia and raised in China before his parents settled in California.

Just as the ebb and flow of America's immigration had shaped the *Drum* officers and crew, so had the Great Depression. For many, the cramped uncomfortable life at sea was, in fact, a step up, promising at least three meals a day. The decade-long economic catastrophe had taught vital lessons about sacrifice, resourcefulness, and endurance to the men who now loaded torpedoes, manned the bow and stern planes, and scanned the horizon for enemy ships. The austere world of a diesel submarine, where sailors went without privacy, showers, and even daylight for weeks at a time was an improvement over the callused childhoods many had endured. One *Drum* sailor had been forced to scavenge coal alongside snowy railroad tracks as a child outside Boston to help heat his family's home. Another watched his father—a stonecutter and polisher—die at just forty-six, his lungs hardened from the granite dust of the tombstones he carved. A pharmacist's mate lived for months in a tent in Texas and later picked avocados for director Victor Fleming of *The Wizard of Oz* and *Gone With the Wind* fame.

The officers who joined Rice on the submarine's bridge each night sensed the enormous pressure the skipper felt. Unlike Burlingame, who palled around with his men, Rice remained distant. A firm believer in the Navy's rigid hierarchy, he seldom ventured past the control room and into the crew's mess and berth. Many officers felt only a little more warmth than the enlisted men. The veteran submariner, who once griped about his obsessive commanders, now found it difficult to delegate responsibility and trust his new subordinates. Much of his reluctance stemmed from an accident aboard *S-30* when his executive officer, during a routine test of the valves used for diving and surfacing, failed to empty the main ballast tanks before yard workers flooded the Pearl Harbor dry dock. Rice had watched in horror from the bridge that day as the rush of water almost swamped his submarine, caught with its hatches and vents wide open. Only his emergency intervention saved the ship. "What embarrassment!" he later wrote. "This near-disaster cured me of placing confidence in my juniors until considerable observation of their performance gave me reason to rely on them."

Rice's autocratic style consisted of blunt evaluations designed to push his men coupled with the occasional raised voice. Though some of the junior officers bristled at his rigidity, many recognized that Rice strove to educate his men about more than just the Navy. "From the first day I met him, he was clearly in charge and he was going to be successful," Rindskopf recalled. "He was a leader in the strictest sense of the word."

The skipper's efforts to shape his men had all been in preparation for this evening in early May. The submarine, some forty miles south of Nagoya, cruised north at six knots, its phosphorescent wake scribbling a sinuous path on the glassy sea. Rice looked up from his makeshift bunk on the bridge at the full moon that radiated in the cloudless sky. *Drum* had arrived in its patrol area at 9:30 that morning, ending a fourteen-day journey across the Pacific. The submarine had encountered only two Japanese flying boats and picked up two other enemy planes on its radar as it cruised toward its destination off Nagoya, one of the principal cities of Japan's aircraft industry and home to Mitsubishi's sprawling engine and aircraft plants, known for its fighters, bombers, and reconnaissance planes. The company's airframe plant—one of the largest in the world—stretched more than four million square feet while its engine works plant totaled 3.8 million square feet. American war planners suspected such an industrial hub would prove rich hunting grounds for *Drum*.

Rice hoped so.

Rice, Burlingame, and other skippers who stalked these waters capitalized on Japan's geographic and economic vulnerabilities. The archipelago consisted of four major islands—Honshu, Hokkaido, Kyushu, and Shikoku—as well as several thousand smaller ones. The diverse islands, with a total landmass comparable to the state of California, stretched almost 2,000 miles, from the icebound harbors of Hokkaido in the north to the azure waters and coral reefs of Okinawa in the south. Mountains crowded as much as 85 percent of Japan with towering ranges that traversed each of the major islands. The rugged terrain had shaped the development of Japan's towns and cities. Many of the nation's seventy-three million men, women, and children squeezed into dense and primitive wooden cities that clung to Japan's narrow shoreline.

This geography had played a crucial factor in the evolution of Japan's transportation systems. The mountains made railroad construction a challenge, demanding tunnels and bridges that proved expensive and vulnerable in wartime. The slow pace of rail construction had left Japan at the outbreak of the war with only two lines that ran the length of the main island of Honshu, home to major cities Tokyo, Osaka, and Kobe. The highway system proved equally primitive with less than 6,000 miles of national roadways, most unpaved. The nation's few paved roads centered around industrial hubs on Honshu and northern Kyushu, but even then Japan lacked important intercity highways. One seventy-seven-mile journey across Honshu after the war would take American surveyors twelve hours.

Japan's dominant means of transportation revolved around the water, a vital maritime highway system that American strategists recognized proved an incredible liability in a submarine war. The concentration of shipyards, aircraft plants, and munitions factories on the central island of Honshu forced Japan to ship vital raw materials from its outer islands. Freighters loaded with coal, steel, and lumber steamed south from Hokkaido, while ships from the southern islands filled with salt, cement, and cane sugar plowed north. Japan's merchant fleet in 1941 contained 18,789 wooden ships, most fewer than 100 tons. These older and more traditional vessels complemented a robust and modern fleet of steel ships—manned by a well-trained and efficient force of 16,000 officers and 60,000 crewmen—that served as the backbone of Japan's international trade. This 6.2-million-ton fleet consisted of 1,250 large passenger and cargo ships of over 1,000 tons, 1,126 smaller ships, and seventy-four tankers.

Japan's inhospitable terrain caused greater strategic problems than just transportation. A critical lack of farmable land handicapped the island nation at the same time Japan had suffered a population explosion, nearly tripling in size since it first opened its doors to the West less than a century earlier. This growth made Japan the densest nation per arable acre in the world with 2,774 people crowded per acre compared to just 230 in the United States. Fishermen sailed as far as Alaska and the Panama Canal to feed the burgeoning populace. "Of all Japanese problems, that of population is the least understood and the most important," noted one newspaper reporter. "It is the driving force behind all Japanese policies, home and foreign. Everything turns on it: emigration, industrialization, social unrest at home, peace or war abroad."

Outside of a few industries, like raw silk, fish oil, and sulfur, Japan had almost no material self-sufficiency, forced to import even its most iconic food, rice. The natural deficiencies became more apparent in the need for war materials. Ships arrived in port loaded down with bauxite to build fighters, rubber to manufacture tires, and cotton to sew uniforms. Japan's largest import need—and the most critical for war—was oil. At the outbreak of the war Japan could produce just two million barrels a year, a figure that equated to just 0.1 percent of the world's oil output. The United States in comparison—

the world's largest producer—delivered 700 times that amount. Until a few months before the war, the United States had supplied some 80 percent of Japan's oil. Investigators even concluded that American fuel likely powered the carriers, bombers, and fighters that had attacked Pearl Harbor. "Napoleon's armies moved on their stomachs," observed a *New York Times* writer. "Modern motorized armies move on gasoline."

Japan's hunger for food and materials laid the foundation for the expansionism that put it on the eventual path to world war. Victory over China in the Sino-Japanese War in 1894–95 had netted Formosa (Taiwan) and broken China's grip on Korea. Japan's defeat of Russia a decade later in the Russo-Japanese War had blocked the czar's expansion into Manchuria and Korea and set up Japan's 1910 annexation of the latter. With China torn by civil war, Russia preoccupied by economic restructuring, and the United States gripped by the Great Depression, Japan seized another chance to expand in 1931 and invaded Manchuria. Control of Manchuria provided rich supplies of nonferrous metals, steel, and coal that would prove the "arsenal of Japanese expansionism." Japan interpreted the failure of major powers to intervene in Manchuria—followed by similar inaction toward Germany and Italy—as a sign that it would meet no major opposition. Troops pushed into northern China in 1937.

These conquests had come at a price. Since Commodore Matthew Perry's arrival in Tokyo Bay in 1853 on a mission to end Japan's isolation, the nation had worked to model itself after the West, drafting a constitution and embracing Western laws, diplomacy, and industrial, commercial, and financial systems. That rapid rise had led to Japan's inclusion as one of five major powers at the 1919 Paris Peace Conference at the end of the Great War and earned Japan a permanent seat on the Council of the League of Nations. Many of the nations that had applauded Japan's success spurned the nation's imperialistic drive. Japanese leaders viewed that as hypocritical given the vast and resource-rich possessions other major powers boasted in Japan's backyard. Britain held Hong Kong, Malaya, Burma, India, and Ceylon. France controlled Indochina, the Dutch ruled the East Indies, and the United States had the Philippines. If these countries could all have possessions in Asia why shouldn't Japan?

These tensions led Japan to quit the League of Nations and triggered a wave of nationalism that swept the country, symbolized by the popular political slogan "Back to Asia." Japan's military successes upended the balance of power. Powerful cliques inside the Army and Navy exerted a strong influence over the nation's domestic and foreign policies, policies endorsed by the bespectacled Emperor Hirohito. Japan's campaign in China, which war planners had viewed as an easy conquest, soon bogged down, costing as much as 40 percent of the nation's oil production. Unable to end the China campaign without losing face—and in desperate need of resources—Japanese leaders looked toward new conquests with a special eye on the oil-rich Dutch East Indies. In preparation for war, Japan stockpiled raw materials, from iron ore and bauxite to copper, zinc, and lead. The government ordered gas rationed in 1938, eventually halting almost all civilian traffic, including buses and taxis. Essential vehicles burned charcoal or wood.

These measures coincided with an aggressive armament program. By the time of the attack on Pearl Harbor, workers punched out more than 550 planes a month, boosting Japan's air forces to some 7,500 aircraft. That figure counted some 2,675 army and navy tactical planes, like fighters and bombers. The propeller-driven Zero—code-named "Zeke" by the Allies—served as Japan's teeth in the skies. Mitsubishi engineers had stripped the single-engine fighter of self-sealing fuel tanks and much of its armor, making the lightweight plane faster and more agile than its American counterparts though vulnerable in dogfights. Japan's muscle spread beyond the skies. Aggressive recruitment would soon swell the army's 1.7 million soldiers to some five million while the navy's register at the war's outbreak listed 381 warships, including ten battleships, ten aircraft carriers, eighteen heavy cruisers, and 112 destroyers. The Japanese navy not only outgunned American forces in the Pacific, but proved more powerful than the combined navies in that ocean of the United States, Great Britain, and the Netherlands.

Japan saw the outbreak of war in Europe as an opportunity and sided with Germany and Italy, forming what President Roosevelt called an "an unholy alliance." Japan seized on the fall of France to move into Indochina, providing important bases for the ultimate capture of Hong Kong, Singapore, and the East Indies. To Japan's surprise, Roosevelt retaliated, ordering Japan's assets frozen. Britain and the Dutch East Indies followed. America increased pressure and shut off exports of oil, demanding Japan's exit from Indochina, Manchuria, and northern China, an untenable position for the nation's military leaders, who refused to appear weak and back down. In an Armistice Day speech delivered at Arlington—and closely studied in Japan—Roosevelt recalled the sacrifice of the men killed in the Great War. "They did not die to make the world safe for decency and self-respect for five years or ten or maybe twenty. They died to make it safe," he said. "The people of America agree with that. They believe that liberty is worth fighting for. And if they are obliged to fight they will fight eternally to hold it."

Japan took him at his word.

The empire's war planners imagined an easy path to victory. Germany's invasion of Russia had eliminated the threat of a Russian attack in Manchuria. Great Britain was on the defensive and would prove unable to fight, much as China would be once Japan severed the Burma Road. Even the United States, war planners believed, posed little threat, despite its size and industrial power. The Japanese banked on a decisive victory at Pearl Harbor that would wipe out America's Pacific strength and buy them as much as two years to seize and fortify resource-rich islands, creating a defensive perimeter across the Pacific. Furthermore, the weakened United States would be pulled into defending Britain and prove unable to fight an offensive war on the opposite side of the ocean. One of America's greatest flaws, in the eyes of the Japanese, was democracy. Strategists believed that the American public would never allow the nation to fight a costly and bloody war against Japan's fanatical soldiers. The United States would have no choice but to make peace and allow Japan to hold on to its territorial gains. But in the exhaustive analysis of America's weaknesses, Japanese strategists failed to spot their own country's critical vulnerability—a vulnerability that would ultimately cost them the war.

Skipper Rice and his men felt anxious to prove themselves, particularly after the Navy aborted *Drum*'s first mission in early April. Ordered to carry some twelve million vitamins to embattled forces on Corregidor island in Manila Bay, *Drum* reached Midway only to learn that Japan would soon seize the Bataan Peninsula and cut off Corregidor, setting the stage for the infamous Death March. *Drum* returned to Pearl Harbor, its torpedo rooms and magazine still stacked with pill bottles. Above the bridge on the periscope shears this evening, lookouts scanned the horizon for the dark silhouettes of enemy ships. Rice closed his eyes and envisioned the ideal attack on the Japanese aircraft carrier he hoped to find at first light; the massive and vital warship was the prize of all submarine skippers. He would track the carrier's course and then maneuver *Drum* ahead. Once in position some 1,500 yards off the carrier, he would fire all six of his bow tubes followed by the four torpedoes loaded in his stern tubes. The Japanese captain, Rice dreamed, would be helpless.

The skipper stirred. Was that an airplane engine, he wondered. He told himself to relax. He likely heard only the rumble of the submarine's small auxiliary engine or "donkey diesel." But Rice couldn't relax. The growl grew louder. He abandoned his bed at 9:24 p.m. and joined the officer of the deck. The men scanned the horizon before a grumble above forced them to look up. The red and green lights of a Japanese plane pulsed just 200 feet overhead. Lookouts had either failed to spot the plane or it had just switched on its lights as a recognition signal. The plane caught *Drum* exposed on the surface on a moonlit night. The klaxon sounded and the lookouts dropped from the shears as the men hustled to clear the bridge before bombs pummeled the submarine. The officer of the deck in the rush to dive failed to collect his pricey binoculars and throat microphone, while Rice abandoned his mattress and pillow. The submarine submerged at such speed that the men barely had time to seal the conning tower hatch before the Pacific washed over *Drum*.

The submarine leveled off at 150 feet as the skipper waited for the aerial bombs to hit. None came. Fifteen minutes later, Rice ordered the submarine up to periscope depth. The moonlit sea filled his eyepiece. The plane had vanished. Rice swiveled the periscope in search of his mattress and pillow, an oceanic billboard that announced the submarine's presence off Japan. The skipper felt that the loss of his mattress—stenciled with *Drum*'s name—mocked his crew's diligence in dumping trash overboard only in weighted bags. His search of the calm sea proved unsuccessful. Forty-six minutes after the plane buzzed *Drum*, Rice ordered the submarine to surface and continue at six knots toward Nagoya. The skipper climbed down to his cabin to rest. Rice had just drifted off again when the general alarm sounded at 11:55 p.m. Dressed only in his underwear and slippers—what a uniform to go into one's first battle, he thought—Rice darted to the control room, grabbed the ladder, and climbed up through the conning tower to the bridge.

He arrived to find that twenty-four-year-old gunnery officer Maurice Rindskopf had just taken over as the officer of the deck for the midnight to

4 a.m. watch. The wiry lieutenant, known as Mike, pointed at the horizon. "Captain, there's a ship," he announced. "I have ordered all the bow tubes made ready for firing."

Drum's four engines now roared as the submarine closed the distance at full speed of almost twenty-one knots. The skipper's eyes had not yet adjusted to the night and he could see only the bright phosphorescence of the bow wave and stern wake, much to his frustration. Finally he spotted a dark silhouette some two miles off the port bow. The 9,000-ton seaplane carrier *Mizuho* steamed at about ten knots from its recent refitting in Yokosuka toward Hashirajima, an island some 300 miles southwest in Hiroshima Bay that provided safe anchorage to Japan's warships. Completed in 1939 after almost twenty-two months of work in Kobe, the Kawasaki-built carrier stretched 602 feet, almost twice the length of *Drum*. Crewed by more than 500 sailors, *Mizuho* could haul up to a dozen floatplanes and twelve midget submarines. The diesel-driven carrier, with a top speed that rivaled that of the stalking submarine, already had played a vital role in Japan's war, providing reconnaissance and air cover for invasion forces in the Philippines and Dutch East Indies. Rice hoped to end that tonight.

Rindskopf dropped down into the conning tower to calculate the best shot, a complex equation given that both *Drum* and *Mizuho* still steamed through the dark night. The fact that a torpedo could take up to several minutes—or even longer—to reach the target complicated the mathematics. The gunnery officer depended on *Drum's* torpedo data computer to help solve the trigonometry. The analog computer operated by hand cranks, knobs, and dials was one of the most sophisticated machines on a submarine where sailors still used the stars to navigate. The computer automatically logged *Drum's* course and speed, but required Rindskopf to manually enter *Mizuho's* estimated speed, bearing, course, and range, data that often came from the periscope in the conning tower or the target-bearing transmitter on the bridge. The computer then tracked *Mizuho's* position and computed the torpedo's course, relaying that information simultaneously to the torpedoes loaded in the bow and stern tubes via a spindle that turned the onboard gyroscopes.

Two dozen Mark 14 torpedoes served as the heart of *Drum's* arsenal. Each of the complex weapons—constructed of some 1,325 parts—cost taxpayers more than $10,000, a sum that could cover the annual salaries of five Navy ensigns in 1942. The twenty-one-inch torpedo functioned much like the

Drum. Once fired by a blast of compressed air, the torpedo's steam engine ignited, powered by burning alcohol. Dual propellers that spun in opposite directions drove the 3,209-pound bomb up to 4,500 yards at forty-six knots or
9,000 yards at the slower and rarely used speed of 31.5 knots. The gyroscope
controlled the rudders to keep the torpedo on course while a depth gauge
guaranteed that the weapon ran at its typical set depth of ten feet below the
target's estimated keel. The torpedo's warhead boasted 507 pounds of TNT,
a charge the Navy would swap later in the war for 668 pounds of the more
powerful explosive Torpex. Engineers designed the torpedo to detonate on
impact or when it detected a change in a magnetic field as it passed beneath a
target's keel, an explosion intended to break a ship in half.

Rice estimated *Mizuho*'s masthead height, course, and range, relaying that
information below to Rindskopf as the submarine closed to 1,200 yards. The
gunnery officer plugged in the data. *Drum* now locked on to *Mizuho*. Sailors
in the forward torpedo room flooded the tubes and wrenched open the outer
doors. Throughout the submarine crewmen who moments earlier had dozed
in bunks stacked three high now stood ready, anxiously waiting to fire *Drum*'s
first torpedoes of the war. At 12:02 a.m.—seven minutes after lookouts spotted the carrier—Rice gave the order, his voice crackling over the conning
tower loudspeaker. Rindskopf eyed the fire control panel bolted to the bulkhead just steps away and verified that all tubes were ready. The gunnery officer
ordered tube one to fire. The fire controlman, still buttoning his pants, mashed
the button. The spindle in the torpedo room that adjusted the gyroscope up
until the second the weapon fired withdrew, followed by the swoosh of compressed air that launched the torpedo. Five seconds later, *Drum* fired another.

The skipper studied the phosphorescent wakes that raced beneath the
waves at fifty-two miles per hour. Submarine doctrine demanded that he
fire at least four torpedoes, but the skipper opted not to shoot any more.
The darkness made it difficult to judge *Mizuho*'s size and value as a target.
Armed with only twenty-four torpedoes—and having traveled some 3,500
miles to use them—Rice was reluctant to waste a single one. Plus he held
out hope that the aircraft carrier he so coveted might soon cross his path. He
watched the torpedoes disappear in the sea until he noted sudden movement
on the surface ahead. The skipper focused his eyes in the dark, before he realized he was staring at the bow wave of a destroyer. The enemy escort appeared
on course to ram *Drum* at an estimated twenty-five knots. Rice ordered his

submarine to dive after firing again, as the destroyer closed to within a 1,000 yards. The men on the bridge dropped through the hatch into the conning tower as Rindskopf computed the shot. The fire controlman slammed the button and a third torpedo launched.

Rice ordered *Drum* down to 100 feet. Seawater flooded the submarine's ballast tanks to make the ship heavier as sailors cranked the bow and stern plane wheels to guide the descent. Throughout the submarine men held on tight. The skipper waited for the submarine to slip beneath the waves when he heard what he later described as a "strange, tinny sound." The submarine submerged and reached its ordered depth. When the baffled Rice later grabbed the ladder and climbed down the dozen rungs to the crowded control room, his men greeted him with grins and a flash of the victory sign as his slippers hit the deck. Thirty-five seconds after firing the second torpedo, the men claimed to have heard an explosion. *Drum* had torpedoed its first ship. Morale soared, but Rice didn't buy it. "The officers and men there insisted that we had hit the target," he recalled. "Convinced that we had sunk a ship, they were full of elation, a feeling I couldn't share."

Rice was wrong. One of *Drum*'s torpedoes had ripped open the side of *Mizuho*. Unknown to the skipper and his men, cold seawater flooded the carrier as the ship listed twenty-three degrees. Damage control crews fought fires and struggled to contain the flooding. The injured *Mizuho* held on for hours as the flooding worsened and the list increased. The crew abandoned ship before *Mizuho* slipped beneath the waves at 4:16 a.m. along with seven officers and ninety-four crewmen. The attack on *Mizuho* injured another thirty-one sailors, seventeen seriously. Japanese Rear Admiral Matome Ugaki, Combined Fleet Commander Admiral Isoroku Yamamoto's chief of staff, recorded the destruction of *Mizuho* in his diary that Saturday afternoon. "This was the greatest loss so far, to my regret," Ugaki wrote. "I am sorry that little can be done against an enemy surprise attack in full moonlight. A warning against enemy submarines was issued in the name of the chief of staff."

Rice ordered *Drum* up to periscope depth at 12:10 a.m., eight minutes after the submarine dove. He swiveled the periscope. The night sky lit up with rockets and flares, an array of reds, blues, whites, and yellows. It reminded him of a Fourth of July celebration. The skipper and his officers mistakenly concluded the distress flares were designed to attract antisubmarine forces. Rice spotted the destroyer 1,500 yards astern. *Drum*'s desperate attempt to hit the charging escort had failed. The destroyer idled in a position Rindskopf felt ideal for attack. Rice relayed the bearing, speed, and range to his gunnery officer. Rindskopf aimed the torpedoes at the middle of the destroyer and set them to strike the target just four feet below the estimated keel depth. Rice ordered him to fire. Three torpedoes launched at twenty-second intervals. The crew waited for the explosions, but none came. All three torpedoes had missed. Rice recorded his frustration in his report. "This attack was on a destroyer lying to—with steady bearing," he wrote. "Misses cannot be explained."

The Japanese escorts, alerted to *Drum*'s presence, turned on the submarine. The skipper ordered the ship down to 300 feet and prepared for silent running. Sailors shut down the air-conditioning, ventilation blowers, and turned off the refrigerator motors. Men stood prepared to seal the watertight doors to limit flooding while other nonessential sailors climbed into the bunks to conserve air and minimize noise. Japanese escorts on the surface above dumped depth charges into the water to target *Drum*. The two-and-a-half-foot cylindrical canisters that rained down typically packed 220 pounds of Type 88 explosive, a charge more powerful than TNT. Water pressure served as the trigger for the rudimentary weapon. A small orifice on each canister allowed seawater to flow into an interior cylinder. Once the cylinder flooded, the charge exploded. The size of the orifice controlled how fast the cylinder filled and dictated the depth of the charge. The simple charges offered only three settings: ninety-eight, 197, and 292 feet—just shy of *Drum*'s maximum depth.

Sailors below braced themselves. A depth charge that exploded within fifty feet of a submarine promised significant damage. If one exploded within twenty-five feet—the kill zone—the submarine would not likely survive. The first depth charge exploded, followed by a second, then a third. Light bulbs and gauge glasses shattered. Cork insulation rained down and sailors reported leaks around the hull fittings. A rattled executive officer Nicholas looked to Rice, who had finally dressed in more than his underwear. "Captain," Nicholas whispered. "They're playing for keeps!" *Drum* sailors throughout the submarine waited for the next explosion, a terrifying ordeal in which the men often could hear the click of the detonator seconds before the blast. The skipper ordered *Drum* to clear the area at 1:55 a.m. The submarine now operated on battery power, meaning it maneuvered at slow speed. If Rice increased the speed, he risked draining the batteries, a dangerous proposition if the escorts did not abandon the attack and allow *Drum* to surface and charge its batteries.

The depth charges grew more sporadic as the escorts rescued *Mizuho's* survivors; the Japanese heavy cruiser *Takao* later transported 472 sailors to Yokosuka. The temperatures on *Drum* rose and the air soured, now heavy with condensation. Winded sailors labored in ten-minute shifts to hand crank the rudders and planes. During a lull between attacks, Rice ordered the smoking lamp lit, signifying that sailors could take a cigarette break. He directed the men in each spot to share one cigarette between them, though the nicotine-deprived sailors discovered the oxygen levels had plummeted so low that matches wouldn't light. Daybreak came and went. The last of the depth charges—thirty-one total over sixteen hours—exploded at 6 p.m. The Japanese stopped hunting at 7:30 p.m. "Throughout the long night and day, my problem as skipper was twofold: first, to maneuver the sluggish *Drum* at two knots in such a way as to confuse and frustrate the succession of attackers and second, to present to my crew a calm and confident demeanor which would conceal from them how scared I was!"

Rice ordered *Drum* up to periscope depth. The skipper had no idea what ships he might find. But he could not stay down any longer or the submarine might not have the power to surface. He ordered all the men to slip on life preservers and assembled the gun crew in the conning tower. Sailors climbed down into the ship's magazine beneath the crew's mess and began passing up shells. If Rice found the Japanese escorts above, the skipper felt he would have no choice but to battle it out. Though not the most devout parishioner, the Episcopalian offered a quick prayer. If God allowed him two hours on the surface to partially recharge his batteries, he would never ask for anything again. *Drum's* periscope broke the surface about 10:30 p.m. Rice grabbed the handles and peered through the eyepiece. The full moon revealed a glassy sea. He swiveled the periscope and scanned the horizon. The empty night greeted him, his prayer answered.

3

SUBMARINES

"Submarine war against merchant shipping is inherently inhuman, and for that reason should be prohibited."

—*New York Times,*
April 13, 1916, editorial

Rear Admiral Charles Lockwood, Jr., bounced in a jeep down a rain-soaked Australian highway late one afternoon in early May. The five-foot, eight-inch Lockwood had just landed in the wintry western corner of Australia as the commander Submarines Southwest Pacific, a job he would hold only briefly before taking over as the principal architect of America's submarine war against Japan. The short time the blue-eyed admiral had spent in Australia was enough to convince him of America's tough road ahead. Japan had overrun the Philippines, Malaya, and the Dutch East Indies. Enemy forces now amassed bases along the Malay Barrier for what Allied war planners feared would be a push into Australia. A glance at the Princess Royal Harbour captured that fear. The only ship Lockwood noted was the American submarine tender *Holland* with a half dozen boats moored alongside. All merchant ships had evacuated. This far corner of Australia had become the new front line of the war.

Lockwood felt bleak as his jeep zipped past the homes and businesses that lined the streets of this wool and cattle town, the flickering of evening lights reminding him of a Kansas boomtown. Australia had become a refuge for the battered remnants of America's Asiatic Fleet, driven from its home base in the Philippines with a great loss of planes, surface ships, and subs. The bombing of Cavite had cost America a supply of 233 precious torpedoes while the assault on Baatan had forced evacuating troops to scuttle the bombed submarine tender *Canopus* rather than risk losing it to the Japanese. The loss of the Philippines had cost more than just planes and ships, but American morale. Grim faces surrounded the man known to most simply as Uncle Charlie. "Must admit I felt pretty well discouraged by all the belly aching I have heard, and seeing so many people so down in the mouth," Lockwood confessed in his personal diary. "I think all this retreating has taken something out of them."

Lockwood knew the best way to guarantee an end to America's retreat was to unleash his submarines. In the wake of the disaster at Pearl Harbor, the United States resorted to a policy that only twenty-four years earlier President Woodrow Wilson had denounced before Congress as immoral and a reason for war when German U-boats carried out unrestricted submarine attacks in the North Atlantic. Chief of Naval Operations Admiral Harold Stark had phoned President Franklin Roosevelt just hours after the attack to read his proposed order. Roosevelt gave him the green light, telling legislative leaders that same day: "The Japanese know perfectly well that the answer to her attack is proper strangulation of Japan—strangulation altogether." At 5:52 p.m. December 7, 1941, in Washington—as the fires still burned 5,000 miles away in Pearl Harbor—Stark fired off an eight-word order that would shape Lockwood's mission and transform the war to come: "Execute against Japan unrestricted air and submarine warfare."

Born in rural Virginia at the end of the nineteenth century, Lockwood had relocated to Missouri when his family settled on a sheep and cattle farm in the small town of Lamar. The boats he built to use on the muddy streams of the Midwest fed his drive to attend the Naval Academy in 1908. The skinny midshipman struggled with academics, but grew into a champion long-distance runner, breaking the school's one-mile record when he charged across the finish line in just four minutes and twenty-nine seconds. Lockwood had shaved off the seconds needed to win only after weeks of arduous training, which had taught him tenacity, endurance, and pace. Those vital skills would shape his combat philosophy and prepare him for a marathon war of attrition measured not in weeks or months, but in years.

Lockwood graduated in 1912, planning to become a battleship sailor. He spent his first two years on the 26,000-ton *Arkansas*, then the most powerful ship in the Navy. Lockwood soaked up the experience. He shoveled coal with soot-stained hands in the battlewagon's boiler room, worked as a junior turret officer in the gunnery department, and served as a signalman on the bridge. He hoped to continue that education when he arrived in the Philippines at the outbreak of the Great War, but instead landed in submarines, regarded by battleship sailors as the Navy's "unwanted stepchildren." He struggled to conceal his disappointment when he climbed aboard the sixty-three-foot-long *A-4* for his orientation cruise in September 1914. The seven-man submarine—built at the turn of the century—had only one torpedo tube and could dive just 100 feet. "Sailor, few people have a built-in affection for submarines," the skipper confided in Lockwood. "They are, like olives and caviar, an acquired habit—but once acquired, hard to give up."

The *A-4* with its top speed of just eight knots headed out into the steamer lanes where Lockwood heard a repetitive thump off the port side. "What's that?"

"That's the propeller of a sizeable ship," the skipper answered.

Lockwood froze and listened as the ship's propeller grew louder. The rhythmic beat reached a crescendo, then faded as the vessel steamed off. Lockwood had imagined himself at that moment in a submarine parked off the coast of war-torn Europe, stalking enemy freighters and battleships. His vision grew even more vivid when the skipper stepped aside and offered to let Lockwood fire a shot, albeit with a torpedo tube filled just with water. The young lieutenant pressed his eye to the periscope and spotted a rusty steamer in the distance. He called out course changes, navigating his submarine to within 800 yards of the target. Lockwood watched as the ship steamed across his eyepiece before he shouted the order to fire. He felt the submarine shudder as a blast of air ejected the water from the tube. Lockwood saw then the awesome potential of the submarine. "At that moment my attitude toward submarines changed," the admiral would later write. "I had felt the urge and thrill of a hunter alerted by the nearness of game."

Lockwood's epiphany in the warm waters off Manila reshaped his career ambitions. He went on to command a half dozen submarines, including a German U-boat surrendered in the Great War. He refined the diplomatic skills necessary for higher command with a tenure as a submarine adviser to the Brazilian navy and later served as naval attaché in London in the months leading up to America's entry into World War II. There Lockwood witnessed the horror of modern warfare on a civilian population as German bombers and fighters crowded the skies each night, pounding the British capital to rubble. Lockwood watched children march down ruined streets to school toting gas masks while another time he witnessed rescue workers pick through the wreckage of a church flattened during the middle of a wedding. The nightly rumble even cracked one of the windowpanes in Lockwood's room at the Dorchester Hotel, where he outlined his mounting frustration in his diary: "I wish to God we would get into this war before it is lost."

His wish soon came true.

Before the smoke had settled over the oily waters of Pearl Harbor, he fired off a letter to the head of the Navy's bureau of personnel, Rear Admiral Arthur Carpender, known to many simply as Admiral Chips. "It has been a fine job and vastly interesting over here in times of peace, but now that we are in it with our little yellow friends I need more space and, besides, I have always had an ambition to bring home a Japanese wishbone. I do not ask for any particular sea job, just so it gives me a chance to get into the scrap," Lockwood wrote in his December 8 letter. "They have drawn first blood but they'll pay for it in plenty of their own." The impatient Lockwood followed up his letter the next day with a Western Union cablegram: "Forgive personal communication but if you need someone for job in Pacific especially submarines Honolulu or westward please consider me."

Lockwood's days of diplomacy were over. He wanted to return to the undersea service with a job in the Pacific. "Submarine warfare was what I had been trained for—and had trained others for—all these years," he wrote. "I certainly did not want to miss this chance to see our training doctrines and techniques put to good use." Inundated by requests from officers hoping for a combat assignment, the Navy opted to make as few changes as necessary to avoid idle sailors in transit between jobs. The frustrated Lockwood had no choice but wait. He spent his days ferrying top secret messages from President Roosevelt to Winston Churchill—whom the president referred to by the code name "A Former Naval Person"—often meeting with the prime minister at dawn at 10 Downing Street as the British leader shaved in his bathrobe. The news arrived on March 5 followed by word of his promotion to rear admiral. "Ordered Home!! Boy, oh Boy!!" he wrote in his diary. "Maybe this will mean subs. Pacific!!"

British Vice Admiral Sir Bruce Fraser offered the attaché some advice before his departure. "Lockwood," he chided him. "Have you heard about the order we've received from the States for thirty thousands kilts?"

"What in the world do we want with thirty thousands kilts?" Lockwood replied.

"So that you people won't get caught with your pants down again!"

Lockwood planned to make sure.

America's war plan devised before the attack on Pearl Harbor—known as Rainbow No. 5—had called for the military to focus first on the defeat of Germany, which analysts considered a greater threat than Japan. "Since Germany is the predominant member of the Axis Powers, the Atlantic and European area is considered to be the decisive theater," the plan stated. "The principal United States Military effort will be exerted in that theatre, and operations of United States forces in other theaters will be conducted in such a manner as to facilitate that effort." America in the meantime would largely play defense in the Pacific, holding Japanese forces at the Malay Barrier, the series of large islands that stretches from the Malay Peninsula east to New Guinea. Loss of those islands would give the enemy access to vital rubber, oil, and bauxite to fuel their war machine. Beyond resources, the fall of the Malay Barrier would put the Japanese within striking distance of Australia and India.

But Japan had not stopped at Pearl Harbor, hitting American forces in the Philippines, Guam, and Wake as well as targeting the British and Dutch from Malaya to the East Indies. Japan had relied on its larger air forces—2,675 tactical planes compared to the 1,290 Allied aircraft—coupled with the element of surprise to overrun opposition. Japanese planes pounded the Marianas island of Guam—ceded from Spain to the United States in 1898—for two days before enemy troops sloshed ashore on December 10. The tiny garrison of some 670 American and local forces—armed only with handguns and .30 caliber machine guns—put up a fight before the governor ordered the flag lowered and surrendered the island. Another battle played out more than 1,300 miles east at Wake, a remote outpost built atop the two-and-a-half-square-mile rim of a submerged volcano that resembled the shape of a wishbone. More than 500 Marines and sailors—aided by 1,200 civilian construction workers—repelled the Japanese from the three-island atoll for fifteen days before finally surrendering December 23.

America's largest forces in the far Pacific had been in the Philippines. Most of America's heavy bombers and fighters crowded the airfields when enemy planes appeared in the skies overhead just hours after the Japanese attacked Pearl Harbor. The ninety-minute assault had destroyed half of America's heavy bomber force, a third of the fighters, and damaged many of the remaining planes. With Japan now in control of the skies, amphibious forces landed, forcing the Navy's retreat to Java and later Australia as forces under Army General Douglas MacArthur made a final effort to defend the Bataan Peninsula and Corregidor. Under orders from President Roosevelt, MacArthur evacuated the Philippines, slipping out with his family in a patrol torpedo boat one night in early March. Bataan fell a month later on April 9. American and local forces would ultimately hold out on the island fortress of Corregidor in Manila Bay until May 6, surrendering just days after Rear Admiral Lockwood landed in Australia.

The British and Dutch suffered similar defeats. Japanese forces landed on the Malay Peninsula, Borneo, and Celebes, sinking the battleship *Prince of Wales* and the battle cruiser *Repulse*. Hong Kong fell, then Singapore. The Japanese army even went so far as to invade Thailand and capture Bangkok. America, England, the Netherlands, and Australia joined forces in a desperate effort to try to hold the Japanese at the Malay Barrier, an alliance plagued by language barriers, communication difficulties, and divergent national interests. The battered Allies struggled to regroup as the Japanese occupied Sumatra, Bali, and Timor. Enemy fighters and bombers launched from four aircraft carriers on February 19, pounding the city of Darwin on the northern coast of Australia, a vital hub for supplying the embattled forces on the Dutch East Indies island of Java. When the enemy strike force finally withdrew, nearly every ship in the harbor sat on the bottom. Australia had no choice but to evacuate the city.

By late February the Japanese noose had tightened around Java, advertised as the "Gem of the Dutch East Indies." The lush equatorial island that served as the heart of the Dutch empire was all that stood between Japan and Australia. Ninety-seven enemy transports loaded with invasion forces steamed toward Java. The Allied forces left to battle the Japanese included just five heavy and light cruisers and ten destroyers. Crews were exhausted and Allied airpower scarce. The February 27 Battle of the Java Sea raged well into the night before the Allies had to retreat. The seven-hour battle cost the Allies two cruisers and three destroyers. The Japanese in contrast had lost nothing. Organized Allied resistance crumbled as Japan completed its conquest of the resource-rich south. America's prewar expectation to hold the Japanese at the Malay Barrier had failed. War planners had underestimated Japanese capabilities. "The United States plan," one postwar report concluded, "had little basis in reality."

Japan had created a defensive perimeter, protecting its conquests in the south as well as its homeland. The free passage of freighters, tankers, and troopships was vital for Japan to transport oil, coal, and other resources as well as to fortify and defend the perimeter. Allied forces faced years of fighting to win back lands Japan had seized in just five months. While forces under General MacArthur in Australia would claw north across the jungles of New Guinea en route back to the Philippines, Admiral Chester Nimitz in Hawaii would push west, fighting the Japanese in the Solomons, the Gilbert and Marshall islands, the Carolines, and the Marianas. The goal was to shatter Japan's perimeter and put the enemy's homeland in reach of Allied bombers. But the disastrous early months of war had wiped out much of America's offensive capabilities. Outside of a few carrier- and land-based air raids, America's offense fell to the submarines, the lone combatants able to sneak into enemy waters and target Japan's supply lines.

Before the war the Navy had assigned submarines to the three major fleets in the Atlantic, Pacific, and Southeast Asia. New London served as the hub for Atlantic Fleet submarines while Pacific Fleet boats operated out of the base at Pearl Harbor. Submarines with the smaller Asiatic Fleet headquartered on the tender *Canopus* in Manila Bay. Japan's invasion of the Philippines had forced the evacuation of those submarines to Australia. There the Navy reorganized the boats as Submarines Southwest Pacific and put Lockwood in charge. The undersea war against Japan now fell to two commands that split the Pacific. Lockwood would oversee the waters from Australia east to the Coral Sea and north to the Philippines. This included New Guinea, Borneo, and Java. Submarines Pacific Fleet under command of Rear Admiral Robert English would patrol the vast central Pacific west of Hawaii that included the strategic areas of the Marianas, Caroline Islands, and the Japanese home waters.

The submarine force was just a small part of the Navy, consisting at the outbreak of the war of 111 submarines with another seventy-three under construction. Fifty-one submarines operated in the Pacific with twenty-two based at Pearl Harbor, including sixteen modern fleet boats plus a half dozen hangovers from World War I, boats ill suited for the long distances this fight would demand. Another twenty-nine submarines—twenty-three modern boats and six older ones—were based in the Philippines. Four of those would be lost before Lockwood took command. New construction in shipyards from Maine to Wisconsin and California would ramp up fleet production to its 1944 peak of ten new boats a month. Even then the force would remain small, never exceeding more than 50,000 officers and enlisted men or just 1.6 percent of the Navy. Only 16,000 of those men would actually serve at sea. To those few fell the responsibility to patrol eight million square miles of ocean, an area more than twice the size of Europe.

The Navy knew that was almost an impossible task. While submarines over the course of the war would help rescue 504 downed aviators, smuggle ammunition to embattled Corregidor, and protect amphibious landings, the principal mission of the force was to destroy to Japan's navy and merchant fleet. To manage the vast seas the Navy created dozens of numbered patrol areas. These areas covered Japan's home islands as well as strategic locations like Formosa, the Marianas, and the Carolines. In creating patrol areas war planners looked not just for enemy naval bases but vital shipping centers. Other patrol areas covered important sea lanes and areas where multiple shipping routes converged, places war planners knew to expect maritime traffic. The Navy assigned submarines headed out on patrol a specific area to hunt. Given the great distances and need for refits and overhauls, only about one third of the fifty-one submarines available at the war's start could be on station at a time.

Lockwood knew that each enemy freighter delivered to the bottom slowed Japan's nimble war machine. Ships required great investments in materials and labor, from the steel required to build the hull down to the maps used to navigate. One 10,000-ton merchant ship required as many as 650,000 rivets while a ship's chronometer cost $200, the engine order telegraph $400, and even an anchor ran more than $1,200. Torpedoed ships not only vanished with experienced officers and crew, but with precious loads of bullets, bauxite, and fuel, a tremendous loss considering a Japanese Zero in combat drank as much as 1,500 gallons of fuel a week while a single tank regiment could burn 2,000 gallons in an hour. "When Japan allied herself with Germany, not only did she join with the chief sponsor of unrestricted submarine warfare but her ships immediately became carriers of men, munitions and war supplies," wrote Lockwood. "Therefore, no longer were there any Japanese merchantmen in the Pacific."

President Roosevelt's shake-up of the Navy after the attack on Pearl Harbor elevated veteran submarine officers to three of the nation's top four admirals. These men understood the pain a submarine war could inflict on Japan. The new commander of the United States Fleet, Admiral Ernest King, who doubled as the chief of naval operations, had served as a submarine division commander. Roosevelt also had initially left Admiral Thomas Hart in charge of the Asiatic Fleet. The sixty-four-year-old Michigan native, during his tenure as director of submarines, had battled to advance the role of submarines in the Navy, pushing to acquire German U-boats after the Great War. Though the fall of the Philippines would spell the end of the Asiatic Fleet—and Allied infighting would lead Roosevelt ultimately to relieve Hart—the veteran admiral would remain influential.

More important to Lockwood was Admiral Nimitz, the new Pacific Fleet commander and mastermind of America's naval war against Japan. The tall and slender admiral with blue eyes and white hair was the son of a cowboy who drove cattle from Texas north to Nebraska. Nimitz's father died before he was born, leaving his grandfather to help raise him, a former German merchant mariner who operated a hotel in Fredericksburg, Texas, shaped like a steamboat, complete with a mast. "The sea—like life itself—is a stern taskmaster," he often told his grandson. "The best way to get along with either is to learn all you can, then do your best and don't worry—especially about things over which you have no control." Nimitz followed that advice. He served as a submarine skipper, traveled to Germany before World War I to study diesel engine design, and helped build the Pearl Harbor submarine base that served as the war's nerve center. On December 31, 1941, Nimitz took command of the battered Pacific Fleet on the deck of the submarine *Grayling*, his four-star flag climbing the submarine's mast that morning. Throughout the war his Pacific Fleet flagship would remain a submarine.

America's submarine force and strategy differed greatly from that of Japan, which started the war with sixty-four submarines. Though America experimented with various-sized boats around the time of the First World War, the decades between the conflicts saw American design coalesce around a long-range fleet boat, perfect for commerce warfare. Japan in contrast boasted a wide range of designs, from two-person midget boats to massive 5,000-ton submarines that could carry seaplanes. That experimentation of design would continue throughout much of the war. The variety reflected a lack of a focused policy. Rather than order submarines to attack merchant ships, Japanese strategists saw the boats as part of a larger fleet action, second-rate to the battleships and aircraft carriers that dominated the surface Navy. Lockwood now hoped to exploit that miscalculation.

The affable admiral's Jeep pulled up outside the Freemasons Hotel in Albany where he planned to have dinner with his chief of staff this early May evening. America's first submarine base in Australia was up in Fremantle on the country's west coast. There the submarine force had leased a couple of fifty-foot-tall wheat-loading sheds, converting them into machine shops. But the small submarine force—and the offensive hope of the United States—was too valuable to risk to a Japanese surprise attack. The Navy had decided to move the submarine tender *Holland* farther south to the harbor in Albany. The 8,100-ton ship functioned like a mobile base, capable of swapping out damaged propellers to resupplying food, fuel, and torpedoes for submarines. The admiral noted that if Albany were to fall, the only place south left to retreat to would be Antarctica.

The winter rains had arrived early in Australia, matching the damp outlook and grim faces on the exiled American forces. The admiral hustled into the lobby of Albany's hotel only to find a chorus of music welcoming him. He peered inside the lounge to discover a dozen submarine officers crowded around a piano singing. The upbeat scene startled the admiral, even more so when he failed to spot empty beer bottles and realized the men were sober. Lockwood's spirit lifted. Unlike all the sulking sailors he had so far encountered, these men were defiant in the face of defeat. This was the enthusiasm American forces needed, the attitude required to fight a long war back across the Pacific. These young officers, Lockwood felt, promised victory. That was confirmed when the admiral paused to listen to the words the men belted out. "Sink 'em all, sink 'em all, Tojo and Hitler and all," the officers roared. "Sink all their cruisers and carriers too. Sink all their tin cans and their stinking crews."

4

SILVERSIDES

"We have just left our ocean and entered theirs, although I don't see any dividing line."

—John Bienia,
May 21, 1943, letter

Silversides cut through the waves off the Japanese stronghold of Rabaul in the South Pacific on the evening of December 22, 1942, just five days into the fourth war patrol. The bearded Burlingame had come a long way in the eight months since his first mission. The skipper had seen his young and inexperienced crew, those the Navy had yet to rotate off, develop into a solid and experienced combat machine. The men had survived depth charges, gun battles, and even an ensnarement in a fishing net that had forced the submarine to finish an attack towing a Japanese flag. The superstitious skipper who had started the war convinced he would die attributed his good fortune to his regular rub of the Buddha's belly, a ritual he practiced so often that his raw finger bled on the statuette.

Burlingame's success, though, depended on a loyal and diverse group of officers who had been on board since the start of the war. Lieutenant Commander Roy Davenport served as the submarine's second in command. A Kansas City native and son of a locomotive engineer, the thirty-three-year-old Davenport was a recent convert to Christian Science. The 1933 Naval Academy graduate opposed gambling and drinking, placing him at odds with his salty Southern skipper, who loved whiskey and welcomed wardroom poker games. The executive officer instead preferred to unwind by playing his trombone, much to the frustration of his fellow officers.

The submarine's next senior officer was Lieutenant Robert Worthington, a twenty-seven-year-old Philadelphian. Worthington had long suffered from a sense of inferiority that fueled an overheated drive to succeed, as evident by his graduating four out of 438 graduates in the Naval Academy's class of 1938, where he was a classmate of *Drum*'s Mike Rindskopf. The gunnery officer had excelled in academics and lettered in gymnastics—the rings were his best event. He also qualified as an expert rifleman and pistol shot. Doctors had recently diagnosed his wife, Dotty, with polio. She was alone in Hawaii—and only home from the hospital one day—when the Japanese attacked, a fact that infuriated Worthington. "Whatever happens," he wrote in a letter just days later. "Bet your boots that we are each determined to get our own personal revenge for Pearl Harbor. It may take a little while, but we'll get it."

Twenty-six-year-old Massachusetts native Lieutenant John Bienia served as the submarine's resident prankster and unofficial biographer, chronicling the exploits of the Silver Lady—as *Silversides* was affectionately known—in letters home to his soon-to-be bride, Alpha. Bienia had graduated in April 1938 from the Massachusetts Nautical School, where he had once received six demerits for failing to wear a complete suit of underwear. He had gone to work as a merchant mariner with the United Fruit Company, traveling throughout Central and South America, a job that had earned him the nickname "Johnny Bananas." Bienia had worked in a rescue crew in a motor whaleboat the day the Japanese attacked Pearl Harbor. A bomb hit the whaleboat's port quarter, cutting all planking from capping to keel. The bomb detonated underwater, throwing Bienia and the others into the harbor.

Burlingame had watched his officers gel, not only in combat, but also in the long hours of downtime that filled patrols. Over cards, cribbage games, and meals around the wardroom table, the men had become close friends, even family. Lieutenant Tom Keegan would even serve as Bienia's best man in his upcoming February 26 wedding in Honolulu, an event celebrated by the Silver Lady's entire wardroom. Much of that camaraderie centered on music, one of the few outlets the men all enjoyed on long patrols in hostile waters. Bienia captured one such recital that began when he and Keegan started harmonizing. "Before we knew it the Captain poked his bearded face into the room and joined us," Bienia wrote in a letter to his fiancée. "He also brought one of those ten cent songbooks along and we three ripped right through them."

The concert, however, had only begun. "We must have sounded pretty good because Gibby and Jerry came in to join us. What a quintet, all we needed was glasses and a bottle," Bienia continued. "Then Bob piled into the room, completing a sextet in our little room—Can you imagine six people in it— why it isn't any bigger than a bathtub. Thank God the other two officers were on watch. We all sang a Southern Rebel song and the Captain left after it was over and went to his room in search of another songbook that his daughter put into his suitcase. While he was gone, we burst into a Yankee (good ole North) Song and we sang it real loud. The Captain yelled gees-Chrise as soon as I leave you fellas get out of hand. We were going to sing 'Marching Through Georgia' but we figured we were fighting one war, no use starting another."

The men hosted a wardroom jam session another night. "There were a guitar, mouth organ, flute, and of all things to play aboard a submarine—a sliding trombone. The Captain played on his homemade bazooka—a comb and a piece of tissue paper. I wish you could have seen the Executive Officer play his trombone. He'd have to slide the handle of the trombone out into the alleyway to get the low notes. Sailors passing to and from the forward torpedo room had to jump lively when they were passing the mad slides of the trombonist. This concert, much to the grief of the rest of the crew, lasted until 11:45 PM," Bienia wrote. "There's ugly talk going about the ship that we won't have to shoot any torpedoes this trip, and that we can slay everyone with our music. Shucks, it seems that there are some people aboard ship who can't appreciate the finer arts."

That camaraderie had become vital—and Burlingame would need it now more than ever as he listened to the grim news from Pharmacist's Mate 1st Class Tom Moore. The young medic had been up since about 5 a.m., caring for Petty Officer 3rd Class George Platter, a nauseated fireman who complained of pain in his upper abdomen. Since *Silversides* had departed Australia, several sailors had suffered similar symptoms, followed a day later by severe diarrhea before the men returned to normal. Moore had suspected Platter battled the same illness and gave him paregoric to ease his pain. But Platter had returned several hours later. His temperature had climbed and his abdomen was rigid and his right lower quadrant tender. The diarrhea that had stricken others had failed to materialize. This was not the same illness that had sidelined others.

This was worse. Much worse.

The skipper listened as Moore outlined his fears. The eighteen-year-old New York native—just one week shy of his next birthday—likely suffered from appendicitis, an illness that could be remedied with a routine abdominal surgery in a shore-based hospital, but proved potentially life-threatening on a submarine at sea. If the appendix ruptures, pus can spill into the abdomen and trigger peritonitis and even sepsis, a severe condition in which bacteria poisons the bloodstream. Time was critical: the appendix can burst less than twenty-four hours after symptoms appear.

Moore was not alone in his fear. The Navy had long worried about the possibility of just such a scenario. "Probably no other single disease," one medical report later noted, "is cause for more anxiety to Submariners than is appendicitis." The Navy's senior medical officers understood that appendicitis promised a host of complications, including the need for a laboratory to confirm diagnosis, a luxury the undersea boats did not have. Submariners, who chow down for months on a diet of canned meats, fruits, and vegetables, notoriously suffered bouts of constipation and other gastric and gastrointestinal discomfort, all symptoms that could easily be mistaken for appendicitis. Even if a pharmacist's mate accurately diagnosed appendicitis, it was vital that the medic recognize that not all cases required immediate surgery.

Submarines did not carry a doctor, only a pharmacist's mate, who functioned as "the medical officer, the dentist, the nurse and the chaplain all rolled into one." The Navy boasted that it applied a "rigorous selection program," but regulations required only that a prospective pharmacist's mate be at least twenty years old, a high school graduate, and "above average intelligence, and, as nearly as can be determined, is an emotionally stable, psychiatrically and physically sound adult." In reality, the typical pharmacist's mate enjoyed only basic medical training, consisting of a sixteen-week program that Moore later described as a "grand slam course." Because of the lack of in-depth instruction, submariners called pharmacist's mates "quacks."

Faced with these challenges, the Navy instructed pharmacist's mates never to resort to surgery, instructions that became an official order near the end of the first year of war. If confronted with a case of suspected appendicitis, the Navy advised pharmacist's mates to withhold giving any food by mouth and allow a patient only the smallest sips of water. In case of dehydration, administer intravenous fluids. Pharmacist's mates should never give a patient a cathartic, but if necessary could administer a low, gentle enema, repeating the procedure if necessary. The Navy instructed that patients remain on absolute bed rest with an icepack over the right lower quadrant and sedatives to ease pain and sulfa drugs to fight infection. This treatment, it was hoped, would slow the infection enough to allow the transfer of a patient to a shore hospital.

But the Navy's conservative approach occasionally collided with medical necessity. That proved the case three months earlier on *Seadragon*. With the submarine submerged to 120 feet to avoid rough swells, Pharmacist's Mate 1st Class Wheeler Lipes sliced open a young sailor on the wardroom table to discover his appendix had turned black and gangrenous. The successful surgery— the first ever on a submarine—required extraordinary creativity, resourcefulness, and a medical instruction book. To ascertain his patient wasn't a hemophiliac, Lipes nicked his ear, placed a drop of blood in an inverted medicine glass, and timed how long it took to clot. He resorted to torpedo alcohol to sterilize his clothes as well as neutralize the carbolic acid used to cauterize the stump. To monitor patient's heart rate during the two-and-a half-hour surgery, Lipes watched blood vessels pulse in the sailor's belly.

Three days before *Silversides* departed Australia for its current patrol, a pharmacist's mate on *Grayback* battled another case of appendicitis. The skipper ordered him to operate. Like Lipes, the Grayback's pharmacist's mate resorted to unorthodox surgical tools, including long-nosed pliers from the engine room, spoons from the galley, and the mouthpiece of a Momsen escape lung to administer ether. The patient, whose appendix already had burst, survived. These successful surgeries generated significant attention in the press. *Chicago Daily News* reporter George Weller would win a 1943 Pulitzer Prize for his graphic account of the *Seadragon* operation. Many submariners viewed the pharmacist's mates as heroes who had overcome incredible odds to save lives. But the surgeries divided the brass.

Silversides pharmacist's mate Moore had paid attention to the scuttlebutt. The twenty-two-year-old Texas native had enlisted in the Navy in August 1938 with a boot camp ambition to become an electrician. Word passed one day of a surprise bag inspection to check uniforms. Two minutes later, another announcement alerted sailors of an exam for prospective hospital corpsmen.

Moore decided he would rather sit through an exam—and flunk—than have his superiors berate him over his uniforms and revoke his liberty privileges. To Moore's surprise, he passed. The Navy sent him to San Diego Naval Hospital for schooling. Moore spent the next three years working at the hospital, much of it on the surgical and genitourinary wards where he became a surgi-cal technician.

Moore's training was intense. To earn his operating room certificate, he later recalled that he had to pass instruments for at least a hundred appendec-tomies, ten gallbladder surgeries, ten laparotomies, a craniotomy, and a speci-fied number of other surgeries. He joked that he made "rear admiral" because the chief nurse made him pass instruments for hemorrhoidectomies every time he became ornery. The Navy transferred Moore to the battleship *Mary-land*, where his schooling continued under a young Mayo Clinic–trained sur-geon who routinely drilled Moore. Following one appendectomy, the surgeon ordered Moore to write a complete description of the operation, including each tissue he cut through, how he removed the appendix, and cauterized the stump. Not until Moore submitted his report would the surgeon authorize his liberty pass.

But Moore's real test came the morning of December 7, 1941. The World War I–era battleship *Oklahoma*, devastated by as many as nine Japanese aerial torpedoes that ripped open much of the ship's port side, capsized in Pearl Harbor next to *Maryland*. Scores of injured sailors, some fished from the oily water, crammed every bunk in the *Maryland* sickbay. Others stretched out on the decks. Moore worked nonstop, describing it as the "fastest day of my life." When he finally climbed up to the afterdeck for a break, it was after dusk. Fires from the attack still burned and smoke blanketed the harbor. Moore, who wanted to fight, soon volunteered for submarine duty. The surgeon who mentored him imparted a final lesson. "If you ever have anything that you have to do surgically," he advised, "remember what I taught you."

Moore did, but had hoped he would never have to use it. Now Moore told Burlingame that Platter's best chance hinged on whether the Navy could dis-patch what was known as a flying boat, a patrol craft that can land in water. *Silversides* sailors could transfer Platter to the plane and the aircrew could fly him back to Australia for emergency surgery. Burlingame agreed to arrange a rendezvous that evening. Moore tried to keep Platter as comfortable as pos-sible, but his condition worsened with each hour. By the afternoon, Moore described Platter as "writhing in pain, all jackknifed up, mo͏̵ or crewmember alike to give him relief." When Moore went radio room, he expected a coded message about that eveni͏̵ None came.

Moore huffed it back to Burlingame's cabin. "Doc, we're not breaking radio silence," the skipper told him. "We're not rendezvousing with another vessel. We are only fifty miles off Rabaul lighthouse. I spotted enemy aircraft all day long, and we are not risking this sub and seventy-one men for one man. We have orders to proceed at all speed ahead to block a strategic shipping lane and that is what we are doing."

"Captain," Moore asked, "what if Platter dies?"

"Son, he might do that, and we might be one man shy at patrol's end," Burlingame told him. "But we will not rendezvous tonight."

The skipper asked for an update on Platter's condition. Moore leveled with him that Platter appeared critical. "If worse comes to worst," the skipper asked, "can you remove his appendix?"

Moore stammered.

"Well, can you or can't you?" Burlingame pressed.

Moore felt his hair stand up. He thought about the idea for a couple of minutes. "I probably can," he finally offered. "But I don't know what the outcome would be."

"If you got to do it," Burlingame told him, "you got to do it," The skipper's demeanor softened. He encouraged Moore, who later described Burlingame as a "con artist from the word go." After about five minutes, Burlingame successfully propped up Moore's confidence so that the young pharmacist's mate felt convinced he could perform the surgery. The skipper said he would take the submarine deep to limit sway and movement. "I'll do anything I can," Burlingame assured him. "You can have any men you want to help you. The whole ship is at your disposal."

The decision to operate was final at 9 p.m. *Silversides* cruised at full speed on its No. 1 and 2 main engines, charging its batteries on the No. 3 and 4 main engines. Fifty-two minutes later, Burlingame ordered the submarine to dive. The klaxon sounded. Lookouts dropped through the narrow hatch into the conning tower and then hustled down the ladder to the control room, manning the bow and stern planes. The chief of the boat opened the main ballast tank vents from forward aft, allowing a rush of cold seawater to flood the forward tanks. *Silversides*, located in the perilous channel off Rabaul, slipped beneath the dark water, leveling off at a depth of 100 feet.

Moore assembled his team. He chose as his chief assistant Petty Officer 1st Class Albert Stegall, a twenty-five-year-old radioman and son of a Tennessee mayor. Moore and Stegall worked together on the coding board and often had chatted about what would happen if the need for surgery ever arose. Stegall sensed that Moore—on only his second war patrol—feared just such an emergency. Stegall had jokingly volunteered to help if needed. Moore remembered. Stegall was cleaning the sound shafts when a winded sailor appeared, delivering news that the pharmacist's mate had sent for him. Stegall hustled to find his friend and ask what he could do. "I'll tell you when the time comes," Moore answered. "Just get cleaned up."

Stegall slipped on an undershirt—what was called a "skivvie shirt"—and reported to the wardroom along with the rest of Moore's small team, including executive officer Davenport, Ensign Donald Finch, signalman Robert Danko, and gunner's mate Robert Detmers. Moore planned to use the cramped wardroom to perform his surgery. A narrow rectangular table, bolted to the floor to weather rough seas, stood in the center where the officers dined using china, silverware, and cloth napkins. Blue padded benches ran along either side of the table and removable chairs sat at each end. Metal lockers and drawers filled with charts, navigation gear, and table linens lined the forward and aft bulkheads. A window along the forward bulkhead allowed stewards to pass trays of hot food from the adjoining officers' galley.

The men immediately discovered a problem: the table was too short for Platter. To remedy it, sailors attached an ironing board to one end and propped it up on nearby lockers. Men yanked the reflectors from the lights, scoured the fixtures, and inserted 150-watt bulbs to provide Moore maximum illumination. Others draped clean sheets over the buffet and seat backs. Moore instructed one of the machinists to bend tablespoons into right angles to make retractors before he sterilized his surgical instruments in a pan of boiling water on the galley stove. Stegall visited Platter in the forward torpedo room, where he shaved his abdomen with a straight razor and swabbed him down with alcohol. Several sailors carried the patient to the wardroom.

The pharmacist's mate, stripped down to a sleeveless undershirt, slipped on his surgical gloves. Stegall did the same. Moore's meager resources lined his surgical tray: a suture kit, scalpel, tweezers, sponge forceps, and little else. He fortunately had requested a spinal needle and a single tube of novocaine—normally not included on a submarine—fearing he might have to treat a severe leg injury. *Silversides* carried cans of ether, but given the close quarters Moore felt it best to use spinal anesthetic. He measured 150 milligrams of novocaine, which he estimated would last an hour and a half, plenty of time to complete the surgery. The men rolled Platter on his side and Danko held him. Moore inserted the needle into Platter's back between the fourth and fifth lumbar vertebrae, watched the clear spinal fluid drip out, and injected the anesthetic, just as he had seen doctors do in the operating room at the San Diego hospital.

The pharmacist's mate eased Platter onto his back and painted his abdomen with Merthiolate to kill germs. He wiped the antiseptic off with pure grain alcohol and draped towels over Platter, who was now numb from about the waist down. One sailor held Platter's feet and another his head. A third stood ready to wipe the sweat from Moore's face as the wardroom temperature soon rose. The nervous pharmacist's mate gripped his scalpel and made his first incision. Moore felt like he "really ripped him open," when in reality his incision stretched about a quarter-inch shorter than the length of a cigarette. Moore explained each step to Stegall. The radioman suspected Moore did so more to prop up his own confidence than to keep Stegall or the others informed. With each incision, Stegall's confidence in his friend increased.

Moore soon found Platter's appendix. The inflamed organ confirmed his diagnosis. Moore tried to lift the appendix only to discover a complication. The organ had adhered to Platter's cecum, part of his large intestine. Moore had to cut it free. Normally a surgeon would use scissors, but the pharmacist's mate felt too timid. Moore instead inserted his needle and ligated his way through it. The added complication, he later recalled, "killed a lot of time." When he finished, Moore still had to remove the appendix and not rupture it in the process. He put a tie around the base of the inflamed organ and walled it off with gauze. He sliced off the sick appendage and cauterized the stump with phenol and alcohol. The thirty-minute surgery appeared a success.

Worthington not only served as the gunnery officer, but the *Silversides* unofficial photographer. He occasionally shot periscope photos, but mostly he snapped pictures of crewmembers on the cigarette deck, developed them at night in the wardroom pantry sink, and gave the sailors copies to mail home to family. No one had ever photographed a submarine appendectomy.

Worthington didn't want to miss the historic opportunity. He popped his head through the forward entrance of the crowded wardroom and leaned against the bulkhead. His Kodak Medalist 620 had no flash and slow film speed of only 25, so he opened the aperture wide to 3.5 and set the shutter speed to one fifth of a second. Worthington eyed the surgeon and his team and squeezed the release. Snap. He wound the film and shot another image. Then another.

Moore believed the danger had passed. Platter's inflamed appendix, no longer a threat to the young fireman, sat atop a white sheet. All I have to do now, the pharmacist's mate thought, is stitch Platter up. Moore remembered that a good surgeon always checked for bleeding. He grabbed a sterile sponge with a forceps and swabbed the inside of Platter's abdomen, confident it would come out clean. He pulled the forceps out and stared at the sponge in disbelief. It was sopping wet with blood. Moore felt he might collapse. Something inside Platter's abdomen was bleeding—and he didn't know what. Platter's survival depended on him figuring that out and fast. "It was a helluva mess," Moore later recalled. "That really took all the aspirations of being a surgeon out of me right quick."

Time complicated Moore's challenge. The novocaine would last only another hour. His timidity in separating Platter's appendix from the cecum, he realized, had cost him precious minutes. He had to find the source of Platter's bleeding, repair it, and stitch him up before the anesthetic wore off. A sailor wiped the sweat from Moore's face as he worked and executive officer Davenport shined a flashlight to provide more light. Moore pulled a portion of Platter's intestine out through the incision and examined it for signs of a nicked blood vessel. He found none. He pulled more of Platter's purplish intestine out, wheeling it slowly in his hands as he searched for the source of the blood. He still found nothing. Ten minutes slipped past, then thirty, and finally an hour. Moore's heart sank.

"Is this operation over yet?" someone asked.

Focused on the finding the source of blood loss, Moore failed to realize the question came from his patient. Platter had begun to wake up.

"I can feel you pulling at my guts," the fireman complained. "Hit me on the head with something."

Platter began to moan and cough as the novocaine wore off. His pain throbbed and he started to fight. Sailors struggled to hold him down on the wardroom table. Platter's thrashing only tore his incision and caused him to bleed more. At one point, his intestines popped back out. Platter began to retch, but he had nothing in his stomach so he dry heaved, further tearing his incision. Davenport, the devout Christian Scientist, repeated the first verses of the forty-sixth Psalm to quiet him: "God is our refuge and strength, a very present help in trouble." But Platter continued to holler. "Give me something to ease the pain, knock me out, hit me over the head with a hammer or something," he cried. "Anything to keep this pain down."

Moore realized he had no choice but to open a can of ether and sedate Platter, a problem on board a submarine since the ventilation system promised to waft the ether through the boat. Moore instructed Davenport to retrieve a can of the anesthetic, a tea strainer, and gauze. Moore told Davenport, who now stood at the head of the table, to place the gauze over the tea strainer and drip the ether into it. Davenport was overly excited and released too much, spilling it onto the patient. Suddenly Stegall, who hovered over Platter's stomach using the bent spoons to hold the incision open, began to feel woozy. Moore had no choice but to take over. He covered Platter's incision with a towel, slipped off his gloves, and showed Davenport how to release just enough ether to keep Platter sedated so that he could finish the surgery. The patient calmed.

Moore regloved and resumed his search for the bleeder, probing Platter's intestine. "We were wheeling that gut about twelve inches at a time," the pharmacist's mate later recalled. "I examined every square inch of that intestine." But still he could not find the source of Platter's bleeding. Moore inspected Platter's guts for so long that December 22 became the 23rd. Davenport opened a second can of ether. The fumes flooded the submarine. Patrick Carswell, who was knocked off the deck gun in the battle with the trawler, could even smell it up in the conning tower. Moore continued his desperate search, but eventually sank in despair. The young fireman, he realized, was going to die. Moore had failed. "I sweated blood until I finally just gave up," he recalled. "I thought, well, hell, I might as well just sew him up and let him die with his skin on."

Moore began to close Platter's peritoneum, the membrane that protects the abdominal organs. He then removed the skin towels so that he could reach the subcutaneous layer, the tissue just beneath Platter's skin. The pharmacist's mate stared down. The source of Platter's bleeding, he discovered, sat right in front of him. A large blood vessel that he had previously tied in Platter's subcutaneous tissue somehow had become loose. Blood now oozed behind the skin towels and down into Platter's wound. He had spent approximately three hours desperately hunting the source of the bleeding, only to find it after he had given up. Moore, who described the surgery as a "lonely endeavor," felt relief wash through him. Unless an infection hit Platter, the fireman would likely survive. Moore could now tie it off and close the wound.

Silversides needed to charge its batteries before dawn. At 1:50 a.m.—three hours and fifty-eight minutes after the boat had submerged for Platter's surgery—Burlingame ordered the submarine to surface. Sailors in the maneuvering room throttled the Nos. 1 and 2 main engines up to full speed and used Nos. 3 and 4 to charge the batteries. Others unsealed the conning tower hatch to allow cool night air to flood the muggy boat as lookouts scrambled up the periscope shears to scan the horizon for enemy ships and planes. Burlingame recorded the topside conditions in his action report: "bright moonlight, unlimited visibility" with a "dead calm, flat sea." The men in the wardroom transferred Platter from the table to a transom bench that doubled as a narrow bunk so the fireman could rest. The rest of the sailors returned to work or bed.

Seventy-five minutes after *Silversides* surfaced, lookouts spotted a darkened ship. All hands topside agreed that it appeared to be a submarine. Given the *Silversides'* position along the western boundary of the patrol area, Burlingame suspected the other boat could be American though he couldn't be certain. The skipper opted to be safe and work around it to the west, a move that forced *Silversides* to cross the moon slick at 3:25 a.m. Lookouts on the other vessel spotted the boat and turned toward *Silversides*, an ominous sign. Burlingame ordered all four engines up to full power to try to outrun the darkened ship. *Silversides* tore across the sea at twenty knots as the bridge crew focused on the trailing vessel. With each minute, the pursuer closed: even at twenty knots the other vessel would overtake *Silversides*.

The skipper ordered his signalman to flash a recognition signal. The approaching vessel failed to answer, charging after *Silversides*. Burlingame ordered his signalman to send a second message. This time the pursuer answered with a green flashing light followed by unidentified characters. The failure to respond in Morse code meant this was no American ship. The skipper ordered the after team to prepare to fire stern torpedoes. The attacker closed to 4,000 yards. Burlingame fired two torpedoes at 3:57 a.m., watching as the first torpedo broke the surface and porpoised before it exploded prematurely 2,000 yards astern. The other torpedo also failed to hit. The enemy continued to close the distance, clawing up the *Silversides'* wake. The skipper had no choice but to dive again and this time rig for depth charges.

The first of four depth charges exploded astern of *Silversides* three minutes later. The sonar watch listened with the headphones for the attacker's propellers as the enemy passed overhead, dropping another barrage of charges that rattled the boat. The attacker then stopped, listening for the submarine 300 feet below. The men on *Silversides* waited for an attack that never came. Burlingame finally ordered *Silversides* up to periscope depth at 6 a.m. The skipper peered through the eyepiece, spotting his attacker illuminated by the dawn light. It wasn't a submarine, but a two-stack destroyer. That explained how it was able to overtake the sub. Burlingame wanted to torpedo the destroyer, but the range was too great. The skipper watched as the destroyer steamed away, vanishing over the horizon.

Exhausted from being up all night, Burlingame retired to his cabin. Lieutenant Robert Worthington swept the horizon with the periscope at 8:56 a.m. No sooner had he finished than a Japanese plane appeared overhead, dropping three bombs. The explosions tossed Burlingame from his bunk. Across the passageway in the wardroom, Platter plunged off the transom to the deck. The explosion shattered every light in the forward and after torpedo rooms as well as the conning tower. Flying glass sliced open sailors while others tumbled out of bed. The attack pried the ship's two barometers off the bulkheads, knocked out the depth gauges, and fried the bridge loudspeaker. The disoriented skipper captured his shock over the violent assault in his report: "I thought the conning tower was being wrenched loose from the pressure hull."

Silversides dove only for Worthington to discover the bow planes had jammed. Sailors struggled to control the submarine's descent as the destroyer returned, dropping four depth charges that shook the boat. Burlingame had no choice but to wait them out. The skipper finally came up for a look at noon. The horizon appeared empty. Rather than risk another surprise attack, Burlingame remained submerged, surfacing after dark to end what the skipper later described as "the most unpleasant day I ever put in."

Burlingame found his humor again when he sat down to write his report:

"The patient convalesced the morning following his amateur appendectomy to the tune of a torpedo firing, two depth charge attacks, two crash dives and an aerial bombing which knocked him out of his bunk on the wardroom transom." The skipper ordered the depth charge alcohol brought out so the crew could celebrate the Silver Lady's survival just hours before Christmas. "We added it to powdered eggs and canned milk," Burlingame wrote, "and with a lot of imagination, it tasted almost like eggnog."

5

DRUM

"Wish I was going to be in a more desirable location for the holidays, but seeing as how I ain't, I just hope we make the best of what we'll have. Get us a carrier or something to celebrate the season with. With no depth charges for a change."

—Eugene Malone,
December 7, 1943, letter

Lieutenant Commander Bernard Francis McMahon woke the morning of December 25, 1942, to the smell of Christmas turkeys roasting in the galley, the largest a twenty-nine-pound bird. The thirty-five-year-old had much to celebrate. Two weeks earlier he had run across a prized target: the 16,700-ton Japanese aircraft carrier *Ryuho*. Workers had hustled to convert the *Ryuho* from its original design as a submarine tender into a carrier when Lieutenant Colonel Jimmy Doolittle's raiders bombed the ship in April. The 707-foot-long carrier had only been commissioned fourteen days before it appeared in McMahon's periscope. The skipper had put a torpedo in its starboard side, watching that morning through his periscope as the carrier rolled so far that he could see the entire flight deck, crowded with dive-bombers. Escorts drove *Drum* down before McMahon could finish off *Ryuho*, but he had sidelined the carrier for months. He would now mock the enemy and celebrate that success over Christmas in the most unlikely of places—just twenty-five miles off the Japanese island of Kyushu.

McMahon had replaced Robert Rice, who skippered the *Drum* for its first three patrols. Rice had followed up his sinking of the seaplane carrier

Mizuho—at the time the largest warship sunk by a submarine—with six more ships for a total tonnage of 33,852. His success had prompted Admiral Chester Nimitz to send a personal note of congratulations to Rice's wife and his father-in-law, Rear Admiral Russell Willson. It wasn't just the brass that lauded Rice. Fellow submariner officer Slade Cutter, destined to become one of the war's top skippers, raved about Rice in a letter to his wife. "Bob Rice did a grand job. His was the most productive patrol yet made," Cutter wrote. "He made the most of his opportunities. I expect him to be one of the most successful of all our skippers."

Unlike Rice, who came from an established New England family, McMahon grew up along Ohio's Lake Erie, surrounded by the Irish and German traditions of his parents. The blue-eyed skipper inherited his father's warmth and gregarious personality and his mother's meticulousness, evaluating decisions on a risk-versus-reward basis. A devout Catholic who loved classical music and opera—particularly Verdi—McMahon enrolled in Ohio University, but quit after a year to work on a lake freighter. He accepted an appointment to the Naval Academy, graduating in 1931 and later marrying his roommate's sister. The five-foot, nine-inch officer had packed on pounds to his then 150-pound frame while his hair had turned a beautiful silver that led his men to dub him the "Great White Father." McMahon was very different from the aristocratic Rice, whom some felt could be intellectually condescending. McMahon was warm, often enjoying games of chess with his officers in the wardroom. His relaxed personality reflected best in his ritual post-attack order: "Take her down, rig for depth charge, and bring me my cigar."

McMahon had inherited a formidable combat machine, thanks in part to the work of Lieutenant Mike Rindskopf, the young gunnery officer just a few years out of the Naval Academy. Ever since the destruction of *Mizuho* that dark May night off Nagoya, Rindskopf had become a fixture in the conning tower. Many of the officers and crew credited *Drum*'s success to his work on the torpedo data computer. The skipper may have given the order to fire, but Rindskopf's calculations made sure the torpedoes hit. Rindskopf had managed to remain focused despite anxiously awaiting news throughout the summer of the birth of his son, Peter, whom he would not meet until after the New Year. "The message came while we were under attack off Truk," he wrote in his unpublished memoir. "Since it was sent once or twice rather than six times as an official message would have been, we failed to receive it." Not until *Drum* moored in Midway in September did Rindskopf receive word. "Son born July twenty five," the message read. "All well."

The good fortune celebrated by Rindskopf and the *Drum's* crew paralleled America's recent victories in the war, victories that promised to make Christmas 1942 better than the previous holiday. Japan's lightning success in the few months following the attack on Pearl Harbor had convinced the nation's leaders of America's weakness. Unlike the United States, with two of its three fleets wrecked, Japan had suffered only the loss of a few destroyers, victims of American submarines. Military and civilian morale boomed. Japanese leaders soon hungered for more conquests, this time to create an outer defensive perimeter. Such a perimeter would help shield Japan from a surprise attack, like Doolittle's April bombing of Tokyo. Japan's first objective: capture Port Moresby along New Guinea's southeastern coast. Control of Port Moresby would allow Japan to rule the skies over northern Australia and New Guinea, endangering America's communications and supply lines with its ally. But Port Moresby was the prelude to a more ambitious goal: the seizure of Midway, the Aleutians, and the total destruction of America's embattled Pacific Fleet.

American intelligence, however, deciphered the plan. Heavy cruisers, destroyers, and the light aircraft carrier *Shoho* would escort about a dozen troop transports to Port Moresby while the larger carriers *Shokaku* and *Zuikaku* would provide cover for the invasion forces. The outgunned American Navy rushed a task force of two aircraft carriers to intercept the Japanese in the Coral Sea, the azure waters off Australia's northeastern coast that are home to the famed Great Barrier Reef. An American search plane pilot spotted the enemy soon after sunrise on May 7—one day after the fall of Corregidor—prompting the carriers *Yorktown* and *Lexington* to launch torpedo and dive-bombers. Pilots soon zeroed in on *Shoho* as Japanese fighters struggled to repel the attack. Thirteen bombs and seven torpedoes capsized and sank the 11,262-ton carrier in just fifteen minutes. A *Lexington* dive-bomber leader crackled over the ship's radio receivers and loudspeakers, summing up the loss of Japan's first carrier of the war with three words that brought cheers to the crew: "Scratch one flattop!"

The battle intensified the next morning when Japanese and American planes bombarded one another. American dive-bombers scored several hits on the *Shokaku*—a veteran of the attack on Pearl Harbor—that started gasoline fires and damaged the flight deck, preventing the carrier from launching planes. A Japanese bomb in turn tore through *Yorktown's* flight deck and detonated below, killing forty sailors and seriously injuring twenty-six others, several of whom later died. Two torpedoes ripped open the port side of *Lexington* while several dive-bomb hits set the carrier ablaze. Crews who only a day earlier had celebrated the destruction of *Shoho* fought to save the Lady Lex. A violent gasoline vapor explosion at 12:47 p.m. rocked the 33,000-ton carrier. Other explosions followed. At 5:07 p.m. the skipper had no choice but order the *Lexington* abandoned. Men lowered the injured into lifeboats while others climbed down ropes to waiting rafts. American ships rescued 2,735 sailors before the destroyer *Phelps* sent the *Lexington* under the waves at dusk with several torpedoes to prevent it from falling into enemy hands.

The Battle of the Coral Sea had proven costly for both sides, but the United States had succeeded in repelling Japan's invasion force. America's success demonstrated that while the Pearl Harbor attack had dealt a significant blow, it was not a knockout punch. The United States had not only benefited from the fortuitous absence of its aircraft carriers at Pearl Harbor, but from the failure of Japanese leaders to order a second strike. Japan had anticipated the loss of as many as three of its six carriers at Pearl Harbor, but the attack had cost it just twenty-nine planes, five midget submarines, and fewer than 100 men. Japanese commanders should have capitalized on that success and ordered pilots to return to the carriers that Sunday morning, rearm, and attack again, spreading the assault over two days. Japan's shortsighted focus on only warships and planes as opposed to the fuel tanks, repair shops, and submarine base allowed America to rebound. The wrecked battleships that littered the oily waters of Hawaii represented a bygone era in a war where battlefields stretched into the heavens and beneath the waves.

Japanese Admiral Isoroku Yamamoto, Combined Fleet commander and architect of the Pearl Harbor attack, saw the seizure of Midway as an opportunity to rectify some of those mistakes. The five-foot, three-inch admiral, who weighed no more than 130 pounds, had studied at Harvard and later served as a naval attaché in Washington. He feared the long-term threat the United States posed to Japan. Yamamoto had watched the celebration that followed Japan's initial successes with horror. "We are far from being able to relax at this stage," Yamamoto wrote to a colleague. "I only wish that they had had, say, three carriers at Hawaii."

The failures at Pearl Harbor and the loss in the Coral Sea only increased the importance of victory at Midway. The two-and-a-half-square-mile atoll made up of two main islands—the largest barely more than a thousand acres—poked only a few feet above the Pacific's blue swells some 1,100 miles northwest of Pearl Harbor. The austere atoll named for its location midway across the Pacific had served as a stopover in the 1930s for weekly transpacific flights of Pan American Airways Clipper seaplane before tensions with Japan prompted the United States to convert the outpost into a naval air station on the eve of the war. Yamamoto's top priority was to destroy America's carriers, which the Doolittle raid had shown could still threaten Japan. The strategic atoll's proximity to Hawaii guaranteed that the United States would have no choice but rush its carriers into battle—and Japan would be ready. Yamamoto knew time was running out: if Japan didn't destroy the Pacific Fleet soon, America's wartime production could make the nation unstoppable.

Japan planned an armada of some 200 ships, including eight carriers, eleven battleships, twenty-three cruisers, and sixty-five destroyers. America in contrast could muster only seventy-six ships, including the aircraft carriers *Enterprise, Hornet,* and *Yorktown,* the latter still damaged from battle in the Coral Sea. More than 1,400 workers at Pearl Harbor had knocked what should have been a ninety-day repair job down to just two days. What America lacked in warships it made up for in intelligence. Cryptanalysts had unraveled much of Japan's plan, which called for dividing its armada into four major task forces. The first would strike north in the Aleutians, a move that would expand Japan's perimeter as well as distract American leaders from the larger objective. A strike group of four carriers would then pound Midway followed by an invasion force of some 5,000 troops. Submarines lurking between Hawaii and Midway would ambush the Pacific Fleet as it charged to defend the atoll while Yamamoto's main force of seven battleships would obliterate any survivors.

Nimitz's plan in contrast proved much simpler: hunker down and defend Midway. The Battle of the Coral Sea, fought solely in the skies, solidified the value of carriers. The aerial brawl had robbed Japan of the use of two of its flattops, the damaged *Shokaku* and the *Zuikaku,* which had suffered heavy pilot and aircraft losses. Despite the overwhelming size and diversity of Japan's armada, the Midway offensive would center on its strike group of four carriers, the tip of the spear. While Japan boasted one more flattop than the United States, the carrier air strength of each nation proved an almost even match. But Nimitz had more than carriers—he had Midway, dubbed an "unsinkable aircraft carrier." The Army, Navy, and Marines crowded the tiny atoll's airfield with some 115 bombers and fighters. Japan did not expect America's carriers to be present at the start of the battle, an opportunity Nimitz could exploit. The admiral ordered his carriers to steam northeast of the strategic atoll, a position outside the enemy's search range that would allow America to ambush the Japanese en route to Midway.

Heavy fog and clouds shielded the enemy strike force from the American search planes that droned in the skies overhead, audible to the sailors on the carriers below. Not until the morning of June 3 did a Navy seaplane spot the approaching invasion force 700 miles from Midway. America scrambled bombers and seaplanes to attack, but managed to damage only a tanker in the predawn hours of June 4. Japanese forces continued to advance through the dark toward Midway, launching more than 100 fighters, torpedo, and dive-bombers before sunrise to attack the atoll. Enemy planes closed to ninety-three miles when radar operators on Midway detected the incoming air strike. Marine fighters outnumbered as much as four to one rose up to intercept the attackers, but fell victim to the superior Japanese Zeros. Enemy bombers unleashed on the island at 6:30 a.m., destroying fuel tanks, the Marine command post, and the power plant on Easter Island. Storehouses and the atoll's hospital burned while the destruction of the aviation fuel system would require future fuelings to be done by hand.

Midway-based bombers that had lifted off moments before the attack on the atoll descended upon the carriers only for the Japanese to destroy wave after wave of the American planes. Japanese Vice Admiral Chuici Nagumo, commander of the carrier strike force, had held back ninety-three airplanes, armed with torpedoes and bombs, to attack ships. Since Japanese forces believed America's carriers remained in Hawaii, the admiral ordered his reserve planes rearmed with incendiary and fragment bombs for another strike against Midway, which had put up more resistance than expected. A search plane then reported about ten American ships to the northeast. The news stunned Nagumo, who had not expected to find any warships. He canceled his order at 7:45 a.m. and demanded his planes again rearm to attack ships. A follow-up report at 8:09 a.m. stated that American forces consisted of five cruisers and five destroyers. Nagumo's concerns subsided at the report of no carriers. He could blast the ships after he wiped out Midway's airpower. But then the news worsened for him eleven minutes later.

The search plane had spotted a flattop.

Two battleships, three cruisers, and eleven destroyers guarded the four Japanese carriers that steamed in two columns. Admiral Nagumo on his flagship carrier the *Akagi* ordered his forces to turn ninety degrees to the left to find and destroy the enemy's ships as crews hustled to rearm and refuel planes. Unknown to the Japanese admiral, planes streaked toward him. American leaders had gambled that Nagumo would organize a second attack on Midway and had ordered a strike, hoping to catch his carriers off guard. Nagumo's course change forced *Hornet*'s fighters and dive-bombers to zoom past the carriers, but not the torpedo bombers. Japanese antiaircraft fire thundered and Zeros swooped down on the defenseless bombers, destroying all fifteen planes. The Japanese next shredded most of *Enterprise*'s fourteen unescorted torpedo bombers followed by twelve from *Yorktown*. The aerial slaughterhouse had cost America thirty-seven out of the forty-one torpedo bombers and had failed to score a single hit. Japanese victory appeared certain—until the dive-bombers arrived.

A straggling Japanese destroyer had led some three dozen dive-bombers straight to the enemy strike force. Japanese fighters had dropped down to target the low-flying American torpedo bombers, leaving the skies unguarded against the dive-bombers that now zeroed in on the Japanese carriers at 10:25 a.m. A bomb hit Nagumo's flagship on the rear rim of the amidships elevator. Another either hit or grazed the after edge of *Akagi*'s flight deck. Fuel and munitions exploded, rocking the 34,364-ton carrier as black smoke flooded the passageways. Captain Mitsuo Fuchida, who had led the air attack on Pearl Harbor six months earlier, served as commander of *Akagi*'s air group. Grounded at Midway because of an attack of appendicitis, the veteran pilot captured the chaos of the attack on the *Akagi*. "There was a huge hole in the flight deck behind the amidship elevator," Fuchida would later write. "The elevator itself, twisted like molten glass, was dropping into the hangar. Deck plates reeled upward in grotesque configuration. Planes stood tail up, belching livid flame and jet-black smoke."

Akagi wasn't the only victim. American planes dove on the 33,693-ton carrier *Kaga*, hitting it with at least four bombs that devastated the bridge, killed the skipper, and set the ship ablaze. *Soryu* turned into the wind to launch fighters. Lookouts scanned the skies as dive-bombers punched through the clouds. Three bombs tore into the carrier. The 18,800-ton flattop erupted in flames and came dead in the water. Within a span of barely six minutes American planes had set three of Japan's carriers ablaze, the tip of the spear blunted. Admiral Nagumo had watched the catastrophic attacks unfold from the bridge of the battered *Akagi*. Black smoke clouded the skies over his wounded carriers. Nagumo's chief of staff urged the reluctant admiral to escape and set up his headquarters on the light cruiser *Nagara*. Nagumo finally caved at 10:46 a.m. Fires blocked the passages below and tickled the bridge, forcing the fifty-five-year-old admiral to climb out of a forward window and down a rope. A boat from *Nagara* pulled alongside *Akagi* to retrieve Nagumo. Escorts moved in to protect *Hiryu*, Japan's one undamaged flattop and last hope for victory.

Hiryu turned into the wind and launched six fighters and eighteen dive-bombers. Enemy pilots trailed the American planes home. Radar operators on *Yorktown* picked up the incoming air strike at a range of forty-six miles. Airborne fighters raced to intercept the Japanese as sailors on *Yorktown* scrambled to prepare for the attack. Crews closed and secured all compartments, drained fuel lines, and ditched an 8,000-gallon tank of aviation fuel in the sea. American fighters pounced on the enemy bombers and antiaircraft fire thundered across the sea. Sailors on *Yorktown* watched Japanese planes fall from the sky on fire. Some of the bombers slipped past and dove to attack *Yorktown*, releasing bombs at just 500 feet. Three hits rocked the carrier, sparking multiple fires and disabling some of the boilers. Crews had the damage under control when enemy torpedo planes arrived, ripping two holes in her port side. *Yorktown* lost all power and rolled twenty-six degrees. Afraid the carrier would capsize, the skipper ordered the ship abandoned.

But the battle was not over.

Just moments before the torpedo attack on the *Yorktown*, an American search plane had spotted Japan's lone remaining carrier. Two dozen dive-bombers roared off the *Enterprise*. Hidden by the afternoon sun, the planes dove, landing four hits on the 20,250-ton *Hiryu* that set the flattop ablaze. All four of Japan's carriers had been hit. The skipper of the burning *Soryu* refused to abandon ship. Sword in hand he sang Japan's national anthem before the carrier sank at dusk with 718 officers and crew. *Kaga* vanished minutes later along with some 800 men. Japanese destroyers torpedoed the crippled *Akagi*, sending Nagumo's former flagship to the bottom moments before sunrise on June 5. *Hiryu* suffered a similar fate several hours later. Before it slipped under the seas around 8:20 a.m. carrier division commander Rear Admiral Tamon Yamaguchi rallied his men, taking responsibility for the loss of *Soryu* and *Hiryu*. "I shall remain on board to the end," he announced. "I command all of you to leave the ship and continue your loyal service to His Majesty, the Emperor."

Yorktown in contrast refused to sink. The skipper along with twenty-nine officers and 141 crewmen returned at dawn on June 6 to salvage the abandoned carrier. Five destroyers circled the wounded flattop to guard against enemy submarines while the *Hammann* moored alongside to supply pumps, water, and electricity. Crews extinguished the fire in the forward rag storeroom and dropped several airplanes overboard on the port side along with a five-inch gun, measures that by around noon had helped reduce the list some two degrees. The Japanese submarine *I-168* slipped through the destroyer screen that afternoon and fired four torpedoes. Two fish ripped into *Yorktown* while another broke *Hammann*'s back, sending the destroyer and eighty-one men down in just four minutes. The other destroyers hunted the Japanese submarine while the salvage party vacated the crippled flattop. In the predawn hours of June 7, sailors on the destroyers lowered flags to half-staff as *Yorktown* capsized around dawn and sank in some 3,000 fathoms, the battle flags still flying.

Midway had proven a success for American carriers, but a wash for the submarine service. Normally tasked to hunt Japanese merchant ships, Midway represented the first time submarines had supported a major fleet battle. Of the twenty-nine boats based at Pearl Harbor, the Navy ordered twenty-five to help defend the coral atoll. This motley crew included six submarines that had never made a war patrol plus eight that had just returned in need of repairs. In preparation for the Japanese attack, the Navy divided the submarines into several groups. The Navy directed the first group of twelve submarines to patrol off Midway. A second group of three submarines—dubbed the "roving short-stops"—would stalk the waters between Midway and Hawaii while a group of four others would patrol 300 miles north of Oahu, an insurance policy against a possible diversionary strike on Pearl Harbor. The Navy directed six submarines returning from patrol, including *Drum*, to intercept the Japanese fleet in retreat.

The submarine force's potential big break came when the skipper of *Nautilus*—alerted via radio of a damaged flattop—spotted smoke on the horizon at 10:29 a.m. on June 4, just minutes after American bombers dove on Japan's carriers. Lieutenant Commander William Brockman, Jr., hungry to get in on the fight, closed the distance, spotting a burning carrier. Brockman identified the wounded flattop as *Soryu*, following repeated checks to guarantee the carrier was not American. The skipper fired three fish that afternoon—a fourth proved unsuccessful—and watched the wakes race across the water. All three fish ripped into the carrier—or so Brockman believed. Postwar analysis would show not only had he misidentified the carrier—he fired on *Kaga*, not *Soryu*—but that his first two fish missed. The third glanced off *Kaga*'s steel hull and broke in half. The torpedo's warhead plunged to the bottom while the air flask floated serving, ironically, as a life preserver for several enemy sailors.

One of the submarine force's few contributions in the battle proved unintentional. Lookouts on the *Tambor* spotted multiple large ships eighty-nine miles off Midway at 2:15 a.m. on June 5. Afraid the ships might be American, the skipper opted to shadow them, firing off a contact report. Lieutenant Commander John Murphy had intercepted four Japanese heavy cruisers and two destroyers tasked to bombard the coral atoll. New Japanese orders arrived—as Murphy tracked the warships—canceling the attack. Soon after the cruisers turned to the northwest, Japanese lookouts spotted the surfaced *Tambor*. The warships executed evasive turns to port, but in the confusion that followed the *Mogami* charged into the *Mikuma*. The glancing blow ruptured a *Mikuma* fuel tank and crushed *Mogami*'s bow. Murphy identified the wounded ships as Japanese, but he struggled to set up a shot and never fired. Carrier-based planes later pounced on the crippled cruisers, scoring six hits on *Mogami* and sending *Mikuma* to the bottom.

But the destruction of *Mikuma* had come at a big price. Murphy's initial contact report stated that he had spotted "many unidentified ships." While the skipper noted the position of the ships, he had failed to report a course. Senior leaders concluded that Japanese invasion forces would soon land on

Midway, deploying America's carriers north of the atoll and ordering all submarines to form a defensive line just a few miles offshore. Not until some four hours later did Murphy fire off a second report, identifying the ships he spotted and noting that the injured cruisers were steaming west. While American ships had hustled to prepare for an invasion, Yamamoto's embattled forces steamed another 100 miles west. Searches that morning by Midway-based planes consumed several more hours—as Japan's forces escaped west at about twenty-five miles an hour—only to confirm the absence of an invasion force. *Tambor*'s vague report had squandered America's chance to pummel Japan's retreating forces.

Midway had cost America the *Yorktown*, but the loss to Japan proved far greater: four of its best carriers and some 250 planes. Combined Fleet Commander Admiral Yamamoto gathered with his staff on the battleship *Yamato*. Despite his superiority in numbers Yamamoto knew that without air cover the battle was over. "But how can we apologize to His Majesty for this defeat?" one officer lamented. "Leave that to me," Yamamoto said. "I am the only one who must apologize to His Majesty." The decisive June 1942 battle would halt Japan's eastward expansion and help tilt the balance of power toward the United States, a realization captured by Yamamoto's chief of staff. "How brilliant was the first stage operation up to April! And what miserable setbacks since Midway in June," Vice Admiral Matome Ugaki would write in his diary at the close of 1942. "The invasions of Hawaii, Fiji, Samoa, and New Caldonia, liberation of India, and destruction of the British Far Eastern Fleet have all scattered like dreams."

America's submarine offensive in contrast had suffered a slower start, in part because of the failure of torpedoes. Since the opening shots of the war, skippers had griped that the fish malfunctioned. The submarine *Sargo*, departing Manila for its first patrol within hours of the attack on Pearl Harbor, had served as the canary in the mine, executing eight attacks in the waters off Indochina only to record thirteen straight misses. Similar problems had plagued *Drum*'s early patrols. The analytical Rindskopf in assisting with *Drum*'s third patrol report went so far as to create a chart, illustrating the duds, premature explosions, and unexplained misses. Out of twenty-three torpedoes fired, his chart showed nine malfunctioned. "Not one of the attacks was hasty; not one was fired from extreme range or from a poor initial position," Rice wrote in his report. "No one likes to blame his tools. I cannot but feel that we accomplished only half of what we earned, and even a smaller fraction of what we were capable of doing."

Rather than investigate the problem, the Bureau of Ordnance blamed the skippers. But Rear Admiral Lockwood refused to shrug off the complaints as simple poor marksmanship. Too many skippers described setting up the perfect shot only to watch the torpedo's trail of bubbles run right under a target and fail to detonate. Lockwood and his staff feared there was only one answer—the fish ran too deep to trigger the magnetic exploder. As boats returned from patrol—*Salmon, Triton, Grenadier, Gudgeon*, and *Skipjack*—the evidence mounted. Morale plummeted as skippers questioned themselves. A few even quit. America's long retreat from the Philippines had temporarily prevented the submarine force from probing the problem, so as soon as Lockwood had unpacked in Australia he set out to solve the crisis. A submarine without torpedoes was as worthless as an aircraft carrier without planes. America was spending too much money and risking too many lives on a weapon that apparently wasn't working.

Lockwood had turned to his trusted chief of staff, Captain James Fife, Jr. The forty-five-year-old Nevada native—and member of the Naval Academy's class of 1918, though the class actually graduated in June 1917 because of the outbreak of the Great War—had a reputation as a dogmatic hard worker and teetotaler. Fife's rigorous style had earned the respect though not always the adoration of his men. "There is a difference," one of his subordinate officers later noted, "between love and respect." Lockwood needed just such a man for this job. Fife knew he had no choice but test a torpedo. The western Australian town of Albany boasted sandy white beaches that from the air looked like snow, a perfect spot to beach a torpedo. All Fife needed was a net—a very large one. Unable to find a net for sale he hired four Portuguese fishermen to fashion one. Lastly, to replicate an actual war shot meant Fife couldn't use an exercise warhead filled with water because its buoyancy differed from the negative buoyancy of a live warhead. Fife and his team improvised, weighting a dummy warhead with a calcium chloride solution.

The men had planned the test for June 20. *Skipjack* torpedomen set the fish to run at a depth of ten feet. With the net in place in Frenchman's Bay, Lieutenant Commander James Coe fired at a distance of 850 yards. The divers' inspection of the net showed that the torpedo had actually run at twenty-five feet, more than double its depth setting. The test continued the next day. *Skipjack* torpedomen set the first fish to run again at ten feet. This one sliced through the net at a depth of eighteen feet. Crews set the second torpedo to run on the surface only for the divers to discover that it pierced the net at eleven feet. Further inspection of the beached torpedo indicated that the fish had actually hit the bottom in sixty feet of water on its initial deep dive out of the tube. The rudimentary test proved that the skippers were right: the fish ran an average of eleven feet too deep. Lockwood and his men fumed. "Here we had this magnificent submarine and we had slipped on the torpedo," Fife recalled. "We had an ineffective torpedo—it was worse than ineffective."

Fixing the run depth magnified other problems, including premature detonations. Such blasts just a few hundred yards into a torpedo's run rattled the crew and ruined the element of surprise, giving a target precious seconds to evade. Escorts used the blasts to home in on the submarine's position and depth-charge the boat. The problem was not as pronounced when torpedoes ran deep, but the turbulent water close to the surface triggered the sensitive exploders. In addition to premature detonations, skippers reported a rise in duds. One watched a fish hit the side of a ship and shoot up out of the water. Lockwood again searched for a remedy. A torpedo fired into a cliff off Hawaii revealed that the firing pin failed to hit the primer with enough force to detonate. The Navy next filled warheads with concrete instead of explosive Torpex, then dropped them ninety feet onto a steel plate, a height designed to replicate a torpedo's force when striking a ship's hull. Out of the ten warheads dropped, seven failed to detonate.

The problems with the Navy's torpedo would stretch on for much of the first two years of the war. Proof of flaws that Lockwood and his staff confirmed in June 1942 buoyed morale. Despite the technical problems that marred the first year, the force had enjoyed some success. Submarines sank 147 ships greater than 500 tons—*Silversides* and *Drum* destroyed ten—and damaged fifty-six others. Skippers fired 1,442 fish in 1942, a number that would more than triple when the force reached its peak strength two years later. Submarine bases had now opened at Midway, Dutch Harbor, and Kodiak and a refueling station at Johnston Island, more than 800 miles southwest of Hawaii. Thirty-seven new fleet boats had reported to Pearl Harbor—an average of about one every other week—since the war's outbreak, bringing America's total fleet boats and World War I–era boats to about ninety. The war to date had cost America eight submarines, a small fraction of the number the conflict would ultimately claim.

Against the backdrop of America's success, McMahon and his crew prepared to celebrate on board the *Drum*. This would prove the first Christmas away from home for many young submariners, while for others it would be the first of several before the war would finally end. Many had learned to handle the long absences from wives, parents, and loved ones by refocusing their priorities. At sea the mission—and only the mission—mattered; its safe conclusion the ticket home. Twenty-four-year-old Lieutenant Ira Dye, Jr., captured that sentiment in a letter days earlier to his wife back home in Seattle. "These patrols sort of do something to a man," he wrote. "For the first week or so, you are in fairly friendly waters, so there is no mental strain. Also, the memories of civilization are very fresh. This seems to make everyone sort of lonesome, wishing for the beach. After a week or so, however, when the strain is on, & the work intensifies, we sort of forget about civilization—how good the one-&-only girl looked, how good that beer tasted, how good it was to sleep in the morning, etc."

Dye and his shipmates were not alone this holiday. Some 1.7 million American service members would spend Christmas 1942 overseas in sixty-five different countries and islands, from the sweltering jungles of New Guinea and the arid deserts of North Africa to Greenland's frozen glaciers. The war had now raged for 383 days and had touched most lives, including that of President Roosevelt, who would celebrate Christmas without any of his five children. The president's four sons—all in the armed forces—served around the world. Travel restrictions barred his daughter from making the trip east from her home in Seattle. The war translated into more than just empty seats at dinner tables. Rationing forced schoolchildren to bake sugarless holiday cookies while tinsel and Christmas trees proved scarce, the latter the result of the loss of manpower and railcars to ship them. The president refused even to light the White House tree in a move to save power as the War Production Board urged families to collect waste fat from ducks, geese, and turkeys that could be converted into medical supplies and gunpowder.

But none of these wartime measures—or the thousands of miles—could dampen the Christmas spirit off the coast of Japan. *Drum* executive officer Lieutenant Commander Nicholas Nicholas had planned ahead, packing a box of holiday decorations. Nicholas had broken out his yuletide bounty and recruited volunteers just a few days earlier. Within a few hours the men had re-decorated the crew's mess and wardroom with red and green streamers, silver bells, and even imitation holly. Nicholas topped it off with Santa Claus masks. "We can hardly eat," Dye wrote in a letter, "without getting tinsel in our tea." *Drum*'s speakers this holiday morning belted out "Jingle Bells" and "White Christmas"—as well as the out-of-season "Good Friday" from the Wagner opera *Parsifal*—while the warm smell of roast turkey, gravy, and vegetables permeated the boat. The ship's unofficial calendar—designed and illustrated by crewmembers—captured the holiday. "Christmas Day is here at last," the calendar stated. "We're fighting for the right to remember the past."

A noontime sonar check and periscope scan of the horizon revealed a sea void of warships, patrol planes, or even sampans. The skipper gave the order and *Drum* slipped down to 150 feet. Christmas had finally arrived. The executive officer played Santa Claus and passed out presents that consisted of small games and noisemakers such as rattles and whistles. "The boat was a madhouse," Dye wrote. "We all kept pretty good faces. What with frequent 'Merry Christmases' to each other, the collective spirits stayed up pretty well." The men then feasted, the sumptuous meal followed by the skipper's favorite, cigars. "It was as if the war had taken a brief recess," Dye concluded. "An hour's interlude of hometown America, just off the enemy's coast."

6

SILVERSIDES

"You said it yourself that when a person's time comes it don't make much difference where they are."

—Gordon Cox,
May 5, 1942, letter

Lieutenant Commander John Starr Coye, Jr., paced the bridge of *Silversides* as the submarine departed Brisbane at 9 a.m. on July 21, 1943. Coye had taken command the day before from Burlingame, a soon to be promoted division commander destined to spend the remainder of the war in Australia and New Guinea to help train others. Burlingame's junior by six years, Coye felt incredible pressure to succeed. Skippers typically commanded a submarine for several patrols before the Navy reassigned them; Burlingame skippered *Silversides* for five, the maximum allowed before the Navy mandated a stateside break to oversee the completion of a new sub or up to a year in a noncombat job. Burlingame had traveled some 34,777 miles on patrols in the waters off Japan, New Ireland, and the Caroline and Solomon islands, firing a total of sixty-five torpedoes. Postwar records show that he sank eight confirmed ships with a combined tonnage of 46,865. He damaged no fewer than ten others, helping to make *Silversides* one of the top performing submarines of the war. The man who had once struggled to become a sailor walked off the *Silversides* with three Navy Crosses, two Silver Stars, and a strong start toward a Presidential Unit Citation.

Burlingame's men adored him. The aggressive skipper had taken a submarineful of boys and made them warriors. He had sipped whiskey with trembling sailors after depth charge attacks, belted out folksongs in the wardroom, and swam with them in the cool waters off the Royal Hawaiian, the Waikiki hotel the Navy leased as a rest camp. With the exception of the loss of Mike Harbin, Burlingame had brought them all home safe, a great feat, as the Navy counted sixteen submarines lost in the first year and a half of the war. Many in the crew had come to revere the bearded Burlingame like a father. "As a man and skipper, there'll never be any finer," John Bienia said in a letter to his wife. "That's just the way the crew feel about him." Executive officer Robert Worthington, who had replaced Davenport as the ship's second in command, echoed Bienia in a letter of his own. "He'll always be the *Silversides'* skipper to us," he wrote. "He belonged to us and we to him." That affection was reflected in the message engraved on the back of the $150 watch the crew presented Burlingame as a farewell gift: "TO THE BEST DAMN SKIPPER ANYWHERE."

Coye had his work cut out for him.

Not only did the new skipper follow a popular and successful leader, but he did so with no real combat record of his own, a fact not lost on his battle-tested crew. The California native had commanded only one vessel prior to *Silversides*, the World War I–era *R-18*. Coye's aged submarine had hunted German U-boats off Bermuda after the war broke out, but failed to spot a single one despite several patrols. He landed in June 1943 in Australia on the staff of Commodore James Fife, Lockwood's trusted former chief of staff and now the commander of a submarine task force. The ambitious Coye recognized his relative inexperience and worked to remedy it as he waited for an assignment. He studied the reports of successful runs and interrogated veteran skippers fresh off patrol. The Navy had planned to ease Coye into Pacific combat by first sending him out with a seasoned skipper, a plan soon scuttled by a shortage of captains. Coye would now have to go it alone. "Burlingame was a hard man to follow," he would later confess. "He was a dynamic leader, and the crew all loved him."

Coye was about the same height as his predecessor, but the similarities between the men stopped there. The big-shouldered Coye grew up the son of Christian Scientists in a home dedicated to education and the arts. His father had studied at the prestigious Massachusetts Institute of Technology and worked as a chemist. Coye's mother was a professional pianist who played the organ for silent films. The rugged blue-eyed Coye acquired her talent, studying at the selective Curtis Institute of Music and under the tutelage of the solo clarinetist in the Philadelphia Orchestra. His thoughtful mother later presented him a leather-bound journal in which she had copied a quotation each day for a year from her favorite poets, including Robert Browning, Ralph Waldo Emerson, and Henry Van Dyke. "Jack dear," she wrote inside. "Mother compiled this long ago. It gave her pleasure, and it would make her still happier if these sentiments and truths find echo in your own thoughts and life."

Coye's personality reflected an equal dose of each parent, strengths he would use to his success when he arrived at the Naval Academy in 1929. The Great Depression that wrecked the economy and ruined families placed a premium on the service academy's free education. Former president of his high school national honor society, Coye joined some of the nation's top minds on the banks of the Severn River. The class of 1933, Coye would later note with pride, would go on to produce the academy's all-time highest percentage of admirals. With curly brown hair and smooth manners that earned him the nickname "DeCoye," the practical jokester proved a solid student in the classroom, graduating 123 out of 432. But the rigid academy failed to break Coye's chief flaw, one that helped him earn forty-one demerits his senior year and a jab in his yearbook bio. "Tardiness is Jack's greatest weakness," his peers wrote in the *Lucky Bag*. "His record of demerits would be as follows: Late formation, Absent formation, Late returning from hop, Late falling in with watch squad, etc."

With thick forearms and strong hands, Coye had boxed under legendary coach Hamilton "Spike" Webb. Though he often joked that he served as "cannon fodder" for more talented boxers, Coye developed quick reflexes that had twice saved him and his submarine. The first calamity occurred in September 1940 when he served as the diving and engineering officer on *Shark*, a Porpoise class submarine that later became the fourth boat lost in the war. During maneuvers with the aircraft carrier *Yorktown* off Honolulu, *Shark* surfaced but the skipper could see only gray through the periscope. He ordered the submarine to dive deep but not before the 19,800-ton carrier tore the shears off at bridge level and flooded the forward battery compartment, a dangerous scenario as saltwater in the cells can generate poisonous chlorine gas. Planesmen struggled to control the submarine—heavy from the flood of seawater—which now plummeted toward the bottom. Coye immediately blew the ballast tanks and forced the crippled *Shark* to the surface, earning a letter of commendation.

Coye garnered a second commendation letter as the skipper of *R-18*, which he dubbed a "pile of rust" after a crewman put a chipping hammer right through the hull. Coye stood on the bridge shortly before dawn one morning as the submarine cruised in a designated safe lane toward Bermuda. The morning light illuminated a friendly Navy plane high above, barreling down on them. Orders barred pilots from bombing submarines inside the safe lane, but just a few months into the war—and with the nation on edge—the cautious Coye still worried. *R-18* flew an American flag from the periscope for identification, but the skipper went further, ordering his signalman to fire a recognition flare. The plane continued straight for them. Coye cleared the bridge and dove just as the plane dropped a depth bomb. The violent explosion flooded the forward trim tanks, knocked out the lights and circuit breakers, and even rattled the needles off the depth gauge. The skipper and his crew fought to save *R-18* and later limped into port, to find the Navy already had given them up for dead.

Coye often quipped that his salvation boiled down to simple good luck though the sailors who served under him attributed it to judgment and keen intellect. He knew when—and more importantly, when not—to take risks. Unlike the gregarious Burlingame who shunned the Navy's rigidity, Coye embraced it, a polished professional more like a corporate executive than a salty sailor. He pushed aside his predecessor's impulsive and instinctive style in favor of an analytical approach to submarine warfare that emphasized thoughtful tactics utilizing a submarine's inherent strengths. He preferred to attack at night—even if it meant trailing a convoy all day or longer—to guarantee the perfect kill shot. When attacking a convoy, Coye would save the coal burners for last, as the black smoke that clouded the horizon made them easy targets to spot for miles. "He was a magnificent leader," recalled Eugene Malone, an officer. "He was not a warrior leader. He was a cool, calm, and analytical leader. He used his head and not his emotions. He did not want to be a hero; he wanted to be successful."

On a personal level, Coye appeared reserved and stoic, reluctant to open up and share his emotions, much to the frustration at times of his wife and children. He chose instead to focus on what he viewed as practical matters: cars, ships, and the Navy. His wife, Betty, had given birth in September 1939 to twins—a boy and a girl—who sadly lived just twenty-four hours in a Honolulu hospital. Their deaths would haunt Coye's wife for the rest of her life. In his unpublished sixty-eight-page memoir, written for family and a handful of close friends, Coye refused even then to open up about the loss, logging the tragedy but without sharing any hint of the emotional toll it took on him. Even at sea with depth charges exploding, Coye never voiced anxiety. Instead he burped to break the tension. The one love he spoke of was the Navy, which he viewed as an "inviolate, almost holy institution." Coye made that clear to his oldest daughter when she returned home one day with several balls she had snatched off a Navy baseball field. Coye spanked her, the only time she ever recalled. "Don't ever steal anything from the U.S. Navy," he scolded her. "It is government property."

Coye's quiet disguised the fact that he was calculating and viewed the world in black and white. Decisions not supported by available facts he trusted to luck, which manifested itself in a Mexican coin he pocketed throughout the war, a superstitious token reminiscent of Burlingame's Buddha. The *Silversides'* new skipper would need both good wits and fortune if he hoped to sink ships and bring his men home alive. He knew that would require that he first gain the respect of the crew, which soon tagged the pudgy skipper with the friendly nickname "Baggy Pants." Executive officer Worthington had been on board from the beginning. Coye planned to lean on him. Following on the heels of the beloved Burlingame, the skipper knew that to be overly assertive and make immediate changes would only invite resentment, something he could not afford. "I made up my mind that this was a successful submarine and that if we were to continue, that I would try to mold myself to the way the crew was doing things," Coye recalled. "I didn't change very much of the routine at all."

Brisbane vanished in *Silversides'* wake. Officers and crew had enjoyed the twenty-day refit in eastern Australia, a welcome return to civilization after a year and a half of war. The combat-weary sailors drank often and too much, dancing the Gypsy trot at the two-shilling town hall dance and nursing headaches in the mornings over greasy breakfasts of steaks and French fries. Burlingame had spent the first night unwinding with his men but then vanished until the end of the rest period, probably off, as one officer noted, in a "tooth and nail battle with some cork and bottle." Inebriated Lieutenant j.g. L. J. Gibson got arrested one night at a club and was hauled back to the submarine tender, where he told off the officer, broke free, and tried to swim ashore. Authorities hospitalized the belligerent sailor for forty-eight hours to check his sanity. The unruly nighttime behavior of Gibby and others earned *Silversides* a poor reputation with the local authorities. That crystallized one night when several military police officers dropped three drunken sailors down the submarine's after battery hatch. John Bienia, the officer on duty that night, protested.

"This is the *Silversides*, isn't it?" the officer asked.

"Yes," Bienia replied.

"Well, here are some drunken sailors for you."

The only problem, Bienia pointed out: these weren't *Silversides* sailors.

With the submarine slicing through the blue water, the officers and crew now focused on the mission ahead, a patrol around the Solomon Islands, the Bismarcks, and New Guinea with operations to be controlled by dispatch. Coye and his crew spent six days at sea practicing night approaches, deep dives, and wolf pack exercises with the submarines *Tuna* and *Growler*, using the 1,800-ton submarine rescue ship *Coucal* as a target. The maneuvers allowed Coye to learn the rhythm of the *Silversides*, a tough task he discovered one day while up on the bridge when the klaxon sounded. The lookouts and bridge personnel dropped through the hatch into the conning tower. The last man down yanked the hatch closed and sealed it as a rush of water flooded the ballast tanks and started the submarine down. Lieutenant Tom Keegan scanned the faces of the men crowded inside the cramped conning tower. The communications officer noticed that *Silversides* appeared one man short. That man was Coye.

"Surface," Keegan screamed. "Surface!"

The men on watch, startled by the change of orders, suddenly froze, a terrible time to do so, as the submarine could dive in less than forty seconds. Veteran John Bienia, the chief engineer and diving officer, took over. He ordered the vents closed and blew compressed air into the main ballast tanks. The submarine's dive halted and *Silversides* returned to the surface. "We came up fast enough so that the Captain—who had a nice cool swim in view—didn't even get his shoes wet," Bienia wrote in a letter to his wife. "After he came down and bawled the hatch closer out, Tom also lit into the poor sailor and told him that if he ever locked the Captain out again on a dive, the Captain would begin to think that we didn't want him aboard. Anyway, we all laughed after it was over, and the Captain is really fast now jumping down the hatch—so fast that he mashed Don's fingers on the next dive. I guess the moral behind that episode could be: 'time, tide, and a diving sub wait for no man.'"

At 4 a.m. on July 28, *Silversides* with Coye in command finally headed back into battle. Topped off with 15,900 gallons of diesel from the *Coucal*, the submarine covered more than 500 miles over the next few days before a puff of smoke appeared on the horizon at 7:15 a.m. on July 31. Coye's first target. The mast of the lead ship came over the horizon seventeen minutes later at a range of about four miles. The skipper ordered the submerged *Silversides* to chase. The sub pushed forward at six knots and 100 feet beneath a calm morning sea. Four ships came into view through the periscope at 7:45 a.m. A medium-sized supply ship that belched dark smoke steamed about 100 yards ahead of a second and larger supply ship. Two destroyers patrolled off either side of the rear ship's bow. Coye observed at least two floatplanes that circled above, providing air coverage. *Silversides* closed to 6,000 yards and flooded all ten torpedo tubes, but did not yet open the outer doors.

Just a few days into his patrol Coye had found his first convoy, a nice change from his uneventful U-boat hunts off Bermuda. The skipper needed to close the distance and set up his shot. Coye took another look through the periscope ten minutes later only to find that the convoy had zigzagged away. The range now increased. Each subsequent periscope observation revealed the convoy growing smaller in the distance. The skipper felt frustrated. If only he could spend fifteen minutes on the surface, he knew he could race ahead of the convoy, submerge, and set up the perfect attack. Within no time these supply ships would be headed to the bottom. But with patrol planes circling above, the cautious Coye refused to risk it. The skipper watched at 8:25 a.m.—seventy minutes after he first spotted the convoy—as the four ships vanished over the horizon. "Did not surface and close due to proximity of enemy air bases," Coye later wrote in his report. "This one was a hard one to miss."

Silversides continued on across the empty ocean, following the convoy's last known course. Morning turned to afternoon and then evening. Another day passed, then another. *Silversides* logged 527 more miles and burned 6,225 gallons of diesel. Finally at 6:56 a.m. on August 2 lookouts spotted an enemy ship dead ahead as the target emerged from a morning rainsquall. Coye ordered the submarine to dive and increase speed to nine knots. Even at a range of almost four miles, Coye recognized the target, the larger of the two ships he had seen days earlier. This time the ship steamed alone with no escorts, an ideal attack scenario. The enemy had offered him a second chance. Coye refused to blow it.

Silversides closed the distance. By 7:47 a.m. only 2,400 yards separated the skipper from his prey. Two minutes later Coye took a final look through the periscope only to discover that the target again had zigzagged away. Coye could not let this ship escape yet again. The increased bow angle made a difficult shot, but the skipper decided to chance it. If he fired a spread of four, he hoped at least one might hit. He gave the order at 7:50 a.m. *Silversides* shuddered as a blast of compressed air ejected a torpedo from tube one. Coye fired a second torpedo nine seconds later followed by two more over the next eighteen seconds, keeping his periscope trained on the target's middle. In the space of just twenty-seven seconds, Coye had fired his first four shots of the war. The anxious skipper now waited as the four fish sped toward the ship at forty-six knots.

He didn't have to wait long. An explosion rattled *Silversides* as the first torpedo prematurely detonated seconds after leaving the tube. The second malfunctioned and exploded. The premature detonations rendered the final two shots worthless. The skipper of the Japanese supply ship spotted the detonations and turned to port, dodging the last two torpedoes. Some $40,000 of American taxpayer money wasted in less than a minute. The supply ship turned on *Silversides*, dropping a depth charge and firing its deck gun at the periscope before it slipped beneath the waves.

Coye ordered the sub to surface at 9:04 a.m. Lookouts could still make out the supply ship as it escaped west on the gray horizon. The skipper now ordered *Silversides* to make a full-speed chase. The four Fairbanks Morse engines roared as the submarine pushed through the calm seas at twenty knots or about twenty-three miles per hour. Coye changed course eighteen minutes later to attempt an end around on the supply ship's starboard side. The target vanished into a heavy rainsquall. Coye felt the reduced visibility would allow him to race ahead unseen. But the squall persisted. Lookouts scanned the horizon while sailors below hovered over the radar. The hours ticked past with no sign of the target. The rainsqualls continued as *Silversides* pushed ahead. Hope faded along with the afternoon. The enemy, yet again, had eluded him.

"Target ducked into a heavy rain squall and contact was not regained," Coye wrote in his report. "We searched for him until dusk."

The tenacious Coye kept up the hunt. Two more days passed before lookouts spotted masts at 5:47 a.m. at a distance of about twenty miles. The men studied the target for the next seven minutes, determining that the ship steamed almost due south. Coye ordered *Silversides* to chase at nineteen knots. Minutes turned into an hour. Then two. The four engines roared as the submarine closed the distance three hours later. Coye ordered *Silversides* to dive dead ahead of the target at 9 a.m. The morning sun illuminated the glassy sea as the target's masts came over the horizon eighteen minutes later. Coye peered through the periscope at 9:34 a.m., concluding from the target's bow that it was likely a destroyer, though in reality it was the 4,000-ton minelayer *Tsugaru*. He maneuvered for a view past the target to determine if it escorted a more valuable target. The calm sea limited his periscope observations—enemy lookouts can better spot periscopes in flat seas—but Coye managed a good look after the target zigzagged, exposing a long flat deck between two masts with a single stack amidships. This was no destroyer.

Tsugaru closed to 1,440 yards at eighteen knots. Sailors cranked open the stern doors. The skipper fired tube seven at 9:47 a.m. followed eight seconds later by tube eight. Coye prepared to fire his third torpedo when he heard the first explode prematurely just fifteen seconds after it left the tube. Coye continued his attack. He fired tube nine, followed eight seconds later by tube ten. The skipper watched through the scope as his third torpedo exploded prematurely sixteen seconds after he fired. Two of his four torpedoes had again malfunctioned. Coye spotted an explosion a minute later near the target's midships. The skipper felt it could have been a hit—postwar records would show that he in fact damaged *Tsugaru*—though at the time he couldn't be certain the torpedo hadn't detonated before impact. *Tsugaru* now swung to ram the submarine. Coye ordered *Silversides* down to 300 feet at 9:50 a.m. "He dropped five depth charges about a minute apart, the first one exploding as we passed 180 feet," Coye wrote in his report. "None of them were close."

Coye's frustration mounted. In the eight days since he'd left the *Coucal*, the new skipper had found a small convoy and two single ships, all viable targets. He had fired eight torpedoes—four of which had exploded prematurely—without a single confirmed hit. Coye recognized that he shared some of the blame. He had fired his first four shots at a minimum range of 2,200 yards—the actual torpedo run distance given the large firing arc was 3,000 yards. That bordered on too far. The skipper also recognized that his second attack could have benefited from a deeper torpedo depth setting than eight feet, but the eighteen-knot speed of the target had left no time for the adjustment. But these errors were small compared to the premature torpedo detonations. He hoped his remaining sixteen torpedoes might fare better.

The days dragged. Coye surfaced, searched, and dove; surfaced, searched, and dove, the only interruption the occasional plane that dotted the skies or the floating tree stump lookouts confused for an enemy submarine. One week turned into two. Then three. Men played cards, read books, and studied for qualification. Some of the homesick officers, having discovered an unnamed mountain on a nautical chart, set out to rename the enemy islands, mountains, and even depth charge alley after missed wives and girlfriends. "The whole chart has been tampered with," John Bienia wrote. "When we have to use it on our way home we'll probably run into some difficulties." Bienia busied himself by tallying the total submerged time over five patrols. "I almost fainted at the sum," the engineering officer wrote to his wife. "We've spent 3,100 hours beneath the surface in the gas-pipe."

Practical jokes helped pass the time. When an enemy plane forced *Silversides* to dive, some of the officers gathered in the wardroom to wait. Executive officer Bob Worthington disappeared to his stateroom and returned with a bottle of Old Crow. The practical jokester Bienia took a sniff of the brown liquor and hatched a plan to fool fellow officer Jerry Clarke. "There was about an eighth of an inch in the bottom of the bottle, and I dabbed a wee bit behind my ears—like you do with perfume. Then, smelling like a boozer, I sauntered into the control room and stood next to Jerry, who was still waiting for bombs. It was the most amazing thing I've ever seen in my life," Bienia wrote to his wife. "Jerry's nose began twitching then twisted in my direction and blushed a deep purple. He grabbed me by the shoulders and asked whether I'd had a shot, and when I told him just a few drops behind the ears, I thought he was going to lick my ears off."

Much of the best entertainment centered on the discovery in the forward and after torpedo rooms of two unlikely stowaways—mice the crew fondly nicknamed Romeo and Juliet. "I get a big kick out of watching the one in the fw'd torpedo room," Bienia wrote in a letter. "The torpedoman on watch there is usually sitting on his chair reading a book and chewing on a sandwich, meanwhile holding a piece of cheese in his other hand for the mouse. Romeo, who's become a regular submariner, just sits there on his little grey duff and nibbles away on the cheese," Bienia went on. "Bob 'the tyrant' has decided to purge these two creatures, and has elected Jerry to be the man behind the axe. But from Jerry's nature I guess the mice have nothing to fear and they will probably grow fatter and smarter as time goes by—who knows, maybe someday we'll have nothing but mice aboard these gas-pipes and we could stay ashore."

Coye decided on August 29 to patrol on the surface, a move he hoped would increase visibility and allow him to receive contact reports. Lookouts spotted smoke on the horizon at 10:12 a.m. at a distance of about twenty-five miles. The puffs appeared to come at ten-minute intervals. Coye ordered the submarine to chase at full speed. By late afternoon *Silversides* had closed to within fifteen miles. Coye ordered *Silversides* to dive. The skipper hoped to silhouette the target against the sunset. If that failed he would wait until after nightfall. *Silversides* surfaced at 7:16 p.m. The target steamed 11,100 yards away, a cargo ship accompanied by a small escort off its bow, another off its stern. Coye ordered an end around as his men kept track by radar.

The night was clear with no moon. Stars shone above. *Silversides* closed the distance to 3,200 yards by 9:53 p.m. The sonar operator reported the high-speed sounds of the escort's screw accompanied by the slower speed of the target, but Coye could not spot the enemy in his periscope. The escort crossed close astern two minutes later. Coye finally spotted the target at 10:03 p.m., but he had missed the shot. He held his fire. *Silversides* surfaced at 10:50 p.m. to make another end around run. Coye started his approach at 12:43 a.m. The clouds had increased and the skipper found it difficult to spot the loaded south-bound freighter with binoculars at a range greater than 6,000 yards. But Coye had learned his lesson. He would set the torpedo depths to eighteen feet and planned to fire fish spread across 150 percent of the target's length.

At 1:06 a.m., the submarine shuddered as Coye fired his first shot. He fired again and again, unleashing six of the one-and-a-half-ton weapons in just fifty-five seconds. The skipper watched as the tracks of three torpedoes disappeared under the target's amidships at 1:08 a.m. He waited for a detonation that would light up the night sky. Nothing happened. He had missed.

A whistle suddenly punctuated the night. Enemy lookouts had spotted the torpedoes and signaled the escorts. Tracer fire from the freighter's 20mm cannon erupted, followed by what sounded like fire from the aft escort's three-inch deck gun. Coye ordered *Silversides* to escape at full power at 1:10 a.m. The skipper heard the first of five explosions a minute and a half later in the distance, explosions he suspected were depth charges.

Coye's third attack had now failed, too. The enemy's draft, he suspected, must have been less than he anticipated. His torpedoes had run right under the target. Time on patrol now wound down. The skipper had been at sea for forty days, burning through as much as 2,000 gallons of diesel every twenty-four hours in his hunt for enemy ships. The galley now ran low on essentials, like butter, sugar, and flour, hampering cooks already plagued by a bad batch of Australian chicken. Coye's chances to redeem himself faded. He had taken over the prized *Silversides* from one of the submarine force's top skippers. He now worried the Navy might relieve him of command for poor performance when he returned to port, his sea career finished.

Coye's thoughts weighed heavy as *Silversides* cruised back to Australia. But the skipper's worries were his own. His men stood watch, played cards, and even scavenged for fresh fish on decks after surfacing, a scene captured by John Bienia, who snagged one. "It was a beauty about 14 inches long, four high and two wide," he wrote. "The top was a light bright green and the belly was creamy colored and it had two bright blue stripes running from head to tail on either side of its body. It tasted very well, fried in the ship's last butter, and I ate it practically all alone while the others munched on pork chops with a strong icebox flavor. I did offer the head and tail to Bob but he stuck to his pork chops, saying that such a bright colored fish would probably be poisonous. Now whenever we surface, everyone on the bridge scans the awash decks for any sign of fish—but I always tell them that they won't taste the same as mine unless fried in butter."

Others sailors looked forward to the end of patrol and a return to Brisbane. Memories of the previous refit there—and all the associated debauchery—remained fresh in the minds of many. The shore patrol would no doubt soon be busy. "There's no excitement of any kind—yet. That is other than the excitement which comes towards the end of a patrol men washing their blues, getting hair cuts, and all the ever present paper work being filled out," Bienia wrote home. "Each man is thinking of what he'll do in port—beer, wine, food, etc. Even Romeo, the mouse, is probably contemplating a shore-piece of cheese and a new mate. Apparently poor Juliet has deserted the ship, via the torpedo express, during a reload and firing. She just ain't anywhere aboard ship—but that's the way with these wimin."

7

SILVERSIDES

"One month from today I will be 21, if I live that long."

—Gilbert Leach,

October 14, 1942, diary

Silversides departed Brisbane for its seventh war patrol at 5:05 a.m. on October 5, ending a three-week refit in Australia. Coye and his men had needed a break after the unsuccessful previous patrol. The skipper demanded his men refreshed and focused. He could afford no more mistakes on his next patrol. The skipper had been self-critical in his report, singling out his errors in range, speed, and torpedo depth setting. His superiors chose not to berate him though his failure to sink or damage a single ship—even though postwar records would later reveal he damaged one—prompted Commodore James Fife to refuse a combat insignia award for the patrol, a mark of pride to submariners whose loss must have stung. The skipper knew his superiors would not tolerate a second patrol like the first; Coye would be replaced with a new skipper, his wartime sea career over. That possibility drove him. From the moment *Silversides* cleared Brisbane he drilled his men to the brink of exhaustion. "Ever since we left port, we've been holding intensive training exercises, firing guns, diving drills, etc.," Bienia griped in a letter. "I've been up all hours of the day and night, sleeping in my clothes whenever I could, and I didn't even bother to take off my shoes."

But Coye faced other challenges, too. The reserved skipper had not yet endeared himself to the *Silversides'* veterans in the same way his swashbuckling predecessor had. "I do wish that we had Capt. Burlingame with us—he was *the* man," Bienia lamented in a letter to his wife, adding in another: "The ship hasn't been the same since he left." Even the new recruits struggled to comprehend Coye. Lieutenant j.g. Eugene Malone compared Coye to his previous skipper, Mike Sellars of the submarine *S-31*. "He isn't as quick as Mike, nor as brilliant, but he's the steadiest human being I've ever seen. Steady, not too slow, aggressive, but not rash, and the most good natured person extant. Kind of fat and a bit sloppy looking, but a hell of a good man for that," Malone wrote. "And in amongst his apparent slowness of motion and thought, he every now and then fools everyone by doing something, or saying something, or figuring something with downright brilliance. Sometimes he baffles me, cause I can't decide whether he's dumb, lazy, or smart and calm. But I've pretty near decided the latter."

The problems ran much deeper than Coye. The war had now slogged on for twenty-two months. The flat-footed Navy devastated at Pearl Harbor and in the Philippines had rebounded, blocking Japanese advances in the battles of the Coral Sea and Midway. While those defeats had thwarted Japan's eastward expansion, the empire had aimed to improve defenses around its massive base at Rabaul. Japan had captured the tiny island of Tulagi in the Solomon Islands on May 3 in the run-up to the Battle of the Coral Sea. Troops had since landed on neighboring Guadalcanal, a 2,500-square-mile island of volcanic peaks, humid jungles, and malarial swamps. Beneath the bruising equatorial sun, crews had labored to build wharves, troop garrisons, and an airfield. Despite America's commitment to defeat Germany first, Admiral Ernest King had refused to play defense. The commander of the United States Fleet knew such a foothold would allow Japan to threaten Australia. America had no choice but to go on the offensive.

The United States landed forces on Tulagi and Guadalcanal in early August, seizing Japan's nearly complete airfield that would become the wellspring of much bloodshed. Japan retaliated in a nighttime sea battle, destroying four Allied heavy cruisers in just thirty-two minutes. The disastrous Battle of Savo Island set an ominous precedent in the struggle for control of the southern Solomons. The opposing navies fought seven major battles—many at night—as summer gave way to fall. A Japanese submarine torpedoed the carrier *Wasp* on September 15, triggering gasoline fires that set the carrier and surrounding seas ablaze and forced evacuation just thirty-five minutes later. A similar fate befell *Hornet* six weeks later when Japanese dive- and torpedo bombers shredded the carrier that only months earlier had launched Jimmy Doolittle's Tokyo raid. Carriers, cruisers, and destroyers plunged beneath the waves off Guadalcanal with such frequency that American sailors dubbed the waters "Ironbottom Sound."

The naval battles at sea rivaled those fought in the jungles. Some 60,000 Marines and soldiers struggled to preserve America's foothold on Guadalcanal against an enemy that offloaded reinforcements night after night under the cover of darkness. The island proved one of America's greatest foes, an illusory paradise whose tropical beauty masked a nightmare for entrenched troops. Swarms of ants, mosquitoes, and screeching birds crowded the dark and sweltering jungles that reeked of rot and slime. Troops sweated all day, then shivered at night as rains turned the earth into knee-deep mud. Men drove jeeps into streams to wash the vehicles and themselves. When hospital attendants finally pulled off Private Ed Carr's shoes after forty-five days, the malarial Marine discovered his socks had rotted away. His mother would later put his mud-caked footwear on display for neighbors in Kansas City. "Life is reduced to essentials," wrote a *New York Times* correspondent. "Guadalcanal's greatest pleasure is still being alive."

Unlike the battles of the Coral Sea and Midway, where victory was decided in a matter of days if not hours, the struggle for Guadalcanal slogged on for weeks, then months, demoralizing both Japanese and American leaders. The stranglehold of the island grew so severe by the middle of October that America refused to risk its valuable tankers to import fuel. Resourceful crews went so far as to siphon gasoline from disabled bombers to keep planes in the air. The Navy transferred submarines from Pearl Harbor to Australia to ramp up attacks on enemy supply ships headed toward Guadalcanal while the submarine *Amberjack* smuggled 9,000 gallons of aviation gasoline—the only time in war when an American submarine hauled fuel in bulk—along with ten tons of bombs to troops on Tulagi. "It now appears we are unable to control the sea in the Guadalcanal area. Thus our supply of the positions will only be done at great expense to us," Admiral Nimitz wrote in October. "The situation is not hopeless, but it is certainly critical."

Combined Fleet commander Admiral Yamamoto shared Nimitz's doubts. The son of a former samurai warrior, Yamamoto had two fingers on his left hand blown off in the Russo-Japanese War. He had warned that America would never give up Guadalcanal—and months of combat had proven him right. Malnourished Japanese troops wracked by swollen joints and chronic diarrhea struggled to survive on what many called "Starvation Island." The muddy war of attrition led Yamamoto to view Guadalcanal as a symbol of Japan's folly when it had sided with Germany and Italy.

America's resolve in the end proved stronger. No one battle would crown the victor at Guadalcanal. Japan simply gave up. With starvation claiming more than 100 lives each day, enemy leaders decided the island warranted no more bloodletting. Under the cover of darkness, Japan evacuated its forces. The six-month campaign had cost the United States more than 400 planes and two dozen warships, including two carriers, eight cruisers, and fourteen destroyers. An equal number of Japanese planes and ships littered the jungles and waters of Ironbottom Sound. But Guadalcanal's real price was in men. America counted almost 7,000 dead sailors, Marines, and soldiers, much less than the roughly 25,000 Japan lost. "Total and complete defeat of Japanese forces on Guadalcanal effected 1625 today," Major General Alexander Patch, commander of the ground forces, radioed to the relief of his superiors on February 9, 1943, after Japan's complete withdrawal. "'Tokyo Express' no longer has terminus on Guadalcanal."

Guadalcanal gave America the runway needed to achieve one of its great symbolic victories two months later. Yamamoto had come to Rabaul to oversee a series of unsuccessful raids on Allied forces in the Solomons, announcing at the operation's end his plan for a one-day tour of frontline bases to help boost troop morale. An encrypted radio message went out the afternoon of April 13, listing Yamamoto's itinerary down to the hour. Many senior officers objected to the trip, particularly after seeing the wide dissemination of the plan that included the precise number of fighter escorts.

Yamamoto's itinerary had an unintended recipient—the United States. The multiple addresses signaled American intelligence that the message was important. IBM machines at Pearl Harbor spit out a rough decryption. Marine Lieutenant Colonel Alva Lasswell and a small team set to work, figuring out crucial details such as geographical codes. The thirty-eight-year-old Lasswell, who had spent several years in Tokyo studying Japanese, soon stared at Yamamoto's complete itinerary. He couldn't believe America's luck. "We've hit the jackpot," Lasswell exclaimed. The Marine officer wasn't the only one who saw the unique opportunity Yamamoto's itinerary presented. Commander Edwin Layton, Nimitz's intelligence officer, strode into the admiral's office at 8:02 a.m. on April 14, clutching a translated copy of the intercept. Layton blurted out just four words as he handed the message to Nimitz: "Our old friend Yamamoto."

"What do you say," Nimitz asked. "Do we try to get him?"

"He's unique among their people," Layton told Nimitz. "Aside from the Emperor, probably no man in Japan is so important to civilian morale."

Nimitz hesitated, questioning whether assassinating Yamamoto might lead to a more effective replacement.

Layton ticked off a list of Japan's senior admirals, none of whom he felt would ever rise to Yamamoto's stature. To hammer home his point, the intelligence officer made it personal. "You know, Admiral Nimitz, it would be just as if they shot you down," Layton concluded. "There isn't anybody to replace you."

Nimitz gave the order. "It's down in Halsey's bailiwick," he said, referring to Admiral William "Bull" Halsey. "If there's a way, he'll find it."

Layton drafted the dispatch for the mission—dubbed Operation Vengeance—that authorized and directed Yamamoto's termination. "There were some qualms of conscience on my part. I was signing the death warrant of a man whom I knew personally," Layton would later write, having served as assistant naval attache in Tokyo in 1937. "It was impossible for me not to feel for Admiral Yamamoto with a certain amount of fondness." Nimitz initialed the dispatch, scribbling a few words of encouragement: "Best of luck and good hunting."

American pilots planned to target Yamamoto over the island of Bougainville as he flew from Rabaul to Ballale on the first leg of his day-long journey. The admiral woke early the morning of April 18, swapping the white dress uniform he had worn in recent days for a green khaki one with airmen's boots. He pulled on a pair of white gloves—the missing index and middle fingers of his left hand tied off with thread—and slipped on a sword given to him by his deceased older brother. In preparation for a long day, Yamamoto pocketed toilet paper, a luxury long missing among the frontline troops. He and his entourage climbed aboard two medium bombers at 6 a.m.—Allies referred to these common planes by the code name "Betty"—lifting off ten minutes later from Rabaul's east airfield. Six fighters followed, just as his itinerary outlined. The sun climbed in the clear morning sky an hour and a half later as Yamamoto's plane flew south along the west coast of Bougainville. At an altitude of some 6,500 feet, the dense jungles of palm and banyan trees appeared below.

Eighteen twin-engine U.S. Army P-38 Lightnings roared to intercept at 210 miles per hour, skimming just thirty feet above the whitecaps. Guided by only a compass and air-speed indicator, the Lightnings reached the projected rendezvous and began to climb.

"Bogey," one of the pilots crackled over the radio just thirty-seconds later. "Ten o'clock high."

Yamamoto was right on time.

The Lightnings jettisoned the belly fuel tanks to improve agility and speed. The tanks refused to drop from one of the four attack fighters, forcing the pilot and his wingman out of the action. That left just a single pair of Lightnings to kill Yamamoto, one piloted by twenty-seven-year-old Captain Thomas Lanphier, Jr., the other by Lieutenant Rex Barber, his wingman and junior by two years. Lanphier and Barber climbed ahead and to the right of the Japanese bombers while the cover fighters zoomed up to 20,000 feet to battle the enemy Zeros. Japanese fighter pilots spotted the Lightnings. The admiral's bombers dove, tickling the treetops in a frantic rush to evade the fighters. Lanphier opened fire on the fighters while Barber pursued Yamamoto. "I was right behind the lead Betty," recalled Barber. "I started shooting across the tail into the right engine. Pieces of the cowling flew up and hit me. The Betty slowed up so much I almost hit it."

Lanphier joined the attack on the admiral. "I spotted a shadow moving across the treetops. It was Yamamoto's bomber. It was skimming the jungle, headed for Kahili. I dived toward him," Lanphier would write in a newspaper article published at the end of the war. "I fired a long steady burst across the bomber's course of flight. The bomber's right engine, then its right wing, burst into flame." Vice Admiral Matome Ugaki, Yamamoto's chief of staff, watched the attack unfold from his cockpit seat in the second bomber. Black smoke and flames engulfed Yamamoto's plane. "My God!" Ugaki said, grabbing the shoulder of an air staff officer. "Look at the commander in chief's plane!" Lanphier continued his dogged pursuit of Yamamoto's plane, the belly of his Lightning brushing the treetops. "Just as I moved into range of Yamamoto's bomber and its cannon, the bomber's wing tore off. The bomber plunged into the jungle. It exploded," Lanphier later wrote. "That was the end of Admiral Isoroku Yamamoto."

Hacking through the tangled jungle of palms, banyans, and rattan vines, Japanese rescuers confirmed Lanphier's observation the next day at dusk. Operation Vengeance was a success. No one had survived the crash of Yamamoto's plane. The second bomber ditched in the sea. Three people, including chief of staff Ugaki, survived. The ambush had cost Japan some twenty lives, including about a half dozen important staff officers. America in contrast had lost only one Lightning. Yamamoto's stopped watch recorded the moment of impact at 7:45 a.m., a crash so violent that it threw the admiral clear of the wreckage. Rescuers found the mastermind of the Pearl Harbor attack strapped in his seat among the trees, ribbons adorning his chest and the three fingers of his left hand curled around his sword. An autopsy later showed that either a bullet fragment or shrapnel had dug into Yamamoto's left shoulder while another piece passed through his lower jaw and exited his temple, killing him in all likelihood before the bomber crashed.

Yamamoto's death was prophetic. The admiral had long resisted war with the United States, believing his nation's limited resources would run out in eighteen months. He voiced those concerns in 1940 to then Prime Minister Fumimaro Konoe when pressed for Japan's chance for success. "If we are ordered to do it," Yamamoto had answered, "then I can guarantee to put up a tough fight for the first six months, but I have no confidence as to what would happen if it went on for two or three years." The war had only realized Yamamoto's fears.

The culture of the *Silversides*, as with many submarines, changed as the war evolved. With workers in Maine, California, and Wisconsin hammering out new submarines each week, the Navy aimed to rotate sailors after several patrols, sending experienced submariners back home to join new boats. Many *Silversides* crewmen, who had remained longer, had recently departed, leaving a dwindling core of veterans. At the end of the previous patrol, officers Don Finch, L. J. Gibson, and Jerry Clarke transferred. All three stood on the pier at dawn to watch *Silversides* depart. Only a handful of men who had joined the Silver Lady at the start of the war remained, including John Bienia, Tom Keegan, and executive officer Bob Worthington. Those left on board felt the absence the moment the pier vanished in the submarine's frothy wake. "We all had lumps in our throats," Bienia wrote to his wife. "One really gets attached to fellows that have been through hell and deep water together."

New officers and crewmen reported aboard after each patrol, plopping down before the bunks cooled. The revolving door occasionally produced friction between fresh arrivals and veterans, who took out frustration over the loss of friends, shared stories, and camaraderie on the new recruits. The twenty-two-year-old Malone, raised on a California cattle ranch, suffered just that under Bienia. Despite having proven himself on three war patrols in the aged *S-31*—a vessel far more challenging to operate than a modern fleet boat—the 1942 Naval Academy graduate found he could do nothing to please Bienia, who described just such an anecdote in a letter to his wife. "I have a new officer under me a Lt. jg from Annapolis. He's a long lanky kid, and when we had some practice clearing the bridge he slowed every dive up," Bienia wrote. "I had him jumping down the hatch so many times that he became almost too pooped to go ashore tonight. But he did anyway—maybe he thought I'd have him practice all night too. So when he left, I told him he could leave some of the lead ballast out of his pants ashore."

Silversides concluded five days of practice approaches, dives, and gun drills before it tied up at 11:30 a.m. on October 10 alongside the *YOG-41*, a gasoline barge moored in Tulagi Harbor in the southern Solomons, the submarine's last stop before starting its seventh patrol. Coye sent for the Seabees—the Navy's construction force—to weld a broken antenna strut as other sailors soap-tested the main induction in search of a small leak that appeared only in the deep.

Crews wrapped up the minor repairs that afternoon and *Silversides* let out a prolonged blast of its whistle, cast off its lines, and headed to sea. The escort turned back at sunset and the submarine increased speed to seventeen knots, its bow slicing through the blue waves. Over the next week, *Silversides* cruised north, passing twenty miles off Feni island in the Bismarcks toward its assigned position between Tanga island and New Ireland. The days were uneventful, interrupted only by the occasional enemy patrol plane or the rogue tree trunk whose branches stood out of the water and appeared from a distance to be a ship's masts. Nighttime searches under a bright full moon with a long slick turned up no targets. Coye welcomed the arrival of new orders on October 13, directing him north to intercept traffic between Japanese bases at Rabaul and Truk.

Lookouts spotted a submarine on the surface after lunch four days later at a range of about ten miles, a submarine Coye surmised was the *Balao*, though he failed to raise the boat on his new radiotelephone. A puff of smoke hung on the horizon at a distance of about twenty-five miles. It appeared that *Balao*, which had now submerged, planned to attack. The skipper decided to track the target. The sun shone down on the calm sea as *Silversides* closed the distance. The sonar operator reported explosions that the skipper believed were *Balao*'s torpedoes. What Coye didn't know was that the convoy had zig-zagged just as *Balao* fired. All six torpedoes had missed, exploding at the end of each run. The sonar operator next reported a string of depth charges, the inevitable outcome of a submarine attack.

Coye decided to join the fight, knowing the escorts would be busy hunting *Balao*. He could just barely see the enemy's masts. The convoy zigzagged at 5:02 p.m. as Coye closed at six knots. The six-ship convoy had departed Palau four days earlier, October 14, bound for Rabaul. The ships steamed in three columns. Two submarine chasers patrolled off the convoy's quarter, likely having returned from the attack on *Balao*. The skipper contemplated a long-range shot, but ruled against it. He ordered *Silversides* to surface and chased at full speed on all four engines, the mast tops in sight. Coye tried to raise *Balao*, but again failed. The skipper ordered *Silversides* to make an end run to the north around the target that radar showed remained some 14,000 yards away. The engines now roared.

Silversides completed its end run through the calm sea at 10:34 p.m. and dove to sixty feet. Moonlight illuminated the convoy in Coye's periscope. *Silversides* passed 1,200 yards abeam of the lead escort and cruised between the convoy's right and center columns. Coye lowered his periscope and swung left, his bow tubes aimed at the lead ship. He raised his scope several minutes later only to discover that the convoy had zigzagged right and his target steamed past. The frustrated skipper hustled to set up a stern shot on the lead ship in the second column, but the range proved too small. Coye realized he was dead ahead of the second ship in the middle column that bore down on him. He ordered *Silversides* to swing left to avoid a collision.

Coye had botched the attack.

The skipper ordered *Silversides* to surface at 12:38 a.m. and chase at full speed on four engines for another end run around the convoy, careful to remain just outside of radar range. *Silversides* submerged at 12:47 a.m., nine miles ahead of convoy. The submarine's radar failed to show the enemy ships so when Coye finally could see them he ordered *Silversides* back down to sixty feet. The moon remained bright—too bright—so Coye decided to wait, all night if necessary. His patience paid off at 5:35 a.m. when the convoy zigzagged, putting *Silversides* on the starboard bow of the lead ship in the right-hand column, the 1,915-ton *Tairin Maru.* "This was the shot we were waiting for," Coye would write. "Leading ship of the starboard column was closest and the largest target. Last ship in center column overlapped its bow, and second ship in right hand column almost overlapped its stern."

Coye fired tube one at 5:37 a.m. He fired again. Then again and again. Thirty-two seconds after he fired his first shot, an explosion rocked *Silversides*, a premature detonation. Coye refused to give up. He fired a fifth torpedo five seconds after the explosion, followed by a sixth just eight seconds later. The skipper spotted an escort 1,000 yards off the starboard bow and ordered *Silversides* deep. He heard an explosion at 5:39 a.m. This one was not a premature detonation. Nine seconds later, a second torpedo crashed into *Tairin Maru*, loaded down with 2,100 tons of trucks, gas pumps, and provisions. The hits under *Tairin Maru*'s bow and bridge blew the gunners off the ship into the water. The escort dumped depth charges, the first one rattling the boat at 5:42 a.m. Thirty seconds later another came. Five more followed over the next minute and twenty-one seconds.

The sonar operator reported the grinding noises of *Tairin Maru* breaking up just before dawn as *Silversides* hid beneath a density layer at 260 feet, a change in the water's temperature and density that helped deflect sonar. Coye's victim had sunk by the stern in just ten minutes. The convoy's remaining five ships had scattered. Coye waited for the escorts to quit searching. The screws faded and vanished in an hour, though sonar still reported distant echo ranging. Coye started up for a look, spotting smoke on the horizon. The skipper waited until the escorts disappeared, then surfaced, hoping to hunt down the rest of the convoy before the ships reached Rabaul. As *Silversides* set off at full speed, sailors discovered a surprise on deck: the remnant of a torpedo warhead case, blown back from the premature explosion. Lookouts spotted debris ahead at 10:56 a.m. Coye ordered crews to man the 20mm gun and pass out pistols and rifles.

Silversides slowed as it entered the debris field. Oil glistened in the water. Two empty clinker lifeboats bobbed in the waves along with several small life rafts and preservers. Four landing barges poked up through the gentle swells.

It was a sea of ghosts. *Tairin Maru* was gone. Coye surmised that the escorts had rescued survivors. To prevent the Japanese from salvaging the barges, the gun crew riddled them with the 20mm, but the wooden boats would not sink. The skipper ordered *Silversides* to pull alongside. Crews leaned over with screwdrivers and stripped one barge of its nameplate, boat box, anchor, steering wheel, and boat hooks. Sailors recovered two ring life preservers stenciled with the ship's name. Several wooden kegs floated in the water. Men pried them open, hoping to find sake, but discovered only pickled onions. Executive officer Worthington's photographs documented the souvenir hunt.

The warm afternoon bled into evening as the sun went down and the stars came out, revealing to the ship's navigator that the submarine likely remained south of the convoy. Worthington spotted the convoy ten miles off the starboard bow at 8:53 p.m. Coye again tried unsuccessfully to raise the *Balao*. The *Silversides* radar worked sporadically and the skipper wanted to wait and use the moonlight to make a submerged periscope attack. The night proved dark and overcast. Lookouts lost sight of the convoy and *Silversides* made an end run around a cloud shadow. Coye fumed. He had intentionally remained far from the convoy to prevent its escorts from detecting the submarine by radar. Now he had lost sight of the convoy. That wouldn't have happened had his radar crew interpreted the contact correctly, a fact the skipper discovered only after a pip he hunted turned out to be an ionized cloud.

Lookouts eventually found the convoy again. The vessels emerged from a haze into bright moonlight off the submarine's port bow at 2:57 a.m. Coye's relief dissipated a minute later when one of the escorts turned on *Silversides*, firing tracer rounds. The skipper had no choice but to head deep. Surfacing an hour before dawn, Coye ordered his third end around. The convoy now steamed in two columns. Coye picked the vessel leading the left-hand column. The bright sun forced Coye to hunt with his sonar. The skipper risked a peek only for the escort to roar over, dropping six charges as *Silversides* dove to 270 feet. "All sounded as if they were set shallow and would have been uncomfortably close if we had been at periscope depth," he would write in his report. "The little rascals seemed unusually persistent today and are showing improvement from the training we had given them."

The rainsquall Coye had hoped for hours earlier now settled over the area at 4:06 p.m., reducing visibility to 500 yards. The weather cleared a little more than an hour later. Coye ordered *Silversides* to surface and chase full speed after the convoy's last bearing, a chase that would take all night. Smoke appeared on the horizon at dawn. Coye had hoped to be about twenty miles ahead, but the convoy had seized on the rainsqualls to steam faster. The convoy commander had outflanked him. He watched as the smoke grew smaller in the distance. Coye had chased this convoy now for three days, four hours, and twenty-one minutes. He could spend the morning closing the twenty-mile distance, but he now cruised near New Guinea's Mussau island. Enemy floatplanes would soon crowd the skies. Chances of getting ahead on the surface vanished. He had no choice but to watch the ships disappear.

Silversides patrolled the next couple of days along the Rabaul shipping lanes without luck. Coye spotted the submarine *Balao* again on October 22 and sought to exchange information, but *Balao* had none. The two submarines agreed to stay ten miles apart to increase the effectiveness of the search. Lookouts spotted smoke on the horizon at 6:50 p.m. Coye ordered *Silversides* to chase. The radar worked spasmodically, leaving the men to track by sight. Coye had found a large convoy that had departed Rabaul for Palau two days earlier. The convoy consisted of six ships that steamed in three columns with two ships to a column. Two submarine chasers escorted the convoy, one ahead, the other astern. Coye radioed *Balao*'s skipper to relay his find. The two captains agreed to attack simultaneously at midnight, *Balao* targeting the convoy's port side, *Silversides* the starboard.

Silversides stalked the convoy through the calm seas. Coye ordered his men to battle stations at 11:47 p.m. and flooded down to decks awash, a move that lowered his profile in the clear and dark night. The radar operator relayed the five-mile range to the convoy at the same time sonar reported hearing *Balao*'s torpedoes running. *Balao*'s skipper had fired all six of his bow torpedoes at three of the ships. He then swung his submarine and fired four more stern shots. The attack had begun. The men on board *Silversides* heard the explosions. The ambitious Coye wanted in on the fight. *Silversides* closed to 5,775 yards at 12:21 a.m. Escorts spotted the submarine two minutes later and turned toward *Silversides* just as one of the ships in the convoy opened fire with its deck gun. Coye had lost the critical element of surprise. The skipper had no choice now but to go deep and wait it out.

Lookouts picked up the convoy again at 5:09 a.m. Coye could not close to within radar range without enemy lookouts spotting him. He ordered *Silver-*

sides to dive for a moonlight periscope attack on the convoy, which steamed at nine knots. The skipper struggled to see through the periscope in the dark as *Silversides* closed to 4,500 yards. Coye fired four stern shots. Five seconds after the last torpedo left, Coye watched one of his fish detonate prematurely. Twelve seconds later, he heard another explosion. Two more followed five minutes later. The anxious skipper instantly knew he had erred. The 4,500-yard range—some two and a half miles—was too far, a distance right at the limit of a steam-powered torpedo. "Should have held fire but having missed earlier in the night went ahead and shot," he later wrote. "The premature put the odds well in the favor of the convoy on this long range shot."

The skipper dove to avoid an escort and waited thirty-three minutes before he returned to periscope depth. He spotted smoke and a stack at 7:09 a.m. headed due west. The skipper waited an hour to be safe and then surfaced. Coye's opportunity to attack had passed as the sun climbed into the morning sky. The skipper decided to track the convoy throughout the day, using its telltale smoke on the horizon to make a gradual end run around its starboard side to set up a nighttime attack. The engines roared as the morning slipped past. Cooks served lunch in the galley and stewards in the wardroom. *Silversides* dove at 12:25 p.m. to avoid an unidentified plane some ten miles off, only to surface fifty-five minutes later and continue the chase. The afternoon faded. Coye radioed the skipper of *Balao* and informed his colleague of his plan to attack at midnight on the starboard side.

Silversides picked up the convoy on radar at 9:51 p.m. at a range of almost five miles. Despite its attack the previous night, *Balao* had no confirmed sinkings. Six ships now steamed due west in two columns at eight and a half knots accompanied by only two escorts. The sea was calm and the night dark—no moon, just stars—and Coye felt the conditions would only improve. He ordered his men to track the convoy by radar and decipher its zigzag plan. The skipper waited. Coye had patiently tracked this convoy the previous night and throughout the day. A few more hours, he knew, made little difference. He had all night, even longer, if necessary. The skipper had already proven that he would hunt a convoy for days. Coye knew that each hour that passed without incident likely only reassured the enemy convoy that all was safe and that maybe tonight an attack would not happen.

Coye ordered his men to battle stations at 11:11 p.m. Men in the forward and after torpedo rooms stood by to crank open the outer doors as sailors in the control room gripped the planes, ready to dive the *Silversides*. The skipper flooded down *Silversides* and began his approach. Coye closed to 3,400 yards off the starboard column, firing his first shot at 12:43 a.m. at the 5,407-ton *Tennan Maru*, the lead ship. He fired five more torpedoes over the next sixty-seven seconds, including two more shots at *Tennan Maru* and three at the ship astern. Coye didn't wait for the results, but dove, hiding beneath a density layer at 275 feet. Two torpedoes ripped into *Tennan Maru*, sending the ship and forty-seven passengers and crew bow-first beneath the waves in just two minutes. "Heard crackling and rumbling noise of a ship breaking up," Coye recorded in his report. "Heard through hull in all compartments."

The skipper ordered *Silversides* to surface at 2:45 a.m. when the sonar operator could no longer hear the escort's screws though still reported pings, sounds Coye used to keep track of the convoy throughout the night. Depth charges exploded in the distance at 4:12 a.m. and again a couple of minutes later, signaling that the escorts still hunted *Silversides*. Coye ordered the submarine to dive at 6:28 a.m. east of the convoy to prevent being sighted in the morning light. One of the escorts and the masts of several ships came into focus through the periscope at 6:44 a.m. Coye closed the convoy and found two stopped ships, one a listing supply ship with its bow blown off, the other a medium-sized cargo ship. Several other cargo ships idled in the calm sea while escorts patrolled around the convoy, dropping sporadic depth charges. The skipper counted a total of only five ships, which meant one was missing. Coye had scored again.

The skipper decided to wait until dark to attack the convoy's remnants. He knew all hands would be alert and everyone would be searching for periscopes and torpedo wakes. The convoy, now made up of three ships and two escorts, continued west at 2 p.m., disappearing over the horizon. Coye eyed the listing ship down by the stern and dead in the water. He ordered *Silversides* to approach. The skipper closed to about 2,000 yards when he observed the other ship dead in the water and in flames. *Silversides* surfaced at 3:32 p.m. about 1,500 yards from the first ship, the 1,893-ton *Kazan Maru*. The skipper saw no sign of life on board and noted the bow been blown off. The ship appeared to be slowly sinking, so he went to investigate the other ship. Eight minutes later, *Kazan Maru* sank, stern first. He could now see that the burning ship was abandoned so he reversed course to investigate the wreckage of *Kazan Maru*.

The top of *Kazan Maru*'s pilothouse floated. Lookouts spotted a 20mm machine gun mounted atop. Sailors rescued the gun—intact with its mount—and hauled it on board. Sailors also scavenged a packing case filled with what appeared to be meteorological instruments. Coye ordered his men to search for charts, but found none, though sailors recovered two more life rings. The skipper decided to reinspect the burning ship at 4:46 p.m. The ship, the 6,182-ton passenger freighter *Johore Maru*, had a large hole amidships on the starboard side that had flooded the engine room. The attack had killed seventy-seven passengers and crew. The superstructure burned furiously, but the ship did not appear to be sinking. Coye ordered the gun crew to open fire. The four-inch .50 caliber roared again and again, firing a total of forty-eight rounds that had little effect. Sailors then resorted to the 20mm, most of which just glanced off the hull.

Coye knew he had to see the ship sink to claim credit, never mind that the ship was abandoned and on fire, so the skipper decided to put another pricey torpedo in *Johore Maru*'s side. He ordered *Silversides* to pull back to 1,050 yards, and at 6:49 p.m. fired a single torpedo amidships in the same spot where the ship had been hit. He felt certain the blast would break the ship's back, but to his amazement the torched ship remained afloat. Sailors stared dumbfounded at the burning ship. Twenty-five minutes later, *Johore Maru* finally broke in half and sank. Coye had hoped to pluck souvenirs from the debris, but the fire had destroyed everything. "Allowed most of the crew to come topside to see torpedo hit and watch ships sink," he later wrote in his report. "Realized this was a bit hazardous, but we were far from enemy bases. The morale value for the crew was high as they had a chance to witness the result of their efforts."

Coye ordered *Silversides* at 7:32 p.m. to chase down the convoy at full speed. He fired off a report to his superiors, alerting them to the patrol's success to date. The night proved dark and squally as *Silversides* cut through the waves on four engines, slowing just once each hour to listen for echo ranging. The hours slipped past as Sunday rolled into Monday. Lookouts spotted smoke at 9:37 a.m. at a range of some twenty miles. Three ships steamed in a single column. The convoy, its numbers cut in half, now zigzagged radically. Coye debated his best approach. Rather than attack during the day, he opted again to wait until nightfall. The skipper had only seven torpedoes left, four forward and three aft. He planned to fire two torpedoes from his bow tubes at the two leading ships, swing *Silversides*, and fire two more at the last targets. He would keep one torpedo in reserve in case he tangled with an escort.

Coye ordered his men to battle stations at 12:19 a.m. He had waited until he had the ideal light for a night surface attack, but the weather had since deteriorated to rough seas beneath an overcast sky with no moon. The convoy steamed just four miles away. The leading escort patrolled off the convoy's starboard bow so Coye maneuvered to attack on the port side only to find the other escort off the convoy's quarter and closer than he preferred. *Silversides* cruised just 2,400 yards off the escort's broadside. Coye knew it was a matter of minutes, maybe sooner, before enemy lookouts spotted the submarine's silhouette. He had to work fast. The skipper disliked the shooting position—a 4,000-yard range—but felt he had no choice. To improve his odds Coye rejected his earlier idea of dividing four torpedoes between the first two ships. He instead planned to send all four fish straight at the lead ship.

Coye fired at 1:10 a.m. and then let loose three more torpedoes at ten-second intervals. The skipper ordered right full rudder to bring his stern tubes to bear. He sighted the last ship in the convoy and fired a fifth and then sixth torpedo, taking no chances that he might miss. Coye's work was now done. He had fired twenty-three of his twenty-four torpedoes, saving his last one in case of an emergency on the long trip back to Pearl Harbor. The skipper ordered ahead full and started to clear the area, but the escort spotted him and turned toward *Silversides*. Then a string of a half dozen explosions rocked the dark night. Coye watched as the final ship in the convoy came dead in the water. The escort would now have more work. "Saw a bright flash and much smoke from the last ship in column which did not have appearance of gunfire," Coye wrote in his report. "Believe one of the stern tubes was a definite hit."

8

DRUM

"Leaving behind 8 pregnant women in exchange for 8 happy sailors. Bon voyage!"

—*Drum* crew calendar,
June 3, 1943

Commander Delbert Fred Williamson trained his binoculars more than ten miles out on the horizon in the waters between the Bismarck Archipelago and the Caroline Islands. It was minutes before dawn on November 11, 1943. Williamson could just make out a convoy of several ships in the morning light—his first targets as the new skipper of the *Drum*. Williamson had replaced McMahon as the submarine's commanding officer, ending the Great White Father's one-year tenure at the helm. McMahon had failed to sink as many ships as his predecessor, Robert Rice, but the cigar-smoking skipper still managed to put four ships on the bottom. McMahon also had sidelined the *Ryuho* just days after the Japanese commissioned the carrier. Williamson inherited *Drum* with a strong record of eleven ships sunk. The pressure was on for him to continue the submarine's success on this eighth patrol.

The thirty-nine-year-old Williamson—known to friends as Bill—was several years older than McMahon. Though born in Missouri, his family had moved to Colorado, settling in the tiny town of Sterling in the plains east of the Rocky Mountains. Williamson had spent half a year at Hastings College in Nebraska before the Naval Academy accepted him into the same class as Rice and Burlingame. The muscular and broad-shouldered Williamson boxed, played football, and served as captain of the lacrosse team. He worked just as hard in the classroom as he did on the athletic field, graduating ninety-three out of 580. Williamson's relaxed nature made him popular with his peers. "He is extremely easy to get along with because he rarely gets angry," stated his profile in the *Lucky Bag.* "When he does, no one has ever known him to use language that would not pass the strictest censorship, which is a restraint which can be especially appreciated by anyone in the Navy."

Williamson served on the cruiser *Omaha* and the destroyers *MacDonough* and *Southard* in the years after graduation. He volunteered for submarine school in 1931 and served in several World War I–era boats, eventually commanding *S-33.* But his academic drive brought him back to the classroom in the years leading up to the war. Williamson studied design engineering at the Naval Postgraduate School and the University of Southern California, eventually earning a master's degree in mechanical engineering. The Navy harnessed his mechanical mind as a teacher in the Diesel Engineering Department at the submarine school in New London, earning the nickname "Diesel Dan." He had spent most of the war not in combat but in a classroom. Williamson knew that test scores and titles would carry him only so far. The war would be the defining benchmark for his generation of officers. If he had any hope to climb the Navy's ladder, Williamson would need to prove himself where it mattered most: at sea.

Drum was his ticket.

Lieutenant Mike Rindskopf greeted his new commanding officer with a healthy dose of skepticism—and he was in a good position to judge. Rindskopf had remained on board *Drum* for eight straight patrols and now through three skippers. He had in that time climbed from gunnery officer to executive officer, the boat's second in command. In comparing his three skippers, Rindskopf rated Williamson last. Old skippers were bad news. Old skippers who worked in classrooms were worse. Just a few months shy of his fortieth birthday, Williamson was in fact old for his first wartime command of a submarine. His fellow 1927 Naval Academy classmates Rice and Burlingame had started the war at the helm. Burlingame had moved up to submarine division commander while Rice would soon join the Bureau of Naval Personnel back in Washington. The all-night attacks, the stress of depth charges, and the incredible pressure to sink ships combined to make wartime skipper a younger man's job.

The war also had revealed the weakness of many of America's older skippers, whose peacetime training had consisted of drills. Real combat had caused some to unravel. One example that made the rounds was *Sailfish* skipper Morton Mumma, Jr., who broke down during a depth charge attack just days into the war. Mumma ordered his executive officer to lock him in his cabin and take command. Younger skippers, who had learned on the job, proved better conditioned. Veteran combat officers knew from experience how to predict an escort's next move or how to hide beneath temperature gradients that would shield a sub from the enemy's sonar. Many had even learned to determine just from the telltale click of a detonator how bad a depth charge blast might be. Williamson had ridden along for one patrol on *Growler* as a prospective commanding officer, but beyond that he lacked the wartime experience of even many of his own officers—men like Rindskopf and others almost half his age who had long since passed the test of battle.

Williamson joined a strong submarine at a time of America's increased success in the undersea war. Victory at Guadalcanal had freed more American submarines to patrol empire waters—three times as many as in the first quarter of 1943. Engineers had finally begun to remedy the torpedo failures that had plagued the force, introducing electric fish. These battery-powered torpedoes ran slower, at twenty-nine knots—compared to forty-six knots for steam-powered weapons—but left no wake for enemy lookouts to spot. Engineers likewise swapped TNT for the more powerful explosive Torpex. Fifty-two new fleet boats would join the fight in the Pacific in 1943, bringing the total to 109 modern submarines—almost three times as many modern boats as America had had when the Japanese attacked Pearl Harbor. Submarines in 1943 would fire 3,937 torpedoes—more than twice as many as the year before—to sink some 300 merchant ships and damage more than 200 others. Japan's shipbuilders could no longer keep up with the losses.

One of the most important advances in the undersea war, however, grew out of communications intelligence. America's efforts to break and read Japan's encrypted communications stretched back more than two decades. A $100,000 slush fund set up at the end of the First World War at Riggs Bank in Washington—under the personal credit of the director of naval intelligence and therefore hidden from congressional oversight—had financed multiple FBI break-ins throughout the 1920s at the Japanese consulate in New York. Operatives cracked the combination safe of the vice consul, who was actually a naval officer, and photographed the Japanese fleet's codebook. Slush funds paid the spousal team of linguists Dr. and Mrs. Emerson Haworth—the husband had served as a missionary and professor at Tokyo University—to translate the capacious codebook, a job that took almost four years. The red buckram that bound the final two-volume translation led analysts to dub Japan's principal naval cryptosystem the "Red Code."

The value of this newfound intelligence crystallized in the spring of 1930 when almost the entire Japanese navy put to sea for fleet maneuvers. In a break from previous protocol, Japan shrouded the operation in secrecy. An American listening post on Guam, however, intercepted the fleet's radio communications. The decrypts stunned American analysts. The five-week operation had revealed Japan's war plan against the United States, a plan that called for the capture of Guam and the Philippines followed by the destruction of the Pacific Fleet. Japan's simulation had even prepared for the possibility of an American carrier raid against Tokyo, just like the one Jimmy Doolittle would lead in April 1942. But the decrypts revealed yet another shock. Japanese intelligence had successfully mapped out America's updated contingency plan for a possible conflict in the Pacific—dubbed War Plan Orange—that strategists in the nation's military colleges had rehearsed that same year.

The intelligence haul America bagged from the 1930 fleet maneuvers led to an even more ambitious experiment three years later when the Japanese navy again put to sea for exercises. Rather than collect communications and forward them for decryption—a process that could take weeks—the Navy wanted to test what could be learned short of cryptanalysis from a real-time examination of message traffic. The test demanded analysts look at message lengths, addresses, call signs, and the frequencies used. The 1933 test proved a great success. Brute grunt work that involved charting the time, date, and sender of each transmission—among other details—as well card indexing every call sign, helped analysts map the entire organization of Japan's naval forces. More than just illuminating Japan's war plans, the test confirmed the value of radio traffic analysis, a technique that would prove invaluable in the years to come as Japan's cryptosystems grew more sophisticated.

Japan changed its naval codes several times in the decade leading up to the war, replacing the so-called Red Code with Blue then Black before finally settling in 1939 on JN-25, the fleet operational code. This complex new cryptosystem would serve as the workhorse of the Japanese navy, handling as much as 70 percent of all message traffic. Compared to previous naval codes,

JN-25 represented a radical departure. Just to operate this cryptologic nightmare required several books, including an instruction manual. An operator preparing to send an encrypted message would first consult a codebook filled with some 30,000 five-digit numbers, representing everything from place names and numbers to Japanese Kana particles. This allowed the operator to convert each word or phrase of a plaintext message into a five-digit numeric code. The Japanese designed the code with a safety mechanism to guard against garbles: the sum of the five numbers in each group was divisible by three.

The operator would next consult a 300-page additive book comprised of random numbers: 100 five-digit groups per page. The operator would add these numbers to the original code groups, but with a catch: no numbers could be carried over. This erroneous arithmetic served to further encipher the original code. Keys hidden inside each message instructed operators on the receiving end the precise page and line to turn to in the additive book to subtract the numbers and reveal the original code. Operators then only needed to look up the corresponding plaintext meaning. The cryptosystem's use of varying additives meant that the one word could be encoded thousands of different ways. American naval cryptanalysts had never seen such a sophisticated system. Japan further exacerbated America's code-breaking challenge, rolling out a new and more expansive version of the code eighteen months later and by issuing eight new additive books before the attack on Pearl Harbor.

America failed to grasp the importance of this new cryptosystem, wasting thousands of hours trying to crack a seldom used flag officers' code. The pursuit of that cryptologic fool's gold along with pressure to read diplomatic messages and a shortage of code breakers sidelined efforts to break the sophisticated system. Largely unable to read messages transmitted in the complex naval code, America depended on traffic analysis to monitor Japan on the eve of the war. But those efforts soon came under attack when Japan changed its naval call signs on November 1, 1941. In what analysts viewed as an ominous sign, Japan changed them again one month later. Traffic analysis ground to a halt for a couple of days until operatives figured out 200 of the most frequently used call signs. Analysts made an alarming observation: none of the recovered radio signs were for Japanese aircraft carriers. No known carrier since November 25, analysts realized, had either sent or been addressed a message.

Where were Japan's flattops?

Pacific Fleet intelligence officer Lieutenant Commander Edwin Layton had struggled to answer that question when he prepared the December 2 intelligence sheet. But the reality proved far worse than Layton or his colleagues could imagine. The Japanese transmitted bogus messages to disguise the departures of almost three dozen carriers, cruisers, and destroyers, most slipping port one by one so as not to arouse suspicion. This massive task force built around six flattops had secretly rendezvoused in a snowy harbor in the Kuril Islands before departing at dawn on November 26 to steam east toward Hawaii. America had actually lost track of Japan's flattops as far back as mid-November. Tasked to keep Pacific Fleet commander Admiral Husband Kimmel apprised of when and where a potential enemy might strike, Layton could only speculate as to the location of Japan's main aircraft carriers, writing simply: "Homeland waters?"

"What?" Kimmel had barked when he read the intelligence sheet. "You don't know where the carriers are?"

"No, sir," Layton had answered, pointing out that he had only guessed homeland waters.

"You mean to say that you, the intelligence officer, don't know where the carriers are?" the admiral pressed.

"No, sir," Layton replied. "I don't."

"You mean they could be coming around Diamond Head, and you wouldn't know it?"

"Yes, sir," the intelligence officer answered, "but I hope they'd have been sighted before now."

The irony of that conversation would haunt Layton.

Cryptanalysts dropped the flag officers' code after the Pearl Harbor attack and focused on cracking JN-25, prying the sophisticated system open in time to decipher details of Japan's plans to capture Port Moresby and Midway. This intelligence tap spilled over to the undersea service, thanks in part to Lieutenant Commander Jasper Holmes. A Naval Academy graduate and former skipper of the submarine *S-30*, Holmes had waged a battle against spinal arthritis that forced him to retire in 1936, ending thirteen years of commissioned service. The Navy recalled him on the eve of the war, but this time as an intelligence officer based at Pearl Harbor. The intelligence community fiercely guarded information derived from cryptology—dubbed Ultra—for fear that leaks or unexpected successes might arouse Japanese suspicions and trigger a code change. But Holmes argued that the submarine force could benefit from America's cryptologic success. "Intelligence, like money, may be secure when it is unused and locked up in a safe," he would write. "It yields no dividends until it is invested."

The veteran submariner succeeded in convincing the head of Station Hypo, Oahu's communications intelligence unit. Armed with decrypted information on aircraft carriers or enemy task force movements, Holmes would pen the longitude and latitude on his palm and walk it over to Vice Admiral Lockwood's chief of staff, careful to scrub his hands of the evidence afterward. Despite Holmes's best intentions, the effort netted little of value, largely because the enemy targets were all well-protected naval ships. Aircraft carriers tended to steam far faster than American submarines, making it difficult for the undersea boats to get into an attack position. Radio intelligence further revealed that when submarines did attack, torpedo and exploder malfunctions often led to failure. "Whatever the causes," Holmes would later write, "in the first two years of the war American submarines sank no aircraft carriers, and the Ultra information on carrier movements that we gave to submarines was all risk for no gain."

But that changed in early 1943 when cryptanalysts cracked what many dubbed the "maru code," the Japanese cryptosystem used to route merchant ships throughout empire waters. Solution of the four-digit code with a superimposed cipher promised to unlock the submarine force's full potential to destroy Japan's economy. The daily noon position reports of each convoy combined with the 8 a.m. and 8 p.m. reports of individual skippers allowed American analysts to plot Japan's freighters, tankers, and transports in real time. This made manageable the undersea service's otherwise impossible task of patrolling eight million square miles. A submarine skipper alerted of a convoy's course could plan to intercept, shadow the ships, and set up the perfect attack, stretching the assault out over hours or even days if necessary. These same decrypts would allow Lockwood and his staff to gauge the success of such attacks, often listing the names of enemy ships sunk and types of cargo lost to the number of troops killed.

Commander Richard Voge served at the time as Lockwood's operations officer. The Chicago native had commanded the first submarine lost in the war: *Sealion*, bombed during an overhaul at Cavite just three days after the attack on Pearl Harbor. Voge helped make the Japanese pay for that loss when he skippered the submarine *Sailfish*, making four patrols into enemy waters in those dark early days of the war. Voge understood the value of the intelligence his old friend Holmes possessed. The two men met at 9 a.m. daily; Voge armed with a chart of the western Pacific that showed the estimated positions of all submarines on patrol. A review of the latest decrypts allowed the officers to update the thin-paper plot with projected convoy routes. Any late-breaking information could be shared via a private phone line that bypassed the switchboard and with hand-crank magneto ringers. The submarine force then used special internal codes—unknown to even American surface ships—to relay target info to submarines at sea.

Code breakers developed fifty-seven possible targets in January 1943. Submarines missed forty of those for various reasons, ranging from failure to receive the message to bad weather or the submarine hunting another target at the time. Of the fifteen targets spotted, submarines attacked eleven, damaging seven and putting four on the bottom. *Silversides* had been one of the first submarines to benefit from this breakthrough in intelligence. On his fourth patrol off the Caroline Islands—as torpedoman George Platter convalesced from his appendectomy—Burlingame received one of his first Ultra messages: "1 freighter to arrive at 07-04N, 151-12E on 4 January 1943 approaching from position 8-01N, 149-29E—speed 10 knots." The brief message had given Burly all he needed: the precise arrival date and position as well as the speed and course of the target. Burlingame peered through the scope at 11:28 that morning. Just as the Ultra predicted, the target arrived on time. The freighter Burlingame hoped to sink, however, turned out to be a marked hospital ship, off limits to attack.

Another Ultra soon reached *Silversides*, alerting Burlingame that the 10,023-ton tanker *Toei Maru* would reach Truk at 10 a.m. on January 18. The message revealed that a single escort guarded this prized target. Burlingame picked up the *Toei Maru* hours ahead of its scheduled arrival, firing four stern tubes at 2:55. The skipper watched as multiple fish crashed into the tanker. "Tremendous explosion and pillar of black smoke 200' high," he recorded in his report, "flame and sparks at its base and out stack." Burlingame's Ultra fortune continued. Intelligence alerted the skipper days later of a four-ship convoy that carried more than 4,000 enemy soldiers, horses, and supplies. Burlingame picked up the freighters on January 20 and fired six torpedoes, hitting the 5,154-ton passenger cargo ship *Sonedono Maru*, the 4,391-ton freighter *Surabaya Maru*, and the 8,230-ton freighter *Meiu Maru*. Code breakers had helped Burly put 17,775 tons of enemy ships on the bottom and kill more than 800 sailors.

But *Silversides* wasn't alone. Submarine successes had continued month after month as code breakers decrypted Japanese intercepts. From January to October 1943 code breakers developed 810 possible targets. Submarines spotted 354 of those, chased down and attacked 120, damaging fifty-six and destroying another thirty-three. "There were nights," Holmes observed, "when nearly every American submarine on patrol in the central Pacific was working on the basis of information derived from cryptanalysis." *Drum* was one of those. Armed with a cup of hot soup from the galley, Rindskopf liked to volunteer for the midnight to 4 a.m. radio room watch, decoding messages. The wiry lieutenant would slip on a garish yellow Aloha shirt when an Ultra arrived. *Drum* would go to battle stations within a few hours and attack a ship. After a few sinkings, the next time *Drum* went to battle stations, Rindskopf looked up to find most of the crew dressed in yellow Aloha shirts.

This November morning *Drum* lookouts had spotted the convoy at 6:05 a.m. Within three minutes, *Drum* dove to attack. Williamson counted three ships guarded by three escorts. One of those that appeared in the skipper's periscope was the *Hie Maru*, an 11,621-ton behemoth. The 535-foot-long vessel had begun its life thirteen years earlier as a transpacific liner, shuttling passengers and cargo between Yokohama and Seattle. One of *Hie Maru*'s earliest voyages had been a mission of peace. The city of Yokohama in 1930 presented Seattle with an eight-ton traditional Japanese stone lantern in appreciation for the city's help after the Great Kanto Earthquake a few years earlier. Seattle reciprocated with a gift of 2,000 rosebushes, many transported in the cargo hold of *Hie Maru*. Requisitioned by the military like so many other ships, *Hie Maru* served as a transport and submarine tender. In place of goodwill and friendship, Williamson saw only his first target—and a very valuable one.

Williamson wasted no time. He may have been a new wartime skipper, but Williamson knew which ship to target: the largest, the *Hie Maru*. The former ocean liner steamed in the middle of the convoy, guarded by an escort off the starboard beam. Williamson watched the ships zigzag across the glassy sea toward him. The skipper fired all six bow torpedoes at 7:10 a.m. Twenty-two seconds later, the first exploded prematurely. With the element of surprise gone Williamson ordered the *Drum* deep. He heard two torpedo explosions, but the run times showed the fish had detonated at about 1,500 yards—250 yards short of *Hie Maru*. Not only did the run times not match, but the explosions sounded reminiscent of the earlier premature detonation. Williamson waited out four depth charges before he started up. Maybe he had damaged the ship and could hunt it down. He surfaced to find only debris and scrum from the depth charges, but no oil or wreckage. His prized target had slipped away.

It would take almost a week of false starts, but *Drum* lookouts finally spotted smoke again six days later on November 17, almost fourteen miles away. The three-ship convoy, guarded by two submarine chasers, had departed Rabaul two days earlier, bound for Truk. *Tamashima Maru* and *Nagoya Maru* accompanied *Hie Maru* through the choppy seas. Williamson had a rare second chance at this massive target. *Hie Maru* had not only escaped *Drum* a week earlier, but had also survived an attack by B-24 bombers that had damaged the former ocean liner. Williamson didn't want to let the ship escape again. The skipper and his men tracked the convoy on the surface, submerging more than eleven miles ahead. Williamson fired four bowshots at 2:40 p.m. and then ordered *Drum* deep. *Hie Maru*'s goodluck had finally run out. The skipper listened beneath the waves as a one-and-a-half-ton torpedo ripped open the *Hie Maru*'s cargo hold that had once carried an American peace offering of roses.

Rindskopf was impressed. He had begun the patrol worried that Williamson, handicapped by age and lack of wartime experience, would be timid. Diesel Dan had so far surprised him, sinking a significant target that would no doubt sting the enemy. Maybe you could teach an old seadog a new trick. Williamson demonstrated his aggressiveness again just five days later when lookouts spotted smoke on the horizon on the morning of November 22. The faint puff of smoke at seventeen miles developed into a four-ship convoy guarded by two escorts. Williamson, once again, didn't hesitate. He ordered *Drum* down and his men to battle stations. Williamson picked the lead freighter in the starboard column as his victim and fired four fish at 11:37 a.m. He didn't stick around, but ordered *Drum* deep. Williamson heard a string of heavy explosions that didn't match the run times. He suspected the blasts weren't hits, but end-of-run detonations.

The skipper ordered *Drum* up to periscope depth more than half an hour later. He spotted the four freighters lying to in the opposite direction in the . rippled sea. He couldn't see any visible damage, but the freighters had not scattered. Maybe he had hit one after all. The escorts hunted *Drum*. Williamson had found few density layers in the waters between Bismarck Archipelago and the Caroline Islands that would shield him from the enemy's sonar. Today was no different: he was naked and exposed. One of the escorts turned toward *Drum*. Williamson ordered his boat back down to 300 feet, but it was too late. The escort zeroed in on *Drum*. The first charge detonated at 12:43 p.m., followed by three more. The violent explosions—the worst Rindskopf had experienced in his eight patrols—shook the submarine. The escort passed directly overhead. The men inside the cramped conning tower hundreds of feet below could hear the rhythmic thump of its propellers through the hull.

There was nowhere for *Drum* to hide. The escort let go four more depth charges. Throughout the boat, men braced themselves. Rindskopf heard the click of a depth charge detonator and knew the blast would be close. The explosion rocked the submarine. The lights flickered as more blasts followed. Chief Petty Officer George Schaedler, who operated the hydraulic manifold in the control room, turned to address the diving officer just as one hit. Insulation blew off the hull and struck him, cutting and bruising his face. Had he not turned away, Schaedler felt certain he would have been blinded. A finger-sized stream of water suddenly shot across the conning tower. Rindskopf looked back to discover the explosion had cracked the after bulkhead between the hinges of the door that led to *Drum*'s main deck. Water streamed in at a rate of three gallons a minute. The water was not the problem as much as the structural integrity, given the incredible sea pressure at 300 feet. One crack could collapse the conning tower.

The battle station auxiliary man appeared, armed with a wrench. Depth charges could loosen glands and cause leaks, problems easily resolved with a few turns of a wrench. This was different. There was nothing the men could do to fix this leak at sea other than head to the surface and decrease the pressure. Rindskopf prepared to evacuate the conning tower. He ordered the quartermaster to grab the chronometers—sensitive clocks—and navigational gear and haul them below to his cabin. Three more depth charges exploded, all distant. Had the escort lost the *Drum*? The men waited, but no more charges followed. Williamson couldn't risk raising his scope too early only to be spotted. Another strong blast might doom *Drum*. The skipper waited. Three hours after the last explosion, he ordered *Drum* up to periscope depth. The freighters and escorts had vanished. Williamson had gotten lucky again. He surfaced *Drum* and began the long trip back to Pearl Harbor, the patrol now over.

9

SILVERSIDES

"The sixteenth depth charge just exploded with no results except to our nerves."

—Robert Worthington,
May 22, 1942, diary

John Coye paced the bridge of *Silversides*. It was 12:58 a.m. on December 29. The skipper, officer of the deck, and lookouts were dressed in waterproofed canvas clothes on this dark and overcast night as *Silversides* cut through the swells on patrol off Palau, a white frothy foam in its bow wake. Unlike some commanders who micromanaged a submarine's operation, Coye preferred to delegate to his junior officers. He didn't meddle with watch schedules, galley menus, or personnel squabbles unless absolutely necessary. Even then he did so only reluctantly. Coye's job was to sink ships. That often meant he spent his downtime in the wardroom or his cabin. "My own personal attitude was that I should try to remain rested, so in case something came up I would be fresh," he once commented. "I spent probably more time in my bunk on patrol than anybody else."

Tonight was different.

The radar had picked up a contact thirteen minutes earlier at a range of more than eleven miles. That initial contact had since developed into nine pips that glowed a soft yellow on the conning tower's green radar screen. The fire control party estimated that those pips represented a six-ship convoy accompanied by three escorts. The southbound ships would reach Palau at daybreak. *Silversides* had only until then to sink them. Coye hungered for an attack. He had been on patrol now for twenty-five days without much luck. Three days earlier, the skipper had fired four shots at a loaded freighter that had just departed a bauxite pier, only to be driven deep by an escort as the torpedoes exploded on a reef, his only reward a depth charge attack that rattled the boat.

Coye felt anxious to follow up on his earlier success. During his previous patrol, he'd sunk four ships in just thirty-four days, half of what the beloved Burlingame had sunk in five patrols. In a private critique, Vice Admiral Lockwood noted that Coye needed to learn to finesse his shots. But that was a minor flaw in an otherwise excellent patrol. Coye's attacks showed that the new skipper seemed still to be a bit anxious, unsure of his relationships with his officers and crew, and rough, a style that mirrored his rumpled appearance. But Coye boasted what some submariners lacked: determination. Plus he learned fast. Lockwood recognized Coye's potential and had high hopes. "This short patrol was aggressively and successfully conducted," the admiral wrote in his endorsement. "*Silversides* carried out two tenacious pursuits of convoys, one of which was sixty four hours duration, and the other eighty five hours. Both of these pursuits and the successive attacks inflicted severe damage on the enemy."

Coye hoped to visit such fury again on the enemy, this time with the aid of new tools. During a recent refit, Pearl Harbor technicians had installed a new high-power transmitter for the radar along with what was known as a plan position indicator. The primitive radar *Silversides* had used up until now would only provide a range and bearing of a target, a challenge to interpret in cases of multiple ships and changing speeds and courses. The plan position indicator in contrast displayed radar returns as a two-dimensional picture presented on a circular scope in the conning tower. *Silversides* occupied the center of the scope surrounded by a web of lines and circles that denoted bearings and increased ranges. The plan position indicator allowed its operators for the first time to use radar to analyze the entire scene in real time, a perfect device for nighttime and foul weather attacks that *Silversides* officer Eugene Malone later wrote would "change the course of submarine warfare."

But the new technology had met with mixed results from some in the submarine force, due in large part to the tendency of the radar to fail. Burlingame had captured that frustration in repeated patrol reports, citing long stretches of radar failure, including his entire third patrol. "It is obviously useless to install such equipment unless it can be made to function properly." Burlingame's harping drew a sharp rebuke from his superiors. Captain John Brown, Jr., who served briefly as the acting commander of the submarines Pacific fleet before Lockwood took over, countered that the new radar technology "must not be belittled." "It is hoped that this will not keep the *Silversides* from becoming radar minded. Many submarines of this force have already used this equipment very successfully. One submarine made a night attack on a convoy in a snowstorm using radar during the entire approach enabling him to get in to advantageous range with subsequent sinkings," Brown wrote. "It is far too valuable a military weapon to overlook."

Six years Burlingame's junior and the son of a scientist, Coye embraced the promise of this new technology. He had shanghaied Malone off *S-31* for just that purpose. The twenty-two-year-old lanky lieutenant, who stood six feet, four inches tall and weighed just 135 pounds, had already enjoyed success with the new plan position indicator, thanks to an unorthodox acquisition. One afternoon in New Caledonia while still the radar officer on *S-31*, Malone had spied crates of cargo—including a plan position indicator—on a wharf designated for Admiral William Halsey's flagship. Malone reasoned that the admiral would no doubt prefer to see his radar installed on a fighting sub than on the flag bridge of a crowded battleship. His skipper agreed. Under the glare of moonlight, Malone and his radar crew hacksawed the scope into several pieces so it would slip through the aged submarine's narrow hatch. Armed with screwdrivers, needle-nose pliers, and soldering irons—not to mention luck—the men reassembled the scope.

It worked.

Malone manned Coye's new scope in the conning tower. Malone relished the newfound comfort of a modern fleet boat compared to his previous World War I–era submarine. "Gosh, this big boat life is wonderful," he wrote to his mother. "A shower we got, even. Of course, the head must perforce be complicated by the usual number of valves and that's a nuisance. But we have staterooms, a wardroom and everything. Wonderful. Such luxury, for a change." But the skinny Malone found his youth soon drew ribbing from *Silversides'* older officers. "Since I made lieutenant I've been absolutely raging most of the time with anger," he wrote. "Everyone insists on calling me to perfect strangers to whom I'm about to be introduced 'the boy lieutenant.'"

Malone and other sailors itched for action tonight, now sixty-six days since the last sinking. Unlike the sixth patrol, which had failed to garner a combat insignia award, the previous run had merited a pier-side ceremony at Pearl Harbor on a warm November day. "Dished out combat insignia to all hands," Malone wrote his family. "Lots of fun. Something else to fill up the front of the uniform with. Be a regular signpost by the time this bloody war is over." That awards ceremony was followed a few nights later by the wedding of communications officer Tom Keegan, a welcome celebration in a time of war. "His in laws had a wondrous reception, with people passing out all over the place, most enjoyable," Malone wrote in a letter. "We all wandered around with our shoes off, danced in fish ponds and had a beauteous time. Best party since the war so everyone said."

The last month at sea had proven largely uneventful for *Silversides*, ordered to patrol the waters around Palau. The United States and its Allies, having blocked Japanese expansion in the battles of the Coral Sea, Midway, and Guadalcanal, now battled the enemy in New Guinea. The second largest island in the world after Greenland, New Guinea stretched some 1,500 miles east to west with some 300,000 square miles of tangled jungles and menacing mountains that had blocked construction of overland roads, requiring that Allied forces execute amphibious land jumps up the coast. Troops slogged through stagnant swamps and fields of razor-sharp kunai grass while battling pythons, rats, and crocodiles that on occasion devoured bathing soldiers. "To die in front of Japanese guns," wrote one war photographer, "sometimes seems easier than to go on living in this strange battlefield where Nature has joined the combat as a vicious third antagonist."

American intelligence had determined that Japan used the Palau Islands as a staging area for troops and supplies headed to repel American forces in New Guinea. Climbing out of the Pacific swells some 500 miles east of the Philippines, Palau served as a major Japanese naval base in the western Carolines. Japan had seized the 110-mile string of islands from Germany as a spoil of the Great War, recognizing that the jagged coral reef that encircled Palau would make one of the Pacific's best fleet anchorages. Japan had worked in the years leading up to the war to convert this Pacific paradise into a fortress, building roads, concrete piers, and airfields. The Navy wanted *Silversides* to target Palau's traffic. "It is believed that convoys of troop-transports and supplies are being assembled for the New Guinea area at Palau," Coye's orders read. "Considerable convoy movements can be expected from the Empire and the coast of China to Palau and from Palau to the new Japanese base at Wewak."

Despite the promise of much traffic, the patrol had proven uneventful, including a reconnaissance of Wake, pummeled by American carrier forces in an October raid. Much of the patrol's excitement instead had stemmed from battles against rough seas that sickened the new recruits, including Lieutenant j.g. Carl Heidel. "He looks green like a plant," John Bienia wrote, "especially when the seas break over him, he sputters, coughs and blows." Conditions proved equally as rough below deck. "Some of the crates have broken open and oranges, apples, pears etc. are rolling all over the deck," one officer wrote. "Looks more like an untidy Greek fruit store than a submarine."

Men hoped to remedy the patrol's boredom on December 29 with an attack on a convoy that now steamed at ten knots toward Palau. Coye knew he had just five hours at best before dawn and the convoy's arrival in port. He had to work fast. The skipper, the officer of the deck, and the lookouts scanned the dark horizon with binoculars as *Silversides* closed the distance, its engines roaring. Rainsqualls peppered the night, perfect conditions for a night surface attack. The submarine's new radar showed the convoy's formation: two columns made up of three ships each and protected by several small escorts. The largest ship—the one Coye planned to target first—led the starboard column. The skipper ordered *Silversides* to approach on the convoy's starboard bow. Executive officer Robert Worthington manned the torpedo data computer in the conning tower just a few feet away from the lanky Malone on the radarscope.

The convoy zigzagged to the right at 1:40 a.m., leaving *Silversides* dead ahead of the starboard column. One of the escorts passed by eleven minutes later at a radar range of just 1,550 yards. The sonar operator heard the escort's pings, but the enemy failed to detect *Silversides*. Rain poured down, obscuring visibility, but Coye could still see the escort's bow waves and stern wake, the bright white of churned-up water standing out against the dark background. Coye judged from the silhouette that the escort was either a torpedo boat or destroyer. Three minutes later, the convoy zigzagged again. Coye surveyed the scene in amazement. *Silversides* now occupied the number two position of the starboard column, right in the heart of the enemy convoy. Malone stared at the radarscope below and reported that it looked like a bull's-eye with *Silversides* dead center. "We were surrounded by ships," Coye wrote. "Maximum range to any ship in convoy was about 2,500 yards, closest range under 600 yards."

Coye struggled for several anxious minutes to extract *Silversides*, clearing the convoy just as enemy lookouts spotted the submarine. Signal lights flashed between the ships as enemy skippers ordered evasive maneuvers. The port column scattered east, the starboard column west. The element of surprise had vanished. Coye had to attack—and fast, before the ships disappeared in different directions. Rain reduced visibility to less than two miles, but Malone reported that the radarscope showed several ships in the line of fire. Coye hustled to set up a snap shot at a freighter 600 yards away. *Silversides* pulled away at full speed, firing two stern shots in twelve seconds at 1:57 a.m. Thirty seconds passed, then a minute. Then two. An explosion lit up the night sky two minutes and twenty seconds after *Silversides* had fired. The skipper realized from the long run that the torpedoes had missed the target but hit and damaged a ship in the far column, the 4,667-ton *Bitchu Maru*. The escorts circled back toward the crippled ship.

The skipper noted that one of the cargo ships now fell in line behind *Silversides*, likely mistaking the submarine's low profile for one of the convoy's escorts. Coye ordered *Silversides* to slow down to let the freighter catch up. The cargo ship closed the distance to 1,600 yards. The skipper fired a stern shot at 2:02 a.m., followed eleven seconds later by another torpedo. The two fish now raced toward the freighter at forty-six knots. Coye watched in frustration as both missed. The skipper heard an explosion in the dark that he suspected was either a depth charge or another torpedo hit in the far column. He couldn't be sure. Coye's orderly attack had suddenly turned chaotic. Now that he had extracted *Silversides* from harm's way, the skipper had to slow down and refocus. Coye still had darkness and the rain. He still had the tactical advantage. The convoy was his to sink.

The skipper surveyed the scene. The starboard column had fanned out. The tanker and another freighter steamed south while the one Coye had just fired on headed west. The escorts appeared confused, patrolling to the east and dropping depth charges on ghost contacts. The skipper hunted for a victim. He spotted what he believed was a tanker—though actually a cargo ship—and ordered *Silversides* to close. Coye fired three shots at 2:46 a.m. and watched from the rain-soaked bridge as the torpedoes sped toward the 1,911-ton *Shichisei Maru* a little more than a mile away. One minute and thirty-eight seconds later, the first torpedo exploded. The second one slammed home five seconds later, followed by the third. The freighter, which carried ammunition and twenty-two small craft, broke in half and plunged to the bottom in minutes, killing thirty-five. "Radar pip disappeared," Coye wrote. "Doubt if there were many survivors."

Coye turned on another target, the 1,970-ton *Tenposan Maru*, which steamed more than two miles away. The rain made it impossible for Coye to use the binoculars affixed to the target-bearing transmitter. The skipper instead had to look down the device's vanes and estimate the target's bearing, a challenge compounded by the fact that he was too close to take accurate readings. Coye fired anyway, unleashing three torpedoes. After several minutes, he knew he'd missed. But half a minute later, Coye heard distant detonations. The skipper may have missed his target, but he'd hit something. He refocused on *Tenposan Maru* and fired again. This time two torpedoes slammed into the freighter, but it didn't sink. Coye spotted flashlights through the smoke as enemy sailors abandoned ship. He opted to fire a final torpedo into the crippled freighter at 4:23 a.m. The skipper watched the torpedo race past the target's stern. He adjusted his shot, but missed again. The frustrated skipper ordered *Silversides* to turn so he could fire his stern tubes. He backed down for a close range shot just as the injured freighter slipped beneath the dark waves.

Coye raced onward. He had only five torpedoes left, one in the forward torpedo room and four aft. The nearest target steamed more than five miles away. Dawn approached. He needed to hurry. Unknown to Coye, the 3,311-ton *Ryuto Maru* carried gasoline, coal, and food—4,300 tons of precious cargo the enemy would surely miss. The skipper didn't have time to set up a stern shot. He needed his final bowshot to hit home. Coye charged *Ryuto Maru* and fired at 5:02 a.m. The violent explosion two minutes later broke *Ryuto Maru*'s back. Coye watched the freighter slip beneath the waves just eight minutes later. "*Silversides* had herself a busy night of it, firing 16 torpedoes in about three hours," Coye wrote in his report. "If time had not been pressing attacks could have been made more deliberately and more hits obtained. Could have 'enjoyed' this convoy more if could have been able to spread this attack over two nights."

Coye had made the most of a hectic night. Rather than allow the alerted convoy to scatter, the skipper had capitalized on the chaos to hunt down ships. He had sunk three freighters in three hours to put a total of 7,192 tons of enemy shipping on the bottom. "Excellent aggressive patrol," Lockwood would later comment in a private critique, "fought all the way." Earlier questions over Coye's leadership among the *Silversides* officers now dissipated. Malone bragged about Coye in letters to his family. "I started out thinking this skipper was sort of a big fat dumb and happy guy, but I've been busy revising my estimate of him all the time. He's big and fat, but he definitely isn't dumb, far from it. He just moves slowly because that's the best way not to get anyone excited," Malone wrote. "He is developing into a cracker jack man on the attack. Calm as all get out which makes the rest of us that much more scared."

The next few days slipped past. Coye peered through the periscope to monitor a life raft that bobbed in the waves with two enemy sailors. Coye hoped to use the men as bait. If the survivors drew a destroyer into a rescue, Coye would have a worthwhile target for his last four torpedoes. But the Japanese knew better and instead sent a small patrol—nothing big enough to warrant attack. The officers and crew used the downtime to relax and usher in the new year. Malone, who stood the midnight to 4 a.m. watch on January 1, recorded the deck log's first entry of 1944 as a poem. "Underway as before, except the year is forty-four," he wrote. "We're making full on all four mains, looking for Nips to give some pains."

Malone climbed up to the bridge to take over the watch as the officer of the deck at noon on January 2. Four lookouts, a quartermaster, and the junior officer of the deck joined him as the submarine zigzagged north in the waters off Palau. The sky was equatorial blue with no clouds, the sea calm with only a few whitecaps generated by a light breeze. The junior officer of the deck and the quartermaster chatted aft on the cigarette deck instead of scanning the air for enemy planes and the horizon for distant ships. Malone decided to break it up at 12:51 p.m., turning back just in time to spot an impulse bubble some 1,200 yards off the starboard beam. The frothy water was a telltale sign: a torpedo had just been fired. A Japanese submarine had caught them off guard. *Silversides* had become the hunted.

"Left full rudder, all ahead emergency," Malone shouted into the bridge microphone. "Make ready the after tubes."

The four Fairbanks Morse engines roared. *Silversides* turned to port, presenting as narrow a target as possible. Malone's adrenaline raced as he tracked the torpedo's wake. A second and third suddenly joined the attack. Three torpedoes now sped through the blue water toward *Silversides*. Malone watched the distance close. *Silversides* completed its turn and charged away from the torpedoes. Malone watched the first fish pass just fifty yards off the starboard beam. A miss. The second passed to the right of the first. Malone waited. The third and final torpedo, fired after *Silversides* began its turn, passed just twenty-five yards off the port side, close enough that Malone could see details of the torpedo and its wake. "Lt. Malone deserves much credit for his prompt and correct action," Coye wrote. "After firing, could see periscope astern. The Jap deserves credit for his periscope handling."

Silversides raced at emergency speed until Coye ordered his crew to dive and reverse course. He planned to reverse roles with the enemy sub when it surfaced that night, but a fire in the maneuvering room suddenly interrupted his plans. Coye's vessel now lost all power to both shafts. Crews fought the blaze, which burned the overhead cork. Smoke and heavy fumes flooded the boat, sickening the damage control crew. Several men were on the verge of collapse as others slipped on rescue breathing apparatus and fought the fire. Damage control crews burned through ten fire extinguishers before finally wrestling control of the blaze twelve minutes later. With the port shaft functioning again, Coye ordered *Silversides* to surface. Crews opened the hatches to ventilate the boat as power returned to the starboard shaft. The crisis had passed. "The words 'fire in the maneuvering room' when heard in enemy controlled waters is a thrill," Coye wrote in his report. "But definitely not a pleasant one."

Radar picked up a convoy at 11:25 a.m. two days later at a range of eighteen miles. *Silversides* tracked the convoy, which steamed east at ten knots throughout the afternoon; one of the lookouts searching with the high scope spotted the mast tops of two large ships. The rough weather made it difficult for *Silversides* to run at periscope depth and ruled out firing torpedoes. The skipper decided to wait until nightfall, hoping the seas would moderate and he could fight on the surface. Coye closed to a little more than eight miles just after sunset. The radar now showed two tankers accompanied by a single escort. The skipper waited. Not long after the moon finally set at 1:30 a.m.,

Coye ordered his men to battle stations. The seas were still rough, prompting the skipper to order the torpedoes set to run at fifteen feet beneath the churning waves. Coye closed the distance and fired his last four fish.

Coye knew within minutes he'd missed. The explosions all came too late—the timing didn't match the distance to his target. The skipper speculated that the weather was still too rough to shoot and that the heavy seas caused at least some of his torpedoes to run erratic. He knew he should have waited a day to attack. Coye sent a contact report at 4:25 a.m., alerting his superiors that he planned to track the convoy even though he was out of torpedoes. He hoped another submarine would join him, but by afternoon a new destroyer had joined the Japanese convoy instead. Coye sent out another contact report. Then another and another. For one interminable week *Silversides* trailed the convoy alone, unable to do anything more than watch and lurk. Coye witnessed with frustration the ship's safe arrival at the Japanese stronghold of Truk. "*Silversides* safely escorted these two tankers for almost seven days and for over 1,400 miles," he wrote. "They must have at least had a bad case of the nerves."

Coye had no choice but to begin the long journey back to Pearl Harbor, a trip made all the more painful by Lieutenant j.g. Brooks Parker's insistence on entertaining the wardroom with the recorder he received as a Christmas gift. "Some utter fool sent one of the other officers a musical, so called, instrument called a recorder," Malone griped in a letter. "It's looks like a post off an old fashioned bed more than anything else, and makes a noise like a sick flute." John Bienia echoed Malone in a letter of his own. "The recorder, incidentally, is the most horrible travesty of a musical instrument that has ever been concocted by some warped brain," he wrote. "It's made of wood, about two feet long, and one inch and a half thick. The instructions that came with it say that the first day the musical instrument should not be played over twenty minutes, and the next day thirty mins. are allowed, and it keeps on like that. But, by jumping if he gets even to the thirty min stage with that ghastly contraption, we'll JAM IT DOWN HIS THROAT."

Word arrived that Bienia would finally be transferred back to the States to join the crew of a new submarine, then under construction in Maine. Such orders promised months of downtime as workers finished construction. Bienia had served on *Silversides* since the start of the war. He had watched almost all of his friends cycle off. Now came his turn—and he felt overjoyed.

"Darling, sit back and relax before you read any further. Here's the good news! You and I are going to the States after this run," he wrote to his wife in Hawaii. "I was going to wait and surprise you when I came home, but this way you can be able to arrange whatever you want in the way of packing, etc." He promised to take her on a cross-country trip east, setting out from San Francisco. "Just a couple of gypsies—and am I going to make love to you, darling," he wrote. "I'll kiss you in trains, planes, buses, hotels, bars & jails. You'll be the most kissed girl in the world."

The ecstatic Bienia prepared for his departure when *Silversides* returned to port. He wrote instructions to his wife for the move, the need to withdraw money, settle debts, and buy steamer trunks. Not until four days later did the usual instigator of practical jokes learn that he had been the victim of a cruel one himself. Bienia felt crushed. He would never send those letters he wrote his wife. "The nasty culprit that had decoded the message, and substituted my name for the real person to get new construction, had decided that maybe it wasn't a joke after all, and in the dead of night reworded the message correctly," Bienia wrote to his wife, explaining what had happened. "It was my habit to read all the messages after I came off watch, and usually I'd read my transfer message before going to sleep, and this night I damn near ground my teeth to my gums when I saw the change. I raised a lot of ELL that night, and wanted to beat the stuffin out of the sadist that did that to me, but no one owned up."

10

TANG

"Sadly, as the *Tang*'s story testifies, in war there can be an inverse moral:
The greater the performance, the harsher the consequence."

—Richard O'Kane,
Clear the Bridge!

The prolonged blast from the USS *Tang*'s whistle echoed across the oily water
of the Pearl Harbor submarine base at noon on January 22, 1944, signaling
the departure of this brand-new submarine's first war patrol. Few noticed the
now common roar that had become a part of everyday life at Pearl; twenty-
six submarines would depart that month for patrols in Japanese-controlled
waters. But for Lieutenant Commander Richard Hetherington O'Kane,
the event was momentous: his first command of a submarine. The thirty-
two-year-old O'Kane—just eleven days shy of his next birthday—didn't dwell
on the accomplishment. He had scores to settle. The two other wartime submarines O'Kane had served on had since departed for patrol never to come
home, joining the growing list of some two dozen American submarines lost
since the war's start just over two years earlier. Entombed inside one was
O'Kane's mentor, the man who had taught him how to sink ships.

Tang eased out of its slip, turned in place, and headed out of the harbor,
escorted this warm winter afternoon by the destroyer *Litchfield*, Oahu's iconic
landmark, the extinct volcano Diamond Head, falling away in the distance.
O'Kane's orders—stamped utmost secret—directed he head to Wake Island,
the tiny coral atoll two thirds of the way between Hawaii and Guam that
Japan had seized soon after the attack on Pearl Harbor. War planners feared

the Japanese would use the three-square-mile sandbar to oppose the planned invasion of the Marshall Islands, code-named Operation Flintlock. American bombers planned to neutralize Wake. Eighteen Catalina patrol bombers—in two waves of nine timed an hour apart—were to lift off between 3 and 4 p.m. from Midway on January 30 for the seven-and-a-half-hour trip to Wake. *Tang*'s orders were that the sub wait thirty-five miles offshore to relay weather reports, help planes navigate, and rescue downed aviators. Only then could O'Kane depart to kill ships.

Nothing in O'Kane's formative years hinted at the fighter he had become; if anything his background suggested a quiet career in science or academia. The blue-eyed New Hampshire native with a ruddy complexion, light brown hair, and large features grew up the son of professor and author, Walter O'Kane, who taught entomology at the University of New Hampshire. Despite his academic father, the younger O'Kane did not excel in the classroom. The prestigious Phillips Academy in Massachusetts kicked him out after he was caught out of town without permission. He ran afoul his first year at the Naval Academy after he cheated and helped a struggling classmate at recitation. The school assigned him 100 demerits and required him to quarter and mess for forty-five days aboard the stationship *Reina Mercedes*. But even in his moral lapse O'Kane showed the loyalty and integrity that would later define his leadership. He didn't hide his guilt, but owned up to it—so much so that he impressed the commandant of midshipmen. "Investigation of this case brought out that this action on the part of Midshipman O'Kane was thoughtless and committed on the spur of the moment and was not of the nature of any premeditated fraud," the commandant wrote. "Attention is particularly invited to his straightforward statement."

Upon graduation in the muggy May of 1934, O'Kane stood in the bottom half of his class, ranked 245 out of 464. He would make up for his lack of academic rigor once he reported for submarine school in January 1938 in New London. O'Kane's class of about thirty officers proved competitive, boasting men who would become some of the war's top submarine skippers: Slade Cutter in *Seahorse*, *Trigger* skipper Robert "Dusty" Dornin, and Norvell "Bub" Ward in *Guardfish*. The young officers sensed war was inevitable; the only question was when. O'Kane pounded the books. He studied diesel engineering, batteries, torpedoes, and torpedo fire control. He reviewed Morse code and practiced dives in Great War–era boats off the Connecticut and Rhode

Island coasts. His self-discipline and drive wowed his classmates. "Everybody was kind of laughing at Dick because all he did was study. And Dick was a fairly bright person," Cutter recalled. "He worked his butt off at submarine school."

O'Kane spent more than three years on board *Argonaut*—a submarine later sunk by the Japanese—before he reported to *Wahoo* in 1942 as the executive officer under Lieutenant Commander Marvin Kennedy, whose reddish hair and fair skin earned him the nickname "Pinky." The thirty-six-year-old Kennedy boasted an exceptional résumé, but Kennedy had gained his experience in peacetime. He proved adept at drills, practice dives, and maneuvers, but struggled to apply them in combat, much to the frustration of O'Kane. That crystallized just thirty-eight days into *Wahoo*'s first patrol in September 1942 when the submarine spotted the *Chiyoda* alone off the Japanese stronghold of Truk, an 11,000-ton seaplane carrier similar to *Mizuho*, which *Drum* destroyed just months earlier. Kennedy's demand that the periscope never rise more than three feet out of the water—a tactic aimed at limiting the submarine's exposure—meant that officers failed to spot *Chiyoda* until too late. Likewise, *Wahoo*'s seven-knot submerged speed proved no match for the seaplane carrier that zigzagged toward safety at eighteen knots. "There were no screens or escorts, and any planes that might have been overhead never came within the periscope field," Kennedy wrote in his report. "The Japs were just begging someone to knock off this Tender, but it was not our lucky day."

O'Kane fumed. He blamed *Wahoo*'s failure on poor tactics and timidity—not bad luck. But a chance for redemption emerged five days later when O'Kane spotted an aircraft carrier shortly past daybreak. Through the periscope the men mistakenly identified the ship as *Ryujo*, an 8,000-ton light carrier American pilots had sunk six weeks earlier off Guadalcanal in the Battle of the Eastern Solomons. Two destroyers escorted the carrier this morning steaming at fourteen knots. The veteran skipper and every man on board knew the potential prize just 11,000 yards ahead. Carriers were rare and coveted targets. Officers made careers off such kills. The pressure mounted. "If we bagged him, it would be the first live, fully commissioned carrier to be sunk by one of our subs," one officer later wrote. "When word went round that the big ship had been spotted, our men were wild with excitement."

O'Kane ordered the *Wahoo* to chase. The sub's speed increased to nine knots, before Kennedy suddenly ordered it cut to one third. The anxious

O'Kane felt the submarine slow to a three-knot crawl as the skipper peered through the periscope, the carrier slipping farther away each minute. *Wahoo* began the chase again, only to slow for another look. Then another. The carrier soon vanished. Kennedy blew it. The crew was crushed. "Made approach which, upon final analysis, lacked aggressiveness and skill," Kennedy confessed. "Watched the best target we could ever hope to find go over the hill untouched."

Alone on the cigarette deck afterward, O'Kane pressed his skipper to request a week's extension to the patrol, scheduled to end in just two days. *Wahoo* still had seventeen torpedoes left, a month's worth of coffee, meat, and vegetables, and more than 16,000 gallons of diesel, enough fuel, O'Kane noted, to cruise back to the United States. With more time and aggressiveness, O'Kane felt *Wahoo* could sink a ship.

Kennedy's answer shocked his executive officer. "No, Dick," he replied. "We're going to take *Wahoo* back to get someone in command who can sink ships; we're never going to win the war this way."

O'Kane respected his skipper's honesty, and believed that Kennedy's tenure on *Wahoo* was over. Back in Pearl Harbor the crew speculated who would replace Kennedy. To the crew's shock, Kennedy returned. O'Kane fumed. Protocol demanded that he go forward and greet his skipper. The executive officer instead rushed to headquarters to see the force chief of staff. In a potentially career-ending move, O'Kane demanded the Navy relieve Kennedy as skipper. He noted that Kennedy had as much asked for that in his candid admission of the first patrol's failures. The chief of staff listened, then noted that Kennedy had once worked for Rear Admiral Robert English, commander of submarine forces. English had given his friend a second chance. To compromise and to help spur Kennedy, the Navy would send Dudley Morton along as a prospective commanding officer.

But Kennedy's poor performance continued on *Wahoo*'s second patrol off the Solomon Islands in the fall of 1942. O'Kane now wrestled with a moral dilemma. Though required to obey his skipper's orders, O'Kane felt doing so only damaged the war effort. The tension between the men worsened to the point it became obvious to the rest of *Wahoo*'s officers and crew.

The skipper's timidity prompted *Wahoo* to muff a nighttime attack on a potential convoy. O'Kane stewed. A week later an Ultra message alerted *Wahoo* to an 18,000-ton loaded tanker, a ship whose precious fuel the enemy would surely miss. But fear of an escort prompted Kennedy to dive and miss the chance to attack. O'Kane could no longer tolerate it. When the captain retired to his cabin to rest, O'Kane consulted a copy of *Navy Regulations*. He looked up his responsibilities as executive officer and regulations for the assumption of command, a bold move that he first contemplated after Kennedy botched the carrier attack. The skipper, whom O'Kane believed had gone to sleep, suddenly climbed up the ladder into the conning tower. Kennedy spotted the open book atop the radar, believing it was a repair manual. He picked it up and began to read. O'Kane waited for the eruption, but none came. "No words were exchanged," he later wrote, "but now each knew exactly where he stood with the other."

When *Wahoo* arrived in Australia, Captain James Fife relieved Kennedy of command. The Navy tapped Dudley Morton, the prospective commanding officer who had witnessed *Wahoo*'s disastrous second patrol.

Morton proved everything Kennedy was not. Three and a half years O'Kane's senior, the Kentucky Baptist radiated physical strength. With blue, wide-spaced eyes, light brown hair, and a ruddy complexion, Morton stood almost six feet tall and weighed more than 170 pounds. He boasted large hands, broad shoulders, and a jaw that *Time* magazine later described as a "boulder." His prominent mouth and ear-to-ear grin earned him the nickname "Mushmouth"—later shortened to just "Mush"—after the character in the popular *Moon Mullins* comic strip. The skipper fueled the name by showing off his trick of stuffing four golf balls in his mouth at once. Morton's physical power defined his athletic career at the Naval Academy where he played varsity football and wrestled all four years until his 1930 graduation. But his fearsome stature camouflaged a warm and gentle nature. He never had to raise his voice; men wanted to follow him. "He was built like a bear, and as playful as a cub," an officer wrote. "The crew loved him."

Wahoo's new skipper approached submarine warfare much as he did his beloved wrestling. You didn't win by avoiding your opponent. Kennedy's tactic of waiting for ships to come to him had clearly failed. So had his timid approach of pursuing ships submerged and pausing for endless periscope searches as faster surface ships disappeared over the horizon. Morton planned to stay on the surface, use more lookouts, cover greater distances. If an attack failed, he would not give up. He would go after his target again and again until he sank the ship. Morton's aggressive new tactics would lead his men to later hail him "Mush the Magnificent"; the press would label him the "maker of Jap widows."

Morton immediately set out to change *Wahoo*'s culture. Kennedy had covered the bulkheads with close-up pictures of Japanese ships, an idea designed to help his lookouts recognize the silhouettes. Morton yanked them down and plastered simple slogans with red block letters that read: "SHOOT THE SONS OF BITCHES." The messages reflected Morton's single-minded view of his job, a view he demanded all men on board share. "In his mind anyone who did not fight the enemy with every bit of his capability was not doing his duty," one officer later wrote, "and he felt nothing but contempt for that person." Morton's aggressiveness rattled some *Wahoo*'s officers, who had grown used to Kennedy's leadership. "Most of us, in calculating the risk, threw in a mental note that we were worth more to the Navy alive than dead—and to our wives and children as well," wrote George Grider, *Wahoo*'s third-ranking officer. "But when Mush expressed himself on tactics, the only risk he recognized was the risk of not sinking enemy tonnage."

O'Kane had found a kindred spirit. Unlike Kennedy, who had refused to delegate responsibility to his executive officer, Morton would come to depend on O'Kane. "You will be my co-approach officer," Morton told O'Kane. "You'll make all observations and fire all torpedoes, but I'll con *Wahoo* to the best attack position." If O'Kane could handle the mechanics of an attack, Morton felt he could focus on the big picture and make faster decisions. Some officers watched the development of this unorthodox method with unease. The doubts these men harbored about Morton only reaffirmed previous concerns about O'Kane, worries that Kennedy's tight leadership had kept in check. Grider, who shared a stateroom with the exec, found O'Kane "overly garrulous and potentially unstable." "He talked a great deal—reckless, aggressive talk—and it was natural to wonder how much of it was no more than talk," Grider wrote. "With Mush and Dick in the saddle, how would the *Wahoo* fare?"

Wahoo would fare exceptionally.

Morton and O'Kane developed in the first half of 1943 into one of the submarine force's top teams, claiming to sink a staggering five ships on *Wahoo*'s third patrol though a postwar review of Japanese records could confirm only three kills. Morton boasted in a radio message to Pearl Harbor that he had destroyed an entire four-ship convoy, a feat no submarine had yet achieved, though he would only be credited after the war with three of the four ships. General Douglas MacArthur even awarded the aggressive skipper the prestigious Army Distinguished Service Cross after Morton clobbered a troop transport, though the ugly manner in which he attacked that ship would come to haunt *Wahoo*'s legacy. *Wahoo*'s fourth patrol claimed another eight ships, a figure postwar review of Japanese records would actually bump up to nine, setting a record for the most ships sunk on a single patrol. When the deck gun jammed in a battle with a trawler, Morton's men lobbed home-made Molotov cocktails. "Morton is the heavy swordsman, the saber," one reporter described of the duo. "O'Kane the quick rapier. Together they are deadly."

The Navy soon realized that *Wahoo* could generate positive press. Newspaper and magazine articles described the submarine returning from patrol with a broom lashed to its periscope, the centuries-old naval symbol of a clean sweep, meaning the boat had fired all of its torpedoes. Morton appeared on the Philip Morris radio program in mid July 1943 with his three-and-a-half-year-old son, Doug. Warner Bros. hired the skipper as a technical adviser for the submarine thriller *Destination Tokyo*—starring Cary Grant—and he even took actor Errol Flynn on a ride. But in letters to friends and family, Morton wrote that he took such great risks, not for celebrity, but to protect his wife, son, and daughter, whose photos he displayed on his desk in his cabin. "Take good care of my family for me," he wrote to his father. "You know that it is for such a grand family that I fight so hard."

Ever the professor's son, O'Kane studied his mentor. He had gone from one extreme under Kennedy to another under Morton, from muffed attacks on aircraft carriers to sinking an entire convoy. The divergence in tactics of these two skippers would prove symbolic of the larger struggle inside the submarine force as older skippers appeared hobbled by outdated tactics and timidity that reflected their peacetime training compared to younger captains, whose experience came during actual war patrols. O'Kane would have to develop his own style as skipper. Were Morton's methods the best? Should he steer a middle course between Kennedy and Morton? Could O'Kane achieve the same success as Morton with less risk to his ship and crew? O'Kane would later wrestle with these questions when the Navy assigned him his own boat—then under construction at Mare Island—after he completed five patrols on *Wahoo*. But Morton still had another lesson to teach.

Malfunctioning torpedoes plagued *Wahoo's* sixth patrol in the Sea of Japan. Morton attacked nine ships and failed to sink any of them, prompting him in his report to quote Rear Admiral David Farragut's famous line: "Damn the torpedoes." The irate skipper returned to Pearl Harbor in a record-breaking eleven-day run and begged Vice Admiral Lockwood to send him back to the Sea of Japan, where targets were plentiful. He wanted a new batch of torpedoes and a second shot. Lockwood relented. How could he refuse his top skipper, a man who had grown so successful that the Navy sat him down between patrols for a series of recorded interviews—both aboard *Wahoo* and in the Operations Office—in which he detailed his patrols, tactics, and exploits. Morton wrapped up his third interview at 11:50 a.m. on September 9, just seventy minutes before *Wahoo's* scheduled departure for its seventh patrol.

Dogged by prostate troubles—a little known fact among his peers—Morton refused to allow his pain to sideline him, though it took its toll. "During our periods in port he would be hospitalized and on patrol have to have semiweekly prostate massages," *Wahoo* Ensign John Griggs III later wrote. "Yet he did not let this deter him from his goal—sink Japs." The chemistry on board *Wahoo* also had changed, as the wardroom became a revolving door of new faces, most of whom knew Morton by reputation. "By now virtually all Mush's old associates in the conning tower were gone, replaced by men who naturally thought of their great and famous skipper as infallible. I believe that, on previous patrols, Mush had come to rely subconsciously on his officers to tell him what not to do," Grider wrote. "Here was a man whose valor blazed up so brightly that at times he could not distinguish between the calculated risk and the foolhardy chance, and now the men who knew him well enough to insist on pointing out the difference were gone."

Wahoo veteran James Allen visited his former sub shortly before departure to see his friend, crewman Kenneth Whipp. Whipp confided over coffee that he had asked for a transfer, but Morton denied it. The crew had grown scared of the skipper, he said, who had grown unstable, driven by his quest to sink more ships. Morton passed through the mess deck as the men chatted. The relaxed skipper Allen recalled, who had washed his skivvies in a bucket of soapy water in the engine rooms, looked haggard and confused. Exhaustion threatened to overwhelm him. "I am going to continue to fight *Wahoo* as I have in the past," Morton had written to his mother in August. "When I begin to slow-up I will turn her over to some kid who has better nerves than I." The weary skipper now seemed unable to follow his own advice. Had Morton the myth finally caught up with Morton the man? Allen watched *Wahoo* back away from the pier and depart for its seventh patrol. He raised his right hand and saluted.

The exhausted Morton had shown previous signs of recklessness, but his popularity and success had prompted his superiors to overlook them. One of the most egregious examples was his attack on the 5,447-ton transport *Buyo Maru*, which carried 1,126 men, including 491 Indian prisoners of war. Japanese and Indian survivors bobbed in the water and crowded aboard twenty small boats. Morton ordered his gun crew to fire across the bow of one boat. "Our fire was returned by machine gun," Morton would later tell the Navy. "Therefore we considered free game to fire not only at the boats but at the troops also. We proceeded to have a field day." The attack, which would earn MacArthur's praise, killed at least eighty-seven Japanese and 195 Indians. The scene shocked some of Morton's men. "Mush, whose biological hatred of the enemy we were only now beginning to sense, looked about him with exultation at the carnage," Grider later wrote. "Combat works its changes in men with chilling speed."

These clouds hung over Morton as he closed in on the enemy's homeland. Japanese radio broadcasts reported in early October that an Allied submarine had boldly slipped into empire waters and torpedoed the loaded passenger steamer *Konron Maru* in the narrow Tsushima Strait between Japan and Korea. The 7,908-ton steamer, ripped open by a single torpedo, sank in seconds. Of the 616 passengers, Tokyo reported that warships and planes rescued only seventy-two. "The Tsushima Straits are Japan's historic doors to the Asiatic mainland," wrote *Time* magazine. "Presumably the submarine knocking on the door last week was American. It had achieved one of World War II's most daring submarine penetrations of enemy waters, a feat ranking with German Günther Prien's entry at Scapa Flow, the Jap invasion of Pearl Harbor, the U.S. raid in Tokyo Bay." Submarine force leaders didn't have to presume. Senior officers knew only one submarine operated in those perilous waters: *Wahoo*.

Morton had regained his touch.

Wahoo's orders demanded that Morton radio the results of his patrol on October 23. That day came and went. Days soon turned into a week, but still no word arrived. None ever would. A Japanese floatplane had spotted *Wahoo* at 9:20 a.m. on October 11 in La Perouse Strait, separating Japan's northern island of Hokkaido from Russia. The plane dropped two bombs. Oil and bubbles surfaced. More planes and ships armed with bombs and depth charges joined the hours-long attack. With only some 200 feet of water to hide, *Wahoo* couldn't dive deep enough to evade. Following a 12:11 p.m. depth charge attack, Japanese forces spotted part of a propeller blade. Lockwood knew none of this at the time; he knew only that something must have gone wrong. Terribly wrong. The three-star admiral waited as long as he could before he reported *Wahoo* overdue on November 9. "It just didn't seem possible that Morton and his fighting crew could be lost," Lockwood would later write. "I'd never have believed the Japs could be smart enough to get him."

O'Kane, having finished his five patrols on *Wahoo*, was overseeing the completion of *Tang* in California when the press reported *Wahoo*'s loss in December. He refused to believe it. Not Morton. Not his friend. Within hours of climbing off *Tang* after it first reported for duty in Pearl Harbor on January 8, O'Kane sought and received confirmation of the reports. The official postwar tally showed that in just ten months Morton had destroyed nineteen ships with a total tonnage of 54,683, making him the third most successful skipper of the war. He held the record at the time of his death for the most ships sunk on a single patrol: nine. The death of the invincible skipper, whose photo adorned the submarine base piano with a Hawaiian lei draped around the frame, reverberated up the chain of command, with Admiral Chester Nimitz calling it "the most serious loss the submarine service has sustained." His loss proved more than just a submarine and its crew, but the first casualty of a new style of submarine warfare. Some questioned whether the risks were worth it.

Not O'Kane.

Morton's death instilled a greater urgency in his protégé, who now devised his own unique methods to drill his men for war. The skipper found that a metronome mounted on a bracket adjacent to the receiver helped his soundmen better track an enemy ship's propeller. He surprised his crew during training off the California coast when he brought a wire recorder on board and placed microphones by the attack periscope, torpedo data computer, plot, and in the control room. O'Kane recorded everything his men said during practice approaches. The skipper then played the recordings between runs, erasing the exclamations, needless orders, and irrelevant conversations. He taught his men how to pare down talk to just the essentials. "The result was amazing—a crisp order, the acknowledgement, and then quiet," O'Kane later wrote. "Three quarters of everything we had said could be erased. We all learned to think before we spoke and to limit what we said to the problem at hand."

But the real test still awaited *Tang*. Naval engineers had designed the Balao class *Tang*—the latest class of submarine—to dive 100 feet deeper than the previous generation of submarines, thanks to a switch from mild steel to high-tensile steel along with an increase in the thickness of the pressure hull plating. O'Kane wanted to push the 400-foot test depth. The skipper knew that with the number of Japanese escorts increasing and antisubmarine measures improving, *Tang's* survival might depend on any extra depth he could squeeze out of his submarine. He ordered crews to man the battle phones in each compartment and stationed officers and senior petty officers throughout the submarine. *Tang* reached 450 feet before the pressure broke a gauge line and a hose to the Bendix pitometer, which measured the submarine's speed. Crews secured the pitometer's valves and jammed a raw potato over the gauge line to plug it until men could find and shut off the stop valve.

Tang dove again. This time the submarine reached 525 feet before the pressure cracked the sound head rollers, part of the submarine's sonar system. *Tang* had to surface. Shopfitters and machinists set to work on improvements. The next free afternoon, *Tang* made it down to 525 feet. Then 550 feet. When the submarine hit 580 feet, flanged joints in the vent risers burst, spraying water at 300 pounds per square inch. *Tang* returned for more repairs. O'Kane set out again the next day. "No one batted an eye till we passed 575 feet, but the very fact that 600 feet was the last figure on the depth gauge did cause some uneasiness, like coming to the edge of the ocean," O'Kane wrote. "The pointer moved to the 600-foot mark and then to the pin three-quarters of an inch beyond. There were no leaks." O'Kane had successfully pushed *Tang's* limit, and he now knew that in an emergency he could safely dive down to 612 feet.

O'Kane's test rattled some of the crew. The chief cook approached executive officer Lieutenant Murray Frazee, Jr., soon after the submarine docked.

He wanted off. *Tang* sailed in the morning for Pearl Harbor and the chief commissary man proved too vital to the ship's operation to lose on short notice. "Well, if you're not going to do anything about it now," the cook threatened, "I just won't show up tomorrow morning."

Frazee turned to the chief of the boat, who stood next to him. "Chief, you heard what he said, didn't you?"

"I sure did," the chief replied.

Frazee turned to the cook and grabbed his shirt. "Listen, you son of a bitch, if you're not here tomorrow morning at 0800 when we sail, I'm going to have you shot for desertion in time of war!" he barked. "Now, have you got that straight?"

Every man showed up the morning *Tang* left for Pearl Harbor. "Never was there such an aggressive submarine officer as Dick O'Kane," Frazee later wrote. "In fact, there were some who doubted his sanity."

11

TANG

"We certainly kept after the bastards until we sank them all. You know I am never satisfied as long as a Jap has a ship still afloat."

—Dudley "Mush" Morton,
February 16, 1943, letter

O'Kane stared at the empty horizon. No warships, no freighters, no trawlers. Nothing. This was not how he envisioned his first patrol as skipper. Lifeguard duty off Wake had proved interesting, but uneventful. Bombers pounded the atoll the night of January 30, 1944, and again on February 5. O'Kane watched from the bridge—his teeth clenched and eyes misty—as the night sky lit up. But the Japanese failed to shoot down any planes and damaged only one, making a rescue by *Tang* unnecessary. *Tang* had since patrolled north of the enemy stronghold at Truk, so far an equally uneventful assignment. With the exception of a February 11 galley fire—a deep-fat fryer ignited and torched the paint and cork on the bulkheads—little had happened. The crew was restless. So was the skipper. "We had been 20 days on patrol without even a puff of enemy smoke to reward the hours of concentration," O'Kane wrote. "It is difficult to inject any levity into such a deadly serious business, but neither is it possible to maintain such a taut routine without some break."

That break arrived in the form of an Ultra message addressed to submarines *Skate* and *Sunfish*—and sent to *Tang* only for information. The message alerted O'Kane that a Japanese convoy planned to depart Gray Feather Bank for Truk at 8 a.m. the following day, February 15. If O'Kane arrived first, the convoy was his, though his theft of a prized target would infuriate his fellow skippers. O'Kane didn't mind. He ordered all four engines online as executive officer Frazee plotted an intercept course. The skipper didn't have long to hunt. His orders had given him until midnight on February 15 to patrol the waters north of the Caroline Islands—an area roughly the size of Connecticut—before he would have to depart and take up his assigned position for the upcoming assault on Truk. The United States planned a carrier strike against the Japanese stronghold and ordered *Tang* and eight other submarines to patrol the waters to intercept fleeing ships and rescue downed American aviators.

The assault on Truk represented another milestone in America's advance across the Pacific. The summer of 1943 saw the United States shift from defense to offense. American forces by that time had driven the Japanese from the Aleutians, captured as part of the attack on Midway. A network of air and naval bases protected supply lines across the south and southwest Pacific, while battles in the Solomons and New Guinea had cost Japan important forward bases and chewed up the country's air and naval forces. America planned to capitalize on its growing strength to capture or neutralize strategic islands across the central Pacific, including the Gilberts and Marshalls, the Carolines, and the Marianas. This maritime march west through Micronesia, coupled with MacArthur's drive north through New Guinea and the Philippines, promised to place the enemy's homeland within reach of America's bombers. War planners calculated that only with Japan's industrial cities reduced to rubble would the emperor surrender.

This road through the central Pacific promised much bloodshed as Japanese leaders depended on Micronesia for defense, providing vital airfields and fleet anchorages to repel invaders. Japan had captured the Marshalls, Carolines, and much of the Marianas from Germany in the Great War. Barring foreign ships and visitors, Japan had spent the interwar years militarizing many of the islands, building barracks, airstrips, and seaplane bases, all under the pretense of cultural improvements. To prevent the possible fall of the islands, Japan designed each group with its own defensive system. The largest atoll in the world with a 839-square-mile lagoon, Kwajalein served as the defensive heart of the Marshalls while Truk played the same role for the Carolines and Saipan for the Marianas.

The United States had set its sights first on the Gilbert Islands, a former British colony more than 2,000 miles west of Hawaii that Japan had grabbed in the days after the attack on Pearl Harbor. Seizure of this string of sixteen tiny equatorial atolls—the largest just fifteen square miles—would give America a foothold to invade the Marshalls, the next island group to the north. Forces from there could advance through the Carolines and on to the Marianas, the ultimate prize, which would provide American bombers the coveted runway to reach Japan. Troops hit the beaches of Tarawa in the Gilberts in late November 1943, fighting hand-to-hand against entrenched Japanese forces that left more than a thousand Americans dead and twice as many injured at the end of the seventy-six-hour battle. Crews readied four airfields in the Gilberts by December with three able to accommodate heavy bombers. American land-based and carrier planes bombed the Japanese in the Marshall Islands, Wake, and Nauru to hold these advances.

The United States next turned to the Marshalls, consisting of twenty-nine coral atolls and five separate islands. The total dry land in the Marshalls added up to just seventy square miles peppered across an area of ocean almost three times the size of Texas. Strategists anticipated better fortifications than in the Gilberts, since the Japanese had controlled the Marshalls before the war. America overlooked no detail in preparation for the January 31, 1944, invasion of Kwajalein and Majuro atolls, from assembling an armada of 217 ships to ferry more than 60,000 troops to including fifty harmonicas and seven ukuleles. The Navy's twelve carriers boasted some 700 planes compared to Japan's 110; American forces wiped out ninety-two of those planes in a single pre-invasion strike. Battleships and heavy cruisers pounded the islands before American troops charged ashore, easily overwhelming the Japanese, as evidenced by the lopsided casualties: the United States suffered 334 killed compared to the more than 8,400 dead Japan counted.

The success of the Marshalls invasion had led the Navy to push up plans to seize Eniwetok, originally scheduled for May. The strategic atoll along the northwestern edge of the Marshalls would play a vital role in the drive through the neighboring Caroline Islands. To protect American forces at Eniwetok, the Navy planned a carrier raid against Truk, dubbed Operation Hailstone. *Tang*'s patrol around this enemy stronghold in the Carolines supported that operation. Home to as many as 11,500 Japanese soldiers, sailors, and airmen, Truk played a similar strategic role for Japan as Hawaii did for America. The press dubbed this fortress built atop the peaks of undersea mountains "Japan's Pearl Harbor" and the "Gibraltar of the Pacific." Nine aircraft carriers and seven battleships, cruisers, and destroyers steamed toward this central Pacific citadel for the February 17–18 attack. War planners hoped *Tang* and other submarines could pick off enemy ships in advance of the strikes and then torpedo escaping vessels afterward.

O'Kane was eager to oblige.

Tang's support of Operation Hailstone represented a larger shift in the undersea service's mission. Submarines had largely operated throughout the war's first two years—with the exception of Midway and some operations in the Solomons—as lone raiders tasked to target Japan's naval and merchant fleets. The invasion of the Gilberts and the launch of America's offensive drive across the Pacific demanded a new role. Submarines would continue to destroy Japan's merchant fleet, but increasingly the Navy called on the undersea service to support major fleet operations. Those tasks assigned to the service played to a submarine's inherent strengths. The boats could slip into Japanese-controlled waters to take important weather readings in advance of air strikes and snap periscope photos of beaches where troops might land. Submarines during an invasion could cripple the enemy's supply lines and intercept warships that might counter an operation as well as pluck downed American pilots from the waves.

Ten submarines deployed for the Gilberts invasion. Since weather in the Pacific moves west to east, America had no way of determining conditions in advance of the assault. Armed with weather balloons and a newly recruited aerologist, former *Drum* skipper Robert Rice parked *Paddle* 300 miles west of Tarawa. At sunset for the five days leading up to the invasion, *Paddle* fired off a report of atmospheric wind direction and velocities. The submarine *Nautilus* reported surf conditions at Tarawa the day before the invasion and landed seventy-eight Marines on Apamama atoll, even bombarding entrenched Japanese forces with its two six-inch deck guns. *Nautilus* and *Plunger* both served as lifeguards for downed aviators while other boats lurked near Truk's entrances and along the major sea routes through the Marshalls to monitor enemy fleet movements that might counter America's invasion. The success of the operation led the Navy to call in submarines for the Marshalls invasion and now for Operation Hailstone.

Frazee wrapped up his calculations at the control room table. *Tang*'s second in command, nicknamed "Fraz," sported dark hair, a medium build, and gentle features that masked a ruggedness developed during an adolescence marred by economic hardship. The Naval Academy offered Frazee four years of stability and a chance to play soccer and lacrosse, though he preferred fifty-cent nine-ball at a local pool hall. Like O'Kane, Frazee had been a mediocre student, graduating in the bottom half of the 1939 class. But the twenty-eight-year-old lieutenant's youth disguised his extensive wartime record. Frazee had already served seven patrols on the submarine *Grayback*, earning a Silver Star for one, before landing as O'Kane's exec on *Tang*.

Frazee shouted his suggested course and speed for the night up to O'Kane in the conning tower. The barometer dropped shortly before midnight and the waves rose. O'Kane polished off a cup of coffee and climbed to the bridge. The skipper and his executive officer studied the whitecaps. The waves stretched to the horizon, disappearing into the black night. The pounding seas cut *Tang*'s eighteen-knot speed by almost two knots and O'Kane knew the situation would only worsen before dawn. If the heavy seas forced *Tang* to miss the plotted intercept point, O'Kane told Frazee he could adjust the course left at dawn and still cut off the convoy later in the morning. That would require *Tang* to run on the surface after daybreak. Such a brazen and exposed chase so close to Japanese operations around Truk exposed *Tang* to the possibility of an air attack. Frazee listened to his skipper's plan. "We can dive faster than a Zeke, Captain," Frazee responded, referring to a Zero fighter.

The seas calmed by morning. The dawn star fix showed that *Tang* remained some forty miles short of the convoy's track. O'Kane ordered the submarine to come left twenty degrees. All four engines roared. Sailors used the aircraft radar sparingly, fearful the Japanese might detect the signal. With each radar check, men noted distant pips, which O'Kane surmised could be island plane traffic or even convoy air escorts. One pip that had remained some eighteen miles out began to close the distance shortly before 9:30 a.m. The radar operator relayed reports as it closed to within twelve miles. O'Kane couldn't risk being spotted. He flashed his exec the thumbs-down sign and the submarine slipped beneath the waves to eighty feet. *Tang* surfaced soon after. This time lookouts failed to spot a Japanese fighter until it appeared right off the port bow, forcing the submarine back down, this time to 300 feet. "All was clear," O'Kane wrote. "But now that we had been sighted, there would be no ships along that course—and most probably along any other course for Truk—on this day."

O'Kane had blown it, not just for *Tang*, but for *Skate* and *Sunfish*, too. Japanese war planners would cancel convoys and reroute others. Escorts and air patrols would increase. The element of surprise had vanished. O'Kane could only hope the convoy had returned to Gray Feather Bank, a move that might allow him to salvage an attack once the Japanese felt the area safe again. *Tang* spent the afternoon submerged as officers swept the horizon with seventeen feet of periscope in the unlikely chance a convoy might risk it, but nothing appeared. Any ship that departed Gray Feather Bank for Truk might vary its course to the north or the south, but it still had to steam in one direction: east. Toward *Tang*. If O'Kane ran north–south legs throughout the night he might intercept a convoy. He ordered *Tang* to patrol on the surface at fifteen knots with its radar to cover as much distance as possible.

No ship appeared that night.

Nor the next day.

The frustrated skipper's luck changed on February 17 at 12:25 a.m. Radar picked up a convoy to the northwest at a range of almost eighteen miles. O'Kane ordered *Tang* to close while the tracking party determined the convoy's course and zigzag pattern. Once armed with that critical information, O'Kane planned to maneuver seven miles ahead to intercept. Sailors soon determined that the convoy steamed east directly into the rising half-moon at 8.5 knots. The convoy had originally departed Yokohama almost two weeks earlier with as many as thirty ships. Most had since split off, bound for other ports. The five remaining vessels, loaded down with munitions and troops, steamed toward Truk, accompanied by four escorts that *Tang*'s radar showed encircled the convoy. "It looked more like a small task force than a convoy," O'Kane noted. "The high ratio of escorts to merchantmen showed what had been happening: Japan's merchant fleet was being sunk at three times the rate of its escorts."

An Ultra message arrived from Pearl Harbor, this time addressed to *Tang* and copied to *Skate* and *Sunfish*. "Convoy will depart Gray Feather Bank at twenty two hundred February sixteen for Truk," the message read. "Note *Skate* and *Sunfish* this is the convoy you were to have attacked but one of you was sighted and convoy ordered to return onto Gray Feather Bank." That convoy—now some two hours into its voyage—loomed in *Tang*'s sights. O'Kane chafed at the writer safely back in Hawaii who—though blaming his fellow sub skippers—had indirectly called him out for being spotted. While he downplayed his foul-up as an occupational risk, his superiors took a dim view: a convoy that should be on the bottom wasn't. O'Kane refocused. Why would a convoy risk such a perilous trip at night? The moon glowed overhead, silhouetting ships and making them easy prey. Lookouts also faced greater challenges spotting submarines in the dark. It didn't make sense. *Tang* approached an attack position at 2:19 a.m. ahead of the convoy that steamed more than eight miles away.

A dark silhouette suddenly appeared 7,000 yards astern—the convoy's starboard flanking escort. The patrol charged after *Tang*. Even with the moonlight O'Kane couldn't believe the escort's lookouts had seen the submarine's low and sleek shape. It must be armed with radar. No wonder it had dared such a risky nighttime transit. *Tang* continued at flank speed, but the escort still closed the distance. The skipper had no choice but to dive. The klaxon sounded and the men on the bridge poured through the hatch. *Tang* slipped seconds later beneath the surface of the dark water. The skipper watched through the periscope as the escort kept coming, its frothy bow wave looming large. O'Kane had to go deep. *Tang* reached 450 feet before the first depth charge exploded. Another blast shook the submarine followed by three more. None caused any damage. "His attack was half-hearted," O'Kane later wrote in his report. "We were able to return to radar depth fifteen minutes after he passed by."

O'Kane refused to be shaken off in his first real test since *Wahoo*. Everyone from the teenage seamen on board *Tang* to the senior officers at Pearl Harbor would judge him. O'Kane ordered full speed submerged, now hidden beneath a temperature gradient that shielded the submarine from the escort's sonar. *Tang* soon climbed back up to radar and then to periscope depth. The convoy, still five miles out, headed O'Kane's way. He waited. The skipper planned to fire his bow tubes, but when the lead freighter reached 3,000 yards, he saw that the ship had turned and would now pass *Tang*'s stern. O'Kane adjusted, ordering the outer doors aft opened. Unlike the manual cranks used on older boats, *Tang*'s operated by a hydraulic system. He watched the leading escort cross to the freighter's opposite bow away from *Tang*. The port escort passed just 100 yards from *Tang*'s bow, oblivious to the lurking submarine. O'Kane had penetrated the escort screen. "We were on the inside," he wrote. "Nothing could stop us!"

The 6,854-ton *Gyoten Maru*—a former British ship once known as the

Empire Moonbeam—closed to just 1,500 yards on track to cross *Tang*'s stern in seconds. O'Kane watched it chug across his scope. "Constant bearing," he said. "Mark!"

"Set."

"Fire!"

Frazee pressed the firing plunger at 3:35 a.m. *Tang* shook as a blast of compressed air ejected a one-and-a-half-ton torpedo from tube seven, its steam-driven propellers kicking on with a whine as it cleared the submarine. O'Kane fired three more times. Petty Officer 1st Class Floyd Caverly, the twenty-six-year-old Minnesotan soundman, listened through his black headphones as the torpedoes zoomed toward the target at forty-six knots. "All hot, straight, and normal," he reported.

"What's the time of the run?" O'Kane asked.

"Fifty-eight seconds, Captain," Frazee replied.

Chief Petty Officer Sidney Jones, *Tang*'s senior quartermaster, called out the time to detonation. Ten seconds passed. Twenty. Then thirty. O'Kane was anxious. He had fired his first shots of the war as skipper. He wanted to be successful. Forty-five seconds after firing, the skipper raised the periscope. He sighted *Gyoten Maru*'s silhouette. Nine seconds later, the ship exploded. O'Kane watched the stern vanish. The next thirteen seconds delivered two more hits. The explosions knocked out *Gyoten Maru*'s radio. The wounded ship's siren rang out as water flooded its bowels. The stunned escorts milled around *Gyoten Maru* before the freighter broke in half and slipped beneath the waves. O'Kane had sunk his first ship. The skipper ordered *Tang* to hide beneath the 375-foot temperature gradient. The submarine leveled off at 575 feet and cleared the area as distant depth charges exploded.

The next few days remained slow for *Tang* as it patrolled sixteen miles off the island of Ulul. Ten submarines now lurked in the waters around Truk. *Darter*, *Searaven*, and *Seal* performed lifeguard duty while *Skate*, *Sunfish*, *Aspro*, *Burrfish*, *Dace*, and *Gato* joined *Tang* to intercept ships. But Operation Hailstone belonged to the aviators, who flew 1,250 sorties, blackening the skies over the sunken mountain range. Five hundred tons of bombs and torpedoes pounded Japanese airfields, ships, and fuel and ammunition depots. The two-day attack cost Japan 270 planes along with twenty-six merchant ships and six combatants for a total tonnage lost of some 200,000. The laconic Pacific Fleet

Commander Admiral Chester Nimitz bragged to the press about Hailstone's success. "The Pacific Fleet has returned at Truk the visit made by the Japanese fleet at Pearl Harbor on Dec. 7, 1941, and effected a partial settlement of the debt."

O'Kane's new orders arrived after dawn on February 20. The fast carrier task force that had reduced Truk to ruins planned to hammer Japanese forces at Saipan. *Tang* and four other submarines from Truk would head some 700 miles north and await additional orders. O'Kane suspected he was the first to learn of the new plan. Submarines could receive fox messages—the nightly broadcasts from Pearl Harbor to boats at sea—only when on the surface to recharge batteries. *Tang* had come up soon after its dawn dive, just in time to pick up the chance message. If he was correct, *Tang* would have a 250-mile head start on the other subs. Furthermore, with all the submarines now around Truk, O'Kane doubted that any patrolled the Marianas, fertile hunting ground. The skipper ordered *Tang*, then running on just one engine, to make eighteen knots. "There had to be ships," he wrote. "*Tang* would have the Marianas all to herself, at least for a time."

Radar showed Japanese planes in the skies, though none closer than twenty miles. O'Kane hoped the planes accompanied a convoy though his searches ten miles on either side of *Tang*'s track failed to spot one. The skies emptied by the afternoon and that evening sailors settled down to watch a movie. The next morning, the repeated appearance of a Japanese bomber sent *Tang* up and down like a yo-yo, slowing the trip. O'Kane finally decided to ignore the plane and continue north. The bomber remained on the horizon as two other planes—one hidden in the sun, the other behind a cloud—suddenly zoomed toward *Tang*. Only at the last second did lookouts spot the planes and send *Tang* safely down yet again. "Twice now we had underestimated the Japanese," O'Kane wrote. "If we were to be successful in our present endeavor, a little more brain power and less reliance on our ship's capabilities was certainly indicated."

The skipper was learning. Not only had the crafty bomber pilot served as a decoy, but now after repeated surveillance the Japanese no doubt knew his course. Rather than risk another trap, he ordered *Tang* to submerge. The submarine surfaced that night after dark and patrolled ten miles south of Aguijan island, hoping to intercept traffic between Saipan and Guam. O'Kane found only a Japanese patrol boat. Bombers crowded the skies the following day, prompting *Tang* again to patrol submerged. Only after dark on February 22 did *Tang* surface. Searchlights from Tanapag Harbor lit up the night sky. O'Kane presumed a convoy had just departed. He ordered the submarine to head north on two engines. Lookouts pulled on rain gear as squalls soaked the bridge, hampering radar performance. But the foul weather also made it easy for *Tang* to patrol unseen on the surface.

O'Kane's instincts paid off. *Tang's* radar picked up a single pip at 10 p.m. at a range of almost eight miles. The radar operator watched the lone signal multiply. One ship morphed into five. The radar showed another possible group of ships to the north. At least five ships, maybe more, loomed ahead. It was a skipper's dream. O'Kane debated how best to attack. Should he charge the convoy, fire a large spread, and retreat from harm's way? That might guarantee hits on multiple ships. German skippers had used that tactic with success against American convoys in the North Atlantic. But that strategy worked only if a convoy's major ships outnumbered the escorts. Japanese convoys often consisted of one or two large ships accompanied by multiple escorts. Armed with limited torpedoes—and with replacements a 6,000-mile round-trip away—O'Kane needed to be precise. "We would hunt out each enemy ship—cargomen of any sort or sizable warships, first come first served—and make every torpedo count."

The bad weather slashed visibility so that even at 4,000 yards O'Kane could not see the convoy in the dark. The skipper ordered the submarine to stop so the sonar operator could listen. Radar showed the lead ship zigzagging toward *Tang* and would pass just a half mile off the bow. O'Kane ordered outer doors three through six in the forward torpedo opened. Chief quartermaster Jones spotted the target just as Caverly picked up its screws over his headphones. Both reported the same: a patrol boat. A worthless target. Not only did patrols not carry war materials, but a missed shot guaranteed a depth charge attack, a scenario that could blow the entire assault and let the convoy escape. O'Kane watched the second pip develop into a patrol or minesweeper; another worthless target. He would bide his time.

The rainsqualls dissipated. A third pip materialized to the north, this one larger than the patrols. O'Kane scanned the dark horizon from the bridge through the 7x50 binoculars atop the target-bearing transmitter, spotting a ship four miles away. A freighter. The ship steamed southwest at nine knots. O'Kane saw two escorts. One patrolled off the target's starboard bow, the other its starboard quarter—good news for *Tang*. The submarine reached its attack position and stopped. Executive officer Frazee down in the conning tower again ordered the outer doors opened. Quartermaster Jones studied the escorts through his binoculars, looking for any sign that *Tang* had been detected. The 3,581-ton *Fukuyama Maru*, a passenger-cargo ship, closed to just 1,500 yards.

"Ten degrees to go," Frazee announced, his voice crackling over the bridge loudspeaker.

"Stand by for constant bearings," O'Kane called back as he focused the reticle of the target-bearing transmitter on the freighter's stack. "Constant bearing—mark!"

"Set."

"Fire!"

Tang shuddered. Three more torpedoes followed in the next twenty-four seconds, aimed at *Fukuyama Maru*'s port side. The skipper ordered full speed and right full rudder, hoping to clear the area before the explosions hit and set the escorts after him. O'Kane wasn't so lucky—nor were the forty-seven enemy sailors who unknowingly stood just seconds away from death. "The enemy literally disintegrated under four hits and sank before we had completed ninety degrees of our turn to evade," the skipper later wrote in his patrol report. "One escort guessed right and closed to 3000 yards, but these boats always seem to find a couple of extra knots for such occasions, and we made a sandblower out of him."

The men relaxed from battle stations long enough for O'Kane to climb down for a much needed visit to the head and a quick cup of coffee in the wardroom. The night was still early. The navigator had charted the convoy's course and O'Kane still had time before dawn to attack again. Thirty minutes after the last explosion—and with the forward tubes reloaded—*Tang* set off to hunt its next victim. O'Kane ordered a thirty-degree course change to starboard and maneuvered ahead of the convoy. When the range to the convoy hit 4,000 yards, O'Kane ordered his crew back to battle stations. Minutes later, a Japanese destroyer emerged from the darkness. The skipper was concerned his torpedoes—set to run at ten feet because of the rough seas—would pass beneath the shallow-draft target. He opted not to attack.

O'Kane retreated. He didn't want the destroyer's lookouts to spot *Tang*, so he moved on to the next target. Scanning the horizon through his binoculars, the skipper saw a sleek and familiar silhouette: a submarine. He felt certain it was Japanese but couldn't chance a shot without positively identifying it first. Then O'Kane spied the silhouette of a freighter, accompanied by bow and stern escorts. The skipper watched the bow escort pull far ahead of the freighter, creating an opening for O'Kane to attack. *Tang* closed on the target's bow. Visibility improved and the skipper studied the 6,776-ton *Yamashimo Maru*. The cargo ship boasted guns forward and aft. A rainsquall had developed in the distance behind *Tang*, hiding the submarine from the target's lookouts as the skipper closed to less than a half mile.

O'Kane fired tubes three, four, five, and six, each at just eight-second intervals. The explosions triggered a shockwave that O'Kane later compared to the detonation of 100 torpedoes. The phosphorescence turned the ocean white. "The first two were beautiful hits in her stern and just aft of the stack, but the detonation as the third torpedo hit forward of his bridge was terrific," O'Kane wrote in his report. "The enemy ship was twisted, lifted from the water as you would flip a spoon on end, and then commenced belching flame as she sank. The *Tang* was shaken far worse than by any depth charge we could remember, but a quick check, as soon as our jaws came off our chests, showed no damage except that the outer door gasket of number five tube, which was just being secured, blew out of its groove."

O'Kane suspected that the target must have served as either an ammunition ship or a submarine or destroyer tender. The detonation of such a ship's cargo would explain the secondary explosion that had rattled *Tang*. One thing was certain: there could be no survivors. The three remaining ships appeared to be escorts, none worth a torpedo. O'Kane ordered his men to hunt the northbound convoy that had appeared on the radar earlier that evening. The skipper stretched out in his cabin at 2:45 a.m. He found sleep impossible. The voices of officers across the passageway in the wardroom rallied him. O'Kane joined them as Ensign Mel Enos, Jr., a graduate of the University of California's Naval Reserve Officers Training Corps program, discussed the waste of torpedoes. Enos believed *Tang* could have sunk each ship with just three, not four fish.

O'Kane had wrestled with whether he'd needed to fire the fourth torpedo in his attacks against *Gyoten Maru, Fukuyama Maru,* and *Yamashimo Maru*. But the skipper considered it his insurance policy. It guaranteed a ship's destruction and allowed him to focus on his escape. "You're right," O'Kane told

Enos. "But they're on the bottom, and that's what counts!" The younger officers cleared the wardroom moments later to head topside, leaving O'Kane and his executive officer. The men relaxed over a game of cribbage. The previous conversation percolated in the skipper's mind, prompting him to share advice with his second in command that Morton had once shared with him—advice that would have haunting consequences for both the Japanese and *Tang*. "Tenacity, Fraz," O'Kane told him. "Stay with 'em till they're on the bottom!"

O'Kane had gone from three weeks without spotting a single target to sinking three ships in seven days. He still had twelve torpedoes and the promise of more success. While not the dramatic start that Morton had enjoyed in his first patrol a year earlier, the skipper knew the difference those twelve months had made in the war. American submarines in 1943 had picked off some 1,360,000 tons of enemy shipping, averaging seventy-seven attacks each month for the first half of the year, a figure that climbed to almost 100 attacks per month by the year's end. The Japanese responded by ramping up escorts, making it harder to pick off convoys. More American submarines—1943 saw new boats commissioned at a rate of more than one a week—crowded the seas, upping the competition. Skippers had to work harder for scalps.

O'Kane planned on it.

Tang patrolled on the surface 150 miles west of Saipan the morning of February 24, searching for targets with its high periscope and radar. An Ultra message from Pearl Harbor delivered good news: the expected noontime coordinates of a Japanese convoy. O'Kane ordered *Tang* to three-engine speed and a slight course change of only twenty degrees to intercept. The submarine sped through the empty ocean as lookouts scanned the horizon for targets. A sailor on the tall search periscope spotted a clue so opaque that only an experienced submariner would recognize what it signified. "A single faint puff of smoke rose off to the north and then blended into the clouds. It was distant, far beyond the horizon," O'Kane would later write. "The enemy had made one mistake, for one bearing was all we needed."

Two targets now appeared on the radar more than a dozen miles away. Jones climbed up the periscope shears with binoculars. The chief quartermaster spotted a freighter, large tanker, and destroyer headed west. O'Kane ordered an end around. The skipper didn't want the convoy's lookouts to spot the stalking sub so he ordered *Tang* to remain on the edge of the convoy's radar range as it raced ahead at eighteen knots. Frazee calculated the course and determined that it would take three hours for *Tang* to arrive at an attack position, but gathering rainsqualls coupled with the convoy's erratic course slowed pursuit. O'Kane suspected the Japanese knew an enemy submarine shadowed them. That possibility made each entrance into a rainsquall more perilous as the downpours reduced *Tang*'s visibility at times to zero.

When sunset approached and the squalls let up, O'Kane ordered the submarine to stop. The fading light silhouetted the distant convoy. The skipper watched the destroyer flash several signals on a searchlight to the other ships that soon lined up behind it. The tanker was now in the rear. Lookouts followed the convoy with binoculars from atop *Tang*'s periscope shears. When the convoy disappeared west over the horizon, O'Kane ordered *Tang* up to full power. He planned to follow the convoy's last true bearing. The skipper surmised the straggling tanker was a ploy—no convoy commander would leave his most valuable charge so exposed for long—and that the convoy in fact planned to circle back. O'Kane wasn't about to be tricked. Lookouts soon picked up the convoy, now headed east toward Saipan, just as O'Kane had suspected. "The enemy zigs were of the wildest sort, sometimes actually backtracking," the skipper wrote in his report. "But their very wildness was his undoing."

Tang continued to track the convoy after dark as sailors sat down for dinner. O'Kane ordered ship identification books passed out in the mess so the lookouts could familiarize themselves with enemy silhouettes over dinner. The attack would prove more challenging than earlier ones since the convoy knew an enemy submarine lurked nearby. But the enemy's wild zigzags not only slowed down the convoy, but seemed almost to guarantee a tactical blunder at some point. O'Kane just needed to wait. The destroyer now patrolled off the tanker's bow. The skipper planned to attack from the stern, trusting that the enemy's aft lookouts would succumb to human nature and stare straight ahead rather than behind. The downside of the plan meant that he would be attacking the freighter first, but could then spend the rest of night hunting the tanker.

O'Kane ordered his crew to battle stations at 8:30 p.m. His hope for an easy shot soon vanished. The 2,424-ton *Echizen Maru*'s erratic zigzags forced O'Kane to botch his early efforts to set up a shot. The third approach appeared much better. If the freighter zigzagged left, it would cross *Tang's* bow, offering a perfect shot, but as the skipper prepared, acrid smoke from the coal-burning freighter descended on the bridge, temporarily blinding O'Kane and his men. But moments later, his luck changed. The freighter zigzagged again and now crossed *Tang's* bow at 1,400 yards. This was the shot that O'Kane had sought. The forward torpedo room's outer doors yawned open as the skipper marked the target's bearing and fired.

Four torpedoes raced toward the *Echizen Maru* and exploded at about 10:30 p.m., killing thirty-five crew members. The skipper colorfully captured the detonation in his report. "We cold-cocked him with the first three of our usual four torpedoes," O'Kane wrote. "The ship went to pieces, and amidst beautiful fireworks sank before we have completed our turn to evade." The tanker opened fire from its forward and aft guns as the destroyer closed, firing shells in all directions. Tracer rounds peppered the waves within 1,000 yards of *Tang.* The skipper ordered *Tang* to cruise out about five miles off the tanker's beam. The destroyer hunted in the area where the freighter sank, convinced that *Tang* had submerged, and dropped a string of harmless depth charges.

O'Kane still coveted the tanker, the convoy's top target. The destroyer now hugged its last charge so close that at times the radar showed only a single pip. Sporadic gunfire and depth charges signaled the destroyer's anxiousness. An immediate attack might be tough. Time and darkness proved O'Kane's tactical advantage, so he decided to wait until dawn. That would give *Tang* time to decipher the enemy's zigzag plan and speed. A few trouble-free hours coupled with the morning light also would cause the enemy to relax. *Tang* could drive ahead, pick the best spot for an attack, and dive. O'Kane turned the ship over to his executive officer for the night and climbed down to his cabin to sleep.

Thirty minutes before dawn, O'Kane climbed out of bed, downed two cups of coffee, and headed to the bridge. *Tang* remained eighty miles west of Saipan and 10,000 yards ahead of the convoy. An Ultra message arrived from Pearl Harbor, reporting that the convoy had been ordered to change course to the north at dawn. O'Kane didn't buy it. He suspected the Japanese had put out misleading information to throw him off. O'Kane ordered *Tang* to dive to radar depth at 5:48 a.m. as the eastern sky grayed. Eighteen minutes later, he spotted his prey. The 18,000-ton tanker O'Kane had so hungered for turned out to be the 1,794-ton freighter *Choko Maru*. *Tang* had only eight torpedoes left, four forward and four aft.

The Japanese destroyer cruised down *Choko Maru*'s starboard side. What struck O'Kane—and what he made special note of in his report—were the lookouts. His attack the night before had clearly rattled the Japanese. "All vantage points," O'Kane wrote, "including guns, bridge, bridge overhead, and rails, were manned with an estimated 150 uniformed lookouts on our side alone." The skipper made his final calculations, careful to use the attack periscope for no more than four seconds at a time and never raising it more than a few inches above the glassy sea. Even if the lookouts spotted *Tang*, there would be no time to take evasive moves. The target loomed just 500 yards away, its fate determined.

O'Kane fired four torpedoes. At a range of just over a quarter mile, the run time was only twenty-three seconds, barely enough for the torpedoes even to arm. O'Kane watched as the Japanese lookouts spotted the torpedo wakes and began to point and shout. Not a single man on the freighter appeared to abandon his post in the final seconds before three of the four torpedoes rammed into *Choko Maru*'s starboard side under the smokestack, bridge, and after superstructure, killing eight. "The explosions were wonderful, throwing Japs and other debris above the belching smoke," O'Kane wrote in his report. "He sank by the stern in four minutes, and then we went deep and avoided. The depth charges started a minute later, but were never close."

12

TANG

"Now I've got my fighting gear on—shorts, sandals and stubble over my face."

—John Bienia,
October 7, 1943, letter

Dick O'Kane looked up in awe. Waves of as many as fifty American planes at a time crowded the dawn sky, engaged in a massive air strike on Truk. O'Kane's mission this morning of April 30 was to rescue downed aviators. Carrier-based fighters and bombers had first pummeled the Japanese stronghold in February. America had since refused to quit. Army B-24 Liberators based in the Marshall and Solomon islands had now pounded the sunken mountain range more than thirty times. Despite the continual bombardment, Japan had managed to reinforce Truk. More than 100 planes crowded four airfields. Pacific Fleet Commander Admiral Chester Nimitz had had enough. He wanted to sideline Truk permanently. That effort was now under way—and O'Kane was impressed. "With the possible exception of a sinking maru," he wrote in his report, "this was the most encouraging sight we've witnessed in this war to date."

O'Kane welcomed the assignment. His patrol to date had been a bust. He had gone forty-five days without a single attack. Despite a similar lackluster start, O'Kane's first patrol had been a stunning success. In just forty-one days at sea the skipper had more than lived up to the expectations set by his mentor, Mush Morton, putting five ships on the bottom. O'Kane had arrived at Midway without a single torpedo left: a clean sweep. He had hoped his superiors would reward him with a patrol in Japan's home waters, where the enemy's dependence on maritime commerce guaranteed a wealth of targets. The skipper had enjoyed such prime missions when he served under Morton, but O'Kane's assignment this patrol in the waters off Palau and now Truk showed that he still ranked low in the skipper hierarchy. Time and fuel now dwindled. No submariner wanted to come home empty-handed.

Especially not O'Kane.

Tang's patrol in the Palau and Caroline islands, while not the assault on the enemy's homeland O'Kane coveted, supported America's drive across the Pacific. The United States had captured Kwajalein, Majuro, and Eniwetok in the Marshall Islands in February, punching a hole through the center of Japan's defensive perimeter. Those victories had planted American forces 2,200 miles west of Hawaii. New anchorages and airfields coupled with a new forward submarine base at Majuro—1,300 miles closer to the fight than Midway—gave the United States a strategic staging area for the march toward the Marianas and Japan. America could amass amphibious forces for future advances, conduct photo reconnaissance, and target enemy forces within range. That success in the Marshall Islands had rendered Truk a liability, prompting the Japanese to pull major naval ships from the Gibraltar of the Pacific back to Palau in the western Carolines some 500 miles southeast of the Philippines.

The United States had chased Japan west, planning a March 30 carrier strike on enemy forces in Palau, dubbed Operation Desecrate. With Douglas MacArthur poised to capture Hollandia along the northern coast of New Guinea, war planners had wanted to pummel Palau to eliminate any threat to the general. Unlike the battles of the Coral Sea, Midway, and Guadalcanal, Japan had chosen not to challenge America's fleet in a sea battle in either the Gilbert or Marshall islands. Strategists suspected the Japanese would not risk a confrontation at Palau and instead would order naval and merchant ships out of port. Submarines *Tullibee*, *Blackfish*, *Bashaw*, and *Archerfish* had joined *Tang* to sink escaping ships. *Tunny*, *Gar*, *Pampanito*, and *Harder* would pluck downed fliers from the waters.

O'Kane had soured at the Palau mission: 3,500 miles was a long haul for what he viewed as a possible one-shot attack. Furthermore, the skipper knew that fleeing ships made tough targets. Japanese skippers would expect submarine attacks and therefore steam at top speeds while zigzagging and echo ranging. The critical element of surprise was lost. But O'Kane's gripes ran deeper than just the Palau mission. Simply put: the skipper didn't like wearing a leash. The push to involve submarines in fleet actions, O'Kane felt, diminished the combat potential of the undersea service. Submarines operated best alone, offensive machines capable of penetrating enemy-controlled waters. The mission off Palau, he predicted, would prove a waste. "There might be torpedoes fired, but it would not be the precise kind of attack that could cold-cock the enemy," O'Kane wrote. "True surprise came days into a voyage, or when the enemy least expected attack, not in a situation like this."

The two-day strike on Palau validated O'Kane's concerns. While carrier-based planes put thirty-six ships on the bottom—a total tonnage lost of 129,807—submarines contributed little other than rescuing downed aviators. Not until the end of the war would America learn why the submarine mission had failed. One night on the eve of the strike *Tullibee* had stalked a three-ship convoy guarded by several escorts en route from Formosa to Palau. The submarine had fired two torpedoes only to be rocked moments later by an explosion. One of the fish had circled back and hit *Tullibee*, sending the submarine to the bottom. *Tullibee's* loss had left a hole in the submarine net around Palau through which the Japanese ships escaped. The Navy learned of *Tullibee's* fate only when the lone survivor, who treaded water all night in a raging storm, walked out of Japan's Ashio copper mine at the end of the war, finally a free man.

Parked in the waters of Truk, O'Kane put Palau behind him, hoping now to save the lives of American fliers. The first call for help crackled over *Tang's* radio at 10:25 a.m., downed fliers in a raft two miles off Truk's southern reef. Lieutenant j.g. Scott Scammell II of Pennsylvania—married less than a year earlier—had piloted his Grumman Avenger when a Japanese shell ripped a four-foot hole in his port wing. The naval pilot finished his run over Truk and turned back out to sea. Flames erupted near the shell hit. Scammell knew the proximity of the fire to his wing tank meant he had little time before the fuel exploded, which would kill him, the radioman, and the turret gunner. He had no choice but to ditch the plane, putting it down hard in the lagoon. "The indicator read 200 knots when we hit the water and we usually land at about 80," recalled Harry Gemmell, Scammell's radioman. "Somehow nobody was hurt."

O'Kane ordered *Tang* to depart immediately at emergency speed. The submarine sliced through the waves toward the reef as American bombers dove through a hole in the clouds above. Antiaircraft fire peppered the sky. With fliers taking such incredible risks above, O'Kane felt the least he could do was rescue any in the water below. Fighters dropped low to guide *Tang* toward Scammell and his men. The aviators opted not to use the raft's bright yellow sail so close to shore for fear the Japanese would target them. Instead the men—two of the three seasick—paddled farther to sea. A *Tang* lookout spotted the raft shortly before noon. O'Kane ordered a man-overboard maneuver—a wide circle that would place the raft upwind of the submarine. *Tang* then eased alongside the raft and sailors pulled the three downed fliers aboard. O'Kane ordered them to bring the raft, too. The baffled men looked at him.

"For my kid," he answered.

The crash had rattled Scammell and his men. O'Kane ordered that his new guests each be served a shot of Lejon brandy, *Tang*'s depth charge medicine. He needed to calm them—so he could put them to work. Technicians at Mare Island had installed Hallicrafter radio receivers in the crew's mess and wardroom. The radios proved powerful enough that *Tang* could receive news broadcasts from as far away as the United States. The addition of a microphone cable meant that *Tang* could do more than just listen. The skipper escorted the fliers to the wardroom, where officers had spread out a large chart of Truk atoll on the dinner table. Scammell and his men not only knew all the call signs, but many of the pilots in the skies above by name. If anyone could interpret what was going on it would be these men. The wardroom would now serve as *Tang*'s Aviation Information Center.

Word arrived at 3:59 p.m. of another downed aviator, this one off the east side of Truk. *Tang* set off again at emergency speed. Another call arrived fifteen minutes later with news of more downed fliers. These aviators were north, near the area where *Tang* rescued Scammell and his crew. O'Kane faced a challenge. The afternoon light had begun to fade. The skipper knew he could reach the second group of aviators during daylight. That almost guaranteed a rescue. He wasn't so sure about the first and was not keen on the idea of a fruitless search in the dark. O'Kane ordered *Tang* to change course and pursue the second group. A twenty-minute search with lookouts and periscopes, however, failed to turn up the raft. *Tang* turned back to find the original group. The skies, crowded all day with American planes, were empty. *Tang* was on its own. "All planes had now been recalled," O'Kane wrote, "leaving us a bit naked."

The skipper didn't have time to dive and skirt Japan's shore-based guns as he paralleled the beach. Instead he summoned *Tang*'s gun crew. He planned to lay down fire that would force the Japanese to take cover rather than target his sub. The gun crew climbed atop the four-inch deck gun and unleashed a mix of common and high-explosive rounds. The first shell exploded in the trees on shore that helped conceal the gun batteries. The shell casing clanged to the deck and the loaders rammed another one in breach. The gun roared again and again. The crew fired twenty rounds before *Tang* had escaped almost five miles away. That proved premature, as the Japanese now returned fire, though the projectiles splashed down more than a half mile astern. O'Kane ordered *Tang* to dive. The submarine remained down for forty minutes before surfacing, setting off again at emergency speed.

Night came. Lookouts had yet to spot the downed aviators. O'Kane ordered *Tang* to begin a zigzag search at ten knots. Sailors fired signal rockets every fifteen minutes at each turn and midway through each leg, hoping the aviators would spot the green flares and respond. But none did. The only light the *Tang* crew saw emanated from a distant runway on nearby Uman island. The night proved a long one for O'Kane and his navigator, neither of whom dared to grab even a few moments of sleep. *Tang*'s search pattern closed in on the reef each hour, forcing the skipper up to the bridge. Fortunately the Japanese, battered after the day's air strikes, left the submarine alone. The frustrated O'Kane finally gave up on the search at 3:30 a.m. and ordered *Tang* to sea in preparation for the second day's strike. He hoped for better luck at daybreak. Somewhere out there, Americans struggled on the waves.

The *North Carolina* steamed about eighty-five miles south of Truk at dawn on May 1. Heavy rainsqualls slashed visibility at times to zero as the 44,800-ton battleship prepared for another day of strikes against the Japanese stronghold. Commissioned just six months before the attack on Pearl Harbor, the 729-foot-long *North Carolina* carried a typical complement of more than 2,300 officers, crewmen, and Marines. The monster battleship was no stranger to the threat posed by the Japanese. An enemy submarine had put a torpedo in its port side in September 1942 in waters southeast of Guadalcanal, killing five sailors. Japanese planes still roamed the skies over Truk; radar had picked up contacts several times in the middle of the night, keeping the battleship crews alert. Private 1st Class Charles Gilbert, part of *North Carolina*'s Marine detachment, captured that watchfulness in his journal. "Bogies were in the area all night," Gilbert wrote in his diary. "Every once in a while one would venture in about ten miles."

The *North Carolina*'s two Kingfisher floatplanes—equipped with pontoons under the fuselage and wings—catapulted off the battleship shortly past 8 A.M. to join the rescue. With a maximum speed of barely 170 miles per hour, the Kingfishers flew toward Truk, where a downed Grumman F6F Hellcat pilot from the carrier *Enterprise* clung to a raft southwest of Ollan island. Lieutenant j.g. Robert Kanze of New Jersey had weathered a rough twenty-four hours. Japanese antiaircraft rounds had ripped holes in his wings and set his fighter ablaze the day before. Kanze had ditched inside Truk's lagoon, perilously close to shore. He had climbed into his raft and put up the sail only to have the Japanese open fire on him from shore. Kanze had yanked down the sail and used it to camouflage himself and the raft until nightfall. He then raised it again and made his way toward open water, crossing the lagoon's reef at high tide. The aviator remained focused throughout the long night. "I wasn't thinking about being rescued," he would later recall. "I was scared stiff I would wash up on Jap shores."

Kanze's all-night effort had paid off. The Kingfisher pilots spotted him soon after liftoff, now more than two miles out in open water. But in the attempt to rescue Kanze, the first floatplane capsized. One downed aviator suddenly turned into three. No one knew how many other airmen might need help that day. Neither *North Carolina* nor a smaller destroyer could steam so close to the enemy's stronghold—within easy range of shore batteries and enemy fighters—to pluck downed fliers out of the water. Even the submarine *Tang* likely couldn't risk such an up-close rescue. The American fighters blasting the Japanese shore batteries would return to their carriers at dark. That meant that any downed fliers not rescued by nightfall would either spend the night adrift at sea—and risk washing up on enemy beaches—or fall prey to enemy boats, venturing out when the skies cleared in search of prisoners.

The only hope for rescue fell to Lieutenant j.g. John Burns, the pilot of the remaining floatplane. The twenty-five-year-old Pennsylvania native turned his Kingfisher into the wind and dropped from the sky. He touched down moments later and taxied over to rescue the three men now in the water. The Kingfisher had only two cockpit seats, one for the pilot, the other for the radioman, so the rescued men had to sit on the wings, to maintain the plane's fragile balance and prevent it from capsizing. But the Kingfisher could not fly with so many men aboard. The floatplane instead would have to serve as a boat. With the men now seated on either wing, Burns turned toward the open water and taxied to find the *Tang*.

O'Kane had received a report at 8:28 a.m. from his new Aviation Information Center of downed fliers in a raft a few miles off Ollan island. The skipper was excited about a second chance to rescue the men from the night before. *Tang* set off at emergency speed with its two largest American flags lashed flat on the deck along either side of the conning tower. Lieutenant Scammell had suggested the flags would make it easier for pilots to identify the submarine as friendly. When *Tang* arrived off Ollan, O'Kane saw something unforgettable: a two-seat floatplane taxiing toward him with men clinging to its wings. American fighters strafed the shore batteries to provide cover as the Kingfisher pulled alongside the submarine. Sailors tossed over a line. There was no need to tie it off; Burns didn't plan to remain long.

Kanze, the fighter pilot who had been the object of the original rescue attempt, and John Dowdle and Robert Hill, the pilot and radioman of the overturned floatplane, hopped from the plane's wing tip to *Tang*'s deck. Burns's floatplane now taxied across the water and took off. But O'Kane's work wasn't done. He still had to dispose of the wrecked floatplane to make sure the Japanese could not salvage it. He summoned *Tang*'s gun crew and destroyed the first target of the patrol: an American plane.

Lookouts spotted a torpedo bomber billowing smoke as it ditched into the sea seven miles to the east. O'Kane ordered emergency speed. The gun crew blasted the shore batteries as the submarine raced past. Enemy forces had removed the trees designed to camouflage their positions the night before, a move that gave *Tang*'s gun crew a clear shot. Fighters and two bombers joined the attack as the Japanese hunkered down, unable to return fire. Lookouts spotted a life raft with survivors at 10:04 a.m. Fighters circled overhead to mark the position. Commander Alfred Matter, Petty Officer 2nd Class James Lenahan, and Petty Officer 2nd Class Tommy Thompson climbed aboard *Tang* sixteen minutes later. "It appeared that the life raft was only a bridge from the bomber to our boat," O'Kane noted. "They were wet only up to their knees."

Meanwhile, the pilot of *North Carolina*'s second floatplane, Lieutenant Burns, was patrolling the skies. Fighter pilots radioed the location of downed aviators and provided cover for the lumbering Kingfisher. Burns spotted several rafts adrift off Truk's eastern reef. Radioman Aubrey Gill dropped dye markers into the water to color each spot as Burns radioed the locations. The rescued aviators who now congregated in *Tang*'s Aviation Information Center relayed the reports to O'Kane. The skipper ordered the submarine to set off again at emergency speed. O'Kane couldn't afford the added time to zigzag, so the fliers in the Aviation Information Center called for air cover. Planes returning from a bombing run dropped down and escorted the submarine. O'Kane paused only long enough to scoop up two more fliers, Lieutenant Harry Hill of Virginia and Lieutenant j.g. James Cole of Texas.

Burns worried that *Tang*—still some fifteen miles away—might take too long to reach the other stranded aviators. He aimed into the wind and guided his Kingfisher down into the waves. Hellcat pilot Lieutenant j.g. Robert Barbor bobbed inside a raft. The Kingfisher taxied toward him. Gill directed the downed pilot from the carrier *Langley* to climb up on the wing next to the fuselage and take a seat. Burns taxied toward a second rubber raft, this one loaded with three torpedo bombers, Lieutenant Robert Nelson, Petty Officer 1st Class Robert Gruebel, and Petty Officer 1st Class James Livingston. A strong gust of wind hit the Kingfisher, lifting one wing and forcing the other under the waves. Gill sprung from his rear cockpit seat onto the elevated wing to balance the plane. The Kingfisher slowly rolled back to an even keel.

The plane's wing had punctured the bomber crew's raft, which deflated and vanished underwater along with the few rations the fliers had salvaged. Gill improvised. He sized up the weight of each flier and advised the men to climb up simultaneously on either side of the fuselage. The aviators did so and took seats along the wing with Hellcat pilot Barbor. Burns had now rescued four men. Half a mile farther out at sea, he spied a third raft; this one also held several men, Ensign Carrol Farrell, Petty Officer 2nd Class Joseph Hranek, and Petty Officer 2nd Class Owen Tabrum. The men's torpedo bomber had died mid-flight, the engine windmilling without power. Pilot Farrell had glided down and landed on the water. The plane floated long enough to allow the men time to inflate the raft and climb aboard with hardly a drop of water on them. "It was a beautiful landing," recalled Hranek, the radioman. "I've landed with more force on carriers."

Gill's job had grown much easier. His existing passengers, equally spaced along the wings, helped to balance the Kingfisher. The remaining men could climb up without the threat of dunking the wings. Three men perched on the port wing, three on the starboard. The seventh crouched next to the cockpit and held on to the fuselage. Burns ordered the men to tie the rubber raft to the plane so the Kingfisher could tow it. If the plane sank, the men might need it. Burns powered up the engine and taxied to sea. O'Kane's rescue of the two other fliers had delayed *Tang*'s arrival, but Burns radioed the skipper that he had ample fuel and the situation well under control. The morning calm gave way to higher swells that battered the floatplane. The men on the wings squirmed to adjust to the propeller blast, but no one complained. Burns taxied for some two hours before *Tang* appeared in the distance.

O'Kane arrived in the middle of the afternoon to find the Kingfisher down by the stern. The heavy seas had smashed the floatplane's tail. The skipper knew it would never fly again. Just as before, *Tang* sailors threw a rope and pulled the plane alongside. The fliers jumped one after the other onto the submarine's deck. O'Kane now met Burns face-to-face. The men had made an unlikely duo, a submarine skipper and a floatplane pilot, but their mutual desire to save lives with the tools available had proven a great success. The exhausted faces of the American aviators who now crowded *Tang*'s wardroom were proof. O'Kane was so impressed with Burns that he planned to recommend him for a Navy Cross once *Tang* returned to Pearl Harbor. But Burns's glory would prove short-lived. He would return to the United States to train as a fighter pilot, only to crash-land in a Hellcat ten months later in Virginia. "Plane total loss," the accident report would state, "injuries to pilot fatal."

Just as he did with the first Kingfisher, O'Kane planned to sink Burns's plane. He didn't want the pilot to watch, so he sent Burns and the others below where depth charge medicine awaited those who wanted a shot. *Tang*'s 20mm gun crew opened fire at 3:15 p.m., setting the Kingfisher ablaze. But *Tang*'s work wasn't over. A final raft with two downed aviators floated south of Ollan island. All the American planes had now been recalled, leaving only *Tang*. Executive officer Frazee mapped out the course. It didn't look good. *Tang* likely would not reach the raft until dark. O'Kane knew from experience how tough it was to locate a raft at night. If he waited until morning, the situation could be worse. Not only would the aviators spend a night at sea—and face possible capture by the Japanese—but the enemy would have time to regroup overnight and could target the *Tang*. O'Kane needed to find them and soon. The skipper knew that would require help from American planes.

Pilots in the Aviation Information Center raised Vice Admiral Marc Mitscher, commander of the task force.

"We'll need two night fighters to locate the last raft, Admiral," O'Kane asked.

"You'll have three," he answered.

Tang set off at twenty-one knots. Three night fighters joined the submarine at sunset to help search, one patrolling ahead and the other two off each bow. With too little light for periscopes, sailors climbed atop the shears, scanning the horizon as the last of the day's light faded. O'Kane's hope dwindled. "The fighters now looking like black albatrosses," he wrote, "as they flew their search patterns ahead and on our beams." The skipper watched one of the fighters suddenly dive and fire flares. Red signal stars answered, lighting up the night sky off *Tang*'s starboard bow. *Tang*'s lookouts spotted the raft. Lieutenant Donald Kirkpatrick, Jr., and Petty Officer 2nd Class Richard Bentley climbed aboard at 6:30 p.m., joining the now crowded wardroom. O'Kane dismissed the fighters. The skipper had enjoyed a successful day. He would return to Pearl Harbor with all twenty-four of his torpedoes, but with a load far more precious: twenty-two rescued American aviators.

13

SILVERSIDES

"Almost all the guys got seasick—but I've ridden Detroit streetcars so much that it didn't bother me any."

—Richard Smith,
undated 1943 letter

Coye paced the bridge of *Silversides* as the submarine departed Brisbane at 1:25 p.m. on April 26 to begin its tenth war patrol. The skipper had come back a hero after the eighth patrol when he had ended up in the number two spot in a Japanese convoy, sinking three ships in a matter of hours. The brass had loved it, raving about Coye's exploits in the patrol endorsements: "For aggressiveness, intelligent conduct, tenaciousness and courageousness and determined actions, this patrol leaves nothing to be desired." Coye had more than lived up to Burlingame's legacy. Word spread throughout the submarine force of the Silver Lady's success. Sailors begged to join the crew. The *Silversides'* officers relished the submarine's newfound fame. "The boat is hot as a firecracker now—fair haired boys with the gold braid," lanky officer Eugene Malone wrote in a letter. "We've been really clicking good."

Officers and crew celebrated their success during the twenty-four-day refit in Pearl Harbor. "I've been leading a most social life the past few days. Dining, dancing, sightseeing, exercising and what have you all day & night every day & evening. Yesterday 3 of us and girls went picnicing, more darn fun. We broiled steaks over a fire—ate sandwiches, tomatoes, celery, olives, loads of things—drove all around," Malone wrote. "Normally, however, we devote the morning to exercise—the captain to take off weight—me to put it on. The afternoon to loafing—and evening to partying. It's been more fun." Beneath the fun and sun, however, the hectic war was taking a toll. "Sure do want to get home for a while. Let my nerves settle down a bit, and maybe get a little saner for a while. After this war is over everyone is going to be considerably nutty I fear," wrote Malone in another letter. "I'm getting tired of playing for keeps."

Coye had followed his successful eighth patrol with a fifty-three-day run west of the Marianas that proved anticlimactic. He had fired seven torpedoes in two attacks, but managed only one kill, the small 1,920-ton cargo ship *Kofuku Maru*, an attack that had at least robbed the enemy of eighty-three infantrymen and fourteen crew. Despite his request for an extension, Coye still returned to port with seventeen torpedoes. He had passed on shooting two cruisers because he lacked a good firing solution and faced an excessive range, a move that drew heat from his superiors in the patrol endorsements. "The decision of the commanding officer in not firing at the cruiser task force is not upheld," wrote Captain John Haines, "as it is considered that such valuable targets are worthy of torpedoes under the circumstances set forth in the report." Coye knew Haines was right; the decision would bother him for years to come. "I probably should have taken a chance," he later said. "We didn't fire, and I regret that we didn't because it would have been worth a shot, even if we had missed."

Coye hoped this tenth patrol would prove better.

Silversides left for the first time without a single one of the seven commissioning officers. The Navy had transferred assistant communications officer Keith Nichols after the eighth patrol, leaving only executive officer Bob Worthington and engineer John Bienia to serve on the ninth patrol. The two men had spent 433 days on patrol and covered 80,911 miles, the equivalent of more than three trips around the earth—and time enough to wear out five 1,000-record needles on the wardroom phonograph. The officers had watched the submarine's internal dynamics evolve from the hell-raising days of Burlingame—a perfect leader for the early frontier period of the war—to the calm and reserved Coye, who reflected the Navy's new calculated strength as it pushed Japan back across the Pacific. The twenty-nine-year-old Worthington had climbed in that time from the gunnery officer to the ship's second in command. The Navy now ordered him home as the executive officer of *Sea Poacher*, a new submarine under construction in Maine. Engineer Bienia had married fourteen months earlier yet had spent barely more than

100 days with his bride. He, too, left *Silversides* for a new assignment, finally packing his sea bag, which included a slender piece of wood he salvaged from the sunken *Kazan Maru*. The *Silversides*, now missing his close friends, was a different place. Rather than look back with sadness, Bienia focused on seeing his wife again. The rest of his life stretched out before him. "Get yourself some new shoes for I understand they're rationed in the States," he wrote to her. "The way I'm going to dance your feet off you'll need shoes—pulenty!"

Brisbane vanished in *Silversides'* frothy wake. No one welcomed the boat's departure more than the shore patrol, as the eighteen-day refit—complete with a mint julep party—had only reaffirmed the submarine's debauched reputation. Eugene Malone had hoped this would be his first patrol as the Silver Lady's new executive officer. Coye had grown fond of the skinny Malone, almost ten years his junior, and with a mind like his, geared toward science and math. The two officers had spent time together between patrols; the lieutenant had even managed to coerce his skipper to attend Mass with him. Coye argued with his superiors that he'd rather have the twenty-three-year-old Malone as his second in command than any of the older and more senior men the submarine force had available. But the Navy brass didn't agree. For his part, Malone feared such an awesome responsibility. "It's a hell of a big job and a vitally important one on these big boats," Malone wrote in a January letter to his mother in California, "and I don't think I'm anywhere near ready for it."

When *Silversides* stopped for fuel on the return to Brisbane after the ninth patrol, Lieutenant Commander Charles Leigh waited pier-side in New Guinea's Milne Bay, clutching orders to replace Worthington as the executive officer. A graduate of the Naval Academy class of 1939, the twenty-seven-year-old Missouri native had spent several years on a World War I–era submarine. The former champion wrestler, who hungered for more wartime experience, had fought his way on board. Coye fumed and Malone felt crushed, though he tried to convince himself otherwise. "If our new exec. hadn't talked his way aboard I'd have gotten that job," Malone wrote. "However, I'm just as glad he did because I don't have any overgreat fondness for either paperwork or paper administration and he now has all that, plus navigation, in hand. I've got all the more active exec. jobs & so I'm happy—if slightly scared. Hope we sink lots of ships again as usual or it might look like my fault if we don't."

Leigh ingratiated himself with Coye as the submarine headed north toward New Guinea en route to the Marianas. Compared to the meticulous Worthington, who took multiple star shots and carefully worked up the equations, Leigh would climb to the bridge, shoot a couple of stars, and deliver the *Silversides* position to the skipper in minutes. "He was most aggressive," Coye recalled. "He was very popular with the crew yet he ruled them with an iron hand." Burlingame, now a division commander, joined the crew for a week as a training officer. Of the sixty-nine sailors on board for the tenth patrol, only a few of the enlisted men who had served under Burly remained. The fishnet Burlingame had run the *Silversides* through on his second patrol off the coast of Japan still adorned the wardroom bulkhead—the same room where he'd pressured Tom Moore to perform his now famous appendectomy. Other than that, little else remained. The former skipper, always a Kentucky gentleman, kept mostly to himself.

Silversides was Coye's boat now.

Like *Tang*, the Silver Lady's orders to sink ships around the Marianas dovetailed with America's drive across the Pacific. War planners looked to capitalize on the success in the Gilbert, Marshall, and Caroline islands and capture the volcanic strategic islands of Guam, Saipan, and Tinian. These islands in the southern Marianas represented Japan's last hope, a natural roadblock to stop America's march toward the homeland. The loss of the islands would shatter Japan's inner perimeter and place industrial cities like Tokyo, Osaka, and Nagoya within reach of American bombers. War planners on both sides saw the Marianas as the fulcrum on which victory balanced. "The war is drawing close to the lines vital to our national defense," Admiral Soemu Toyoda, commander of the Japanese navy, wrote in May 1944. "The issue of our national existence is unprecedentedly serious; and unprecedented opportunity exists for deciding who shall be victorious and who defeated."

Silversides arrived in Milne Bay at 11:40 a.m. on May 1, mooring alongside the 7,600-ton submarine tender *Eurayle*. This Allied outpost had changed dramatically in the two years since American and Australian forces had hacked a base and airfield out of an old coconut plantation on the southern tip of New Guinea. Burlingame disembarked with little fanfare this humid morning as tender crews climbed aboard to make minor repairs. Others took advantage of the overnight laundry service. *Silversides* let out a blast of its whistle the next afternoon and departed for patrol. The next few days slipped past as the submarine cruised more than 1,000 miles north, arriving off Guam at 3:15 a.m. on May 8. *Silversides* dove two hours later to inspect for possible targets in Apra Harbor, a deep-water port on the Guam's west coast. Several Japanese bombers and fighters buzzed the harbor around daybreak, a trend that continued throughout the day as planes lifted off from an airfield on Orote Peninsula, which formed the southern edge of the harbor. Coye counted seven ships in the harbor at 7:30 a.m., including several large transports. He contemplated shooting them in the harbor, but a shot over the reef appeared impractical.

The skipper decided to wait. He had just started his patrol and knew the seven ships would leave at some point. A single large sampan emerged at 9:40 a.m. and stood out northward along the coast, a departure followed later by a half dozen distant depth charges or bombs. Eventually, the skipper spotted masts through the periscope that soon developed into a convoy of six or seven ships roughly assembled in three columns. Five escorts guarded the harbor-bound convoy. Coye had precious few minutes to attack before the ships reached port. He could tell from the enemy's frequent sonar pings that the escorts sensed his presence. With the range too great to fire, Coye headed toward the convoy's center, all tubes ready. The convoy zigzagged right. Coye let the escort pass by 1,000 yards. He swung right and set up a stern shot at what he estimated was a 5,000-ton freighter that brought up the rear of the port column.

Coye fired four torpedoes, spreading them from a quarter length ahead of the freighter's bow to a quarter length astern. He hoped at least one of his torpedoes would hit. The soundman reported all four of the wakeless electric torpedoes ran hot, straight, and normal at twenty-nine knots toward the freighter less than a mile away. The quartermaster ticked off the time. Seventy-seven seconds later, the skipper heard an explosion. The sonar operator reported the target's screws stopped followed by increase in speed of the escorts' screws. Coye ordered *Silversides* deep at 2:34 p.m. Three distant depth charges exploded six minutes later. The soundman reported faint noises reminiscent of a ship breaking up, though Coye did not see it sink to confirm. Investigators after the war would find no proof of the ship's loss. The skipper returned to periscope depth in time to watch the convoy safely enter the harbor.

Planes buzzed overhead the rest of the afternoon and into the evening, the running lights glowing like shooting stars. With at least eleven ships in Apra Harbor, Coye radioed his superiors that it would be an opportune time for an air strike, but someone, somewhere, must have disagreed because no air strike materialized. The Japanese rewarded Coye's patience the next morning. A seven-ship convoy guarded by up to five escorts departed port and steamed north toward the empire. Coye was excited. He would have plenty of time to hunt and attack—days if necessary. The convoy zigzagged southwest, splitting into three columns. The skipper decided to trail the convoy throughout the day. "All seven ships appear to be good sized," he noted. "One is a four goal poster."

Coye kept his eye on the convoy's smoke, the telltale dark clouds that hung above the horizon. He felt eager to surface and chase as the smoke grew faint, knowing that the eight-knot convoy pulled farther ahead each minute. But Guam with its crowded enemy airfields remained in sight just thirty miles astern, too close for him to risk a surface chase. The skipper waited until 5:01 p.m. and then surfaced, the submarine's 252 battery cells depleted. The engines roared as *Silversides* sliced through the swells. Lookouts spotted the convoy's smoke on the horizon once again. "Closed until head masts in sight with high periscope," Coye wrote. "With all the planes available at Guam it seems a miracle this convoy had no air cover."

Coye ordered the speed increased at sunset to gain radar contact only to learn his radar had failed. A full moon shone above, prompting the skipper to order an end around down-moon. Clouds moved in at 9:15, by which time Coye realized he had lost contact. The convoy had zigzagged at sunset and *Silversides*—absent its radar—had spent the last few hours chasing a cloud shadow. Coye ordered a retiring search curve at full speed along the convoy's last known position. Lookouts finally spotted the convoy at 11:11 p.m. at a distance of ten miles. Not long after Malone and his men restored the radar, one of the escorts spotted *Silversides*, challenging it to identify itself with a signal light. The element of surprise had vanished.

Coye put the escort astern as the ships switched on red lights. He heard multiple explosions that he speculated might be gunfire though were more likely depth charges. The skipper worked for hours to gain a favorable attack position. He finally dove right before daybreak, studying the convoy through his periscope. Five overlapping ships paraded past: a skipper's dream shot. Coye fired. Within just fifty-seven seconds, he unleashed six fish, two aimed at the large transport leading the center column and one each at four other ships. Five crashed into the convoy as *Silversides* started deep. Seven depth charges shook the boat. "These were too close for comfort," Coye wrote. "Screws were heard to pass over forward torpedo room."

The sonar operator heard the grinding noises of bulkheads collapsing as two ships sank, the 2,631-ton converted gunboat *Choan Maru No. 2* and the 2,254-ton freighter *Okinawa Maru*. Sixty-eight enemy passengers and crew-members vanished with them. Coye returned to periscope depth and spotted a ship on fire about three miles away. Dark smoke curled skyward and several escorts milled around. Coye took pictures and let the crew have a look at the crippled ship. More smoke appeared on the horizon to the north and twice the skipper spied the masts of two ships, but he needed visual confirmation to claim credit. Four dozen depth charges punctuated the morning, none of them close. "Japs sounded awful mad," Coye wrote in his report. "Charges were distant but full sized and made a swish in superstructure."

The escorts departed after noon, following the decimated convoy as it returned to Guam. *Silversides* approached the 4,319-ton passenger cargo ship *Mikage Maru No. 18*, which had appeared on the verge of sinking all morning yet had somehow remained afloat, albeit now emptied of survivors. Coye thought about surfacing and shooting it with the deck gun, but a Japanese bomber appeared on the horizon and dampened his enthusiasm. He could see that the torpedo had broken the ship's back and each swell tugged at the bow and stern. Debris swirled around the wounded ship—oil drums, wood, and even a whaleboat that forced the skipper to duck his periscope to avoid a collision. Coye decided at 3:40 p.m. that he could wait no longer. Just as Coye's impatient torpedomen prepared a final shot, the *Mikage Maru No. 18* slipped beneath the waves, leaving only a metal landing barge that floated off to mark the spot where the ship and fourteen crewmen went down.

Silversides spent the next week hunting, cruising some 138 miles north to prowl the waters of Saipan, where enemy planes too numerous to count crowded the skies. Despite the dense air traffic, the seas remained largely empty, minus the occasional sampan or patrol. The one viable target Coye encountered on May 17—what appeared to be a 4,000-ton freighter accompanied by four escorts—he passed on firing, as the two-mile range meant enemy lookouts would spot his torpedo wakes and take evasive measures. The skipper circled back to Guam. There he picked off the 998-ton converted gunboat *Shosei Maru* on May 20, but the small boat came with a big price. "Four escorts and planes turned on us with a vengeance," he wrote. "Sixty one charges were dropped, which included one salvo of twenty four dropped in rapid succession."

At 5:24 on the morning of May 28, lookouts spotted a Mavis at a range of eight miles, a Japanese flying boat often used for patrol. Coye surmised the plane was guarding a convoy and ordered *Silversides* to close. When the plane finally vanished two hours later, *Silversides* surfaced and lookouts spotted smoke on the horizon. A convoy steamed southeast at seven knots from the home islands to Saipan. Coye tracked the convoy through the calm sea, diving after lunch when the Mavis returned. He closed before sunset to inspect the convoy, which consisted of the 1,949-ton cargo ship *Shoken Maru* and 1,999-ton freighter *Horaizan Maru*, guarded by four escorts that patrolled off the bow, each beam, and astern. The skipper decided he would attack that night, when the moon had set and the enemy lookouts had relaxed.

Coye ordered all ten tubes made ready to fire at 1:15 a.m. as the torpedomen in both rooms wrenched open the outer doors. The escorts blocked *Silversides* from approaching too close but Coye slipped in to about 3,400 yards. He fired six fish, three at each freighter—the iconic torpedo whine signified that the eighteen-hour-and-seven-minute hunt neared its completion. The quartermaster ticked off the time. Two minutes and twenty-five seconds later, Coye saw the first explosion, followed by three more. The torpedoes hit with such violence that night turned into day—even for the men below deck. "The explosion lit up the whole conning tower as if the sun had suddenly moved right over the hatch," recalled Malone. "There was a bright yellow, orange, fire-color illumination—incredible—a blast of heat and the god-awfullest noise you ever heard."

The two vaporized freighters—along with fifty-nine passengers and crew—vanished from *Silversides'* radar. Coye ordered *Silversides* to clear out, the four engines roaring. The skipper remained on the bridge and watched the enemy escorts close, dropping a total of twenty-six erratic depth charges that proved no threat to the sub. "Escorts were probably blinded by the holocaust which was now raging astern," Coye speculated in his report. "It is doubtful that any of the crews survived. Ships were apparently loaded with gasoline and a million or so gallons burning is truly an awe-inspiring sight." The crew secured from battle stations at 2:10 a.m., but up until daybreak—and even from a distance of more than thirty miles—men watched the flames tickle the sky. "Every 4th of July I am reminded of this attack," Coye would later write, "but I have yet to see any fireworks that surpass it."

14

TANG

"There will be widows in Tokyo tonight."

—Donald Sharp,
June 30, 1944, diary

Tang let out a prolonged blast of its whistle, turned in place, and headed out into the channel at Pearl Harbor. It was 1:30 p.m. on June 8, 1944, two days after American and Allied forces stormed the beaches at Normandy for the D-Day invasion. The twenty-four days in port had proven hectic—and not just in preparation for patrol. The submarine force's steam-driven fish ran off alcohol—dubbed torpedo juice—to which the Navy wisely added the purgative croton oil to dissuade thirsty sailors. Some figured out how to strain out the obtrusive additive with a loaf of stale bread. Other more crafty sailors constructed makeshift stills, boiling the alcohol, then capturing the steam. Once in port sailors cut the potent booze with pineapple and grapefruit juice. The homemade cocktail proved so strong that it would not only burn lips, but would eat the wax lining out of a paper cup, forcing the bottom to drop out after just a few drinks.

Sailors guzzled it by the gallon.

Tang radarman Floyd Caverly had become one of the boat's resident distillers, setting up shop in the radio shack. The twenty-six-year-old Minnesota native and his cohorts had found all the materials and tools needed to build a still on board, from the transmitter's output coil to the Silex coffeemaker. The men even rigged up a small fan to waft away fumes. After settling in at the Royal Hawaiian after *Tang*'s second patrol, Caverly and his roommate fired up the still in the bathroom. The volatile contraption exploded, shattering the full-length mirror on the bathroom door and totaling the toilet. Caverly watched in horror as water flooded his hotel room, the same one where actress Mae West had once stayed and autographed all the lamp shades. "The troops had left sex behind when we passed through the Golden Gate," O'Kane would later joke when he learned of Caverly's ingenuity, "but that was just about all."

Tang bustled this warm afternoon. Fourteen new sailors—two officers and twelve enlisted men—had reported aboard. Sailors hung additional bunks to accommodate the new crew, including one that dangled almost seven feet above the wardroom passageway that was now home to Ensign Richard Kroth. O'Kane had used the refit to manage the installation of two new antennas as well as to rest in the luxury of the Royal Hawaiian, sharing a second-floor oceanfront suite with Frazee. As O'Kane set out on his third patrol, the remains of the battleship *Arizona* slipped past the starboard side, a rusting reminder of the dangers O'Kane faced. "I could never give it more than a glance," he later wrote, "and still keep the clear eye my job demanded."

Despite returning to port with all twenty-four torpedoes, *Tang's* second patrol had been a great success, described by the *New York Times* in a front-page story as "the most dramatic and productive cruise of her career." *Tang* sailors had fished twenty-two downed aviators out of the perilous waters off Truk in the two-day assault on Japan's stronghold. The Navy immediately recognized—as it had with Mush Morton and *Wahoo*—the positive headlines the rescue could generate. O'Kane, with Lieutenant Burns and the other rescued aviators, sat down two days after arriving in Pearl Harbor for a press conference that triggered stories and photos in newspapers and magazines nationwide. A full-page photo of the grinning O'Kane—surrounded by all the rescued fliers on *Tang's* deck—even appeared in *Life* magazine.

But O'Kane was eager to hunt ships, the mission of a submarine. The skipper had spent his first two patrols—much to his frustration—tethered to the fleet as carriers pounded Japanese forces at Wake, Truk, and Palau. Those patrols had supported America's offensive push across the central Pacific, a push whose momentum would continue to build as Allied forces pressed multiple pressure points along Japan's frazzled front lines.

Tang's latest set of orders promised a welcome change. No more lifeguard duty or carrier raids. O'Kane would patrol area twelve, the East China and

Yellow seas—right in the heart of the empire. The second *Sealion* and *Tinosa* would join *Tang* in that area, though the boats would operate independently, every man for himself. "Considerable important enemy shipping passes through area twelve en route between the Japanese Empire and Shanghai and other Chinese ports, and en route between the Japanese Empire and Indo-China, Philippines, and Dutch East Indies," *Tang's* orders stated. "Traffic between Shanghai and Nagasaki and Sasebo is believed to be routed close up the China coast to about latitude thirty-three degrees north, then due east to the empire. Shipping along west shore of Chosen is believed to stay fairly close to the coast, taking advantage of shallow water and coastal islands."

O'Kane knew the area well. He had patrolled the same waters just sixteen months earlier with Morton. That was the patrol where *Wahoo* sank nine ships. The skipper knew enemy shipping might have changed since then, but the geography hadn't. He had a tactical advantage, something he would need since two other submarines would hunt the same waters. The competitive O'Kane knew *Sealion* and *Tinosa* could affect how he conducted his own patrol. Frazee, chief quartermaster Sidney Jones, and Lieutenant Frank Springer used the refit at Pearl Harbor to feel out colleagues on the other boats for clues to how their skippers planned to operate. O'Kane had even recruited wardroom steward Howard Walker to hunt down information from fellow stewards.

The skipper settled on his own plan about the time *Tang* entered the channel at Midway at 8 a.m. on June 12. O'Kane felt that *Tinosa* and *Sealion* would likely patrol on the surface in the vast open waters, a move that guaranteed enemy planes would eventually spot one or both. That would force the Japanese to reroute convoys close to shore. If *Tang* could remain undetected in shallow waters, enemy war planners might deliver convoys directly to him. To help guarantee that interception, O'Kane counted on William Leibold, his trusted chief boatswain's mate. Known to most simply as "Boats," Leibold had become a fixture on the bridge. The twenty-one-year-old California native, who had convinced his father to sign a waiver so he could enlist at seventeen, had hoped to become a submariner. He had landed instead on *Pruitt*, a World War I–era destroyer the Navy had converted into a minelayer. After a storm off the Aleutians parted *Pruitt's* mast lines, Leibold braved the ice to climb atop and secure new lines. The Navy rewarded him with orders to the undersea service.

Tang cruised northwest for almost ten days. The men executed practice and trim dives, serviced the torpedoes, and watched movies at night. The submarine passed some 450 miles off the Marianas and later the volcanic island of Sofu Gan, a giant peak known to mariners as Lot's Wife, which marked the entrance to empire waters. The skipper used the uninhabited rock as a radar target and navigational fix. Eventually, *Tang* closed in on Japan and paralleled the south coast of Honshu, the enemy's main island. Much to the skipper's surprise, *Tang* encountered no planes. He surmised that enemy ships used the safer Inland Sea, but the lack of aircraft surprised him. O'Kane wondered if maybe the enemy had picked up on *Tinosa* and *Sealion* and now focused on them. The radio delivered the news that American forces had invaded Saipan and secured the beachhead, the same waters O'Kane had hunted only four months earlier on *Tang*'s first patrol—and a more likely explanation for the empty skies.

Tang slipped through Colnett Strait—the passageway south of Kyushu and the Ryuku islands—the evening of June 22, cruising at eight knots so that on radar the submarine might appear to be a trawler. At 3:50 a.m. *Tang* rendezvoused with *Sealion*. With dawn just hours away, the submarines could only exchange signals and agree to meet the following night. *Tang* spent the day submerged, a departure from the tactic that Morton had deployed so well. It frustrated O'Kane, but was necessary. "The East China and Yellow seas held everything to be found in the open-ocean areas and the close-in Empire areas except one thing, deep water. Only in the region directly to the west of the Nansei Shoto and lower Kyushu was it possible to dive deep and evade below a temperature gradient," O'Kane wrote. "Elsewhere our submarine would be fortunate to have 100-foot depth of water for attack and could not expect over 200 feet in which to hide."

The crew enjoyed a relaxed Sunday as the submarine patrolled underwater. Sailors broke open crates of oranges, napped, and played cards. Others sat through a lesson about how the Kleinschmidt stills converted salt to fresh water. The crew counted twelve distant explosions, but no one could be sure if they had been torpedoes or depth charges. A search with periscopes showed nothing. Late in the day, *Tang* surfaced briefly to ventilate the submarine. O'Kane scanned the horizon from the bridge when the loudspeaker crackled: an Ultra message had just arrived from Pearl Harbor. Such messages often promised news of a target. The skipper climbed down to the control room, where the men read the tape. "Damaged battleship proceeding from Ryukyus through Nansei Shoto to Kobe or Sasebo Next Thirty Hours," the message stated. "Weiss in *Tinosa* position submarines to intercept Sasebo passage."

The skipper smarted about the message. Even 4,000 miles from Pearl Harbor, O'Kane felt under the thumb of his superiors. Though he conceded that if the information proved valid—and he could add a battleship to his résumé of sinkings—he wouldn't gripe. *Tinosa* skipper Don Weiss, the senior of the three captains, contacted *Tang* and demanded a meeting. His coded message ordered *Tang* and *Sealion* to rendezvous at Danjo Gunto, a ninety-mile run north and farther out to sea. *Tang* set off shortly past sunset, much to the frustration of the skipper. O'Kane disliked abandoning his spot, feeling that each mile took him farther away from any possible action. Over cups of hot coffee, O'Kane and Frazee talked. The skipper felt that the best spot to intercept the wounded battleship would be off the Koshiki Islands.

Frazee left *Tang* at 1:15 a.m. joined by Petty Officer 3rd Class Dante Cacciola—known to his shipmates simply as the Dago—in a yellow rubber raft, carrying ten movies the crew wanted to swap, infrared signaling apparatus, and the code for the coordinated attacks. Cacciola paddled across the dark, pulling alongside *Tinosa* for almost a half hour. Frazee disembarked and climbed down to *Tinosa*'s wardroom to meet with Weiss. Back on *Tang*, O'Kane eyed the clock and stewed. If he was going to make it south to the Koshikis, he needed to leave soon. Dawn approached. He would need as much time as possible to run on the surface or else the trip would be pointless. The skipper gritted his teeth when he finally spotted the yellow raft returning through the darkness.

Frazee had barely dropped through the hatch when *Tang* set off on all four engines at flank speed. The executive officer changed into dry clothes and joined O'Kane in the wardroom for another cup of coffee. The twenty-eight-year-old lieutenant appeared tired. "OK, Fraz," O'Kane asked. "What's our spot?"

"Any one we want, Captain," he answered. "We've got the islands and the straits all to ourselves." Frazee explained that *Tinosa* and *Sealion* would patrol two lanes to the west, thirty miles wide. "Captain Weiss got pretty mad at my insistence, but finally told us to go to our 'goddammned islands.'"

Tang dove shortly past daybreak to avoid a Japanese patrol. The submarine would have to remain submerged throughout the day, running at six knots. If

Tang continued at its present course it wouldn't reach the strait until 10 p.m., too late to catch the enemy. Frazee adjusted *Tang*'s course to head farther north and use the radar to catch the ships leaving the strait at dusk. The men spent the day studying and killing time. O'Kane reviewed officer fitness reports, but struggled to focus. He wanted to attack. *Tang* surfaced at twilight and fired off two main engines to charge the batteries and two more plus the auxiliary to run at seventeen knots, dodging the sampans that bobbed in the waves. *Tang* passed the 100-fathom curve and added another engine to propulsion. Ensign Dick Kroth flipped on the bridge speaker at 9:45 p.m. to deliver the good news: "Radar contact, bearing one five zero, range twenty thousand yards!"

The young officer's announcement validated O'Kane's predictions. The skipper had been confident that *Tang*'s position would generate targets. He believed the Japanese had no option but to run ships up the coast to Nagasaki, a congested industrial hub of 285,000 residents that was home to Mitsubishi's steelworks and arms plant as well as a massive dockyard. But it still surprised O'Kane that he had found a possible target so fast. The skipper studied the chart in the conning tower and anxiously awaited an updated radar report on the ship's location. Either the ship exited the strait—and headed north toward *Tang*—or it entered the passage and steamed south and away. The veteran skipper believed it had left the strait. The narrow passage could prove difficult to navigate at night, a fact that would prompt a cautious captain to anchor until dawn. Petty Officer 1st Class Edwin Bergman stared at the green radar screen. "A mess of ships," he called out. "Range twenty thousand!"

O'Kane pushed Bergman aside and stared at a jumble of pips. No single pip appeared large enough to be a battleship, but the number of them shocked O'Kane. Japanese convoys tended to be small; a couple of ships, three at the most. This defied conventional enemy tactics. O'Kane fired off a one-word message to the other American submarines: "convoy." *Sealion* acknowledged, but not *Tinosa*. *Tang*'s limited radar use made it difficult to pinpoint the convoy's exact course and speed, but sailors determined it zigzagged northwest. *Tang* fired off another message. When the convoy settled on a westerly course at twelve knots, he sent a third and final report. O'Kane knew he should probably wait for his colleagues to arrive and attack as a proper wolf pack. But such patience wasn't a part of his makeup. He would take his men to battle alone. "*Tang* had done what she could to bring the other boats in," O'Kane later wrote. "This was pure business, and our business was sinking ships; we meant to do just that."

Tang loomed off the convoy's port bow with a three-day-old moon about to set, ideal conditions for a night surface attack. Quartermaster Jones and boatswain's mate William Leibold joined the skipper on the bridge. The decreasing range helped clarify the convoy's composition, first on the radar and then through the 7x50 binoculars. O'Kane spied at least six large ships steaming in two columns, the two leaders likely large escorts. That meant that convoy boasted at least four large targets. Six escorts formed a circular screen around the convoy. Another screen also comprised of six escorts formed a second layer of protection. Additional escorts patrolled ahead and astern of the two screens. More than a dozen patrol craft guarded the convoy. No one had seen such a protective ring around a few ships. Quartermaster Jones captured the thoughts of everyone on the bridge with his one-word exclamation: "Christ!"

The swarm of escorts that guarded the convoy demonstrated the toll America's unrestricted submarine war had now taken on Japan. Merchant ships loaded with everything from oil and coal to bauxite and rubber now went down faster than shipbuilders could hammer out new ones, starving Japan's wartime industry of precious raw materials vital to construct fighters, warships, and munitions. American submarine skippers in 1944 would average 137 attacks each month, firing more than 500 torpedoes. The success of those attacks came down to more than just talented skippers, like O'Kane. Thirty months of war had revealed the failure of Japan's antisubmarine strategy, a major problem since maritime transportation served as the backbone of the island nation's civilian and military economies. Inferior technology and poor prewar planning coupled with a reluctance to adapt to new tactics now threatened not only Japan's war effort but the nation's ability to survive.

One of Japan's biggest weaknesses was poor technology. Japan had proven slow to embrace the promise of radar, instead emphasizing lookouts. Though lookouts are valuable for spotting large surface ships, American submarines presented a much greater challenge. The low and sleek design of submarines coupled with improved camouflage paint introduced in 1943 made submarines difficult to spot at great distances. The preference of many skippers to hunt late at night further complicated that challenge. Skippers like O'Kane routinely seized such opportunities to pick off targets under the watchful eye of lookouts. Japanese technicians in advance of Midway had installed two experimental radar sets, not on the frontline carriers, but on the battleships *Hyuga* and *Ise*, both relegated to guard the Aleutians invasion. Even as radar appreciation grew, escorts remained a low priority. Not until at least September 1944 would technicians install radar on escorts with any regularity.

But Japan's problems ran deeper than just technology. While Japan provided some antisubmarine protection to large combatant ships and vital convoys, military leaders had failed to adequately anticipate the threat from American submarines. Many ships in the early days of the war often steamed through the open seas unescorted, easy prey for lurking subs. The only time ships enjoyed protection was when leaving or arriving in port. The responsibility of that protection then fell to local commanders, each of whom had varying resources. Exacerbating the problem was the failure of the Japanese to accurately gauge the effectiveness of its antisubmarine measures. Antisubmarine efforts, according to a Navy postwar tally, cost America just three submarines in 1942. The next three years saw the likely losses of fifteen, fourteen, and eight submarines respectively. Japanese forces in contrast claimed as many as 500 American submarines destroyed, a figure ten times higher than reality.

Japan's antisubmarine failures were rooted in an outdated view of naval warfare that centered on fleet actions and surface battles. Military leaders did not view submarines as independent fighters, but as auxiliaries to the fleet, much as American leaders had viewed submarines two decades earlier. This frustrated the Germans, who unsuccessfully pressured Japan to adopt America's strategy of targeting merchant ships. "The Japanese Navy thought always of the U.S. carriers. They talked about how many were building, and how many were in the Pacific and that these must be sunk; but it was always carriers they talked about. Next after that they would attack battleships and lesser ships but never the merchantmen except under most favorable conditions," Vice Admiral Paul Wenneker, who had served as an attaché in Japan, would tell American investigators after the war. "The mission was the American carriers and they could not be changed on this principle."

As much as military leaders resisted change, Japan could no longer ignore America's submarine war. Too many ships were going down. The Japanese in November 1943 finally formed the Grand Escort Fleet to protect ships that steamed between the empire and vital locales, including the Marianas, Philippines, and the East Indies. Within a year the fleet grew to include some sixty vessels, including destroyers, sub chasers, patrol boats, and about forty-five frigates. Many of these frigates could carry as many as 300 depth charges. The Grand Escort Fleet also depended on air patrols that would reach a maximum size of 170 planes, many of them obsolete and only one third equipped with radar. In March 1944 Japan also issued its first operation order, outlining no fewer than ten formations escorts should use when driving convoys. The general plan called for a convoy to steam in a block formation encircled by a ring of escorts. On the bridge of *Tang* this evening, O'Kane saw not just one ring, but two.

O'Kane could not shoot from outside the escort screen and hope to hit any of the freighters. He would have to penetrate the double-layered screen, a job better suited for a magician than a sailor. He had no chance at an undetected approach on the convoy's bow, but he hoped he could slip in for a broadside attack, a move that would allow him to fire a split salvo at two ships. Jones and Leibold studied the patrols through binoculars, looking for any sign that the escorts had spotted the submarine. *Tang* cruised across the phosphorescent wake of the leading port escort only to find that the submarine would pass the bow of the inner escort, a move that guaranteed the lookouts would spot *Tang*. O'Kane retreated. The skipper tried a second time but again found the inner escort blocked his path. The broadside attack, he realized, wouldn't work. He needed a new strategy, one the Japanese would never anticipate. O'Kane decided to attack from the stern.

Tang eased across the wake of the rear port escort, expecting to find a starboard patrol right alongside. The men scanned the dark waters before Leibold spotted it, far off the starboard flank. O'Kane hopped down into the conning tower, where the radar confirmed the visual observation. The skipper ordered Frazee to calculate the distance between the two rear escorts. The executive officer delivered the news to O'Kane on the bridge seconds later—2,300 yards or a little over a mile. O'Kane had found what he needed: a hole in the net. *Tang* crossed the convoy's wake and turned to follow the same course, planning to slip between the escorts. The skipper ordered a third engine online, and *Tang* roared ahead in the darkness, closing in on the rear escorts. O'Kane slowed to sixteen knots, fearful *Tang*'s motion might draw the eye of the enemy's lookouts.

The scenario reminded O'Kane of a night on *Wahoo* eighteen months earlier under then skipper Pinky Kennedy. On its second patrol off the Solomon Islands *Wahoo* had encountered a large freighter in the middle of the night accompanied by a single escort. The freighter had just passed *Wahoo*, zigzagging frantically. The target's stern still loomed large on the horizon and its erratic course slowed its pace, making it easy prey that *Wahoo* could sneak up on from behind. Though skippers generally preferred a broadside attack, in war ideal setups were rare. O'Kane told Kennedy that *Wahoo* had no choice but to pursue and attack the freighter from the stern. The skipper's reaction shocked and humiliated O'Kane. "Don't be stupid," Kennedy had shouted in front of several other officers and crewmembers. "A submarine can't attack from here."

O'Kane planned to prove him wrong.

Tang inched up on the convoy's rear. Jones focused his binoculars on the port escort while Leibold studied the starboard. Neither would say a word unless the patrols turned toward *Tang*. Communication had been reduced to whispers. The men on the bridge could now clearly see the patrols that flanked either side of the submarine, two destroyer escorts with guns mounted fore and aft. The Japanese ships towered over *Tang*, and though intimidating, their height worked to O'Kane's advantage. The elevated vantage points meant enemy lookouts would not see a submarine silhouetted against the sky. In fact, to spot the *Tang*, lookouts would actually have to look down, where the submarine would blend into the dark waters. Furthermore, no lookout would ever suspect an American skipper would be stupid or bold enough to try to penetrate the narrow swath between them. They hadn't met Dick O'Kane.

"Come up here, Fraz," the skipper called. "This you've got to see!"

Frazee was there before the skipper finished his sentence. The two officers surveyed the scene. The silhouette of the destroyer escorts now fell behind *Tang*'s stern. A glance to either side revealed the sleek outlines of other craft, encircling the convoy. Directly off *Tang*'s bow steamed the massive freighters. Like a virus that penetrates a cell's defensive membrane, O'Kane had punctured the convoy's protective shield. He was now on the inside, a traveling member of a Japanese convoy, protected from the outside world by the enemy's own escorts—as long as he wasn't spotted. O'Kane was thrilled. The skipper dropped down into the conning tower for one last look at the chart. Nagasaki remained another twenty-five miles to the north. The skipper had plenty of time. O'Kane considered how best to attack. Should he target the port or starboard column?

O'Kane settled on the starboard column. *Tang* increased speed to seventeen knots. The men on the bridge could see the two closest targets through binoculars as *Tang* maneuvered off the convoy's starboard side: a large four-masted freighter with a high composite superstructure topped by a short stack led the starboard column, followed by what appeared to be a modern tanker. Both rode low in the water and likely were loaded. O'Kane planned to shoot a spread of three torpedoes from *Tang*'s bow at each of the two closest ships. "Make all tubes ready for firing."

"All tubes ready," Frazee answered.

"Open outer doors forward."

"Outer doors are open."

O'Kane had waited months for this exact moment, a loaded convoy dead ahead, oblivious to his lethal presence.

"Any time, Captain."

The skipper watched the lead freighter chug across the scope of the target-bearing transmitter, centering the reticle on the ship's after mast. "Constant bearing—mark!"

"Set," crackled over the bridge loudspeaker.

"Fire!"

Tang shuddered as the first torpedo left the tube, followed seconds later by two more. O'Kane then turned to the tanker and fired three torpedoes.

"Torpedo run one minute forty-eight seconds, Captain."

O'Kane ordered *Tang* to turn north, all four engines online for evasion once the skipper had the required visual confirmation of the Japanese losses.

"Thirty seconds to go."

The freighter's stern exploded followed by a blast amidships that lit up the night sky. "The explosion appeared to blow the ship's sides out, and he commenced sinking rapidly," O'Kane wrote in his report. "On schedule, our fourth and fifth torpedoes hit under the stack and just forward of the after superstructure of the tanker. His whole after end blazed up until extinguished as he went down by the stern."

The Japanese escorts hurled depth charges as additional explosions rocked the night. *Tang* seized on the chaos to escape, just slipping past one stunned escort. A low-hanging cloud of smoke marked the dark sky where the ships sank. O'Kane climbed below at midnight for a visit to the head in the forward torpedo room. Wardroom steward Howard Walker greeted the skipper afterward with a cup of hot coffee. "How many did we get," Captain?"

"Why, both of them," O'Kane said, taking a sip. "We saw them go."

"I think there was more, sir."

Explosions often outnumbered ships, O'Kane explained, making it impossible for sailors below deck to tally losses.

"Oh, I wasn't down here," Walker confessed. "You were topside so long, I brought your coffee to the bridge. It was so exciting, I dropped your coffee down into the superstructure."

Walker was right, though O'Kane didn't know when he logged just two ships sunk in his report that night. A postwar review of Japanese records would double that number, revealing that O'Kane had destroyed the freighters *Tainan Maru* and *Kennichi Maru* along with passenger cargo ships *Nasusan Maru* and *Tamahoko Maru*, the latter taking down with it 560 Allied captives en route to prison in Japan, a tragedy that would prove all too common in the war. Six torpedoes fired in the two-hour-and-eight-minute attack had destroyed 16,292 tons of Japanese ships. O'Kane's approach from the stern—ridiculed eighteen months earlier by Kennedy—had produced the most successful single attack of the war, an attack Petty Officer 2nd Class Donald Sharp summed up afterward with four simple words in his diary: "Tonight the fireworks started."

O'Kane scanned the horizon at 8 p.m. the night of June 27 when the bridge loudspeaker crackled with the news that an Ultra message had arrived. O'Kane preferred such messages contain specific information on convoy movements. This one in contrast provided only coordinates for offshore enemy shipping routes. O'Kane was suspicious. Good information was rare in this area yet American war planners some 4,000 miles away in Pearl Harbor had suddenly cracked a message about a new secret shipping route. O'Kane didn't buy it. *Tang* had just obliterated four ships. The weary skipper suspected the enemy had put out bogus leads to throw off the American submarines that now hunted in Japan's home waters.

The Ultra directed *Tinosa* skipper Don Weiss to take charge again and position the three submarines to intercept the enemy convoys. O'Kane fumed. He was tired of Pearl Harbor's micromanagement of this patrol, particularly the insistence that the three submarines work together. The effort so far had proven futile. *Tinosa* had never even responded to *Tang*'s messages during its attack on the convoy a few nights earlier. *Sealion* had at least responded, but failed to get in on the action. The time had come for them to part ways. Weiss ordered another meeting off Danjo Gunto. Frazee climbed back into the yellow raft and paddled over to *Tinosa*. When he returned to *Tang*, he headed to the wardroom to deliver the news. "We've been banished."

Tinosa would operate south of the enemy shipping lane, *Sealion* to the north. *Tang* would patrol north of both, at least forty miles above the shipping lane.

"And the other boundaries?" O'Kane asked.

"Well, Captain Weiss didn't get around to that," Frazee answered. "I didn't think we would want to bring it up."

The skipper digested the news. Weiss had only limited *Tang*'s southern boundary. O'Kane had no restrictions to the north, east, or west. The whole Yellow Sea was now his. Some of his crew in contrast greeted the news with trepidation. "The water is mighty shallow," Don Sharp wrote in his diary. "May god & luck still be with us, we'll need plenty."

Heavy fog swept across the waves at dawn on June 29 as *Tang* patrolled submerged near the southwest coast of Korea. The cold water and the humid air fogged the two periscopes, forcing the officers on watch to alternate between them, dunking one to clear the lens as the officer peered through the other. *Tang* compensated with periodic radar sweeps.

The loudspeaker crackled near noon with the news that a freighter steamed west. O'Kane peered through the periscope—still clutching his lunchtime drumstick—and could just make out the major details of the ship, a mast-funnel-mast-freighter. O'Kane could not overtake it submerged, so *Tang* surfaced early that afternoon and paralleled the freighter through rough seas. Once O'Kane was ahead of the freighter, he ordered *Tang* to dive again. The skipper would wait for his prey to come to him.

O'Kane ordered his crew to battle stations at 5:30 p.m. and fired two torpedoes. Frazee announced a forty-seven-second run time. O'Kane raised the scope to watch. The skipper spied the smoke from the torpedo's wakes; both raced ahead just as aimed, but disappeared beneath the ship. Both had run too deep and missed.

The freighter turned on the *Tang*. O'Kane ordered the submarine deep. Two depth charges exploded as *Tang* reached 200 feet, just fifty feet off the shallow bottom. The failed attack—the second in as many days—infuriated O'Kane. "To bring torpedoes pushing on toward 5,000 miles, and to have six in a row, six out of our first 12 fail us," he wrote. "That wasn't quite fair."

Tang surfaced, allowing the watch to track the freighter's last known course. The smell of steaks wafted through the compartments. The skipper re-hashed the failed attack over dinner. How at ten feet had the torpedo passed beneath the target? Then it hit him: the China-bound freighter was empty, carrying just enough weight for ballast. He'd missed because the ship rode high in the water. The draft of an empty ship was only eight feet. His torpedo had slipped right beneath.

The wardroom phone interrupted a post-dinner cribbage game at 8:30. The conning tower reported a radar contact due north. O'Kane climbed to the bridge. The skipper suspected it was the same ship he had missed earlier, a mistake he planned to remedy before dawn. O'Kane decided to attack after moonset, still a few hours away. The darkness would allow *Tang* to slip in so close that the freighter would have no time to evade. The skipper climbed down to his bunk, slipped off his shoes, and closed his eyes.

Wardroom steward Walker woke the skipper a few hours later with a cup of hot coffee. O'Kane downed a second one moments later in the wardroom beneath the glow of the red night-vision lights. "We going to get her this time, Captain?"

"That's right," O'Kane told his steward. "One pickle right in her middle."

The skipper climbed to the bridge, where Frazee pointed out the *Nikkin Maru* to O'Kane, whose eyes had not yet adjusted to the dark. The 5,707-ton freighter that had left the Japanese port of Moji bound for Woosung proved far from empty. Some 3,400 passengers crowded aboard, all oblivious to the lurking submarine. Across the dark and rough seas, O'Kane studied his target. "Let's go to battle stations," he ordered. "Set all torpedoes to run at six feet. I'll take the con."

Frazee dropped below.

"Constant bearing—mark!"

"Set!"

"Fire!"

This time O'Kane hit the ship with one shot. The one-and-a-half-ton weapon—packed with more than 500 pounds of the explosive Torpex—doomed 3,150 passengers and sixty-nine crewmembers. "The explosion amidships, just thirty seconds after firing, was as beautiful as it was reassuring," O'Kane wrote in his report. "It broke the freighter's back, his stern sinking with a down angle, his forward section with an up, in a cloud of fire, smoke, and steam."

O'Kane planned for an easy day following *Tang*'s day-long chase of and attack on *Nikkin Maru*. At dawn some forty miles off Ko-To on the west coast of Korea, Lieutenant Hank Flanagan spotted a Chinese junk. *Tang* battle-surfaced alongside. The Chinese sailors trimmed the sails to escape—no doubt stunned by the sub's sudden appearance—as *Tang*'s gun crew fired four rounds across the bow. The junk lowered its sails. O'Kane hoped he might collect some intelligence about enemy ships, but communication proved difficult. Lookouts scanned the horizon for any sign of ships as *Tang* sailors struggled to communicate. A distant puff of smoke curled above the horizon: a real target. *Tang*'s sailors tossed a bunch of canned goods that the labels had washed off over to the Chinese and set off.

The day of rest would wait.

The skipper ordered *Tang* to chase at full power, using the raised high periscope to increase visibility along the distant horizon. The single puff of smoke morphed into two. Lookouts watched as the masts of two ships came over the horizon, the 868-ton tanker *Takatori Maru* and the 998-ton freighter *Taiun Maru No. 2*. The ships zigzagged west. *Tang* chased for three hours, pounding the seas at full power to reach a position ahead of the targets. The submarine dove at 1:22 p.m. for a submerged attack. O'Kane ordered key battle station personnel to step aside and allow each position's understudy to take charge. The Navy's practice of rotating a percentage of sailors after each patrol, O'Kane believed, had played a role in the loss of his first subs, *Argonaut* and *Wahoo*. Too many experienced hands had left at once. He didn't want to risk the same with *Tang*.

The convoy zigzagged toward *Tang*. O'Kane raised the periscope to check the progress every four to six minutes. With each observation, the ships drew closer. The skipper spied a hefty deck gun mounted on the bow of the tanker, which patrolled ahead like an escort. The bridge, superstructure, and smokestack all stood aft along with a large—and loaded—depth charge rack perched on the portside of the stern. The skipper presumed the tanker boasted an identical rack on the starboard side. O'Kane decided to eliminate the tanker first with a salvo of electric torpedoes. The wakeless weapons ran at almost half the speed of gas torpedoes, but proved much harder for enemy lookouts to spot—ideal for daylight attacks. The slower speed also would give him an extra minute to set up his shot on the freighter.

"Up scope," O'Kane ordered.

Quartermaster Jones raised the scope and the skipper marked the *Takatori Maru*, now just 1,500 yards off the freighter's starboard bow. Frazee mashed the firing plunger twice. O'Kane braced for detonation. Three. Two. One. Nothing. The furious skipper, who felt he had just botched his third attack of the patrol, cursed his faulty torpedoes. O'Kane ordered the periscope up and pressed his eye to the scope just as an explosion rocked the tanker. The wounded ship's stern rose in the air before it slipped beneath the waves in just two minutes and twenty seconds, killing all twenty-eight on board.

The freighter that had trailed the tanker turned back. O'Kane did not have a solid shot and refused to waste a precious torpedo. There was no need to rush. One hundred miles of open water separated the freighter from the Korean coast and the ship's escape route led him straight toward the submarines *Tinosa* and *Sealion*. O'Kane dashed off a contact report and ordered *Tang* to trail the freighter, keeping its smoke in sight. The skipper bragged in his log that the target had nowhere to go: "We had the freighter caught between third base and home."

O'Kane ordered the sub to surface around sunset. He climbed to the bridge and studied the coal-black smoke that hung on the otherwise empty horizon. *Tang* dove that night ahead of the freighter and just a mile and a half from the island of Ko-To. He waited as the target steamed toward him, closing to just 500 yards. He noted that the freighter had slowed—likely feeling safe so close to land—as he fired two torpedoes.

"Both hot, straight, and normal," soundman Caverly reported.

O'Kane asked for the run time. The executive officer calculated out loud, but before Frazee could finish, a massive explosion vaporized much of the freighter and its crew of twenty and shook the submarine. Merely twenty seconds had passed. The skipper peered through the periscope to see that only a short section of *Taiun Maru's* bow remained. The second torpedo, trailing seconds behind, had nothing to hit. *Tang* surfaced four minutes later. "There could have been no survivors," O'Kane would later write. "We would have seen them in the moonlight."

O'Kane was learning that to guarantee a hit he needed to get in tight, an aggressive tactic few skippers embraced. "There were submariners who frowned at getting so close underfoot, where an enemy zig in the closing minutes could drive a submarine down," O'Kane later wrote. "By and large, they were not the ones who sank many ships." In the past seven days, O'Kane had more than made up for his previous patrol, putting 23,873 tons of Japanese ships on the bottom. He'd all but forgotten his earlier frustrations at his long string of missed shots. "How could anybody feel other than satisfaction at the way this patrol was now developing?" he wrote. "Five ships down and we still have five steam torpedoes plus two electrics waiting for targets."

Tang failed to encounter many vessels over the next few days. O'Kane surmised that the recent attacks meant the Japanese would hold up shipping bound for China. The sudden lack of targets would prompt an enemy submarine to move on within a few days and shipping could resume. That had been the case in 1943 when O'Kane hunted this area on *Wahoo*. But the ships already at sea or those headed toward Japan—often loaded with much needed materials—would continue, hugging the coast in hope that the shallow waters would protect them from submarines. A counterclockwise search of the Yellow Sea would guarantee that *Tang* intercepted them.

O'Kane didn't have to wait long. Lookouts spotted the heavy masts of a ship on the morning of July 4. The skipper climbed to the bridge for a look. More than a dozen fishing trawlers bobbed in the waves between *Tang* and its target: a morning traffic jam on the Yellow Sea. *Tang* wove between the trawlers, O'Kane hopeful the fishing boats would camouflage his sub. The submarine dove and the skipper studied the 6,886-ton freighter *Asukazan Maru* through the periscope. He liked what he saw: a massive bow, broad superstructure and bridge, and towering masts—and just as O'Kane had suspected—the freighter was bound for Japan. What he didn't know was that it had departed China's Tung Ting Lake area for the Japanese port of Yawata, loaded down with 11,400 tons of precious iron ore.

The freighter zigzagged, spoiling O'Kane's shot. The ship steamed toward shore with *Tang* taking up the chase. O'Kane and Frazee studied the chart. The water grew shallower with each minute. The ten-fathom curve—

signifying just sixty feet of water—ran fifteen miles offshore. O'Kane knew his next move would depend on what the ship did when it reached that spot. The skipper ordered *Tang* to full power, which meant his batteries would last only an hour. Caverly called out the depth. Only twenty-four feet of water separated *Tang*'s keel from the sea bottom, a depth that dropped moments later to just eighteen feet. Frazee announced that the ship had reached the ten-fathom curve.

"Up scope," O'Kane ordered. "All ahead full. She's turning right!"

The ship presented its starboard side to *Tang* as O'Kane closed the distance. Eighteen feet of water beneath *Tang*'s keel dropped to twelve then six feet. The fathometer stopped working. O'Kane ordered *Tang* to stop as the submarine came to rest on the muddy sea floor. The skipper shot a glance at the depth gauge to discover that his submarine sat aground in just fifty-eight feet of water, leaving no room for the boat to operate. O'Kane ordered the submarine to back up into deeper water as he took a final look through the scope, marked the target, and fired three torpedoes.

The explosion rocked the *Tang*. The skipper looked through the periscope. Only the bow, stern, and masts rose out of the water as the rest of the *Asukazan Maru* settled on the bottom, sixty-five passengers and crew now dead. A huge cloud of smoke loomed overhead. *Tang* surfaced five minutes after firing. O'Kane counted thirty-four fishing boats milling around, apparently awestruck by the blast. Some fifty survivors bobbed in the water and crowded in life rafts, far more the skipper noted than otherwise should have been needed on such a ship. The men watched as the bow tip slipped under amid the bubbling water before *Tang* departed for deeper seas.

The men feasted on salmon loaf and peas—the skipper's New England Independence Day tradition—as *Tang* cruised slowly that afternoon. The only interruption came from distant depth charges that rumbled more than fifty miles away. The wardroom phone rang before sunset, delivering news of smoke on the horizon to the north. That meant O'Kane would have to return to where he had sunk *Asukazan Maru* that morning, an area likely still crawling with Japanese antisubmarine forces. The skipper took a final periscope sweep of the horizon in preparation to surface when he spotted a faint wisp of smoke to the west—another ship.

Tang surfaced after sunset and began to chase, the full moon illuminating the seas. Excitement filled the boat at the prospect of two attacks in one day. O'Kane dove at 8:41 p.m., leveling off at forty-seven feet so the crew could track the ship by radar. The skipper watched the 6,932-ton *Yamaoka Maru* develop in his periscope, noting its raked bow, tripod mast, and king posts forward and aft. A mushroom-topped bridge structure towered over the deck. The combined speeds of the target and the *Tang* meant that the distance closed at 400 yards a minute. The target zigzagged into position. "We'll fire on this leg," O'Kane ordered. "Standby for a quick setup."

Yamaoka Maru chugged across O'Kane's periscope seconds later, the range now just a half mile. O'Kane fired two shots, watching thirty seconds later as the torpedoes tore into the freighter. The explosions broke *Yamaoka Maru*'s back. The masts collapsed in toward one another as the ship sank by the middle, taking down fifty-eight enemy crewmembers. O'Kane ordered the sound piped over the submarine's loudspeaker. The entire crew now listened to grinding sound of the target's bulkheads collapsing under the pressure of the water as it plummeted toward the sea bottom. O'Kane stepped back seconds later to let chief quartermaster Sidney Jones take a peek. "She's gone," the quartermaster exclaimed. "Christ, all of her!"

Tang surfaced. Debris littered the dark water. Lookouts spotted a lone survivor, who ducked beneath a capsized lifeboat. Boatswain Leibold grappled the boat and pulled it toward *Tang* while Petty Officer 1st Class James White coaxed the enemy sailor out with a few rounds from his machine gun, *Tang*'s first prisoner. Sharp captured the Independence Day excitement in his journal. "If I hadn't been on this ship & experienced it with my own eyes, I would never have believed it, the way we celebrated the 4th out here today," he wrote. "I can say not many people had the fireworks we did. Today we sank two *ships*, both damn big ones."

O'Kane had managed in just twenty-six days to sink nine ships—and tie Mush Morton's record. His hope of breaking it depended on what he could accomplish with his last two torpedoes. The skipper didn't have to wait long. Lookouts spotted smoke the next morning from a ship steaming south, hugging the Korean coast. The ship's course meant that it eventually would round Choppeki Point, a promontory that offered deep water—a welcome change—and the promise of even more coastal traffic. *Tang* surfaced at sunset and began a three-hour run to Choppeki Point.

The skipper's instincts again proved correct. Radar picked up a ship more than fifteen miles away that steamed north. The skipper ordered an end around at 10:57 p.m. The full moon shone down as *Tang* raced across a rippleless sea, reaching an attack position seven miles ahead of the 1,469-ton freighter *Dori Maru* several hours later. *Tang* dove and waited. The still fogging periscopes showed that *Dori Maru* chugged toward him, oblivious to the lurking submarine. Morton's record was his. O'Kane pulled the trigger at 3:20 a.m.

The skipper stepped back to allow Frazee and Jones to look. The men alternated dunking the submarine's two periscopes to clear the fog. The first torpedo tore into *Dori Maru* beneath the mainmast.

"Her whole side's blown out!" one of the men hollered.

The second torpedo crashed seconds later into the freighter under the foremast. *Dori Maru* was finished. "She's capsizing!"

The sky turned pink with the approach of dawn as *Tang* surfaced to inspect the damage only to find no survivors and little remaining of the freighter that had vanished along with sixteen passengers and crew. "Both torpedoes hit exactly as aimed," O'Kane wrote in his report. "There was only floating wreckage and broken life boats in sight."

15

DRUM

"I don't know where we are going to go, nor do I know what we are going to do, but I hope that they send us where the Japs are good and thick."

—Slade Cutter,
December 11, 1941, letter

Lieutenant Commander Maurice Rindskopf stared through his binoculars at two motor sampans cruising five miles northwest on the afternoon of July 29. Rainsqualls gathered on the horizon and he would soon lose sight of the first targets he had seen in days, a far cry from the crowded seas his orders had promised he would find off Palau. "The Japanese are fighting desperately and will exert every effort to maintain Palau as their primary advanced base," the orders stated. "Traffic between the Empire and Palau and Palau and other advanced outlying bases is expected to be heavy." The only heavy traffic Rindskopf had seen were American carrier forces—and he'd spotted just the mast tops of those on the horizon—that had pounded Japanese forces in recent days. Enemy traffic proved equally light; just the two sampans.

Two measly sampans.

A conning tower leak had required *Drum* to return to Pearl Harbor for immediate repair. On a New Year's Day test trial in the cool waters off Hawaii, Rindskopf looked up from his seat on the chart table at 225 feet below the surface and saw the cork in the conning tower crack. The executive officer ordered *Drum* to surface immediately. Crews ripped the cork off to discover that the water pressure had deformed the steel as much as an inch, the possible prelude to a catastrophic collapse. The Navy had ordered *Drum* to Mare

Island for sixty-six days so shipfitters could install a new conning tower. The good fortune Diesel Dan Williamson had enjoyed on the eighth patrol, when he sank the prized former ocean liner *Hie Maru*, failed to materialize for the ninth. The seas around the Bonin Islands proved empty of worthwhile targets. After fifty-two days at sea and covering 12,641 miles, Williamson returned to port with all twenty-four of his torpedoes. The patrol had proven a bust.

So had Williamson.

Not only did the bespectacled skipper learn via a message at sea that his ill wife had died, but he suffered a painful gallbladder attack that had forced him to spend much of the patrol in his bunk, leaving Rindskopf to command the submarine. When *Drum* moored in Majuro for refit, Williamson hopped a plane for Pearl Harbor. Doctors there diagnosed him with gallstones and recommended surgery. Williamson's tenure at the helm of *Drum* was over. With the submarine's refit now complete, *Drum* was ready for patrol. The Navy offered Rindskopf two options. He could await the arrival of a new skipper—his fourth—or he could replace Williamson, a move that would allow Rindskopf to forgo prospective commanding officer school and the traditional first job as captain of an aged World War I–era submarine. Rindskopf didn't hesitate. In a June 23 ceremony on the submarine's deck, the twenty-six-year-old became the youngest fleet boat skipper fighting in the Pacific.

No one was better qualified. Unlike some submarines such as *Tang* and *Silversides*, where a single skipper remained in command beyond the customary several patrols, the Navy had regularly rotated *Drum*'s top officer. That revolving door had allowed Rindskopf to learn from each man he had saluted as captain, captains who had proven varied in personality, style, and tenor and whose backgrounds reflected some of America's cultural diversity. *Drum*'s first skipper, Robert Rice, the cerebral Massachusetts Episcopalian and gifted fencer, had taught Rindskopf periscope work and finesse. The Great White Father McMahon, the Ohio Catholic of Irish and German descent, had shown him how to build a strong combat team, while the Colorado native and Presbyterian Williamson had taught him the importance of training. These lessons would prove invaluable to Rindskopf, a Brooklyn Jew and the son of a chemical engineer, as he charted his own legacy at the helm of *Drum*.

Compared to O'Kane, who had witnessed the extreme leadership differences of Pinky Kennedy and Mush Morton, Rindskopf had enjoyed a progression of solid and aggressive skippers who had helped him grow. None of his predecessors would top the list of the war's most successful skippers, in part because the men didn't serve at the helm long enough to sink the vast number of ships credited to Morton, O'Kane, and Coye. But each of *Drum*'s skippers had performed well. Postwar records would show that Rice had destroyed seven ships and McMahon four. Even though Diesel Dan Williamson had sunk just one ship in his two patrols, the *Hie Maru* would prove *Drum*'s largest victim of the entire war. The aggregate tonnage of these ships—coupled with what Rindskopf would add—would make *Drum* one of the war's top fighters. Unlike the brazen *Wahoo*, which tallied great scores in a short time but ended in tragedy, *Drum*'s success was built on consistent performance.

More than any other skipper, Rindskopf symbolized the *Drum*. Though the Navy had remained vigilant in its rotation of officers, it had left Rindskopf on board for ten straight patrols. The wiry lieutenant junior grade, who had joined the wardroom a few years out of the Naval Academy and twenty-five days before the Japanese attacked Pearl Harbor, had fought the entire war on *Drum*, climbing in that time from gunnery officer to skipper. Rindskopf had eaten almost every meal for nearly three years at the green wardroom table, had helped fire more than 100 torpedoes, and now closed in on *Drum*'s 1,000th dive, many in hostile waters, from the Japanese stronghold at Truk to the enemy homeland of Honshu. He had seen the once pristine submarine, commissioned on a blustery fall morning in New England 965 days earlier, weathered by more than 80,000 miles of salty ocean water and battered by depth charges that had shattered lights, busted glass gauges, and sprung leaks.

Rindskopf felt an awesome responsibility. The American government had trusted him with one of the most sophisticated and expensive submarines ever built, to say nothing of the lives of some eighty young men. The fate of *Drum*'s original officers would illustrate the danger Rindskopf faced as skipper. Of the seven men who had joined him each night for dinner at the wardroom table, the war would claim two, including Manning Kimmel. The former *Drum* engineering and executive officer had died just three days earlier when the submarine he commanded, *Robalo*, struck a mine two miles off the coast of Palawan island in the Philippines. *Drum*'s original communications officer, John Harper, would die in late October as the executive officer aboard the second submarine *Shark* when a depth charge attack sent it to the bottom.

Rindskopf felt confident he could handle the job in part because he enjoyed the support of his men. Unlike *Drum*'s older and rigid previous skippers, all of whom had come to the ship with a wealth of experience earned elsewhere, Rindskopf was homegrown. He had stood watches with the enlisted men, was the first to pick up the basketball with the crew at the Royal Hawaiian, and had left his door open for anyone who needed to talk. The crew felt a unique sense of connection and ownership over Rindskopf, who came of age as a warrior alongside many of the sailors who now saluted him. Rindskopf's rise to become the Pacific war's youngest fleet boat skipper not only reflected his hard work, skill, and determination, but that of the entire fighting crew, from the lookouts and torpedomen to the cooks and quartermasters. "He never appeared superior to us," recalled Robert White, a machinist's mate who served eleven patrols. "He was just another man doing his job the best he could."

That job had proven a challenge this patrol. The skipper had dreaded *Drum*'s mission off Palau, as much of the fight now focused around the Marianas. American forces had invaded the strategic island of Saipan in June. The Japanese fleet had failed to challenge the United States for control of the Gilbert and Marshall islands, but American war planners knew the Marianas would prove the pressure point to trigger a fight not seen since the Solomons slugfest in Ironbottom Sound. Japanese naval leaders, who still clung to the unrealistic idea that a single decisive battle could destroy America's Pacific Fleet, had hoped to set a trap. The Japanese reinforced the Marianas and Carolines with several hundred land-based planes while the fleet's carriers, battleships, and cruisers converged at Tawi-Tawi in the southern Philippines. The Japanese plan called for luring the Pacific Fleet to the waters off Palau in the western Carolines. There the combined carrier- and land-based planes would overwhelm America's superior forces.

But Japan misjudged America's next move. Rather than drive west and strike Palau, the United States turned north and invaded Saipan, forcing Japan to modify its plan. America had grown much stronger since the two navies last tangled, boasting fifteen carriers, seven battleships, twenty-one cruisers, and sixty-nine destroyers. Japan in contrast could muster just nine carriers, five battleships, thirteen cruisers, and twenty-eight destroyers. America's 956 fighters, bombers, and floatplanes doubled Japan's airpower, already handicapped by inexperienced pilots. But Japan enjoyed several advantages, including planes based on Guam, Rota, and Yap. The easterly trade wind allowed Japanese carriers to launch aircraft en route to battle, while the lack of armor and self-sealing fuel tanks gave the enemy's lighter planes a greater reach. One of Japan's biggest advantages in this operation, however, came down to focus. Unlike the American Navy, which had to protect the invasion force, the Japanese had one mission: annihilate the Pacific Fleet.

In preparation for the Marianas invasion, America called up twenty-eight submarines. The United States wanted no surprises. About a dozen boats patrolled around Tawi-Tawi and Mindanao and in the Luzon, Surigao, and the San Bernardino straits, covering all possible approaches from the Philippines. Five more submarines lurked north of the Marianas to guard against forces sent down from the empire while nine other boats west of the Marianas blocked the route up from Palau. The heavy investment of boats paid off. Submarines *Harder, Redfin, Flying Fish, Seahorse,* and *Cavalla* tracked the departure of Japan's forces from Tawi-Tawi en route to battle. America now knew what to expect. Admiral Raymond Spruance, commander of the Marianas operation, postponed the invasion of Guam, ordering his fleet to assemble June 18 in the waters west of Tinian. "Our air will first knock out enemy carriers, then will attack enemy battleships and cruisers to slow or disable them," he directed. "Action against the enemy must be pushed vigorously by all hands to ensure complete destruction of his fleet."

The sun rose at 5:42 a.m. on June 19, climbing into a sky almost free of clouds that boasted unlimited visibility and fourteen-knot winds. American commanders suspected the Japanese planned to use Guam-based planes in battle—just as the United States had used Midway—and organized an air strike that morning on the Marianas island. American carrier pilots bagged some thirty-five planes over Guam when radar detected an inbound strike 150 miles west. Japan's flattops had joined the fight. General quarters sounded as the American carriers turned into the wind, sending fighters into the skies to intercept the enemy while bombers pounded ground-based planes on Guam and Rota. U.S. pilots shot down forty-five of the sixty-nine inbound planes, then destroyed ninety-eight of the 130 planes in a second Japanese strike. American pilots continued to chew up waves of Japanese planes—346 by the day's end. Aviators dubbed the aerial slaughter the "The Great Marianas Turkey Shoot."

Unlike at Midway where submarines had proven woefully ineffective, the Battle of the Philippine Sea represented a reversal as the undersea boats claimed some of the biggest prizes. *Albacore* skipper Lieutenant Commander James Blanchard stared through his scope at 7:55 a.m. at two flattops, an embarrassment of riches. The skipper zeroed in on the second, the 29,300-ton flagship *Taiho* or "Great Phoenix." Commissioned less than four months earlier, *Taiho* was Japan's newest and largest carrier, designed with an armored flight deck to allow the flattop to better withstand aerial attack. Despite problems with the torpedo data computer, Blanchard fired six fish, then dove deep. One torpedo tore into *Taiho*, flooding the forward aircraft elevator pit with water, gasoline, and fuel oil. Efforts to ventilate the ship only spread the dangerous fumes, triggering a massive explosion that afternoon that crumpled the armored flight deck and blew the hangar's sides out. The flaming Phoenix capsized and sank.

Albacore wasn't the only submarine to score such an impressive kill. *Cavalla* skipper Lieutenant Commander Herman Kossler peered through the periscope at 10:52 a.m. at the 29,800-ton *Shokaku*, a veteran of the attack on Pearl Harbor and the Coral Sea. "When I raised my periscope at this time the picture was too good to be true," Kossler wrote in his report. "I could see four ships, a large carrier with two cruisers ahead on the port bow and a destroyer about one thousand yards on the starboard beam." Several planes circled above the carrier, then landed. No fewer than thirty, Kossler counted, crowded the flight deck. The skipper fired six torpedoes; several tore into the carrier. Japanese destroyers turned on Kossler, dropping 106 depth charges over the next three hours. But the enemy's fury could not save *Shokaku*. The carrier's bow settled so low that waves rushed over the flight deck and into the hangar. *Shokaku's* stern rose into the air as the carrier dove bow first, taking down more than 1,250 souls.

The battle continued the next day as three of America's four carrier groups hunted the retreating enemy. A pilot spotted the Japanese the afternoon of June 20 at a range of 275 miles, right at the limit of how far American planes could fly. Ten carriers turned into the wind. In the span of just ten minutes, 216 planes roared into the sky. The planes closed in at sunset, sinking the 24,140-ton carrier *Hiyo* with two torpedoes and damaging the flattops *Zuikaku*, *Chiyoda*, and *Junyo*. Planes returning that night faced the dangerous prospect of landing in the dark until Vice Admiral Marc Mitscher, commander of the Pacific Fleet's fast carrier forces, ordered all ships to ignore antisubmarine doctrine and light up. The two-day Battle of the Philippine Sea cost America 130 planes. Japan in contrast had lost three aircraft carriers and almost 500 planes. America's victory in what many describe as the greatest carrier battle of the war destroyed Japan's naval air forces and paved the wave for the July invasions of Guam and Tinian.

The focus on the Marianas meant that Rindskopf's assigned area in the waters off Palau would be void of targets. America had guaranteed that with strikes against Japanese positions in the western Carolines, where he now hunted. The most excitement Rindskopf had seen in his thirty-five days at sea had come watching American Liberators pummel Yap while he performed lifeguard duty. Japanese fighters had chased twenty-three bombers before one peeled off and strafed *Drum* as the submarine dove. Rindskopf surfaced to find that projectiles had hit the deck, the conning tower fairwater, and the submarine's three radio antennas. Fortunately the nicked antennas still worked. The skipper had celebrated Independence Day with a thirty-five-minute gun attack on Fais island, pouring 1,530 rounds into shore installations. His only torpedo attack had come just five days earlier against a 700-ton oiler. He had set up the perfect shot only to watch as his four torpedoes ran right under the shallow draft target.

Rindskopf hoped his luck would improve as he struggled to pursue the two motor sampans through an afternoon rainsquall. While not a prized enemy warship or tanker, sampans often served as intelligence collectors. An attack would deprive the enemy of a valuable set of eyes and ears. Rindskopf radioed the submarine *Balao* with the news of his find, alerting skipper Lieutenant Commander Marion F. Ramirez de Arellano that he planned to leave his radar on so that *Balao* could track the signal while *Drum* pursued. Once the submarines picked up the sampans, Rindskopf would dive and attack from the target's quarter. *Balao* could charge in and attack from the bow. Rindskopf spotted the sampans at 3:06 p.m., more than seven miles out. He ordered *Drum* down and studied the targets through his periscope. The boats resembled schooners, but without masts. Both appeared unarmed and small; too small to justify a torpedo. A gun battle would prove best.

The skipper ordered the gun crews ready. Unlike the nighttime assault on Refinery Point, today's attack would occur in the middle of the afternoon with ample light to aid the Japanese in counterfire. Nervous sailors strapped on helmets and climbed up into the conning tower. Others dropped down into the magazine beneath the crew mess and handed up gun shells, forming an ammunition train that ran through the submarine. The men had good reason to feel anxious. Submarines would fight 939 gun battles throughout the war, sinking 722 vessels. But many of those attacks would come with a price: ten deaths. Dozens of other sailors suffered injuries, ranging from gunshot and shrapnel wounds to compound fractures, frostbite, and even hernias from hefting heavy shells.

Drum battle-surfaced at 4:34 p.m. still two miles from what Rindskopf estimated as a twenty-five-ton sampan. The gun crews charged out on the wet deck and manned the four-inch .50 caliber and the 20mm and .30 caliber machine guns. The gunners sighted the starboard sampan and fired the massive deck gun. The spent shell casing clanged to the deck as a loader rammed in another. The gun roared again and again. Projectiles straddled the target. Rindskopf watched the rounds splash at the sampan's waterline as *Drum* continued to close the distance. Then a shot struck home, tearing into the motor sampan. Enemy crews failed to return fire. Sailors on *Drum*'s 20mm and .30 caliber guns joined the fight once the target came in range, the quiet afternoon suddenly transformed by a cacophony of barking guns. Four-inch projectiles smashed one after the other into the sampan's wooden hull and deckhouse. Rindskopf watched as wood timbers flew, but the sampan kept going.

Japanese sailors began to jump overboard. The skipper counted as many as twenty-five bobbing in the water. The shredded sampan turned toward *Drum* at a range of about 1,000 yards. Gunners fired again, smashing the sampan's deckhouse with two more four-inch shells. The final shot came at a range of just 500 yards. Rindskopf and his men watched the sampan stop and erupt in flames, the dark smoke wafting skyward. The skipper ordered his men to cease fire, ending the forty-one-minute battle. Petty Officer 2nd Class John Meyer, a 20mm gunner, looked down on the sailors in the water. The nineteen-year-old Arizonan, who normally loaded torpedoes, surveyed the carnage. "That was a first time that we ever saw what we had done," Meyer recalled. "There were Japs floating in the water as far as you could see. It didn't mean a thing to me. They were the enemy and we were doing what we could to stop the war. They were the ones who started it and that was their tough luck."

Balao zeroed in on the lead sampan, raking it with gunfire as enemy sailors dove overboard. The Americans pulled up to the sampan with its bow along the target's starboard side. Two sailors climbed aboard to search the enemy vessel. Dead bodies littered the deck. The sailors found no charts or radio gear, but grabbed all the ditty boxes, later found to contain opium pipes, pay accounts, diaries, fishing gear, and photographs of parents and family of the dead sailors. The boarding party entered the bunkhouse—described in the report as a "charnel house"—only to find more dead, a total of fourteen. The men returned to *Balao*. The submarine backed away before gunners fired a shell into the oil drums stacked on deck. The sampan exploded. To the surprise of the skipper, six more enemy sailors leaped out of a rear bunkhouse, bringing the total in the water to thirty-six. None would come aboard. Sailors dropped bread and a five-gallon can of water overboard before *Balao* pulled away.

Rindskopf looked down upon the two dozen enemy sailors treading water alongside *Drum*. Their destroyed sampan would be reduced in a matter of hours to little more than charred timbers and ash, debris *Balao* would find two days later when the submarine returned to investigate the attack scene. Rindskopf hoped to take a couple of prisoners for future interrogation. He ordered his men to fire machine guns over the heads of the sailors in the water, a move designed to frighten the men into surrender. *Drum* sailors threw a line over the starboard side and waited. "Captain," Meyer finally called out. "We got one here." A lone Japanese sailor paddled over and grabbed the line. The *Drum* crew hauled him on board. Another followed. The rest refused. Rindskopf ordered *Drum* to depart shortly before sunset.

Sailors escorted prisoners Chono Natsumoro and Keiei Shimochi below. For hygienic reasons the crew shaved their heads with electric clippers—the captives had to trim their own genitalia—and dusted them with flea powder. Pharmacist's Mate 1st Class Ralph McFadden cleaned Shimochi's shrapnel wounds in a bunk in the forward torpedo room. The other prisoner, whom the men simply called Chono, settled in the after torpedo room. Chono confessed that he had served as a crewmember on *Nissho Maru No. 1*, the sampan *Drum* destroyed. Shimochi worked as a fisherman. The crew rotated watch over them, but the regimen soon proved unnecessary. Shimochi's injuries kept him confined to a bunk, but Chono, despite not knowing any English, soon endeared himself to his captors, quelling the crew's initial fear that the prisoners might attempt to sabotage the submarine. Within days, crewmembers stopped viewing the men as prisoners and practically as guests.

The crew put Chono to work in the galley, peeling potatoes and washing dishes. The men reveled at the skinny prisoner's ravenous appetite and his love for *Drum*'s ice cream machine. "Top notch chow hounds," Hubert Wheeler wrote in his diary. "Chono finally made mess cook third class." Sailors showed Chono pictures of family, let him flip through magazines, and set out to teach him English. He soon greeted each compartment along his route to galley with a shout of "good morning." Another favorite the crew taught him: "Fuck Tojo." When *Drum* reached Pearl Harbor on August 14, the crew felt sad to turn Chono over to the Marines. But the sailors had taught him a special song and shouted for Chono to sing it as the jeep pulled away, chuckling as he belted out the final line: "Fuck the Marines."

16

TANG

"Goodnight my sweetest of parents, pleasant dreams, say a few dozen assorted effective prayers that all Jap depth charges are distant duds."

—Eugene Malone,
December 1, 1943, letter

O'Kane hustled to prepare *Tang* for its fifth war patrol in late September 1944. Recently promoted to the rank of commander, O'Kane had spent the past three weeks in Pearl Harbor, overseeing *Tang*'s refit so that he could again return to sea. Commissioned less than a year earlier, *Tang* already showed the wear of America's submarine war effort. In addition to greasing the torpedo tube rollers, checking battery cells for gravity and electrical circuits for grounds, shipyard workers dry-docked the *Tang* to scrape, wire-brush, and blast the marine life from its bottom before repainting the hull with anti-fouling paint, a move that would help the submarine maintain its top speed and endurance. O'Kane noted with pride that in just nine months his submarine had already logged some 40,000 miles, almost twice the circumference of the earth.

Tang's third patrol had been one for the record books. Though O'Kane claimed in his report to sink eight ships, postwar analysis would bump that number to ten. The thirty-six-day patrol ultimately would prove to be the greatest run of the entire war by the number of ships sunk, a particularly impressive feat since *Tang* spent only sixteen of those days in its patrol area. Vice Admiral Lockwood raved about the mission's success in his patrol endorsement. "This patrol was an outstanding example of excellent judgment, expert area analysis, bull-dog tenacity, and severe damage to the enemy," the admiral wrote. "Each attack was carefully planned and brilliantly executed."

Tang had barely arrived in Midway for refit before the ecstatic admiral turned O'Kane around and sent him back, this time to the waters off Honshu. The skipper's orders had come with a personal note. "I want to tell you why I am sending you and your *Tang* right back to the Empire, with hardly a breather," the admiral wrote. "We have had two poor, and now a dry patrol in these areas, the boats reporting a dearth of shipping. Intelligence reports indicate that the merchant traffic must be there, and I am certain that *Tang* can rediscover it." The aggressive skipper did just as ordered. Despite malfunctioning torpedoes that plagued the thirty-four-day patrol, O'Kane still sank two ships—with a total tonnage of 11,463—and set a patrol boat ablaze in a fifty-three-minute surface battle on *Tang*'s return to port.

Tang prepared to depart for its fifth patrol without O'Kane's trusted executive officer, Murray Frazee, who had been promoted to lieutenant commander. O'Kane had come to depend on Frazee much as Morton had once relied on O'Kane. But the time had arrived for Frazee to advance. O'Kane typed a one-page letter, recommending him for command of his own submarine. O'Kane noted that Frazee had made eleven war patrols, likely more than any of his contemporaries. Furthermore, the skipper wrote, the Navy would only do the Japanese a favor by holding him back. O'Kane recommended Frazee attend prospective commanding officers' school in New London, not because he felt his exec needed more training, but with the hopes that the four-week course would give him much needed time off and that others in his class might learn from him.

Frazee looked forward to the break. *Tang*'s fourth patrol had made him jittery. The Navy's policy of rotating a quarter of the crew after each patrol had left *Tang* with young and inexperienced officers that Frazee feared might fumble in an emergency. His worries had forced him to stay up every night on patrol to back up his men. It had exhausted the twenty-eight-year-old; he joked that the intensity of *Tang*'s four patrols should make them count double. But O'Kane had educated the grateful Frazee. "Going to sea with you was a revelation," he later wrote in a letter to his skipper. "I learned that taking some real risks was in order; that the Japanese were not supermen; that our submarines were hard to detect and harder to damage if we operated intelligently; and that seeking out the enemy with real determination yielded great rewards."

Much of the crew shared Frazee's exhaustion. O'Kane had pushed his boat and men to the limit. In four patrols totaling 171 days he had destroyed seventeen confirmed ships, more than many submarines would sink during the entire war. O'Kane now averaged a ship sunk for every ten days on patrol. Though his taut routine had made *Tang* a legend, Frazee noted, it had come at the expense of the crew. O'Kane even pushed to cut rest periods so he could return to the fight, a tactic Morton, too, had embraced to his men's frustration. "O'Kane liked to run back to base on the surface at full speed, with lookouts all over the place, just so he could load up more torpedoes and get back out there—sink more ships, kill more Japs," Frazee would later write. "That did not thrill many people in the crew." But O'Kane was not blind to his crew's fatigue. If his men needed a break, he would make it happen. The crew had earned it.

Allied forces had carved two routes toward Japan. Admiral Nimitz's forces had fought through the Gilbert and Marshall islands, the Carolines, and the Marianas while General MacArthur's troops had battled the Japanese across the malarial jungles of New Guinea and isolated the enemy's once mighty base at Rabaul. The September 15 invasions of the Palaus and Morotai island merged these divergent paths. MacArthur now planned his triumphant return to the Philippines. Carrier air strikes would wipe out Japanese supply lines and reinforcements while submarines would target cargo and warships.

War planners expected a ferocious fight. Japan's only hope to prolong the day when enemy warships appeared off its shores hinged on stalling America's westward advance. Reinforcements and supplies shipped out for the Philippines. Troops came from as far away as Manchuria while freighters loaded with tanks, horses, and ammunition steamed down from Formosa and aircrews flew in from Burma. Anemic Japan had few resources to spare, a fact reflected in the decision to escort one convoy of aircraft personnel and supplies with battleships.

The undersea service planned a choke hold around the Philippines that when coupled with the destruction wrought by American aviators would destroy Japan's merchant fleet. Fourteen Australian-based submarines would hunt the archipelago's waters, guarding the Palawan Passage, the west coast of Luzon, and the approaches to Manila. Lockwood intended to contribute another twenty-six Hawaii-based boats, including *Tang*, *Drum*, and *Silversides*. These would crowd the waters north of the Philippines, covering the approaches from Formosa and Japan. These forty subs that created what Lockwood later described as a "watertight blockade" approached the total number of boats America had had to cover the entire Pacific at the start of the war. To make it all work, however, the admiral needed *Tang* in place—and fast.

O'Kane had power to bargain.

"How soon could you be ready to head west?" Lockwood asked the skipper. "All the way west."

"Four days, sir," O'Kane replied. "But there is one thing I request in return." The admiral listened.

"I'd like something to take back to my crew," he said. "I'd like our next upkeep scheduled for Mare Island."

O'Kane had asked for a real plum. A California overhaul would sideline one of America's top submarines for up to three months at a critical time when the Navy hoped to capitalize on its momentum. But for the eighty-seven officers and crew who served on *Tang*, Mare Island would give them a chance to visit family and enjoy a real break from the war, not just the couple of weeks on the beach in front of the Royal Hawaiian, but a chance to enjoy San Francisco, the wine country, and a taste of American life. The added incentive of an extended visit to the West Coast would give O'Kane's crew motive to fight extra hard on this next patrol.

"I appreciate what you say," Lockwood said, extending his hand to O'Kane. "I'll take care of it."

O'Kane and his crew departed four days ahead of schedule. A sudden torpedo shortage had hit Pearl Harbor, forcing *Tang* to scavenge a load of electric fish from *Tambor*, waylaid from patrol by a propulsion problem. *Tang*'s officers and crew paused only long enough from fueling and stashing canned vegetables, meat, and coffee for Pacific Fleet Commander Admiral Nimitz and Lockwood to present medals honoring *Tang*'s third patrol, including a second Navy Cross for O'Kane. The departing Frazee received his third Silver Star, while new executive officer Lieutenant Frank Springer received his first.

The entire crew also received the coveted Presidential Unit Citation—the highest award a ship or combat unit can receive—in honor of the submarine's first three patrols.

With the food all loaded and the crew on board, *Tang* let out a prolonged blast of its whistle at 1 p.m. on September 24, signaling its departure for its fifth patrol. O'Kane marveled at how Pearl Harbor—decimated by the Japanese two years, nine months, and seventeen days earlier—largely had returned to its pre-attack condition. Salvage crews had righted the capsized battleship *Oklahoma* and moved it into dry dock for repairs. Other ships had already returned to battle. The bombed and scorched battleship *Tennessee*, which had bombarded the Japanese in the Gilbert, Marshall, and Mariana islands, would soon fight in the Leyte campaign that *Tang* now supported, while the torpedoed *Nevada*'s deafening guns had just three months earlier pounded German defenses during the Allied landings on D-Day. Crews had stripped the sunken battleship *Arizona*'s topside structure and armament, leaving the hull as a tomb on the harbor's murky bottom.

One of the newer faces on board *Tang* belonged to Lieutenant Lawrence Savadkin, a tall and lean engineering officer who had joined the wardroom before the fourth patrol. The twenty-four-year-old Savadkin, known to friends as Larry, grew up in a Jewish household in the small town of Easton in Pennsylvania's Lehigh Valley midway between Philadelphia and New York City. The former captain of the Lafayette College track team, Savadkin was once the half mile champion for the Middle Atlantic Association. Savadkin had served on the destroyer *Mayrant*, bombed by the Germans a year earlier off Palermo in the assault on Sicily. The explosion had hurled Savadkin out of the forward engine room just seconds before it flooded, but he brushed off his injuries and fought to save the ship, actions that earned him the Silver Star.

O'Kane was particularly fond of the athletic Savadkin, whom he felt brought a wealth of knowledge and experience to the *Tang* even though he was new to the submarine service. Savadkin soaked up the opportunity. The young officer on his first patrol had felt curious to see what it looked like when a torpedo hit a ship. After *Tang* fired on a moored patrol boat, Savadkin asked permission to climb to the bridge. O'Kane invited him up. Savadkin stepped onto the deck just forty-five seconds after the explosion to find the enemy ship obliterated. "There was still glowing bits of debris coming down from the heavens," Savadkin recalled. "That was all that was left of our target. There was a blotch of smoke on the surface, no evidence of any solid mass there at all and these bits of glowing debris falling from the sky."

Tang arrived at Midway at 7 a.m. three days later to top off fuel. The boat had spent seventeen days there between its third and fourth patrols. O'Kane had soured on how the two-square-mile atoll in the middle of the Pacific had developed. The former stopover for China-bound Pan Am Clippers had morphed into a bustling naval base and air station, bringing with it the crushing formality that permeated the Navy. Crews had constructed a separate bar to allow junior officers to drink apart from senior leaders. O'Kane felt that that move ruined one of the greatest war patrol schools in the Navy, a place where junior and senior officers swapped patrol stories over beers, unencumbered by rank. No more. "The gooneys would not change, but Midway had," O'Kane observed. "The island was no longer a frontier."

Tang departed Midway five hours after its arrival and aimed west toward Formosa, battling eight-foot waves that forced perennially seasick radarman Floyd Caverly to strap a child's toilet onto his belt. O'Kane joked that Caverly's crapper more accurately predicted the weather than the submarine's barometer. During a pre-storm inspection O'Kane stepped into an open hatch in the forward engine room and plummeted some five feet below. His left foot snagged on the ladder's lower rung. The skipper felt a wave of nausea wash over him and sweat on his brow. Pharmacist's mate Chief Petty Officer Paul Larson examined O'Kane and informed the skipper he had broken some of the small bones in his foot. The skipper stretched out in his bunk and commanded *Tang* via the squawk box, his foot secured in a size fourteen sand shoe laced tight to serve as a splint.

Days later a swell out of the southwest developed into crashing seas that battered the bridge crew. The injured skipper, who listened to the storm's fury over the Voycall in his cabin, ordered his men below. A violent roll tossed the skipper to the deck. Executive officer Springer appeared in the cabin seconds later with pharmacist's mate Larson. The exec needed help. O'Kane's convalescence would have to wait. Larson gave O'Kane an injection in his foot and the skipper hobbled toward the conning tower. The submarine rolled again. O'Kane landed by the inclinometer, which measured the submarine's list. It read seventy degrees. He began to wonder if *Tang* would roll back to port and right itself or capsize. "Jesus Christ," the skipper blurted out. "Is she ever coming back?"

"Sometimes they don't, you know," Springer replied.

The seas moderated by October 8 and O'Kane ordered a third engine online as the submarine headed toward the Formosa Strait, the narrow body of water that divided China from the island of Formosa. The typhoon had pushed the submarine off course by as much as sixty miles. The towering mountains of Formosa, many of which climbed over 10,000 feet, loomed dead ahead at noon on October 10. O'Kane ordered a fourth engine online to enter the strait that night. The afternoon faded to evening as *Tang* powered ahead, rounding the northern tip of Formosa after dark and entering the strait. Crews found calmer seas now that Formosa, which translates to "beautiful island" in Portuguese, shielded *Tang* from the Pacific. The skipper stretched out on his bunk when at 4 a.m. on October 11 the duty officer appeared at the door.

"We've got a ship, Captain."

The radar showed the ship almost ten miles away, steaming up the coast from Pakusa Point. The target's fourteen-knot speed made the skipper question whether it was just a large patrol craft. Whatever it was, the shallow waters would force O'Kane to attack from a seaward position. He wouldn't have Formosa's dark backdrop to camouflage *Tang*'s silhouette. To get in close as he preferred—under 1,000 yards—the skipper would have no choice but to attack submerged. O'Kane and Leibold climbed up to the bridge and scanned the horizon for the target. Leibold spotted it in seconds, a large modern diesel freighter, heavily loaded and boasting a low silhouette. *Tang* maneuvered onto the freighter's track as the first gray light of dawn began to show on the horizon. Two blasts of the diving alarm took *Tang* down.

The 1,658-ton *Joshu Go* cargo ship closed to 800 yards. The skipper raised the scope for a final look, placing the reticle on the freighter's aft well deck. "Constant bearing—mark!"

"Set!"

"Fire!"

Three electric torpedoes sped through the water at twenty-nine knots toward the target, which was barely more than a quarter mile away. Springer called out a run time of forty-seven seconds. Caverly flipped the speaker switch and the men listened to the rhythmic thump of the freighter's propeller coupled with the whine of the torpedoes, the sound of death's approach. "The first two hit exactly as aimed sinking this overloaded freighter immediately," O'Kane wrote in his report of the attack, which killed eight enemy sailors. "Surfaced as soon as the smoke had cleared away to find no survivors and only wreckage and several empty landing craft half-swamped, drifting about in the water."

O'Kane ordered a full-power run down the coast toward Pakusa Point, a spot that would offer the submerged submarine clear views north and south. The Japanese had covered the west coast of Formosa with airfields. *Tang* needed to clear the area before enemy air support arrived. The towering mountains that crowded Formosa blocked the morning sun and gave *Tang* a few more minutes of precious darkness to escape. The skipper surveyed the shore that raced past, noting the lush mountains and valleys. "The view brought home the importance of this great island to the enemy as both a strategic frontier and a rice bowl," O'Kane would later write. "It suddenly became all the more evident that every torpedo must count."

Tang cruised south. The skipper climbed up to the conning tower around noon for a look through the periscope. A northerly wind battled the prevailing current and whipped up the seas, conditions that made depth control difficult but also camouflaged the periscope. O'Kane spotted the masts of a northbound freighter. The zigzagging ship hugged the coastline, staying inside sixty feet of water. O'Kane considered his options. *Tang* could run submerged at high-speed and catch the target by mid-afternoon. That would force O'Kane to attack in shallow water with nearly depleted batteries, a dangerous scenario since it would still be daylight. The skipper opted instead to track the ship until nightfall and attack on the surface under cover of darkness.

The seas picked up after lunch, making depth control difficult. *Tang* slipped down to eighty feet to avoid the rough water and pick up speed. The occasional trip up to periscope depth showed that *Tang* still closed in on the 711-ton *Oita Maru*. The unloaded freighter rode high in the water, its screws churning up heavy foam. At sundown the *Oita Maru* passed directly overhead. The officers sat down in the wardroom for dinner and listened to the thump of the target's propeller through the hull at seventy beats a minute. "We could work better on a full stomach," Savadkin recalled. "It made us feel sort of odd to sit down to a very sumptuous dinner, planning this fellow's doom immediately after we had finished."

Tang now trailed the cargo ship, a move that allowed the tracking party to precisely determine the target's course, speed, and zigzag pattern. The lookouts zipped on foul weather gear and *Tang* climbed to the surface. The target loomed 4,000 yards ahead in the dark. Two engines powered *Tang* as it veered off the target's track to race ahead. The radar detected two escorts. O'Kane now ordered *Tang* to pass abeam. The skipper spotted the spume of *Oita Maru* as the radar operator reported that the escorts had dropped back. O'Kane studied the ship through the target-bearing transmitter, noting its large black bow. "The 400-foot ship looked enormous as she started across our stern," O'Kane wrote, "mainly due to her proximity but perhaps amplified by this somewhat eerie stormy night."

The skipper watched *Oita Maru* parade across his reticle before he ordered *Tang* to fire a single wakeless torpedo. The explosion some thirty seconds later rocked the submarine as a pillar of fire streamed skyward. The torpedo must have exploded the ship's boilers. Shore-based antiaircraft fire lit up the night sky, as the Japanese mistakenly blamed American bombers for the attack, which had claimed the lives of twenty-six of *Oita Maru*'s crew. O'Kane ordered *Tang* to clear the area south before the enemy realized its mistake. *Tang*'s crew was at the top of its game. "Our experience of the morning was not a mistake. We were clicking," O'Kane wrote in his report. "Only the first few members of the fire-control party to reach the bridge saw any of the ship before it went down."

But *Tang*'s explosive start fizzled. The monotony of the next few days was interrupted only by the furious fires around Kiirun, the result of American air strikes on Formosa. O'Kane ordered *Tang* to cross the strait and patrol off the coast of China, but even there the skipper found only empty seas. He returned two days later to the center of the strait. Still, other than one fruitless chase after a cruiser and two destroyers, O'Kane had found little to do. The skipper stretched out to take the weight off his injured foot when the duty chief burst into his cabin at midnight on October 23. "We've got a convoy, Captain," he blurted out. "The chief says it's the best one since the Yellow Sea."

O'Kane climbed out of his bunk, laced up his makeshift splint, and headed to the conning tower. Radarman Floyd Caverly first thought the cluster of blips eight miles ahead must be an island chain until a check of the chart showed no such land. This was none other than a large convoy. The skipper debated two possible attack plans. He could trail the enemy through the night and attack submerged at dawn. O'Kane's second option was a night surface attack. He cringed at the thought of penetrating a dense escort screen. But this convoy appeared smaller than the previous one and with fewer escorts. Plus, O'Kane had the advantage of time. The skipper could attack tonight, and if necessary hit the convoy again at dawn.

Tang closed the distance. The four-ship convoy guarded by no less than two destroyers steamed from China toward Takao, a port city on the southern coast of Formosa. O'Kane looked for an opening. The lead escort abandoned its position and began a two-mile inspection sweep around the convoy. The skipper saw his chance, a bold move he knew the enemy would never expect. O'Kane ordered *Tang* to charge in and assume the destroyer's spot as the convoy's leader. The American submarine now mimicked the convoy's moves so that on radar *Tang* would appear just like an escort. The skipper then maneuvered his submarine to the convoy's wayward side, a move that would allow the ships to overtake *Tang*.

"All stop."

O'Kane turned the submarine to bring on the bow tubes. The 1,944-ton *Tatsuju Maru*, the 1,915-ton *Toun Maru*, and the 1,920-ton *Wakatake Maru* chugged ahead through the darkness.

"Everything checks below. Any time now, Captain."

O'Kane fired his first two shots at the *Tatsuju Maru* at a range of just 300 yards, aiming at its stack and engine room. The skipper fired a third fish at the stern of the *Toun Maru*, then turned to the *Wakatake Maru*, shooting two more torpedoes at the stack and engine room. Two tore into *Tatsuju Maru's* stern, exploding the freighter's boilers and engine room and killing seven. A single torpedo set the *Toun Maru* ablaze, dooming another 164 passengers, gunners, and crew. Fires now silhouetted *Tang*. The skipper darted aft to set up a fourth shot when Leibold grabbed him and pulled him forward. The *Wakatake Maru* raced to ram *Tang*. "We were boxed in by the sinking tankers, the transport was too close for us to dive, so we had to cross his bow," O'Kane wrote in his report. "It was really a thriller-diller."

The skipper rang up flank speed. Black smoke poured from *Tang's* diesels. *Wakatake Maru's* bow towered over *Tang* less than 100 yards away. With under thirty seconds until impact, O'Kane ordered left full rudder, hoping the ship might glance off *Tang* and not puncture the pressure hull. *Tang* passed down the side of *Wakatake Maru* as the two ships' combined speeds totaled some forty knots. Japanese gun crews opened fire. The skipper cleared the bridge before he realized the wild shots had no chance of hitting and ordered the dive halted. He now watched *Wakatake Maru* continue its turn in an effort to avoid colliding with the 1,339-ton *Kori Go*, which also had come in to ram the *Tang*. O'Kane knew the enemy's effort was hopeless. He jumped to the after target-bearing transmitter. "Stand-by aft!"

"Set below."

O'Kane watched as *Wakatake Maru* closed in, about to ram *Kori Go*'s stern. He marked a bearing on the center of the two ships and fired a spread of four torpedoes, aimed along the lengths of both targets. Small caliber enemy gunfire popped as *Tang* pulled away from the impending disaster. The ships collided as the torpedoes hit home. Hit in the engine room, *Wakatake Maru* snapped in half, sinking in just forty seconds with the loss of 176 passengers and crew. *Kori Go* suffered a bruising fate, though the extent of the ship's damage remains unclear. "At a range of 400 yards the crash coupled with four torpedo explosions was terrific, sinking the freighter nose down almost instantly while the transport hung with a 30° up angle," O'Kane wrote. "Only 10 minutes had elapsed from the time of firing our first torpedo until that final explosion when the transport's bow went down."

Gunshots rattled in the distance as *Tang* cleared the area at full power. Only the convoy's escorts remained, firing wild shots at random. *Tang*'s officers retired to the wardroom, too wound up to sleep. The men discussed the enemy's brave attempts to ram the submarine. O'Kane excused himself at 3:50 a.m. and climbed to the bridge for a final last venture topside. In the dark and moonless night, the skipper studied the submarine's phosphorescent wake, which to him appeared brighter than the stars. The patrol so far had gone quite well. *Tang* had now fired thirteen of its twenty-four torpedoes. O'Kane planned for each man to swap his battle station position with his understudy before the next attack.

That came less than forty-eight hours later when a messenger appeared at his cabin door. O'Kane slipped on his shoes, the swelling in his injured foot having finally subsided. The skipper downed a cup of coffee before he climbed to the conning tower. The convoy remained too far away to see, but the men buzzed over the radar operator's initial reports. The convoy appeared big. Real big. "It was the biggest convoy that I—and I believe most of the other people in the submarine—had seen," recalled engineering officer Larry Savadkin. "As a matter of fact, the radar operator, when he picked it up, thought it was land. There were pips all over the screen, almost a solid line of pips across the screen. There wasn't supposed to be any land there."

O'Kane studied the radar alongside the perennially seasick Floyd Caverly. The twelve-ship convoy had departed the Japanese port of Sasebo less than a week earlier, bound for western Borneo. No fewer than five escorts guarded the convoy. O'Kane suspected that a large single blip shoreward of the convoy carried the commander. The convoy size awed the skipper. He correctly judged that the convoy did not appear to be a formation of warships, but a large supply line. O'Kane now regretted using the four torpedoes on the first two ships of the patrol. Those two ships had steamed toward Japan for domestic use while this convoy likely was headed to reinforce Japanese troops. O'Kane planned to disrupt that plan. He ordered the crew to battle stations.

The convoy rounded the northeast tip of Turnabout Island in the Formosa Strait. The skipper ordered the submarine slow so that the tracking party could determine the convoy's course. The column of ships hugged the ten-fathom curve, closing in on *Tang* at 400 yards a minute. The skipper watched the ships take shape in the darkness. Why had the commander strung his convoy out in this long column? He would have been wiser to make two or more columns and create dual escort screens. The skipper surmised that the commander hoped the distance might limit a submarine picking off one ship at a time, giving the others a chance to flee. O'Kane didn't have time to dwell on it. He ordered all ten tubes readied for firing.

One of the escorts detected *Tang* and signaled the other ships with a searchlight, a move that illuminated the dark convoy for O'Kane. The skipper used the light to pick his first target: the 6,956-ton *Ebara Maru*. The 7,024-ton freighter *Matsumoto Maru* trailed behind it followed by what appeared to be a large modern tanker. Enormous crates crowded the decks of the loaded ships. The skipper planned to target all three. With his element of surprise now blown—and before the escorts could drive him off—O'Kane ordered *Tang* to race ahead at full speed. The submarine then turned and slowed for the shot. The skipper marked three bearings on the *Ebara Maru* at 12:05 a.m. as gunfire erupted off *Tang*'s starboard side.

"It all checks below," crackled Springer's voice over the bridge loudspeaker. "Anytime, Captain."

Tang let loose two torpedoes in quick succession, then raced between the convoy and its escorts so O'Kane could focus on *Matsumoto Maru.* The skipper was shocked. None of the ships so far had taken evasive measures. He fired two more shots. O'Kane then aimed at his third target, the range just 900 yards. He shouted the order and felt the familiar shudder of the submarine as blasts of compressed air launched two more fish. The skipper watched as a trail of phosphorescence lit up the dark water. He ordered right full rudder to bring on the stern tubes. "The order was smothered by the first detonation," O'Kane later wrote. "The detonations continued, like a slow-motion string of monstrous firecrackers."

One of O'Kane's torpedoes ripped open the port side of *Ebara Maru* near the stern and destroyed the engine room. The freighter slowed to a stop as the second torpedo hit the No. 3 hold. Cold seawater flooded the cargo ship, pulling it down by the stern along with fourteen enemy sailors. The *Matsumoto Maru* skipper ordered the ship to turn hard to port and rang up full speed to evade. Lookouts spotted *Tang.* Japanese machine gunners on the freighter's bridge opened fire on the submarine as the *Matsumoto Maru* turned to try to ram the *Tang.* The cargo ship charged seconds later into the path of *Tang*'s torpedoes. The explosion forced *Matsumoto Maru*'s bow beneath the waves and the ship came dead in the water.

O'Kane believed he had hit his third target as well. Chaos erupted as fires raged off either beam, a scene O'Kane would later describe as a "holocaust." The skipper's earlier shock over the enemy's lack of countermeasures vanished. The Japanese were convinced a wolf pack hunted the convoy. The five coastal defense ships that served as escorts turned on *Tang.* Depth charges exploded and machine guns rattled. The skipper hustled on to other targets. *Tang* passed just 600 yards abeam of a medium freighter before turning to target what O'Kane suspected was a tanker. The executive officer reported the outer doors aft were open. O'Kane watched his fourth target of the night steam across the reticle.

The skipper fired a single torpedo aimed under the suspected tanker's stack some 600 to 700 yards away. O'Kane focused the target-bearing transmitter on the next ship, which he believed was either a transport or a passenger freighter. He fired a shot at the foremast and another at the mainmast. The bow of an escort entered the skipper's binocular view as he fired his last shot. The escort turned toward *Tang*. Time was up. O'Kane ordered all ahead flank. "Things were anything but calm and peaceful now, for the escorts had stopped their warning tactics and were directing good salvos at us and the blotches of smoke we left," he wrote in his report. "Just exactly what took place in the following seconds will never be determined."

Tang cleared the area, slowing to eliminate the smoke from the diesels that the escorts could follow. Sporadic gunfire and flames on the water illuminated the scene, which soon fell several miles astern. Men grabbed quick cups of coffee and relaxed as torpedomen used the next half hour to check and load the final two torpedoes. The night was not over. Nor was O'Kane's attack. *Tang* turned around at 1:25 a.m. and headed back to sink what O'Kane believed was a disabled transport, though in all likelihood was *Matsumoto Maru*. Two escorts patrolled the seaward side of the crippled ship, forcing the skipper to do an end around so that he could attack from the shore side, where the destroyers had left a hole in the protective screen.

O'Kane ordered his men back to battle stations when *Tang* closed to just two miles. The hydraulic outer doors on tubes three and four opened. Darkness settled over the disabled ship. O'Kane scanned the deck, but saw no one. He wondered if the sailors were working below deck to stop the flooding. The disabled vessel appeared to sit lower in the water, but O'Kane could not be sure if it was sinking. He suspected it wasn't or the escorts would have towed it to shore to salvage its cargo. "Tenacity, Dick," Morton had once advised him. "Stay with the bastard till he's on the bottom." O'Kane planned to do just that tonight. *Tang* closed at 200 yards a minute, reaching an attack position 900 yards out at 2:30 a.m. "Stand by below!"

"Ready below, Captain."

"Fire!"

The submarine shuddered as it launched its twenty-third torpedo of the patrol. O'Kane watched the phosphorescent wake zoom ahead. He estimated one minute until detonation, plenty of time for him to set up another shot and fire before the first exploded. The skipper again focused the reticle on the disabled ship. This was his last torpedo of the patrol. It would be another clean sweep. Only a few minutes stood between *Tang* and a victorious return trip, a trip all the way home to the West Coast of California, to waiting wives, children, and parents. It would be a well-earned break from the 1,052 days of war, from the depth charges, aerial bombs, and gun battles. His men would finally get a respite from fear.

O'Kane fired.

The spindle that controlled the torpedo's onboard gyroscope withdrew a fraction of a second before a blast of compressed air ejected the 3,154-pound torpedo. The electric motor kicked on with a high-pitched whine. O'Kane and Leibold watched the torpedo race ahead in the dark night, the crippled ship only a half mile away. The skipper needed only to await visual confirmation of the sinking to guarantee credit, to earn another Japanese meatball for *Tang*'s battle flag, the expression used by sailors to describe the enemy's ensign, featuring a red sun on a white background. Throughout the submarine, men felt the familiar vibration and relaxed. The patrol was now over. Cooks thawed turkeys and put out several apple pies in anticipation of a celebration feast. Several sailors enjoyed coffee in the crew's mess while another yelled: "Let's head for the barn."

But it wasn't over yet.

O'Kane and Leibold watched in horror as the weapon suddenly surfaced in a spume of bright phosphorescence just yards in front of *Tang*'s bow. The torpedo then dove, but broke the surface again seconds later. O'Kane had fired enough fish to recognize immediately what had happened: an erratic torpedo, every skipper's nightmare. The weapon surfaced and dove, surfaced and dove, a white foam chasing it through the dark water like a comet's tail. The porpoising projectile pulled to port, skipping along the waves. Like a boomerang, the out-of-control bomb now circled back toward *Tang*, each second growing closer. "All ahead emergency!" O'Kane shouted. "Right full rudder!"

The skipper's only hope was to fishtail *Tang* outside of the torpedo's turning radius. It would be tough. The submarine crawled at a jogger's pace of just six knots. He needed speed to swing his submarine out of harm's way. "The problem was akin to moving a ship longer than a football field," O'Kane would later write, "and proceeding at harbor speed clear of a sudden careening speedboat." Men raced *Tang*'s four Fairbanks Morse engines. The massive diesels—capable of producing a combined 6,400 horsepower—now roared below. The skipper could see the frantic efforts of his men. *Tang*'s screws churned up the seas and black smoke from the engines wafted skyward.

The torpedo's dual manganese bronze propellers now drove some 570 pounds of explosive Torpex—the equivalent of 850 pounds of TNT—

through the water at thirty-three miles an hour. Engineers had designed the warhead to arm after 200 yards or twelve seconds, a safety feature intended to prevent a torpedo from exploding too soon after leaving the tube and jeopardizing the sub. But that time had now passed. The skipper watched as his armed bomb galloped through the waves. The erratic torpedo passed just sixty feet off the submarine's port beam before it turned straight for *Tang*. O'Kane estimated he had ten seconds to swing the 311-foot submarine out of the way. "Left full rudder!"

17

SILVERSIDES

"If we make it tonight, I'll be a *Christian*."

—Donald Sharp,
July 8, 1944, diary

The prolonged blast of the *Silversides* whistle reverberated across the waters at Pearl Harbor at 1:30 p.m. on the afternoon of September 24, 1944, just half an hour after *Tang*'s departure—signifying the start of the Silver Lady's eleventh war patrol, the sixth under the command of Jack Coye. The skipper's previous patrol off Guam and Saipan in advance of the Marianas invasion had been one for the record books. In just forty-six days, *Silversides* had sunk a half dozen ships for a total of 14,150 tons, ranking the patrol as the sixth top run of the entire war. The eager yet inexperienced skipper who had taken command fourteen months earlier now joined a select club of elite submarine skippers, a club that included men like Dick O'Kane of *Tang*, Slade Cutter on *Seahorse*, and Eugene Fluckey, skipper of *Barb*. Vice Admiral Charles Lockwood made that clear in his endorsement: "The tenth war patrol of the *Silversides* makes her one of the outstanding submarines of the Submarine Force."

The officers and crew celebrated that successful run with a return to Mare Island, the California Navy yard where shipbuilders had hammered out *Silversides* on the eve of the war. The rust-streaked submarine had since covered 92,210 miles and burned through 988,840 gallons of diesel. On patrols that ranged from Japan and the Marianas to the Solomon and Caroline islands, *Silversides* had fired 157 torpedoes, sinking twenty-two enemy ships. The Silver Lady had endured more action than most submarines. So had her men.

The seventy-seven-day overhaul gave the officers and crew a welcome break from the war, a chance to visit family and friends, and soak up being back in America. Coye flew to New York, where he and his wife, Betty, laughed through the musical *Oklahoma!*, danced, and traveled up to Massachusetts so the skipper could visit his daughter, Beth, and son, Johnny, marveling at how big his young children had grown in his absence.

The news over the summer of 1944 proved far different than the headlines that had gripped the nation when the Navy had commissioned *Silversides* eight days after the attack on Pearl Harbor. Allied forces successful in the June D-Day invasion swept across former Great War battlefields on the path to Berlin. Bombers and fighters crowded the skies over Europe by the thousands, pounding German oil refineries, rail yards, and war plants. Virginia representative Clifton Woodrum, chairman of the House Select Committee on Post-War Military Policy, went so far as to predict that the Army might finish its job against Germany by October. American lawmakers prepared for the end of war in Europe and the return to a peacetime economy, a challenge that would involve ending military contracts, liquidating surplus ships, tanks, and planes, and responding to the sudden unemployment of millions of wartime workers.

The Office of War Information predicted the Pacific fight could stretch on as much as two years past Germany's defeat because of greater logistical challenges. U.S. forces needed to move close enough to bomb Japan's cities to ruin. Furthermore, Navy secretary James Forrestal told reporters that Japan's pullback from bases across the Pacific to its own islands, the Philippines, and China meant that it could amass its airpower in a smaller theater of action. "The United States Navy will face Jap air power in the coming year that will be stronger both quantitatively and qualitatively," Forrestal said. "The fight will be a long and hard one." But the men who fought did not doubt America's gains. "The news over the radio tonight sounds good to my weary ears," officer Eugene Malone wrote. "Pretty soon I guess the Jap will be plenty sorry he tangled with us, if he isn't already. That's my motto, sink more Jap ships quicker. Then it will be time to go home. And I want to go home. I'm getting fed up with this war."

Silversides had returned to Pearl Harbor on September 12, allowing time for voyage repairs and training before departure with the submarines *Salmon* and *Trigger*. The three subs would operate as a wolf pack; *Tang* had been invited to join, but the fiercely independent O'Kane had opted to hunt alone. The senior of the three skippers, Coye would lead the pack, dubbed "Coye's Coyotes." Just as the name implies, wolf packs consisted of multiple submarines hunting in tandem. Rather than one submarine attacking a six-ship convoy and hoping to sink one or two freighters, a wolf pack could attack the same convoy from multiple positions, create confusion for the escorts, and sink them all. The Germans had used wolf packs with great success against Allied shipping in the North Atlantic early in the war, sinking 1,094 merchant ships for a total of some six million tons put on the bottom in 1942 alone. That one-year tonnage lost rivaled the size of Japan's entire merchant fleet at the start of the war.

The United States in contrast had been slower to adopt the same tactics, largely because the Navy didn't have the resources. The sprawling Pacific Ocean was too vast—and with too many strategic spots to cover—for the Navy to double and triple up submarines. That situation changed as the war progressed and new submarines joined the fight. Japanese antisubmarine tactics also had improved, prompting American leaders to reconsider the value of wolf packs. The easy prey had disappeared. Gone were the unarmed and unescorted Japanese merchant ships. Japan had launched an expansion of its long-lagging escort fleet and by 1944 more vessels were deployed to guard enemy convoys, making it harder for a lone submarine to penetrate and sink multiple ships. Skippers reported improved depth charge attacks and convoy commanders now knew to scatter immediately after the first explosion, forcing American submarines to spend much of the night hunting down individual ships.

But one of the most important factors in the decision to employ wolf packs was the collapse of Japan's merchant fleet. American submarine captains were victims of their own success. They were running out of targets. Submarines in the first six months of 1944 sank almost double the number of enemy ships destroyed in the same period the year before, averaging 115 attacks each month and reaching a peak of 250,000 tons of enemy shipping destroyed in May. The second half of 1944 would prove the most destructive time of the war with submarines ramping up attacks each month to an average of 172, many of them along the coasts of China and the Philippines. Those numbers would spike in October and November with 423 attacks—and 1,574 torpedoes fired—that put 549,000 tons of merchant ships on the bottom. Submarines could team up and inflict greater damage on the few targets that existed. "The total area for submarines was becoming less and less," Coye recalled. "We were getting new boats out; we were getting more and more submarines, so you had to put them in wolf packs."

Despite their benefits, wolf packs created an uncomfortable role for many submarine skippers. Undersea warfare was inherently independent. Working in tandem raised a host of challenges, many of them involving communication. The radios used between submarines didn't work well—as Coye had discovered when he attempted to work with *Balao*—and required that submarines be on the surface to use them, which was not always possible. Communication between submarines required a certain creativity. Submarines flipped their radar on and off to communicate via Morse code or simply pulled alongside one another to allow skippers to shout through a megaphone. Coye in particular disliked the added responsibility. "It has its advantages and disadvantages," he later said. "I didn't like it as much because you are not only concerned about the safety and whatnot of your own submarine, but you had the problems of the other submarines that were with you."

The three submarines arrived in recently captured Saipan on October 3. *Silversides* swapped out a defective torpedo and topped off its diesel before the wolf pack set off again at 5:15 p.m. the next afternoon. The subs passed two days through a severe typhoon with heavy seas that forced them to slow to seven knots to avoid sloshing dangerous amounts of water down the conning tower hatch. A wave crashed over the bridge and almost washed Lieutenant Carl Heidel overboard, leaving him with a severe head wound for six days. The seas moderated by October 8 and *Silversides* increased to three-engine speed as the submarines approached the northeastern coast of Formosa. In preparation for the invasion of the Philippines, America planned massive air strikes on the island to cripple the enemy's air strength. Carrier pilots flew 1,378 sorties on October 12 followed by 974 the next day and 146 on the third, destroying more than 500 Japanese planes as well as hangars, ammo depots, and industrial plants.

American war planners had expected the Japanese navy to put up a fight for the Philippines, as in the Marianas, but how much of a battle remained to be seen. The once feared Japanese navy had become a shell of its former self. While it still boasted a sizable surface fleet—including nine battleships, one shy of the ten available at the war's start—Japan lacked the fuel to fight.

Years of war had chewed up Japan's pilots and planes, leaving its few remaining carriers with empty hangars. The Battle of the Philippine Sea had only exacerbated Japan's woes, robbing the nation of three carriers and almost 500 planes. For the defense of the Philippines the navy cobbled together a force of four carriers, nine battleships, fifteen cruisers, and twenty-nine destroyers. The United States in contrast boasted an armada Admiral Nimitz could have only dreamed of at Midway, including forty-six fleet, light, and escort carriers, twelve battleships, twenty-three cruisers, and 178 destroyers.

Similar to the Battle of Midway, Japan had devised an overly complicated plan designed to trap American forces. Timed to coincide with General Mac-Arthur's invasion of Leyte, the plan called for the Japanese to divide into three forces: northern, central, and southern. The northern force, centered around four carriers, would steam down from the Inland Sea. These flattops had a combined total of only 116 planes, which because of inexperienced pilots had to be hoisted on the carriers with cranes. These tempting targets, Japan hoped, would lure Admiral Halsey and America's powerful carriers on a chase to the north, leaving the invasion forces vulnerable. Japan's central and southern forces would approach from Borneo, steam through the Philippine Islands, and encircle the invasion force in a pincer movement. The battleships, cruisers, and destroyers would wipe out America's amphibious forces and then escape before Halsey's hoodwinked carriers returned.

America's deployment of submarines throughout Philippine waters paid off. The skippers of the submarines *Darter* and *Dace* discussed how best to patrol together in a midnight rendezvous October 23 in the Palawan Passage when *Darter* picked up Japan's central force of five battleships, twelve cruisers, and fifteen destroyers. "We have radar contact," Commander David McClintock shouted through his megaphone. "Let's go." McClintock fired off repeated contact reports as the submarines shadowed the warships until dawn, *Darter* targeting the convoy's western column, *Dace* the eastern. McClintock fired ten torpedoes at the first two cruisers, watching as the explosions rocked the enemy. "Whipped periscope back to the first target to see the sight of a lifetime," he wrote. "She was a mass of billowing black smoke from number one turret to the stern. No superstructure could be seen. Bright orange flames shot out from the side of the main deck from the bow to the after turret."

Four torpedo hits sent the 15,781-ton heavy cruiser *Atago*—the flagship of central force commander Vice Admiral Takeo Kurita—to the bottom along with some 360 officers and crew. Two more torpedoes rocked *Takao*, sidelining the heavy cruiser for the rest of the war. *Dace* skipper Commander Bladen Claggett watched his colleague's attack unfold. "*Darter* is really having a field day. Can see great pall of smoke completely enveloping spot where ship was at last look," he wrote in his report. "Ship to the left is also smoking badly. Looks like a great day for the *Darter*." Claggett hurried to set up a shot, watching the parade of cruisers and battleships. "This is really a submariner's dream," he wrote, "sitting right in front of a task force." Claggett fired six torpedoes, scoring four hits and sinking the 15,781-ton heavy cruiser *Maya*. "Heard tremendous breaking up noises. This was the most gruesome sounds I have ever heard," Claggett wrote. "Sounded as if she was coming down on top of us."

"We better get the hell out of here," *Dace's* diving officer quipped.

Submarines had destroyed two heavy cruisers and damaged a third. *Darter's* contact reports proved equally as important, warning American forces of the enemy's approach. Carrier-based planes roared into the skies, hammering Admiral Kurita's central force in some 259 sorties. Pilots singled out the battleship *Musashi*. The 70,000-ton monster and its sister ship, *Yamato*, held the title for the largest battleships ever built, boasting almost twice the displacement of the United States' *North Carolina* class battlewagon. Wave after wave of pilots from the carriers *Intrepid, Cabot, Essex, Lexington, Franklin*, and *Enterprise* drilled *Musashi*, scoring by some estimates as many as twenty torpedo hits, seventeen bomb hits, and eighteen near misses. The goliath battleship capsized and sank with more than 1,000 officers and crew. The aerial attack prompted Kurita to reverse course beyond the range of American planes, a move that led Admiral Halsey to conclude Japan's central force was in retreat.

Carrier planes had spotted Japan's southern force the morning of October 24. Two battleships, one cruiser, and four destroyers planned to slip through the narrow Surigao Strait into Leyte Gulf that night, followed a half hour later by a support force of three cruisers and four destroyers. The United States built an impenetrable defense line. More than three dozen torpedo boats crowded the fifteen-mile-wide strait, backed up by several destroyer squadrons. Any ships fortunate enough to make it past them would collide with a battle line of six battleships and eight cruisers. The lopsided numbers promised not a fight but a slaughter—and America delivered, sinking both battleships, three of the four destroyers, and crippling the cruiser, later lost to carrier planes. The carnage triggered the trailing support force to abort the operation. "Most beautiful sight I ever witnessed," one destroyer squadron commander remarked. "The arched line of tracers in the darkness looked like a continual stream of lighted railroad cars going over a hill."

The Japanese trap sprang. The mission of Vice Admiral Jisaburo Ozawa, commander of the northern force, was to lure Halsey far from Leyte Gulf, a mission Ozawa knew if successful would lead to the annihilation of his own four carriers. The Japanese admiral hoped to bait Halsey with a strike against America's carriers October 24. Bad weather forced some of the Japanese planes to land on Luzon while others splashed down. Of Ozawa's 116 planes, just twenty-nine remained. But Halsey was snared. The ambitious admiral ordered his forces north to battle Japan's toothless carriers, leaving a hole in the defensive net. Pilots roared into the skies at first light on October 25, pounding Ozawa's sacrificial flattops in 527 sorties. The *Chitose* vanished at 9:37 a.m., followed that afternoon by the 29,800-ton *Zuikaku*, the last survivor of the six carriers that attacked Pearl Harbor. The crippled *Zuiho* dove next, followed by the *Chiyoda*, finished off by blazing guns of American cruisers.

Ozawa had accomplished his mission. Kurita's central force, which Halsey had believed was whipped, doubled back, slipping unmolested through San Bernardino Strait. Gone was the threat of Halsey's ten carriers, six battleships, eight cruisers, and forty-one destroyers, all now steaming north. Despite the earlier bruising, Kurita's force remained formidable, including four battleships, eight cruisers, and eleven destroyers. The tall masts of Kurita's battlewagons that crested the horizon minutes after sunrise on October 25 must have terrified the unsuspecting American lookouts of Taffy 3, a small force of six escort carriers guarded by just three destroyers and four destroyer escorts. These "baby flattops" resembled the Navy's powerful fleet carriers in name only. Often converted tankers and freighters, escort carriers hauled only twenty-seven planes, tasked to cover amphibious forces and provide combat air and antisubmarine patrols. Such ships boasted so little defensive armament that sailors joked the escort carrier's designation CVE stood for "Combustible, Vulnerable, Expendable."

Rear Admiral Clifton Sprague, commander of Taffy 3, sized up his chances. Not only were all of Halsey's forces far beyond range—a fact few realized—but the warships that throttled the Japanese in Surigao Strait had to first take on ammo. Sprague knew the five-inch guns of his escort carriers would prove powerless against Kurita's battleships and cruisers. His only hope: run. Two other escort carrier groups operated south of Taffy 3. These sixteen flattops mustered 143 torpedo planes and 235 fighters. Until that help arrived, Sprague was on his own. The outgunned admiral ordered his carriers up to flank speed as planes shot into the skies. Sprague's forces poured out smoke to provide cover, but not enough as the Japanese guns zeroed in on the American ships. "The enemy was closing with disconcerting rapidity and the volume and accuracy of fire was increasing," Sprague wrote in his report. "At this point it did not appear that any of our ships could survive another five minutes of the heavy-caliber fire being received."

Sprague refused to go down without a fight, ordering his escorts to attack the Japanese with torpedoes as the carriers escaped into a rainsquall. The attacks created diversions that slowed pursuit and drew enemy fire away from the carriers but came at great sacrifice. The skipper of *Hoel* later estimated in his report that the Japanese fired more than 300 two- and three-gun salvos at his ship, including armor-piercing shells that punched through the destroyer's steel skin. Demolished by more than forty hits—and with the engineering spaces flooding—*Hoel* capsized and sank at 8:55 a.m. The destroyer escort *Samuel B. Roberts* suffered a similar fate seventy minutes later. Enemy cruisers and destroyers likewise encircled *Johnston* and unleashed what the senior surviving officer described as an "avalanche of shells." The destroyer rolled over at 10:10 a.m. Survivors reported that a Japanese officer, watching *Johnston* vanish from the bridge wing of a nearby destroyer, raised his hand and saluted.

American planes from all three escort carrier groups bore down on the pursuers with torpedoes, bombs, and machine guns. Pilots out of ammo even executed dry runs just to distract enemy gunners. Four cruisers, despite interference from escorts and planes, pulled ahead. The skipper of *Gambier Bay*, who dodged the enemy's salvos for half an hour, watched the cruisers creep closer. The escort carrier soon fell under the enemy's guns, dropping out of formation as the Japanese pounced like piranhas. *Gambier Bay* capsized and sank at 9:07 a.m. American torpedo bombers and fighters retaliated and pounded *Chokai* and *Chikuma*, forcing the Japanese later to scuttle the crippled cruisers. Just as his warships nipped at the heels of the flattops, Admiral Kurita ordered the chase halted at 9:11 a.m. His initial plan to reassemble his scattered forces and press on toward Leyte Gulf crumbled under the realization that he faced certain defeat. American sailors watched in shock as the enemy warships retired.

"Goddammit, boys," shouted a signalman on the bridge of the carrier *Fanshaw Bay*. "They're getting away!"

The war's first kamikaze attacks would hours later claim the escort carrier *St. Lo*, but the organized surface fight off the island of Samar had ended. The Battle of Leyte Gulf had robbed Japan of twenty-six warships, including four carriers, three battleships, ten cruisers, and nine destroyers. The United States in contrast lost just six ships, though the destruction could have been far greater. Not until Kurita's forces collided with Sprague's escort carriers did many senior leaders realize Halsey had left not a single ship to guard the San Bernardino Strait. Despite Ozawa's postwar admission to interrogators that his force had served as a decoy, Halsey still argued he had made the right choice. "My decision was to strike the Northern Force," he wrote in 1952. "Given the same circumstances and the same information as I had then, I would make it again." Halsey's first face-to-face encounter with Sprague, however, appeared to indicate the brash admiral harbored doubts. "I didn't know," Halsey confessed, "whether you would speak to me or not."

Sprague criticized Halsey in a letter to his wife as "the gentleman who failed to keep his appointment," though in person he appeared inclined to forgive. "Why Admiral Bill," Sprague answered. "I'm not mad at you."

"I want you to know," Halsey then declared, "I think you wrote the most glorious page in American naval history that day."

Coye had listened to radio communications of the October 25 battle that raged east of the Philippines. In contrast, his patrol to date had dragged. *Trigger* had at least rescued a downed pilot from the carrier *Bunker Hill* and stalked a force of cruisers before the Japanese drove off the boat, even firing a torpedo that streaked past the submarine's starboard side. The news over the radio, however, promised a possible remedy. Coye ordered *Silversides* south to intercept the enemy's retiring forces, picking up *Trigger* and *Salmon* that night. *Trigger*'s high periscope revealed the tops of two battleships at 8:36 a.m. at a range of twenty-five miles. Coye's Coyotes gave chase with *Trigger* hoping to execute an end around to the east. The enemy warships increased speed and pulled ahead. *Trigger* skipper Commander Frederick

Harlfinger II could only watch in frustration as the tops of the enemy's prized battlewagons grew smaller on the horizon, replaced by puffs of smoke that soon vanished.

The next few days proved anticlimactic as the submarines searched for targets. That changed at 4:01 a.m. on October 30. *Salmon*'s radar picked up a large tanker escorted by as many as four escorts. Skipper Lieutenant Commander Harley Nauman alerted the others and dove to begin its approach at 5:45 a.m. *Silversides* spotted the target—the massive 10,021-ton *Takane Maru*—an hour later at a distance of fourteen miles. Coye ordered his submarine to dive minutes later. *Trigger* picked up the tanker soon after. All three submarines, like wolves hunting cattle, moved in on the *Takane Maru*. Coye closed to just under two miles and fired six torpedoes in the span of just fifty seconds. "Ten seconds after last torpedo had been fired, heard and felt an explosion that jarred our back teeth," Coye would write in his report. "As nearest escort was about 1200 yards away this could only have been a premature."

Coye ordered *Silversides* deep as the depth charges started, a total of fourteen. None detonated as close as the premature torpedo. *Silversides* surfaced and started to chase. The skipper of *Takane Maru*—alerted by the premature torpedo—had taken evasive measures and now knew at least one submarine hunted him. The enemy skipper sought shelter in rainsqualls and executed dramatic course changes. That afternoon *Trigger* moved in to attack, firing six torpedoes, all of which missed. But the submarine scored with another round of torpedoes five minutes later. Coye spotted the tanker emerging from a late afternoon haze more than ten miles away and saw it rocked by at least two of *Trigger*'s torpedoes. The shots blew off *Takane Maru*'s stern and left the tanker afloat but dead in the water. Escorts swarmed and began dropping depth charges—seventy-eight total—on *Trigger*.

Salmon and *Silversides* prepared to finish off the crippled *Takane Maru* as the setting sun and bright moon illuminated the moderate seas. *Salmon* closed at 7:40, the enemy tanker about fourteen miles away and drifting with the wind at a speed of one and a half knots. Four escorts patrolled on either side of the tanker at a range of about 1,000 yards, searching for enemy submarines. *Salmon* closed to about four and a half miles and dove to attack. Lieutenant Commander Nauman, who had first detected the tanker fifteen hours earlier, now hoped to put it on the bottom. *Salmon* closed to 3,300 yards at 8:01 p.m. and fired four torpedoes. A sonar operator on board *Silver-*

sides reported the high-pitch whine of torpedo screws now speeding through the dark water toward the tanker at forty-six knots. An attack was under way. Four minutes and ten seconds after firing, the first torpedo hit *Takane Maru*. A second followed ten seconds later, lighting up the night sky.

Nauman had seen three of his torpedoes breach the surface, leaving a phosphorescent trail straight back to *Salmon*. Japanese escorts turned on the submarine. The skipper had planned to fire his stern tubes, but the escorts forced him to stop the attack. He ordered *Salmon* deep and passed 310 feet one minute later. Four sets of depth charges—each consisting of six to eight charges—exploded close overhead. The blasts shut down auxiliary power and the steering and stern planes failed. Light bulbs shattered, the fathometer fried, and the magnetic compass lost all direction. Seawater flooded the electric ranges in the galley and hull fittings started to leak in the engine rooms and in the air and hydraulic systems. The pumps struggled to keep up with the rush of water and the bilges filled up. "The conning tower vibrated up and down so violently that I thought the ship was going to shake herself apart," Nauman would later write. "I remember bending my knees to ease the shock."

The depth charges continued, each explosion forcing *Salmon* deeper. The skipper ordered all ahead emergency, and a twenty-degree up angle on the boat stopped the plummet at 400 feet—150 feet past *Salmon*'s designed operating depth. *Salmon* climbed to 300 feet. The skipper ordered the boat to level off and reduce speed, but that move caused the submarine to again drop, this time to 500 feet. The skipper brought *Salmon* back up to 150 feet, but another attempt to level the boat sent the submarine plunging to 578 feet before the crew could stop the descent. But the depth in the after torpedo room, given the angle of the boat, approached some 620 feet. Nauman knew at that depth the pressure hull could collapse. The boat was in serious trouble. Complicating the challenge, the batteries were empty. The water level in the engine rooms continued to rise and had now reached the main motor casing. *Salmon* had run out of options. The skipper recorded his decision in his report: "Our only hope is to surface and take our chances."

Seventeen minutes after *Salmon* dove, Nauman ordered his submarine to surface. The skipper had no way to know what he might find above in the dark. He knew only that his chances below were worse. Crews raced to the guns as luck prevailed. The closest escort appeared down-moon almost four miles away. The crew was safe for the moment, but *Salmon* was in bad shape.

Water washed over the decks and the submarine suffered a fifteen-degree list to starboard. The depth charge attack had cracked the binoculars on the target-bearing transmitter and the sights on the four-inch deck gun. Sailors found the wood decking and steel frame of the superstructure warped and broken. Crews hustled to make repairs. Nauman ordered the No. 3 engine and battery put on for propulsion. Engineers restored the fourth engine eighteen minutes later, cranking open the exhaust vents by hand. Electricians started the low-pressure blowers, blew the ballast tanks, and killed the list, helping to level the submarine in the water.

The escorts made no attempt to close in on the crippled submarine, which gave damage control crews time to make repairs. But the submarine was not alone for long. An escort searchlight illuminated the *Salmon* at 9 p.m. from a distance of about three miles. A few wild salvos followed, likely from a three-inch deck gun. Nauman found his radio antennas destroyed but crews rigged an emergency wing antenna. The skipper ordered an emergency message sent out to the wolf pack. He relayed *Salmon*'s position and let the others know the submarine could not dive and had no choice but take on the escorts with gunfire. *Salmon* needed help immediately. The other three escorts about five miles south of *Salmon* began firing in the direction of the first escort. Confusion followed and gave *Salmon* precious minutes. The skipper ordered his gun crew to use ammunition sparingly. He did not know how long he would have to fight. With the four-inch gun sight telescopes destroyed, crews would have to use the open sights. If he hoped to hit the escorts, the skipper would have to get in close.

Salmon got a third engine running, giving it a maximum speed of about sixteen knots—an improvement certainly, but still not fast enough to outrun the escort. Nauman watched as the escort repeated the same tactic. The enemy skipper would charge *Salmon*'s port quarter, sheer out to expose its after gun, and fire a few rounds at the crippled submarine. *Salmon*'s gun crew learned to wait until the escort sheered out, then fired five rounds of the four-inch gun. *Salmon* missed, but gunners registered a few near splashes. But the enemy's rounds landed even closer, splashing water on the bridge and decks. The skipper spotted a rainsquall to the southwest. Before he could make it, the escort attacked again, passing within 2,000 yards off *Salmon*'s port beam. The submarine's gun crew opened fire, landing a few small caliber hits. The escort now prepared to cut across *Salmon*'s bow. The skipper knew this was his best—and only—chance to go on the offensive. Nauman ordered all guns trained off the starboard side.

The escort moved to cut across the Salmon's course, but the skipper ordered hard left rudder. *Salmon* swung to port and headed straight toward the escort, passing alongside at a distance of just fifty yards. Gun crews opened fire. The submarine's four-inch deck cannon roared again and again, hitting the escort's bridge at least once. Smaller .30 and .50 caliber automatic weapons rattled in the dark, raking the escort from bow to stern, killing as many as five enemy sailors and wounding twenty more. The escort returned fire, hitting Petty Officer 3rd Class Troy Adams just below the knee. Sailors carried Adams below, where the pharmacist's mate gave him morphine, tied off the bleeders, and applied compress dressings over sulfanilamide powder. He would later pluck ten bone fragments from his leg. The startled escort stopped firing and fell astern of *Salmon*. A second escort closed in on the submarine, but the gun crew again opened fire and repelled the escort. The battered submarine aimed for the rainsquall at 12:15 a.m., one escort ahead and the others falling astern.

Salmon disappeared into the heart of the dark swirling showers. All Nauman and his crew could do was wait and hope. Ten minutes passed without an attack. The submarine pushed onward. Half an hour later it became clear the escorts had vanished. The battle for *Salmon* was over. The submarine had beaten the odds. Unable to dive, the injured *Salmon* had held off four Japanese escorts for five hours. The desperation of the battle showed in the gun crew's tally of ammunition fired: 7,760 tracer, incendiary, and armor-piercing rounds from the submarine's smaller guns and fifty-seven of the larger four-inch shells. The submarine *Sterlet*, lured by the frantic radio calls, arrived and put the final shot into the 10,500-ton *Takane Maru*. *Salmon* spent the night making emergency repairs and sent out a message around dawn to *Silversides* and *Trigger*, alerting them to the submarine's position, course, and speed. "It was a relief to get a message from her," Coye would later write. "At this point we were not too certain that she was still afloat."

Orders arrived, directing the crippled *Salmon* to return for repairs, its patrol now over. *Silversides*, *Trigger*, and *Sterlet* would escort the injured submarine. Coye positioned *Trigger* ten miles ahead to warn of patrol boats while *Sterlet* and *Silversides* cruised 1,000 yards off each bow because *Salmon* still could not dive. Coye refused to leave one submarine alone on the surface as a target.

If an enemy plane or ship approached, he ordered all boats to remain on the surface and fight it out. The next few days passed without incident as the four submarines cut south through the waves, arriving in Saipan on November 3. *Silversides* would spend the next week in Saipan before departing for another two weeks to help hunt down patrol boats, an extension that would not lead to any sinkings. The Silver Lady wrapped up its eleventh patrol at Midway on November 23.

The eleventh patrol would be Coye's last as skipper. He relinquished command six days later in a quiet ceremony at Midway, turning *Silversides* over to his friend Commander John Nichols. The Silver Lady would make three more war patrols in the East China Sea and off the Japanese home islands of Kyushu and Honshu. But the lack of enemy targets translated into just one more victim, a 4,500-ton cargo ship in late January 1945. In Guam undergoing refit when the war ended, *Silversides* would conclude its service as a naval trainer and auxiliary, destined never again for combat. Commissioned just eight days after the Japanese attack on Pearl Harbor, *Silversides* over the course of the war would consume more than 1.5 million gallons of diesel fuel and cover more than 141,000 miles on war patrols. The 183 torpedoes *Silversides* fired would claim twenty-three confirmed kills, earning the coveted Presidential Unit Citation. For his part Coye had earned three Navy Crosses, a Bronze Star, and the Legion of Merit.

The Navy reassigned Coye as the top instructor at the prospective commanding officer school in New London, where he could apply his wartime expertise to train others in the dwindling days of the war and after. Coye had served as the skipper for six patrols, one more than the Navy policy normally allowed. But Coye was good. Real good. His superiors no doubt felt reluctant to interrupt his stream of destruction. Coye had begun his tenure sixteen months earlier worried he might not live up to Burlingame's record. He now departed with the record of having sunk fourteen ships, putting a total of 38,659 enemy tons on the bottom. He had nearly doubled the number of ships Burlingame sank and would rank the tenth top skipper of the war by the number of ships sunk. "That was really the highlight of my career, the patrols on *Silversides*," Coye would later recall. "That's what I figured I was trained for and what I did as well as I could."

18

TANG

"We knew when we went aboard the submarine that we might end up with this iron cylinder being our tomb."

—Clay Decker,
Tang survivor

O'Kane watched in horror as his twenty-fourth torpedo of the patrol now circled back toward *Tang*. The skipper estimated he had just ten seconds to turn his submarine—a ship almost the length of a football field—before the torpedo crashed into his stern. He had rung up emergency speed and left full rudder, hoping to fishtail *Tang* out of the torpedo's path. Black diesel smoke poured from the submarine as *Tang*'s four engines roared. Sailors throughout the submarine had prepared to head for California after the final shot, but the euphoria of another successful patrol was interrupted by the frantic bells of the engine order telegraph and shouts from the bridge. O'Kane and boatswain's mate William Leibold watched the armed torpedo porpoise closer and closer, its phosphorescent wake aimed straight at *Tang*.

O'Kane's hope dimmed.

The torpedo ripped open the port side of *Tang* at around 2:30 a.m., just twenty seconds after the skipper had fired his last shot. The violent explosion near the bulkhead that divided the maneuvering and after engine rooms destroyed the submarine's propulsion plant and blew the tops off the only regular ballast tanks aft. *Tang*'s forward momentum halted in seconds. Cold seawater immediately flooded the after torpedo, maneuvering, and after engine rooms, drowning any men who may have survived the blast. Sailors inside the adjacent and half-flooded forward engine room struggled to seal the watertight door against the pressure of streaming seawater, the added weight of three flooded compartments pulling the submarine's stern underwater like a giant pendulum.

The explosion ruptured high-pressure air lines, jarred watertight doors, and popped up steel deck plates throughout the submarine. Loose equipment, gear, and fittings crashed to the deck as men struggled to grab anything in reach. The detonation's shock hurled unsuspecting sailors as far forward as the control room against the deck, bulkheads, and equipment with enough force to rip skin and break bones. Signalman Petty Officer 3rd Class John Accardy plunged through the conning tower hatch to the control room deck some eight feet below, snapping his arm. Another sailor nearby suffered a broken leg. The shock tossed Lieutenant j.g. Mel Enos headfirst, leaving several deep gashes that poured blood.

Up on the bridge, the torpedo's detonation jolted O'Kane and Leibold, who struggled to maintain their balance. The men watched a spray of water rise up in the dark night in what looked to Leibold like a big cloud of black smoke. The telltale sign of destruction the men had seen so many times to mark a torpedoed enemy ship now hovered over *Tang*, the tragic result of its malfunctioning weapon. The skipper ordered the conning tower hatch sealed as *Tang*'s flooded stern began to dive underwater. He scanned the horizon for the two Japanese destroyers that had guarded what he thought was an injured transport though was likely *Matsumoto Maru*. Enemy lookouts had no doubt heard and possibly seen the explosion. The injured *Tang* would make easy prey. "Do we have propulsion?" the skipper demanded, his voice crackling over the loudspeaker. "Do we have propulsion at all?"

"We have no communication with the maneuvering room," replied executive officer Frank Springer, who stood at the foot of the hatch.

"We're coming to a stop," O'Kane yelled. "Any report of damage?"

"No."

O'Kane asked if *Tang* had steering.

"The rudder is locked," Springer shouted up the ladder. "We are trying to shift to hand steering."

"Radar, I want information on the two destroyers," O'Kane called out, turning his attention to the enemy. "Where are they?"

Radarman Floyd Caverly had listened to the whine of the torpedo's propellers through the sonar operator's headphones, a whine that vanished a second before impact. The explosion had wiped out much of the submarine's internal communications. Caverly could hear O'Kane's orders broadcast over the conning tower speakers, but nothing happened when the radarman keyed his microphone to answer. Caverly twice shouted that his last radar reading before the system crashed showed one of the destroyers about 3,000 yards away, the other about 4,200.

"Radar, I want information on the two destroyers," the skipper barked again. "Where are they?"

Caverly realized O'Kane couldn't hear him. He stepped beneath the hatch. "Captain, this is Caverly," he shouted. "I want permission to come to the bridge."

This was no time for formality. Springer grabbed Caverly by the nape of his neck and the seat of the pants and shoved him up the ladder. The radarman clambered up as cold seawater drenched him. He stepped onto the bridge to find water up to his knees and looked back to see the strong current flow down through the open hatch he just exited. Some eight men—the executive officer, engineering officer, helmsman, plotters, soundman, and another radarman—remained trapped below. The water climbed to Caverly's waist.

"Captain, this boat is sinking," Leibold shouted in the dark. "We're going down."

The sea swallowed *Tang*'s stern. The rising water washed O'Kane off the bridge just as the twenty-third torpedo blasted the crippled enemy ship. Caverly feared the sinking submarine might pull him down with it. The radarman stepped off the bridge into the water and swam away from *Tang*, pulling his body through the water, one stroke after the other. The bridge vanished seconds later, leaving only the air-filled bow to bob above the waves. "The people on the bridge were left standing there treading water," recalled one survivor. "The ship just dropped out from underneath them."

Leibold didn't fare as well. The boatswain's mate held his breath as the submarine plummeted beneath the dark waters, accelerating as the stern plunged toward the seafloor. Darkness enveloped him. Leibold felt what he surmised was either a secondary explosion or *Tang*'s stern striking the bottom of the Formosa Strait. He pushed off and kicked up, pulling himself toward the surface, his adrenaline pumping as he fought against the weight of his metal binoculars, submarine jacket, and shoes.

• • •

Larry Savadkin operated the torpedo data computer in the rear of the conning tower when the explosion rocked *Tang*. He felt the submarine bounce up and down, but the wiry lieutenant kept his footing. Savadkin heard the skipper ask whether *Tang* still had propulsion and started forward to check the pitometer log. He spotted it just as the lights went out, forcing him and others to struggle in total darkness. Water raced through the open hatch into the conning tower as the stern dove. "No one was able to close the hatch to the bridge, sufficient time just didn't exist," Savadkin recalled. "Water rushed through the hatch with terrific force, knocking down practically everybody in the conning tower, just sweeping them off their feet, tangling them all up and making it impossible for them to do anything to help themselves."

Savadkin grabbed the No. 2 periscope shaft. The downward angle of the boat coupled with the rush of water washed loose gear and men past, bumping into him. Savadkin held on tight. The water level rose, lifting him with it. The former college track star found a small pocket of air—just large enough for his nose and mouth—in an indentation between the overhead cork and hull. He sucked in air. The conning tower, buzzing moments before, fell silent. Gone were the voices of the executive officer, radarmen, and plotters, all now drowned, their lungs filled with salty seawater. Savadkin breathed the precious air. The torrent of water coupled with the sudden darkness disoriented Savadkin, who felt the submarine was upside down. He feared if he continued up the periscope well he would end up in the pump room. The air soured.

The engineering officer took a deep breath and ducked beneath the cold water. Like a blind man, he ran his hands over the equipment to orient himself. He popped up into another air bubble in the forward end of the conning tower near the hatch that led to the bridge, the air bubble this time large enough to accommodate his entire head. Savadkin again fingered the equipment, grasping the engine order telegraph. The knob clicked as Savadkin spun it over the various engine speeds—standard, full, flank—speeds the legendary *Tang* never again would make. The young officer took another deep breath, dropped under the water, and pulled himself up through the hatch, popping up in yet another air bubble, this time underneath the forward cowling on the bridge.

"Who is it?" a voice called out in the dark.

"Mr. Savadkin," he answered. "Who are you?"

"Bergman," replied Petty Officer 1st Class Edwin Bergman, the soundman who had stood opposite the torpedo data computer. "Do you know where we are?"

"I think we are under the bridge."

"What are you going to do?"

Savadkin told him that they had to get to the surface.

"Can I go with you?" Bergman asked.

"Sure," Savadkin replied.

"How?"

Savadkin instructed Bergman—a veteran of all five of *Tang*'s patrols—to grab hold of his legs. He would lead them out, just as the former captain and champion runner had once led his Lafayette College teammates to victory. The officer took a deep breath and pushed down to clear the cowling, but Bergman let go. Savadkin later speculated that he must have been confused though Bergman had sounded fine in the brief conversation the men shared. Savadkin kicked off toward the surface. He would never see Bergman again. "I began to swim up, using both hands, as hard as I could—the whole idea was to get up," he recalled. "I wanted air and lots of it."

Tang's bridge hovered underwater at a distance roughly equal to the height of a six-story building. Savadkin remembered from submarine training that he needed to exhale as he ascended to prevent his chest from ballooning as the water pressure decreased. Rather than slowly breathe out, he blew all of his air out at once. The surface loomed far above. The lieutenant clawed his way up, his oxygen-depleted body desperate for air. Savadkin feared he wouldn't make it; every instinct in his body screamed at him to breathe, but he knew he would only fill his lungs with saltwater. Just when Savadkin couldn't resist any longer, he broke the surface and sucked in the cool night air.

Petty Officer 3rd Class Pete Narowanski knew the hell a submarine could inflict on a ship—and not just because he worked as a torpedoman. The twenty-six-year-old Marylander previously served on *Hugh L. Scott*, a 12,500-ton former passenger liner the Navy had converted into an attack transport. *Scott* offloaded supplies in November 1942 near Casablanca off the coast of Morocco when a German submarine penetrated its protective screen at sunset and slammed two torpedoes into its starboard side. The explosions turned wooden partitions into arrows that skewered sailors in the mess deck. Concrete used to reinforce the bridge crashed through the lower decks and one of the boilers exploded, spraying scalding steam throughout the engine room. The attack killed eight officers and fifty-one crewmen. Landing craft rescued Narowanski and other survivors before the crippled transport slipped beneath the waves.

The loss of the *Scott*, followed by a stint shoveling snow off the decks of battleship *Alabama*, prompted Narowanski to volunteer for submarines. He made two patrols on *Halibut*—that submarine's eighth and ninth—before it docked in San Francisco for a three-month overhaul and crew rest. *Halibut* arrived in Pearl Harbor just four days before *Tang* left for its fifth patrol. Narowanski learned that *Tang* planned to return to Mare Island for a refit after its next patrol. The promise of several more months in San Francisco prompted him to swap duty with one of *Tang*'s exhausted lookouts. Narowanski had counted the days until the patrol's end. He felt the familiar shudder of *Tang*'s final torpedo before he stepped out from between the tubes with an announcement for his fellow sailors. "Hot dog, course zero nine zero," he howled, his course suggestion due east. "Head her for the Golden Gate."

The torpedo explosion seconds later knocked Narowanski to the deck. The torpedoman recovered to find ten men—all equally shocked—huddled in the forward room, including the reload crew, fire controlman, torpedo officer, and chief petty officer in charge of the compartment. The sailors knew from the violent lurch that *Tang* had sustained a severe hit but did not know where or what damage the explosion had caused. The pitometer log showed *Tang* suffered an immediate loss of forward motion seconds before the stern sank. Narowanski and the others reached out for anything to grab as loose gear and men tumbled toward the rear bulkhead. The stern struck the muddy bottom. The sailors in the buoyant bow heard air rush through the main ballast tank blowers and suspected survivors in the control room hoped to blow *Tang* to the surface. But the flooded stern refused to budge.

Sailors sealed the watertight door that divided the forward torpedo room from officers' country. The man on the sound-powered phones tried unsuccessfully to raise other compartments while another sailor triggered the emergency lights. The bow plane rigging and tilting motor ran uncontrollably, burning out ten minutes later. The men debated an escape through the empty torpedo tubes, but decided against it for fear the Japanese destroyers might shell the bow. They chose to wait and use the escape chamber. Chief Petty Officer Leland Weekley, in charge of the forward room, climbed up and opened the chamber's lower hatch. "Since it was quite possible the conning tower might be flooded and we were sure the after torpedo room was, that left only the forward torpedo room for escape purposes," one survivor recalled. "Therefore, we couldn't escape without waiting for everyone left alive to get to the forward room."

The torpedo's ferocious detonation moved Petty Officer 3rd Class Clay Decker less than four inches. The twenty-three-year-old motor machinist, seated on a bench with the bow plane operating wheel right in front of him and a bulkhead behind, gripped the steel wheel the second of impact. The married father of a two-year-old son, Decker had served on board *Tang* since its commissioning almost a year earlier. The Navy figured since Decker had once worked in a mine—a job no one with claustrophobia could stomach—that he would be a perfect fit for submarines.

Decker surveyed the control room. He had escaped injury, but others around him had not. He counted at least two men who had plummeted through the control room hatch, each suffering broken limbs. The sharp metal edges of various pumps, equipment, and the chart table had sliced open others, including chief of the boat Bill Ballinger, who bled from a head wound. But the watertight hatch that led to the conning tower presented a greater concern. A hunk of wood tied to a lanyard used to pull the hatch closed had gotten wedged in the rubber gasket, preventing the men from sealing it. Seawater from the flooded conning tower rained down, frying the lighting motor generators and forcing the men to rely on the faint glow of emergency lights that fed off the batteries. Survivors would have no choice but to leave—and soon.

Tang's shredded stern sat on the seafloor off the Formosa Strait some 180 feet underwater. The air-filled bow still jutted like a knife blade as much as twenty-five feet above the dark seas. Decker and the other roughly fourteen survivors in the control room could hear the waves slosh against the exposed bow, an easy target for the Japanese escorts that by now no doubt were hunting *Tang*. Naval engineers had designed the submarine with two escape hatches, one in the after torpedo room, the other in the forward torpedo room. The survivors in the control room knew, based on the sinking of the stern, that the after torpedo room had flooded. The forward torpedo room— two compartments away—offered their only hope.

Tang's sharp forty-degree angle from stern to bow meant survivors faced an uphill climb, a tough task for men with broken limbs. The steel doors that divided the compartments would further complicate the climb. The doors closed forward to aft, meaning survivors would have to fight gravity to push them open, a job Decker figured would require the use of a hydraulic jack. The injured Ballinger muttered to Decker that the men had only one option: level the boat. If the flooded stern couldn't float, Decker would have to sink the bow, a task that required releasing the air from the main ballast tanks. Because the explosion had knocked out the hydraulic power, Decker would have to do it manually. He spied a large lever in the overhead that would allow him to manually open the vent valves for the ballast tanks. Decker crawled up on the chart table, removed a pin, and wrapped his legs around the lever to give him added strength. He pulled. The valves yawned open and air bubbled out. Seawater flooded the tanks, pulling *Tang*'s bow beneath the waves for the last time.

Injured sailors moaned. The able-bodied men untangled a pile of wounded at the bottom of the conning tower ladder and loaded them into blankets that could double as stretchers. Assuming all the sailors aft of the control room had died—either from the explosion or by drowning—the survivors set out for the forward torpedo room, carrying the injured along the narrow passageway into officers' country. There the sailors found communications officer Mel Enos, his head still bleeding from several deep gashes, in the skipper's cabin, struggling to torch *Tang*'s codebooks in a wastebasket. "Mr. Enos, you can't do that! We need every bit of air we've got," Decker told the officer, snatching the codebooks from his grip. "Besides, the batteries are right below us—you can't have any sort of spark near them!"

"But we have to destroy the codebooks," replied Enos, refusing to budge from Navy protocol.

"Stuff 'em in the batteries," barked Ballinger.

Decker yanked open a hatch in the deck and dropped down inside the forward battery well that held half of *Tang*'s 252 cells. He popped the top of one of the battery cells and dumped the codebooks in the sulfuric acid. Decker hopped out and the survivors continued on to the forward torpedo

Silversides slices through the waves off California's Mare Island Navy Yard on August 21, 1944. *U.S. Navy*

Silversides sailors rush to reload and fire the deck gun during a surface battle while on patrol in 1942. *U.S. Navy*

A Japanese picket vessel, a victim of *Silversides*, burns in 1942, as viewed through the submarine's periscope. *U.S. Navy*

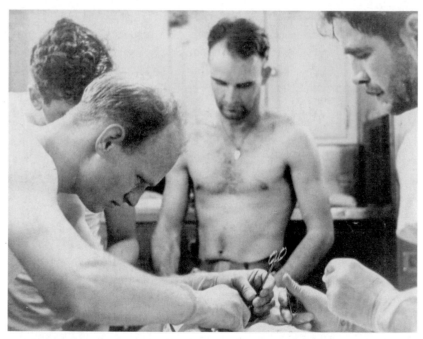

Pharmacist's Mate 1st Class Thomas Moore removes Petty Officer 3rd Class George Platter's appendix on *Silverside's* wardroom table in an emergency surgery at sea on December 22–23, 1942. *U.S. Navy*

Petty Officer 1st Class Cornell Scanlan, Seaman 1st Class Thomas Burke, Petty Officer 2nd Class Robert Vehmeier, and Chief Petty Officer Floyd Hoaglin play records in the crew's mess. *U.S. Navy*

Silversides skippers Jack Coye (left) and Creed Burlingame. The two skippers combined sank twenty-two confirmed ships. *Photo courtesy of John Bienia*

Lieutenant Eugene Malone stands watch on the bridge as *Silversides* departs for its tenth war patrol. *U.S. Navy*

Silversides officers on the seventh patrol. Top row, left to right: Lieutenant Tom Keegan, Lieutenant Bob Worthington, and Ensign Andrew Smiley. Bottom row: Lieutenant John Bienia, Lieutenant Keith Nichols, Lieutenant Commander Jack Coye, Lieutenant Commander Cyrus Cole, and Lieutenant j.g. Eugene Malone. *U.S. Navy*

Drum officers and crew display a life ring from the freighter *Oyama Maru*, sunk on *Drum*'s fifth patrol, after *Drum*'s return to port on May 13, 1943. Top row, left to right: Chief Petty Officer Dock Eller, Lieutenant Mike Rindskopf, Lieutenant John Harper, Chief Petty Officer Audly Crowe, and Chief Petty Officer Kenneth Armstrong. Bottom row: Chief Petty Officer Joseph Ryan, Petty Officer 1st Class Donald Vaughn, Petty Officer 2nd Class Jack Rich, and Petty Officer 1st Class Clarence Pyle. *National Archives*

Enemy sailors, victims of an attack by *Drum,* cling to debris. *National Archives*

Executive officer Lieutenant Dick O'Kane (left) chats on the bridge of *Wahoo* with his friend and mentor, Lieutenant Commander Dudley "Mush" Morton, around February 1943. *U.S. Navy*

Wahoo sends the cargo ship *Nittsu Maru* to the bottom on March 21, 1943. *U.S. Navy*

Downed aviators crowd the wings of Lieutenant j.g. John Burns's Kingfisher floatplane off Truk on May 1, 1944. *National Archives*

Tang sailors would rescue a total of twenty-two downed aviators off the Japanese stronghold of Truk on April 30 and May 1. *U.S. Navy*

Emaciated prisoners of war, many of whom suffered malnutrition and nutritional diseases, gather belongings and prepare to depart prisoner of war camp Omori. *National Archives*

Excited Allied POWs
at camp Omori greet
American rescuers
on August 29, 1945.
U.S. Navy

President Harry Truman congratulates *Tang* skipper Dick O'Kane on the White House
lawn following his presentation of the Medal of Honor on March 27, 1946. *U.S. Navy*

room, reaching the compartment at least fifteen minutes after the torpedo hit. The explosion had ruptured the high-pressure air lines to the forward torpedo room, meaning a great difference in pressure existed between the two compartments. Opening the doors and equalizing that pressure could prove dangerous. Survivors had no choice but to unseal the watertight door, a move that seconds later sent them airborne. "There was such a difference in air pressure between the compartments," recalled one survivor, "that it literally blew the men into the forward room."

Petty Officer 2nd Class Jesse DaSilva had spent much of the night in the after engine room, manning the sound-powered phones. The nineteen-year-old Los Angeles native—and son of a Portuguese immigrant from the Azores—needed a cup of coffee. DaSilva reached the crew's mess to find two friends perched on a nearby bunk, one listening to the final attack unfolding over headphones and relating the details to the other. DaSilva joined them. *Tang* fired its twenty-third torpedo followed a few seconds later by its last, the familiar vibration signaling the end of another productive patrol. The men waited for the news that *Tang* would be heading home. Instead the sailor on the phones reported the skipper had ordered all ahead emergency. An explosion seconds later whipped the ship "like a giant fish grabbed by the tail," forcing DaSilva to cling to the ladder under the after battery hatch. "My God," he cried. "What happened?"

Sailors inside the half-flooded forward engine room struggled to dog-down the watertight hatch that led to the after engine room. That would prevent the rest of the submarine from flooding but guaranteed that any survivors trapped inside the stern compartments would die. Water poured through the open door that ran from the control room into the crew's mess, cutting off any escape. DaSilva felt certain he would drown in the same compartment where for the last three patrols he had swapped stories over dinners of chicken, canned vegetables, and fruit. He wondered how long it would take. The cold water that climbed his legs triggered DaSilva's survival instincts. The men needed to seal the door. DaSilva and several sailors seized the door and tried to force it shut. Seawater pushed back. The sailors heaved, fighting against the torrent. The rush of water slowed and finally stopped as the door clanged shut.

Some twenty men now gathered in the crew quarters and mess, a dangerous place to loiter in a flooded submarine. Just beneath the steel deck sat 126 battery cells, each made of lead plates submerged in a water and sulfuric acid solution. Saltwater was a critical threat to the batteries, a fact hammered into sailors in submarine school. Seawater mixed with sulfuric acid created chlorine gas, a yellow-green fog that filled a victim's lungs with fluid and drowned him. The poisonous gas was so deadly that the Germans killed hundreds—if not thousands—of French soldiers in minutes during the spring of 1915 in what is widely considered the first significant use of weaponized gas. "We knew we couldn't stay here," DaSilva said. "This meant opening the control room door and for all we knew, it might be flooded. Yet, we had to risk it."

Water had indeed flooded the control room up to the eye port in the door. The trapped sailors tested the bulkhead flappers in the ventilation piping above and discovered the water had not yet climbed that high. A good sign. Opening the door would let the water disperse throughout the two compartments—lowering the overall level—and allow the men to trudge through the control room toward the forward torpedo room. DaSilva decided to divert the water further. He yanked open the deck hatch that led to the voluminous refrigerator and freezer space beneath the crew mess; no one planned to stay on board long enough to need the food. To avoid the flood of water, sailors scrambled atop the four rectangular tables. One of the men cracked the door. Seawater again charged inside. The men waited as the water climbed ankle deep. The force of the water soon dissipated and the surge slowed, leveling off at DaSilva's knees.

The men sloshed one after the other into the control room. DaSilva eyed the depth gauge and saw it read 180 feet. The bottom of the Formosa Strait. He knew his only chance of survival hinged on reaching the forward torpedo room and the escape chamber. One of the officers demanded the sailors stop and destroy secret equipment and records, an order DaSilva privately questioned. He doubted the Japanese—now struggling against American advances across the Pacific—would ever recover *Tang*. The anxious sailors obeyed, smashing the radar and radio equipment with rifle butts, then waded forward, passing from the control room into officers' country, the wardroom on the left, the skipper's stateroom on the right. Smoke filled the narrow passageway. One of the officers again ordered the men to stop and torch classified papers before resuming the trip, the path forward illuminated by faint emergency lights.

The last of the survivors reached the sealed forward torpedo room almost an hour after *Tang* sank. The escape chambers—the only hope for survival—sat just a few feet behind the sealed door. Torpedoman Petty Officer 2nd Class Hayes Trukke and Rubin Raiford, one of *Tang*'s black stewards, feared a repeat of what happened when the first group of survivors opened the door. With the voice communication system fried, men tapped out a warning to crack the door. That would allow the pressure to equalize. Survivors outside failed to understand. Were the men in the forward room deliberately keeping them out? Tension and fear escalated as sailors pushed the door. That raw force coupled with tremendous air pressure rammed the door open. Trukke looked in horror as Raiford dropped. "It struck the negro in the face," Trukke recalled. "His lips were smashed, nose pushed over to one side and eyes closed."

O'Kane treaded water in the cold. As the seas charged up the stern and washed him overboard, the skipper had taken small consolation in watching the *Matsumoto Maru* explode, the victim of his twenty-third torpedo. His heart went out to the men trapped inside *Tang* and to the eight lookouts and bridge personnel topside who, like him, now faced the sea alone. He watched for the first few minutes after *Tang*'s stern sank as the bow swayed in the current, reminding him of a buoy anchored in a seaway. O'Kane tried to swim to *Tang*, but the strong current coupled with the depth charges kept him back. "She appeared to be struggling like a great wounded animal, a leviathan, as indeed she was," he wrote. "*Tang*'s bow suddenly plunged on down to Davy Jones's locker, and the lonely seas seemed to share in my total grief."

O'Kane grabbed hold of what resembled a wooden door that likely had blown off a Japanese ship and used it as a makeshift floatation. The skipper, once caught between the timid Pinky Kennedy and the aggressive Mush Morton, had embraced the latter, following Morton's creed to pursue the Japanese at all costs. That advice had paid off. In just nine months, O'Kane had sunk twenty-four confirmed ships, a tally that would make him the greatest skipper of the war by the number of ships destroyed. He had won praise, fame, and a place in history, but he now shared Morton's tragic fate, albeit not at the hands of the enemy, but his own malfunctioning weapon. Morton had at least died with his men. O'Kane would have to live with killing his.

If he survived.

Larry Savadkin bobbed in the cold water, cut off from his skipper. When he surfaced after his sixty-foot ascent from the flooded conning tower, he spotted *Tang*'s bow jutting above the waves. The former college athlete swam for it but found the current too much. He gave up and floated, hoping to conserve energy. Savadkin's waterlogged clothes weighed him down so he slipped off his shirt, socks, and long pants, tying them around his waist as he drifted in his skivvies. Somewhere in his desperate ascent, he had lost his watch. A small price to pay. The cold water forced him to shiver uncontrollably and made him swallow some saltwater. "I felt alone—screamed bloody murder—no answer," he recalled. "I got the impression that I was the only person who had gotten off the boat."

The engineering officer collected himself and focused on survival. He remembered his submarine school training. Savadkin removed his trousers from around his waist, tied the ends, and inflated them, creating a makeshift lifebelt. To his surprise, the trick worked, though he had to reinflate them every fifteen minutes. Then he remembered an island about ten miles away. Savadkin tried to swim for it, using the stars to head west, but he struggled to navigate and gave up. He hoped he could stay afloat until dawn and try again in the daylight. Savadkin alternated between his back and stomach. Japanese patrols hunted for *Tang* in the dark waters, sporadically dropping depth charges. He felt the first explosion rumble through the seas, but learned to arch his back when the bombs exploded.

Bill Leibold broke the surface moments after *Tang* sank. Like Savadkin, he, too, disrobed. The boatswain's mate dropped his 7x50 binoculars and kicked off his shoes and heavy submarine coat. He slipped off his trousers, tied the ends, and tried unsuccessfully to inflate them, eventually letting them drop beneath the waves. Then he heard Petty Officer 3rd Class Darrell Dean Rector, the gunner's mate who had survived the first successful appendectomy operation on a submarine, call out in the darkness. He heard quartermaster Sidney Jones, too. Others had made it off the bridge. The men drifted. The voices grew faint and eventually stopped. Leibold treaded water in the cold, the only landmark the bow of a sunken enemy ship that rose above the waves.

Radarman Floyd Caverly had seen only one other sailor since *Tang*'s sinking. Lieutenant j.g. John Heubeck swam past him, pausing just long enough to ask if Caverly knew the direction toward land. "Straight down about 180 feet," replied Caverly. The radarman watched Heubeck swim away, never to be seen again. Hours slipped past before he heard splashing. He looked up to see Leibold swimming toward him. The men felt relief to have one another as company. Caverly had been floating on his back, swallowing water each time a wave broke over him. Leibold instructed him to time his breathing with the motion of the waves. Caverly returned the favor by sharing a trick of his own to keep warm: turn into the current and urinate.

About forty-five sailors crowded in *Tang*'s forward torpedo room at 3:30 a.m., roughly one hour after the sinking. The men remained upbeat, despite the circumstances. The last radar bearing showed that *Tang* had gone down just a few miles from shore and most felt the chances of reaching the surface and swimming it were good. Sailors parceled out the scant few life preservers. Others grabbed Momsen lungs: the escape devices strapped on much like life preservers. The four-liter rubberized bag, complete with a nose clip and mouthpiece, allowed sailors to breathe recycled air, filtered through a can of soda lime to remove excess carbon dioxide. The men reviewed how to operate the lung: more than half had long since forgotten.

The Japanese escorts still prowled above, hunting the wounded *Tang*. A barrage of about ten depth charges rattled the boat, but caused no damage. The sailors below, who had prepared to escape, froze and waited, sitting silently in the glow of the emergency lights. Smoke and fumes generated from the torched documents made the air thick. The heat and humidity in the overcrowded compartment climbed, coupled with higher than normal air pressure that added to the discomfort. Minutes turned to hours. When the Japanese patrols departed sometime close to dawn, Mel Enos decided the men should attempt to blow the water from the tanks and flooded compartments, a move that would refloat *Tang* and make it easier and faster for them to escape. The lieutenant organized a party of six men to trudge back to the control room.

The men cracked the sealed door. Black acrid smoke from an electrical fire in the neighboring compartment poured into the torpedo room. The men immediately slammed the door, but not before thick fumes penetrated the compartment. The smoke slashed visibility so that even the emergency lights appeared only as a dim glow in the haze that stank of torched rubber, an indication that the batteries now burned. Some of the sailors—throats burning—gagged and choked. Desperate for fresh air, men slipped on Momsen lungs, using them as makeshift respirators. The fire now trapped the almost four dozen survivors in the crowded forward torpedo room. All options to salvage

Tang had vanished. The men had no choice but to slip on lungs, climb up into the escape chamber, and swim some 180 feet to the surface.

The men decided an officer should lead the first escape. Enos volunteered, accompanied by chief of the boat Ballinger and Petty Officer 1st Class John Fluker, a torpedoman. The threesome strapped on lungs—Enos also report-edly grabbed a couple of pistols and a bayonet—and climbed up into the cylindrical chamber mounted in the overhead at about 6 a.m., some three and a half hours after *Tang* sank. The sailors below then handed up a rubber lifeboat. If any of the crew escaped, the men would need it. Once sealed inside the chamber, the sailors would flood it with seawater and pressurized air. The men would then open the side door, release a buoy attached to an ascending line, and head to the surface. The last man out would tap an alert to the men below that all had left. A lever in the torpedo room allowed the sailors there to close the side door and drain the chamber so another party could enter.

Enos and his party crowded inside the chamber, just large enough for four men. The men squabbled over how to operate the chamber before success-fully flooding it with water. The sailors opened the side door, but struggled to attach a rope to the buoy that would allow them to ascend hand over hand to the surface. Just below the chamber in the forward torpedo room, anxious sailors waited for the signal. Thirty minutes passed with no word. Inside the chamber, Enos grew frustrated. He gave up waiting on the buoy and dove out alone into the cold water. No one would ever see him again. The men below waited ten more minutes, then finally pulled the lever that closed the cham-ber door and drained the tank. Sailors unsealed the hatch and found Ballinger and Fluker still inside. The latter climbed down and announced that he would not try again.

Ballinger did, but this time without the bulky lifeboat that crowded the chamber. Torpedo officer Lieutenant j.g. Hank Flanagan climbed inside along with Leland Weekley, the chief in charge of the forward room. Ballinger asked for volunteers. Clay Decker knew the chief of the boat had survived a half dozen patrols on the submarine *Tunny* before he made all five runs on the *Tang*. If anyone knew what to do, Decker figured, it had to be Ballinger. He would ride the chief's coattails. Decker turned to his close friend, twenty-four-year-old Petty Officer 1st Class George Zofcin. The two men's wives and young sons had shared a small house on a hill at 67 Stoneyford Avenue in San Francisco while Decker and Zofcin roomed together between patrols at the Royal Hawaiian. Zofcin helped Decker strap on his Momsen lung. Decker reciprocated.

"You go ahead and go with this wave," Zofcin told his friend.

"Why, George?" Decker replied. "Come on, go with us."

"No."

"Why?"

"I have a confession to make."

A confession, Decker thought, what the hell? The men had to get off the boat.

"Clay," his friend said. "I can't swim."

Zofcin's confession stunned Decker, who told his friend he didn't need to know how to swim. He could use his lung as a life preserver when he reached the surface.

"You go ahead," Zofcin told him. "I'll come up with the next wave."

Decker climbed up into the chamber, carrying a shark knife and a pistol and bullets. One of *Tang*'s young ensigns took Zofcin's place. Ballinger handed the escape buoy to Decker. He told him to let it out when the men opened the door, careful to count each knot that slipped through his hands. Tied every six feet—one-fathom intervals—the knots functioned like a rudimentary depth gauge. The men flooded the chamber up to their armpits and opened the door. Decker released the buoy. He counted ten knots, then fifteen, followed by twenty. The knots still passed through his hands. When he reached thirty, he felt the rope jerk. The buoy had broken the surface and bobbed on the waves. Decker tied the rope to the top rung of the ladder, using several knots to make sure it didn't come undone.

One hundred and eighty feet of dark water stood between Decker and survival. The motor machinist wrapped his arms and legs around the line and started up, his hands running along the rope. He wanted to let go and kick for the surface, but held himself back. Decker remembered from his training that he had to pause at each knot to exhale and inhale to equalize the pressure in his lungs. He watched the air bubbles he released race past him toward the surface somewhere above. Decker ascended, the rope slipping through his hands, the surface just striking distance away. He popped through the waves into the morning light. He unclipped his nose clamp only to find blood in his hand. He wiped his cheek and found it also bled. The pressure change had popped blood vessels in his cheek and nose.

Decker spit out the mouthpiece before he remembered to reach down and turn the valve. The Momsen lung flooded with seawater, making it worthless as a life preserver. He slipped it off and held the soccer ball–sized buoy, still tethered to the stricken submarine on the seafloor. He could feel the heavy tide trying to pull him out to sea. When Ballinger broke the surface moments later, Decker stared in horror. Blood poured from his face. The chief of the boat screamed and vomited. He thrashed in the water just a few feet away. Decker started to reach out for him, but something told him to stop. Ballinger would pull him down and drown them both. The men locked eyes. "I could hear him screaming," recalled Decker, the last man to see the chief alive. "He was flowing with the tide then. It just carried him on out to sea."

Inside the torpedo room, time inched past. The men grew worried. Forty minutes had elapsed with still no signal. Moans emanated from the chamber. The sailors pulled the lever to close the escape door and drain it. Men unsealed the hatch and found Flanagan and the ensign inside. Weekley had escaped like Decker and Ballinger but would never be seen again. Flanagan had become tangled in the unused ascending line, forcing the sailors to cut him loose and lower him to the deck below wrapped in blankets. The ensign floated in and out of consciousness, likely the result of his inability to withstand the high partial pressures and increased carbon dioxide. The young officer regained consciousness and announced that he would not attempt another escape, but said there was no reason why the other sailors shouldn't try.

Depth charges once again rattled the submarine, forcing the men to halt their escape. Morale began to plummet. Escape proved far more difficult than many had envisioned. The heat and humidity inside the crowded torpedo room climbed as the smoke-and-carbon-dioxide-filled atmosphere deteriorated, sapping the energy and motivation of many sailors. The confidence and enthusiasm most felt only hours earlier faded. Some men stretched out on the bunks; others ignored protocol and chatted even as enemy patrols circled above. Defeat settled over the room. Some of the sailors bordered on unconsciousness. "Many of the men did not care whether they escaped or not," recalled one survivor. "The constantly increasing pressure, smoke, and heat seemed to affect everyone's thinking."

Hayes Trukke refused to die on the *Tang*. The exhausted torpedoman climbed up into the chamber to lead a third escape attempt. Torpedoman Pete Narowanski and another motor machinist joined him. Even torpedoman Fluker rallied and crawled up through the hatch, ready, finally, to try again. The sailors worried that the effort to free Flanagan from the tangled line might have cut the buoy loose, prompting them to grab a life ring salvaged from the freighter *Yamaoka Maru*, sunk on *Tang*'s third patrol. The men sealed the hatch and flooded the chamber. Trukke tried the door, but found it jammed. The men pushed and it finally opened. The torpedoman then attempted to fill his Momsen lung from the air manifold only to discover there was no oxygen.

Trukke explained that the men could breathe into the lungs to inflate them, but his reasoning failed to assuage the fear that gripped the others. The oxygen-starved torpedoman began to feel light-headed and confused. He knew he teetered on passing out as he struggled to rig the buoy as a lifeline. His motor skills and thought process slowed. Fifteen minutes ticked past. Trukke had planned to release the life ring, let it float to the surface, then rise up the line, just as he would have done on the rescue buoy. But in his groggy haze, he stumbled out of the hatch, still clutching the life ring. "I felt very exhausted—like I couldn't get any oxygen into my lungs and began to get dizzy, so I knew I had better get out while I could," Trukke recalled. "The other men in the trunk would have escaped if only they had stepped out."

The buoyant life ring shot toward the surface with Trukke in tow. He had gone up only about twenty feet when he felt the line jerk. Narowanski tugged the rope to slow Trukke's ascent so he could equalize the pressure in his lungs. But the jerking caused Trukke to lose his Momsen lung, forcing him to blow out his air as he rode the ring up, his sandals lost somewhere in the furious ascent. Trukke broke the surface exhausted and sick. He vomited for much of the next half hour. The torpedoman heard Decker call out to him. Trukke spotted the motor machinist clinging to the rescue buoy about fifty yards away. He paddled over and the men tied the buoys together. The morning light illuminated the coast in the distance as well as what appeared to be the masts of two sunken ships and the bow of *Tang*'s final victim jutting above the water.

The three men inside the escape chamber climbed down into the torpedo room to find that conditions had worsened. The fire in the adjacent compartment raged with such ferocity that the paint on the torpedo room bulkhead had melted and had begun to run down the wall. Increased air pressure seeped into the room through the drain in the sink. Sailors tried to stop the intrusion with wooden plugs from the depth charge kits. Not only did sailors battle extreme heat and humidity but Navy calculations would later show that after only four hours—by about 6:30 a.m.—carbon dioxide had reached a poisonous level. Only those men driven to save themselves now worked. Others lay in the bunks or on the deck resigned to die. Conversation that had earlier focused on escape and survival turned toward family and loved ones.

Fluker and the motor machinist decided not to attempt another escape, but Narowanski refused to give up. He had come too close to quit. The exhausted Flanagan, who had gotten tangled in the ascending line, joined him. DaSilva worked his way over toward the ladder that led up into the escape chamber. The emergency lights in the compartment faded as the batteries died, forcing the men to switch on battle lanterns. The four-man chamber had room enough for two more men. DaSilva urged his close friend Petty Officer 2nd Class Glen Haws to go with him. Unlike the young and unwed DaSilva, Haws had a wife and a son he had never seen, born while *Tang* was at sea on its fifth patrol. "He had everything to live for," DaSilva later recalled. "I had nothing."

"We need somebody else," Flanagan called down.

"Hell," DaSilva said. "I'm not afraid."

The motor machinist's mate scrambled up the ladder. DaSilva called down to Haws to join them, but he again refused. Another sailor stepped forward and climbed up in his place. DaSilva shot a glance at the clock on the bulkhead and saw it was 8 a.m., six and a half hours after *Tang* had sunk. The men closed the hatch and flooded the trunk. DaSilva felt the air pressure increase, making the men's voices sound high. When the water reached the top of the side door, the men tested the Momsen lungs and opened the hatch, finding the buoy line still attached. Narowanski went first, dressed just in his swim shorts. Flanagan followed three minutes later. DaSilva waited the same, then wrapped his arms and legs around the rope and rose up ten feet, pausing long enough to count to ten. He repeated the process, watching as the water around him lightened.

DaSilva broke the surface to find Decker, Trukke, Narowanski, and Flanagan clinging to the buoy. Narowanski dry heaved, but DaSilva felt fine. The sun climbed in the morning sky. Two Japanese escorts swept the water between the buoy and the coast. Pharmacist's mate Larson, who had cared for the injured in the torpedo room, popped to the surface about an hour later. DaSilva watched as he spit up blood and appeared to choke. One of the survivors held Larson's head above water. Rubin Raiford, the injured mess steward, surfaced some fifty feet away. He flailed for a few seconds, then slipped beneath the water. DaSilva swam to help him, but he had disappeared. "He drowned while we watched him, floating away with his head just under the surface of the water," recalled a survivor. "None of us could possibly have reached him."

Leibold and Caverly watched a Japanese escort approach, picking up survivors from the ships *Tang* had torpedoed the night before. Leibold didn't believe the lookouts had spotted them and urged the men to swim toward the Chinese coast rather than let the Japanese take them prisoner, but the exhausted Caverly feared he couldn't make it. The escort lowered a whaleboat and sailors rowed toward the survivors, tossing them a rescue line. The time to escape had passed. After almost eight hours in the frigid water, Caverly was so weak the rope slipped from his swollen hands. The sailors hauled him and Leibold on board and started back before spotting another survivor. The men recognized O'Kane, clinging to what resembled a wooden door. Leibold reached down to help his skipper. "Good morning, Captain," he said. "Do you want a ride?"

Leibold instantly regretted his comment. The Japanese didn't understand much English—the sailors repeatedly asked if Leibold and Caverly were "Deutsche"—but instantly recognized the word "captain." The skipper of an enemy ship would be a prized intelligence asset. The Japanese singled out O'Kane, forcing him to sit near the stern as the whaleboat returned to the escort, its hull marked *P-34*. Caverly spotted a watch on one sailor's arm when the men disembarked. The radarman turned the man's wrist and read the 10:30 a.m. time—eight hours after *Tang* had sunk—only to have the sailor punch Caverly in the face. The Japanese tied up the prisoners, hauled them to the port side of the main deck, and sat them down in the hot sun. Larry Savadkin soon joined them.

The six *Tang* sailors who clung to the rescue buoy watched a Japanese escort circle them with its guns manned. The survivors could not mount a defense. Decker and the others who had escaped from the *Tang* with pistols, ammunition, and shark knives stuffed in their pockets had long since abandoned the cumbersome weapons along with their waterlogged shirts, shoes, and pants. Most now floated in little more than their underwear. The struggle to survive against the horrific conditions below coupled with the grueling escape had left them all exhausted and sick. The patrol circled a second and third time, then stopped. The gunners turned the weapons on the survivors in the water. "Well this is it," DaSilva thought to himself. "They're going to shoot us."

The Japanese instead lowered a whaleboat with five sailors, who rowed out to retrieve the last of the *Tang*'s men, ushering them with rifles to the boat's stern. One of the Japanese sailors tried to retrieve the buoy, failing to realize that it was anchored to a submarine on the bottom. No one volunteered to explain. Pharmacist's mate Larson stopped breathing as the whaleboat pulled alongside the escort, the likely result of a pulmonary embolism. He lay in the bottom of the boat, his face blue. The Japanese forced the other survivors to climb aboard while the men slapped and kicked Larson to revive him before lifting him on deck. The *Tang* crew pleaded to help Larson, who at one point appeared to stir and rise up, but the Japanese refused. When Leibold later asked about Larson's fate, a guard motioned that he had been tossed overboard.

The five survivors from the life buoy joined the other four *Tang* sailors as prisoners on board the escort *P-34*. Nine men were all that remained of a crew of eighty-seven. By the time the Japanese off-loaded the last survivors from the whaleboat, it is probable that every man still on board the *Tang* had died.

The Japanese of *P-34* took no chances with the *Tang* survivors—not that the exhausted men posed any threat. The captors tied each man's biceps to his chest, then lashed his wrists. Leibold tried but couldn't move either his arms or hands. The Japanese then sat all nine together on the port side of the main deck in the hot sun. "We were trussed up like a chicken," recalled Savadkin. "Then they asked us our name, our rank and the name of the vessel from which we had come. Failure to answer the questions brought severe socks on the jaw, to be perfectly blunt about it, they just hauled off and whacked us, and we decided it wouldn't hurt too much to tell them our name and what ship we were from. They also wanted to know what job we had aboard. We balked at this and they didn't press the point too much."

The men were thirsty after a long night at sea. The Japanese offered them hot seawater to drink, served in a can of Campbell's vegetable soup Trukke brought up from the *Tang*. The harassment escalated. Guards made DaSilva sing and dance while men clubbed him. The executive officer struck Caverly on the head with his samurai sword, knocking him unconscious while the crew kicked Flanagan in the ribs and kidneys and stomped on his bare feet. O'Kane's refusal to reveal the name of his submarine or answer whether others lurked in the area prompted guards to punch him in the face and thrash his back with clubs that resembled baseball bats. "O'Kane received the worst beating of us all," Caverly would later tell war crimes investigators. "They beat and kicked him from head to rump, with fist, feet and bamboo clubs."

Burned Japanese sailors covered in bandages and coated in a white salve gathered around, slapping and kicking the manacled Americans. Others shoved lit cigarettes up their nostrils, in their ears, and used the prisoners' necks to grind out butts, the pain excruciating. The skipper again drew most of the torment, his skin peppered with burns. The *Tang* survivors understood the hostility. The bandaged tormentors were survivors of the ships *Tang* had destroyed. The *Tang* men had come face-to-face with their victims. "When we realized our clubbings and kickings were being administered by the burned, mutilated survivors of our own handiwork," O'Kane would later write, "we found we could take it with less prejudice."

19

DRUM

"We did not care one way or another whether the ship sank or not as we had suffered greatly and felt that if the ship did go down, our suffering would be at an end."

—Philip Brodsky, war crimes testimony
September 5, 1946

Sergeant Calvin Graef couldn't slake his thirst on the Japanese prison ship *Arisan Maru*, which steamed through the dark toward Formosa on the night of October 23, 1944. The twenty-nine-year-old New Mexico native—one of some 1,800 prisoners on board—had endured twelve days in the ship's crammed cargo hold. Graef had watched in that time as dehydration and disease had claimed the lives of some prisoners and driven others mad. The journey threatened to break even the most hardened men, including Graef, who had survived the infamous Bataan Death March and more than 900 days in Japanese captivity. The father of a two-year-old he had never met had passed those lonely days in prison speculating about his son's birth date. Graef had settled in his mind on April 9; a day he would never forget, the fall of Bataan. Not until he received his wife's first letter shortly before *Arisan Maru* had departed—accompanied by two photographs of his son—did Graef learn he had guessed three days too early.

Graef's experience on *Arisan Maru* had only confirmed why prisoners called such freighters "hellships." The Japanese had crammed some 1,200 prisoners into bunks hammered together out of planks and stacked several high that reminded Graef more of shelves than beds. Prisoners lacked room to stretch out or even roll over. "To try and describe an allotment of space that was given per person is about like putting marbles into a bottle," he would later recall. "When there are so many marbles in the bottle, you just can't put any more in." Guards forced the remaining 600 captives down ropes into the freighter's coal hold. Prisoners rode atop piles of coal that tumbled about in the rough seas, burying the captives and forcing them to dig out. "The oil and coal dust got smeared on our bodies and caused infection. There was no way of stopping it, in the wallow of filth and dirt," recalled prisoner Donald Meyer. "The coal dust worked deeper and deeper into the lesions of these sick men until they cried and prayed to die."

Rations aboard the *Arisan Maru* consisted of less than a fistful of rice twice a day coupled with a few ounces of rust-flavored water, far less than the men needed to battle the tropical heat. Guards taunted the emaciated captives and nibbled chocolate pilfered from the Red Cross packages intended for the prisoners. "Food was lowered to us in buckets, and no attempt was made by the Japs to ration or apportion the food," recalled prisoner Philip Brodsky. "If you wanted any, you had to get there fast." A handful of five-gallon cans served as latrines—emptied only once a day at night—but in the overcrowded quarters few ventured to find them, a wending journey through the throngs of prisoners that could take up to two hours. Many of the sick, suffering from malaria, dysentery, and pneumonia, defecated on themselves, the feces and blood dripped between bunks. "We waded in fecal matter," Graef would write. "Most of the men went naked. The place was alive with lice, bedbugs, and roaches."

Conditions had deteriorated soon after the 448-foot-long freighter had departed Manila's Pier 7 on the afternoon of October 11 amid air strikes in advance of MacArthur's return. The ship steamed south and anchored in a sheltered bay, a move prisoners presumed was devised to wait out the attacks. The days at sea had provided a breeze that vanished once the ship anchored. Temperatures soared during the day as the sun beat down on the steel decks. The sun-side bulkhead grew too hot even to touch. Heat blistered the prisoners, turning skin the texture of raw hamburger. Tempers flared and fights broke out. Others suffered breakdowns or sank into lethargy. "If you fell down," Graef recalled, "you just suffocated." Many did, their bodies tossed overboard. "While men were dying of thirst, Jap guards—heaping insults upon us—would empty five gallon tins of fresh water into the hold," Graef later wrote. "Men caught the water in pieces of clothing and sucked the cloth dry. Men licked their wet skin."

The horror Graef endured on *Arisan Maru* proved all too common. Japan's conquests had netted thousands of prisoners, many of whom now cleared jungles, toiled in factories, and shoveled coal. Crammed and filthy hellships throughout the war would shuttle by some estimates more than 126,000 prisoners around the empire. Absent the wooden hulls and canvas sails, these modern slave ships were little different from their centuries-old ancestors. In the bowels of one such ship that had just unloaded horses, prisoners crowded atop hay soaked with urine and sticky with manure. Emaciated captives picked through the soiled hay beneath a swarm of blowflies to scavenge seeds left over from the millet the Japanese fed the horses. When temperatures topped 120 degrees below deck on another ship, men drank urine while others slashed fellow prisoners for a taste of blood. Some went mad, as described by one former prisoner: "As a guy goes crazy he starts to scream—not like a woman, more like the howl of a dog."

The 6,886-ton *Arisan Maru*, much to the relief of the prisoners, had returned to Manila once the air strikes ended. In the days since Graeff had first boarded the hellship, the harbor had been transformed. Sunken ships littered the waters. Graef hoped what he saw proved the Japanese equivalent of Pearl Harbor. But he would have to wait and wonder. *Arisan Maru* remained in port only long enough for crews to load bananas, sugar, rice, and water before the freighter departed again just before midnight on October 20 as part of a large convoy of ships that the Japanese hoped to move beyond the reach of American fighters and bombers. Twelve ships steamed north toward Formosa's port city of Takao, hauling everything from raw rubber and manganese to aviation fuel. Five escorts guarded convoy MATA-30, including three destroyers, a fleet supply ship, and a submarine chaser. With a top speed of just seven knots *Arisan Maru* set the convoy's slow pace through waters infested with American submarines.

Graef and other captives understood the danger the *Arisan Maru* faced at sea because the Japanese refused to mark such freighters as prisoner of war ships, forgoing the illuminated crosses typically used to denote hospital ships. Through a bombardier's eyepiece or a skipper's periscope, *Arisan Maru* looked no different from any other cargo ship that might otherwise haul coal, bauxite, or iron ore. Attacks on prisoner ships had occurred throughout the war.

But the concentration of American carrier forces and submarines in waters close to Japan—coupled with the enemy's harried effort to evacuate prisoners ahead of Allied advances—saw those numbers reach a crescendo in September, killing by some estimates up to 9,000 POWs, almost half of the war's total of 21,000. *Sealion* had torpedoed the 9,418-ton *Rakuyo Maru* September 12 off the coast of Luzon. Of the 1,318 Allied prisoners—most former laborers on the infamous Burma Railway—only 159 men survived. North of Subic Bay just nine days later, Allied bombers obliterated the *Hofuku Maru*, killing more than a thousand Dutch and British prisoners.

But the worst such attack had occurred just twenty-three days before *Arisan Maru* set sail. That afternoon the 5,065-ton *Junyo Maru* steamed from Java to Sumatra with 2,200 Allied and Indonesian prisoners along with another 4,320 Javanese slave laborers. The British submarine *Tradewind* picked up a plume of smoke on the horizon, chased down *Junyo Maru*, and fired four torpedoes. Explosions rocked the ship. The bow rose up out of the sea so that the crippled ship appeared to stand upright, like a skyscraper. Prisoners in the water spied two twenty-five-foot holes in the ship's steel side. Others saw men, trapped on the bow, plummet toward the bridge. Against the backdrop of a fiery sunset, *Junyo Maru* dove beneath the waves, taking with it 5,640 Allied prisoners and Javanese conscripts.

As the misery below deck on *Arisan Maru* increased en route toward Formosa, Graef noted, many of the prisoners crowded around him now prayed aloud to meet a similar fate.

"If the Navy would sink us we'd—"

"Come on, Navy!" begged others.

Maurice Rindskopf scanned the dark horizon for convoy MATA-30 on the night of October 23. *Drum*'s radarman had detected the seven-knot convoy at sunset at a distance of almost fifteen miles. The skipper had ordered his men to start the hunt. Rindskopf needed a good target. He had been at sea for forty-five days and had yet to fire a single torpedo. He may have been the youngest skipper in the Pacific, but he knew the Navy demanded that he perform just as well as his older colleagues. Rindskopf had fared well on his first patrol as skipper off Palau despite hunting in waters void of worthwhile targets. He had demonstrated his aggressiveness in blasting Refinery Point followed by his destruction of the sampan and capture of two prisoners. He felt he had made the most of the empty seas. Vice Admiral Lockwood agreed, deeming the patrol successful so as to earn the coveted combat insignia. The convoy MATA-30 that steamed through the dark ahead offered Rindskopf the promise of a much better patrol.

The war Rindskopf now fought as skipper proved far different from the one he entered as a young lieutenant junior grade in the frightful days after Pearl Harbor. America had hacked away at Japan's empire with 1944 on track to be a decisive year for the enemy. American troops had invaded Saipan in June followed by Guam and Tinian in July. Emperor Hirohito needed only to look to Germany for a glimpse of his nation's future. Allied bombers that October would drop more than two tons of explosives every minute. The importance of the Marianas was reflected not only in the 50,000 troops Japan sacrificed to defend the islands, but also in the ouster of Premier Hideki Tojo and his cabinet following the loss. More telling were the four words uttered by Fleet Admiral Osami Nagano, Hirohito's supreme naval adviser: "Hell is on us."

For the Japanese, the news only worsened.

Three days earlier American troops had hit the beaches of the Philippines accompanied by an armada of some 700 ships, the most powerful naval force yet assembled. The invasion held special importance for Douglas MacArthur, who had escaped with his wife and young son from the Philippines in a patrol torpedo boat the night of March 11, 1942. After his arrival in Australia he vowed that he would return to liberate the Pearl of the Pacific. The fall of the Philippines had haunted MacArthur, who only spoke of it in public to mark the anniversary, as he fought his way back across the Pacific. "Bataan is like a child in a family who dies," he confided in fellow officers. "It lives in our hearts." Two years, seven months, and nine days after his escape, MacArthur sloshed ashore through the knee-deep surf in an event designed for maximum press exposure. "People of the Philippines," he declared in a radio broadcast. "I have returned."

Allied victories had robbed the empire of its conquests as submarines strangled the island nation. Captured airfields coupled with increased carrier power helped tighten America's blockade, forcing Japan to abandon major sea lanes as well as some coastal routes through home island waters. Skippers like O'Kane, Coye, and Rindskopf helped slash Japan's former first-class merchant fleet by some 75 percent, from 6.6 million tons to just 1.5 million. The few vessels that remained afloat proved small and inefficient, if not inoperable. The destruction of Japan's merchant fleet halted the flow of the raw materials that fed and fueled Japan. As stockpiles of iron ore, rubber, and bauxite vanished, Japan turned to desperate measures. Workers collected scrap copper and lead, recycled cotton, and slashed the amount of nickel used in armor plating and gun barrels. With scrap aluminum totaling 80 percent of the aircraft industry's supply, engineers even experimented with wooden planes.

More than any other import, the loss of oil proved catastrophic. Japan could produce only 10 percent of the oil needed to power its fighters, tanks, and aircraft carriers, importing the rest from territories conquered in the south. America's blockade had cut Japan's imported oil from fifteen million barrels in 1943 to just five million in 1944. In the final year of the war only a handful of tankers would brave the blockade to deliver just a few thousand barrels. The Japanese would grow so desperate in 1945 that engineers would extract oil from peanuts, soy beans, and coconuts to use for industrial purposes and would convert fat and vegetable oils into lubricants. Workers built almost 40,000 small distilleries, including some on the golf courses of tony Tokyo clubs, to harvest oil from pine roots. Engineers battled gasoline shortages with substitutes of ethanol, methanol, and acetone while others converted confiscated rice, sweet potatoes, and sugar to alcohol. Even precious bottles of sake vanished from store shelves.

Few of these measures helped. While military trucks puttered around base powered by charcoal, battleships and even aircraft carriers lay at anchor, relegated to port and antiaircraft duty. Japan struggled to keep its fighters in the air, slashing gasoline quality from 92 octane to 87 as technicians modified engines to burn alcohol. Pilots who had once received 100 hours of basic training now got as little as thirty and no navigation. Fliers would follow one another into combat as mission losses soared as high as 70 percent. Fuel scarcity would force leaders to devise the kamikaze attacks. "There was no prospect of victory in the air by the employment of orthodox methods. Suicide attacks were more effective because the power of impact of the plane was added to that of the bomb," recalled Lieutenant Colonel Naomichi Jin, an air army operations staff officer. "Suicide attack was the only sure and reliable attack by airmen whose training hand been limited because of the shortage of fuel."

As Japan foundered, America strengthened. The vast Pacific gains had

opened up new fueling depots and advance bases where crews could refit submarines and sailors could unwind closer to the fight. No longer did boats need
to travel thousands of miles back to Hawaii and Australia. Saipan opened as
a fuel station at the end of July while Guam would host a submarine refit
and rest camp in November. The war moved so fast that some bases became
obsolete within months. The Australian town of Brisbane that the *Silversides*
crew so loved proved little more than a ghost town. One hundred and fifty-six
subs—an increase of thirty-three from the previous year—now operated in
the Pacific, serviced by fourteen tenders. So heavy was the concentration at
times that two submerged boats off the coast of Indochina would actually collide in February 1945. That unlikely accident seemed only to reaffirm a common expression—reported by an enemy prisoner of war—that a person could
walk from Singapore to Japan on the tops of American submarine periscopes.

One consequence of America's success: a lack of worthwhile targets, a
frustrating reality now faced by Rindskopf and other young skippers who
had waited the entire war to take command. Even mediocre captains could
earn solid records early in the war while the best of skippers in late 1944 were
left with little more to shoot at than trawlers and sampans. Postwar records
would show the devastating toll America's submarine force exacted on Japan's
merchant and naval fleets. Submarines in 1942 sank fewer than two hundred
Japanese naval and merchant ships compared to two years later when the
boats destroyed 526 merchant ships over 500 tons and 105 warships ships,
including one battleship, seven aircraft carriers, nine cruisers, and thirty-two
destroyers. But those days neared the end. By January 1945, fighters and
bombers would sink more ships than submarines as targets vanished and the
war moved from the sea to the air. Postwar records showed that many of the
warships destroyed by American submarines and planes in early 1945 were
little more than 800-ton coastal defense frigates while many merchant ships
ranged from 500 tons down to twenty-ton sampans.

Against these deteriorating odds, Rindskopf felt pressure to succeed. He
knew the rest of his career would hinge on the record he produced now.
Command of a wartime submarine alone would not guarantee future promo-
tions and success. He needed to demonstrate that he was a competent, determined, and aggressive fighter. The Navy quantified such attributes one way:
ships on the bottom. *Drum*'s eleventh patrol so far had not offered Rindskopf
a chance to seal his future. He had just missed an opportunity to attack three

destroyers on October 22. The warships had steamed at more than twenty-five knots and zigzagged three times in just eight minutes. Rindskopf had been unable to set up a shot in time and dove as the closest one passed just 200 yards astern. The skipper had fumed. "These were the first targets worthy of torpedoes that the *Drum* has seen since November 22, 1943," Rindskopf wrote in his report. "The epitome of frustration!"

He hoped the night of the 23rd would be different.

One of the empire's last major sea routes ran through the South China Sea from the Philippines past Formosa to Japan. Japan's war machine depended on shipping from Hong Kong, Singapore, the East Indies, Manila, and Formosa. Ships that steamed this backdoor route often would pass through the Luzon Strait, which separated the Philippines from Formosa and the Formosa Strait, which divided that island from mainland China. This route had grown increasingly vital in recent months as Japan struggled to reinforce the Philippines in advance of America's invasion and now as a way to pull its few precious merchant ships from harm's way. Submariners relished assignments in this target-rich environment, which had earned the nickname "Convoy College." The seas throughout September and October had crawled with submarine wolf packs, boasting colorful names like Donk's Devils, Ed's Eradicators, and Ben's Busters. Rindskopf's orders directed him to patrol the waters off the Luzon Strait with the submarines *Icefish* and *Sawfish* to form a wolf pack led by Commander Alan Banister, Banister's Beagles.

The Japanese knew the dangers American submarines posed in these waters, a fact confirmed at 6 a.m. on the 23rd when convoy MATA-30 first detected signals from American submarines. More intercepts followed three hours later. The convoy commander ordered five of the faster ships to steam at top speed through the Luzon Strait. *Sawfish* first picked up convoy MATA-30 hours earlier when mast tops and smoke appeared in Banister's periscope. The thirty-nine-year-old skipper had chased down the convoy and set his sights on the last ship, the *Kimikawa Maru*, loaded down with bauxite, crude oil, and aviation gas as well as some 300 passengers. Banister fired five torpedoes. An explosion ripped open the port side aft of the tender, flooding the No. 7 cargo hold. The skipper ordered abandon ship as *Kimikawa Maru* sank by the stern, disappearing beneath the waves in just two and a half minutes along with eighty-one passengers and twenty-four crewmembers. Escorts hunted *Sawfish* with depth charges. The sonar operator on *Drum* heard eleven explosions at 5:32 p.m. *Icefish* sailors detected three. By the time *Sawfish* escaped the escorts, surfaced, and fired off a report to the wolf pack, *Drum* had already found the rest of the convoy and picked up the hunt.

The submarine *Snook*, which had just wrapped up a wolf pack patrol with *Pomfret* and *Cobia*, radioed the Beagles. Commander George Brown wanted in on the action. He ordered his submarine to run at three-engine speed to close the seventy-five-mile distance. Like sharks following the scent of blood, four submarines zeroed in on the convoy's eleven remaining ships. The moon would set at 11:20 p.m., making an ideal time for a surface attack. The submarines would have much of the night to work. *Snook* approached from the bow, *Drum* the starboard flank, *Sawfish* and *Icefish* the port. Wolf pack commander Banister studied the radar at 10:43 p.m. Despite the destruction of *Kimikawa Maru*, convoy MATA-30 remained well organized. The radar showed a tight cluster of ships that steamed north between six and seven knots. A single large ship lagged behind while escorts swept across the dark water. Banister fired off a message at 10:59 p.m. to the wolf pack: "Attacking from port flank."

For the second time, Banister closed the convoy. The skipper had only five fish left. He planned to fire four at the last ship in the convoy and save his last one in case he needed to escape. *Sawfish* crossed astern of one of the destroyers and charged what Banister surmised was a tanker. The skipper fired four torpedoes at 11:21 p.m., watching as the second and third breeched the surface. The third launched so high out of the water that Banister feared it might land back on deck. The frustrated skipper had come too far to botch this attack. He immediately fired his last torpedo, then put the convoy astern at flank speed. Banister heard a single explosion followed by a string of depth charges. His radar confirmed his fear that his attack had failed. The pip still glowed on the screen as the target steamed onward. Banister fired off a message to the rest of the wolf pack. "Attack completed," the skipper radioed. "All torpedoes expended trailing until *Snook* joins."

Snook and *Icefish* moved in to attack. Commander Richard Peterson in *Icefish* fired six torpedoes at 12:52 a.m. His one hit on *Shinsei Maru No. 1* proved a dud, but it forced the 5,878-ton passenger cargo ship to slow so damage control crews could repair a hole. Commander Brown in *Snook*, hoping to draw the escorts off of *Icefish*, charged the convoy's starboard quarter. He set his sights on the closest and largest ship he could find, the 7,369-ton *Kokuryu Maru*, a passenger ship with a roster this night of 1,357. Brown fired four torpedoes at 12:56 a.m. Three minutes later, the first torpedo hit, ripping open the starboard side of No. 2 cargo hold. Water flooded inside and the ship listed. A second torpedo crashed into the engine room seconds later. Brown watched flames dance beneath a cloud of smoke that rose into the dark night. Passengers hustled into lifeboats and rafts as the ship's list worsened. Half an hour after the first torpedo hit, *Kokuryu Maru* capsized and sank bow first, taking with it 392 passengers and crew.

The submarines returned to the convoy again and again, probing for weak spots. One would attack from the port side, the next the starboard or the bow. The tightly clustered convoy began to unravel as ships scattered, hoping to make it hard for the attackers to pursue. The convoy's five escorts, unsure of where to depth-charge, plucked survivors from the cold sea. Rindskopf, now operating on battery power to increase *Drum*'s stealth, seized on the chaos and charged the convoy's port flank. The young skipper fired tube seven at 2:03 a.m. at a range of almost two miles. The electric torpedo streaked toward the target. Rindskopf fired again ten seconds later. Then again and again. Up on the bridge in the dark, he struggled to watch. A minute passed. Then two. All four of his torpedoes had missed. The skipper dropped back behind the convoy to allow *Snook* another attack.

Snook roared in again and fired six torpedoes at 3:10 a.m. Lookouts on the 3,887-ton tanker *Kikusui Maru* spotted wakes off the starboard side, but without enough time to evade. The first hit failed to explode, but the second ripped open the bow. The third struck the boiler room, sending the ship down in flames stern first. "The resulting explosion was only a shade less than spectacular," Brown, *Snook*'s commander, wrote, "the whole after end of the target appearing to disintegrate." The tenacious skipper refused to let up, setting his sights next on *Tenshin Maru*, a 4,236-ton cargo ship loaded down with bauxite. Brown fired five torpedoes at 5:59 a.m., watching from the bridge as the fish streaked toward the target. One torpedo tore open the port side of cargo hold No. 2. The ship came dead in the water just as a second torpedo exploded. The dual hits snapped the ship in half. Brown watched as *Tenshin Maru*—along with 6,250 tons of bauxite and fifty-two men—vanished under the swells in just two minutes.

Sawfish and *Icefish* had each sunk one ship while *Snook* had destroyed three. Rindskopf's one attack had failed. The sun rose and with it went the other submarines. Out of torpedoes, *Sawfish* had quit. A plane kept *Icefish* submerged and *Snook* had bowed out. But Rindskopf refused to give up. He scanned the horizon through the periscope at 7 a.m., spotting the 4,725-ton *Shikisan Maru* loaded down with rubber, manganese, and general war goods. A destroyer patrolled off the target's opposite bow while three other freighters steamed in a rough column another mile and a half beyond. Rindskopf fired four torpedoes at 7:57 a.m. Lookouts spotted wakes at 600 yards and *Shikisan Maru* turned to evade. The first torpedo streaked just five yards past the bow. The next three ripped the side of the ship open, from the foremast to the stern. *Shikisan Maru* plunged to the bottom in just a minute and a half with the loss of fifteen men. Rindskopf had sunk his first major ship of the war.

The submarines *Shark*, *Blackfish*, and *Seadragon*, operating as another wolf pack, waited to pick off the remnants. *Seadragon* skipper Commander James Ashley, Jr., watched the three freighters Rindskopf had spotted come into view through his periscope at 9:20 a.m. He fired four torpedoes at the 4,620-ton *Taiten Maru*. Lookouts spotted the wakes and the ship turned to evade. Two fish zoomed past the bow. The third crashed into the engine room on the starboard side while the fourth tore open No. 4 cargo hold. *Taiten Maru*'s bow rose skyward, plunging beneath the waves at noon. *Seadragon* circled back and fired again at 12:14 p.m., destroying *Shinsei Maru No. 1*, the ship damaged by a dud the night before. *Seadragon* then targeted the 1,847-ton *Eiko Maru*, which had plucked survivors of the other ships from the cold water. The skipper watched as a torpedo severed the ship's bow, sending *Eiko Maru* to the bottom with its screws in the air. At this rate the entire convoy would soon vanish.

Drum's attack, however, was now over. Rindskopf and his crew relaxed. The twenty-seven-year-old skipper would sink two more freighters two days later, the 6,886-ton *Taisho Maru* and 6,886-ton *Taihaku Maru*, concluding his final patrol with three kills totaling 18,497 tons. His final two victims alone took down more than 3,000 Japanese soldiers. Rindskopf would relinquish command the next month at Majuro after serving eleven war patrols, a duration matched only by two of the boat's enlisted men. *Drum* would make two more patrols, but would never sink another ship, ending the war with fifteen confirmed kills for a total tonnage of 80,580. At sea when the Japanese surrendered, *Drum* would conclude its service as a Naval Reserve ship with the Potomac River Naval Command, struck from the register in 1968, just one year before *Silversides*. Like the Silver Lady, *Drum*, over the course of the war had logged enough miles to cover more than five trips around the earth. Rindskopf in that time had made more than 1,000 dives, helped fire 125 torpedoes, and survived no fewer than 300 depth charge attacks, one of which put a hole in the conning tower. He would return to the submarine school as a torpedo and gunnery instructor, having earned a Navy Cross, Silver Star, Bronze Star, and a Letter of Commendation.

Arisan Maru steamed onward toward Formosa. It had been a slaughter. Submarine wolf packs in less than twenty-four hours had devoured nine of the convoy's twelve ships, tearing apart ship after ship and sending loads of bauxite, crude oil, and aviation gasoline beneath the waves along with hundreds of lives. Some of the prisoners on board surmised the fate of the other vessels from the debris that bobbed in the water. Sergeant Calvin Graef had even spotted a few lifeboats crammed with survivors, though the hellship made no effort in these submarine-infested waters to help. The slowest freighter in the convoy—the one with the Allies' most precious cargo—had somehow defied odds and made it through the long night and morning.

Graef and a half dozen others topside prepared water and steamed rice for the prisoners late in the afternoon, a task Graef relished for its brief promise of fresh air. The Japanese guards would crack the prisoners over the head for looking over the rail, but Graef couldn't resist the urge and stole glances at the rough seas that tossed below. Half of the prisoners had been fed at about 5 p.m. when some of the Japanese guards sprinted down the deck. Graef peered over the side and saw the wake of a torpedo streak past *Arisan Maru*'s stern. Another fish missed the bow. The ship's general alarm rang out. Guards drove Graef and the other prisoners back into the cargo hold with rifle butts, sealing the hatch covers to prevent escape.

"What gives?" prisoners prodded.

"Submarines," Graef replied. "School of fish."

The submarine *Shark* had found *Arisan Maru* and Commander Edward Blakely was hungry. *Shark*'s thirty-two-year-old skipper, a Naval Academy classmate of Dick O'Kane's, had yet to sink a ship on this patrol. Now he bore down on his target, unaware of the 1,800 prisoners crowded aboard the unmarked hellship, the majority of them Americans. The prisoners trapped in *Arisan Maru*'s cargo holds listened to the footfalls of the Japanese on deck above. The hellship's deck gun roared again and again. To the men trapped below, liberation appeared at hand, an end to the horrors endured at the hands of the Japanese. Many of the prisoners cheered the *Shark*. "Sink us, Navy!" men cried. "Please God, don't let 'em miss!"

Blakely didn't.

A one-and-a-half-ton torpedo ripped open the starboard side of No. 3 cargo hold. Another tore into *Arisan Maru*'s stern. Coal dust and rust clouded the air as cold seawater rushed inside the freighter. Prisoners who only moments before had begged aloud for an American attack suddenly fell silent, their prayers answered. The prisoners recovered from the shock and charged up the ladder, shoving the hatch covers open. Men poured out onto the deck and inhaled the cool air as healthier captives helped haul up the sick. Most of the Japanese had abandoned the crippled ship, leaving the prisoners to fend for themselves. One Japanese guard, who had taunted the captives with water, had failed to escape. Prisoners pounced on him, crushing him with a hatch cover.

Graef watched as a deranged pandemonium seized some prisoners, a result of years of abuse and starvation coupled with the sudden shock of the attack. Rather than strap on a life preserver and abandon the sinking ship, some prisoners started looting. One captive appeared on deck dressed in the Japanese skipper's tropical white uniform, the pant bottoms at his knees and the coat too tight to button. Others ransacked the ship's galley. "They ate like savages grabbing great handfuls of rice and sugar," Brodsky would later tell American investigators. "They even drank bottles of catsup." One such man appeared on deck next to Graef, feasting on a papaya. "Want a bite?" he asked. "They've got vitamins and everything."

Graef felt the explosion of the boilers and watched as the stern started to sink. The ship would not remain afloat much longer. He grabbed a life preserver and canteen and plunged over the side. He hit the water, surfaced, and started to swim toward a Japanese destroyer on the horizon. The wind and the waves carried him toward the warship. He could see Japanese sailors lining the rails, armed with long poles. The sailors throttled the prisoners in the water and pushed others down under the waves, drowning the starved and exhausted captives. Graef tried to turn back, but the waves pushed him closer. The poles soon came down on him. "They took at least five pokes at me," he would later tell investigators, "one of them nipping off a piece of my right ear."

Corporal Donald Meyer, who had survived the voyage by drinking dirty bilge water that had run off the coal and into the scuppers, likewise was shocked by the reactions of other prisoners. The twenty-four-year-old California native, down in the coal hold when the torpedoes hit, grew enraged when the Japanese cut the rope ladders. Rather than drown in the hold, Meyer shimmied up the stanchion. He and others found a rope, lowered it into the hold, and hoisted the severed ladder back up, tying it off so that others could climb up. Not all the prisoners shared his drive to survive. "Some felt that the end had come and appeared to be greatly relieved," Meyer would later write. "They seemed to just want to be left alone and go down with the ship. Freedom for them had come too late. They sat and waited. A few of them smoked cigarettes."

Not Meyer.

He and another prisoner grabbed a hatch cover and dropped it overboard. The men jumped in and paddled out toward the destroyers *Harukaze* and *Take*, which rescued the Japanese crewmen. Meyer realized as he paddled closer that the Japanese refused to pull the prisoners on board, pushing the captives underwater with long poles. He had no choice but to make it on his own, and clung to the hatch cover. Others joined him. The sun dropped beneath the horizon and dusk settled over the waves. Men watched the crippled *Arisan Maru* slip beneath the waves around 7:40 p.m. "There were still many men aboard her when she went down," one survivor would later tell American investigators. "I could see them silhouetted against the sky."

Hundreds of men bobbed in the waves, clinging to planks, crates, and oil cans. One even clung to a toilet. The hatch cover that Meyer and others held began to sink so he let go and grabbed a wooden plank that floated past. After days of sweating in the coal hold, he now shivered in the water. Faint stars glowed in the sky. He could see no one in the dark, but he could hear the voices of the men around him. Some called out for friends. Others cried. "Men were going down now. The sea was getting rougher. It was a strange bereft feeling with so many of my friends drowned all about me, and a great numbness came over me and I felt for a moment as though I would be better off just to let it go. A sinking feeling took possession of me as I felt myself slipping. This only lasted a second. I shook it off and began to swim to get my circulation started."

Graef, too, wrestled with despair. He and several others that afternoon lassoed floating debris into a raft with ropes, belts, and wires stripped off crates. Graef had spotted two bamboo poles drifting nearby. He had struck out at sunset to retrieve them, but when he seized the poles and turned back, he found that he couldn't find his companions in the dark. The waves rose and fell as a bitter wind stung. He felt lost and alone. "Clinging to my precious bamboo poles, I thought of my boyhood, my school days, my marriage to lovely Bobbie, my enlistment, Bataan, the son I had never seen. Everything came back, to pass in review on the gray waves," he would later write. "In the hours before dawn I lived an eternity."

The waves washed over Meyer, threatening his grip on the plank. The board split in two, leaving him hanging on to one half. The debris field from the vanished hellship had begun to disperse, carried away by the wind and the waves. He had been unable before sunset to see land in any direction and knew that by ship he was at least a day away from Formosa, too far to swim. Meyer recalled a prayer from childhood. Though he could only remember a few words, he ran through it over and over again in his head. Meyer needed no less than a miracle—and in the meantime a new float. He scanned the water for more debris and spotted some bamboo poles. He paddled over to find Graef and a sense of relief that he was no longer alone.

"What kind of chance do you think we have?" Graef asked.

"About fifty-fifty," Meyer replied.

The men assembled another raft. Graef tied the bamboo poles together as Meyer paddled around to retrieve wreckage, from brooms and planks to crates. With the raft secure, the men climbed atop, struggling to stay afloat as the waves throttled them. "The yelling and screaming had grown fainter and fainter. It had been a long time since we heard anything but the pounding of the waves. Would we go down too with the rest of them? What would happen to us out here?" Meyer wrote. "As we got deeper into the night, the sea grew steadily wilder. Three times we were completely under—the raft partly broken and gone—clutching wildly at nothing. Each time we thought it was the end, then some how we would come back. We couldn't think clearly now—just struggle blindly. We hadn't talked for hours. Words were a waste of strength."

Eventually, the gray light of dawn began to glow on the horizon. Graef and Meyer had made it through the night. Meyer spotted a boat less than 100 yards away, bobbing on the waves. Impossible, he thought. Surely he had gone mad.

"Say, bud," Meyer asked. "Is that a boat?"

"Sure it's a boat," Graef answered. "Come on let's go."

The exhausted men paddled the raft toward the boat, one of the discarded lifeboats the Japanese crew had used the day before to reach the destroyers. "Hey boat!" Graef shouted as the men approached. "Anybody there?"

Several men sat up. The survivors reached down and plucked Graef and Meyer from the raft. Too exhausted to move, the men lay in the boat. Civilian Robert Overbeck, Corporal Anton Cichi, and Sergeant Avery Wilbur waited for the new arrivals to rally. After a round of introductions, the men began to bail water from the boat. The Japanese had stripped the boat of its oars and sail, but Overbeck had managed to fish a sail out of the water. The Japanese had fortunately failed to toss the mast, boom, and tiller overboard. Rations consisted of a sealed can of dry biscuits. Though the Japanese had opened the water barrels to drain—even filling one with salt water—the survivors found enough fresh water to last several days with rationing. Meyer contributed his full canteen, which he had tied to his leg when he abandoned ship.

The men unfurled the sail when a Japanese destroyer appeared on the horizon, aimed straight for them. Would the Japanese take them prisoner again or machine-gun them? The men had worked too hard to fall prisoner again. But there was nowhere to go. The destroyer closed the distance, the bow wake slicing through the waves. The survivors had one option: play dead. The men dropped to the deck and froze. The destroyer circled the lifeboat at a range of just 100 yards. The men could see Japanese sailors crowding the destroyer's deck, studying the survivors through binoculars. No one moved. The destroyer circled the lifeboat again. Then to the amazement of the survivors, the enemy warship steamed off, disappearing over the horizon.

"Where's China?" one of the men asked.

"West," answered another.

The five survivors raised the sail. The afternoon wind grabbed it and propelled the boat west with Overbeck at the tiller. These five men along with four others that the Japanese rescued would be the only survivors among the 1,800 prisoners aboard *Arisan Maru*, making it one of the worst hellship disasters of the war. The men picked up by the Japanese—dehydrated, plagued by open sores, and with one man completely naked—had endured days at sea. Only three of those four would live long enough to see the end of the war. Another eighty-seven Americans died on board the submarine *Shark*, sunk during a depth charge attack by the *Arisan Maru*'s escorts. The predator had become the prey.

Graef, Meyer, and the other three survivors crowded in *Arisan Maru*'s discarded lifeboat put the horror and tragedy of the hellship astern and sailed toward China. A few Japanese planes zipped through the skies high overhead, too high, the men surmised, to spot them. Afternoon gave way to evening as the boat sliced through the waves. The darkness brought out the stars, allowing Overbeck to navigate by the North Star. "There was a lot of phosphorescence in the water and in my imagination, probably brought on by mental strain and lack of sleep, I kept seeing lights and hearing the familiar voices of friends on the ship calling my name and screaming for help," he would later write. "When dawn broke it was like coming back to life."

The sun climbed high the next morning. The survivors munched on hardtack and sipped water, each hour taking them closer to freedom. The dark silhouette of the Chinese coast appeared on the horizon that afternoon. Chinese fishing junks bobbed in the water. Rather than risk the heavy surf near shore, Overbeck pulled alongside one of the junks. The Chinese fishermen welcomed the survivors with a reception of hot tea, rice, and fish while crews dismantled and sank the lifeboat. Handed over to the Americans, the survivors began the journey home, flying to India, North Africa, and on to the United States. Meyer looked down out of the plane at the bright lights below. "This was our country," he wrote. "This was Mom and Dad—home."

20

TANG

"Dear All, Am prisoner of war in Japan. Feel alright. Miss you very much.... Will see you when the war is over."

—Gordon Cox,
undated postcard

The October sun beat down on O'Kane and his crew, hogtied on the deck of *P-34*. The nine exhausted men could see off the port side as the Japanese plucked more survivors from the water, all victims of the ships *Tang* had torpedoed. The guards moved the prisoners at dusk into a deckhouse fireroom that housed a locker, stove, and the ship's traditional bath. The cramped compartment proved little bigger than a bathroom, allowing only four men to sleep at a time while the others stood. Guards ordered the survivors to knock to use the head. "When we would knock on the door," Leibold would later tell investigators, "the Jap guard would shove his bayonet through the space about the door and swing it about maliciously, making it very hard for us to dodge the bayonet." Narowanski improvised. "I'll be damned," the blond torpedoman griped, urinating in the bath heater's ash pot. "I've got to take a leak."

Sparse rations only added to the crew's discomfort. Despite the ship's visible stores of fish, rice, and squash, the Japanese fed the survivors just a few hardtack crackers accompanied by a cup of hot water. The only solace these meager meals offered was a fifteen-minute reprieve from the hand ties. The Japanese continued to harass the men—albeit not as bad as the first day—including the ship's executive officer, who repeatedly tried to pry a diamond ring off Leibold's finger. Unable to remove it, the officer settled for punching him. The terrific heat from the neighboring galley made the men's nightly 6 p.m. to 8 a.m. confinement unbearable as the bulkheads grew too hot to even touch. "Our men would pass out," Caverly would later tell war crime investigators. "We would have to carry the men to the door, which was locked and try to revive them with the little air that seeped through the door-jambs."

Tang's malfunctioning twenty-fourth torpedo had brought a tragic end to one of the war's greatest runs. Postwar records would show that in just thirty-one days O'Kane had sunk seven ships for a total of 21,772 tons, making it the third most successful patrol of the war by the number of ships sunk. The final run added to O'Kane's already impressive list of sinkings. In just nine months at the helm of *Tang*, the thirty-three-year-old skipper had sunk a confirmed twenty-four ships with a total of 93,824 tons, solidifying his rank as the top skipper of the war. But none of that mattered now. The war was over for O'Kane and his men. They had one goal: survive. "Anything that the Japs ask you, answer them," O'Kane ordered his men. "Don't tell them a lie. Don't let them catch you in a lie. Anything you know, be assured they know. I am the guy they are after."

P-34 arrived a few days later in Formosa's Takao. The Japanese hauled the blindfolded Americans ashore, threatened to behead them, and imprisoned them for the night in an old warehouse. The guards chained the men's hands to rings set high on the cell walls, leaving them defenseless throughout the night as a swarm of mosquitoes feasted on them. The Japanese guards paraded the prized American submariners through town the next morning for the locals to see. Hayes Trukke's shaggy blond hair hung down in front of his mouth—the product of the lax submarine force regulations—and reminded O'Kane of the character Hairless Joe in the Al Capp comic strip. With each step, his locks swayed, prompting the locals to holler and jeer, turning what should have been a display of Japanese military might into a circus.

The guards issued the half-naked sailors ragged white clothes, blindfolded them again, and loaded them on a train, each handcuffed prisoner tethered with a lanyard to a guard. The train pulled away from the station and chugged north, following the same valley the men had seen from the sea. The exhausted prisoners—with blindfolds removed and train car shades opened—sat largely in silence for the eight-hour trip, content to watch the verdant landscape slip past the window beneath gray and drizzly skies, the farms and rudimentary tools a throwback to an earlier century. "We watched their primitive agricultural methods, hand-powered water wheels for irrigational purposes, thatched garments for shedding rain," Savadkin recalled. "We also noted that all the people, civilians, school children and everyone seemed to be in some sort of uniform. They all wore leggings of some type and a uniform hat."

The train ended its 150-mile journey that evening on the northeastern tip of Formosa in the port city of Kiirun. The Japanese guards marched the *Tang* survivors through the now dark rain to the city jail, a decrepit and primitive fortress the Americans dubbed the "Kiirun Clink." The guards marshaled the prisoners—three to a cell—into small wooden pens. "The cells are like the cages you see in the zoo, the floor of the cell being raised above the floor of the corridor that leads between the cells," recalled Savadkin. "There are bars in the front of the cell running from ceiling to deck. They were wooden bars about four inches in diameter, there was a very small door in the forward portion of the cell through which we entered and left it. The door was very narrow and small and you had to stoop down and double up to get in and out of it. The head was nothing more than a recess in the wall and a slit in the deck."

The Japanese fed the prisoners a couple baseball-sized rice balls, cucumbers, and a few small fish that reminded the prisoners of shiners or minnows often used as bait. The meal came served in a corn or cane husk accompanied by bamboo chopsticks wrapped in paper, much like soda straws found at any local pharmacy counter. Guards passed out blankets—one per prisoner—when the men finished dinner. That night the exhausted prisoners slept for the first time since the loss of the *Tang*. The men passed a few days in the cells, swapping stories and sleeping. The only highlight came when a conscripted guard entered Savadkin's cell and announced that he was a Christian and had brought presents for the men. He handed the lieutenant—the only one awake—several melting popsicles. Savadkin hid them behind his back. "Hey, fellows!" he announced, rousing his cellmates. "Guess what I've got for you—ice cream on a stick!"

"Take it easy, Mr. Savadkin," griped a groggy sailor—no doubt convinced the lieutenant had lost his mind—until Savadkin produced a "long, cool, drippy, and wonderfully sticky popsicle on a stick for each of us."

The guards returned a few days later, hauled the men out of the wooden cells, and loaded them on a convoy bound for Japan; the three officers went on separate destroyers, while the six enlisted men piled on top of sugar sacks in the cargo hold of a cruiser. The destroyer captain escorted O'Kane to his cabin, where he was provided shoes, warm clothes, and food. An armed guard stood watch at the door through which O'Kane observed the ship's drills, marveling at the speed of the destroyer's gun crew. The destroyer's skipper, a lieutenant commander about the same age as O'Kane, visited his prisoner that evening. The two officers chatted in English about naval tactics, the progress of the war—the men agreed a battleship confrontation was no longer possible given Japan's losses—and even literature. "How is it, Commander, that you speak no Japanese, but seem to understand my English?" asked the Japanese officer. "How could we expect to understand each other's problems when you made no attempt to learn even a word of our language?"

The destroyer captain soon returned to the bridge, leaving O'Kane alone to replay the loss of his submarine, questioning why the Navy had removed anti–circular run devices from torpedoes. That mechanism forces a torpedo to dive if it turns too far. Such a device would have saved seventy-eight lives and O'Kane's submarine. *Tang* could have continued fighting, sunk more ships, and helped bring an end to the war. Instead O'Kane and eight other survivors steamed north toward Japan and an uncertain future.

Savadkin and Flanagan enjoyed similar warm treatment on board the other destroyers. The Japanese allowed the officers to bathe and issued them clean clothes, blankets, and a pillow, offering the wardroom transom as a bed. Two guards armed with bayonets sat day and night, occasionally attempting conversation. The ship's doctor visited Savadkin, giving the lieutenant an English-Japanese dictionary. Savadkin and the doctor, armed with his own bilingual dictionary, discussed the similarities between American and Japanese destroyer crews. "I ate with the Japanese officers," recalled Savadkin. "However, they provided me a plate and a set of silverware, a regular knife, fork and spoon inscribed with the Japanese naval emblem. The officers used chopsticks, each had his own set of very beautifully-formed chopsticks and kept in a highly polished and extremely well decorated personal case, something like a toothbrush kit."

Four days and three nights passed as the convoy steamed some 700 miles north through the East China Sea toward Kobe, Japan's bustling port on the southeastern side of the main island of Honshu. The *Tang* survivors arrived at a Kobe naval base to find Formosa's more tropical climate had given way to a bitter November rain mixed with sleet. With the promise that fresh clothes awaited him and his men on shore, O'Kane returned the shoes, shirt, and pants issued at the start of the trip, thanking the destroyer captain for his hospitality. O'Kane paused at the top of the gangway to ask the captain one last question. Why had he and the others been treated so harshly on the *P-34* compared to the civility enjoyed on this voyage? "That ship and the escort force," the captain replied, "are not part of the Imperial Navy."

Barefooted and dressed in little more than rags, the reunited survivors slogged through the rain and sleet to a naval training station, where guards sat them down, backs against a fence. A Japanese rear admiral arrived with his entourage after an hour to inspect the soaked and shivering sailors. The admiral walked down the line, pausing when he reached Leibold. "How old are you?"

"Twenty-one," the boatswain's mate replied, surprised at the admiral's command of English.

"You look thirty-five," the admiral answered, noticing that Leibold's teeth chattered. "Frightened?"

"No," Leibold answered. "I'm cold."

The admiral dropped his eyes to Leibold's wet and muddy feet. "Of course, stupid," he barked. "No shoes."

The Japanese admiral turned and left. The men hoped his comments meant guards might provide them shoes and clothes, a hope that never materialized. The Japanese loaded the sailors on a train north, no handcuffs but each accompanied by a personal guard. O'Kane's heart sank as he watched the enemy homeland rush past. Despite thirty-four months of war—and the efforts of American submarines, bombers, and fighters to starve the empire of its precious raw materials—Japan appeared far from defeat. "The countryside may have been beautiful, but the fast, loaded trains, the hydroelectric lines coming down out of the mountains, and the buzzing industry were depressing to us indeed. This was particularly so at Nagoya, where we disembarked for a time. It was dark, but the factories were booming like Kaiser's shipyards, the bluish light of arc-welding spread out through the city," he wrote. "Here I knew that Japan, with her routes to China quite defensible, could be defeated only by invasion."

The survivors disembarked about 8 p.m. the night of November 3. Guards marched the men in the dark some 1,500 meters down a muddy road to the

Ofuna Naval Interrogation Center, a nonregistered prison administered by the Yokosuka Naval Station. The Japanese built the secret camp just south of Tokyo on the site of a former school at the junction of two valleys, opening its doors on April 7, 1942. An eight-foot-high board fence enclosed the primitive prison, constructed of little more than unpainted planks and tarpaper roofs that American investigators later measured at just seventy-five yards long and sixty-eight yards wide. "The camp was built of flimsy wood and consisted mainly of three plain, crackerbox structures called One, Two, and Three—*Ichi, Ni,* and *San,*" recalled former prisoner Louis Zamperini, an American Army bombardier forced to ditch in the Pacific because of engine trouble. "The layout looked like the letter E. Each barrack was set apart from the other by twenty yards; all were connected to a main building that housed the officers' headquarters, the latrines, and the kitchen."

Prisoners crowded into approximately ninety small cells, each six feet wide and nine feet long, the floors covered with two grass mats—*tatamis* in Japanese—on which the men bedded down at night. Wooden bars guarded the small windows. Lieutenant Commander John Fitzgerald, skipper of the sunken submarine *Grenadier,* who arrived in Ofuna in May 1943, would later tell war crimes investigators how prisoners locked in these austere cells battled the frigid winters with nothing more than worn blankets and tattered clothes. Many even suffered frostbite. "No heat of any description was furnished for these quarters. Their construction was very poor, so poor in fact that the weather aged the boards forming the walls and floors of the building so they would no longer overlap thus forming large cracks in both walls and floors," Fitzgerald would recall in his 1946 affidavit. "When snow fell, accompanied by a wind, the cracks in the building were large enough to permit snow to be blown into some of the rooms."

But the physical conditions at Ofuna, as the *Tang* men would learn, proved only part of the struggle. Nonregistered captives received less food than official prisoners of war. Typical rations consisted of a teacup of rice and barley—counted out almost grain by grain—and a thin soup made of hot water mixed with a teaspoon of soya bean paste and a few carrot tops and potato peels served three times a day, a diet of just a few hundred calories. Prisoners received a sliver of meat or fish on rare occasions—and even then the meat was often rotten. Bombadier Zamperini, who endured a year in Ofuna before the Japanese transferred him to another camp a month before the men from the

Tang arrived, would later recount one such event to war crimes investigators. "One day I walked over and looked in a wagon in which fish were being brought into the camp for our food. The fish were covered with maggots which were swarming all over," Zamperini recalled. "Later that same night, fish were served as the meal but I lost my appetite."

"Eat!" one of the guards ordered the aviator.

"I can't eat it."

"You eat," the guard demanded and pressed the tip of his bayonet into the muscle behind Zamperini's ear, drawing blood. "You eat."

Zamperini did as ordered.

Portion sizes fluctuated, but rarely did quantities increase, in part to help wear down prisoner resolve, but also because the camp's thieving cook operated a black market for the local population. Prisoners suffered chronic diarrhea, body sores, and malnutrition; the latter coupled with neglected wounds would lead to at least eight deaths. Many others battled beriberi, a painful thiamine deficiency associated with malnutrition that causes the loss of muscle function in the legs. The diet proved so poor in nutritional value that some prisoners would go as long as six weeks without a bowel movement. Food became an obsession. Men lulled themselves to sleep at night remembering favorite childhood meals. Chief Petty Officer Carl Quarterman, a *Grenadier* quartermaster who spent nine months at Ofuna, recorded a list in his diary of "new experiences" he endured as a prisoner, much of it dedicated to the horrible things he ate to survive, including fish and animal guts, horse blood, and even weeds and tree leaves. "Eating soup with worms floating on top," Quarterman penciled on his list. "Living from day to day."

But prisoners suffered more than starvation.

With every able-bodied Japanese man fighting on the front lines, Zamperini observed, Ofuna's guards proved little more than "moronic farm kids and misfits not fit for combat." Trivial offenses like talking, spilling rice, or failing to show respect translated into beatings. Other times guards invented charges. Staff made a special sport of slipping into cells in the middle of the night to pummel sleeping prisoners. The midnight groans of the injured reverberated throughout the barracks. The sadism went beyond just clubbings. The prisoners nicknamed one guard the Lover because he enjoyed unzipping the flight suits of captives, reaching inside and then pulling them around by the penis. The same guard on another occasion held a gun on a prisoner and made him masturbate while he watched. Other guards masturbated with an injured duck. Prisoners recalled with horror how guards drilled one day using the body of a deceased B-24 pilot as a bayonet target. "We lived in eternal constant dread of beatings and punishment," recalled one prisoner. "It affected many of these men mentally and all of us physically. Some of the American prisoners through this constant dread of beatings and inhumane treatment could not even eat and digest their rations."

The worst of the guards—a man the *Tang* sailors would come to despise—was the camp's ruthless medical orderly, Sueharu Kitamura. The thirty-one-year-old medic thrived on other people's pain. Born in Tokyo's Ushigome ward, Kitamura grew up the middle of five children. His father died when he was eight years old, leaving Kitamura's impoverished mother to raise him, his two sisters, and two brothers. The married father of a newborn daughter, he had enlisted in the Navy when he was twenty-one, climbing the ranks to the American equivalent of petty officer 1st class. He landed at Ofuna in March 1944. Kitamura's light skin, square face, and chiseled jaw and general hand-some looks disguised a maniacal fury that he liked to vent on Allied prisoners. Compared to the other Japanese guards that prowled Ofuna, Kitamura was a giant, standing almost six feet tall and weighing about 180 pounds, much of it muscle. "He was very heavily built," recalled one prisoner. "Very wide shoulders, hard as a rock."

Kitamura had a feminine high-pitched laugh that could spark terror in the prisoners, who alternately dubbed him "the Quack" and "the Butcher." He carried a small black book in one hand to log alleged prisoner infractions and a bat in the other that he used to thrash captives. Other times Kitamura simply punched prisoners in the face and then kicked them when they fell to the ground. The medic at times forced prisoners to squat on the balls of their feet while holding their hands above their heads in a tortuous position the captives called the "Ofuna Crouch." Kitamura other days made them stoop over and push wet rags down the floors while he and other guards whipped them. When the passageways iced over in winter, Kitamura forced the men to do it barefoot, punishment that tore the skin off the bottoms of the prisoners' feet. No one was safe from his violence, not even his young bride, Kazue, whom American prosecutors would later learn he often beat at home.

The increase in Japanese battle losses in the summer and fall of 1944 coincided with a rise in beatings. One prisoner noted that a glance at Kitamura's face served as "a barometer to us of the Allied progress in the war." The violence at Ofuna reached a crescendo one afternoon just weeks before the *Tang* crew's arrival. Fitzgerald recorded that brutal September 9 beating after the Butcher caught Marine Lieutenant Bill Harris and Navy Lieutenant George Bullard trying to translate headlines in a week-old Japanese newspaper. "Kitamura called Bullard out of the formation of POW's and started striking him with a club approximately 1½" in diameter and 4' long across the back of his legs and buttocks. Bullard was struck approximately 15 times," Fitzgerald recalled. "Kitamura then turned on Harris. By this time, Kitamura had become a raving maniac, he was screaming and jabbering Japanese intermixed with a few words of English to such an extent that none of us could understand what he was talking about. He then started striking Lt. Harris with the same club he had used on Bullard but in a more vicious manner. After about 10 or 12 blows Harris fell to the ground."

To the men's horror, the beating continued. "Kitamura started kicking him about the body and face and made him stand up again. He then continued beating him with the club. Harris was again knocked down and was unable to rise. After being again brutally kicked about the back and body he forced two American prisoners to lift Harris up and hold him in an erect position while he, Kitamura, struck Harris repeatedly in the face with his fists. After many blows in the face Harris was again knocked down whereupon Kitamura started kicking him again in the face and body. He then drew a circle about three feet in diameter, after a few minutes Harris had revived to a certain extent, whereupon he was forced to stand on his feet in his dazed condition within the limits of this small circle," Fitzgerald said. "A P-38 pilot and a B-17 pilot passed out as a result of the psychological effect upon them and had to be carried to their rooms. As a result of this severe beating Harris had a lapse of memory for about three days."

For the nine survivors of *Tang*—cold, wet, and filthy—Ofuna was now home. The guards ordered the new arrivals to wash their feet, dirty from walking through mud. The Japanese then issued them fresh clothing that included a dry shirt, pants, and shoes several sizes too small. Narowanski still wore the Hawaiian shorts he had had on when he escaped from the *Tang*, while the barefooted DaSilva sported only dungarees. Personal toiletries doled out included a toothbrush, tooth powder, and a towel that was little larger than a handkerchief. Guards escorted the new arrivals to individual cells, each with a stack of tattered blankets in the corner, a stack whose size would diminish throughout the winter as new prisoners arrived. The exhausted men slurped down a small bowl of soup and warm rice before stretching out for the night on the *tatami* mat, eager for rest. Morning loomed just a few hours away, promising the men a first glimpse of what life was really like in Ofuna.

Vice Admiral Lockwood stewed in his Pearl Harbor office. *Tang* had departed for its fifth war patrol on September 24, arriving in Midway three days later to top off fuel before leaving that afternoon for the coast of Formosa. *Tang*'s orders called for O'Kane to depart his patrol area November 8 and return to Midway ten days later. That day came and went. Skippers of *Silversides, Trigger*, and *Salmon*—all on patrol in the same area—had heard nothing from O'Kane. Repeated attempts to raise the *Tang* by radio had so far been greeted with silence. Lockwood waited as long as he could before he forwarded his four-page report to Admiral Nimitz. "It is with the deepest regret that the Commander Submarine Force, Pacific Fleet, reports that the U.S.S. *Tang* is overdue from patrol and must be presumed to be lost," Lockwood wrote. "The area assigned to the *Tang* was at the request of the Commanding Officer of that vessel, who fully realized the dangers involved. However, it was the nature of Commander O'Kane to ask for the most difficult assignments and then to carry them out to perfection."

Western Union telegrams went out the same day to the families of the *Tang*'s officers and crew, a three-sentence message families hoped never to receive. "The Navy Department deeply regrets to inform you that your husband William Rudolf Leibold, Chief Boatswains Mate USN, is missing following action while in the service of his country," read one such message. "The Department appreciates your great anxiety but details not available now and delay in receipt thereof must necessarily be expected to prevent possible aid to our enemies and to safeguard the lives of other personnel. Please do not divulge the name of his ship or station or discuss publicly the fact that he is missing." Most knew that the odds were against the *Tang* crew's survival. Lockwood had captured that anxiety in a personal letter a year earlier to Mush Morton's wife after *Wahoo*'s failure to return. "The words 'missing in action' are, in our service, misleading," the three-star admiral wrote. "We all know when a Submarine is reported over due how slim is the chance that any of her gallant crew has survived."

Lockwood had grown tired of such messages. American submarine losses had continued to climb; the Navy counted some forty boats as presumed lost. The same day *Tang* was lost, so were two other submarines, *Darter* and *Shark*, the latter following its destruction of the *Arisan Maru* hellship. The famous *Tang*'s loss shocked the submarine community and the nation. The *New York Times* reflected on the *Tang* and the inherent risks faced by submariners in an editorial titled simply "Overdue." "The undersea craft and the men who take them down are in a class by themselves. They fight far from the warming spotlights of public attention. In the far reaches alone, unaccounted by fellow fighting ships, they go in for the attack, often on the very threshold of the enemy domain," the paper wrote. "The *Tang* and her men have gone to join the gallant and honored company—and company it is, for submarine losses are relatively higher than in any other category of fighting ship."

The gravity of the *Tang* crew's predicament crystallized the morning after arrival when an American prisoner under the supervision of a Japanese guard informed the men that Ofuna functioned as a secret interrogation camp unknown to the Allies and international relief agencies. "We were all warned that we were special captives of the Japanese, and that we were not prisoners of war, and that we would not be entitled to the privileges of prisoners of war. We were to be held strictly off the books," recalled Marine pilot Major Gregory Boyington. "In other words, the Japanese did not notify our government through the Swiss that we were alive. To our people back home or anyone else we remained missing in action or dead." Bombardier Zamperini outlined what that meant in blunt terms. "There would be no Red Cross supervision, no improved treatment. No humanity," he wrote. "Men left the camp to be either executed or relocated. If you died there, no one would know but your brothers in arms."

"We pulled you out of the water," camp officials threatened new arrivals, "and can drop you back in."

The *Tang* men witnessed Ofuna's horror at 8:30 a.m. on the morning of November 6, just three days after arrival. Guards marched the survivors— kept in isolation on the camp's west side—across the compound, where the rest of the prisoners stood at morning formation. Kitamura opened his dreaded black book and called out eight captives for punishment, all over trivial offenses. One man had failed to jump fast enough when a guard demanded he move a bench. The staff had caught two other captives talking. Another prisoner had complained that the men scrubbing the barracks had needed a break. Lastly, the Butcher singled out *Grenadier*'s Fitzgerald, who had only five days earlier celebrated a grim anniversary: eighteen months in Ofuna. Guards demanded that the thirty-six-year-old Missouri native—as the camp's senior prisoner—be punished alongside the others as an example. O'Kane watched his fellow submarine skipper step forward, a man who looked so shriveled he resembled a walking skeleton, and who as a captain and captive had endured the unimaginable.

Guards lined Fitzgerald and the other seven men up five paces in front of the rest of the prisoners, ordering the men to raise their hands above their heads. Armed with two-foot clubs Kitamura and other guards beat the captives as O'Kane and the *Tang* crew watched. "Every blow was as vicious as possible resembling an attempt to hit a 'home run.' They fell anywhere between the shoulder blades and knees of the prisoners, knocking them down, and in three cases unconscious," O'Kane would later testify. "I counted the blows administered to Lieutenant Commander Fitzgerald. They were twenty seven in number. He must have been 'out on his feet' about half way through this torture when Kitamura knocked him clear of them and then to the ground. This beating was so severe that I fully expected several of the prisoners would be killed."

Kitamura had before the morning formation smiled and promised O'Kane and his men an important lesson that day in Japanese. The Butcher's brutal instruction horrified the *Tang* crew. Caverly, a former professional boxer, vomited. Leibold watched the blows fall on Fitzgerald with such force he feared the *Grenadier* skipper's back would shatter. To the shock of the crew, guards hoisted the unconscious men back up and held them so the beatings could continue. None of the Japanese officials present—including the camp's commander—intervened to stop the assault. Only when the winded and exhausted guards finally tired did the blows stop. Fitzgerald would later tell war crimes investigators that it was the eighteenth blow—a direct hit to his spine—that finally toppled him. "As a result of this beating each of us remained stiff and sore for about a week," he would testify. "The discolored condition of our flesh where the blows fell remained black and blue for fully two weeks."

Fitzgerald wasn't the only familiar face the *Tang* crew found in Ofuna. Marine Major Gregory Boyington—known to most as Pappy—worked in the prison's galley. The hard-charging fighter ace and leader of the famed Black Sheep Squadron had become a celebrity as he closed in on the then-top record of twenty-six shoot-downs, a record jointly held by Guadalcanal hero Major Joe Foss and former World War I fighter ace Eddie Rickenbacker, both recipients of the Medal of Honor. A thirty-one-year-old divorced father of three young children, Boyington boasted an outsized personality and bravado the American public loved, even as he battled severe alcoholism that forced him at times to fly combat missions hung over. A former star college wrestler at the University of Washington, Boyington once circled above an enemy airfield, daring the Japanese to send someone up to fight him. "Major Boyington," the Japanese radioed as he flew over Kahili. "What is your position?"

"Right over your damn airport, you yellow bellies," the major barked, "Come up and fight!"

The major claimed four Zeros over Rabaul two days before Christmas 1943, upping his total victory credits to twenty-four planes. He blasted his twenty-fifth days later, bringing him one plane shy of the record. On the morning of January 3, Boyington lifted off for another attack on Rabaul. As seventy Japanese fighters rose up, Boyington dove toward them, blasting the first plane he spotted. He watched seconds later as the enemy pilot bailed out, his plane on fire. His twenty-sixth victim. Enemy planes swirled around Boyington, as many as twenty by his estimate. The Corsair flown by his wingman Captain George Ashmun started to smoke and glide down as the Japanese zeroed in on him. Boyington moved in to protect his wingman, but he was too late. Ashmun's plane erupted in flames and plunged into the water. The Japanese turned on Boyington. "I could feel the impact of the enemy fire against my armor plate, behind my back, like hail on a tin roof," he would later write. "I could see the enemy shots progressing along my wing tips, making patterns."

Far outnumbered and with his wingman dead, Boyington dove at full speed to try to evade when a 20-mm cannon shell tore into his Corsair's belly. Shrapnel from the explosion riddled his left leg, ripping a large gash in his thigh. Other smaller pieces lacerated his forearm and lodged in his jaw, ear, and scalp. With his plane crippled and surrounded by enemy fighters, Boyington felt he had no choice but to ditch. He hoped that a coast watcher on New Ireland's nearby Cape St. George might rescue him. His plane skimmed just a few hundred feet above the water when Boyington released his safety belt, grabbed the ripcord, and kicked the stick all the way forward. His head jerked as his chute caught the air. He crashed seconds later into the Pacific. Afraid to inflate his life raft and give the Japanese a target, the battered pilot treaded water, stripping off his shoes and fatigues to make it easier before he gave up and decided he had no choice but to inflate his raft. He climbed inside naked, now at the mercy of the waves.

Rescued by an enemy submarine, Boyington landed in Rabaul then Truk before the Japanese eventually transferred him to Ofuna in late March, seven months before the arrival of the *Tang* crew. Boyington had spent his first six months as a prisoner battling his infected wounds, stretched out in the corner of his cell atop his own soiled bandages. The shrapnel in the major's thigh pained him so much that bombardier Zamperini massaged his leg each morning and he limped with the aid of a makeshift crutch. Kitamura finally decided to remove Boyington's shrapnel, recruiting captives to hold Boyington down—Ofuna's version of anesthetic. "The pharmacist's mate cut a criss-cross incision over the wound, but failed to extract the shrapnel," Grant Butcher later testified. "The pharmacist's mate cut another deep criss-cross incision over the shrapnel and squeezed to get the metal. The Major passed out because of the excruciating pain, but before this man proceeded with the operation he had the Major revived by having water thrown on him. He then proceeded with his torture."

Boyington fit the profile of the high-value prisoner the Japanese interred at Ofuna. So did Fitzgerald and now O'Kane. The camp's roster included not only American aviators and submariners, but Australians, British, and other Allied nationalities. Interrogation of the *Tang* crew began immediately in a small room with just two chairs and a table. Unlike the poorly educated guards, Ofuna's visiting interrogators from the *Gunreibu*—the intelligence division of the Japanese navy—spoke fluent English. Most had attended American schools, like James Sasaki, a graduate of the University of Southern California and a former classmate and friend of bombardier Zamperini's. Ofuna's chief interrogator Yuzuru Sanematsu boasted to prisoners that he had studied at Princeton—he spent a term there while assigned to the Japanese embassy—and had toured the United States in a Buick before the war broke out. One even claimed to have taught American history at the University of Rhode Island. Prisoners dubbed the interrogators the "Quiz Kids."

Interrogators dressed in Western clothes and some carried matchbooks from Hot Springs, the mountain resort area in Virginia where America interned many Japanese diplomats before repatriation. The Japanese pressed the *Tang* crew on operational matters. What areas did submarines patrol? How many did America have? What number had been lost or damaged? Interrogators also focused on mechanical and technical questions about radio gear, radar, and a submarine's engineering department. Other times inquisitors probed prisoners for mundane details about recreational programs, facilities, and what previous jobs the men had worked. The sailors remembered O'Kane's admonition not to lie about facts that could be found in references like *Jane's Fighting Ships*, valuable advice Decker recalled when an interrogator quizzed the machinist's mate for two hours about *Tang's* Fairbanks Morse engines—only to produce the manual afterward. "If I had told him a falsehood," Decker said, "he would have caught me."

The prisoners realized that knowing when to tell the truth made the Japanese more inclined to believe the men's fabrications. Fitzgerald went round after round with interrogators over what submarine bases America had in Australia. "We became terrific liars," the *Grenadier* skipper recalled, "and usually got away with it." The men also learned to bend the truth, obfuscate, and play dumb. "I kept telling the interrogators that I was just a 'prospective' engineering officer, I really didn't know much about the submarine," Savadkin recalled. "It didn't seem to matter what you told the questioner, just so they could keep filling out papers to send back to Tokyo. I made some of the wildest statements about the speed and power of our ship. My machinist made wild statements in the other direction." When the interrogators pressed Savadkin's subordinate over inconsistencies, the machinist's mate covered for him. "Well you know, Mr. Savadkin," he answered. "Just a greenhorn, doesn't know a thing."

The days at Ofuna marched past as O'Kane and his men learned the prison's rhythm, outlined in detail in Fitzgerald's diary. Guards required the men to rise early, fold their blankets, and wash at an outdoor spigot. Prisoners then scrubbed the passageways, using a mop that consisted of a thick rope about three feet long with no handle that the men pushed up and down the corridor in what one prisoner described as a "bear walk." Captives could earn a cigarette for helping a local farmer dubbed the "honey dipper" scoop feces from the camp's primitive outhouses that the farmer used as fertilizer. Interrogation and idle time ate up the rest of the day. "Conversation was prohibited and books were negligible. As a result we were forced to stand around like a bunch of animals—and in our captors' minds we were probably no more than that," Fitzgerald wrote. "Everyone was always glad when night time came along for in that way we could forget the days past and obtain ever needed rest."

O'Kane and his men remained in isolation, cut off from the camp's other prisoners as the Japanese interrogated them daily, though some of Ofuna's crafty captives managed to communicate via notes scribbled on scrap paper and left in the bathrooms. Guards set out to teach the new arrivals Japanese, starting with numbers one through ten, an essential skill the men would need for the prison's morning head count. Other lessons involved basic expressions, like *konichiwa* and *konbanwa*, respectively "good morning" and "good evening." "We had to greet them every morning with the proper salutation and had to bow to them and treat them with great respect," recalled Savadkin. "This saved us considerable unhappiness." Even with interrogations, chores, and language training, the men grew restless. "Most of the day there was nothing to do, so in our little compound we just walked back and forth, back and forth," Savadkin remembered. "Walking was a good way to keep warm."

Guards over time moved the *Tang* crew from the No. 1 barracks— designated for the camp's newcomers—to the camp's No. 2 and later No. 3 barracks as more new prisoners arrived. With each move came fewer interrogations and greater liberties. O'Kane and his men again enjoyed conversation and mingled with the camp's veteran prisoners, including Boyington, who used his job in the kitchen to dole out larger portions of rations to the hungry submariners. The greatest privilege of the new quarters, Savadkin discovered, was access to the prison's few worn and tattered books, a reported holdover from some merchantmen captured at the start of the war and whose shipboard libraries the Japanese had pilfered. "The rest of our time we spent just talking about food which was foremost in our minds and wondering how long it would be before the war was over," Savadkin recalled. "We got tired of telling one another our experiences in the war and gradually, by common consent, that was never even discussed."

Prisoners received a welcome gift on November 23—one week before Thanksgiving—when guards distributed Red Cross food packages. The starving Fitzgerald itemized the contents of the packages in his diary: two twelve-ounce cans of Spam, one twelve-ounce can of corned beef, one eight-ounce can of salmon, one six-ounce can of Rose Mill Paté, one six-ounce can of jam, two four-ounce bars of ration "D" chocolate, five to seven packages of either Camel or Chesterfield cigarettes, two packs of Wrigley's Doublemint gum, powdered milk, and coffee, a half pound of cheese, raisins, prunes, and two bars of soap. "The usual concoctions of desserts, etc., plus ways of mixing up the food is going on, 'how do you make so and such?' Well how much of the chocolate, sugar, jam etc. to do it," the skipper wrote, "and of course the exchange market among us, some liking one thing more than another and an exchange being made so that both parties are most satisfied—or so they think."

December 4 brought the camp's first freeze followed several days later by as many as four small earthquakes, strong enough to splash the water out of the pool used to collect water to fight fires. The first snow—just a half inch—fell December 13. The men celebrated Christmas two weeks later with a service that morning based on the Gospel of Luke and Psalm 23, a fitting message for Ofuna: "Though I walk through the valley of the shadow of death, I will fear no evil." The prisoners sang "Silent Night," "O Come, All Ye Faithful," and "O Little Town of Bethlehem" before concluding with a series of silent prayers for an end to the war, the safety of friends still fighting, comfort for the families back home, and for the strength to overcome the bitterness and hatred. "If it be thy will that we return safely to our beloved homeland," the men prayed, "grant that we return not broken, spiritless, but infinitely better sons, husbands, friends and citizens tempered by the ordeals we have passed through."

Snow blanketed Ofuna again after the first of the year. The *Tang* men convinced guards to allow a few of them to crowd into a single cell to share body heat. Pete Narowanski dwelled on the turkeys cooks had thawed for the trip home—before the torpedo ripped open the *Tang*—while Jesse DaSilva recalled the three apple pies he had spied on the counter as he trudged past the flooded galley. The men's hunger now manifested in physical ailments. "Still in our tattered whites and with rags for shoes, although we were each allowed a blanket, we walked incessantly in the snow to keep warm and as an antidote for the creeping paralysis of beriberi," wrote O'Kane, who dropped fifty-four pounds and suffered painful scurvy ulcers. "Our conversations ranged from boyhood to shipboard just to keep our thoughts from our stomachs, and now having shared tasks we had never dreamed of, the barriers our different ranks had imposed were steadily dropping away. I doubt that any skipper has ever learned more about his ship from the viewpoint of the troops than did I."

Caverly even confessed to bootlegging.

The men watched with elation in February as American planes pummeled Japan. O'Kane interpreted carrier operations so far north as a sign MacArthur had secured the Philippines. Guards beat any prisoner who dared a peek skyward at the torpedo bombers buzzing overhead, a beating O'Kane felt worth the risk. The increased air strikes translated into new prisoners, including twenty-three-year-old bomber pilot Lieutenant Richard Hunt, Jr. A former winner of the high school Missouri State Golf Championship, Hunt had enlisted in the Navy in February 1942 during his senior year at the University of Kansas City. During his first tour overseas in the fall of 1943, the torpedo bomber pilot was wounded near the Gilberts. Hunt returned home to recuperate before he deployed again in fall 1944. Along with another bomber pilot, Hunt was credited with sinking a Japanese battleship off the Philippines. On a mission over Hong Kong on January 16, 1945, Hunt collided with another plane and was forced to bail out. The burned and injured aviator arrived thirteen days later at the gates of Ofuna in a wheelbarrow.

Guards dumped Hunt into a cell adjacent to Bill Leibold's. *Tang's* boatswain's mate worked as Kitamura's assistant in the dispensary, a job he landed after he successfully constructed a model airplane that the medic had requested. Leibold knew firsthand what kind of treatment the flier could expect at the hands of the Butcher. Rather than remove shrapnel from a B-24 gunner's groin, Kitamura once punched the prisoner's wound to drain pus. Another time the medic only gave a few bandages to a flying boat pilot who had been shot down and burned—his wounds later became so infected that maggots ate his flesh. When one airman arrived with a clean bullet hole in his right thigh, Kitamura delighted in reopening the wound, day after day for some five months. "He would run a swab completely through the hole, a dry cotton swab. This would break through the part of the wound that was healed," Grant Butcher would later testify. "Many of the men who got this treatment passed out, but I was so unfortunate as to remain conscious throughout the ordeal."

In between cleaning the medic's quarters and shining his shoes, Leibold studied Kitamura. The Butcher hoarded rolls of fresh dressings, vitamins, and B_1 vials in a four-foot-long trunk, supplies he refused to administer to sick prisoners, but traded with local villagers, one time returning to camp with carpenter tools he had coveted. Kitamura over the course of a month treated a young village girl, carefully washing her eyes out. Other times he treated the cook's wife for beriberi and even performed house calls for her twice a week, taking precious camp supplies with him. His care for the local villagers was so common that many showed up and walked unescorted through the camp straight to the treatment room. Prisoners in contrast received almost no care. Kitamura's treatment for diarrhea was to withhold food. He forced prisoners to wear recycled bandages that helped spread infection, bandages Kitamura made Leibold wash of blood and pus. As one prisoner noted: "A man being treated for a sore throat had the same rag used on his throat as a man who was treated for hemorrhoids." The only time Leibold ever saw Kitamura use a fresh gauze bandage was to shine his samurai sword.

The pale and exhausted Hunt had arrived at Ofuna in rough shape. Third-degree burns ran from his feet to his knees on both legs and the skin had begun to rot. Additional burns peppered his chest, back, and shoulders. Pus oozed from facial burns and dried tracks marked his skin, like tears. Hunt suffered from a compound and comminuted fracture between the elbow and shoulder of his left arm. A wire splint offered the only support for the unset and shattered arm, which drained dark pus from a hole in his punctured skin. His bandaged right arm hung limp and useless. The day after his arrival at Ofuna, guards ordered the burned and broken aviator—covered in bloodied bandages from the hips down and with a blanket thrown over his head as a makeshift blindfold—to trudge at least fifty yards from his cold cell to Kitamura's office. "He staggered most of the way," Leibold would later testify. "His wounds were poorly bandaged and blood was running out of the bandages on his legs."

Leibold witnessed the Butcher examine Hunt only a handful of times, eventually allowing the *Tang* boatswain's mate and a fellow prisoner Charles Rogers of the British Royal Navy to carry the pilot to Kitamura's office on a

stretcher. On that first visit Kitamura ordered Leibold and Rogers to position the stretcher alongside a bench. The Butcher then rolled Hunt off the
stretcher so that the carrier aviator landed on his broken arm. Kitamura then
ordered the prisoners to wait outside for forty-five minutes, leaving the medic
alone with Hunt. The prisoners knew the Butcher seemed to reserve his
harshest treatment for aviators, payback no doubt for the increased bombings of Japan. Hunt experienced Kitamura's torment on his first visit. When
Leibold returned to retrieve him some forty-five minutes later, Hunt confided
that the Butcher had "worked him over," even jerking his broken arm. Kitamura hurt him again on his next visit. Hunt begged Leibold not to take him
back.

Hunt spent his days alone in his cell, unable even to feed himself. Leibold
watched from his nearby cell as guards and fellow prisoners delivered his
food, then returned later to retrieve the uneaten rice and soup. One of those
food carriers was Hayes Trukke, *Tang*'s blond-haired torpedoman. Hunt's
condition pained the submariner, who noted that every time Hunt moved
he left a trail of blood. "A guard stood by me as I placed his soup and rice
by his bed and Hunt asked me would I help him eat it. I started to tell him I
couldn't and the guard gave me the usual growl and slapped me, pushing me
from his cell," Trukke would later testify. "At the end of a week Hunt hadn't
eaten anything and his cell smelled terrible, also it was evident he was losing his mind. He told me there was a man hiding behind his door and other
things on that order. A couple of days later one of the newer guards let me
stay in Hunt's cell and feed him but he ate only a small portion of rice and
soup and then vomited it a little later."

The *Tang* men knew food—even Ofuna's meager rations—offered Hunt
his only chance of survival. He needed to eat and build up his strength to
heal. Kitamura's refusal to allow fellow prisoners to feed Hunt prompted
O'Kane to go over him. The skipper appealed to Ofuna chief interrogator
Yuzuru Sanematsu, a man prisoners dubbed the "Little Captain." O'Kane's
request was denied. Hunt began to starve alone in his cell just as the February temperatures plummeted. Snow blew through the cracks in the walls and
even healthy prisoners struggled to keep warm in unheated cells. Leibold
refused to sit idle, even if it meant suffering the Butcher's wrath. "Some of the
other prisoners and I sneaked into Hunt's cell several times when the guards
were not looking to cover him and try to make him comfortable, as it was

very cold and Hunt was unable to keep covers on himself," Leibold recalled. "Hunt was given no medical attention and had to lay in his own excretion as he was too weak to go to the head."

Guards refused to touch Hunt, whose cell stank of burned skin, infection, and feces. Few even dared to venture into his cell. The only time guards did so was to pound a bat on the floor at night and laugh at Hunt, now delirious with pain, reliving his crash over and over again. Kitamura finally relented and allowed Leibold twice to enter Hunt's cell, but only to clean his filthy dressings. "When I tried to wash these bandages there were bits of flesh and matter clinging to them that I was unable to get off," Leibold would later testify. "Consequently I had to take them out and bury them." The prisoner in the cell next to the burned pilot heard his delirium finally fall silent. Hunt died at 9:40 p.m. on February 25. "Kitamura and Commander Sanematsu were directly responsible for his death," Leibold testified. "I firmly believe that with a little care Hunt would have survived."

Hunt's death would not be the last at Ofuna.

The Allied assault on Japan had now reached the homeland and bombers crowded the skies over major cities. Interrogators pressured guards to break the will of prisoners who could provide intelligence that might help Japan counter the furious attacks. Guards ramped up the beatings and slashed the already meager diets. The *Tang* men were not immune. Guards liked to force O'Kane—who became Ofuna's senior prisoner when Fitzgerald was transferred—to punch fellow captives. Other times guards thrashed him, including a Kitamura-ordered attack in April that cost the skipper some teeth. "After five full swings from the six-foot guard with closed fists to my jaw and ear, I was still standing mainly because of the wall behind me," O'Kane would later testify. "Kitamura who was standing in back of the guard watching each blow then ordered him to hit me five more times in spite of blood coming from my mouth and chips of my teeth falling out."

Prisoners began to unravel. One man repeatedly sang a line from the song "Freight Train Blues" while others obsessed over the camp's policy of a cigarette in exchange for 100 dead flies. "One of the more pathetic sights I witnessed at Ofuna was seeing full grown men, all of varying degrees of sanity or insanity, salvaging dead rats and garbage out of the dump. These items would be placed in a choice spot in the sunlight to attract the flies, which were swatted," one prisoner would later testify. "The dead flies would then be picked up by the fingers and placed in a can containing dead flies, filled with maggots." Starving prisoners withered. Beriberi ravaged many by spring, leaving some unable to walk. Others stumbled. "Naval intelligence had obviously expected that the physical terror and the starvation diet would break men down, but that the food would be sufficient until the prisoners were transferred to registered camps," O'Kane observed. "They had miscalculated and now took alarm."

When a diet swap of bread for barley coupled with shots to fight dysentery failed to improve prisoner health, the Japanese decided to transfer nineteen captives to a camp in Tokyo, including Boyington and *Tang*'s six enlisted sailors. *Tang* officers O'Kane, Savadkin, and Flanagan would remain in Ofuna until late July. The *Tang* enlisted men bid farewell on April 5 and hiked up the dirt road that had delivered them to Ofuna 155 days earlier. Boyington led the crew. The fighter ace had first arrived at the camp in late March 1944, marveling at the beauty of the Japanese countryside as he approached Ofuna's gate. A year of beatings, torture, and starvation had changed Boyington's perspective. "I looked back over my shoulder at the closed gates of Ofuna with no nostalgia," Boyington would later write. "When we walked back the same road I came in on originally, I wasn't conscious of the quiet wooded scenery in the same way, for I saw no beauty in looking back anyplace."

21

TANG

"Recurrently I am homesick, but even home and the loved ones there seem so distant—so indistinct and far off that even my homesickness is instinctive rather than voluntary."

—Ernest Norquist,
July 14, 1943, diary

Boyington, the six enlisted *Tang* survivors, and twelve other former Ofuna captives climbed aboard a streetcar that wound down out of the hills toward Tokyo, a trip the fighter ace estimated at about twenty-five miles. The men disembarked upon arrival and marched the rest of the way, crossing a narrow bridge that led to a small island that housed Omori prison. Guards lined up the new arrivals in front of the camp's administration building for orientation. The men prayed the transfer to Omori would mark the end of their status as special prisoners. They hoped that the American government—and more importantly, the men's families—would now learn the truth that they were still alive. The captives stood at attention all day before the camp's gray-haired commander emerged at dusk amid the profuse bows from his subordinates. The colonel turned to address the new arrivals with the aid of an interpreter. "You are to remain in this camp as 'special prisoners,'" he barked. "If any of you try to escape you will be killed."

Omori served as the main prisoner of war camp for Tokyo and Yoko-hama. American investigators would discover at the war's end that there were twenty-one branch camps, including Ofuna, which housed a combined 6,050 prisoners. Unlike Ofuna, where the Japanese imprisoned men in individual cells, Omori's unheated barracks resembled human stables. Some 600 captives crowded each night into the shotgun-style quarters. A dirt path bisected each barracks with two raised sleeping platforms along either side, one stacked about five feet above the other. Newcomers slept up top while veterans stretched out below. Lice, fleas, and bedbugs feasted on them all. Many prisoners worked at rail yards, wharves, and warehouses, promising opportunities to steal everything from rice and canned goods to dried fish and grain alcohol, the contraband hidden in pant cuffs, false pockets, and even in socks suspended inside trouser legs. Stolen sugar served as Omori's illicit currency. Prisoners swapped sugar for food with captives on different work details while others bartered with the guards for cigarettes. Some even forked over a half canteen of sugar as payment for a night with one of the camp's homosexuals.

Work not only supplemented the men's diets, but helped prisoners pass the days faster, though some jobs proved better than others. Men scooped feces from the pit latrines into wooden buckets, then hauled them dangling from bamboo poles to dump into a beachside pit just outside the prison. Others worked in the camp's leather shop, stitching ammunition pouches for the military, or lugged sacks of coal across Omori's causeway from the mainland. Most prisoners labored offsite, sorting steel in scrap yards and unloading lumber and coal from railcars and ships. Other captives hauled steel rails and plates to help build air raid shelters. Prisoners used these glimpses of the enemy's homeland and the daily lives of Japan's citizenry to chart the war's progress. "Disappointed with what I see of Tokyo," American Ernest Norquist, who survived the 1942 Bataan Death March, wrote in his diary. "It is decrepit. Trucks and cars run on charcoal and are all over age. Houses and shops are ramshackle and in need of repairs. Factories are like junk heaps."

Most captives—except the special prisoners—enjoyed greater freedoms than in Ofuna. British prisoners captured in Hong Kong entertained the camp at night with jazz and orchestra concerts while a Red Cross phonograph belted out tunes such as "Queenie, the Strip-Tease" and "Don't Sit Under the Apple Tree." Captives even produced a New Year's Eve play, a spin-off of Shakespeare's *The Tempest*. "The change to Omori was like surfacing after an all day dive," O'Kane wrote, "for the 500 prisoners made it impossible for the guards to single out individuals." But the effort needed to hold out hope for the war's end wore down many prisoners. "The waiting seems more than a man can stand. I even hate to be with people at times. I crave both solitude and open spaces—and freedom," Norquist wrote. "I've worn ruts into my memory thinking the same thoughts over and over. Even my plans for the future have grown stale with the long anticipation."

The bombing that helped buoy prisoner morale intensified—bombing that came at the hands of one of America's deadliest new weapons, the B-29 Superfortress. Boeing's aeronautical monster more than lived up to its name, boasting the largest propellers ever fitted on a plane along with a sprawling 141-foot wingspan—twenty feet longer than the distance of the Wright brothers' first successful flight. Constructed out of some 55,000 parts, twelve miles of wiring and tubing, plus 600,000 rivets, the four-engine bomber could haul ten tons of ordnance and fly some 4,000 miles across the ocean, a task that demanded a railroad tanker car's worth of oil and fuel. Engineers spared nothing, from pressurized cabins that allowed fliers to operate free of oxygen masks at altitudes as high as seven miles to built-in ashtrays for the standard eleven-member crew. Hailed by the *New York Times* as a "magnificent instrument of destruction," the Superfortress ushered in the air war "against the heart of the Japanese Empire."

The horror that this new air war would bring to Japan became clear in the predawn hours of March 10, 1945. Some 300 bombers had lifted off from Guam, Saipan, and Tinian at sunset, aimed at Japan's capital of Tokyo, the world's third-largest city. B-29s dropped 1,667 tons of incendiary bombs on the city's center, an area crowded with as many as 100,000 people per square mile. The fires proved so intense that bombers en route used them to navigate from 200 miles out while airmen as high as 20,000 feet over the city could read their watch dials. Soot even blackened the bombers' bellies. Recon photographs taken hours later would reveal 15.8 square miles of homes, shops, and industry had burned as the fires reached the edge of the emperor's palace. The attack killed 83,793 people, injured another 40,918, and left one million homeless. "I have never seen such a display of destruction," wrote a *Boston Globe* journalist who flew in one of the B-29s. "I not only saw Tokyo burning furiously in many sections, but I smelled it."

American Frank Fujita, imprisoned in Tokyo, described the horrific attack in his diary. "Almost instantly it seemed as if the entire city burst into flames," wrote Fujita, who had been captured in 1942 in Java. "Fires created other fires and then their up-drafts would join and create monstrous 'fire storms' that

sent flames thousands of feet into the air. It was awesome." The true destruction greeted the Japanese and Allied prisoners at daybreak. "We saw such a
sight as I have never seen in all my life," Omori's Norquist wrote in his diary.
"Even we as prisoners, who have suffered so much, did not glory in what we
saw—miles of destruction, block after block of charred ruins, as far as the
eye could see, where just yesterday the flimsy dwellings and shops had stood.
Twisted metal, smoldering wood, household goods and what not else, lay in
black heaps. There was the stench of burnt flesh and the suffocating smell
of smoke in the air. Women stood weeping, with children on their backs.
Ragged, tired-looking men pushed carts or carried bundles that held all their
rescued earthly possessions."

Tokyo proved only the start. Bombers returned night after night, pounding the major cities of Nagoya, Osaka, and Kobe. In just ten days B-29s flew
1,595 sorties, dropping 9,373 tons of bombs on Japan's arsenals, factories,
and shipyards. More than thirty-one square miles vanished. The size of these
airborne armadas only grew as new $600,000 Superfortresses rolled off as-
sembly lines each week at plants in Washington, Kansas, and Georgia. The
same military that could muster only 111 bombers in November 1944 for the
first Tokyo attack since Jimmy Doolittle's raid now sent five times that many
planes. On a mission in late May more than 550 bombers—with over 6,000
fliers crowded inside them—pummeled Tokyo in a nearly two-hour attack in
which about forty tons of bombs dropped each minute. Reconnaisance photos revealed that the fifteen square miles leveled in March jumped to fifty-one
square miles of charred ruins in less than three months, an area more than
double the size of Manhattan island.

Prisoners at the Tokyo area camps sat ringside to this holocaust. The
scream of air raid sirens—dubbed the "music" by the prisoners—would send
guards scurrying into shelters. The exposed captives could do little more than
watch and pray to survive as bombers darkened the skies. Australian Captain
John Woodward, a surgeon with the Indian Medical Service captured after
the British surrendered Hong Kong on Christmas Day 1941, described an
attack on Yokohama that left standing little more than scorched chimneys.
"We went to a top window to see the raid. From 12 till 2 B-29s accompanied
by fighters came over in unwavering formation and the sound of their bombs
on the distant Yokohama was like the continuous roll of a drum. After we
had counted 200 planes, both planes, city and sun were obscured by smoke

and we saw no more," Woodward wrote. "The following morning when the smoke had cleared Yokohama had vanished and in its place were blackened smouldering ruins."

The merciless pounding at times brushed right up against the gates of Omori—one attack even destroyed the causeway—where prisoners waited and wondered how much more Japan could tolerate. "Shrapnel from incendiaries whizzed into our camp," Norquist wrote in his diary in late May. "Scraps of burnt paper fluttered in all day from huge blazes. What a sight!" Boyington and the *Tang* sailors, though sequestered from the other prisoners in a special barracks, watched the attacks, too. To the starving prisoners, Boyington would later write, the silver B-29s looked beautiful. "The ground would shake. The windows would tremble and shake, and the sills on the doors would creak back and forth," Boyington wrote. "Yet this was not so bothersome as at night, when the B-29s came over low, at around four to six thousand feet. We could hear them swoop down and dive, the engines roaring. We didn't know where they were, didn't know when to duck. We could just put our faces down into our cotton blankets—and hope."

The Japanese ordered Omori's special prisoners to sift through the debris of American bombings. "We would walk to these outskirts in areas where houses had been burned out. There would be bodies, dead bodies hither and yon," recalled *Tang*'s Clay Decker. "They had flat bed trucks. We had to load the dead bodies on these flat bed trucks. Then we would clean up the rest of the debris." Weakened by beriberi and chronic diarrhea, the *Tang*'s Jesse DaSilva made tea for the men, using a five-gallon water can he carried. The rest of the time he scavenged for garbage the men could eat, like discarded vegetables and fish heads. "When you're starving, anything tastes good," DaSilva said. "Another time when we were all on a tea break and sitting around talking, a stray old dog came around. We immediately discussed the possibility of eating this animal if only someone had the nerve to kill it. But of course, nobody would."

The men labored in the rubble one day when a Japanese woman approached their guard, a gentle man with a limp the prisoners had nicknamed Gimpy. The filthy and emaciated prisoners horrified the woman. She left and returned. When she departed the second time, Gimpy summoned the prisoners. The woman had given them a ball of *mochi*, a pounded rice cake. As the senior-ranking prisoner and group leader, Boyington cut up the ball into nineteen pieces, a tiny sliver for each man. The woman returned the following day and brought the men candy carrots. Work not only promised the occasional bite of food, but also in Boyington's case helped with his nicotine fix. The fighter ace scavenged the ruins for discarded cigarette butts, which he smuggled back into camp. He collected the tobacco and rolled his own cigarettes, using any paper he could find. When the light came through the cell window at the right time of day, he would use a convex flashlight lens to light the first one. He would then chain-smoke them all, lighting a new one off the last.

The work coupled with the lack of food took its toll on the *Tang* survivors as spring turned to summer. Given lesser rations than official prisoners of war—and cut off from Omori's illicit bartering system—submariners who had once enjoyed the Navy's finest meals slowly starved to death. The six-foot-tall DaSilva, who weighed 168 pounds when he joined the submarine service, dropped to just 100 pounds. His feet swelled up, making it too painful to walk. He stopped laboring in the rubble with the others. Machinist's mate Decker's weight plummeted from almost 170 pounds to just 102 pounds. Leibold suffered hepatitis and a beating from a guard left his foot and leg infected. O'Kane turned bright yellow from jaundice. Recently transferred from Omori to another camp, Norquist captured in his diary the plight of many such prisoners on the eve of the war's end. "I'm so weak I can hardly walk. How long can we keep on this schedule?" he wrote. "We work day and night now. Lord, deliver us soon!"

The wait for the war's end would prove too much for some. Stronger prisoners began to contemplate how the conflict might end. Would troops storm the beaches, as they did at Guadalcanal, Saipan, and Iwo Jima? What would the Japanese do with the thousands of captives—many weak and infirm—crowded in flea-infested prisons like Omori? March them inland for a final stand? Kill them? Let them go? Other prisoners looked past the war's end. What would life be like, the return home to parents, wives, sons and daughters? How had the beatings, torture, and starvation shaped them? Twenty-two-year-old Frank Fujita, forced to make propaganda radio messages, wrestled with these questions in his diary. "If we are to be free, we will emerge emaciated, weary fragments of humanity into a strange world; endowed with nothing but a few measly dollars, an unsurpassed knowledge of human nature and such a morbid philosophy on life that it will serve to ostracize us from society, should we put it to use," Fujita wrote. "We will be easy to please and hard to fool."

Prison gave other captives a chance to reflect on life's priorities and hopes for the future. Many looked forward to leaving the service, marrying and starting families, thoughts reflected in Minnesota native Norquist's diary. "I dream of home again and again and again. I dream, too, of the home that is to be—God grant that it may! The home that the one I love shall plan and build and live in. Shall I someday know a little one who will call me 'Daddy' and climb on my knee? A little bit of my own self in miniature," Norquist wrote. "I want to enjoy life as never before and find in each day an adventure. I want to be known as hospitable always by every friend and acquaintance. And yet, I want to be alone at times too—to fish in streams and lakes, and wander through the old familiar countryside with perhaps just a faithful hound to accompany me. I want to get away from the Army—to be a civilian again—to wear the clothes I want to wear when I want to wear them and be my own master again."

Colonel Paul Tibbets, Jr., throttled up his B-29 bomber in the muggy predawn darkness of August 6. The veteran pilot of more than two dozen combat missions over Europe and North Africa couldn't help but feel nervous as he stared down the chipped coral runway on the tiny Pacific island of Tinian. America's relentless pounding of Japan had so far failed to force the enemy to surrender even though bombers had burned up almost 160 square miles of Japan's urban centers. Secured in the bomb bay just a few feet away from Tibbets sat what American leaders hoped would be a persuasive new weapon. Experts estimated that the 9,000-pound atomic bomb—nicknamed "Little Boy"—packed the punch of more than 20,000 tons of TNT, a horrific force equivalent to what 2,000 B-29s would carry. Tibbets released the brakes at 2:45 a.m. The newly christened *Enola Gay*—named in honor of his red-haired mother back home in Miami—roared down the runway at 155 miles per hour and lifted off into the dark.

Tibbets puffed his Kaywoodie Briar pipe as the *Enola Gay* with its twelve-member crew droned across the empty ocean, reaching Iwo Jima at 5:55 a.m. He looked down a few hours later on Hiroshima 30,700 feet below—pleased at the lack of fighters and antiaircraft fire—and noted its streets, buildings, and waterfront piers. A 7 a.m. air raid alarm had sent many of the city's

250,000 residents into shelters, only to emerge an hour later after the all clear signal. Families sat down to breakfast. Businessmen and shopkeepers rushed to work this Monday morning. Overhead, the *Enola Gay*'s pneumatic bomb bay doors yawned open. At 8:15 a.m. the bomb dropped. Tibbets turned the plane 155 degrees, the engines roaring. Forty-three seconds later, Little Boy detonated. A blue-white light lit up the plane's cabin. The plume rose 45,000 feet in the air as the copilot Robert Lewis jotted down on the back of War Department forms he used as a makeshift log: "My God, what have we done?"

American investigators after the war estimated that the attack killed approximately 80,000 men, women, and children, some charred black. As many as 100,000 others suffered injuries. The blast leveled more than four square miles and destroyed 65,000 of Hiroshima's 90,000 homes, schools, and factories. Clothes erupted in flames and clay roof tiles bubbled when temperatures surpassed 3,200 degrees. Radiation not only exposed X-rays housed in the concrete basement of a hospital but made the fillings in Tibbets's teeth tingle miles overhead. In a statement issued sixteen hours after the attack, President Harry Truman warned that Hiroshima was only the start. Failure to surrender would invite a "rain of ruin from the air, the like of which has never been seen on this earth.

"The force from which the sun draws its power has been loosed against those who brought war to the Far East," Truman declared. "Let there be no mistake; we shall completely destroy Japan's ability to make war."

Bombers carried the president's threat directly to the Japanese people, dropping millions of leaflets that begged residents to evacuate urban areas and pressure the government to surrender. "We are in possession of the most destructive explosive ever devised by man," stated the translation of one such leaflet. "We have just begun to use this weapon against your homeland. If you still have any doubt, make inquiry as to what happened to Hiroshima when just one atomic bomb fell on that city." The pressure intensified as Russia declared war, steamrolling across Japanese-held Manchuria. On the Thursday morning of August 9, a second B-29 shot down Tinian's darkened runway. Hours later the atomic bomb dubbed "Fat Man" plummeted toward the congested city of Nagasaki. The explosion that muggy summer morning flattened 1.8 square miles. Postwar investigators estimated that the attack killed approximately 45,000 people and injured as many as 60,000.

Japan could take it no longer. A radio announcer informed the Japanese public at 7:21 a.m. on August 15 that Emperor Hirohito would deliver an address over the airwaves at noon. Officials planned to provide power to blacked-out districts and ordered receivers set up at government buildings, train stations, and post offices. Only hours earlier the emperor had read his entire speech into a microphone, 625 words when later translated into English, allowing audio engineers to capture it on a gramophone record. It took two tries before engineers felt the emperor—with tears in his eyes—successfully recorded the words designed to end the war that for America had started at Pearl Harbor three years, eight months, and eight days earlier.

At noon throughout Japan millions of men, women, and children crowded around radios to hear for the first time the voice of the Sacred Crane. Even Hirohito, secure in an underground shelter after a failed military coup, tuned in with a portable RCA radio. Captives watched at one of the prison camps as guards dressed in formal uniforms—complete with swords—bowed to the radio. O'Kane and other prisoners from Omori, forced to dig bomb shelters, paused to listen as guards piped the broadcast over the worksite loudspeaker. The announcer asked listeners to please stand. Japan's national anthem played. In Studio 8 of the NHK building, engineers cued the recording; the emperor's voice now crackled over the airwaves. "To our good and loyal subjects," Hirohito began. "After pondering deeply the general trends of the world and the actual conditions obtaining in Our Empire today, we have decided to effect a settlement of the present situation by resorting to an extraordinary measure."

That extraordinary measure was, of course, Japan's surrender, though Hirohito's four-minute-and-forty-two-second recording was ambiguous. Rather than admit defeat, the emperor told his subjects that the "war situation has developed not necessarily to Japan's advantage." The war had never been about territorial gains, he argued, but Japan's self-preservation, something the atomic bomb now threatened. "The enemy has begun to employ a new and most cruel bomb, the power of which to damage is indeed incalculable, taking the toll of many innocent lives," the emperor said. "Should we continue to fight, it would not only result in an ultimate collapse and obliteration of the Japanese nation, but also it would lead to the total extinction of human civilization. Such being the case, how are we to save the millions of our subjects; or to atone ourselves before the hallowed spirits of our imperial ancestors? This is the reason why we have ordered the acceptance of the provisions of the Joint Declaration of the Powers."

The news of Japan's surrender reverberated around the war-weary world. Fleet Admiral Chester Nimitz broadcast a message to all naval forces in the Pacific to cease operations, but continue searches, patrols, and remain vigilant. Vice Admiral Charles Lockwood fired off a message of his own to the submarine force. "The long awaited day has come and ceasefire has been sounded. As force Comdr I desire to congratulate each and every officer and man of the submarine force upon a job superbly well done. My admiration for your daring skill, initiative, determination, and loyalty cannot be adequately expressed. Whether you fought in enemy waters or whether you sweated at bases or in tenders you have all contributed to the end which has this day been achieved. You have deserved the lasting peace which we all hope has been won for future generations," Lockwood wrote, ending with a reminder of those destined never to come home. "May God rest the gallant souls of those missing presumed lost."

Following Hirohito's broadcast, guards ordered O'Kane and the other prisoners to stop work, gather up the tools, and march back to camp. Other work parties streamed through Omori's gates that afternoon, including a group of British captives who sang. Some of the Japanese at Omori slaughtered a horse, then left with the meat, though Omori's crafty cooks salvaged the horse's intestines, chopped them up, and mixed them with gyp corn that would serve as part of a makeshift celebratory feast for the prisoners. Boyington stretched out on his back on his straw mat, suffering from jaundice and unable to work. One of the guards, an elderly man the fighter ace respected, summoned the major. He informed Boyington of Japan's surrender. The major had learned enough Japanese to understand the guard, but after twenty months in captivity the gravity of his words failed to register. Boyington's blank stare prompted the guard to repeat the news. "The war is over," he declared. "It was over fifteen minutes ago."

The special prisoners gathered that night for the evening formation, led as always by Boyington. "Hey, fellows," the major called out. "We don't know whether this is over, but I would like to suggest something."

"What is it?" came the chorus.

"Let's stay in formation and all repeat the Lord's Prayer."

And so they did.

The guards burned many of the compound's records that night, a move the *Tang*'s Savadkin felt signified that the war had truly ended. The shock of the emperor's surrender message drove many of Omori's guards to drink. Boyington, O'Kane, and the *Tang* crew woke up to a banging on the barracks door. The on-duty guard warned the men that some of his inebriated colleagues had debated killing the Americans. The guard handed Boyington a hammer and nails to seal the door. The prisoners peered through the cracks as a drunken noncommissioned officer stumbled and shouted, slicing the air with his sword. Despite the on-duty guard's efforts to restrain him, the drunken guard pounded on the door. The prisoners feared he would break it down. Boyington gripped the hammer and perched next to the door, planning to crush the drunk's skull should it open. "Let me at the captives," the drunk barked. "I am going to kill all of them. I'll prove to them that Japan is greater than the United States. Let me at them."

The drunks had sobered up—or passed out—by the morning. The prison commander accompanied by an interpreter visited the *Tang* crew's barracks and asked about the quality of the living conditions, a visit that surprised the men since the commander had never before shown any interest in Omori's special prisoners. The commander's visit preceded an issuance of new clothes along with multivitamins, iron tablets, and cod-liver oil pills. Medics began sick call for the special prisoners and increased the meager food rations, improved treatment many greeted with cynicism. "It seems as if the Japanese were trying in a few days of kindness to make up for the years of deprivation and cruelty," Norquist wrote in his diary. "I have no desire or plans for revenge. I want to go home and forget about Japan and everything here. I'll be so very happy to be truly free that I won't be able to be mad at anybody at all. Just let me be free, and everything else will take care of itself. May God grant it soon."

American planes soon appeared in the skies above Omori. British prisoner Harry Berry, captured in 1942 in Singapore, described the euphoria that seized prisoners during one such flyover. "We all stood out in the open, rain or no rain, stripped to the waist standing on roofs or anything else available and cheered and waved like mad," Berry wrote in his diary. "One pilot must have seen one of our Yanks who was standing on the roof signaling him to dive. He dived straight towards him and just skimmed the fence." Frank Fujita climbed atop one of the latrines as a pilot buzzed the camp, tossing down his half empty pack of cigarettes with a note that read: "Hang on! It won't be long now!" "When he came over we all waved and I was going to shout or let out a big yell for joy but no sound would come out," Fujita later wrote. "There was a lump in my throat about the size of a grapefruit and the harder I tried to yell the worse it hurt. I was so emotional and elated that I almost burst out in tears."

The B-29s that had for months rained fire down on Japanese cities returned, but now hauling 10,000-pound loads of medicine, canned food, and clothes. The massive bombers, with "P.W. Supplies" painted beneath the wings in three-foot-high block letters, slowed to just 165 miles per hour and buzzed as low as 500 feet over the camps, parachuting fifty-five-gallon drums. America planned the loads for three-, seven-, and ten-day drops, the first and most important containing medical supplies, soups, and juices; foods that starving prisoners could easily digest. The seven-day drops delivered more substantive foods and extra medicines, while the ten-day drops consisted largely of canned foods. During the twenty-four days beginning on August 27, bombers would fly some 900 sorties, dropping 4,470 tons of food, clothes, and medicine to captives at some 158 camps scattered across Japan, China, Korea, and Formosa. These supplies would help the prisoners survive until America could evacuate them.

Prisoners climbed atop Omori's barracks and used Japanese tooth powder mixed with water to paint messages on the rooftops, including a three-word communiqué that would appear as a photo in the *New York Times*: "Pappy Boyington Here!" Supplies soon rained down, from toothbrushes and razors to soap, cigarettes, and chewing gum. Prisoners devoured ham sandwiches and popped handfuls of sugarcoated vitamins, sucking the sweet layer off them like candy. "This is better," Harry Berry wrote in his diary, "than any Christmas I have had." Some of the drums dropped into the bay while others tore free of the parachutes and crashed to the ground, including one that busted through an office window. "Everyone ran for cover just in time," Fujita wrote of one such scare. "When the steel drums hit the ground, the tackwelds broke loose and here came all the little cans of food, shooting out like shrapnel."

Boyington watched the B-29 drops from the safety of a bomb shelter. "Why don't you stay out here and get some of this stuff," one prisoner asked the major.

"After living through all I have," the fighter ace fired back, "I'm damned if I'm going to be killed by being hit on the head by a crate of peaches."

22

TANG

"I have been dead 2½ years while the world has passed me by—just existing from day to day a slave for the Japs."

—Carl Quarterman,
September 15, 1945, letter

Commodore Joel Boone climbed on board a Navy landing craft shortly before 3 p.m. on August 29 in Tokyo Bay. The mission this muggy afternoon of Boone's fifty-sixth birthday: liberate the prisoners of war at Omori. A former physician to presidents Warren Harding, Calvin Coolidge, and Herbert Hoover, the mustached Boone's job was to help identify and evacuate the most critical prisoners first. No one was better suited for the job. The Pennsylvania native in July 1918 had repeatedly braved enemy fire and gas on a French battlefield to treat wounded Marines, heroism that earned him the Medal of Honor. American forces had spent the nine days since Hirohito's broadcast of Japan's surrender planning the rescue of thousands of Allied prisoners. The Navy had trained special medical units, assembled portable communication sets, and prepared landing forces. Boone and others had pored over intelligence reports and studied maps and aerial photographs of the prisons in preparation for their mission.

Supreme Commander for the Allied Powers General Douglas MacArthur had ordered the Navy to wait for the Army before liberating prisoners. A picket boat patrolling near shore south of Tokyo the night of August 27 had rescued two escaped British prisoners who recounted gruesome stories of captivity, stories Boone had confirmed the next day in a briefing with a Swiss doctor with the International Red Cross. Admiral Halsey felt he couldn't wait. Liberation must begin immediately. He fired off a plea to MacArthur, alerting him that local emissaries reported some 6,125 prisoners in Tokyo area camps with 417 of them bedridden. Halsey informed MacArthur that he had three hospital ships along with thirty doctors, ninety corpsmen, and enough food and clothes for 3,000 men with enough medical personnel and supplies on the way to accommodate up to 4,000 more. "I propose for most expeditious action," he urged. "All of the facilities under my command are available to you."

Most of Halsey's Third Fleet at the time lay at anchor twenty-five miles south of Tokyo in scenic Sagami Bay near the emperor's summer palace and with a view of iconic Mount Fuji on the distant horizon. The colorful admiral known as Bull, who made headlines after he boasted of his plan to ride through the capital on Hirohito's white horse, weighed anchor and steamed into Tokyo Bay the morning of August 29, followed a few hours later by the cruiser *San Juan* and the hospital ship *Benevolence*. Halsey's 9:40 a.m. meeting with Boone and other senior officers on board the battleship *Missouri* only reconfirmed his belief that the Navy needed to begin evacuations immediately—with or without MacArthur's blessing. Halsey outlined the dire scenario to Fleet Admiral Nimitz, the commander in chief of the Pacific Fleet and Pacific Ocean areas, moments after the five-star admiral touched down on board a seaplane from Guam at 2:20 p.m. and climbed aboard the battleship *South Dakota*, Nimitz's flagship.

"Go ahead," Nimitz replied. "General MacArthur will understand."

The landing craft pulled away from *San Juan* just forty minutes later, cutting through the water toward Omori. Boone moments earlier had dashed off a note to *Benevolence*'s senior medical officer to prepare to screen and care for the prisoners, but hospitalize only the sick. Able-bodied prisoners would be sent on to other ships. The surgeon also had forwarded color-coded tags he'd created to help classify the returning prisoners. On board the landing craft with Boone sat Commodore Rodger Simpson, commander of the rescue operation, and his chief of staff, Commander Harold Stassen, who had resigned as governor of Minnesota in 1943 to go on active duty in the Navy. The *Missouri*'s chaplain accompanied the men as an interpreter. Two other landing craft with Red Cross officials and additional medical officers and hospital corpsmen followed. Navy planes buzzed overhead, guiding the three boats some four miles across the bay toward Omori on this muggy summer afternoon.

Prisoners on the beach at Omori had watched America's massive warships steam into Tokyo Bay with great excitement. The promised liberation appeared at hand. For the nine survivors of *Tang*, the war's end had arrived just in time. The reduced rations given to the special prisoners had pushed O'Kane and his crew to the brink of starvation. None weighed over 100 pounds and beriberi had crippled most of them. Motor machinist's mate Jesse DaSilva could hardly walk, while Clay Decker could press on his ravaged muscles and make them dimple. The hepatitis that had racked Leibold had now hit O'Kane, the suspected culprit a dirty needle the Japanese had used to inoculate the prisoners. Jaundice had turned him ocher, a color that reminded Leibold of a Philip Morris cigarette pack. O'Kane was so weak he needed help just to get off his *tatami* mat. He struggled even to eat. The Navy's arrival in the bay had buoyed morale. Many of the prisoners collected around the beach, including *Tang*'s Clay Decker and Pete Narowanski, waiting to see what would happen.

"What's that?" a prisoner shouted around 4 p.m.

The prisoners stared out as the landing crafts roared toward them, a scene British captive Harry Berry captured in his diary. "Nobody doubted that they were anything else but a landing party and everybody was right. As they drew near we could see three launches, the last one flying the Stars and Stripes. Everybody went mad. From out of nowhere came the home-made Union Jacks, Stars and Stripes and the Dutch flag. Everyone dashed along the beach shouting and guiding the barges in. Some men swam out to meet them," he wrote. "The camp was in an uproar." Everyone that is except Boyington, who after twenty months in captivity felt empty. "All these months I had been wondering what my reaction would be on being rescued. I could imagine myself crying, maybe laughing and jumping around, doing practically anything. As I looked around, all these prisoners were now doing these things," the major wrote. "But for my own part I was numb. I just couldn't feel. I couldn't cry. I couldn't laugh."

Frank Fujita jumped in the water and began to swim out to the boats, still dressed in his clothes and shoes. Fujita swam some forty yards before he found his strength depleted. He sucked in a mouthful of water as his head slipped beneath the waves. Fujita struggled back to the surface, took a deep breath, and tried to arch his back to remain afloat. He saw one of the landing craft headed toward him and feared the propeller would chop him to pieces. The exhausted Fujita again slipped underwater. Why had he been so foolish in his weakened state, he thought, to attempt to swim out to the boats? "I had ended my own life just at the moment of liberation," he wrote, making one last kick toward the surface. "The next thing I knew, two large hands had me by the head and were pulling me out of the water, and then another sailor helped lay me on the deck of the landing craft," he wrote. "As the other landing craft plucked up the rest of the swimmers, I lay on the deck too exhausted to move."

Boone's landing craft pulled up to a sewer pipe supported by pilings that extended out into the channel. Excited prisoners lined the edge of the camp's bulkhead, shouting with joy at the liberators. A Navy photographer snapped pictures, including one that showed the *Tang*'s Decker, shirtless and dressed only in a pair of tattered shorts, at the forefront, his arms raised in excitement. A few feet to Decker's left stood submariner Denny Landrum of *Grenadier*, waving an American flag he had made from a bedsheet and hung on a fireman's pole. Boone, Simpson, Stassen, and the others climbed up on the sewer pipe and onto the beach, with Boone the first ashore, a distinction he wrote in his report that he could not be mindful of given the starving and suffering captives who now mobbed the rescuers. "The excitement of the prisoners was a never-forgettable sight," Boone wrote in his report. "Many of them were unclad, some clad merely with a G-string, others with trunks, while some others were dressed in non-descriptive apparel."

Senior prisoner Commander Arthur Maher, who had served as gunnery officer on the cruiser *Houston* when the Japanese sank it off Java in 1942, approached Boone along with an Army major. The prisoners informed the surgeon that the Japanese guards—armed with fixed bayonets—demanded that the rescuers enter through Omori's main gate. Guides then led Boone, Simpson, Stassen, and the others around the prison's waterfront to where the men found the Swedish Red Cross representative. The Japanese had barred him from entering Omori, so he had waited for the rescuers for several hours at the camp's entrance. The Japanese escorted the Americans to the office of the Omori's commanding officer. Simpson told the Japanese colonel that his party had arrived to rescue the prisoners. The colonel protested through an interpreter that he did not have orders from his war department to release them. Simpson and Boone countered that Admiral Halsey had ordered the immediate liberation of the prisoners.

"I have no authority to release them," the colonel stammered.

"You have no authority, period!" Stassen fired back.

Rescuers pushed the colonel aside and entered Omori. The officers announced to the prisoners who crowded around them that the camp was now liberated. No longer would captives have to bow to Japanese officers. Rescuers entered Omori's dispensary to find emaciated prisoners, deprived even of simple comforts like sheets, blankets, and pillows, stretched out atop bare wooden platforms. Other than a small dressing room with a few drugs and bandages, Boone found nothing that indicated the building served as a dispensary. He ordered one of the medical officers to assemble all of Omori's sick in the dispensary and prepare them for immediate evacuation, a total of eighteen stretcher-bound patients and 125 ambulatory. Rescuers gave senior prisoner Maher a portable communications set and instructed him to help organize the rest of the prisoners for evacuation. All afternoon and evening rescue boats would run, ferrying 707 prisoners to *Benevolence* moored five miles offshore.

To the nine survivors of *Tang*, the *Benevolence* resembled a luxury liner. The 15,400-ton ship stretched over 500 feet and spread out over seven decks. Staffed with a typical complement of about seventeen medical officers, thirty nurses, and 238 corpsmen, *Benevolence* boasted a surgical suite with several operating rooms plus dental, dermatology, and eye, ear, nose, and throat clinics. Patients even could enjoy whirlpools and massages in the physical therapy clinic. The floating hospital was designed to care for 802 officers and crewmen, but if pressed could accommodate up to a 1,000. There were bunks equipped with reading lamps and a five-channel radio system that offered a choice of educational shows, religious services, or the ship's entertainment program. Staff pushed around library carts and showed movies topside while the band belted out the ship's theme song, "Sentimental Journey." "It was just magnificent," recalled Alice Bruning, a nurse. "It was a brand new hospital."

Crews on *Benevolence* immediately began processing the throngs of former captives who climbed on board. Clerks interviewed and tagged each prisoner. The men stripped, showered, and slipped on clean pajamas, bathrobes, and slippers; crews destroyed all the lice- and flea-infested clothes. Doctors gave each man a physical exam to determine who required hospitalization. The Navy then issued new white uniforms including underwear, socks, shoes, and a hat. Eighty-five percent of the prisoners, in Boone's estimation, suffered serious malnutrition. Many battled tuberculosis, beriberi, and pellagra while others suffered infected wounds and even fractures. "All were to a fair degree emotionally disturbed and had a marked expression of fright," Boone observed. "All showed evidence of intense suffering."

The medical staff sympathized with the hundreds of traumatized prisoners who cycled through *Benevolence.* "These men were right from the camps and it was a psychological shock to suddenly be safe on this beautiful, immaculate hospital ship. They just couldn't believe what had happened to them," recalled Madge Gibson, a nurse on *Benevolence.* "Here were these poor, emaciated, filthy dirty, horribly smelling men crawling with lice in a state of disbelief and ecstatic euphoria. They had had no showers, no delousing, and were starving. Some were carrying small tattered cloths, perhaps containing a picture of a wife and a few precious things they had been able to hold onto all those years. Many were wearing stiff, unwashed dungarees that had recently been dropped by our planes. I will always remember those unwashed dungarees on those poor dirty bodies. They had to put their little possessions into an autoclave on the fantail because everything was so contaminated."

The first order of business for the *Tang* survivors: food. After ten months of starvation in Ofuna and Omori with little more to eat than rice, barley, and broth, the men hungered for calories, fat, and flavor. Much to the frustration of the ship's medical staff, the skipper of *Benevolence* ordered that the prisoners be allowed to eat as much as they wanted, even though their shrunken stomachs would no doubt struggle. The cooks answered the call. Prisoners gorged on plates of fried eggs, bacon, and ham. Others dove into bowls of fruits and grains, chasing the fine meal with endless cups of juice and coffee. Prisoners marveled over the ship's "mechanical cow" that could convert powdered milk into forty gallons of frothy liquid every hour, while others lined up at the automatic ice cream machine. "Boy, what a meal," Harry Berry wrote in his diary. "Real ham and eggs. Fruit, cereals, coffee, milk. Everything. I shall never forget it."

Tang engineer Larry Savadkin couldn't stop himself once he sat down.

He pounded down one egg after the other, trying to make up for 309 days of missed meals in a single sitting. "I personally accounted for 15 fried eggs, about a quarter of a pound of ham and I don't know how much milk and ice cream. I got sick a few hours afterwards. I think all of us did the same thing," recalled Savadkin. "It is my opinion that the doctors felt that they could handle an upset stomach, and the effect on our morale would far offset the effect of our upset stomachs after we were all finished with it." Pappy Boyington rivaled Savadkin, devouring five plates of ham and eggs to the shock of a bomber pilot across the table. "My God," the pilot declared. "I wish I could put all the stuff away that you do." A corpsman rolled Bill Leibold to the mess hall in a wheelchair, where the *Tang*'s boatswain's mate had the opposite reaction of Savadkin and Boyington. "I got some food," he recalled. "All I could do was sit there and look at it."

Life aboard *Benevolence* and other Navy ships came with its shocks for the *Tang* men and other prisoners, something the nurses recognized. "The men would go through stages you could identify. At first everything was wonderful—like a miracle. And then after a while, nothing was right," nurse Gibson recalled. "At first, they couldn't believe having sheets on the bunks and things like that. Then they would hoard food because they weren't sure they would get any more. When you made up their bunks you'd find bread stuffed under the pillows as though they figured there might not be any food tomorrow." Other former captives simply wanted to talk. "We were the first women they had seen in years," Gibson remembered. "They wanted to tell you what they had been through. I guess it was a catharsis for them. And they wanted to talk to us because they thought we, as women, would be more sympathetic. We represented their wives, their girlfriends, their mothers, or whatever."

Some captives proved in worse shape than others, including *Tang* motor machinist's mate Jesse DaSilva. Beriberi had largely robbed him of his ability to walk. "I was in no condition to be flown home," DaSilva wrote. "I was put to bed and given blood and other medication." Worse than DaSilva was *Tang* skipper Dick O'Kane. Emaciated and jaundiced, he suffered a high fever. Doctors placed the skipper in isolation and sedated him, but he would survive. Vice Admiral Charles Lockwood, grateful to see seventeen submarine officers and 141 enlisted men freed from Japanese prisons, was shocked when he first saw his prized skipper. "He was just skin and bones. His arms and legs looked no bigger than an ordinary man's wrists," the three-star admiral recalled. "His eyes were yellow with jaundice, but that's the only yellow in O'Kane's make up. Nothing ever had, nor will anything ever, daunt him."

The Navy had learned from intercepted communications that O'Kane and eight others had survived the loss of the *Tang*, a fact kept secret even from the families. The public's first news of the men's survival and the details of what happened that tragic October night off Formosa now appeared in newspapers nationwide. "The saga of the submarine *Tang* and her nine survivors cannot be retold too often," the *New York Times* wrote. "It ranks among the epics of American naval history." Ernestine O'Kane sent a copy of that article to the families of the *Tang* crew. "Words are inadequate to tell you what a great part your loved one took in helping to bring the war to its end. I pray each of you may find peace of mind with His help," she wrote. "There will be months of recuperation of body and soul for my husband and I am asking you not to write him for the present, since his pain for the gallant men who went out with him and for their loved ones, is one of the scars I shall try to help him heal."

New prisoners poured in each day from other liberated camps in the region, prompting the Navy to cycle the healthier ones off of *Benevolence* as fast as possible to free up beds. This included Leibold, who landed on board the *Ozark* after his strength returned following his battle with hepatitis. One of the corpsman told him that O'Kane was on board. Leibold visited his sedated skipper and found him the lone occupant of a two-person room. He promptly moved in with him. The *Tang* survivors one by one departed for home, excited to see family and friends. Savadkin in a trip typical of most of the crew flew first to Guam, Pearl Harbor, and then back to California, met at each stop by representatives from the submarine force, who offered to assist in any way. Jesse DaSilva took a different and slower route. The Navy transferred him to the hospital ship *Rescue*, where he would steam for weeks across the Pacific. A corpsman appeared in the door one day and announced that Leibold's turn to depart had finally arrived.

"What about the old man here?" he asked.

"He's not ready to leave yet," the corpsman replied.

Leibold was reluctant to leave his skipper. He had commissioned the *Tang* with O'Kane almost two years earlier. The skipper had in just five patrols spread out over nine months managed to sink more ships than most submarines did in the entire war. Leibold had been on the bridge right next to O'Kane—a pair of binoculars pressed to his face, searching for enemy escorts—for almost every one of those attacks. The men had endured the loss of the *Tang*, the cold night at sea, and ten subsequent months in Japanese prisons that had almost forced them to suffer the same fate that befell their seventy-eight shipmates at the hands of a malfunctioning torpedo. But the pair had survived. The corpsman told Leibold he had no choice now. The Navy had arranged his air evacuation. The boatswain's mate knew that O'Kane—unconscious and sedated—would heal and follow him soon. Leibold's wife now waited for him in California along with the promise of a new start. It was time to go home.

The war was over.

Finally over.

EPILOGUE

"Please take care of yourself, honey, & just stand by. I'll be back some day."

—Ira Dye,
January 15, 1943, letter

Dick O'Kane stood on the south lawn of the White House alongside President Harry Truman at 12:30 p.m. on Wednesday, March 27, 1946. The former skipper of the ill-fated *Tang*, who in February had celebrated his thirty-fifth birthday, dressed for the occasion in his formal blue uniform. The requisite winter Navy blue cap hat hid his buzzed head. His wife, Ernestine, and the couple's six-year-old son, James, and nine-year-old daughter, Marsha, looked on along with O'Kane's sister and parents. Secretary of the Navy James Forrestal and Fleet Admiral Chester Nimitz attended along with the architect of the submarine war, Vice Admiral Charles Lockwood. O'Kane had earned over the course of the war three Navy Crosses, three Silver Stars, the Navy Commendation Medal, the Legion of Merit, and the Purple Heart. To that collection this afternoon would be added the Medal of Honor, the nation's highest award for heroism.

The seven months since Emperor Hirohito announced Japan's surrender had proven a period of adjustment for O'Kane and the other eight survivors of *Tang*. Bill Leibold had come home to recover in the arms of his wife, while Clay Decker had returned to find his wife had given him up for dead and remarried. Fearful that his gaunt frame would frighten his family, O'Kane had delayed his homecoming, hoping to pack on a few extra pounds. His mentor, Mush Morton, had died alongside his men. O'Kane had suffered the loss of seventy-eight of his, a grief so strong that he would spend his final days before Alzheimer's and pneumonia claimed him in 1994 desperate to swim out to rescue them.

O'Kane was not yet done with the horrors of the war. He would return to Japan along with Leibold to testify in the war crimes trials against their captors, including Sueharu Kitamura, the notorious Butcher of Ofuna. The tribunal would ultimately convict Kitamura for causing the death of Norman Imel—a naval aviator O'Kane and the *Tang* crew buried—and contributing to the deaths of three others. The tribunal determined that he had beat no fewer than a hundred other prisoners. "It was the opinion of the prosecutor," one memo stated, "that he was one of the most vicious beaters ever tried in the Tokyo area." The tribunal sentenced the Butcher to hang on February 26, 1948, prompting his mother, brothers, and sisters to break down in tears, his entire family with the notable exception of his wife.

But the Butcher's neck would never swing at the end of a rope. Kitamura's file would soon swell with the impassioned pleas of his family to spare his life, including a letter Kitamura's mother wrote to the wife of General Douglas MacArthur, begging her to intervene. Sixteen months after Kitamura was sentenced to hang, MacArthur signed an order commuting his sentence to thirty years of hard labor. Commutations and clemencies soon followed as former guards and others walked free. December 1958 would see the release of the last Japanese war criminals. None served more than thirteen years. The rise of the Cold War had changed the geopolitical equation. America needed Japan as an ally, a check to help balance the power of the Soviet Union and China.

Postwar records would show that *Tang* had destroyed a confirmed twenty-four Japanese ships, earning two Presidential Unit Citations and O'Kane the title of the war's top skipper. Only the submarine *Tautog* sank more, putting twenty-six enemy warships and merchantmen on the bottom. But that was the work of three skippers spread out over three years. O'Kane had done it in just nine months. *Silversides* sank just one ship fewer than *Tang*, making it the third highest-performing submarine of the war. Creed Burlingame and Jack Coye accounted for twenty-two of the Silver Lady's twenty-three victims; Coye sank fourteen to Burlingame's eight. *Drum* destroyed fifteen ships. These three submarines sank a confirmed sixty-two freighters, tankers, and transports for a total of 264,484 tons, the equivalent tonnage of more than seven Essex class aircraft carriers.

Engineers, welders, and electricians at shipyards from Maine and Connecticut to Wisconsin and California had hammered out new submarines week after week, month after month, year after year, displaying the awesome industrial might that Admiral Yamamoto had so feared. The United States had begun the war that Sunday morning in December 1941 with just fifty-one submarines in the Pacific—tasked to cover more than eight million square miles—but would count 182 on duty when the Navy broadcast the cease-fire order 1,347 days later, the majority of them modern fleet boats designed to take the fight to the enemy's shores. All told some 288 submarines served in the war, skippered by a small club of just 465 officers, a diverse group of men like O'Kane, Coye, and Rindskopf. The thirty-two patrols of *Silversides*, *Drum*, and *Tang* totaled just 2 percent of the 1,570 war patrols submarines made in the Pacific, patrols that covered some 16.5 million miles, a quarter of that submerged.

American submarines over the course of the war attacked some 4,112 merchant ships, firing 14,748 torpedoes from the Aleutians to the Solomons to Japan's home island waters. A postwar comparison of American and Japanese records revealed that U.S. submarines sank 1,113 of those ships with a tonnage of 4,779,902. The undersea boats destroyed another 201 warships with a total tonnage of 540,192, including one battleship, eight carriers, and eleven cruisers. Authorities listed dozens of other merchant and warship losses as the probable victims of American submarines. Merchant ship crews suffered gravely, particularly those who worked aboard Japan's more modern fleet of steel ships that steamed to the far corners of the vast empire. Japan had counted at the start of the war some 16,000 officers and 60,000 crew in its highly trained and efficient merchant fleet. The submarine war would claim the lives of 16,200 of those sailors and leave another 53,400 wounded, ill, or marooned.

But the United States also paid a steep price. America lost fifty-two submarines, or almost one out of every five boats. The Japanese plucked 196 sailors from just seven of the lost submarines, tossing some back into the water, executing a few others, and marching the rest off to wretched prison camps. Only 158 of those starved and tortured souls would come home. Of the

16,000 sailors who served on submarines, the war claimed 374 officers and 3,131 enlisted men. The casualty rate among submariners not only topped all military branches, but proved a staggering six times higher than the surface Navy. In comparison to the enemy, however, America's losses seemed limited. The Italians lost eighty-five submarines, the Japanese 130, and the Germans 781.

Japan's dependence on shipping had proven the Achilles' heel of the nation's war machine, a critical vulnerability that had allowed America to ravage an empire that had once dominated one tenth of the world. Each ship torn apart by torpedoes ferried cargoes of rubber and bauxite, oil and coal to the muddy seafloor. The sweltering summer heat and rains rotted loads of cereals that piled up on Korean docks. The desperate Japanese in the end tried to make butter from silkworms as the starving populace ate chaff, acorns, and even sawdust. Antigovernment and antimilitary graffiti covered buildings and fights broke out over the tattered belongings of enemy prisoners of war. The fabric of Japanese society began to unravel. "The war against shipping," the United States Strategic Bombing Survey concluded, "was perhaps the most decisive single factor in the collapse of the Japanese economy and the logistic support of the Japanese military and naval power."

Japanese military leaders, who had rehearsed for possible war against the United States more than a decade before Pearl Harbor, had failed to anticipate and guard against a war on the nation's shipping. Even after American submarines began to destroy merchant ships, Japan proved slow to organize a convoy system. The resulting effort, handicapped by inferior antisubmarine equipment and a belated effort to arm merchant ships, was destined to fail. The American submarine service, which benefited from the breaking of Japan's maru code, continued to decimate the nation's merchant fleet. Blinded by an outdated desire to fight decisive sea battles, Japanese leaders failed to grasp the danger of America's submarines. "It must be stated as a fact that the results obtained by your submarines against our naval craft and against our shipping far exceeded anything we had expected," Vice Admiral Shigeru Fukudome later told interrogators. "It served to weaken our fighting strength and to speed up the termination of hostilities."

But the United States wrestled with its own struggles. Though engineers had designed the perfect submarine for a commerce war, the Navy had failed to adapt its tactics for just such a fight, in part because the United States adhered to treaty provisions that forbade unrestricted submarine warfare. Many skippers who had trained during peacetime, like Pinky Kennedy, proved too timid in combat, failing to maximize a submarine's inherent strengths. Valuable merchant and naval targets escaped in those early months, a time when many Japanese ships steamed unescorted, easy prey for submarines. One of the greatest problems, however, was torpedo failures. The battle between the leaders of the submarine service, who were convinced the weapon was faulty, and the officers in the Bureau of Ordnance, who wanted to blame the skippers as bad shots, only demoralized the undersea service, led talented skippers to quit as skippers, and delayed the search for a remedy. "The torpedo scandal of the U.S. submarine force in World War II," wrote historian Clay Blair, Jr., "was one of the worst in the history of any kind of warfare."

But those problems now drifted into the past. The president this afternoon in Washington prepared instead to celebrate O'Kane's success, one of only seven submariners in the war to receive the Medal of Honor. O'Kane saluted as Truman read the citation for his medal, describing the final actions that would wreak havoc on the Japanese and ultimately claim his submarine and most of his men. The president then placed the five-pointed star around the skipper's neck. "The Medal of Honor," O'Kane would later write, "represents great success my crew and I had in the midst of horrendous warfare." Truman captured the beliefs of many in his remarks. "This, in my opinion, is the most pleasant and the most honorable job that a President of the United States has to do, to pin the medals on the heroes who have made the country great," he told attendees. "I have said it time and again, and I will keep on saying it, that I would rather have a Medal of Honor than be President of the United States."

ACKNOWLEDGMENTS

Only through the tremendous help provided by scores of veterans and family members—many of whom sat for hours of interviews and provided me with letters, diaries, and personal writings—was I able to research and write the stories of *Silversides*, *Drum*, and *Tang*. To tell the tale of *Silversides* I am indebted to Patrick Carswell, Albert Stegall, Howard Calver, Jerry Bocian, Charles Swendsen, Tom Ross, Roland Fournier, Jack Flebbe, Joe Allison, Willis Chandler, James Allen, John Schumer, Owen Mehringer, John Bienia, Barbara Smith, Bob Clark, Mike Dowell, Robin Worthington, Robert Worthington, Anson Burlingame, John Burlingame, Paul Burlingame, Bonnie Byhre, Beth Coye, John Coye, Miriam Malone, Jane McFarren, and Gene Malone, Jr. My friend and former journalism colleague Fred Tannenbaum, who worked as a docent on the Silver Lady years ago, shared scores of photographs from his personal collection as well as the personal letters he exchanged over the years with officers from *Silversides*. I want to thank Fred as well for his thoughtful review of the manuscript. The late Gene Malone went above and beyond, graciously giving of his time through countless hours of interviews, phone calls, and e-mails as well as his poring over various drafts of the manuscript to improve its accuracy. Gene sadly passed away in February 2012; he was a rare gem of a man whom I count lucky to have called a friend.

I likewise owe a tremendous debt to the veterans and family members of those who served on *Drum*, including Dave Schmidt, Verner Utke-Ramsing, Phillip Williamson, James Eubanks, Eugene Pridonoff, Al Galas, Gerard

DeRosa, Joe Ireland, Bob White, Bill Lister, Ralph McFadden, George Schaedler, Wayne Green, Norman Style, Hubert Wheeler, Sammy Kess, Ron and Regina Thibideau, John Meyer, Donald Kronholm, Melvin Etheridge, Rosamond Rice, Elizabeth Rindskopf Parker, Amy Rindskopf, Bernard McMahon, Ferrall Dietrich, and Craig Dye. I owe a special thanks to the late Admiral Mike Rindskopf, the young junior officer who over the course of the war rose to become *Drum*'s skipper. Admiral Rindskopf not only sat for hours of interviews and provided me with volumes of personal records, but graciously reviewed chapters of the manuscript for accuracy before his passing in July 2011. He was a joy to work with and I consider it a privilege and honor to share his story. I also wish to extend my appreciation to *Tang* veterans and family members Bill Leibold, Floyd Caverly, Jim O'Kane, Barbara Lane, Barbara Siegfried, and Skip Frazee, all of whom proved invaluable in helping me tell the story of that ill-fated boat. I want to add a special thanks to Bill Leibold, who generously shared with me his time and personal records as well as tirelessly edited the manuscript and offered invaluable insight and corrections. Others who provided me important assistance to tell these stories include Aubrey Gill, Charles Sullivan, Bob Gerle, Paul Crozier, Michael Dolder, Jerry Landrum, Duane Stofan, Janice Cox, Wayne Dow, Calvin Graef, and Charles Overbeck.

I am indebted to an army of archivists and researchers who assisted me over the years. Those include Denise Herzhaft and Paul Garzelloni with the USS *Silversides* Submarine Museum, who were a tremendous help in telling the story of that great boat. Likewise, Tom Bowser and Lesley Waters at Battleship Memorial Park, who have done an amazing job restoring *Drum*, hosted me for several days, giving me one of the best tours anyone could hope for of a diesel boat. I am also indebted to Tom for his careful review of this manuscript for errors. I want to thank Charles Hinman at the USS *Bowfin* Submarine Museum in Honolulu and the Navy's Christy Hagen and Josh Thompson, who graciously welcomed me for a visit and tour of the Pearl Harbor submarine base. Others I owe thanks to include Nate Patch at the National Archives; Dave Winkler with the Naval Historical Foundation; the Bureau of Medicine and Surgery's André Sobocinski; Evelyn Cherpak at the Naval War College; the Naval Academy's Jennifer Bryan; Stephen Moore, author of the terrific book *Presumed Lost*; and historian Bruce Gamble, who wrote the excellent book *Black Sheep One*; my good friend Tim Frank; and

John Hodges with the Naval History and Heritage Command; the Navy Department Library's Davis Elliott; Nathan Matlock at the Regis University Center for the Study of War Experience; the Australian War Memorial's Jane Robertson; and Mary Ames Booker and Kim Robinson Sincox with the Battleship *North Carolina* Memorial and Museum. Few people know their way around the prisoner of war records at the National Archives better than Katie Rasdorf.

Writing a book is never easy. I am indebted as always to my great friend Craig Welch, a fantastic journalist and author who pored over countless drafts to help me shape the manuscript. I also want to extend my sincere appreciation to John Alden, an unrivaled World War II submarine expert and author who graciously reviewed the manuscript for accuracy. I owe a tremendous debt to my wonderful agent Wendy Strothman, a tireless advocate for her writers. I also want to thank my terrific editor at Simon & Schuster, Bob Bender, who has been an absolute joy to work with these past five years, as well as the always patient and helpful associate editor Johanna Li. Thanks as well go to Fred Chase for the manuscript's excellent copyediting and Simon & Schuster's superb marketing and publicity departments. Last but certainly not least, I want to thank my amazing wife, Carmen Scott, who not only served as my sounding board, but an invaluable editor and critic. I am especially grateful to her and our two wonderful children, Isa and Grigs, for the support and encouragement needed to tell this tale.

NOTE ON SOURCES

The *Silversides* and *Drum* live on today as museums—in Muskegon, Michigan, and Mobile, Alabama, respectively—that help tell the important story of the submarine service's role in winning World War II. I depended on both to research this book along with almost three dozen other archives, libraries, and museums scattered across several continents. Each submarine returning from a war patrol prepared a roughly thirty-page report, the final touches often finished as the crews moored the submarine in the waters of Pearl Harbor, Brisbane, and other bases across the Pacific. Patrol reports from more than 1,500 war patrols conducted by American submarines in the war total over 60,000 pages. The reports for *Silversides, Drum,* and *Tang* total 1,012 pages and cover just thirty-two patrols. These reports provide exhaustive details, including ship contacts, tides, weather conditions, food, and often the exact second each torpedo was fired. The patrol reports coupled with the deck logs on file in the National Archives provide a wonderful day-to-day—and in many cases, minute-by-minute—accounting of life on board each submarine.

The Navy provided skippers with ship recognition manuals to help them identify targets damaged and sunk on patrol. But these manuals left much to interpretation. "After an attack, the officers would come show you the recognition book," observed Slade Cutter, one of the war's top skippers. "So you and they picked the biggest ship that looked like that silhouette—just human nature." To more accurately tally Japanese naval and merchant ship losses, the military created the Joint Army-Navy Assessment Committee. This committee compared American and Japanese records, producing a report of its findings in February 1947. Often referred to by the acronym JANAC, the report revised downward the tallies of almost all skippers. The JANAC report was not perfect—particularly in the eyes of many submarine skippers—but the record remains an unbiased benchmark to help chart Japanese losses.

I consulted other important references, including John Alden and Craig McDonald's *United States and Allied Submarine Successes in the Pacific and Far East During World War II*, a vital reference that charts every successful attack throughout the war. Another excellent reference that I depended on was a privately translated copy by William Somerville of the Japanese *Senji Yuso Sendan Shi*, a compilation of many of Japan's wartime convoys that includes convoy compositions, departure and arrival times and dates, cargoes, and the outcomes of attacks by American and Allied forces. The stealth nature of submarine warfare makes tallying precise losses a virtual impossibility and with so many sources there naturally are differences. In general, I relied on JANAC for overall tallies, given the report's status as the only official governmental tabulation. In the case of discrepancies, however, I explain the differences in the notes.

I conducted more than a hundred interviews with World War II submarine veterans—cooks, electricians, engineers, torpedomen—to learn about life on a diesel boat. Many skippers later wrote about the war, including Richard O'Kane, whose published book, *Clear the Bridge!*, proved an invaluable resource for information on *Tang*. The memoirs of many others I depended on are unpublished, including those of Jack Coye, Robert Rice, Mike Rindskopf, and Murray Frazee, Jr. Rosamond Rice, daughter of Vice Admiral Robert Rice, recorded a series of interviews with her father in the 1970s. She copied the tapes for me, allowing me to hear him narrate his own story. Beyond interviews I collected more than 3,000 pages of letters, journals, telegrams, personal writings, and photos. So voluminous were the records in some cases, like that of *Silversides*' engineering officer John Bienia, that I had to create a chronology and bind them to keep copies organized. These personal records beautifully captured the daily rhythms of life on board, the camaraderie and friendships, the fear, the longing for the war to end, and the horror of life in prisoner of war camps.

ARCHIVES, LIBRARIES, AND MUSEUMS

American Heritage Center (AHC), University of Wyoming, Laramie, Wyoming
Arkansas Inland Maritime Museum, North Little Rock, Arkansas
Australian War Memorial, Canberra, Australia
Battleship *North Carolina* Archives & Collections, Wilmington, North Carolina
Center for the Study of War Experience, Regis University, Denver, Colorado
Charleston County Public Library, Charleston, South Carolina
Congressional Medal of Honor Society, Mount Pleasant, South Carolina
Daniel Library, The Citadel, Charleston, South Carolina
Harry S. Truman Library and Museum, Independence, Missouri
Kansas City Public Library, Kansas City, Missouri
Kentucky Library and Museum, Western Kentucky University, Bowling Green, Kentucky
Library of Congress, Washington, D.C.
Marlene and Nathan Addlestone Library, College of Charleston, Charleston, South Carolina
National Archives, Kew, United Kingdom
National Archives and Records Administration (NARA), College Park, Maryland
National Museum of the Pacific War, Fredericksburg, Texas
Naval Historical Foundation, Washington, D.C.
Naval History and Heritage Command (NHHC), Washington, D.C.
Naval War College Library (NWCL), Newport, Rhode Island
Navy Bureau of Medicine and Surgery (NBMS), Falls Church, Virginia
Navy Department Library (NDL), Washington, D.C.
Nicholas Murray Butler Library, Columbia University, New York, N.Y.
Nimitz Library, U.S. Naval Academy (USNA), Annapolis, Maryland

North Dakota State University Library, Fargo, North Dakota
Sterling Memorial Library, Yale University, New Haven, Connecticut
U.S. Military Academy Library, U.S. Military Academy, West Point, New York
U.S. Naval Institute, Annapolis, Maryland
USS *Alabama* Battleship Memorial Park, Mobile, Alabama
USS *Bowfin* Submarine Museum and Park (BSMP), Honolulu, Hawaii
USS *Silversides* Submarine Museum, Muskegon, Michigan (formerly Great Lakes Naval Memorial and Museum)
William Henry Smith Memorial Library, Indiana Historical Society, Indianapolis, Indiana
Willis Library, University of North Texas, Denton, Texas

ABBREVIATIONS

AHC	American Heritage Center, University of Wyoming, Laramie, Wyoming
Alden and McDonald	John D. Alden and Craig R. McDonald, *United States and Allied Submarine Successes in the Pacific and Far East During World War II*, 3rd Ed. (Jefferson, N.C.: McFarland, 2009)
BSMP	USS *Bowfin* Submarine Museum and Park, Honolulu, Hawaii
JANAC	Joint Army-Navy Assessment Committee, *Japanese Naval and Merchant Shipping Losses During World War II by All Causes* (Washington, D.C.: U.S. Government Printing Office, 1947)
LOC	Library of Congress
NARA	National Archives and Records Administration, College Park, Maryland
NBMS	Navy Bureau of Medicine and Surgery, Falls Church, Virginia
NDL	Navy Department Library, Washington, D.C.
NHHC	Naval History and Heritage Command, Washington, D.C.
NWCL	Naval War College Library, Newport, Rhode Island
RG	Record Group
Senji Yuso Sendan Shi	Shinshichiro Komamiya, *Senji Yuso Sendan Shi* (Wartime Transportation Convoys History), part 1, trans. William G. Somerville (Tokyo: Shuppan Kyodosha, 1987)
USNA	Nimitz Library, U.S. Naval Academy, Annapolis, Maryland
USSBS	United States Strategic Bombing Survey

NOTES

Chapter 1. *Silversides*

1 *"No one knows"*: Slade Cutter letter to Esther Cutter, Feb. 9, 1942, Slade D. Cutter Papers, Navy Department Library (NDL), Washington, D.C.

1 *at 9:51 a.m.*: *Silversides* deck log, April 30, 1942; *Silversides* Report of First War Patrol, June 21, 1942.

1 *The thirty-seven-year-old*: Creed C. Burlingame Navy Bio, Oct. 26, 1955, NDL; Anson Burlingame, Jr., "Being a Burlingame," unpublished memoir, 2009, p. 36; "The Empire Builders," *Time*, Nov. 22, 1943, pp. 65–66.

2 *The Army belatedly ordered*: "Army to Dim Shore," *New York Times*, April 27, 1942, p. 1.

2 *Two days earlier*: "Great Signs Dark as Gay White Way Obeys Army Edict," *New York Times*, April 30, 1942, p. 1; photoplay advertisements, *New York Times*, April 28, 1942, p. 25.

2 *Draft registration*: "13,000,000 Registered in 4th Draft, Including 911,630 in New York City," *New York Times*, April 28, 1942, p. 1; "1,000 a Minute Sign in Draft; 588,752 Are Enrolled Here," *New York Times*, April 27, 1942, p. 1.

2 *The press predicted*: "Washington Wire: A Special Report from the Wall Street Journal's Capital Bureau on Six Months of War—and the Six Months Ahead," *Wall Street Journal*, June 5, 1942, p. 1.

2 *$100 million a day*: "The Price for Civilization Must Be Paid in Hard Work and Sorrow and Blood," Fireside Chat to the Nation, April 28, 1942, in Samuel I. Rosenman, comp., *The Public Papers and Addresses of Franklin D. Roosevelt*, 1942 volume, *Humanity on the Defensive* (New York: Harper & Brothers, 1950), pp. 227–38.

2 *The burned-out:* Homer N. Wallin, *Pearl Harbor: Why, How, Fleet Salvage and Final Appraisal* (Washington, D.C.: U.S. Government Printing Office, 1968), pp. 253–80; "Report on Infamy," *Time*, Dec. 14, 1942, pp. 75–80; Robert Trumbull, "'Dead' Ships Rise at Pearl Harbor; Miracle in Salvage Cuts Loss to 3," *New York Times*, May 23, 1943, p. 1.

2 *Workers salvaged:* "Salvage Pearl Harbor Greetings," *New York Times*, Feb. 4, 1942, p. 5; Salvage Officer to the Commandant, Navy Yard, Pearl Harbor, Report of the Salvage of the USS *West Virginia*, June 15, 1942, in Wallin, *Pearl Harbor*, p. 349.

2 *"Japanese forces":* Operational Order No. 46-42, April 26, 1942, Box 294, RG 38, Records of the Office of the Chief of Naval Operations, Plans, Orders and Related Documents, National Archives and Records Administration (NARA), College Park, Maryland.

3 *a compound that housed:* Theodore Roscoe, *United States Submarine Operations in World War II* (Annapolis, Md.: Naval Institute Press, 1949), pp. 7–8.

3 *Likewise, nearby:* Chester Nimitz, "Pearl Harbor Attack," undated observations, Naval War College Library (NWCL), Newport, Rhode Island.

3 *twenty million square miles:* Max Hastings, *Retribution: The Battle for Japan, 1944–45* (New York: Alfred A. Knopf, 2007), p. 9; Richard B. Frank, "An Overdue Pacific War Perspective," *Naval History*, vol. 24, no. 2, April 2010, pp. 14–17.

3 *The son of a receiver:* Details are drawn in part from: Creed Burlingame's Naval Academy midshipman file on microfilm in the Special Collections and Archives Department of the Nimitz Library, U.S. Naval Academy (USNA), Annapolis, Maryland; Anson Burlingame e-mail to author, Aug. 12, 2009; John Burlingame e-mail to author, Aug. 12, 2009.

3 *The Naval Academy rejected:* M. S. Tisdale letter to Creed Burlingame, Sept. 29, 1922, USNA.

4 *He took classes:* Creed Burlingame Declaration Sheet, Examination for Admission to the United States Naval Academy, Feb. 7, 1923, USNA.

4 *"Upon examination":* O. G. Martin to Superintendent, U.S. Naval Academy, May 26, 1926, USNA.

4 *he graduated:* Transcript of Scholastic Record of Creed Cardwell Burlingame, USNA.

4 *preferring his coffee:* Patrick Carswell interview with author, August 23, 2009; Charles Swendsen interviews with author, June 23, 2009, and June 26, 2009.

4 *The only formality: The View from the Bridge*, Oral History of RADM C. C. Burlingame, produced by Paul Knutson, 1976. Compact Disc, USS *Silversides* Submarine Museum, Muskegon, Michigan.

4 *"You are not":* Ibid.

4 *"There were people":* Thomas A. Moore oral history interviews with Jan K.

Herman, March 24, 1993, March 29, 1993, and April 30, 1993, Navy Bureau of Medicine and Surgery (NBMS), Office of Medical History, Falls Church, Virginia.

4 *He shared a prejudice:* Anson Burlingame, Jr., "Being a Burlingame," p. 37; Henry H. Lesesne, *A History of the University of South Carolina: 1940–2000,* Columbia: University of South Carolina Press, 2001, p. 142.

4 *A healthy dose:* Creed Burlingame interview with Clay Blair, circa 1972, Box 96, Clay Blair, Jr., Papers, American Heritage Center (AHC), University of Wyoming, Laramie, Wyo.; Robert Trumbull, *Silversides* (New York: Henry Holt, 1945), pp. 26, 91.

4 *a bottle of Chanel #5:* John Bienia letter to Alpha Bienia, July 16, 1943.

5 *"I drink more":* The View from the Bridge.

5 *Burlingame privately doubted:* Anson Burlingame, Jr., "Being a Burlingame," p. 39.

5 *"Lord knows":* Robert Worthington letter to mother, Dec. 13, 1941.

5 *"Press home":* General Instructions for Patrol, Operational Order No. 46-42, April 26.

5 *These dangers:* Naval History Division, Office of the Chief of Naval Operations, *United States Submarine Losses: World War II* (Washington, D.C.: U.S. Government Printing Office, 1963), p. 1.

5 *"We hate those":* Slade Cutter letter to Esther Cutter, Dec. 11, 1942, Slade D. Cutter Papers, NDL.

5 *German U-boats surrendered:* Gary E. Weir, "The Search for an American Submarine Strategy and Design, 1916–1936," *Naval War College Review,* vol. 44, no. 1, Sequence 333, Winter 1991, pp. 34–48; Charles A. Lockwood, *Down to the Sea in Subs* (New York: W. W. Norton, 1967), pp. 100–103.

6 *Engineers wrestled:* Charles Lockwood, *Hell at 50 Fathoms* (Philadelphia: Chilton Company, 1962), pp. 141–89.

6 *Filled with 280,000:* Jessie W. Kohl, "History of the Medical Research Department, U.S. Submarine Base, New London, 7 December 1941 to 7 December 1945," Medical Research Department, U.S. Submarine Base, New London, Connecticut, p. 7.

6 *Veterans challenged:* Weir, "The Search for an American Submarine Strategy and Design, 1916–1936," pp. 34–48.

6 *Workers at Mare Island:* James L. Mooney et al., eds., *Dictionary of American Naval Fighting Ships,* vol. 6 (Washington, DC.: U.S. Government Printing Office, 1976), pp. 508–9.

7 *$6 million:* J. R. "Kacy" Ward, "Giant Sub Launched at Mare Island Yard," *Berkeley Daily Gazette,* Aug. 27, 1941, p. 1.

7 *473 days:* This date is calculated from Nov. 4, 1941, when the workers laid the

keel, through Feb. 20, 1942, which Robert Worthington noted in his journal as *Silversides'* official completion date.

7 *Eight watertight compartments:* Detailed descriptions of modern fleet submarines are drawn in part from: *The Fleet Type Submarine*, NavPers 16160, June 1946, Standards and Curriculum Division, Training, Bureau of Naval Personnel, pp. 6–16, 22–38; Larry Kimmett and Margaret Regis, *U.S. Submarines in World War II: An Illustrated History* (Seattle: Navigator Publishing, 1996), pp. 16–21.

8 *The heart of the submarine's:* Synopsis of Machinery and Hull Data, in Board of Inspection and Survey, Report of Official Trial of U.S.S. *Silversides* (SS-236), April 24, 1942, Box 2076, RG 19, Bureau of Ships General Correspondence, 1940–1945, NARA; *The Fleet Type Submarine*, NavPers 16160, June 1946, Standards and Curriculum Division, Training, Bureau of Naval Personnel, pp. 62–71.

8 Silversides *could submerge:* John D. Alden, *The Fleet Submarine in the U.S. Navy: A Design and Construction History* (Annapolis, Md.: Naval Institute Press, 1979), p. 101.

8 *Despite the advanced technology:* Ivan F. Duff, *Medical Study of the Experience of Submariners as Recorded in 1,471 Submarine Patrol Reports in World War II*, Bureau of Medicine and Surgery, Navy Department, Washington, D.C., 1947, pp. 1–2, 21–27.

8 *One such tragedy: Tullibee* Report of Third War Patrol, Feb. 10, 1944.

8 *An accidental discharge: Blueback* Report of Third War Patrol, July 21, 1945.

8 *Every torpedoman's worst fear: Pollack* Report of Ninth War Patrol, April 11, 1944.

8 *Seventeen submariners:* Duff, *Medical Study of the Experience of Submariners as Recorded in 1,471 Submarine Patrol Reports in World War II*, pp. 2, 23–25.

8 *"bridal suite":* Tom Bowser interview with author, Dec. 9, 2009; Fred Tannenbaum e-mail to author, Jan. 11, 2013.

9 *The ship's desalination plant:* Board of Inspection and Survey, Report of Official Trial of U.S.S. *Silversides* (SS-236), April 24, 1942.

9 *Sailors often bathed:* Author interviews with Roland Fournier (Aug. 3, 2009), Phillip Williamson (Sept. 2, 2009), Verner Utke-Ramsing (Aug. 20, 2009), and George Schaedler (Oct. 29, 2009).

9 *Off-duty sailors:* Author interviews with Roland Fournier (Aug. 3, 2009), Alexander Galas (Sept. 1, 2009), James Eubanks (Aug. 28, 2009), Verner Utke-Ramsing (Aug. 20, 2009), and Eugene Pridonoff (Aug. 31, 2009); *Silversides* Report of First War Patrol, June 21, 1942.

9 *Fresh fruits and vegetables:* David Schmidt interviews with author, Aug. 11, 2009, and Aug. 14, 2009; Gerard DeRosa interview with author, Aug. 7, 2009.

9 Silversides *boasted:* Board of Inspection and Survey, Report of Official Trial of U.S.S. *Silversides* (SS-236), April 24, 1942.

9 *Men stashed crates:* David Schmidt interviews with author, Aug. 11, 2009, and Aug. 14, 2009.

9 *Rather than clutter: Silversides* Report of First War Patrol, June 21, 1942.

9 *The same rationale:* Roy M. Davenport, *Clean Sweep* (New York: Vantage, 1986), p. 26.

9 *preserved fruits helped:* Thomas Withers, "The Preparation of the Submarines Pacific for War," *U.S. Naval Institute Proceedings*, April 1950, pp. 387–92.

9 *Veterans learned:* David Schmidt interviews with author, Aug. 11, 2009, and Aug. 14, 2009; Gerard DeRosa interview with author, Aug. 7, 2009.

10 *Burlingame's cramped: Silversides* Report of First War Patrol, June 21, 1942.

10 *Burlingame's youngest brother:* Background on Paul Burlingame comes from: Anson Burlingame, Jr., "Being a Burlingame," pp. 36, 48–50; United States Military Academy, *Seventy-Second Annual Report of the Association of Graduates of the United States Military Academy at West Point, New York, June 10, 1941* (Newburgh, N.Y.: Moore Printing Company), pp. 417–18.

10 *At 8:15 a.m.:* Details of the crash that killed Paul Burlingame come from the following news reports: "11 Killed in Crash of 2 Bombers Here," *New York Times*, June 18, 1940, p. 3; "Sky-Watchers Filled with Horror as Army Bombers Crash and Burn," *New York Times*, June 18, 1940, p. 3; "Air Crash Burns Fatal to Woman," *New York Times*, June 19, 1940, p. 19; "11 Army Fliers Killed When Two Planes Collide in Mid-Air and Fall in Flames," *St. Petersburg Times*, June 18, 1940, p. 1; "Twelve U.S. Fliers Die as Army Planes Crash," *Ludington Daily News*, June 17, 1940, p. 1.

11 *Foul weather:* Robert Worthington diary, May 10, 1942, Robert Worthington Papers (NWCL).

11 *The lookouts perched: Silversides* deck log, May 10, 1942; Trumbull, *Silversides*, p. 130.

11 *The skipper pressed:* John D. Alden and Craig R. McDonald, *United States and Allied Submarine Successes in the Pacific and Far East During World War II*, 3rd Ed. (Jefferson, N.C.: McFarland, 2009), p. 37.

11 *These trawlers:* Commander Submarine Force, U.S. Pacific Fleet, *Submarine Operational History World War II*, vol. 1, unpublished, pp. 264–65, NDL; Roscoe, *United States Submarine Operations in World War II*, pp. 110–11.

11 *$10,000 torpedo:* Roscoe, *United States Submarine Operations in World War II*, p. 252.

12 *the thirty-four-pound rounds:* Tom Bowser e-mail to author, Jan. 12, 2013.

12 *Petty Officer 3rd Class Patrick Carswell:* Patrick Carswell interview with author, Aug. 23, 2009.

12 *Five years older:* Muriel H. Wright, "Oklahoma War Memorial—World War II," part 2, *The Chronicles of Oklahoma*, vol. 22, no. 1, Spring 1944, p. 26; Trumbull, *Silversides*, p. 26.

12 *firing thirteen-pound projectiles:* John Campbell, *Naval Weapons of World War Two* (Annapolis, Md.: Naval Institute Press, 1985), p. 145.

12 *Carswell hopped:* Patrick Carswell interviews with author, Aug. 23, 2009, Aug. 26, 2009, and June 8, 2010.

13 *One missed Burlingame's head:* Creed Burlingame oral history interview with Richard Stone, March 9, 1978, Kentucky Library and Museum, Western Kentucky University, Bowling Green, Kentucky.

13 *One of the loaders:* Trumbull, *Silversides*, pp. 34–35.

13 *A wave hit Carswell:* Patrick Carswell interviews with author, Aug. 23, 2009, Aug. 26, 2009, and June 8, 2010.

14 *"Suddenly he realized":* Creed Burlingame oral history interview with the Navy, Jan. 4, 1944, Box 5, RG 38, Records of the Office of the Chief of Naval Operations, World War II Oral Histories, 1942–1946, NARA.

14 *"It broke the strap":* David LeMieux, "Brush with Death: Loader Witnessed Only Combat Fatality Aboard Sub," *Muskegon Chronicle*, Aug. 14, 2005, p. 1.

14 *His red blood splattered:* Trumbull, *Silversides*, pp. 36–37.

14 *"Get back":* Patrick Carswell interview with author, Aug. 23, 2009.

14 *"His mouth":* Albert Stegall interview with author, Aug. 12, 2009.

14 *the submarine* Scorpion: Alden and McDonald, p. 77.

15 *"He was on fire:"* *Silversides* Report of First War Patrol, June 21, 1942. Alden and McDonald's account records that the attack killed seven enemy sailors and injured two others.

15 *Carswell climbed down:* Patrick Carswell interviews with author, Aug. 23, 2009, Aug. 26, 2009, and June 8, 2010.

15 *The gun crew's tally:* *Silversides* Report of First War Patrol, June 21, 1942.

15 *Sailors carried Harbin:* Patrick Carswell interviews with author, Aug. 23, 2009, Aug. 26, 2009, and June 8, 2010.

16 *The men tied a gun shell: The View from the Bridge.*

16 *The skipper clutched:* Trumbull, *Silversides*, pp. 40–42.

16 *"We therefore commit":* Ibid.

16 *The rest of the men:* Patrick Carswell interview with author, June 8, 2010.

16 *"It was a stupid": The View from the Bridge.*

17 *The sun faded:* Trumbull, *Silversides*, pp. 40–42.

17 *"It was quite a problem":* Creed Burlingame oral history interview with the Navy, Jan. 4, 1944.

17 *The skipper gathered:* Trumbull, *Silversides*, pp. 40–42.

17 *"The first fish":* Ibid.

17 *"Wherever you lead":* Ibid.

17 *"Underway as before":* *Silversides* deck log, May 10, 1942.

Chapter 2. *Drum*

PAGE

18 *"We have every type":* Dudley Morton radio interview transcript, "Johnny Presents: The New Philip Morris Program," July 13, 1943, Dudley Morton Family Papers, USS *Bowfin* Submarine Museum and Park (BSMP), Honolulu, Hawaii.

18 *Lieutenant Commander Robert Henry Rice: Drum* Report of First War Patrol, June 12, 1942; Operational Order No. 38–42, April 14, 1942, Box 294, RG 38, Records of the Office of the Chief of Naval Operations, Plans, Orders and Related Documents, NARA; "The Up-Angle Cake," transcript of an undated speech by Robert Rice.

18 *"It is now your privilege":* H. R. Stark letter to Robert Rice, Oct. 25, 1941, USS *Alabama* Battleship Memorial Park, Mobile, Alabama.

18 *The two-star admiral:* Raymond P. Schmidt, "Ciphers, Subs, Sacrifice, and Success: The Wilson and Rice Navy Families in Two World Wars," *Cryptolog*, Winter 2005, pp. 7–12.

19 *"We'll either get":* Eugene Pridonoff interview with author, Aug. 31, 2009.

19 *Unlike* Silversides*'s rowdy skipper:* Eunice W. Rice, "Thirty Years in the Navy: The Memoirs of Robert H. Rice, Vice Admiral, United States Navy (Ret.)," unpublished, pp. 29–30; Rosamond Rice e-mail to author, May 11, 2010.

19 *His hard work:* R. E. Heise letter to the University Club of Syracuse, Sept. 26, 1958, Robert Rice midshipman file, USNA.

19 *"Bob is quiet":* J. S. Heavilin, ed., *The Lucky Bag of 1927: The Annual of the Regiment of Midshipmen* (Annapolis, Md.: USNA, 1927), p. 201.

19 *But Rice's academic:* Robert H. Rice Navy Bio, Sept. 9, 1957, NDL; Rice, "Thirty Years in the Navy," pp. 2–41; Robert Rice handwritten draft memoir, pp. 1–40.

20 *The half dozen officers:* "The Up-Angle Cake," transcript of an undated speech by Robert Rice; Maurice Rindskopf unpublished memoir, pp. 1–4; Maurice Rindskopf comments on Robert Rice unpublished memoir, June 9, 1993.

20 *But Ensign Eugene Pridonoff:* Eugene Pridonoff did not join *Drum* until its second war patrol, but Rice always included him in his speeches about the wardroom's diversity that are framed around the submarine's first patrol.

21 *One* Drum *sailor:* Ron Thibideau interview with author, Nov. 5, 2009.

21 *Another watched:* George Schaedler interview with author, Aug. 28, 2009.

21 *A pharmacist's mate:* Ralph McFadden interview with author, Oct. 28, 2009.

21 *Unlike Burlingame:* Details on Rice's leadership style are drawn from the following author interviews: Maurice Rindskopf (Aug. 14, 2009); Eugene Pridonoff (Aug. 31, 2009, and Sept. 3, 2009); Verner Utke-Ramsing (Oct. 30, 2009, and Nov. 10, 2009).

21 *"What embarrassment!":* Robert Rice handwritten draft memoir, pp. 29–31.

21 *"From the first day":* Maurice Rindskopf interview with author, Aug. 14, 2009.

22 *The submarine had encountered:* "The Up-Angle Cake," transcript of an undated speech by Robert Rice; *Drum* Report of First War Patrol, June 12, 1942.

22 *one of the principal cities:* The United States Strategic Bombing Survey (USSBS), *The Japanese Aircraft Industry* (Washington, D.C.: U.S. Government Printing Office, 1947), pp. 2, 16.

22 *several thousand smaller ones:* Robert P. Porter, *Japan: The New World-Power* (London: Humphrey Milford/Oxford University Press, 1915), p. 264.

22 *Mountains crowded:* USSBS, *The War Against Japanese Transportation, 1941–1945* (Washington, D.C.: U.S. Government Printing Office, 1947), p. 13.

22 *Many of the nation's:* "Population of Japan up 6.4% in Five Years," *New York Times,* April 18, 1941, p. 7; USSBS, *The Effects of Strategic Bombing on Japan's War Economy* (Washington, D.C.: U.S. Government Printing Office, 1946), p. 13; USSBS, *The War Against Japanese Transportation, 1941–1945,* p. 17.

22 *The slow pace:* USSBS, *The War Against Japanese Transportation, 1941–1945,* p. 1.

22 *The highway system:* Ibid., p. 29.

23 *The concentration of shipyards:* Ibid., pp. 17–18.

23 *Japan's merchant fleet:* Ibid., p. 31.

23 *a population explosion:* "Four Babies a Minute, Japanese Birth Rate," *New York Times,* Dec. 25, 1932, p. E7; "Birth Rate Gaining Rapidly in Japan," *New York Times,* July 19, 1931, p. N4; "Birth Control in Japan," *New York Times,* June 5, 1921, p. 77; "Population of Japan up 6.4% in Five Years," *New York Times,* April 18, 1941, p. 7.

23 *This growth made Japan:* Herbert Adams Gibbons, "Japan Feels Her Way Toward a Dominant Role in Asia," *New York Times,* Jan. 24, 1932, p. XX3.

23 *"Of all Japanese problems":* "Japan's Record Crop of Babies Adds to Her Grave Problems," *New York Times,* Dec. 10, 1933, p. XX3.

23 *Outside of a few industries:* USSBS, *The War Against Japanese Transportation, 1941–1945,* p. 13.

23 *At the outbreak of the war:* USSBS, *Oil in Japan's War* (Washington, D.C.: U.S. Government Printing Office, 1946), p. 11.

23 *The United States in comparison:* Ibid.; Harold Callender, "Oil: Major Factor in Another War," *New York Times,* Aug. 13, 1939, p. E4.

24 *Investigators even concluded:* USSBS, *Oil in Japan's War,* p. 1.

24 *"Napoleon's armies":* Arno Dosch-Fleurot, "Oil to Dominate Next World War," *New York Times,* June 19, 1938, p. E5.

24 *Victory over China:* USSBS, *The Effects of Strategic Bombing on Japan's War Economy,* pp. 5–9; "Japan Is About to Annex Korea," *New York Times,* Aug. 18, 1910, p. 4.

24 *"arsenal of Japanese expansionism":* USSBS, *The Effects of Strategic Bombing on Japan's War Economy,* p. 7.

24 *Japan interpreted:* Ibid., p. 8.

24 *Since Commodore Matthew Perry's:* George E. Sokolsky, "Japan Ponders Her Role in the World," *New York Times*, March 27, 1932, p. SM3; Herbert Adams Gibbons, "Japan Feels Her Way Toward Modernity," *New York Times*, Jan. 23, 1932, p. XX3; Hugh Byas, "What Japan Thinks of America," *New York Times*, Jan. 22, 1933, p. SM1.

24 *These tensions led:* Hugh Byas, "Japan Quits League to 'Insure Peace,'" *New York Times*, March 28, 1933, p. 1; Hugh Byas, "'Back to Asia!' Japan's New Cry," *New York Times*, Oct. 2, 1932, p. SM1; "'Manifest Destiny' Stirs Japan," *New York Times*, Nov. 24, 1935, p. SM1.

25 *Japan's military successes:* USSBS, *Summary Report (Pacific War)*, pp. 1–2; USSBS, *The Effects of Strategic Bombing on Japan's War Economy*, pp. 6–10; USSBS, *Oil in Japan's War*, pp. 29–31.

25 *In preparation for war:* USSBS, *The Effects of Strategic Bombing on Japan's War Economy*, pp. 13, 29, 52.

25 *The government ordered:* USSBS, *Oil in Japan's War*, p. 1.

25 *By the time of the attack:* USSBS, *The Effects of Strategic Bombing on Japan's War Economy*, p. 13.

25 *That figure counted:* USSBS (Pacific), Military Analysis Division, *Japanese Air Power* (Washington, D.C.: U.S. Government Printing Office, 1946), pp. 4–5, 28–29; USSBS, *Summary Report (Pacific War)*, p. 9.

25 *Mitsubishi engineers:* "Science: What Adds up to a Zero," *Time*, Sept. 28, 1942, p. 46.

25 *Aggressive recruitment:* USSBS, *Summary Report (Pacific War)*, p. 12.

25 *while the navy's register:* Ibid., pp. 10–11; David M. Kennedy, ed., *Library of Congress World War II Companion* (New York: Simon & Schuster, 2007), p. 257.

25 *The Japanese navy not only:* Samuel Eliot Morison, *The Two-Ocean War: A Short History of the United States Navy in the Second World War* (Boston: Atlantic Monthly Press/Little, Brown, 1963), p. 39.

25 *"unholy alliance":* Turner Catledge, "Roosevelt Calls for Greater Aid to Britain," *New York Times*, Dec. 30, 1940, p. 1.

25 *Japan seized:* USSBS, *The Effects of Strategic Bombing on Japan's War Economy*, p. 9.

25 *To Japan's surprise:* Ibid.; "British Empire Joins Our Action; Canada and Netherlands in Move," *New York Times*, July 26, 1941, p. 1; "Batavia Risks War," *New York Times*, July 29, 1941, p. 1; "Japanese Trade with U.S. to End," *New York Times*, July 26, 1941, p. 5; "Japan to Allow Americans to Go; Tokyo Trade Hit," *New York Times*, Aug. 23, 1941, p. 1; "Oil Policy Changes," *New York Times*, Aug. 2, 1941, p. 1; "U.S. Solidifies Far East Policy," *New York Times*, Aug. 17, 1941, p. E5; "Vast Trade Curbed," *New York Times*, July 26, 1941, p. 1; "Washington Retaliates," *New York Times*, Aug. 3, 1941, p. E1.

26 *"They did not die":* "Text of the President's Armistice Day Speech," *New York Times,* Nov. 12, 1941, p. 3.

26 *Germany's invasion:* USSBS, *The Effects of Strategic Bombing on Japan's War Economy,* pp. 10–11; USSBS, *Summary Report (Pacific War),* pp. 1–4.

26 *Ordered to carry:* Operational Order No. 28–42, March 29, 1942, Box 294, RG 38, Records of the Office of the Chief of Naval Operations, Plans, Orders and Related Documents, NARA.

26 *Rice closed his eyes:* "The Up-Angle Cake," transcript of an undated speech by Robert Rice.

28 *The wiry lieutenant:* Maurice Rindskopf unpublished memoir, pp. 4–43; Maurice Rindskopf e-mail to author, May 22, 2010; Joseph Dana Allen letter to A. H. Rooks, March 7, 1934, Maurice Rindskopf midshipman file, USNA; USNA, *Annual Register of the United States Naval Academy* (Washington, D.C.: U.S. Government Printing Office, 1938), p. 52.

28 *The 9,000-ton:* The Joint Army-Navy Assessment Committee (JANAC), *Japanese Naval and Merchant Shipping Losses During World War II by All Causes* (Washington, D.C.: U.S. Government Printing Office, 1947), p. 2; Anthony J. Watts and Brian G. Gordon, *The Imperial Japanese Navy* (Garden City, N.Y.: Doubleday, 1971), pp. 213–14; Hansgeorg Jentschura, Dieter Jung, and Peter Mickel, *Warships of the Imperial Japanese Navy, 1869–1945,* trans. Antony Preston and J. D. Brown (Annapolis, Md.: Naval Institute Press, 1977), pp. 65–66; Paul S. Dull, *A Battle History of the Imperial Japanese Navy (1941–1945)* (Annapolis, Md.: Naval Institute Press, 1978), pp. 66–67.

28 *Rindskopf dropped:* Maurice Rindskopf interviews with author, Aug. 19, 2009, and May 27, 2010.

28 *The analog computer:* Maurice Rindskopf interview with author, May 27, 2010; *Torpedo Data Computer,* Ordnance Pamphlet No. 1056, Arma Corporation Prepared for the Bureau of Ordnance, June 1944, pp. 56–57.

28 *Each of the complex weapons:* E. W. Jolie, "A Brief History of U.S. Navy Torpedo Development," Technical Document No. 5436, Sept. 15, 1978, Naval Underwater Systems Center, Newport Laboratory, Newport, Rhode Island, pp. 34, 45, 81; Roscoe, *United States Submarine Operations in World War II,* pp. 250–52; Frank Thone, "Speeding Torpedo Production," *Science News-Letter,* vol 37, no. 23, June 8, 1940, pp. 362–64.

29 *Rice estimated:* Robert Rice handwritten draft memoir, pp. 45–46; "The Up-Angle Cake," transcript of an undated speech by Robert Rice; Maurice Rindskopf interviews with author, Aug. 19, 2009, and May 27, 2010; Maurice Rindskopf e-mail to author, June 1, 2010.

29 *The skipper studied:* Robert Rice handwritten draft memoir, p. 46; "The Up-Angle Cake," transcript of an undated speech by Robert Rice.

30 *"strange, tinny sound"*: Robert Rice handwritten draft memoir, p. 46.

30 *"The officers and men"*: "The Up-Angle Cake," transcript of an undated speech by Robert Rice.

30 *"This was the greatest"*: Matome Ugaki, *Fading Victory: The Diary of Admiral Matome Ugaki, 1941–1945*, ed. Donald M. Goldstein and Katherine V. Dillon, trans. Masataka Chihaya (Pittsburgh: University of Pittsburgh Press, 1991), pp. 118–19; JANAC, p. 12 of the appendix; Alden and McDonald, p. 36. Alden and McDonald note a discrepancy among sources over *Mizuho's* actual tonnage; the two figures they list are 9,000 tons and 10,930 tons. JANAC records *Mizuho's* tonnage as 9,000.

31 *"This attack was"*: *Drum* Report of First War Patrol, June 12, 1942.

31 *The two-and-a-half-foot*: *Submarine Report: Depth Charge, Bomb, Mine, Torpedo and Gunfire Damage Including Losses in Action, 7 December, 1941 to 15 August, 1945*, vol. 1, War Damage Report No. 58, Preliminary Design Branch, Bureau of Ships, Navy Department, January 1, 1949, pp. 10–12.

31 *A depth charge that exploded*: Kimmett and Regis, *U.S. Submarines in World War II*, p. 87.

31 *"Captain"*: "The Up-Angle Cake," transcript of an undated speech by Robert Rice.

32 *the Japanese heavy cruiser* Takao: Ugaki, *Fading Victory*, pp. 118–19; Janusz Skulski, *The Heavy Cruiser Takao* (Annapolis, Md.: Naval Institute Press, 1994), p. 10.

32 *The last of the depth charges*: *Drum* Report of First War Patrol, June 12, 1942.

32 *"Throughout the long night"*: "The Up-Angle Cake," transcript of an undated speech by Robert Rice.

Chapter 3. Submarines

PAGE

33 *"Submarine war against"*: "War on Neutral Shipping," editorial, *New York Times*, April 13, 1916, p. 12.

33 *Rear Admiral Charles Lockwood, Jr.*: Charles A. Lockwood, *Sink 'Em All* (New York: E. P. Dutton, 1951), pp. 13–14.

33 *The five-foot, eight-inch Lockwood*: Andy Lockwood e-mail to author, May 21, 2011.

33 *Japan had overrun*: Lockwood, *Sink 'Em All*, p. 13.

34 *"Must admit"*: Charles Lockwood diary, May 3, 1942, Box 1, Charles Lockwood Papers, (LOC), Washington, D.C.

34 *"The Japanese know"*: Samuel Flagg Bemis, "Submarine Warfare in the Strategy of American Defense and Diplomacy, 1915–1945," unpublished paper, Dec. 15, 1961, Box 65, Samuel Flagg Bemis Papers, Manuscripts and Archives, Yale University Library, New Haven, Connecticut.

34 *"Execute against Japan":* Ibid.

34 *Born in rural Virginia:* Background on Lockwood is drawn from the following sources: Lockwood, *Down to the Sea in Subs*, pp. 11–32; Charles Lockwood, Jr., midshipman file, USNA; Charles A. Lockwood, Jr., Navy Bio, March 22, 1957, NDL; William R. Denslow and Harry S. Truman, *10,000 Famous Freemasons from K to Z, Part Two* (1957; repr., Whitefish, Mont.: Kessinger Publishing, 2004) p. 98.

35 *"unwanted stepchildren":* Lockwood, *Down to the Sea in Subs*, p. 26.

35 *"Sailor, few people":* Ibid., p. 34.

35 *"At that moment":* Ibid., p. 39.

35 *There Lockwood witnessed:* "Diary of Captain (Later Vice Admiral) C. A. Lockwood for the Period 20 March 1941 to 22 March 1942, Inc. While Serving as U.S. Naval Attache, London," Box 1, Charles Lockwood Papers, LOC; Lockwood, *Down to the Sea in Subs*, pp. 242–45.

36 *"I wish to God":* Charles Lockwood diary, April 22, 1941, Box 1, Charles Lockwood Papers, LOC.

36 *"It has been a fine job":* C. A. Lockwood, Jr., to Arthur S. Carpender, Dec. 8, 1941, Box 12, Charles Lockwood Papers, LOC.

36 *"Forgive personal communication":* C. A. Lockwood, Jr., to Detail Officer, Dec. 9, 1941, ibid.

36 *"Submarine warfare":* Lockwood, *Down to the Sea in Subs*, p. 257.

36 *Inundated by requests:* A. H. Gray to C. A. Lockwood, Jr., Dec. 27, 1941, Box 12, Charles Lockwood Papers, LOC.

36 *He spent his days:* Lockwood, *Down to the Sea in Subs*, p. 263.

36 *"A Former Naval Person":* Ibid., p. 248.

36 *The news arrived:* Ibid., pp. 264–65.

36 *"Ordered Home!!":* Charles Lockwood diary, March 5, 1942, Box 1, Charles Lockwood Papers, LOC.

37 *"Lockwood":* Charles A. Lockwood and Percy Finch, "We Gave the Japs a Licking Underseas," part 1, *Saturday Evening Post*, July 16, 1949, p. 23.

37 *"Since Germany":* U.S. Congress, Joint Committee on the Investigation of the Pearl Harbor Attack, *Pearl Harbor Attack: Hearings Before the Joint Committee on the Investigation of the Pearl Harbor Attack*, part 32, *Proceedings of Navy Court of Inquiry*, 79th Cong., 1st Sess. (Washington, D.C.: U.S. Government Printing Office, 1946), p. 70.

37 *America in the meantime:* Morison, *History of the United States Naval Operations in World War II*, vol. 3, *The Rising Sun in the Pacific, 1931–April 1942*, pp. 51–52, Morison, *The Two-Ocean War*, p. 86; USSBS, *Summary Report (Pacific War)*, p. 4.

37 *Japan had relied:* USSBS, *Japanese Air Power*, pp. 4–5, 28–29; USSBS, *Summary Report (Pacific War)*, pp. 2–3.

37 *Japanese planes pounded:* Morison, *History of the United States Naval Operations in World War II*, vol. 3, *The Rising Sun in the Pacific, 1931–April 1942*, pp. 184–86.

37 *Another battle played out:* Ibid., pp. 223–54.

38 *America's largest forces:* Ibid., pp. 164–83; Morison, *The Two-Ocean War*, pp. 77–86; USSBS, *The Campaigns of the Pacific War*, pp. 26–28.

38 *The British and Dutch:* Morison, *The Two-Ocean War*, pp. 82–89; USSBS, *The Campaigns of the Pacific War*, pp. 28–30, 41; Robert J. Cressman, *The Official Chronology of the U.S. Navy in World War II* (Annapolis, Md.: Naval Institute Press, 2000), pp. 61–80.

38 *Enemy fighters and bombers:* USSBS, *The Campaigns of the Pacific War*, p. 30; "Darwin Is Raided," *New York Times*, Feb. 19, 1942, p. 1; "Darwin Raids Rank with London Blitz," *New York Times*, Feb. 22, 1942, p. 3; "Java Seen Most Involved," *New York Times*, Feb. 21, 1942, p. 3.

38 *"Gem of the Dutch East Indies":* Lillian Dow Davidson, "Java—Gem of the Dutch East Indies," *The Rotarian*, Sept. 1931, pp. 28–31, 48–50.

38 *Ninety-seven:* Morison, *The Two-Ocean War*, pp. 88–98; USSBS, *The Campaigns of the Pacific War*, p. 31.

39 *"The United States plan":* USSBS, *Summary Report (Pacific War)*, p. 4.

39 *Japan had created:* Ibid., pp. 1–4; USSBS, *The Campaigns of the Pacific War*, pp. 2–4.

39 *the Navy had assigned:* Roscoe, *United States Submarine Operations in World War II*, pp. 16, 119–20; Richard G. Voge, ed., "Submarine Commands," vol. 1, unpublished, 1946, No. 170a of the series *U.S. Naval Administrative Histories of World War II*, pp. 1–12, NDL.

39 *The submarine force:* Roscoe, *United States Submarine Operations in World War II*, p. 4; Voge, ed., "Submarine Commands," vol. 1, pp. 47–50; Lockwood, *Sink 'Em All*, p. 18.

40 *New construction in shipyards:* Lockwood and Finch, "We Gave the Japs a Licking Underseas," part 1, p. 116.

40 *While submarines:* Commander Submarine Force, U.S. Pacific Fleet, *Submarine Operational History World War II*, vol. 1, p. 11.

40 *To manage the vast seas:* Roscoe, *United States Submarine Operations in World War II*, p. 50.

40 *One 10,000-ton merchant ship:* Mark P. Parillo, *The Japanese Merchant Marine in World War II* (Annapolis, Md.: Naval Institute Press, 1993), p. 159; Roscoe, *United States Submarine Operations in World War II*, pp. 491–92.

40 *a Japanese Zero:* Parillo, *The Japanese Merchant Marine in World War II*, p. 41.

40 *"When Japan allied herself":* Lockwood and Finch, "We Gave the Japs a Licking Underseas," part 1, p. 23.

41 *President Roosevelt's shake-up:* Roscoe, *United States Submarine Operations in World War II*, pp. 42–43.

41   *The new Commander:* Ernest J. King Navy Bio, July 21, 1965, NDL.

41   *The sixty-four-year-old:* Thomas C. Hart Navy Bio, July 29, 1960, NDL; James L. Mooney et al., eds., *Dictionary of American Naval Fighting Ships*, vol. 7 (Washington, D.C.: U.S. Government Printing Office, 1981), p. 141.

41   *The tall and slender:* Chester W. Nimitz Navy Bio, June 21, 1948, NDL; Noel F. Busch, "Admiral Chester Nimitz," *Life*, July 10, 1944, pp. 82–92; Chester Nimitz, *The Reminiscences of Admiral Chester W. Nimitz* (New York: Columbia University Oral History Research Office, 1967), p. 1; Roscoe, *United States Submarine Operations in World War II*, p. 43; E. B. Potter, *Nimitz* (Annapolis, Md.: Naval Institute Press, 1976), pp. 26–36.

41   *"The sea":* Potter, *Nimitz*, p. 32.

41   *On December 31, 1942:* Potter, *Nimitz*, p. 23; Edwin T. Layton with Roger Pineau and John Costello, *"And I Was There": Pearl Harbor and Midway—Breaking the Secrets* (New York: William Morrow, 1985), p. 354; "Nimitz Takes Charge of U.S. Pacific Fleet; Command Shifted with Minimum Fanfare," *New York Times*, Jan. 1, 1942, p. 7.

41   *sixty-four submarines:* Morison, *The Two-Ocean War*, p. 496.

42   *Japan in contrast:* Carl Boyd and Akihiko Yoshida, *The Japanese Submarine Force and World War II* (Annapolis, Md.: Naval Institute Press, 1995), pp. 8–35; Charles Lockwood, "The Misuse of the Japanese Submarine During World War II," undated memo, Box 17, Charles Lockwood Papers, LOC; Roscoe, *United States Submarine Operations in World War II*, pp. 7, 449–50.

42   *Rather than order submarines:* Interrogation of Vice Admiral Shigeyoshi Miwa, Oct. 10, 1945, in USSBS (Pacific), Naval Analysis Division, *Interrogations of Japanese Officials*, vol. 2 (Washington, D.C.: U.S. Government Printing Office, 1946), pp. 291–95; Interrogation of Vice Admiral Paul Wenneker, Nov. 11, 1945, in USSBS (Pacific), Naval Analysis Division, *Interrogations of Japanese Officials*, vol. 1 (Washington, D.C.: U.S. Government Printing Office, 1946), pp. 284–86.

42   *The affable admiral's:* Charles Lockwood diary, May 5–8, 1942, Box 1, Charles Lockwood Papers, LOC; Lockwood, *Sink 'Em All*, pp. 13–14; Roscoe, *United States Submarine Operations in World War II*, pp. 95–96.

42   *The 8,100-ton ship:* Clayton F. Johnson et al., eds., *Dictionary of American Naval Fighting Ships*, vol. 3 (Washington D.C.: U.S. Government Printing Office, 1968), p. 348–49.

42   *"Sink 'em all":* Lockwood, *Sink 'Em All*, pp. 13–14.

Chapter 4. *Silversides*

PAGE

43 *"We have just left":* John Bienia letter to Alpha Bienia, May 21, 1943.

43 Silversides *cut: Silversides* Report of Fourth War Patrol, Jan. 31, 1943; *Silversides* deck log, Dec. 22, 1942.

43 *The men had survived:* Details are drawn from *Silversides'* patrol reports.

43 *The superstitious skipper: The View from the Bridge.*

43 *Lieutenant Commander Roy Davenport:* Background on Davenport is drawn from the following sources: Roy Davenport Navy Bio, June 30, 1955, NDL; Roy Davenport midshipman file, USNA; Roy Davenport oral history interview with the Navy, April 18, 1945, Box 7, RG 38, Records of the Office of the Chief of Naval Operations, World War II Oral Histories, 1942–1946, NARA; Roy Davenport interview with Clay Blair, circa 1972, Box 97, Clay Blair, Jr., Papers, AHC; Creed Burlingame interview with Clay Blair, circa 1972, Box 96, Clay Blair, Jr., Papers, AHC; Davenport, *Clean Sweep*, pp. 6, 19; Bonnie Byhre interview with author, Jan. 4, 2010; John Bienia letter to Alpha Drury, Dec. 14, 1942.

44 *Lieutenant Robert Worthington:* Background on Worthington is drawn from the following sources: Robert Worthington Navy Bio, May 27, 1957, NDL; Robert Worthington midshipman file, USNA; USNA, *Annual Register of the United States Naval Academy* (Washington, D.C.: U.S. Government Printing Office, 1938), p. 54; Robert Worthington letter to Fred Tannenbaum, Nov. 18, 1985; Robert Worthington, Jr., and Robin Worthington joint interview with author, Jan. 2, 2010.

44 *"Whatever happens":* Robert Worthington letter to mother, Dec. 13, 1941.

44 *Lieutenant John Bienia:* Background on Bienia is drawn from the following sources: Massachusetts Nautical School/Massachusetts Maritime Academy cadet file, Massachusetts Maritime Academy, Buzzards Bay, Massachusetts; R. Dudley to Commander Train Squadron SIX, Dec. 9, 1941, Report of Particulars After Battle of Sunday, Dec. 7, 1941; Trumbull, *Silversides*, pp. 83–84; John Bienia letter to Alpha Drury, Feb. 25, 1943; John Bienia interview with author, Jan. 4, 2010.

44 *"Before we knew it":* John Bienia undated letter to Alpha Bienia.

45 *"There were a guitar":* John Bienia letter to Alpha Drury, July 19, 1942.

45 *The young medic: The Silversides Album: A Living History*, written and produced by Paul Knutson in cooperation with the Great Lakes Naval Memorial and Maritime Museum, 1985 (USS *Silversides* Submarine Museum, Muskegon, Michigan) audio cassette.

46 *If the appendix:* Mark H. Beers, ed., *The Merck Manual of Medical Information*, 2nd home edition (Whitehouse Station, N.J.: Merck Research Laboratories, 2003), pp. 781–82; Donna Olendorf, Christine Jeryan, and Karen Boyden, eds.,

The Gale Encyclopedia of Medicine, vol. 1 A–B (Farmington Hills, Mich.: Gale Research, 1999), pp. 313–18.

46 *"Probably no other"*: C. W. Shilling and Jessie W. Kohl, *History of Submarine Medicine in World War II*, May 25, 1947, U.S. Naval Medical Research Laboratory, U.S. Naval Submarine Base, New London, Conn., pp. 103–5.

46 *"the medical officer"*: Ibid., p. 96.

46 *"rigorous selection program"*: Duff, *Medical Study of the Experience of Submariners as Recorded in 1,471 Submarine Patrol Reports in World War II*, p. 220.

46 *"above average intelligence"*: Shilling and Kohl, *History of Submarine Medicine in World War II*, pp. 96–97.

46 *"grand slam course"*: Thomas A. Moore oral history interviews with Jan K. Herman, March 24, 1993, March 29, 1993, and April 30, 1993.

46 *"quacks"*: Roscoe, *United States Submarine Operations in World War II*, p. 167.

46 *the Navy instructed:* Shilling and Kohl, *History of Submarine Medicine in World War II*, pp. 104–5.

47 *three months earlier: Seadragon* Report of Fourth War Patrol, Oct. 20, 1942.

47 *Pharmacist's Mate 1st Class Wheeler Lipes:* Wheeler B. Lipes oral history interview with Jan K. Herman and Robert Bornmann, March 3, 1993, NBMS; Franz Hoskins oral history interview with Jan K. Herman and Robert Bornmann, Aug. 27, 1997, NBMS.

47 *Three days before: Grayback* Report of Fifth War Patrol, January 23, 1943.

47 Chicago Daily News: George Weller, " 'Doc' Lipes Commandeers a Submarine Officers' Wardroom," *U.S. Navy Medicine*, July–Aug. 1986, pp. 13–15. This is a reprint of Weller's original story, which was published in the *Chicago Daily News* on Dec. 14, 1942.

47 Silversides *pharmacist's mate Moore:* Thomas A. Moore oral history interviews with Jan K. Herman, March 24, 1993, March 29, 1993, and April 30, 1993.

48 *"fastest day"*: Ibid.

48 *"If you ever"*: Ibid.

49 *"writhing in pain"*: *The Silversides Album*.

49 *"Doc, we're not"*: Ibid.

49 *Moore felt: Nautilus*, Episode No. 3, "Hunters and the Hunted," directed by Ian Potts, BBC, 1995. Videocassette.

49 *"I probably can"*: Thomas A. Moore oral history interviews with Jan K. Herman, March 24, 1993, March 29, 1993, and April 30, 1993.

50 *He chose:* Albert H. Stegall oral history interview with the Navy, Nov. 9, 1944, Box 27, RG 38, Records of the Office of the Chief of Naval Operations, World War II Oral Histories, 1942–1946, NARA; Albert Stegall interview with author, Aug. 12, 2009.

50 *"I'll tell you":* Albert H. Stegall oral history interview with the Navy, Nov. 9, 1944.

50 *To remedy it:* Ibid.; Trumbull, *Silversides*, p. 74.

50 *Moore instructed:* Thomas A. Moore oral history interviews with Jan K. Herman, March 24, 1993, March 29, 1993, and April 30, 1993.

50 *Stegall visited:* Albert H. Stegall oral history interview with the Navy, Nov. 9, 1944.

50 *The pharmacist's mate:* Thomas A. Moore oral history interviews with Jan K. Herman, March 24, 1993, March 29, 1993, and April 30, 1993.

51 *"really ripped him open": Nautilus,* Episode No. 3, "Hunters and the Hunted."

51 *"killed a lot of time": The Silversides Album.*

51 *Worthington not only:* Robert Worthington oral history interview with Jan K. Herman, April 13, 1993, NBMS.

52 *"It was a helluva mess":* Thomas A. Moore oral history interviews with Jan K. Herman, March 24, 1993, March 29, 1993, and April 30, 1993.

52 *"Is this operation":* Ibid.

52 *"I can feel you":* Walter B. Clausen, "Sub Officer Performs His First Appendectomy, Taking 5 Hours," *The Palm Beach Post,* Feb. 17, 1943, p. 6.

53 *"God is our refuge":* Robert Trumbull. "Pharmacist's Mate, 22, Operates on an Appendix in a Submarine," *New York Times,* Feb. 14, 1943, p. 34; Roy Davenport speech, Feb. 6, 1979, National Museum of the Pacific War, Fredericksburg, Texas; Davenport, *Clean Sweep,* pp. 8–20.

53 *"we were wheeling":* Thomas A. Moore oral history interviews with Jan K. Herman, March 24, 1993, March 29, 1993, and April 30, 1993.

53 *"I sweated blood":* Ibid.

53 *"I thought, well, hell": Nautilus,* Episode No. 3, "Hunters and the Hunted."

54 *"lonely endeavor":* Thomas A. Moore oral history interviews with Jan K. Herman, March 24, 1993, March 29, 1993, and April 30, 1993.

54 *At 1:50 a.m.: Silversides* Report of Fourth War Patrol, Jan. 31, 1943; *Silversides* deck log, Dec. 23, 1942.

54 *"bright moonlight": Silversides* action report, December 23, 1942, Box 742, RG 38, Records of the Chief of Naval Operations, World War II Action and Operational Reports, NARA.

55 *"I thought": Silversides* Report of Fourth War Patrol, Jan. 31, 1943.

55 Silversides *dove: Silversides* deck log, Dec. 23, 1942; Robert Worthington diary, Dec. 23, 1942.

55 *"the most unpleasant day":* Creed Burlingame oral history interview with the Navy, Jan. 4, 1944.

56 *"The patient convalesced": Silversides* Report of Fourth War Patrol, Jan. 31, 1943.

56 *"We added it to powdered eggs"*: Clay Blair, Jr., *Silent Victory: The U.S. Submarine War Against Japan* (1975; repr., Annapolis, Md.: Naval Institute Press, 2001), p. 347.

Chapter 5. *Drum*

PAGE

57 *"Wish I was going"*: Eugene Malone letter to Elinor Ives, Dec. 7, 1943.

57 *a twenty-nine-pound bird:* Ira Dye letter to Evelyn Dye, Dec. 28, 1942.

57 *Two weeks earlier: Drum* report of Fourth War Patrol, Jan. 23, 1943; Alden and McDonald, p. 56.

57 *Workers had hustled:* Norman Polmar, *Aircraft Carriers: A History of Carrier Aviation and Its Influence on World Events*, vol. 1, *1909–1945* (Washington, D.C.: Potomac Books, 2006), p. 208; Paul E. Fontenoy, *Aircraft Carriers: An Illustrated History of Their Impact* (Santa Barbara, Calif.: ABC-CLIO, 2006), p. 247.

57 *The skipper had put: Drum* report of Fourth War Patrol, Jan. 23, 1943.

57 *just twenty-five miles:* Ira Dye, "Christmas off Kyushu: The U.S.S. *Drum* in 1942," unpublished article.

57 *Rice had followed up:* JANAC, p. 12 of the appendix. JANAC lists one of those ships as probably sunk, though that ship and the tonnage are included in the *Drum*'s overall totals of ships sunk.

58 *send a personal note:* Chester Nimitz letter to Russell Willson, June 26, 1942.

58 *"Bob Rice did a grand job"*: Slade Cutter letter to Frances Cutter, June 24, 1942, Slade D. Cutter Papers, NDL.

58 *McMahon grew up:* Details on McMahon's background are drawn from the following sources: B. F. McMahon interview with author, Nov. 9, 2009; Bernard McMahon Navy Bio, March 25, 1958, NDL; Bernard McMahon midshipman file, USNA.

58 *"Great White Father"*: George Schaedler interview with author, Oct. 29, 2009; Norman Style interview with author, Nov. 2, 2009.

58 *McMahon was warm:* Background on McMahon's leadership is drawn from author interviews with Verner Utke-Ramsing (Oct. 30, 2009, and Nov. 10, 2009), George Schaedler (Oct. 29, 2009), Eugene Pridonoff (Aug. 31, 2009), and Phillip Williamson (Sept. 2, 2009).

58 *"Take her down"*: Maurice Rindskopf unpublished memoir, p. 76.

58 *"The message came"*: Ibid., p. 69.

59 *"Son born"*: COMINCH to USS *DRUM*, July 27, 1942.

59 *Japan's lightning success:* USSBS, *The Campaigns of the Pacific War*, p. 32.

59 *Japan's first objective:* Ibid., pp. 52–53; Morison, *The Two-Ocean War*, pp. 137–41.

59 *American intelligence, however, deciphered:* Morison, *The Two-Ocean War*, pp. 141–47; USSBS, *The Campaigns of the Pacific War*, pp. 52–57; Watts and Gordon, *The Imperial Japanese Navy*, pp. 184–86.

59 *"Scratch one flattop!"*: "There Were the Japs," *Time*, June 22, 1942, pp. 25–28.

59 *The battle intensified:* Morison, *The Two-Ocean War*, pp. 145–47; USSBS, *The Campaigns of the Pacific War*, p. 53; Interrogation of Captain Mineo Yamaoka, Oct. 19, 1945, in USSBS, *Interrogations of Japanese Officials*, vol. 1, pp. 53–55.

60 *A Japanese bomb:* Elliot Buckmaster to Chester Nimitz, May 25, 1942, Report of Action of *Yorktown* and *Yorktown* Air Group on May 8, 1942.

60 *Two torpedoes ripped:* Frederick C. Sherman to Chester Nimitz, May 15, 1942, Report of Action—The Battle of the Coral Sea, 7 and 8 May 1942.

60 *The Battle of the Coral Sea:* USSBS, *The Campaigns of the Pacific War*, p. 53.

60 *Japan had anticipated:* Interrogation of Captain Mitsuo Fuchida, Oct. 10, 1945, in USSBS, *Interrogations of Japanese Officials*, vol. 1, pp. 122–31; Hiroyuki Agawa, *The Reluctant Admiral: Yamamoto and the Imperial Navy*, trans. John Bester (New York: Kodansha International, 1979), p. 264; Joint Committee on the Investigation of the Pearl Harbor Attack, *Investigation of the Pearl Harbor Attack*, pp. 65, 166.

60 *Japanese commanders should have:* Chester Nimitz, "Pearl Harbor Attack," undated observations, NWCL.

60 *The five-foot, three-inch:* Agawa, *The Reluctant Admiral*, pp. 2, 73, 82–86.

60 *"We are far from":* Ibid., pp. 285–86.

61 *Yamamoto's top priority:* Morison, *The Two-Ocean War*, pp. 147–78.

61 *Japan planned an armada:* Henry F. Schorreck, "Battle of Midway, 4–7 June 1942: The Role of COMINT in the Battle of Midway," SRH-230, June 1972, NDL.

61 *America in contrast:* Morison, *The Two-Ocean War*, pp. 148–49.

61 *More than 1,400:* Ibid., p. 149; Norman Polmar, *Aircraft Carriers*, vol. 1, *1909–1945*, p. 227.

61 *Cryptanalysts had unraveled:* Schorreck, "Battle of Midway," 4–7 June 1942; Morison, *The Two-Ocean War*, pp. 148–50; Polmar, *Aircraft Carriers*, vol. 1, *1909–1945*, pp. 225–30.

62 *"unsinkable aircraft carrier":* Morison, *The Two-Ocean War*, p. 149.

62 *Heavy fog and clouds:* Ibid., pp. 151–57; Polmar, *Aircraft Carriers*, vol. 1, *1909–1945*, pp. 231–39; Chester Nimitz to Ernest King, June 28, 1942, Battle of Midway; USSBS, *The Campaigns of the Pacific War*, pp. 58–60.

63 *A bomb hit:* Jonathan Parshall and Anthony Tully, *Shattered Sword: The Untold Story of the Battle of Midway* (Washington, D.C.: Potomac Books, 2005), pp. 241–42; Mitsuo Fuchida and Masatake Okumiya, *Midway: The Battle That Doomed Japan, The Japanese Navy's Story* (Annapolis, Md.: Naval Institute Press, 1992), p. 213.

63 *Captain Mitsuo Fuchida:* Fuchida and Okumiya, *Midway*, pp. xxi, 142.

63 *"There was a huge":* Ibid., p. 213.

64 *American planes dove:* Parshall and Tully, *Shattered Sword,* pp. 248–52; Polmar, *Aircraft Carriers,* vol. 1, *1909–1945,* p. 239; Fuchida and Okumiya, *Midway,* pp. 219–23; Morison, *The Two-Ocean War,* pp. 156–57.

64 *Nagumo's chief of staff:* Fuchida and Okumiya, *Midway,* pp. 213–15.

64 Hiryu *turned:* Ibid., pp. 226–27.

64 *Radar operators on* Yorktown*:* Elliot Buckmaster to Chester Nimitz, June 18, 1942, Report of Action for June 4, 1942 and June 6, 1942.

64 *an American search plane:* Chester Nimitz to Ernest King, June 28, 1942, Battle of Midway.

64 *Two dozen dive-bombers:* Ibid.; George Murray to Chester Nimitz, June 8, 1942, Report of Battle of Midway Island, June 4–6, 1942; Marc Mitscher to Chester Nimitz, June 13, 1942, Report of Action—4–6 June 1942; Morison, *The Two-Ocean War,* p. 157.

64 *Hidden by the afternoon sun:* Fuchida and Okumiya, *Midway,* pp. 231–33; Parshall and Tully, *Shattered Sword,* pp. 324–27.

65 *Sword in hand:* Fuchida and Okumiya, *Midway,* pp. 223–24.

65 Kaga *vanished:* Ibid., p. 221.

65 *Japanese destroyers torpedoed:* Ibid., pp. 217–18.

65 Hiryu *suffered:* Ibid., pp. 232–35.

65 *"I shall remain":* Ibid., p. 233.

65 Yorktown *in contrast:* Elliot Buckmaster to Chester Nimitz, June 18, 1942, Report of Action for June 4, 1942 and June 6, 1942; Arnold True to Chester Nimitz, June 16, 1942, Action Report, 4–6 June, 1942.

65 *The Japanese submarine:* Ibid.; Fuchida and Okumiya, *Midway,* pp. 257–60; Morison, *The Two-Ocean War,* pp. 161–62; Chester Nimitz to Ernest King, June 28, 1942, Battle of Midway.

65 *In the predawn hours:* Morison, *The Two-Ocean War,* p. 162; Elliot Buckmaster to Chester Nimitz, June 18, 1942, Report of Action for June 4, 1942 and June 6, 1942; Chester Nimitz to Ernest King, June 28, 1942, Battle of Midway.

65 *Midway had proven a success:* Commander Submarine Force, U.S. Pacific Fleet, *Submarine Operational History World War II,* vol. 1, pp. 174–89.

66 *The submarine force's potential big break:* Ibid., pp. 184–85; *Nautilus* Report of First War Patrol, July 16, 1942.

66 *Postwar analysis:* Fuchida and Okumiya, *Midway,* pp. 219–20, 224.

66 *Lookouts on the* Tambor*:* Ibid., pp. 255–57, 262, 264–68; Commander Submarine Force, U.S. Pacific Fleet, *Submarine Operational History World War II,* vol. 1, pp. 186–88; *Tambor* Report of Third War Patrol, June 17, 1942; Parshall and Tully, *Shattered Sword,* pp. 345–48, 369–72, 375–81.

66 *"many unidentified ships":* Tambor Report of Third War Patrol, June 17, 1942.

66 *While the skipper:* Ibid.; Commander Submarine Force, U.S. Pacific Fleet,

Submarine Operational History World War II, vol. 1, p. 187; Blair, *Silent Victory*, pp. 246–47.

67 *Midway had cost:* USSBS, *The Campaigns of the Pacific War*, p. 60.

67 *Despite his superiority:* Fuchida and Okumiya, *Midway*, pp. 250–53.

67 *"But how can we apologize":* Ibid, p. 252.

67 *"Leave that to me":* Ibid.

67 *The decisive June 1942 battle:* USSBS, *The Campaigns of the Pacific War*, p. 60.

67 *"How brilliant":* Matome Ugaki diary, Dec. 31, 1942, in Ugaki, *Fading Victory*, pp. 318–19.

67 *The submarine* Sargo*:* Commander Submarine Force, U.S. Pacific Fleet, *Submarine Operational History World War II*, vol. 2, pp. 697–710; *Sargo* Report of First War Patrol, Jan. 29, 1942; History of the USS *Sargo* (SS-188), Sept. 27, 1957, Navy Department, Office of the Chief of Naval Operations, Division of Naval History (Op-29), Ships' Histories Section; *The Reminiscences of Admiral James Fife* (New York: Columbia University Oral History Research Office, 1962), pp. 247–50.

67 *"Not one of the attacks":* Drum Report of Third War Patrol, Nov. 16, 1942.

68 *Rather than investigate:* Lockwood, *Sink 'Em All*, pp. 20–22.

68 *As boats returned:* Commander Submarine Force, U.S. Pacific Fleet, *Submarine Operational History World War II*, vol. 2, pp. 716–21.

68 *Morale plummeted:* Ibid., pp. 727–30.

68 *The forty-five-year-old:* Admiral James Fife, Jr., Navy Bio, Nov. 14, 1957, NDL; James Fife, Jr., midshipman file, USNA; *The Reminiscences of Rear Admiral Charles Elliott Loughlin., U.S. Navy (Retired)* (Annapolis, Md.: Naval Institute Oral History Department, 1982), pp. 149–51.

68 *"There is a difference":* The Reminiscences of Rear Admiral Charles Elliott Loughlin, pp. 113–14.

68 *Fife knew:* The Reminiscences of Admiral James Fife, pp. 283–85.

68 *Fife couldn't use:* Ibid.; Commander Submarine Force, U.S. Pacific Fleet, *Submarine Operational History World War II*, vol. 2, pp. 721–27; Charles Lockwood letter to W. H. P. Blandy, July 11, 1942, Box 12, Charles Lockwood Papers, LOC.

69 *"Here we had":* The Reminiscences of Admiral James Fife, p. 248.

69 *Fixing the run depth:* Commander Submarine Force, U.S. Pacific Fleet, *Submarine Operational History World War II*, vol. 2, pp. 730–42; Roscoe, *United States Submarine Operations in World War II*, pp. 256–61.

69 *Submarines sank:* Commander Submarine Force, U.S. Pacific Fleet, *Submarine Operational History World War II*, vol. 1, pp. 34–35; JANAC, pp. 12, 43 of the appendix.

69 *Skippers fired:* USSBS, *The War Against Japanese Transportation, 1941–1945*, p. 134.

69 *Submarine bases had now:* Commander Submarine Force, U.S. Pacific Fleet, *Submarine Operational History World War II*, vol. 1, p. 35.

69 *Thirty-seven new fleet boats:* Ibid.; Roscoe, *United States Submarine Operations in World War II*, p. 187; Voge, ed. "Submarine Commands," vol. 1, p. 50.

70 *"These patrols":* Ira Dye letter to Evelyn Dye, Dec. 16, 1942.

70 *Some 1.7 million:* "Keep Us Strong in Our Faith That We Fight for a Better Day for Humankind," Christmas Eve Fireside Chat on Tehran and Cairo Conferences, Dec. 24, 1943, in Samuel I. Rosenman, comp., *The Public Papers and Addresses of Franklin D. Roosevelt*, 1943 volume, *The Tide Turns* (New York: Harper & Brothers, 1950), pp. 553–62; Hanson W. Baldwin, "Our Troops 'Line' Guards the World," *New York Times*, Dec. 7, 1942, p. 5.

70 *including that of President Roosevelt:* W. H. Lawrence, "Axis Faith Fades, Roosevelt Says," *New York Times*, Dec. 25, 1942, p. 1.

70 *Rationing forced:* Ibid.; Catherine Mackenzie, "Christmas as Usual," *New York Times*, Dec. 20, 1942, p. SM19; "Christmas Tree Supply Here to Be 'Limited,' But Some Dealers Say It Will Meet Demand," *New York Times*, Dec. 8, 1942, p. 31; "City Christmas Tree Quota Cut Two-Thirds by Shortages of Manpower and Shipping," *New York Times*, Dec. 25, 1942, p. 20; "'Save Turkey Fats' Plea Runs into a Dilemma," *New York Times*, Dec. 25, 1942, p. 20; "Many Depict War Themes and Draw Crowds of Service Men—Several Openings of New Displays Are Scheduled," *New York Times*, Dec. 10, 1942, p. 32; "Joy of Christmas Yields to Thoughts of the Men at War," *New York Times*, Dec. 26, 1942, p. 1.

70 Drum *executive officer:* Ira Dye letter to Evelyn Dye, Dec. 20, 1942.

71 *"We can hardly eat":* Ibid.

71 *"Christmas Day is here":* Drum crew calendar, Dec. 25, 1942.

71 *"The boat was a madhouse":* Ira Dye letter to Evelyn Dye, Dec. 28, 1942.

71 *"It was as if the war":* Ira Dye, "Christmas off Kyushu: The U.S.S. *Drum* in 1942," unpublished article.

Chapter 6. *Silversides*

PAGE

72 *"You said it yourself":* Gordon Cox letter to Nellie Cox, May 5, 1942.

72 *Lieutenant Commander John Starr Coye, Jr.:* Silversides Report of Sixth War Patrol, Sept. 12, 1943.

72 *the maximum allowed:* Voge, ed., "Submarine Commands," vol. 1, pp. 198–99.

72 *Burlingame had traveled:* This is based on data recorded in *Silversides'* first five patrols.

72 *Postwar records:* JANAC, p. 43 of the appendix.

72 *He damaged:* This is based on damage figures credited by the Navy for *Silversides'* first five patrols.

72 *The man who:* Creed C. Burlingame Navy Bio, Oct. 26, 1955, NDL.

73 *a great feat:* Naval History Division, Office of the Chief of Naval Operations, *United States Submarine Losses*, p. 8.

73 *"As a man and skipper":* John Bienia letter to Alpha Bienia, Oct. 1, 1943.

73 *"He'll always be":* Robert Worthington letter to Fred Tannenbaum, Nov. 18, 1985.

73 *"TO THE BEST":* John Bienia letters to Alpha Bienia, Sept. 25, 1943, and Oct. 1, 1943.

73 *The California native:* John Starr Coye, Jr., Navy Bio, Aug. 30, 1968, NDL; John Coye, Jr., *The Reminiscences of Rear Admiral John S. Coye, Jr., U.S. Navy (Retired)* (Annapolis, Md.: Naval Institute Oral History Department, 1983), pp. 9–57; John S. Coye, Jr., unpublished memoir, pp. 11–13.

73 *"Burlingame was a hard man":* John S. Coye, Jr., unpublished memoir, p. 13.

73 *"He was a dynamic":* The Reminiscences of Rear Admiral John S. Coye, Jr., p. 57.

73 *The big-shouldered Coye:* Ibid., pp. 1–5; Beth Coye interview with author, Jan. 5, 2010; Beth Coye letter to author, Jan. 3, 2010; John Coye midshipman file, USNA; John Coye, Jr., Ancestral Genealogy.

74 *"Jack dear":* Mabel Coye journal.

74 *"DeCoye":* E. P. Lee, Jr., ed., *The Lucky Bag of 1933: The Annual of the Regiment of Midshipmen* (Annapolis, Md.: USNA, 1933), p. 165; John Coye midshipman file, USNA.

74 *graduating 123:* USNA, *Annual Register of the United States Naval Academy* (Washington, D.C.: U.S. Government Printing Office, 1933), p. 24.

74 *"Tardiness is Jack's":* Lee, ed., *The Lucky Bag of 1933*, p. 165; John Coye midshipman file, USNA.

74 *"cannon fodder":* The Reminiscences of Rear Admiral John S. Coye, Jr., p. 8.

74 *The first calamity:* Ibid., pp. 30–33; John S. Coye, Jr., unpublished memoir, pp. 9–11.

75 *"pile of rust":* The Reminiscences of Rear Admiral John S. Coye, Jr., p. 40. Information on the attack on *R-18* is also drawn from John S. Coye, Jr., unpublished memoir, pp. 11–13.

75 *"He was a magnificent":* Eugene Malone interview with author, Aug. 5, 2009.

75 *On a personal level:* Beth Coye interview with author, Jan. 5, 2010; Beth Coye letter to author, Jan. 3, 2010.

76 *Even at sea:* Eugene Malone interview with author, Jan. 7, 2010.

76 *"inviolate":* Beth Coye letter to author, Jan. 3, 2010.

76 *"Don't ever steal":* Ibid.

76 *Coye's quiet disguised:* Beth Coye interview with author, Jan. 5, 2010.

76 *"Baggy Pants":* John Bienia letter to Alpha Bienia, Dec. 5, 1943.

76 *"I made up my mind":* The Reminiscences of Rear Admiral John S. Coye, Jr., p. 57.

76 *Officers and crew:* John Bienia letters to Alpha Bienia, July 4, 1943, July 6, 1943, July 7, 1943, July 8, 1943, July 9, 1943, July 13, 1943, July 14, 1943, and July 18, 1943.

76 *"tooth and nail":* John Bienia letter to Alpha Bienia, July 7,1943.

77 *"This is the* Silversides*":* John Bienia letter to Alpha Bienia, July 19, 1943.

77 *"We came up fast":* John Bienia letter to Alpha Bienia, Aug. 3, 1943.

78 *Topped off with: Silversides* Report of Sixth War Patrol, Sept. 12, 1943; *The Reminiscences of Rear Admiral John S. Coye, Jr.,* pp. 57–64.

78 *"Did not surface": Silversides* Report of Sixth War Patrol, Sept. 12, 1943.

80 *"Target ducked":* Ibid.

80 *"He dropped five":* Ibid.; Alden and McDonald, p. 92.

81 *"The whole chart":* John Bienia letter to Alpha Bienia, Aug. 3, 1943.

81 *"There was about":* John Bienia letter to Alpha Bienia, Aug. 13, 1943.

81 *"I get a big kick":* John Bienia letter to Alpha Bienia, Aug. 11, 1943.

83 *He now worried:* John S. Coye, Jr., unpublished memoir, p. 13.

83 *"It was a beauty":* John Bienia letter to Alpha Bienia, Sept. 6, 1943.

83 *"There's no excitement":* Ibid.

Chapter 7. *Silversides*
PAGE
85 *"One month from today":* Gilbert Leach diary, Oct. 14, 1942.

85 Silversides *departed Brisbane: Silversides* Report of Seventh War Patrol, Nov. 8, 1943.

85 *Coye and his men:* Details of the time in Australia are drawn from: John Bienia letters to Alpha Bienia, Sept. 25, 1943 (there are three letters that share this date), Sept. 26, 1943, and Oct. 1, 1943.

85 *"Ever since we left":* John Bienia letter to Alpha Bienia, Oct. 7, 1943.

85 *"I do wish":* John Bienia letter to Alpha Bienia, Oct. 1, 1943.

86 *"The ship hasn't":* John Bienia letter to Alpha Bienia, Oct. 2, 1943.

86 *"He isn't as quick":* Eugene Malone letter to family, Dec. 7, 1943.

86 *While those defeats:* USSBS, *The Campaigns of the Pacific War,* p. 105.

86 *Japan had captured:* Morison, *The Two-Ocean War,* p. 165.

86 *Troops had since landed:* Ibid.; James D. Hornfischer, *Neptune's Inferno: The U.S. Navy at Guadalcanal* (New York: Bantam, 2011), pp. 1–5.

86 *Despite America's commitment:* Morison, *The Two-Ocean War,* pp. 164–77.

86 *The opposing navies:* Hornfischer, *Neptune's Inferno,* p. xxi.

86 *A Japanese submarine:* Ibid., pp. 132–33; U.S.S. *Wasp* (CV-7), Loss in Action Report, Sept. 15, 1942.

86 *A similar fate:* Morison, *The Two-Ocean War,* pp. 193–96.

87 *"Ironbottom Sound":* Hornfischer, *Neptune's Inferno,* p. xxi.

87 *Some 60,000:* Ibid.

87 *The island proved:* Details of life on Guadalcanal are drawn from: F. Tillman Durdin, "It's Never Dull on Guadalcanal," *New York Times*, Sept. 18, 1942, p. 1; "Solomons Menus of Marines Good," *New York Times*, Oct. 15, 1942, p. 5; Frank L. Kluckhohn, "West and East—Two Kinds of Warfare," *New York Times*, Oct. 17, 1943, p. SM12; Morison, *The Two-Ocean War*, pp. 166–67.

87 *When hospital attendants:* "'Guadalcanal Mud' Goes on Exhibit," *Reading Eagle*, April 24, 1943, p. 14.

87 *"Life is reduced":* F. Tillman Durdin, "It's Never Dull on Guadalcanal," *New York Times*, Sept. 18, 1942, p. 1.

87 *Resourceful crews:* Morison, *The Two-Ocean War*, pp. 188–89.

87 *The Navy transferred:* Commander Submarine Force, U.S. Pacific Fleet, *Submarine Operational History World War II*, vol. 1, pp. 189–92, and vol. 2, pp. 886–87.

87 *"It now appears":* Morison, *The Two-Ocean War*, p. 189.

87 *The son of a former samurai:* Agawa, *The Reluctant Admiral*, pp. 2, 17–18, 333, 338.

88 *"Starvation Island":* Ibid., p. 338.

88 *No one battle:* Hornfischer, *Neptune's Inferno*, p. 396.

88 *With starvation claiming:* Ibid., p. 404–8.

88 *Under the cover:* Ibid.; Morison, *The Two-Ocean War*, p. 212.

88 *The six-month campaign:* Hornfischer, *Neptune's Inferno*, pp. xxi, 437.

88 *"Total and complete":* Morison, *The Two-Ocean War*, p. 214.

88 *Yamamoto had come:* Agawa, *The Reluctant Admiral*, pp. 345–46.

88 *The multiple addresses:* David Kahn, *The Codebreakers: The Story of Secret Writing* (New York: Macmillan, 1968), p. 595.

88 *"We've hit the jackpot":* Donald A. Davis, *Lightning Strike: The Secret Mission to Kill Admiral Yamamoto and Avenge Pearl Harbor* (New York: St. Martin's, 2005) pp. 226–27.

89 *"Our old friend Yamamoto":* Potter, *Nimitz*, pp. 284–85.

89 *"What do you say":* Ibid., p. 284.

89 *"He's unique":* Ibid.

89 *"You know, Admiral Nimitz":* Ibid.

89 *"It's down in Halsey's bailiwick":* Ibid.

89 *"There were some qualms":* Layton, *"And I Was There,"* p. 475.

89 *"Best of luck":* Ibid.; Edwin T. Layon, "Admiral Kimmel Deserved a Better Fate," in Paul Stillwell, ed., *Pearl Harbor!: Recollections of a Day of Infamy* (Annapolis, Md.: Naval Institute Press, 1981), p. 276.

89 *American pilots planned:* Thomas G. Lanphier, Jr., "Flier Who Shot Down Yamamoto Says White House Baited the Trap," *New York Times*, Sept. 12, 1945, p. 2; Thomas G. Lanphier, Jr., "Yamamoto's Killer Arrived on the Dot," *New York Times*, Sept. 13, 1945, p. 5.

89 *The admiral woke early:* Matome Ugaki diary, April 18, 1943, and April 18, 1944, in Ugaki, *Fading Victory*, pp. 330, 352; Agawa, *The Reluctant Admiral*, pp. 347–48, 357–60.

90 *Eighteen twin-engine:* Thomas G. Lanphier, Jr., "Yamamoto's Killer Arrived on the Dot," *New York Times*, Sept. 13, 1945, p. 5.

90 *"Bogey":* Ibid.

90 *The Lightnings jettisoned:* Ibid.; Robert D. McFadden, "Thomas G. Lanphier Jr., 71, Dies," *New York Times*, Nov. 28, 1987, p. 41; Richard Goldstein, "Rex T. Barber, Pilot Who Downed Yamamoto, Dies at 84," *New York Times*, Aug. 1, 2001, p. A15; "WWII Ace Rex Barber Dead at 84," *The Register-Guard*, July 28, 2001, p. 2B.

90 *Japanese fighter pilots:* Matome Ugaki diary, April 18, 1944, in Ugaki, *Fading Victory*, pp. 353–54.

90 *Lanphier opened fire:* Thomas G. Lanphier, Jr., "Yamamoto Died in Flaming Crash," *New York Times*, Sept. 14, 1945 p. 7.

90 *"I was right behind":* Richard Goldstein, "Rex T. Barber, Pilot Who Downed Yamamoto, Dies at 84," *New York Times*, Aug. 1, 2001, p. A15.

90 *"I spotted a shadow":* Thomas G. Lanphier, Jr., "Yamamoto Died in Flaming Crash," *New York Times*, Sept. 14, 1945, p. 7.

90 *Vice Admiral Matome Ugaki:* Matome Ugaki diary, April 18, 1944, in Ugaki, *Fading Victory*, pp. 353–54.

90 *"My God!":* Ibid., p. 354.

90 *"Just as I moved":* Thomas G. Lanphier, Jr., "Yamamoto Died in Flaming Crash," *New York Times*, Sept. 14, 1945, p. 7.

91 *Hacking through:* Agawa, *The Reluctant Admiral*, pp. 356–60.

91 *The second bomber:* Matome Ugaki diary, April 18, 1944, in Ugaki, *Fading Victory*, pp. 353, 355–60.

91 *America in contrast:* Thomas G. Lanphier, Jr., "Yamamoto Died in Flaming Crash," *New York Times*, Sept. 14, 1945, p. 7.

91 *Yamamoto's stopped watch:* Agawa, *The Reluctant Admiral*, pp. 358–59, 362.

91 *An autopsy:* Ibid., pp. 384–85; Davis, *Lightning Strike*, pp. 299–300.

91 *The admiral had long resisted:* Agawa, *The Reluctant Admiral*, pp. 186–93, 232–33.

91 *"If we are ordered":* Ibid., p. 189.

91 *"We all had lumps":* John Bienia letter to Alpha Bienia, Oct. 7, 1943.

92 *The twenty-two year-old Malone:* Eugene Malone interview with author, Aug. 5, 2009.

92 *"I have a new officer":* John Bienia letter to Alpha Bienia, Oct. 2, 1943.

92 *Crews wrapped up:* Unless otherwise noted, the remainder of this chapter is drawn from the following sources: *Silversides* Report of Seventh War Patrol,

Nov. 8, 1943; John S. Coye, Jr., unpublished memoir, pp. 14–15; *The Reminiscences of Rear Admiral John S. Coye, Jr.*, pp. 64–78.

93 *What Coye didn't know: Balao* Report of Second War Patrol, Nov. 16, 1943.

94 *the 1,915-ton* Tairin Maru: JANAC, p. 43 of the appendix; Alden and McDonald, p. 106.

94 *loaded down with 2,100 tons:* Shinshichiro Komamiya, *Senji Yuso Sendan Shi* (Wartime Transportation Convoys History), part 1, trans. William G. Somerville (Tokyo: Shuppan Kyodosha, 1987). This is a privately translated document and pagination varies among versions. As a result I have chosen not to include references to specific page numbers and in subsequent citations refer to this work solely by its Japanese title. Much of this same information can be found in Alden and McDonald's book, which also depended on Somerville's translation.

96 Balao's *skipper had fired: Balao* Report of Second War Patrol, Nov. 16, 1943.

98 *the 5,407-ton* Tennan Maru: JANAC, p. 43 of the appendix; Alden and McDonald, p. 107.

98 *Two torpedoes ripped: Senji Yuso Sendan Shi.*

98 *the 1,893-ton* Kazan Maru: JANAC, p. 43 of the appendix; Alden and McDonald, p. 107.

99 *the 6,182-ton passenger freighter* Johore Maru: JANAC, p. 43 of the appendix; Alden and McDonald, p. 107; *Senji Yuso Sendan Shi.*

Chapter 8. *Drum*

PAGE

101 *"Leaving behind": Drum* crew calendar, June 3, 1943.

101 *Commander Delbert Fred Williamson: Drum* Report of Eighth War Patrol, Dec. 5, 1943.

101 *McMahon had failed:* JANAC, p. 12 of the appendix.

101 *The thirty-nine-year-old Williamson:* Details on Williamson's background are drawn from the following sources: Delbert Williamson oral history interview with the Navy, Aug. 18, 1944, Box 30, RG 38, Records of the Office of the Chief of Naval Operations, World War II Oral Histories, 1942–1946, NARA; Delbert Williamson midshipman file, USNA.

102 *"He is extremely":* J. S. Heavilin, ed., *The Lucky Bag of 1927: The Annual of the Regiment of Midshipmen* (Annapolis, Md.: USNA, 1927), p. 138.

102 *Williamson served:* Delbert Williamson oral history interview with the Navy, Aug. 18, 1944; "Delbert Fred Williamson '27," *Shipmate*, vol. 51, no. 8, October 1988, p. 92; Verner Utke-Ramsing interviews with author, Aug. 20, 2009, and Nov. 10, 2009.

102 *Lieutenant Mike Rindskopf:* Maurice Rindskopf unpublished memoir, pp. 80–81; Maurice Rindskopf interview with author, Aug. 28, 2009.

103   *One example:* Blair, *Silent Victory*, pp. 143–44.

103   *Veteran combat officers knew:* Eugene Malone e-mails to author, June 22, 2011.

103   *Victory at Guadalcanal:* Commander Submarine Force, U.S. Pacific Fleet, *Submarine Operational History World War II*, vol. 1, p. 36.

103   *Engineers had finally:* Ibid., p. 50; Jolie, "A Brief History of U.S. Navy Torpedo Development," pp. 35–36, 85.

103   *Fifty-two new fleet boats:* Voge, ed., "Submarine Commands," vol. 1, p. 51.

103   *Submarines in 1943:* Commander Submarine Force, U.S. Pacific Fleet, *Submarine Operational History World War II*, vol. 1, p. 50; USSBS, *The War Against Japanese Transportation, 1941–1945*, pp. 37–38, 134; Roscoe, *United States Submarine Operations in World War II*, pp. 298–99.

103   *America's efforts:* Frederick D. Parker, *Pearl Harbor Revisited: United States Navy Communications Intelligence, 1924–1941*, United States Cryptologic History, Series IV, World War II, vol. 6 (Fort George G. Meade, Md.: Center for Cryptologic History/National Security Agency, 1994), p. 7; "Pearl Harbor Revisited—Linguists," www.nsa.gov; Layton, *"And I Was There,"* pp. 28–32.

104   *The value of this newfound intelligence:* Layton, *"And I Was There,"* pp. 34–35; "The Origination and Evolution of Radio Traffic Analysis: The Period Between the Wars," *Cryptologic Quarterly*, vol. 6, nos. 3–4, Fall–Winter 1987–88, p. 25.

104   *The intelligence haul:* "The Origination and Evolution of Radio Traffic Analysis: The Period Between the Wars," pp. 27–35.

104   *Japan changed:* Parker, *Pearl Harbor Revisited*, p. 18.

104   *This complex new cryptosystem:* Ibid., pp. 19–21; Robert J. Hanyok and David Mowry, *West Wind Clear: Cryptology and the Winds Message Controversy—A Documentary History*, United States Cryptologic History, Series IV, World War II, vol. 10 (Fort George G. Meade, Md.: Center for Cryptologic History/National Security Agency, 2008), pp. 5–6, 9; Layton, *"And I Was There,"* pp. 77–78; Stephen Budiansky, *Battle of Wits: The Complete Story of Codebreaking in World War II* (New York: Touchstone, 2002), p. 319; W. J. Holmes, *Double-Edged Secrets: U.S. Naval Intelligence Operations in the Pacific During World War II* (Annapolis, Md.: Naval Institute Press, 1979), pp. 54–55; Duane L. Whitlock, "The Silent War Against the Japanese Navy," *Naval War College Review*, vol. 48, no. 4, Autumn 1995, pp. 43–52.

105   *America failed to grasp:* Layton, *"And I Was There,"* p. 77.

105   *The pursuit:* Parker, *Pearl Harbor Revisited*, pp. 20–21, 23–25, 30, 34–35, 45, 49–51.

105   *Largely unable to read:* Ibid., p. 42.

105   *In what analysts viewed:* Ibid.; Holmes, *Double-Edged Secrets*, pp. 27–28.

106   *"Homeland waters?":* Layton, *"And I Was There,"* p. 18.

106   *Cryptanalysts dropped:* "Pearl Harbor Review—JN-25," www.nsa.gov; Freder-

ick D. Parker, *A Priceless Advantage: U.S. Navy Communications Intelligence and the Battles of Coral Sea, Midway, and the Aleutians*, United States Cryptologic History, Series IV, World War II, vol. 5 (Fort George G. Meade, Md.: Center for Cryptologic History/National Security Agency, 1993), pp. 20–28, 41–58.

106 *A Naval Academy graduate:* Holmes, *Double-Edged Secrets*, pp. 9–10.

106 *The intelligence community:* Ibid., pp. 23, 75, 126–28.

107 *"Intelligence, like money":* Ibid., p. 128.

107 *The veteran submariner:* Ibid., pp. 63–64, 103–5, 124–26.

107 *"Whatever the causes":* Ibid., p. 127.

107 *But that changed:* Ibid., pp. 125–27; Layton, *"And I Was There,"* pp. 471–72.

107 *These same decrypts:* C. A. Lockwood, June 17, 1947, COMINT Contributions, Submarine Warfare in WWII, SRH-235, NDL.

107 *The Chicago native:* Richard G. Voge Navy Bio, Jan., 24, 1964, NDL; Naval History Division, Office of the Chief of Naval Operations, *United States Submarine Losses*, pp. 8, 13; History of the USS *Sailfish* (SS-192), July 1948, Office of Naval Records and History, Ships' Histories Section, Navy Department.

108 *The two men met:* Holmes, *Double-Edged Secrets*, pp. 125–26; C. A. Lockwood, June 17, 1947, COMINT Contributions, Submarine Warfare in WWII.

108 *Code breakers developed:* The Role of Communication Intelligence in Submarine Warfare in the Pacific, January 1943–October 1943, vol. 1, Nov. 19, 1945, SRH-011, p. 1, NDL.

108 *"1 freighter to arrive":* Ibid., p. 2.

108 *Burlingame peered: Silversides* Report of Fourth War Patrol, Jan. 31, 1943.

108 *Another Ultra:* The Role of Communication Intelligence in Submarine Warfare in the Pacific, January 1943–October 1943, vol. 1, Nov. 19, 1945, SRH-011, p. 7.

108 *Burlingame picked up: Silversides* Report of Fourth War Patrol, Jan. 31, 1943; Alden and McDonald, p. 62.

108 *Intelligence alerted:* The Role of Communication Intelligence in Submarine Warfare in the Pacific, January 1943–October 1943, vol. 1, Nov. 19, 1945, SRH-011, pp. 8–9; *Senji Yuso Sendan Shi*; JANAC, p. 43 of the appendix; Alden and McDonald, p. 62.

109 *From January to October 1943:* The Role of Communication Intelligence in Submarine Warfare in the Pacific, January 1943–October 1943, vol. 1, Nov. 19, 1945, SRH-011, p. ix.

109 *"There were nights":* Holmes, *Double-Edged Secrets*, p. 128.

109 *Armed with a cup:* Maurice Rindskopf unpublished memoir pp. 75–76; Maurice Rindskopf as told to Dr. Karel Montor, "Case Study of Leadership at Sea," unpublished report, USNA.

109 *Drum lookouts had spotted: Drum* Report of Eighth War Patrol, Dec. 5, 1943.

109 *the* Hie Maru: JANAC, p. 12 of the appendix; Robert J. Cressman, *The Official*

Chronology of the U.S. Navy in World War II (Annapolis, Md.: Naval Institute Press, 2000), p. 193.

109 *The 535-foot-long vessel:* E. Mowbray Tate, *Transpacific Steam: The Story of Steam Navigation from the Pacific Coast of North America to the Far East and the Antipodes, 1967–1941* (New York: Cornwall Books, 1986), pp. 124–25.

109 *The city of Yokohama:* "Cherry Blossoms Taiko-Gata Stone Lantern and Roses," *Seascope,* No. 180, June 2002.

109 *Requisitioned by the military:* Roger Jordan, *The World's Merchant Fleets, 1939: The Particulars and Wartime Fates of 6,000 Ships* (Annapolis, Md.: Naval Institute Press, 2006), p. 541.

109 *The skipper fired: Drum* Report of Eighth War Patrol, Dec. 5, 1943.

110 *The three-ship convoy: Senji Yuso Sendan Shi.*

110 *Hie Maru had not only escaped:* Jürgen Rohwer, *Chronology of the War at Sea, 1939–1945: The Naval History of World War II,* 3rd rev. ed. (Annapolis, Md.: Naval Institute Press, 2005), p. 285.

110 *The skipper listened: Drum* Report of Eighth War Patrol, Dec. 5, 1943; JANAC, p. 12 of the appendix; Alden and McDonald, p. 113.

110 *Rindskopf was impressed:* Maurice Rindskopf unpublished memoir, p. 81.

110 *Williamson demonstrated: Drum* Report of Eighth War Patrol, Dec. 5, 1943.

111 *Williamson had found:* Ibid.

111 *Rindskopf heard:* Maurice Rindskopf unpublished memoir, p. 81.

111 *Chief Petty Officer George Schaedler:* George Schaedler interview with author, Nov. 5, 2009.

111 *A finger-sized stream:* Maurice Rindskopf unpublished memoir, p. 81; Maurice Rindskopf interview with author, Aug. 28, 2009.

111 *Water streamed in: Drum* Report of Eighth War Patrol, Dec. 5, 1943.

111 *The battle station auxiliary man:* Maurice Rindskopf unpublished memoir, p. 81; Maurice Rindskopf interview with author, Aug. 28, 2009.

112 *Three hours after: Drum* Report of Eighth War Patrol, Dec. 5, 1943.

Chapter 9. *Silversides*

PAGE

113 *"The sixteenth depth charge":* Robert Worthington diary, May 22, 1942.

113 *John Coye paced: Silversides* Report of Eighth War Patrol, Jan. 15, 1944; Eugene Malone interview with author, Jan. 7, 2011; Operational Order No. 285–43, Dec. 3, 1943, Box 297, RG 38, Records of the Office of the Chief of Naval Operations, Plans, Orders and Related Documents, NARA.

113 *Coye preferred:* Eugene Malone interview with author, Jan. 7, 2011.

113 *"My own personal attitude": The Reminiscences of Rear Admiral John S. Coye, Jr.,* p. 72.

114 *he'd sunk four ships:* JANAC, p. 43 of the appendix.

114 *In a private critique:* E. W. Grenfell to John Coye, Jr., Nov. 11, 1943.

114 *"This short patrol":* C. A. Lockwood, Jr., to the Commander-in-Chief, United States Fleet, Nov. 13, 1943.

114 *The plan position indicator in contrast:* Blair, *Silent Victory*, p. 448; Roscoe, *United States Submarine Operations in World War II*, p. 290; Eugene Malone interview with author, Jan. 7, 2010.

114 *"change the course":* Eugene Malone, *"Silversides'* Great Eighth."

114 *"It is obviously useless":* Silversides Report of Third War Patrol, Nov. 25, 1942. Burlingame repeated this same line in his fourth patrol report.

115 *"must not be belittled":* J. H. Brown, Jr., to Submarine Force, Pacific Fleet, Feb. 3, 1943.

115 *"It is hoped":* Ibid.

115 *He had shanghaied:* Eugene Malone interview with author, Aug. 5, 2009.

115 *lanky lieutenant:* Eugene Malone interview with author, Jan. 7, 2011.

115 *One afternoon in New Caledonia:* Eugene Malone, "Fighting World War II in a World War I Submarine"; Eugene Malone, *"Silversides'* Great Eighth"; Eugene Malone interview with author, Jan. 7, 2011.

115 *"Gosh, this big boat life":* Eugene Malone letter to Helen Malone, Nov. 9, 1943.

115 *"Since I made lieutenant":* Eugene Malone letter to Helen Malone, Dec. 1, 1943.

116 *"Dished out combat insignia":* Eugene Malone to Elinor Ives, Nov. 25, 1943.

116 *"His in laws":* Eugene Malone letter to Helen Malone, Dec. 1, 1943.

116 *New Guinea stretched:* USSBS, *The Campaigns of the Pacific War*, p. 173; Frank L. Kluckhohn, "West and East—Two Kinds of Warfare," *New York Times*, Oct. 17, 1943, p. SM12; Merlin Spencer, "Monotony Foe in New Guinea," *Telegraph-Herald*, May 31, 1943, p. 6; Pat Robinson, "I Saw War in New Guinea," *St. Petersburg Times*, March 18, 1943, p. 10.

116 *"To die in front":* Frank Prist, "Nature Is Third Antagonist for Yanks in 'Green Hell,'" *Palm Beach Post*, Jan. 25, 1943, p. 2.

116 *Climbing out of the Pacific:* Samuel Eliot Morison, *History of the United States Naval Operations in World War II*, vol. 12, *Leyte, June 1944–January 1945* (Boston: Atlantic Monthly Press/Little, Brown, 1970), pp. 30–32; "Advance in the Pacific," editorial, *New York Times*, Sept. 16, 1944, p. 12.

116 *"It is believed":* Operational Order No. 285-43, Dec. 3, 1943.

117 *"He looks green":* John Bienia letter to Alpha Bienia, Dec. 7, 1943.

117 *"Some of the crates:* John Bienia letter to Alpha Bienia, Dec. 5, 1943.

117 *The skipper, the officer:* unless otherwise noted, the remainder of this chapter is drawn from the following sources: Silversides Report of Eighth War Patrol, Jan. 15, 1944; John S. Coye, Jr., unpublished memoir, pp. 15–16; *The Reminiscences of Rear Admiral John S. Coye, Jr.*, pp. 78–87.

118 *the 1,911-ton* Shichisei Maru: JANAC, p. 43 of the appendix; Alden and Mc-
       Donald, p. 122; *Senji Yuso Sendan Shi.*
119 *the 1,970-ton* Tenposan Maru: Ibid.
119 *the 3,311-ton* Ryuto Maru: Ibid.
120 *"Excellent aggressive patrol":* E. W. Grenfell to John Coye, Jr., Jan. 26, 1944.
120 *"I started out thinking":* Eugene Malone letter to Helen Malone, Jan. 16, 1944.
120 *"He is developing":* Eugene Malone letter to Anna Maria Ives, Jan. 16, 1944.
120 *Malone climbed up:* Eugene Malone interview with author, Aug. 6, 2009; Eugene
       Malone, "Submarine Versus Submarine."
121 Silversides *raced:* Ibid.; *Silversides* Report of Eighth War Patrol, Jan. 15, 1944.
122 *"Some utter fool":* Eugene Malone letter to Anna Maria Ives, Jan. 16, 1943.
122 *"The recorder":* John Bienia letter to Alpha Bienia, Jan. 17, 1944.
123 *"Darling, sit back":* John Bienia letter to Alpha Bienia, Dec. 26, 1944.
123 *"The nasty culprit":* John Bienia letter to Alpha Bienia, Jan. 17, 1944.

Chapter 10. *Tang*

PAGE

124 *"Sadly":* Richard H. O'Kane, *Clear the Bridge! The War Patrols of the U.S.S. Tang*
       (Chicago: Rand McNally, 1977), p. 19.
124 *The prolonged blast: Tang* Report of First War Patrol, March 3, 1944; *Tang* deck
       log, Jan. 22, 1944; O'Kane, *Clear the Bridge!*, pp. 55–56.
124 *twenty-six submarines:* Blair, *Silent Victory*, pp. 942–43.
124 Tang *eased out:* Operational Order No. 30–44, Jan. 21, 1944, and Charles Lock-
       wood to Richard O'Kane, Jan. 22, 1944, Box 297, RG 38, Records of the Of-
       fice of the Chief of Naval Operations, Plans, Orders and Related Documents,
       NARA; O'Kane, *Clear the Bridge!*, pp. 55–56.
125 *Nothing in O'Kane's formative years:* Background on O'Kane comes from the
       following sources: Richard O'Kane Navy Bio, March 15, 1967, NDL; Richard
       O'Kane midshipman file, USNA; Jim O'Kane interview with author, Jan. 22,
       2010; William Leibold interview with author, July 8, 2009; Floyd Caverly inter-
       view with author, July 16, 2009.
125 *"Investigation of this":* C. P. Snyder to Superintendent, Feb. 10, 1931, USNA.
125 *Upon graduation:* USNA, *Annual Register of the United States Naval Academy*
       (Washington, D.C.: U.S. Government Printing Office, 1934), p. 38.
125 *O'Kane's class:* Slade Cutter, *The Reminiscences of Captain Slade D. Cutter, U.S.
       Navy (Retired)*, vols. 1–2 (Annapolis, Md.: Naval Institute Oral History De-
       partment, 1985), pp. 143–62 (vol. 1), 512–23 (vol. 2); *The Reminiscences of Rear
       Admiral Charles Elliot Loughlin*, pp. 44–49.
126 *"Everybody was kind of laughing": The Reminiscences of Captain Slade D. Cutter*,
       vol. 2, pp. 512–13.

126 *Lieutenant Commander Marvin Kennedy:* Background on Kennedy comes from the following sources: Marvin Kennedy Navy Bio, Jan. 14, 1953, NDL; Marvin Kennedy midshipman file, USNA; George Grider as told to Lydel Sims, *War Fish* (Boston: Little, Brown, 1958), p. 23; Richard H. O'Kane, *Wahoo: The Patrols of America's Most Famous World War II Submarine* (New York: Bantam, 1989), p. 11.

126 *Kennedy's demand:* O'Kane, *Wahoo*, pp. 55–58; Grider, *War Fish*, pp. 56–57.

126 *"There were no screens":* Wahoo Report of First War Patrol, Oct. 17, 1942.

126 *Through the periscope:* James L. Mooney et al., eds., *Dictionary of American Naval Fighting Ships*, vol. 8 (Washington, D.C.: U.S. Government Printing Office, 1981), pp. 29–33.

126 *"If we bagged":* Grider, *War Fish*, p. 56.

127 *"Made approach":* Wahoo Report of First War Patrol, Oct. 17, 1942.

127 Wahoo *still had:* Ibid.

127 *"No, Dick":* O'Kane, *Wahoo*, p. 58.

127 *O'Kane fumed:* O'Kane, *Wahoo*, pp. 68–69.

127 *The skipper's timidity:* Wahoo Report of Second War Patrol, Dec. 26, 1942; O'Kane, *Wahoo*, pp. 77–81.

128 *"No words":* O'Kane, *Wahoo*, p. 81.

128 *When* Wahoo *arrived:* Marvin Kennedy undated letter to Clay Blair, Jr., Box 68, Clay Blair, Jr., Papers, AHC.

128 *Three and a half years:* Background on Morton comes from the following sources: Dudley Morton Navy Bio, August 28, 1957, NDL; Dudley Morton midshipman file, USNA; David A. Stretch, ed., *The Lucky Bag of 1930: The Annual of the Regiment of Midshipmen* (Annapolis, Md.: USNA, 1927), p. 165; Grider, *War Fish*, pp. 60, 68–69; O'Kane, *Wahoo*, p. 73.

128 *"boulder":* "Must Be Presumed . . . ," *Time*, Dec. 13, 1943, p. 68.

128 *stuffing four golf balls:* John Griggs III letter to Clay Blair, May 29, 1972, Box 67, Clay Blair, Jr., Papers, AHC.

128 *"He was built":* Grider, *War Fish*, pp. 68–69.

129 *"Mush the Magnificent":* Ibid.

129 *"maker of Jap widows":* "Skipper of *Wahoo* Tells of Sinking 19 Jap Ships," *Los Angeles Times*, June 29, 1943, p. 3.

129 *Kennedy had covered:* O'Kane, *Wahoo*, pp. 109–11.

129 *"In his mind":* John Griggs III letter to Clay Blair, May 29, 1972.

129 *"Most of us":* Grider, *War Fish*, p. 69.

129 *"You will be":* O'Kane, *Clear the Bridge!*, p. 17.

129 *"overly garrulous":* Grider, *War Fish*, p. 23.

129 *"He talked a great deal":* Ibid., p. 70.

129 *claiming to sink:* Wahoo Report of Third War Patrol, Feb. 7, 1943; JANAC, p. 54 of the appendix.

129   *Morton boasted:* Lockwood, *Sink 'Em All*, p. 66.

130   *after Morton clobbered:* Ibid. p. 65; Dudley Morton Navy Bio, August 28, 1957; "Submarine Record in Pacific Honored," *New York Times*, May 23, 1943, p. 18; Dudley Morton oral history interview with the Navy, Sept. 9, 1943, Box 20, RG 38, Records of the Office of the Chief of Naval Operations, World War II Oral Histories, 1942–1946, NARA.

130   *Wahoo's fourth patrol: Wahoo* Report of Fourth War Patrol, April 6, 1943; JANAC, p. 54 of the appendix.

130   *"Morton is the heavy swordsman":* Bill Ewing, undated draft article, Dudley Morton Family Papers, BSMP.

130   *Newspaper and magazine articles:* Robert Trumbull, "U.S. Submarine Flaunts a Broom for Clean Sweep off New Guinea," *New York Times*, Feb. 10, 1943, p. 4; "Clean Sweep," *Time*, Feb. 22, 1943, p. 24.

130   *Morton appeared:* Dudley Morton radio interview transcript, "Johnny Presents: The New Philip Morris Program," July 13, 1943, Dudley Morton Family Papers, BSMP.

130   *Warner Bros. hired:* "On the Set with the Warner Crew Filming 'Destination, Tokyo,'" *New York Times*, Oct. 24, 1943, p. X3; Dudley Morton letter to mother, August 1943, Dudley Morton Family Papers, BSMP.

130   *whose photos he displayed:* Walter B. Clausen, untitled Associated Press wire story, Feb. 9, 1943, Dudley Morton Family Papers, BSMP.

130   *"Take good care":* Dudley Morton letter to father, February 1943, Dudley Morton Family Papers, BSMP.

131   *Malfunctioning torpedoes: Wahoo* Report of Sixth War Patrol, Aug. 29, 1943.

131   *The irate skipper:* Lockwood, *Sink 'Em All*, pp. 116–17; Lockwood, *Down to the Sea in Subs*, pp. 292–93.

131   *a man who had grown so successful:* Dudley Morton oral history interview with the Navy, Sept. 9, 1943.

131   *"During our periods":* John Griggs III letter to Clay Blair, May 29, 1972.

131   *"By now virtually":* Grider, *War Fish*, p. 124.

131   *Wahoo veteran James Allen:* James Allen interview with author, Nov. 4, 2009; James Allen letter to Richard O'Kane, June 15, 1988, Dudley Morton Family Papers, BSMP.

132   *"I am going to":* Dudley Morton letter to mother, August 1943, Dudley Morton Family Papers, BSMP.

132   *One of the most egregious:* James F. DeRose, *Unrestricted Warfare: How a New Breed of Officers Led the Submarine Force to Victory in World War II* (New York: John Wiley & Sons, 2000), pp. 77, 94; JANAC, p. 54 of the appendix; Alden and McDonald, p. 64. Alden and McDonald's figures for those killed on *Buyo Maru* are slightly higher: eighty-six army, eight crew, and 269 Indians.

132 *"Our fire was returned"*: Dudley Morton oral history interview with the Navy, Sept. 9, 1943.

132 *"Mush, whose biological"*: Grider, *War Fish*, p. 101.

132 *Japanese radio broadcasts*: Charles Lockwood, Jr., to the Commander-in-Chief, U.S. Fleet, Loss of U.S.S. *Wahoo* (SS-238), Nov. 9, 1943, Box 743, RG 38, Records of the Office of the Chief of Naval Operations, World War II Action and Operational Reports, NARA.

132 *Of the 616*: Alden and McDonald, p. 103. Alden and McDonald's figures are slightly higher than those broadcast by the Japanese in 1943. Alden and McDonald report that the attack killed 445 of 479 passengers and 137 of 176 crewmembers.

132 *"The Tsushima Straits"*: "Knock at the Door," *Time*, Oct. 18, 1943, p. 36.

133 *A Japanese floatplane*: O'Kane, *Wahoo*, pp. 300–301, 320–22; Commander, U.S. Pacific Fleet Public Affairs, "Navy Says Wreck Found off Japan Is Legendary Sub USS *Wahoo*," Oct. 31, 2006; Thomas A. Logue, Jr., and Bryan MacKinnon, "The Journey to Find USS *Wahoo*," *Undersea Warfare*, Spring 2007, pp. 22–27.

133 *The three-star admiral waited*: Charles Lockwood, Jr., to the Commander-in-Chief, United States Fleet, Loss of U.S.S *Wahoo* (SS-238), Nov. 9, 1943.

133 *"It just didn't seem possible"*: Lockwood, *Sink 'Em All*, p. 131.

133 *the press reported*: "Must Be Presumed . . . ," *Time*, Dec. 13, 1943, p. 68.

133 *Within hours*: O'Kane, *Clear the Bridge!*, p. 50.

133 *The official postwar*: JANAC, p. 54 of the appendix.

133 *making him the third*: Blair, *Silent Victory*, p. 984.

133 *whose photo adorned*: COMSUBPAC undated telegram to USS WAHOO, *Wahoo* File, BSMP.

133 *"the most serious loss"*: Charles Lockwood, Jr., letter to Mrs. Dudley Morton, Dec. 1, 1943, Dudley Morton Family Papers, BSMP. Lockwood relates Nimitz's comments in his letter to Mrs. Morton.

133 *The skipper found*: O'Kane, *Clear the Bridge!*, p. 300.

133 *He surprised his crew*: Ibid., pp. 33–40.

134 *"The result was"*: Ibid., p. 39.

134 *Naval engineers had designed*: Alden, *The Fleet Submarine in the U.S. Navy*, pp. 101, 105; O'Kane, *Clear the Bridge!*, pp. 39–40.

134 *"No one batted an eye"*: O'Kane, *Clear the Bridge!*, p. 40.

135 *"Well, if you're not"*: Murray B. Frazee, Jr., "We Never Looked Back," *Naval History*, July–August 1994, pp. 47–51; O'Kane, *Clear the Bridge!*, p. 42.

135 *"Never was there"*: Murray Frazee, Jr., unpublished memoir, pp. 51–52.

Chapter 11. *Tang*

136 *"We certainly kept":* Dudley Morton letter to George Clarke, Feb. 16, 1943, Dudley Morton Family Papers, BSMP.

136 *O'Kane stared:* Unless otherwise noted, information in this chapter is drawn from the following sources: *Tang* Report of First War Patrol, March 3, 1944; *Tang* deck log; O'Kane, *Clear the Bridge!*, pp. 55–109. All dialogue comes from O'Kane's book.

137 *The summer of 1943:* USSBS, *The Campaigns of the Pacific War*, p. 191; Morison, *The Two-Ocean War*, pp. 295–96.

137 *This road through:* Samuel Eliot Morison, *History of the United States Naval Operations in World War II*, vol. 7, *Aleutians, Gilberts and Marshalls, June 1942–April 1944* (Boston: Atlantic Monthly Press/Little, Brown, 1975), pp. 69–79.

137 *To prevent:* Morison, *History of the United States Naval Operations in World War II*, vol. 7, *Aleutians, Gilberts and Marshalls, June 1942–April 1944*, pp. 69–70, 230; William Hughes, *The Geography of the British Colonies and Dependencies, Physical Political, Commercial*, rev. ed., *Philip's Geographical Manuals* (London: George Philip & Son, 1907), p. 212.

138 *Troops hit the beaches:* USSBS, *The Campaigns of the Pacific War*, pp. 191–93; "The Fight for Tarawa," *Life*, vol. 15, no. 24, Dec. 13, 1943, pp. 27–35; John Wukovits, *One Square Mile of Hell: The Battle for Tarawa* (New York: NAL Caliber, 2006), pp. 217–18.

138 *The United States next turned:* Gordon L. Rottman, *The Marshall Islands 1944: Operation Flintlock, the Capture of Kwajalein and Eniwetok* (Oxford: Osprey Publishing, 2004) p. 11.

138 *Strategists anticipated:* Philip A. Crowl and Edmund G. Love, *Seizure of the Gilberts and Marshalls*, in the series *United States Army in World War II: The War in the Pacific*, Center of Military History Publication 5-6 (Washington, D.C.: U.S. Government Printing Office, 1955), pp. 177, 206–18.

138 *America overlooked:* USSBS, *The Campaigns of the Pacific War*, pp. 193–94; Burton Wright III, *Eastern Mandates*, in the series *The U.S. Army Campaigns of World War II*, Center of Military History Publication 72-73 (Washington, D.C.: U.S. Government Printing Office, 1993), pp. 9–13.

138 *Battleships and heavy cruisers:* Crowl and Love, *Seizure of the Gilberts and Marshalls*, pp. 222–23; Wright, *Eastern Mandates*, p. 14.

138 *the United States suffered:* Crowl and Love, *Seizure of the Gilberts and Marshalls*, pp. 301, 331.

138 *The success of the Marshalls:* USSBS, *The Campaigns of the Pacific War*, p. 194.

138 *"Japan's Pearl Harbor":* Robert Trumbull, "Bold Blow at Truk Amazed News Men," *New York Times*, Feb. 21, 1944, p. 3; "The Attack on Truk," editorial, *New*

York Times, Feb. 18, 1944, p. 16; Morison, *History of the United States Naval Operations in World War II,* vol. 7, *Aleutians, Gilberts and Marshalls, June 1942–April 1944,* pp. 315–32.

138 *Submarines had largely:* Commander Submarine Force, U.S. Pacific Fleet, *Submarine Operational History World War II,* vol. 1, pp. 174–76.

139 *Ten submarines:* Ibid., pp. 192–99; Robert Rice handwritten draft memoir, p. 53; *Nautilus* Report of Seventh War Patrol, Dec. 4, 1943; History of Ships Named *Nautilus,* Aug. 28, 1962, Office of the Chief of Naval Operations, Naval History Division, Ships' Histories Section.

139 *Tang's second in command:* Background on Murray Frazee, Jr., comes from the following sources: Murray Frazee, Jr., midshipman file, USNA; Murray Frazee, Jr., unpublished memoir, pp. 1–51; V. T. Boatwright, ed., *The Lucky Bag of 1939: The Annual of the Regiment of Midshipmen* (Annapolis, Md.: USNA, 1939), p. 182; Murray Frazee III interview with author, Aug. 30, 2009.

142 *The 6,854-ton Gyoten Maru:* JANAC, p. 48 of the appendix; Alden and McDonald, p. 135; *Senji Yuso Sendan Shi.*

143 *Ten submarines:* Roscoe, *United States Submarine Operations in World War II,* p. 363; Commander Submarine Force, U.S. Pacific Fleet, *Submarine Operational History World War II,* vol. 1, pp. 198–205.

143 *But Operation Hailstone:* USSBS, *The Campaigns of the Pacific War,* p. 194; JANAC, pp. 9–10, 49–51.

144 *"The Pacific Fleet has returned":* George F. Horne, "Japanese Stunned," *New York Times,* Feb. 21, 1944, p. 1.

146 *The 3,581-ton Fukuyama Maru:* JANAC, p. 48 of the appendix; Alden and McDonald, p. 137.

147 *the 6,776-ton Yamashimo Maru:* Ibid.

148 *American submarines in 1943:* USSBS, *The War Against Japanese Transportation, 1941–1945,* pp. 37–38, 48–49; Roscoe, *United States Submarine Operations in World War II,* p. 300.

149 *the 2,424-ton Echizen Maru's:* JANAC, p. 48 of the appendix; Alden and McDonald, p. 138.

151 *the 1,794-ton freighter Choko Maru:* Ibid.

Chapter 12. *Tang*

PAGE
152 *"Now I've got":* John Bienia letter to Alpha Bienia, Oct. 7, 1943.
152 *Waves of as many:* O'Kane, *Clear the Bridge!,* pp. 168–70.
152 *Carrier-based fighters:* Morison, *History of the United States Naval Operations in World War II,* vol. 7, *Aleutians, Gilberts and Marshalls, June 1942–April 1944,* pp. 315–32.

152 *Army B-24 Liberators:* "Truk Bombed 35th Time," *New York Times,* May 1, 1944, p. 1; "Second Carrier Attack on Truk," *New York Times,* May 3, 1944, p. 2.

152 *Despite the continual:* Samuel Eliot Morison, *History of United States Naval Operations in World War II,* vol. 8, *New Guinea and the Marianas, March 1944–August 1944* (Boston: Little, Brown, 1953), p. 38.

152 *"With the possible exception":* Tang Report of Second War Patrol, May 15, 1944.

152 *In just forty-one days:* JANAC, p. 48 of the appendix.

152 *He had hoped:* O'Kane, *Clear the Bridge!,* p. 136; Operational Order No. 91–44, March 13, 1944, Box 298, RG 38, Records of the Office of the Chief of Naval Operations, Plans, Orders and Related Documents, NARA.

153 *The United States had captured:* USSBS, *The Campaigns of the Pacific War,* pp. 204–5.

153 *The United States had chased:* Ibid., p. 207; Morison, *History of United States Naval Operations in World War II,* Vol. 8, *New Guinea and the Marianas, March 1944–August 1944,* p. 140.

153 *Strategists suspected:* Commander Submarine Force, U.S. Pacific Fleet, *Submarine Operational History World War II,* vol. 1, pp. 207–8; Roscoe, *United States Submarine Operations in World War II,* pp. 165, 365.

154 *"There might be torpedoes fired":* O'Kane, *Clear the Bridge!,* p. 141.

154 *While carrier-based planes:* Morison, *History of United States Naval Operations in World War II,* vol. 8, *New Guinea and the Marianas, March 1944–August 1944,* p. 33.

154 *One night on the eve:* Commander Submarine Force, U.S. Pacific Fleet, *Submarine Operational History World War II,* vol. 1, p. 208; Roscoe, *United States Submarine Operations in World War II,* pp. 320–21; Naval History Division, Office of the Chief of Naval Operations, *United States Submarine Losses,* pp. 85–86; *Senji Yuso Sendan Shi.*

154 *The first call:* Tang Report of Second War Patrol, May 15, 1944; Tang deck log, April 30, 1944.

154 *Lieutenant j.g. Scott Scammell II:* Larry McManus, "Rescue off Truk," *Yank,* August 11, 1944, p. 8; "Milestones, Jun. 21, 1943," *Time,* June 21, 1943, p. 79.

154 *"The indicator":* McManus, "Rescue off Truk," *Yank,* August 11, 1944, pp. 8–9.

155 *O'Kane ordered:* Tang Report of Second War Patrol, May 15, 1944; O'Kane, *Clear the Bridge!,* pp. 170–71.

155 *"For my kid":* Larry McManus, "Rescue off Truk," *Yank,* August 11, 1944, pp. 8–9.

155 *O'Kane ordered:* Tang Report of Second War Patrol, May 15, 1944; O'Kane, *Clear the Bridge!,* pp. 170–71.

156 *"All planes":* Tang Report of Second War Patrol, May 15, 1944.

156 *The skipper didn't have time:* Ibid.; *Clear the Bridge!,* pp. 171–78.

156 *The* North Carolina: USS *North Carolina* War Diary, April 29–30, 1944, Battleship *North Carolina* Archives and Collections, Wilmington, North Carolina: U.S.S. *North Carolina* deck log, April 30, 1944, ibid.; Deaths on BB55, fact sheet, ibid.; Ben W. Blee, *Battleship North Carolina* (Wilmington, N.C.: USS *North Carolina* Battleship Commission, 2005), pp. 82–93, 150–51.

157 *Japanese planes:* USS *North Carolina* War Diary, April 30, 1944.

157 *"Bogies were":* Charles Gilbert diary, April 30, 1944, Battleship *North Carolina* Archives and Collections.

157 *Lieutenant j.g. Robert Kanze:* Larry McManus, "Rescue off Truk," *Yank,* August 11, 1944, pp. 8–9.

157 *"I wasn't thinking":* Ibid.

157 *He touched down:* Aubrey Gill interviews with author, Oct. 20–22, 2010.

158 *O'Kane had received: Tang* Report of Second War Patrol, May 15, 1944; O'Kane, *Clear the Bridge!,* p. 181.

158 *destroyed the first target: Tang* Report of Second War Patrol, May 15, 1944; O'Kane, *Clear the Bridge!,* pp. 181–82.

158 *"It appeared":* O'Kane, *Clear the Bridge!,* p. 182; Larry McManus, "Rescue off Truk," *Yank,* August 11, 1944, pp. 8–9; Aubrey Gill interviews with author, Oct. 20–22, 2010.

159 *Lieutenant Burns:* Aubrey Gill interviews with author, Oct. 20–22, 2010.

159 *O'Kane couldn't afford: Tang* Report of Second War Patrol, May 15, 1944; O'Kane, *Clear the Bridge!,* pp. 182–83; Larry McManus, "Rescue off Truk," *Yank,* August 11, 1944, pp. 8–9; Aubrey Gill interviews with author, Oct. 20–22, 2010.

159 *Burns worried:* Larry McManus, "Rescue off Truk," *Yank,* August 11, 1944, pp. 8–9; Aubrey Gill interviews with author, Oct. 20–22, 2010.

159 *Gill improvised:* Aubrey Gill interviews with author, Oct. 20–22, 2010.

160 *"It was a beautiful":* Larry McManus, "Rescue off Truk," *Yank,* August 11, 1944, pp. 8–9.

160 *Gill's job:* Ibid.; Aubrey Gill interviews with author, Oct. 20–22, 2010.

160 *O'Kane arrived:* Ibid.; *Tang* Report of Second War Patrol, May 15, 1944; O'Kane, *Clear the Bridge!,* p. 184.

160 *O'Kane was so impressed:* O'Kane, *Clear the Bridge!,* p. 192.

160 *He would return:* Lt. (jg) John A. Burns, U.S.N.R., memo prepared by Charles J. Sullivan, Nov. 18, 2003, Battleship *North Carolina* Archives and Collections; Charles J. Sullivan interview with author, Oct. 20, 2010.

160 *"Plane total loss":* F. E. Deam to ComNavAirBases, 5ND, War Diary, February 1945, March 3, 1945, Battleship *North Carolina* Archives and Collections.

160 *Just as he did: Tang* Report of Second War Patrol, May 15, 1944; O'Kane, *Clear the Bridge!,* pp. 184–85; Larry McManus, "Rescue off Truk," *Yank,* August 11, 1944, pp. 8–9.

161 *"We'll need two"*: O'Kane, *Clear the Bridge!*, p. 184.

161 *"The fighters"*: Ibid., p. 185; Larry McManus, "Rescue off Truk," *Yank*, August 11, 1944, pp. 8–9.

Chapter 13. *Silversides*

PAGE

162 *"Almost all the guys"*: Richard Smith undated 1943 letter to parents.

162 *"For aggressiveness"*: Frank T. Watkins to Commander-in-Chief, United States Fleet, Jan. 24, 1944.

162 *"The boat is hot"*: Eugene Malone letter to Anna Maria Ives, Jan. 30, 1944.

162 *"I've been leading"*: Ibid.

163 *"Sure do want to get home"*: Eugene Malone letter to Elinor Ives, Feb. 4, 1944.

163 *Coye had followed:* *Silversides* Report of Ninth War Patrol, April 8, 1944; JANAC, p. 43 of the appendix; Alden and McDonald, pp. 142–43.

163 *"The decision of the commanding officer"*: J. M. Haines to the Commander in Chief, United States Fleet, April 17, 1944.

163 *"I probably should have"*: *The Reminiscences of Rear Admiral John S. Coye, Jr.*, p. 88.

163 *The two men had spent:* These figures are drawn from the first nine patrol reports; John Bienia letter to Alpha Bienia, Feb. 26, 1944.

163 *The Navy now ordered:* Robert Worthington Navy Bio, May 28, 1957; Mooney et al., eds., *Dictionary of American Naval Fighting Ships*, vol. 7, p. 406.

164 *"Get yourself some new shoes"*: John Bienia letter to Alpha Bienia, May 1, 1944.

164 *The two officers had:* Eugene Malone letter to Anna Maria Ives, Jan. 30, 1944; Eugene Malone letter to Helen Malone, May 1, 1944.

164 *"It's a hell of a big job"*: Eugene Malone letter to Helen Malone, Jan. 28, 1944.

164 *waited pier-side:* John Bienia letter to Alpha Bienia, April 4, 1944.

164 *A graduate of the Naval Academy:* Charles F. Leigh midshipman file, USNA.

164 *Coye fumed:* Eugene Malone letter to Helen Malone, April 12, 1944.

164 *"If our new exec"*: Eugene Malone letter to Anna Maria Ives, April 17, 1944.

165 *"He was most aggressive"*: *The Reminiscences of Rear Admiral John S. Coye, Jr.*, p. 93.

165 *The loss of the islands:* USSBS, *The Campaigns of the Pacific War*, pp. 209–11.

165 *"The war is drawing close"*: Soemu Toyoda, Combined Fleet Ultrasecret Dispatch 041213, May 4, 1944, in USSBS, *The Campaigns of the Pacific War*, pp. 211, 233.

165 *Burlingame disembarked:* *Silversides* Report of Tenth War Patrol, June 11, 1944; John S. Coye, Jr., unpublished memoir, p. 17; *The Reminiscences of Rear Admiral John S. Coye, Jr.*, pp. 92–100.

167 *"All seven ships"*: *Silversides* Report of Tenth War Patrol, June 11, 1944.

167 *"Closed until"*: Ibid.

168 *"These were too"*: Ibid.

168 *the 2,631-ton converted gunboat:* JANAC, p. 43 of the appendix; Alden and McDonald, p. 156.

168 *"Japs sounded":* *Silversides* Report of Tenth War Patrol, June 11, 1944.

168 *the 4,319-ton passenger cargo ship* Mikage Maru No. 18: Ibid.

169 *998-ton converted gunboat* Shosei Maru: JANAC, p. 43 of the appendix; Alden and McDonald, p. 158.

169 *"Four escorts":* *Silversides* Report of Tenth War Patrol, June 11, 1944.

169 *the 1,949-ton cargo ship* Shoken Maru: JANAC, p. 43 of the appendix; Alden and McDonald, p. 161.

169 *"The explosion":* Eugene Malone interview with author, Aug. 8, 2009.

169 *"Escorts were probably":* *Silversides* Report of Tenth War Patrol, June 11, 1946.

170 *"Every 4th of July":* John S. Coye, Jr., unpublished memoir, p. 17.

Chapter 14. *Tang*

PAGE

171 *"There will be widows":* Don Sharp diary, June 30, 1944, BSMP.

171 Tang *let out:* Unless otherwise noted, information in this chapter is drawn from the following sources: *Tang* Report of Third War Patrol, July 14, 1944; *Tang* deck log; O'Kane, *Clear the Bridge!*, pp. 195–278. All dialogue comes from O'Kane's book.

171 *The submarine force's steam-driven fish:* William F. Halsey and J. Bryan III, *Admiral Halsey's Story* (New York: Whittlesey House/McGraw-Hill, 1947), p. 23.

171 *Other more crafty sailors:* John Meyer interview with author, Nov. 6, 2009.

171 Tang *radarman Floyd Caverly:* Floyd Caverly interview with author, July 16, 2009; O'Kane, *Clear the Bridge!*, pp. 464–65.

172 *"The troops had left":* O'Kane, *Clear the Bridge!*, p. 465.

172 *"the most dramatic":* George F. Horne, "22 U.S. Fliers Rescued by a Submarine at Truk," *New York Times*, May 18, 1944, p. 1.

172 *A full-page photo:* "U.S. Submarine Saves Airmen," *Life*, May 29, 1944, p. 40.

172 *Those patrols had supported:* USSBS, *The Campaigns of the Pacific War*, pp. 181–82, 210–11; Morison, *The Two-Ocean War*, pp. 321–27.

173 *"Considerable important enemy":* Operational Order No. 198-44, June 7, 1944, Box 299, RG 38, Records of the Office of the Chief of Naval Operations, Plans, Orders and Related Documents, NARA.

173 Wahoo *sank nine ships:* JANAC, p. 48 of the appendix; Blair, *Silent Victory*, pp. 682–83.

173 *Known to most:* William Leibold interview with author, July 8, 2009.

175 *"Damaged battleship":* O'Kane, *Clear the Bridge!*, p. 217.

175 *Frazee left:* O'Kane states in his book that Frazee was joined by Darrell Rector. The deck log, however, shows it was Dante Cacciola.

176 *Nagasaki, a congested:* USSBS, *Summary Report (Pacific War)*, p. 24.

177 *American submarine skippers in 1944:* USSBS, *The War Against Japanese Transportation, 1941–1945,* p. 134.

177 *Thirty months of war:* Unless otherwise noted, details on the failure of Japan's antisubmarine strategy are drawn from: Commander Submarine Force, U.S. Pacific Fleet, *Submarine Operational History World War II,* vol. 1, pp. 242–80.

178 *Japanese technicians:* Fuchida and Okumiya, *Midway,* pp. 93, 281–82; Gordon W. Prange with Donald M. Goldstein and Katherine V. Dillon, *Miracle at Midway* (New York: McGraw-Hill, 1982), p. 33.

178 *Japanese forces in contrast:* Interrogation of S. Kamide, Nov. 12, 1945, in USSBS, *Interrogations of Japanese Officials,* vol. 2, pp. 309–12.

178 *"The Japanese Navy":* Interrogation of Paul Wenneker, Nov. 11, 1945, in USSBS, *Interrogations of Japanese Officials,* vol. 1, pp. 284–86.

180 Wahoo *had encountered:* O'Kane, *Wahoo,* pp. 89–91.

182 *A postwar review:* JANAC, p. 48 of the appendix; Alden and McDonald, p. 169.

182 *the latter taking down:* Gregory F. Michno, *Death on the Hellships: Prisoners at Sea in the Pacific War* (Annapolis, Md.: Naval Institute Press, 2001), pp. 166–71.

182 *"Tonight the fireworks started":* Don Sharp diary, June 24, 1944.

183 *"The water is":* Don Sharp diary, June 27, 1944.

184 *the* Nikkin Maru*:* JANAC, p. 48 of the appendix; Alden and McDonald, p. 171.

185 *the 868-ton tanker* Takatori Maru*:* JANAC, p. 48 of the appendix; Alden and McDonald, p. 172.

187 *the 6,886-ton freighter* Asukazan Maru*:* JANAC, p. 48 of the appendix; Alden and McDonald, p. 173.

189 *the 6,932-ton* Yamaoka Maru*:* Ibid.

189 *"If I hadn't been":* Don Sharp diary, July 4, 1944.

190 *the 1,461-ton freighter* Dori Maru*:* JANAC, p. 48 of the appendix; Alden and McDonald, p. 174.

Chapter 15. *Drum*

PAGE

191 *"I don't know where":* Slade Cutter letter to Esther Cutter, Dec. 11, 1941, NDL.

191 *Lieutenant Commander Maurice Rindskopf:* Drum Report of Tenth War Patrol, August 14, 1944.

191 *"The Japanese":* Operational Order No. 215–44, June 23, 1944, Box 299, RG 38, Records of the Office of the Chief of Naval Operations, Plans, Orders and Related Documents, NARA.

191 *On a New Year's Day test trial:* Maurice Rindskopf unpublished memoir, p. 82; Maurice Rindskopf interview with author, Aug. 28, 2009.

192 *After fifty-two days:* Drum Report of Ninth War Patrol, May 31, 1944.

192 *Not only did:* Maurice Rindskopf unpublished memoir, pp. 81–84; Maurice Rindskopf interviews with author, Aug. 28, 2009, and Sept. 4, 2009.

192 *In a June 23 ceremony: Drum* Report of Tenth War Patrol, August 14, 1944; Maurice Rindskopf interview with author, Sept. 4, 2009.

192 Drum's *first skipper:* Maurice Rindskopf interview with author, March 3, 2011.

193 *Postwar records:* JANAC, p. 12 of the appendix.

193 Drum's *1,000th dive: Drum* Report of Tenth War Patrol, August 14, 1944.

193 *weathered by more than:* This is based on data recorded in *Drum*'s first nine war patrols.

193 *The former* Drum *engineering:* Mooney et al., eds., *Dictionary of American Naval Fighting Ships,* vol. 6, p. 120.

193 Drum's *original communication officer:* Ibid., pp. 467–68; Naval History Division, Office of the Chief of Naval Operations, *United States Submarine Losses: World War II,* p. 114.

194 *Unlike* Drum's *older:* Background on Rindskopf's leadership is drawn from author interviews with Verner Utke-Ramsing (Aug. 20, 2009, and Oct. 30, 2009), Eugene Pridonoff (Aug. 31, 2009), Robert White (Nov. 5, 2009), Donald Kronholm (Jan. 8, 2010), George Schaedler (Oct. 29, 2009), John Meyer (Nov. 6, 2009), and Phillip Williamson (Sept. 2, 2009).

194 *"He never appeared":* Robert White interview with author, Nov. 5, 2009.

194 *The skipper had dreaded:* Maurice Rindskopf unpublished memoir, p. 84.

194 *The Japanese fleet:* Commander Submarine Force, U.S. Pacific Fleet, *Submarine Operational History World War II,* vol. 1, pp. 209–10.

194 *Japanese naval leaders:* Morison, *The Two-Ocean War,* pp. 330–31.

194 *But Japan misjudged:* USSBS, *The Campaigns of the Pacific War,* p. 213.

194 *America had grown:* Morison, *The Two-Ocean War,* pp. 333–34.

195 *In preparation for:* Commander Submarine Force, U.S. Pacific Fleet, *Submarine Operational History World War II,* vol. 1, pp. 211–18.

195 *Admiral Raymond Spruance:* Morison, *The Two-Ocean War,* pp. 331–36.

195 *"Our air will first":* Ibid., p. 336.

195 *The sun rose:* USSBS, *The Campaigns of the Pacific War,* p. 214; Morison, *The Two-Ocean War,* pp. 338–43.

195 *Unlike at Midway:* Commander Submarine Force, U.S. Pacific Fleet, *Submarine Operational History World War II,* vol. 1, pp. 209, 219–21.

196 Albacore *skipper: Albacore* Report of Ninth War Patrol, July 16, 1944.

196 *"Great Phoenix":* Mark Stille, *Imperial Japanese Navy Aircraft Carriers, 1921–45* (Oxford: Osprey Publishing, 2005), pp. 35–36; Morison, *The Two-Ocean War,* p. 339.

196 *One torpedo tore:* Morison, *History of United States Naval Operations in World War II,* Vol. 8, *New Guinea and the Marianas, March 1944–August 1944,* pp. 281–82.

196   Cavalla *skipper: Cavalla* Report of First War Patrol, Aug. 3, 1944.

196   *The carrier's bow settled:* Stille, *Imperial Japanese Navy Aircraft Carriers, 1921–45,*
      p. 20.

196   *The battle continued:* Morison, *The Two-Ocean War,* pp. 342–45; USSBS, *The
      Campaigns of the Pacific War,* pp. 214–15, 243–44.

197   *America had guaranteed:* USSBS, *The Campaigns of the Pacific War,* p. 218.

197   *The most excitement: Drum* Report of Tenth War Patrol, August 14, 1944.

197   *Nervous sailors:* Ibid.; John Meyer interview with author, Nov. 13, 2009; Robert
      White interview with author, Oct. 27, 2009.

198   *Submarines would fight:* Duff, *Medical Study of the Experience of Submariners as
      Recorded in 1,471 Submarine Patrol Reports in World War II,* pp. 2, 27–30.

198   Drum *battle-surfaced: Drum* Report of Tenth War Patrol, August 14, 1944;
      Maurice Rindskopf unpublished memoir, pp. 84–85; Maurice Rindskopf in-
      terview with author, Sept 4, 2009; John Meyer interviews with author, Nov. 6,
      2009, and Nov. 13, 2009; Donald Kronholm interview with author, Jan. 8, 2010.

198   *"That was a first time":* John Meyer interview with author, Nov. 13, 2009.

198   Balao *zeroed in: Balao* Report of Sixth War Patrol, August 22, 1944.

199   *"Captain":* John Meyer interview with author, Nov. 13, 2009.

199   *Ralph McFadden:* Ralph McFadden interviews with author, Oct. 28, 2009, and
      Jan. 6, 2010.

199   *Chono confessed: Drum* Report of Tenth War Patrol, August 14, 1944; Alden and
      McDonald, p. 184.

199   *The crew rotated:* Ron Thibideau interviews with author, Nov. 5, 2009, and
      Nov. 12, 2009, John Meyer interview with author, Nov. 13, 2009; Hubert
      Wheeler interview with author, Nov. 3, 2009; Robert White interview with au-
      thor, Oct. 27, 2009.

200   *"Top notch chow hounds":* Hubert Wheeler undated letter to parents.

200   *"Fuck the Marines":* John Meyer interview with author, Nov 13, 2009.

Chapter 16. *Tang*

PAGE

201   *"Goodnight my sweetest":* Eugene Malone letter to parents, Dec. 1, 1943.

201   *O'Kane hustled:* Unless otherwise noted, information in this chapter is drawn
      from the following sources: *Tang* Report of Fifth War Patrol, Sept. 10, 1945,
      completed after O'Kane's release from a Japanese prisoner of war camp; O'Kane,
      Clear the Bridge!, pp. 367–456. All dialogue comes from O'Kane's book.

201   *postwar analysis:* JANAC, p. 48 of the appendix; Blair, *Silent Victory,* p. 988.

201   *"This patrol was":* Charles A. Lockwood, Jr., to the Commander-in-Chief,
      United States Fleet, July 24, 1944.

202 *"I want to tell you":* O'Kane, *Clear the Bridge!*, p. 301.

202 *Despite malfunctioning torpedoes: Tang* Report of Fourth War Patrol, Sept. 3, 1944; JANAC, p. 48 of the appendix; Alden and McDonald, pp. 189, 195–96.

202 *Tang's fourth patrol:* Murray Frazee, Jr., unpublished memoir, pp. 55–56.

202 *"Going to sea":* Murray Frazee, Jr., letter to Richard O'Kane, Nov. 6, 1986, Dudley Morton Family Papers, BSMP.

203 *"O'Kane liked to run":* Murray Frazee, Jr., "We Never Looked Back," *Naval History,* July–August 1994, pp. 47–51.

203 *Allied forces had carved:* Charles R. Anderson, *Leyte,* in the series *The U.S. Army Campaigns of World War II,* Center of Military History Publication 72-27 (Washington, D.C.: U.S. Government Printing Office, 1994), p. 3.

203 *The September 15 invasions:* Morison, *The Two-Ocean War,* pp. 421–28; Blair, *Silent Victory,* p. 693; USSBS, *The Campaigns of the Pacific War,* pp. 282–83.

203 *Japan's only hope:* USSBS, *The Campaigns of the Pacific War,* pp. 280–81; Edward J. Drea, *In the Service of the Emperor: Essays on the Imperial Japanese Army* (Lincoln: University of Nebraska Press, 1998), pp. 128–29; *Senji Yuso Sendan Shi.*

203 *The undersea service planned:* Commander Submarine Force, U.S. Pacific Fleet, *Submarine Operational History World War II,* vol. 1, pp. 225–26; Roscoe, *United States Submarine Operations in World War II,* p. 410.

204 *Lockwood intended to:* Lockwood, *Sink 'Em All,* pp. 225–26; Roscoe, *United States Submarine Operations in World War II,* p. 410; Operational Order No. 326–44, Sept. 24, 1944, Box 299, RG 38, Records of the Office of the Chief of Naval Operations, Plans, Orders and Related Documents, NARA.

205 *Lieutenant Lawrence Savadkin:* Lawrence Savadkin oral history interview with the Navy, Jan. 30, 1946, Box 24, RG 38, Records of the Office of the Chief of Naval Operations, World War II Oral Histories, 1942–1946, NARA; O'Kane, *Clear the Bridge!,* pp. 201, 432; "Athlete on Missing Submarine," *New York Times,* Feb. 7, 1945, p. 12; Barbara Lane interview with author, Dec. 19, 2010.

205 *"There was still":* Lawrence Savadkin oral history interview with the Navy, Jan. 30, 1946.

207 *The 1,658-ton* Joshu Go: JANAC, p. 48 of the appendix; Alden and McDonald, p. 215.

208 *the 711-ton* Oita Maru: Ibid.

208 *"We could work":* Lawrence Savadkin oral history interview with the Navy, Jan. 30, 1946.

210 *The 1,944-ton* Tatsuju Maru: JANAC, p. 48 of the appendix; Alden and McDonald, pp. 220–21; *Senji Yuso Sendan Shi.* Alden and McDonald report that the Japanese towed *Toun Maru* to Formosa, but repairs proved impossible, resulting in the breakup of the ship. Sources are mixed as to whether *Kori Go*

actually sank. JANAC does not record the loss, though Alden and McDonald report that some sources do. Alden and McDonald conclude the ship was likely damaged in the collision that O'Kane witnessed.

212 *"It was the biggest":* Lawrence Savadkin oral history interview with the Navy, Jan. 30, 1946.

212 *the 6,956-ton* Ebara Maru*:* JANAC, p. 48 of the appendix; Alden and McDonald, p. 223; *Senji Yuso Sendan Shi.* The final attacks of *Tang* are difficult to decipher with total accuracy. O'Kane claimed more sinkings than Japanese and postwar accounts record. Both JANAC and Alden and McDonald report two ships destroyed. I have tried to balance the various accounts as best possible.

215 *Cooks thawed turkeys:* Cindy Adams, "Tang Survivors Recall World War II Ordeal," *Patrol,* Sept. 5, 1980, pp. 4–6.

215 *Several sailors:* Jesse B. DaSilva, "Survivor of the Mighty Tang," *American Submariner,* July–September 2001, pp. 16–18.

215 *"Let's head":* Duff, *Medical Study of the Experiences of Submariners as Recorded in 1,471 Submarine Patrol Reports in World War II,* p. 251.

215 *O'Kane and Leibold watched:* William Leibold interview with author, July 10, 2009.

215 *The torpedo's dual:* ComdtNY Mare Island to Senior Member, Board of Inspection and Survey, Nov. 19, 1943, Synopsis of Machinery and Hull Data for SS306, Box 2134, RG 19, Bureau of Ships General Correspondence, 1940–1945, NARA; Navy Department, Bureau of Ships, *Submarine Report: Depth Charge, Bomb, Mine, Torpedo and Gunfire Damage Including Losses in Action 7 December, 1941 to 15 August, 1945,* vol. 1, 1 January 1949, p. 112.

Chapter 17. *Silversides*

PAGE

217 *"If we make it":* Don Sharp diary, July 8, 1944.

217 *The prolonged blast: Silversides* Report of Eleventh War Patrol, Nov. 23, 1944.

217 *In just forty-six days:* JANAC, p. 43 of the appendix; Blair, *Silent Victory,* p. 988.

217 *"The tenth war patrol":* C. A. Lockwood, Jr., to the Commander-in-Chief, United States Fleet, June 19, 1944.

217 *The rust-streaked submarine:* These figures are drawn from the first ten patrol reports.

218 *Coye flew to New York:* John S. Coye, Jr., unpublished memoir, p. 18.

218 *Allied forces:* Drew Middleton, "Enemy Route Grows," *New York Times,* Aug. 27, 1944, p. 1; Drew Middleton, "U.S. Tanks Race On," *New York Times,* Aug. 30, 1944, p. 1; "Battle of Europe," *New York Times,* Aug. 6, 1944, p. E1.

218 *Bombers and fighters:* "2,200 U.S. Planes Smash at Germany, *New York Times,* Oct. 3, 1944, p. 4; Richard J. H. Johnston, "2,000 U.S. Planes Rip Reich Targets,"

New York Times, Aug. 6, 1944, p. 25; David Anderson, "Big Bombers Strike Destroys Nazi Oil," *New York Times*, June 19, 1944, p. 5; Sydney Gruson, "3,000 U.S. Planes Rock Nazi Targets," *New York Times*, Aug. 1, 1944, p. 8.

218 *Virginia representative:* "Oct. 1 'Tentative' Date for Nazi Defeat; War in Pacific 'at Least Until End of '45,'" *New York Times*, Aug. 26, 1944, p. 2.

218 *American lawmakers:* C. P. Trussell, "Transition Problems Crowd Upon Congress," *New York Times*, Aug. 6, 1944, p. E6; "Congress Bogged Down by Disputes over Legislation to Shift Nation from War to Peacetime Production," *Wall Street Journal*, Aug. 21, 1944, p. 10; John F. Fennelly, "The Shift from War to Peace Economy," *New York Times*, Sept. 3, 1944, p. SM11.

218 *The Office of War Information:* "Long Pacific War Seen by the OWI," *New York Times*, Sept. 28, 1944, p. 13.

218 *"The United States Navy":* "Forrestal Sees Long, Hard Fight with Japs," *Lewiston Evening Journal*, Sept. 6, 1944, p. 1; "Tougher Japan in Air Is Seen by Forrestal," *New York Times*, Sept. 7, 1944, p. 13.

218 *"The news over the radio":* Eugene Malone undated letter to Anna Maria Ives.

218 *The three subs:* Coordinated Patrol Report, 24 September–3 November 1944, Box 98, RG 38, Records of the Office of the Chief of Naval Operations, Plans, Orders and Related Documents, NARA.

219 *The Germans:* David T. Zabecki, ed., *World War II in Europe: An Encyclopedia* (New York: Grand Publishing, 1999), p. 1086.

219 *The United States in contrast:* Lockwood, *Sink 'Em All*, pp. 35–36, 122–24.

219 *Submarines in the first six months:* USSBS, *The War Against Japanese Transportation, 1941–1945*, pp. 36–41, 47, 134.

220 *"The total area":* The Reminiscences of Rear Admiral John S. Coye, Jr., p. 104.

220 *Working in tandem:* Ibid., pp. 104–7.

220 *"It has its advantages":* Ibid., p. 166.

220 *The three submarines arrived:* Silversides Report of Eleventh War Patrol, Nov. 23, 1944; Coordinated Patrol Report, 24 September–3 November 1944.

220 *Carrier pilots flew:* Morison, *The Two-Ocean War*, pp. 428–29.

220 *While it still boasted:* Hastings, *Retribution*, pp. 132–33.

221 *Similar to the Battle of Midway:* USSBS, *The Campaigns of the Pacific War*, pp. 280–84; Morison, *The Two-Ocean War*, pp. 436–39; Hastings, *Retribution*, pp. 133–34; James D. Hornfischer, *The Last Stand of the Tin Can Sailors: The Extraordinary World War II Story of the U.S. Navy's Finest Hour* (New York: Bantam, 2004), pp. 94–97.

221 *The skippers:* Darter Report of Fourth War Patrol, Nov. 5, 1944; Dace Report of Fifth War Patrol, Nov. 6, 1944; Kennedy, ed., *The Library of Congress World War II Companion*, p. 596.

221 *"We have radar contact":* Darter Report of Fourth War Patrol, Nov. 5, 1944.

221 *"Whipped periscope":* Ibid.

221 *Four torpedo hits:* Dull, *A Battle History of the Imperial Japanese Navy (1941–1945),* pp. 315–16.

222 *Two more torpedoes:* Ibid.; Commander Submarine Force, U.S. Pacific Fleet, *Submarine Operational History World War II,* vol. 1, p. 227.

222 *"Darter is really having":* Dace Report of Fifth War Patrol, Nov. 6, 1944.

222 *"This is really":* Ibid.

222 *Claggett fired six torpedoes:* Ibid.; Commander Submarine Force, U.S. Pacific Fleet, *Submarine Operational History World War II,* vol. 1, p. 227.

222 *"Heard tremendous":* Dace Report of Fifth War Patrol, Nov. 6, 1944.

222 *"We better get":* Ibid.

222 *Darter's contact reports:* Darter Report of Fourth War Patrol, Nov. 5, 1944; Dace Report of Fifth War Patrol, Nov. 6, 1944; Morison, *The Two-Ocean War,* pp. 439–40.

222 *The 70,000-ton:* Thomas J. Cutler, *The Battle of Leyte Gulf, 23–26 October 1944* (New York: HarperCollins, 1994), p. 64.

222 *Wave after wave:* Morison, *History of the United States Naval Operations in World War II,* vol. 12, *Leyte, June 1944–January 1945,* p. 186; Ugaki, *Fading Victory,* p. 523; Kennedy, ed., *The Library of Congress World War II Companion,* p. 596.

222 *The aerial attack:* Hastings, *Retribution,* p. 141.

222 *Carrier planes had spotted:* Morison, *The Two-Ocean War,* pp. 441–42; USSBS, *The Campaigns of the Pacific War,* p. 285.

222 *The United States built:* Morison, *The Two-Ocean War,* p. 442; Craig L. Symonds, *The Naval Institute Historical Atlas of the U.S. Navy* (Annapolis, Md.: Naval Institute Press, 1995), p. 180.

222 *The lopsided numbers:* USSBS, *The Campaigns of the Pacific War,* p. 285.

223 *"Most beautiful sight":* Morison, *The Two-Ocean War,* p. 447.

223 *The mission of Vice Admiral:* Interrogation of Vice Admiral Jisaburo Ozawa, Oct. 30, 1945, in USSBS, *Interrogations of Japanese Officials,* vol. 1, pp. 219–27.

223 *The Japanese admiral:* Ibid.; Morison, *The Two-Ocean War,* pp. 463–70.

223 *The Chitose vanished:* Cutler, *The Battle of Leyte Gulf,* pp. 235–36; Morison, *History of the United States Naval Operations in World War II,* vol. 12, *Leyte, June 1944–January 1945,* pp. 325–28.

223 *Kurita's central force:* Morison, *The Two-Ocean War,* pp. 451–54.

223 *Gone was the threat:* Hastings, *Retribution,* p. 160.

223 *Despite the earlier bruising:* E. B. Potter, ed., *Sea Power: A Naval History* (Englewood Cliffs, N.J.: Prentice Hall, 1960), pp. 790–92.

223 *The tall masts:* Morison, *The Two-Ocean War,* pp. 451–55.

223 *"baby flattops":* Ibid., p. 455.

223 *Often converted tankers:* Ibid.; Cutler, *The Battle of Leyte Gulf*, pp. 57–58; Hastings, *Retribution*, p. 150.

223 *Rear Admiral Clifton Sprague:* Morison, *The Two-Ocean War*, pp. 451–57.

224 *"The enemy was closing":* C. A. F. Sprague to Commander in Chief, United States Fleet, Oct. 29, 1944, Special Report of Action Against the Main Body off Samar Island, 25 October 1944.

224 *The skipper of* Hoel*:* Leon Kintberger to the Secretary of the Navy, Nov. 15, 1944, Combined Action Report and Report of Loss of U.S.S. *Hoel* (DD-533) on 25 October, 1944.

224 *The destroyer escort* Samuel B. Roberts*:* Roscoe, *United States Destroyer Operations in World War II*, p. 429.

224 *"avalanche of shells":* R. C. Hagen to Commander in Chief, United States Fleet, Nov. 14, 1944, Action Report—Surface Engagement off Samar, P.I., 25 October 1944.

224 *Survivors reported:* Cutler, *The Battle of Leyte Gulf*, p. 248.

224 *American planes:* Morison, *The Two-Ocean War*, pp. 459–60.

224 *The skipper of* Gambier Bay*:* USS *Gambier Bay* (CVE-73), Action Report, Narrative by Captain W. V. R. Vieweg, USN, Commanding Officer.

224 Gambier Bay *capsized:* Morison, *The Two-Ocean War*, p. 460.

224 *American torpedo bombers:* Ibid.; Dull, *A Battle History of the Imperial Japanese Navy (1941–1945)*, p. 326.

224 *Just as his warships:* Morison, *The Two-Ocean War*, p. 461–62

225 *"Goddammit, boys":* Ibid., p. 461.

225 *The war's first kamikaze attacks:* Ibid., pp. 462–63.

225 *The battle of Leyte Gulf had robbed:* Hastings, *Retribution*, p. 163.

225 *Not until Kurita's forces:* Morison, *The Two-Ocean War*, pp. 454, 466–67.

225 *Despite Ozawa's postwar admission:* Interrogation of Vice Admiral Jisaburo Ozawa, Oct. 30, 1945, in USSBS, *Interrogations of Japanese Officials*, vol. 1, pp. 219–27.

225 *"My decision":* William F. Halsey, Jr., "The Battle for Leyte Gulf," *Proceedings*, vol. 78, no. 5, May 1952, p. 490.

225 *"I didn't know":* John F. Wukovits, *Devotion to Duty: A Biography of Admiral Clifton A. F. Sprague* (Annapolis, Md.: Naval Institute Press, 1995), p. 206.

225 *"the gentleman":* Ibid.

225 *"Why Admiral Bill":* Ibid.

225 *Coye had listened:* Unless otherwise noted, details of the patrol are drawn from: *Silversides* Report of Eleventh War Patrol, Nov. 23, 1944; *Trigger* Report of Tenth War Patrol, Nov. 3, 1944; *Salmon* Report of Eleventh War Patrol, Nov. 29, 1944; Coordinated Patrol Report, 24 September–3 November 1944.

226 *10,021-ton* Takane Maru*:* JANAC, p. 74; Roscoe, *United States Submarine Operations in World War II*, p. 564; Alden and McDonald, p. 226.

227 *Nauman had seen:* Navy Department, Bureau of Ships, *Submarine Report: Depth Charge, Bomb, Mine, Torpedo and Gunfire Damage Including Losses in Action 7 December, 1941 to 15 August, 1945*, vol. 1, 1 January 1949, pp. 61–81; H. K. Nauman to Stephen Towne, Information on damage to U.S.S. *Salmon* (SS-182), March 21, 1947, Box 76, RG 19, War Damage Reports and Related Records, 1942–1949, NARA.

227 *"The conning tower":* H. K. Nauman to Stephen Towne, March 21, 1947.

227 *"Our only":* *Salmon* Report of Eleventh War Patrol, Nov. 29, 1944.

229 *"It was a relief":* Coordinated Patrol Report, 24 September–3 November 1944.

230 *He relinquished command:* *Silversides* Report of Twelfth War Patrol, Feb. 12, 1945.

230 *The Silver Lady would make:* Mooney et al., eds., *Dictionary of American Naval Fighting Ships*, vol. 6, pp. 508–9.

230 *But the lack of enemy targets:* JANAC, p. 43 of the appendix.

230 *Commissioned just eight days:* Statistics are drawn from a review of *Silversides'* fourteen war patrol reports.

230 *Coye had earned:* John Starr Coye, Jr., Navy Bio, Aug. 30, 1968.

230 *The Navy reassigned Coye:* Ibid.; *The Reminiscences of Rear Admiral John S. Coye, Jr.*, pp. 118–19.

230 *He now departed:* JANAC, p. 43 of the appendix; Blair, *Silent Victory*, p. 984.

230 *"That was really":* *The Reminiscences of Rear Admiral John S. Coye, Jr.*, p. 118.

Chapter 18. *Tang*

PAGE

231 *"We knew":* Bill Nichols and Andrea Stone, "'You Never Lose Hope,' Sub Survivor Recalls," *USA Today*, Aug. 16, 2000, p. 16A.

231 *The skipper estimated:* O'Kane, *Clear the Bridge!*, p. 456; *Tang* Report of Fifth War Patrol, Sept. 10, 1945, including Report of the Loss of the U.S.S. *Tang* (SS-306); William Leibold interview with author, July 10, 2009.

231 *The torpedo ripped:* O'Kane, p. 456; *Tang* Report of Fifth War Patrol; Navy Department, Bureau of Ships, *Submarine Report: Depth Charge, Bomb, Mine, Torpedo and Gunfire Damage Including Losses in Action 7 December, 1941 to 15 August, 1945*, vol. 1, 1 January 1949, pp. 112–13; Duff, *Medical Study of the Experiences of Submariners as Recorded in 1,471 Submarine Patrol Reports in World War II*, pp. 252, 255–56.

232 *Up on the bridge:* William Leibold interview with author, July 10, 2009.

232 *"Do we have propulsion?":* "Five War Patrols," Floyd Caverly's story as told to David A. Jones; Floyd Caverly interviews with author, July 16, 2009, and July 30, 2009.

233 *Leibold didn't fare as well:* William Leibold interview with author, July 10, 2009.

234 *Larry Savadkin operated:* Details of Lawrence Savadkin's escape from the conning tower are drawn from the following sources: Lawrence Savadkin oral history interview with the Navy, Jan. 30, 1946; Shilling and Kohl, *History of Submarine Medicine in World War II*, pp. 203–4; Duff, *Medical Study of the Experiences of Submariners as Recorded in 1,471 Submarine Patrol Reports in World War II*, pp. 251–52.

235 *Petty Officer 3rd Class Pete Narowanski:* Details on Pete Narowanski and the men in the forward torpedo room are drawn from the following sources: Cindy Adams, "Tang Survivors Recall World War II Ordeal," *Patrol*, Sept. 5, 1980, pp. 4–6; Johnson et al., eds., *Dictionary of American Naval Fighting Ships*, vol. 3, p. 386; Rick Atkinson, *An Army at Dawn: The War in North Africa, 1942–1943* (New York: Henry Holt, 2002), pp. 152–56; Shilling and Kohl, *History of Submarine Medicine in World War II*, pp. 203–4; Duff, *Medical Study of the Experiences of Submariners as Recorded in 1,471 Submarine Patrol Reports in World War II*, pp. 252, 255.

237 *"Since it was quite possible":* Duff, *Medical Study of the Experiences of Submariners as Recorded in 1,471 Submarine Patrol Reports in World War II*, p. 252.

237 *The torpedo's ferocious detonation:* Details on Clay Decker and the men in the control room, unless otherwise noted, are drawn from the following sources: Clay Decker video oral history interview with Dan Clayton, March 2002, Center for the Study of War Experience, Regis University, Denver, Colorado; Clay Decker undated video oral history interview with Clark M. Brandt, Fitzsimons Army Medical Center, Aurora, Colorado; Clay Decker video oral history interview with the Rocky Mountain Base, United States Submarine Veterans, Inc., 2003.

238 *The injured Ballinger:* Flint Whitlock and Ron Smith, *The Depths of Courage: American Submariners at War with Japan, 1941–1945* (New York: Berkley Caliber, 2007), pp. 320–21.

238 *"Mr. Enos, you can't do that":* Ibid., p. 322.

239 *"There was such":* Duff, *Medical Study of the Experiences of Submariners as Recorded in 1,471 Submarine Patrol Reports in World War II*, pp. 252–53.

239 *Petty Officer 2nd Class Jesse DaSilva:* Details on Jesse DaSilva and the men in the crew's mess, unless otherwise noted, are drawn from the following sources: Jesse DaSilva oral history interview with Douglas E. Clanin, Sept. 4, 1992, Indiana Historical Society, Indianapolis, Indiana; Jesse B. DaSilva, "Survivor of the Mighty Tang," *American Submariner*, July–September 2001, pp. 16–18; Cindy Adams, "Tang Survivors Recall World War II Ordeal," *Patrol*, Sept. 5, 1980, pp. 4–6.

239 *"like a giant fish":* Cindy Adams, "Tang Survivors Recall World War II Ordeal," *Patrol*, Sept. 5, 1980, p. 4.

239 *"My, God":* Jesse DaSilva oral history interview with Douglas E. Clanin, Sept. 4, 1992.

240 *Just beneath: The Fleet Type Submarine,* NavPers 16160, June 1946, Standards and Curriculum Division, Training, Bureau of Naval Personnel, p. 71; Norman Friedman, *U.S. Submarines Through 1945: An Illustrated Design History* (Annapolis, Md.: Naval Institute Press, 1995), pp. 263–64.

240 *The poisonous gas:* R. Everett Langford, *Introduction to Weapons of Mass Destruction: Radiological, Chemical, and Biological* (Hoboken, N.J.: Wiley-Interscience, 2004) pp. 214–15; Eric A. Croddy, James J. Wirtz, and Jeffrey A. Larsen, eds., *Weapons of Mass Destruction: An Encyclopedia of Worldwide Policy, Technology, and History* (Santa Barbara, Calif.: ABC-CLIO, 2005), pp. 327–58.

240 *"We knew we couldn't stay here":* Jesse B. DaSilva, "Survivor of the Mighty Tang," *American Submariner,* July–September 2001, p. 16.

240 *DaSilva decided:* DeRose, *Unrestricted Warfare,* p. 219; "Trapped at Thirty Fathoms," Jesse DaSilva's story as told to Bill Hagendorn, Indiana Historical Society.

240 *smashing the radar:* Lawrence Savadkin oral history interview with the Navy, Jan. 30, 1946.

241 *With the voice communication:* DeRose, *Unrestricted Warfare,* p. 219.

241 *"It struck the negro":* Duff, *Medical Study of the Experiences of Submariners as Recorded in 1,471 Submarine Patrol Reports in World War II,* p. 253.

241 *O'Kane grabbed hold: Tang* Report of Fifth War Patrol, Sept. 10, 1945, including Report of the Loss of the U.S.S. *Tang* (SS-306); O'Kane, *Clear the Bridge!,* p. 456; William Leibold interview with author, July 10, 2009.

241 *In just nine months:* JANAC, pp. 48–49 of the appendix; Blair, *Silent Victory,* p. 984.

241 *Larry Savadkin bobbed:* Lawrence Savadkin oral history interview with the Navy, Jan. 30, 1946; Duff, *Medical Study of the Experiences of Submariners as Recorded in 1,471 Submarine Patrol Reports in World War II,* pp. 251–52.

242 *Bill Leibold broke:* William Leibold interview with author, July 10, 2009.

242 *Radarman Floyd Caverly:* Floyd Caverly interview with author, July 16, 2009; "Five War Patrols," Floyd Caverly's story as told to David A. Jones.

243 *About forty-five sailors:* Navy Department, Bureau of Ships, *Submarine Report: Depth Charge, Bomb, Mine, Torpedo and Gunfire Damage Including Losses in Action 7 December, 1941 to 15 August, 1945,* vol. 1, 1 January 1949, p. 115; Duff, *Medical Study of the Experiences of Submariners as Recorded in 1,471 Submarine Patrol Reports in World War II,* p. 253.

243 *Momsen lungs:* NBMS, *Submarine Medicine Practice* (Washington, D.C.: U.S. Government Printing Office, 1956), pp. 317–20.

243 *The Japanese escorts:* Navy Department, Bureau of Ships, *Submarine Report: Depth*

Charge, Bomb, Mine, Torpedo and Gunfire Damage Including Losses in Action 7 December, 1941 to 15 August, 1945, vol. 1, 1 January 1949, pp. 115–16; Duff, *Medical Study of the Experiences of Submariners as Recorded in 1,471 Submarine Patrol Reports in World War II,* pp. 253–55.

244 *Clay Decker knew:* Clay Decker video oral history interview with Dan Clayton, March 2002; Clay Decker undated video oral history interview with Clark M. Brandt.

244 *George Zofcin:* Barbara Siegfried e-mail to author, Dec. 12, 2010.

245 *"You go ahead":* Clay Decker video oral history interview with Dan Clayton, March 2002.

246 *"I could hear him screaming":* Ibid.

246 *Inside the torpedo room:* Navy Department, Bureau of Ships, *Submarine Report: Depth Charge, Bomb, Mine, Torpedo and Gunfire Damage Including Losses in Action 7 December, 1941 to 15 August, 1945,* vol. 1, 1 January 1949, pp. 116–17; Duff, *Medical Study of the Experiences of Submariners as Recorded in 1,471 Submarine Patrol Reports in World War II,* pp. 254–55.

246 *Depth charges:* Ibid.

246 *"Many of the men":* Duff, *Medical Study of the Experiences of Submariners as Recorded in 1,471 Submarine Patrol Reports in World War II,* p. 255.

246 *Hayes Trukke refused:* Navy Department, Bureau of Ships, *Submarine Report: Depth Charge, Bomb, Mine, Torpedo and Gunfire Damage Including Losses in Action 7 December, 1941 to 15 August, 1945,* vol. 1, 1 January 1949, pp. 117–18; Duff, *Medical Study of the Experiences of Submariners as Recorded in 1,471 Submarine Patrol Reports in World War II,* pp. 254–56.

247 Yamaoka Maru: O'Kane, *Clear the Bridge!,* p. 459.

247 *"I felt very exhausted":* Duff, *Medical Study of the Experiences of Submariners as Recorded in 1,471 Submarine Patrol Reports in World War II,* p. 254.

247 *The three men:* Navy Department, Bureau of Ships, *Submarine Report: Depth Charge, Bomb, Mine, Torpedo and Gunfire Damage Including Losses in Action 7 December, 1941 to 15 August, 1945,* vol. 1, 1 January 1949, pp. 118–19; Duff, *Medical Study of the Experiences of Submariners as Recorded in 1,471 Submarine Patrol Reports in World War II,* pp. 254–56; *Tang* Report of Fifth War Patrol, Sept. 10, 1945, including Report of the Loss of the U.S.S. *Tang* (SS-306).

248 *DaSilva urged:* Jesse DaSilva oral history interview with Douglas E. Clanin, Sept. 4, 1992; Alex Kershaw, *Escape from the Deep: The Epic Story of a Legendary Submarine and Her Courageous Crew* (New York: Da Capo, 2008), pp. 124–25.

248 *"He had everything":* Jesse DaSilva oral history interview with Douglas E. Clanin, Sept. 4, 1992.

248 *"We need somebody else":* Ibid.

248 *"Hell":* Ibid.

248 *The motor machinist's mate scrambled:* Ibid.; Jesse B. DaSilva, "Survivor of the Mighty Tang," *American Submariner,* July–September 2001, p. 16.

248 *DaSilva broke the surface:* Jesse DaSilva oral history interview with Douglas E. Clanin; Duff, *Medical Study of the Experiences of Submariners as Recorded in 1,471 Submarine Patrol Reports in World War II,* pp. 254–57.

249 *"He drowned":* Duff, *Medical Study of the Experiences of Submariners as Recorded in 1,471 Submarine Patrol Reports in World War II,* p. 257.

249 *Leibold and Caverly:* William Leibold interview with author, July 10, 2009; Floyd Caverly interview with author, July 30, 2009.

249 *The six* Tang *sailors:* Clay Decker video oral history interview with Dan Clayton, March 2002; Clay Decker undated video oral history interview with Clark M. Brandt; Jesse DaSilva oral history interview with Douglas E. Clanin, Sept. 4, 1992; Jesse B. DaSilva, "Survivor of the Mighty Tang," *American Submariner,* July–September 2001, p. 16

250 *"Well, this is it":* Jesse B. DaSilva, "Survivor of the Mighty Tang," *American Submariner,* July–September 2001, p. 16.

250 *The Japanese instead:* Deposition of Henry James Flanagan, March 22, 1946, Box 1454, RG 153, Records of the Office of the Judge Advocate General (Army), War Crimes Branch, Case Files, 1944–1949, NARA; Clay Decker video oral history interview with Dan Clayton, March 2002; Clay Decker undated video oral history interview with Clark M. Brandt; Duff, *Medical Study of the Experiences of Submariners as Recorded in 1,471 Submarine Patrol Reports in World War II,* pp. 256–58.

250 *He lay in the bottom:* Details on the death of Paul Larson are drawn from the depositions of William Rudolph Leibold (Oct. 26, 1945), J. N. DaSilva (April 26, 1946) C. O. Decker (April 24, 1946), and Henry James Flanagan (March 22, 1946), Box 1454, RG 153, Records of the Office of the Judge Advocate General (Army), War Crimes Branch, Case Files, 1944–1949, NARA.

250 *Nine men:* Navy Department, Bureau of Ships, *Submarine Report: Depth Charge, Bomb, Mine, Torpedo and Gunfire Damage Including Losses in Action 7 December, 1941 to 15 August, 1945,* vol. 1, 1 January 1949, p. 118–119.

250 *The captors tied:* William Leibold interview with author, July 10, 2009.

250 *"We were trussed up":* Lawrence Savadkin oral history interview with the Navy, Jan. 30, 1946.

250 *The Japanese offered:* William Leibold interview with author, July 10, 2009; Deposition of Lawrence Savadkin, June 13, 1946, Box 1454, RG 153, Records of the Office of the Judge Advocate General (Army), War Crimes Branch, Case Files, 1944–1949, NARA.

251 *Guards made DaSilva:* Deposition of William Rudolph Leibold, Oct. 26, 1945.

251 *The executive officer struck:* Deposition of Floyd Murel Caverly, May 22, 1946, Box 1454, RG 153, Records of the Office of the Judge Advocate General (Army), War Crimes Branch, Case Files, 1944–1949, NARA.

251 *the crew kicked Flanagan:* Deposition of Henry James Flanagan, March 22, 1946.

251 *O'Kane's refusal to reveal:* Deposition of William Rudolph Leibold, Oct. 26, 1945.

251 *"O'Kane received":* Deposition of Floyd Murel Caverly, May 22, 1946.

251 *Burned Japanese sailors:* Deposition of William Rudolph Leibold, Oct. 26, 1945; Deposition of C. O. Decker, April 24, 1946; William Leibold interview with author, July 10, 2009; Clay Decker video oral history interview with Dan Clayton, March 2002; Lawrence Savadkin oral history interview with the Navy, Jan. 30, 1946.

251 *"When we realized": Tang* Report of Fifth War Patrol, Sept. 10, 1945, including Report of the Loss of the U.S.S. *Tang* (SS-306).

Chapter 19. *Drum*

PAGE

252 *"We did not care":* Testimony of Philip Brodsky, Sept. 5, 1946, Box 1431, RG 153, Records of the Office of the Judge Advocate General (Army), War Crimes Branch, Case Files, 1944–1949, NARA.

252 *Sergeant Calvin Graef:* Background on Calvin Graef is drawn from the following sources: Calvin Robert Graef with Harry T. Brundidge, "We Prayed to Die," *Cosmopolitan*, vol. 118, no. 4, April 1945, pp. 52–55, 177–80; Calvin Graef, Jr., interview with author, April 21, 2011.

252 *Graef's experience:* Details of the conditions aboard *Arisan Maru* are drawn from the following sources: depositions of Martin Binder (Nov. 8, 1946), Glenn Oliver (Dec. 3, 1946), Anton Cichy (April 30, 1946), Philip Brodsky (Jan. 25, 1946, and Sept. 5, 1946), Avery Wilber (May 1, 1946) Donald Meyer (May 22, 1946), Calvin Graef (Dec. 6, 1944, and April 27, 1946), and Robert Overbeck (June 13, 1946), Box 1431, RG 153, Records of the Office of the Judge Advocate General (Army), War Crimes Branch, Case Files, 1944–1949, NARA; Joint Statement of Calvin Graef, Donald Meyer, Robert Overbeck, Anthony Cichy, and Avery Wilber, Dec. 6, 1944, ibid.; Escape in the China Sea, Mr. Robert S. Overbeck, Report No. 483, Dec. 26, 1944, ibid.; Oral Reminiscences of Master Sergeant Calvin R. Graef, U.S. Army, Oct. 1, 1971, RG 49, D. James Clayton Collection, General Douglas MacArthur Memorial Archives and Library, Norfolk, Virginia; Donald Meyer, "Five Came Back," personal narrative, American Defenders of Bataan and Corregidor Museum, Brooke County Public Library, Wellsburg, West Virginia; Robert Overbeck, "Voyage to China," unpublished article.

253 *"To try and describe"*: Oral Reminiscences of Master Sergeant Calvin R. Graef, Oct. 1, 1971.

253 *"The oil and coal dust"*: Donald Meyer, "Five Came Back," personal narrative.

253 *"Food was lowered"*: Deposition of Philip Brodsky, Jan. 25, 1946.

253 *"We waded"*: Calvin Robert Graef with Harry T. Brundidge, "We Prayed to Die," *Cosmopolitan*, vol. 118, no. 4, April 1945, p. 177.

253 *"If you fell down"*: Oral Reminiscences of Master Sergeant Calvin R. Graef, Oct. 1, 1971.

253 *"While men were dying"*: Calvin Robert Graef with Harry T. Brundidge, "We Prayed to Die," *Cosmopolitan*, vol. 118, no. 4, April 1945, p. 177.

254 *Crammed and filthy hellships:* Michno, *Death on the Hellships*, pp. 280–82.

254 *In the bowels:* Review of the Staff Judge Advocate in the case of *The United States of America vs. Junsaburo Toshino*, Headquarters Eighth Army, United States Army, Office of the Staff Judge Advocate, Yokohama, Japan, May 4, 1948.

254 *When temperatures topped:* Ibid.

254 *"As a guy goes crazy"*: Donald L. Miller, *The Story of World War II* (New York: Touchstone/Simon & Schuster, 2001), p. 596.

254 *In the days since:* Calvin Graef as told to Melissa Masterson, *Ride the Waves to Freedom* (Kearney, Nebr.: Morris Publishing, 1999), p. 72.

254 *Twelve ships: Senji Yuso Sendan Shi*; Alden and McDonald, p. 221.

254 *Graef and other captives:* Oral Reminiscences of Master Sergeant Calvin R. Graef, Oct. 1, 1971.

255 *killing by some estimates:* Michno, *Death on the Hellships*, pp. 225–44, 280.

255 *Sealion had torpedoed:* Ibid., pp. 202–21; James E. Wise and Scott Baron, *Soldiers Lost at Sea: A Chronicle of Troopship Disasters* (Annapolis, Md.: Naval Institute Press, 2004), pp. 162–65.

255 *North of Subic Bay:* Michno, *Death on the Hellships*, pp. 242–44.

255 *But the worst such attack:* Ibid., pp. 235–41; Wise and Baron, *Soldiers Lost at Sea*, pp. 165–67.

255 *"If the Navy"*: Calvin Robert Graef with Harry T. Brundidge, "We Prayed to Die," *Cosmopolitan*, vol. 118, no. 4, April 1945, p. 178.

255 *Maurice Rindskopf scanned:* Drum Report of Eleventh War Patrol, Oct. 26, 1944.

256 *American troops had invaded:* USSBS, *The Campaigns of the Pacific War*, pp. 210–20.

256 *Allied bombers:* Sydney Gruson, "New Records Set in Air in October," *New York Times*, Nov. 4, 1944, p. 4.

256 *The importance of the Marianas:* Potter, ed., *Sea Power*, pp. 769–70; USSBS, *The Campaigns of the Pacific War*, p. 220.

256 *"Hell is on us"*: Interrogation of Fleet Admiral Osami Nagano, Nov. 20, 1946, in USSBS, *Interrogations of Japanese Officials*, vol. 2, pp. 352–56.

256 *Three days earlier:* Morison, *History of the United States Naval Operations in World War II*, vol. 12, *Leyte, June 1944–January 1945*, pp. 113–38.

256 *The fall of the Philippines:* "MacArthur Marks Fall of Bataan by New Vow to Retake Philippines," *New York Times*, April 9, 1943, p. 1; "M'Arthur Renews Philippines Pledge," *New York Times*, March 18, 1944, p. 7; William B. Dickinson, "Bataan Torturers Trapped on Leyte," *New York Times*, Oct. 21, 1944, p. 3; Eric Larrabee, *Commander in Chief: Franklin Delano Roosevelt, His Lieutenants, and Their War* (Annapolis, Md.: Naval Institute Press, 1987), p. 321.

256 *"Bataan is like a child":* "MacArthur Marks Fall of Bataan by New Vow to Retake Philippines," *New York Times*, April 9, 1943, p. 1.

256 *Two years, seven months:* "Beachheads Won," *New York Times*, Oct. 20, 1944, p. 1; Morison, *History of the United States Naval Operations in World War II*, vol. 12 *Leyte, June 1944–January 1945*, pp. 136–37.

256 *"People of the Philippines":* "M'Arthur Appeals for Filipinos' Aid," *New York Times*, Oct. 21, 1944, p. 3.

256 *Captured airfields:* USSBS, *The Effects of Strategic Bombing on Japan's War Economy*, pp. 41–42.

256 *Skippers like:* Ibid.

257 *As stockpiles:* USSBS, *The War Against Japanese Transportation, 1941–1945*, p. 112; USSBS, *The Effects of Strategic Bombing on Japan's War Economy*, p. 24.

257 *Workers collected:* USSBS, *The War Against Japanese Transportation, 1941–1945*, pp. 108, 112–13.

257 *With scrap aluminum:* Ibid., p. 112.

257 *More than any other import:* USSBS, *Oil in Japan's War*, opening page, pp. 50–57.

257 *The Japanese would grow:* Ibid., pp. 6, 61–62.

257 *While military trucks:* Ibid., pp. 1, 6.

257 *Japan struggled to keep:* Ibid., pp. 6, 85–87.

257 *"There was no prospect":* Ibid., p. 86.

257 *The vast Pacific gains:* Roscoe, *United States Submarine Operations in World War II*, pp. 324, 432–33.

258 *So heavy was the concentration:* Commander Submarine Force, U.S. Pacific Fleet, *Submarine Operational History World War II*, vol. 4, pp. 1353–55.

258 *many of the warships:* JANAC, pp. 19–25, 78–87.

259 *"These were the":* Drum Report of Eleventh War Patrol, Oct. 26, 1944.

259 *One of the empire's last:* Roscoe, *United States Submarine Operations in World War II*, pp. 410–11; Commander Submarine Force, U.S. Pacific Fleet, *Submarine Operational History World War II*, vol. 1, pp. 72–75.

259 *The seas throughout:* Operational Order No. 304–44, Sept. 8, 1944, Box 299, RG 38, Records of the Office of the Chief of Naval Operations, Plans, Orders and Related Documents, NARA.

259 *Rindskopf's orders:* Ibid.; Maurice Rindskopf unpublished memoir, p. 85.

259 *a fact confirmed: Senji Yuso Sendan Shi.*

259 Sawfish *first picked up: Sawfish* Report of Eighth War Patrol, Nov. 8, 1944.

259 *The thirty-nine-year-old:* Alan Banister Navy Bio, March 4, 1971, NDL.

259 *the* Kimikawa Maru: Alden and McDonald, pp. 213, 221; *Senji Yuso Sendan Shi.*

260 *The sonar operator: Drum* Report of Eleventh War Patrol, Oct. 26, 1944.

260 Icefish *sailors: Icefish* Report of First War Patrol, Nov. 13, 1944.

260 *The submarine* Snook: *Snook* Report of Seventh War Patrol, Nov. 18, 1944; Operational Order No. 326-44, Sept. 24, 1944, Box 299, RG 38, Records of the Office of the Chief of Naval Operations, Plans, Orders and Related Documents, NARA.

260 *Wolf pack commander Banister: Sawfish* Report of Eighth War Patrol, Nov. 8, 1944.

260 *"Attacking from port flank":* Ibid.

260 *"Attack completed":* Ibid.

260 *Commander Richard Peterson: Icefish* Report of First War Patrol, Nov. 13, 1944.

260 *His one hit:* Alden and McDonald, pp. 221–22; *Senji Yuso Sendan Shi.*

260 *Commander Brown in* Snook: *Snook* Report of Seventh War Patrol, Nov. 18, 1944; Alden and McDonald, p. 221; *Senji Yuso Sendan Shi;* JANAC gives *Seadragon* credit for the sinking of *Kokuryu Maru;* however, *Seadragon's* patrol report shows that the submarine did not join the fight until much later.

261 *The tightly clustered convoy: Senji Yuso Sendan Shi.*

261 *Rindskopf, now operating: Drum* Report of Eleventh War Patrol, Oct. 26, 1944.

261 Snook *roared in: Snook* Report of Seventh War Patrol, Nov. 18, 1944.

261 *Lookouts on the 3,887-ton tanker:* Alden and McDonald, pp. 221–22; *Senji Yuso Sendan Shi;* JANAC, p. 45 of the appendix.

261 *"The resulting explosion": Snook* Report of Seventh War Patrol, Nov. 18, 1944.

261 *The tenacious skipper:* Ibid.; Alden and McDonald, p. 222; *Senji Yuso Sendan Shi;* JANAC gives *Hoe* credit for the sinking of *Tenshin Maru;* however, *Snook* is the more likely submarine.

262 *Out of torpedoes: Sawfish* Report of Eighth War Patrol, Nov. 8, 1944; *Icefish* Report of First War Patrol, Nov. 13, 1944; *Snook* Report of Seventh War Patrol, Nov. 18, 1944.

262 *He scanned the horizon: Drum* Report of Eleventh War Patrol, Oct. 26, 1944; Alden and McDonald, p. 222; *Senji Yuso Sendan Shi;* JANAC, p. 12 of the appendix.

262 *The submarines* Shark: Roscoe, *United States Submarine Operations in World War II,* p. 411; *Seadragon* Report of Eleventh War Patrol, Nov. 8, 1944.

262 Seadragon *skipper: Seadragon* Report of Eleventh War Patrol, Nov. 8, 1944; Alden and McDonald, pp. 222–23; *Senji Yuso Sendan Shi;* JANAC, p. 40 of the appendix.

262 *the 6,886-ton* Taisho Maru: JANAC, p. 12 of the appendix; Alden and McDonald, pp. 224–25; *Senji Yuso Sendan Shi.*

262 *Rindskopf would relinquish command: Drum* Report of Twelfth War Patrol, Jan. 17, 1945; Maurice Rindskopf unpublished memoir, p. 86.

262 Drum *would make:* Harold P. Deeley, Jr., et al., eds., *Dictionary of American Naval Fighting Ships,* vol. 2 (Washington, D.C.: U.S. Government Printing Office, 1963), pp. 301–2; JANAC, p. 12 of the appendix.

263 *Like the Silver Lady:* Maurice Rindskopf unpublished memoir, p. 86.

263 *He would return:* Maurice Rindskopf Navy Bio, Nov. 15, 1972, NDL.

263 *Some of the prisoners:* Deposition of Calvin Graef, April 27, 1946.

263 *Half of the prisoners:* Calvin Robert Graef with Harry T. Brundidge, "We Prayed to Die," *Cosmopolitan,* vol. 118, no. 4, April 1945, p. 178.

263 *"What gives?":* Ibid.

263 Shark's *thirty-two-year-old:* Edward Blakely Navy Bio, Feb. 5, 1958, NDL, JANAC, p. 43 of the appendix.

264 *"Sink us, Navy!":* Calvin Robert Graef with Harry T. Brundidge, "We Prayed to Die," *Cosmopolitan,* vol. 118, no. 4, April 1945, p. 178.

264 *A one-and-a-half-ton:* Alden and McDonald, p. 223; *Senji Yuso Sendan Shi.*

264 *Coal dust:* Robert Overbeck, "Voyage to China," unpublished article.

264 *Prisoners who only:* Calvin Robert Graef with Harry T. Brundidge, "We Prayed to Die," *Cosmopolitan,* vol. 118, no. 4, April 1945, p. 178.

264 *"They ate like savages":* Deposition of Philip Brodsky, Sept. 5, 1946.

264 *"Want a bite?":* Calvin Robert Graef with Harry T. Brundidge, "We Prayed to Die," *Cosmopolitan,* vol. 118, no. 4, April 1945, p. 178.

265 *"They took at least five pokes":* Deposition of Calvin Graef, April 27, 1946.

265 *Corporal Donald Meyer:* Donald Meyer, "Five Came Back," personal narrative; Deposition of Donald Meyer, May 23, 1946.

265 *"Some felt":* Donald Meyer, "Five Came Back," personal narrative.

265 *"There were still":* Deposition of Glenn Oliver, Dec. 3, 1946.

265 *"Men were going down":* Donald Meyer, "Five Came Back," personal narrative.

266 *Graef, too:* Calvin Robert Graef with Harry T. Brundidge, "We Prayed to Die," *Cosmopolitan,* vol. 118, no. 4, April 1945, p. 179.

266 *"Clinging to my":* Ibid.

266 *"What kind of chance":* Donald Meyer, "Five Came Back," personal narrative.

266 *"The yelling":* Ibid.

267 *"Say, bud":* Ibid.

267 *"Hey boat!":* Calvin Robert Graef with Harry T. Brundidge, "We Prayed to Die," *Cosmopolitan,* vol. 118, no. 4, April 1945, p. 180.

267 *The Japanese had stripped:* Ibid.; Robert Overbeck, "Voyage to China," unpublished article.

267 *Meyer contributed:* Donald Meyer, "Five Came Back," personal narrative.

267 *The men unfurled:* Ibid.; Calvin Robert Graef with Harry T. Brundidge, "We Prayed to Die," *Cosmopolitan*, vol. 118, no. 4, April 1945, p. 180; Robert Overbeck, "Voyage to China," unpublished article; Deposition of Calvin Graef, April 27, 1946.

267 *"Where's China?":* Calvin Robert Graef with Harry T. Brundidge, "We Prayed to Die," *Cosmopolitan*, vol. 118, no. 4, April 1945, p. 180.

267 *The five survivors:* Robert Overbeck, "Voyage to China," unpublished article.

268 *The men picked up:* Depositions of Martin Binder (Nov. 8, 1946), Glenn Oliver (Dec. 3, 1946), and Philip Brodsky (Jan. 25, 1946, and Sept. 5, 1946).

268 *Another eighty-seven:* Naval History Division, Office of the Chief of Naval Operations, *United States Submarine Losses*, pp. 114–15.

268 *"There was a lot of phosphorescence":* Robert Overbeck, "Voyage to China," unpublished article.

268 *"This was our country":* Donald Meyer, "Five Came Back," personal narrative.

Chapter 20. *Tang*
PAGE

269 *"Dear All":* Gordon Cox undated postcard to family.

269 *The October sun:* O'Kane, *Clear the Bridge!*, pp. 459–60; William Leibold interview with author, July 10, 2009.

269 *The cramped compartment:* Details of the time aboard *P-34* are drawn from the depositions of Henry James Flanagan (March 22, 1946), William Rudolph Leibold (Oct. 26, 1945), C. O. Decker (April 24, 1946), Floyd Murel Caverly (May 22, 1946), and J. N. DaSilva (April 26, 1946); Lawrence Savadkin oral history interview with the Navy, Jan. 30, 1946.

269 *"When we would knock":* Deposition of William Rudolph Leibold, Oct. 26, 1945.

269 *"I'll be damned":* Floyd Caverly interview with author, July 30, 2009.

270 *"Our men would pass out":* Deposition of Floyd Murel Caverly, May 22, 1946.

270 *Postwar records:* JANAC, p. 48 of the appendix; Blair, *Silent Victory*, p. 988.

270 *"Anything that the Japs ask you":* Clay Decker video oral history interview with Dan Clayton, March 2002.

270 *P-34 arrived:* O'Kane, *Clear the Bridge!*, p. 460; Lawrence Savadkin oral history interview with the Navy, Jan. 30, 1946.

270 *The guards issued:* O'Kane, *Clear the Bridge!*, p. 460; Lawrence Savadkin oral history interview with the Navy, Jan. 30, 1946; Jesse B. DaSilva, "Survivor of the Mighty Tang," *American Submariner*, July–September 2001, pp. 16–18; "Saga of POWs," *All Hands*, June 1946, pp. 18–19.

271 *"We watched":* Lawrence Savadkin oral history interview with the Navy, Jan. 30, 1946.

271 *The train ended:* O'Kane, *Clear the Bridge!*, p. 460; Jesse B. DaSilva, "Survivor of the Mighty Tang," *American Submariner*, July–September 2001, pp. 16–18.

271 *"The cells are like the cages":* Lawrence Savadkin oral history interview with the Navy, Jan. 30, 1946.

271 *The Japanese fed the prisoners:* Ibid.; O'Kane, *Clear the Bridge!*, p. 460.

271 *"Hey, fellows!":* "Saga of POWs," *All Hands*, June 1946, p. 18.

271 *The guards returned:* Lawrence Savadkin oral history interview with the Navy, Jan. 30, 1946.

272 *The destroyer captain:* O'Kane, *Clear the Bridge!*, p. 460–62.

272 *"How is it":* Ibid., p. 461.

272 *"I ate with the Japanese officers":* Lawrence Savadkin oral history interview with the Navy, Jan. 30, 1946.

272 *Four days and three nights passed:* Ibid.

273 *"That ship":* O'Kane, *Clear the Bridge!*, p. 462.

273 *"How old are you?":* Ibid.; William Leibold interview with author, July 10, 2009; Lawrence Savadkin oral history interview with the Navy, Jan. 30, 1946; William Tuohy, *The Bravest Man: The Story of Richard O'Kane and U.S. Submariners in the Pacific War* (Gloucestershire: Sutton Publishing, 2002), pp. 355–56.

273 *"The countryside":* O'Kane, *Clear the Bridge!*, p. 462.

274 *The Japanese built the secret camp:* Descriptions of Ofuna are drawn from: Robert H. Dolder to HQ XI Corps, Report of Recovery Team 56, Sept. 23, 1945; Louis Zamperini with David Rensin, *Devil at My Heels: A World War II Hero's Epic Saga of Torment, Survival, and Forgiveness* (New York: William Morrow, 2003), pp. 134–35.

274 *"The camp was built":* Zamperini, *Devil at My Heels*, p. 134.

274 *"No heat of any description":* Affidavit of John Fitzgerald, July 11, 1946, Papers of Rear Admiral John A. Fitzgerald, 1943–1945, Naval History and Heritage Command, Washington, D.C.; Deposition of Donald Curry Stanley, April 12, 1947, Box 700, RG 153, Records of the Office of the Judge Advocate General (Army), War Crimes Branch, NARA.

274 *Nonregistered captives received:* William Leibold interview with author, July 13, 2009; O'Kane, *Clear the Bridge!*, p. 463; Gregory "Pappy" Boyington, *Baa Baa Black Sheep* (New York: G. P. Putnam's Sons, 1958), pp. 275, 296–97; John Fitzgerald introduction to diary; copies of Fitzgerald's diary are on file with his papers at the Naval History and Heritage Command and in Box 17 of Charles Lockwood's papers at the Library of Congress. Both copies appear to be missing pages. Author Stephen Moore graciously provided me with what appears to be a complete copy of Fitzgerald's diary.

275 *"One day I walked":* Notes of the deposition of Louis Zamperini, provided by Stephen Moore.

275   "Eat!": Zamperini, *Devil at My Heels*, pp. 136–37.

275   *Portion sizes fluctuated:* Review of the Staff Judge Advocate in the case of *The United States of America vs. Tatsumi Hata*, Headquarters Eighth Army, United States Army, Office of the Staff Judge Advocate, Yokohama, Japan, Dec. 21, 1948.

275   *Prisoners suffered:* Deposition of Sage M. Johnston, March 18, 1948, Box 700, RG 153, Records of the Office of the Judge Advocate General (Army), War Crimes Branch, NARA; John Fitzgerald introduction to diary; Jesse DaSilva oral history interview with Douglas E. Clanin, Sept. 4, 1992.

275   *at least eight deaths:* Review of the Staff Judge Advocate in the case of *The United States of America vs. Yuzuru Sanematsu et al.* Headquarters Eighth Army, United States Army, Office of the Staff Judge Advocate, Yokohama, Japan, Feb. 15, 1949. Records show that at least six confirmed prisoners died at Ofuna. At least two others died shortly after being transferred to other camps, those deaths a direct result of treatment received at Ofuna.

275   *Men lulled themselves to sleep:* Boyington, *Baa Baa Black Sheep*, p. 297.

275   *"Eating soup with worms":* Carl Quarterman diary, undated entry titled "New Experiences as P.O.W."; Carl Quarterman letter to family, Sept. 15, 1945.

275   *"moronic farm kids":* Zamperini, *Devil at My Heels*, p. 140.

275   *Trivial offenses:* Affidavits of Arthur Maher, Nov. 28, 1945, and Oct. 17, 1946, Box 1, Papers of Rear Admiral Arthur L. Maher, 1926–1984, NHHC: Affidavit of John Fitzgerald, July 11, 1946; John Fitzgerald diary, Nov. 6, 1944; O'Kane, *Clear the Bridge!*, p. 463; William Leibold interview with author, July 13, 2009.

275   *The prisoners nicknamed one guard:* Affidavit of George F. Rumrill, Oct. 19, 1945, Box 590, RG 153, Records of the Office of the Judge Advocate General (Army), War Crimes Branch, NARA.

276   *Other guards masturbated:* Boyington, *Baa Baa Black Sheep*, p. 279.

276   *Prisoners recalled with horror:* Zamperini, *Devil at My Heels*, p. 140.

276   *"We lived in eternal":* Affidavit of Richard M. Smith, Oct. 24, 1945, Box 590, RG 153, Records of the Office of the Judge Advocate General (Army), War Crimes Branch, NARA.

276   *The worst of the guards:* Background on Sueharu Kitamura is drawn from the following sources: Kitamura undated handwritten biographical sketch, Box 1227, RG 331, Supreme Commander for the Allied Powers, Legal Section, Administrative Division, Misc. Subject File, 1945–50, NARA; Deposition of John Ross Benge, April 11, 1946, Box 2, RG 125, Records of the Office of the Judge Advocate General (Navy), War Crimes Branch, Records Re. Pacific Area War Crimes Cases, 1944–1949, NARA; Petitions of Taki Ota (June 22, 1948) and Kato Kitamura (June 22, 1948), Box 1644, RG 331, Supreme Commander for

the Allied Powers, Legal Section, Prosecution Division, USA Versus Japanese War Criminals, Case File, 1945–49, NARA; Kato Kitamura letter to Douglas MacArthur, April 13, 1949, ibid.; Depositions of Charles Miller Bransfield (Jan. 29, 1946), Charles Valentine August (Sept. 20, 1945), William Adelbert Dixon (Jan. 7, 1946), and Gordon Francis Bennett (Oct. 10, 1945), ibid.

276 *"He was very heavily built"*: Deposition of Grant Leslie Butcher, Sept. 12, 1945, Box 1644, RG 331, Supreme Commander for the Allied Powers, Legal Section, Prosecution Division, USA Versus Japanese War Criminals, Case File, 1945–49, NARA.

276 *feminine high-pitched laugh:* Deposition of Charles Miller Bransfield, Jan. 29, 1946.

276 *"the Quack":* Review of the Staff Judge Advocate in the case of *The United States of America vs. Sueharu Kitamura*, Headquarters Eighth Army, United States Army, Office of the Staff Judge Advocate, Yokohama, Japan, Feb. 4, 1949, Box 1644, RG 331, Supreme Commander for the Allied Powers, Legal Section, Prosecution Division, USA Versus Japanese War Criminals, Case File, 1945–49, NARA.

276 *He carried:* Deposition of William Adelbert Dixon, Jan. 7, 1946.

276 *Other times Kitamura:* Review of the Staff Judge Advocate in the case of *The United States of America vs. Sueharu Kitamura.*

276 *"Ofuna Crouch":* Ibid.

276 *Kitamura other days:* Ibid.

276 *When the passageways iced over:* Ibid.; Deposition of Richard O'Kane, Aug. 15, 1946, Box 1644, RG 331, Supreme Commander for the Allied Powers, Legal Section, Prosecution Division, USA Versus Japanese War Criminals, Case File, 1945–49, NARA.

276 *No one was safe:* R. T. Brunckhorst to Alva C. Carpenter, Aug. 13, 1948, Box 1644, RG 331, Supreme Commander for the Allied Powers, Legal Section, Prosecution Division, USA Versus Japanese War Criminals, Case File, 1945–49, NARA.

277 *"a barometer to us":* Deposition of Arthur J. Walker, Nov. 18, 1946, Box 1644, RG 331, Supreme Commander for the Allied Powers, Legal Section, Prosecution Division, USA Versus Japanese War Criminals, Case File, 1945–49, NARA.

277 *"Kitamura called Bullard":* Affidavit of John Fitzgerald, July 11, 1946.

277 *For the nine survivors:* William Leibold interview with author, July 13, 2009; Lawrence Savadkin oral history interview with the Navy, Jan. 30, 1946; O'Kane, *Clear the Bridge!*, pp. 462–63; Cindy Adams, "Tang Survivors Recall World War II Ordeal," *Patrol*, Sept. 5, 1980, pp. 4–6.

278 Tang *had departed:* Tang *Report of Fifth War Patrol*, Sept. 10, 1945.

278 Tang's *orders:* Operational Order No. 326-44, Sept. 24, 1944, Box 299, RG 38, Records of the Office of the Chief of Naval Operations, Plans, Orders and Related Documents, NARA.

278 *"It is with the deepest regret":* C. A. Lockwood, Jr., to Commander in Chief, United States Fleet, Nov. 27, 1944, Box 744, RG 38, Records of the Chief of Naval Operations, World War II Action and Operational Reports, NARA.

278 *"The Navy Department":* Randall Jacobs telegram to Grace Clara Leibold, Nov. 27, 1944.

278 *"The words 'missing in action' ":* C. A. Lockwood, Jr., letter to Mrs. Dudley Morton, Dec. 1, 1943, Dudley Morton Family Papers, BSMP.

279 *American submarine losses:* Naval History Division, Office of the Chief of Naval Operations, *United States Submarine Losses,* pp. 8, 112–15.

279 *"The undersea craft":* "Overdue," editorial, *New York Times,* Feb. 16, 1945, p. 22.

279 *"We were all warned":* Boyington, *Baa Baa Black Sheep,* p. 275.

279 *"There would be no":* Zamperini, *Devil at My Heels,* p. 131.

279 *"We pulled you":* Arthur L. Maher undated speech outline, Box 1, Papers of Rear Admiral Arthur L. Maher, 1926–1984, NHHC.

279 *The* Tang *men witnessed:* O'Kane, *Clear the Bridge!,* p. 463; William Leibold interview with author, July 13, 2009; Affidavit of John Fitzgerald, July 11, 1946; John Fitzgerald diary, Nov. 6, 1944; John Fitzgerald Navy Bio, June 2, 1958, NDL.

280 *O'Kane watched:* O'Kane, *Clear the Bridge!,* p. 463.

280 *"Every blow":* Deposition of R. H. O'Kane, Oct. 29, 1947, Box 1287, RG 331, Supreme Commander for the Allied Powers, Legal Section, Administrative Division, Tokyo Case File, 1945–48, NARA.

280 *Kitamura had before:* Deposition of Hayes O. Trukke, Aug. 1, 1946, Box 1644, Supreme Commander for the Allied Powers, Legal Section, Prosecution Division, USA Versus Japanese War Criminals, Case File, 1945–49, NARA.

280 *Caverly, a former professional boxer:* O'Kane, *Clear the Bridge!,* p. 463.

280 *Leibold watched:* Deposition of William Leibold, Oct. 21, 1947, Box 1644, Supreme Commander for the Allied Powers, Legal Section, Prosecution Division, USA Versus Japanese War Criminals, Case File, 1945–49, NARA.

280 *None of the Japanese officials:* Deposition of R. H. O'Kane, Oct. 29, 1947.

280 *"As a result":* Affidavit of John Fitzgerald, July 11, 1946.

281 *The hard-charging fighter ace:* Background on Gregory "Pappy" Boyington is drawn from: "Boyington Bag at 24; Nears Plane Record," *New York Times,* Dec. 27, 1943, p. 3; "Highest Award for Boyington," *New York Times,* April 13, 1944, p. 5; "Boyington Holiday Due When He Fell," *New York Times,* Jan. 9, 1944, p. 37; "Boyington Missing; Downed 26 Planes," *New York Times,* Jan. 7, 1944, p. 1; " 'Pappy' Boyington Credited with His Twenty-sixth Plane," *Spokane Daily-Chronicle,* Jan. 6, 1944, p. 1; Richard Goldstein, "Joe Foss, Ace, Dies at 87," *New York Times,* Jan. 2,

2003, p. B8; "Hoover Pins Medal on Rickenbacker," *New York Times*, Nov. 7, 1930, p. 16; Boyington, *Baa Baa Black Sheep*, p. 321; Bruce Gamble, *Black Sheep One: The Life of Gregory "Pappy" Boyington* (Novato: Presidio, 2000), pp. 39–46, 266–68, 289–309.

281 *"Major Boyington":* Gamble, *Black Sheep One*, p. 266.

281 *The major claimed:* "Boyington Bag at 24; Nears Plane Record," *New York Times*, Dec. 27, 1943, p. 3; Gamble, *Black Sheep One*, pp. 289–93.

281 *He blasted:* "Marine Ace," *New York Times*, Jan. 5, 1944, p. 4; Gamble, *Black Sheep One*, pp. 295–97.

281 *On the morning:* Boyington, *Baa Baa Black Sheep*, pp. 229–31; Gamble, *Black Sheep One*, pp. 303–9.

281 *"I could feel":* Boyington, *Baa Baa Black Sheep*, p. 231.

281 *Far outnumbered:* Ibid., pp. 231–77; Gamble, *Black Sheep One*, pp. 305–9.

282 *The shrapnel in the major's thigh:* Zamperini, *Devil at My Heels*, p. 139.

282 *"The pharmacist's mate cut":* Deposition of Grant Leslie Butcher, Sept. 12, 1945.

282 *Boyington fit the profile:* Deposition of Max L. Parnell, Aug. 23, 1946, Box 1644, RG 331, Supreme Commander for the Allied Powers, Legal Section, Prosecution Division, USA Versus Japanese War Criminals, Case File, 1945–49, NARA.

282 *The camp's roster:* Roster of Allied POWs Transferred from Ofuna (Navy) to Army POW Camps, as of 15 Aug. 1945, Box 1305, RG 331, Supreme Commander for the Allied Powers, Legal Section, Administrative Division, Misc. File, 1945–48, NARA.

282 *Interrogation of the* Tang *crew:* Jesse B. DaSilva, "Survivor of the Mighty Tang," *American Submariner*, July–September 2001, pp. 16–18.

282 *like James Sasaki:* Zamperini, *Devil at My Heels*, pp. 131–34.

282 *Ofuna's chief interrogator:* Hugh S. Taylor to Bertram W. Tremayne, Jr., Feb. 7, 1946, Box 2, RG 125, Records of the Judge Advocate General (Navy), War Crimes Branch, Records Re. Pacific Area War Crimes Cases, 1944–1949, NARA; Depositions of George Estabrook Brown, Jr. (July 10, 1946), and George Clough Bullard (Jan. 23, 1946), Box 2, RG 125, Records of the Judge Advocate General (Navy), War Crimes Branch, Records Re. Pacific Area War Crimes Cases, 1944–1949, NARA.

283 *One even claimed:* Lawrence Savadkin oral history interview with the Navy, Jan. 30, 1946.

283 *Interrogators dressed:* Ibid.

283 *The Japanese pressed:* John Fitzgerald introduction to diary; Lawrence Savadkin oral history interview with the Navy, Jan. 30, 1946.

283 *"If I had told":* Clay Decker undated video oral history interview with Clark M. Brandt.

283 *"We became terrific liars":* John Fitzgerald introduction to diary.

283   *"I kept telling the interrogators":* "Saga of POWs," *All Hands,* June 1946, p. 18.

284   *"honey dipper":* Clay Decker undated video oral history interview with Clark M. Brandt.

284   *"Conversation was prohibited":* John Fitzgerald introduction to diary.

284   *Ofuna's crafty captives:* Ibid.

284   *Guards set out to teach:* O'Kane, *Clear the Bridge!,* pp. 462–63; Clay Decker undated video oral history interview with Clark M. Brandt; "Saga of POWs," *All Hands,* June 1946, pp. 18–19; William Leibold interview with author, July 13, 2009.

284   *"We had to greet them":* Lawrence Savadkin oral history interview with the Navy, Jan. 30, 1946.

284   *"Most of the day":* "Saga of POWs," *All Hands,* June 1946, pp. 18–19.

284   *Guards over time:* Lawrence Savadkin oral history interview with the Navy, Jan. 30, 1946.

284   *"The rest of our time":* Ibid.

285   *"The usual concoctions of desserts":* Fitzgerald diary, Nov. 23, 1944.

285   *December 4 brought:* Fitzgerald diary, Dec. 4, 1944, and Dec. 7–8, 1944.

285   *"If it be thy will":* Christian Program, Ofuna, Japan, 1944, included as appendix 2 to Fitzgerald's diary.

285   *Snow blanketed:* Fitzgerald diary, Jan. 6, 1945.

285   *The* Tang *men convinced:* Jesse B. DaSilva, "Survivor of the Mighty Tang," *American Submariner,* July–September 2001, pp. 16–18.

285   *Pete Narowanski dwelled:* Cindy Adams, "Tang Survivors Recall World War II Ordeal," *Patrol,* Sept. 5, 1980, pp. 4–6.

285   *"Still in our tattered whites":* O'Kane, *Clear the Bridge!,* p. 464; Review of the Staff Judge Advocate in the case of *The United States of America vs. Tatsumi Hata,* Headquarters Eighth Army, United States Army, Office of the Staff Judge Advocate, Yokohama, Japan, Dec. 21, 1948.

286   *The men watched with elation:* O'Kane, *Clear the Bridge!,* p. 465.

286   *A former winner:* Background on Hunt is drawn from: Richard L. Hunt, Jr., Bio and the Gold Star Mother's Legion scrapbook (SC68), pp. 54–55, both on file at the Missouri Valley Special Collections, Kansas City Public Library, Kansas City, Missouri; *The Paseon,* vol. 12 (Kansas City, Mo.: Paseo High School, 1938), pp. 23, 48, 121; "Richard L. Hunt Missing," *Kansas City Star,* Feb. 1, 1945, p. 4; "Dies in a Jap Prison," *Kansas City Star,* Sept. 18, 1945, p. 7.

286   *On a mission over Hong Kong:* Report on Death of Prisoner of War, Feb. 28, 1945, Box 1305, RG 331, Supreme Commander for the Allied Powers, Legal Section, Administrative Division, Misc. File, 1945–48, NARA. Some records state that Hunt arrived at Ofuna on or about January 26.

286   *Tang's boatswain's mate worked:* Deposition of William Leibold, Oct. 21, 1947.

286 *Rather than remove:* Review of the Staff Judge Advocate in the case of *The United States of America vs. Sueharu Kitamura,* Headquarters Eighth Army, United States Army, Office of the Staff Judge Advocate, Yokohama, Japan, Feb. 4, 1949.

286 *"He would run a swab":* Deposition of Grant Leslie Butcher, Sept. 12, 1945.

287 *In between cleaning:* Deposition of William Leibold, Oct. 21, 1947.

287 *"A man being treated":* Deposition of John Ross Benge, April 11, 1946, Box 2, Records of the Office of the Judge Advocate General (Navy), War Crimes Bnrach, Records Re. Pacific Area War Crimes Cases, 1944–1949, NARA.

287 *The only time:* Kitamura in his deposition after the war surprisingly admitted using fresh gauze to clean his sword, though he denied using bandages.

287 *The pale and exhausted Hunt:* Commanding Officer, Yokosuka Naval Garrison Unit, to Commanding Officer, Yokosuka Naval Base, Report on Death of Prisoner of War, Feb. 28, 1945, Box 1305, RG 331, Supreme Commander for the Allied Powers, Legal Section, Administrative Division, Misc. File, 1945–48, NARA; Deposition of Sueharu Kitamura, undated, Box 1281, RG 331, Supreme Commander for the Allied Powers, Legal Section, Administrative Division, Investigation and Interrogation Reports, 1945–48, NARA; Review of the Staff Judge Advocate in the case of *The United States of America vs. Kakuzo Iida et al.,* Case No. 291, Headquarters Eighth Army, United States Army, Office of the Staff Judge Advocate, Yokohama, Japan, May 19, 1949.

287 *"He staggered":* Deposition of William Leibold, Oct. 21, 1947.

287 *Leibold witnessed:* Ibid.

288 *The prisoners knew:* Deposition of Arthur J. Walker, Nov. 18, 1946.

288 *"worked him over":* Deposition of William Leibold, Oct. 21, 1947.

288 *"A guard stood":* Deposition of Hayes O. Trukke, Aug. 1, 1946.

288 *Kitamura's refusal:* Deposition of R. H. O'Kane, Oct. 29, 1947.

288 *Snow blew:* Review of the Staff Judge Advocate in the case of *The United States of America vs. Kakuzo Iida,* Case No. 291, Headquarters Eighth Army, United States Army, Office of the Staff Judge Advocate, Yokohama, Japan, May 19, 1949.

288 *"Some of the other prisoners":* Deposition of William Leibold, Oct. 21, 1947.

289 *The only time guards:* Deposition of Frederick Dewitt Turnbull, Sept. 19, 1947, Box 1644, RG 331, Supreme Commander for the Allied Powers, Legal Section, Prosecution Division, USA Versus Japanese War Criminals, Case File, 1945–49, NARA.

289 *"When I tried to wash":* Deposition of William Leibold, Oct. 21, 1947; William Leibold e-mails to author, Aug. 5, 2010.

289 *The prisoner in the cell:* Deposition of William R. Eustis, Nov. 14, 1946, Box 1644, RG 331, Supreme Commander for the Allied Powers, Legal Section, Prosecution Division, USA Versus Japanese War Criminals, Case File, 1945–49,

NARA; Commanding Officer, Yokosuka Naval Garrison Unit, to Commanding Officer, Yokosuka Naval Base, Report on Death of Prisoner of War, Feb. 28, 1945, Box 1305, RG 331, Supreme Commander for the Allied Powers, Legal Section, Administrative Division, Misc. File, 1945–48, NARA.

289 *"Kitamura and Commander Sanematsu":* Deposition of William Leibold, Oct. 21, 1947.

289 *Interrogators pressured guards:* Review of the Staff Judge Advocate in the case of *The United States of America vs. Sueharu Kitamura*; Deposition of Anthony Warren Dawson-Grove, Oct. 4, 1947, Box 1644, RG 331, Supreme Commander for the Allied Powers, Legal Section, Prosecution Division, USA Versus Japanese War Criminals, Case File, 1945–49, NARA; Deposition of R. H. O'Kane, Oct. 29, 1947.

289 *Guards liked to force:* Deposition of Gordon Grant Johnson, Aug. 14, 1946.

289 *"After five full swings":* Deposition of R. H. O'Kane, Oct. 29, 1947.

289 *"Freight Train Blues":* Deposition of Louis Temple Vance, April 2, 1947, Box 1744, RG 331, Supreme Commander for the Allied Powers, Legal Section, Prosecution Division, USA Versus Japanese War Criminals, Case File, 1945–49, NARA.

289 *"One of the more pathetic":* Deposition of Charles Valentine August, Jan. 28, 1948, Box 700, RG 153, Records of the Office of the Judge Advocate General (Army), War Crimes Branch, Case Files, 1944–1949, NARA.

290 *"Naval intelligence":* O'Kane, *Clear the Bridge!*, p. 465.

290 *the Japanese decided to transfer:* Deposition of William Leibold, Oct. 26, 1945, Box 583, RG 153, Records of the Office of the Judge Advocate General (Army), War Crimes Branch, Case Files, 1944–1949, NARA.

290 *"I looked back":* Boyington, *Baa Baa Black Sheep*, p. 2.

Chapter 21. *Tang*
PAGE

291 *"Recurrently I am homesick":* Ernest Norquist diary entry, July 14, 1943, in Ernest O. Norquist, "Three Years in Paradise: A GI's Prisoner-of-War Diary, 1942–1945," *Wisconsin Magazine of History*, Autumn 1979, pp. 12–13.

291 *Boyington, the six enlisted:* Boyington, *Baa Baa Black Sheep*, p. 322.

291 *Omori served:* Lt. Robert H. Dolder to HQ XI Corps, Report on Omori POW camp, Sept. 25, 1945.

291 *Unlike Ofuna:* Robert R. Martindale, *The 13th Mission: The Saga of a POW at Camp Omori, Tokyo* (Austin, Texas: Eakin Press, 1998), pp. 79–83; William Leibold interview with author, July 13, 2009.

292 *Many prisoners worked:* Alfred A. Weinstein, *Barbed-Wire Surgeon* (New York: Macmillan, 1956), pp. 235–36; Zamperini, *Devil at My Heels*, pp. 153–54.

292 *Stolen sugar served:* Weinstein, *Barbed-Wire Surgeon*, p. 236.

292 *Men scooped feces:* Ibid., pp. 237–39; Martindale, *The 13th Mission*, pp. 83, 97.

292 *Most prisoners labored:* Ernest Norquist diary, Oct. 9, 1943, Oct. 11, 1943, Oct. 30, 1943, in Ernest Norquist, *Our Paradise: A GI's War Diary* (Hancock, Wisc.: Pearl-Win Publishing, 1989), pp. 284, 286.

292 *"Disappointed with":* Ernest Norquist diary, Oct. 13, 1943, in ibid., p. 285.

292 *British prisoners:* Weinstein, *Barbed-Wire Surgeon*, p. 246.

292 *Captives even produced:* Ernest Norquist diary, Jan. 1, 1945, in Norquist, *Our Paradise*, pp. 294–95.

292 *"The change to Omori":* O'Kane, *Clear the Bridge!*, p. 465.

292 *"The waiting seems":* Ernest Norquist diary, May 13, 1945, in Ernest O. Norquist, "Three Years in Paradise: A GI's Prisoner-of-War Diary, 1942–1945," *Wisconsin Magazine of History*, Autumn 1979, p. 26.

293 *Boeing's aeronautical monster:* Background on the B-29 comes from the following sources: Foster Hailey, "Superfortress Is Largest and Swiftest Bomber in the World," *New York Times*, June 16, 1944, p. 4; Hanson W. Baldwin, "The Tokyo Raids—1," *New York Times*, Nov. 27, 1944, p. 12; "B-29 Device Ends Oxygen Mask Use," *New York Times*, June 22, 1944, p. 11; "The Mighty B-29," *New York Times*, Aug. 5, 1945, p. 67; "Five New U.S. Planes Get into the Fight," *Popular Science*, August 1944, p. 57.

293 *"magnificent instrument":* "B-29 Anniversary," editorial, *New York Times*, June 10, 1945, p. E8.

293 *"against the heart":* Sidney Shalett, "B-29s Make Debut," *New York Times*, June 16, 1944, p. 1.

293 *The horror that:* Details of the B-29 raid come from the following sources: Bruce Rae, "Record Air Attack," *New York Times*, March 10, 1945, p. 1; Martin Sheridan, "Giant Tokyo Fires Blackened B-29's," *New York Times*, March 11. 1945, p. 14; Warren Moscow, "City's Heart Gone," *New York Times*, March 11, 1945, p. 1; "Tokyo in Flames," editorial, *New York Times*, March 12, 1945, p. 18; USSBS, *Summary Report (Pacific War)*, pp. 16–17; Wesley Frank Craven and James Lea Cate, eds., *The Army Air Forces in World War II*, vol. 5, *The Pacific: Matterhorn to Nagasaki, June 1944 to August 1945* (Washington, D.C.: U.S. Government Printing Office, 1983), pp. 614–17.

293 *"I have never seen":* Martin Sheridan, "Giant Tokyo Fires Blackened B-29's," *New York Times*, March 11, 1945, p. 14. Sheridan was a *Globe* journalist whose story appeared in the *Times* as part of the Combined American Press.

293 *"Almost instantly":* Frank Fujita, *Foo: A Japanese-American Prisoner of the Rising Sun* (Denton: University of North Texas Press, 1993), p. 264.

294 *"We saw such a sight":* Ernest Norquist diary, March 10, 1945, in Norquist, *Our Paradise*, p. 301.

294 *Bombers returned:* USSBS, *Summary Report (Pacific War)*, pp. 16–17.

294 *The size:* Foster Hailey, "Superfortress Is Largest and Swiftest Bomber in the World," *New York Times*, June 16, 1944, p. 4; "Tokyo Laid Waste by B-29's, Royal Palaces Devastated; Fighters Smash at Kyushu," *New York Times*, May 27, 1945, p. 1.

294 *The same military that could:* Emmett O'Donnell, Jr., Air Force Bio, undated.

294 *On a mission:* Bruce Rae, "Peak Japan Blow," *New York Times*, May 24, 1945, p. 1.

294 *Reconnaissance photos:* Warren Moscow, "51 Square Miles Burned Out in Six B-29 Attacks on Tokyo," *New York Times*, May 30, 1945, p. 1.

294 *"music":* Boyington, *Baa Baa Black Sheep*, pp. 326–27.

294 *"We went to a top":* J. J. Woodward, "Report of Service from December 1941 to September 1945 of Capt. J. J. Woodward IMS/IAMC," 1946, PR83/032, Australian War Memorial, Canberra, Australia.

295 *one attack even destroyed:* Deposition of William Laughlin Connell, Oct. 29, 1948, Box 743, RG 153, Records of the Office of the Judge Advocate General (Army), War Crimes Branch, Case Files, 1944–1949, NARA.

295 *"Shrapnel from incendiaries":* Ernest Norquist diary, May 30, 1945, in Ernest O. Norquist, "Three Years in Paradise: A GI's Prisoner-of-War Diary," *Wisconsin Magazine of History*, vol. 63, no. 1, Autumn 1979, p. 26.

295 *"The ground would shake":* Boyington, *Baa Baa Black Sheep*, p. 330.

295 *"We would walk":* Clay Decker undated video oral history interview with Clark M. Brandt.

295 *"When you're starving":* Jesse B. DaSilva, "Survivor of the Mighty Tang," *American Submariner*, July–September 2001, p. 18.

295 *The men labored:* William Leibold interview with author, July 13, 2009.

296 *The fighter ace scavenged:* Clay Decker video oral history interview with Dan Clayton, March 2002.

296 *The six-foot-tall DaSilva:* Jesse DaSilva oral history interview with Douglas E. Clanin, Sept. 4, 1992; Jesse B. DaSilva, "Survivor of the Mighty Tang," *American Submariner*, July–September 2001, pp. 16–18.

296 *Machinist's mate Decker's weight:* Clay Decker undated video oral history interview with Clark M. Brandt.

296 *Leibold suffered hepatitis:* William Leibold interview with author, July 13, 2009; O'Kane, *Clear the Bridge!*, p. 466.

296 *"I'm so weak":* Norquist diary, June 12, 1945, in Ernest O. Norquist, "Three Years in Paradise: A GI's Prisoner-of-War Diary," *Wisconsin Magazine of History*, vol. 63, no. 1, Autumn 1979, p. 28.

296 *The wait for the war's end:* Boyington, *Baa Baa Black Sheep*, p. 324; William Leibold e-mail to author, Aug. 12, 2010; Arthur Gill, Certificate of Death,

July 6, 1945, Box 1305, RG 331, Supreme Commander for the Allied Powers, Legal Section, Administrative Division, Misc. File, 1945–1948, NARA; Deposition of Gregory Boyington, in Martindale, *The 13th Mission*, p. 207.

296 *"If we are to be free":* Fujita diary, Aug. 11, 1945, in Fujita, *Foo*, pp. 301–2.

297 *"I dream":* Norquist diary, July 14, 1943, in Norquist, *Our Paradise*, pp. 133–34.

297 *Colonel Paul Tibbets, Jr.:* Details on the mission of the *Enola Gay*, unless otherwise noted, are drawn from the following sources: Paul W. Tibbets, Jr., *Return of the Enola Gay* (Columbus, Ohio: Mid Coast Marketing, 1998), pp. 196–244; W. H. Lawrence, "5 Plants Vanish," *New York Times*, Aug. 8, 1945, p. 1; Paul W. Tibbets, Jr., Air Force Bio, May 1964.

297 *America's relentless pounding:* W. H. Lawrence, "Air Might Clinched Battle of Japan," *New York Times*, Aug. 15, 1945, p. 11.

297 *Experts estimated:* Notes of the Interim Committee Meeting, May 31, 1945, Misc. Historical Documents Collection, Harry S. Truman Library and Museum, Independence, Missouri; Statement by the President of the United States, Aug. 6, 1945, Subject File, Ayers Papers, ibid.; Translation of leaflet dropped on the Japanese (AB-11), Aug. 6, 1945, Miscellaneous Historical Documents Collection, ibid.

297 *A 7 a.m. air raid:* The United States Strategic Bomb Survey, Medical Division, *The Effects of the Atomic Bombs on Health and Medical Services in Hiroshima and Nagasaki* (Washington, D.C.: U.S. Government Printing Office, 1947), p. 3.

298 *"My God":* "Hiroshima: A Diary," *Time*, 1973, p. 14.

298 *American investigators after the war:* Precise casualties from the attacks on Hiroshima and Nagasaki are difficult to estimate; figures even vary within reports prepared by the United States Strategic Bombing Survey. The figures used here come from the following sources: USSBS, *The Effects of the Atomic Bombs on Health and Medical Services in Hiroshima and Nagasaki*, p. 57; USSBS, *The Effects of the Atomic Bombs on Hiroshima and Nagasaki* (Washington, D.C.: U.S. Government Printing Office, 1946), p. 15.

298 *The blast leveled:* USSBS, *The Effects of the Atomic Bombs on Hiroshima and Nagasaki*, pp. 3–10, 25; USSBS, *Summary Report (Pacific War)*, pp. 22–25; Tibbets, *Return of the Enola Gay*, p. 231.

298 *"rain of ruin":* Statement by the President of the United States, Aug. 6, 1945, Subject File, Ayers Papers, Harry S. Truman Library and Museum, Independence, Missouri.

298 *"We are in possession":* Translation of leaflet dropped on the Japanese (AB-11), Aug. 6, 1945, Miscellaneous Historical Documents Collection, ibid.; "Leaflets and Radio Tell Japanese Bad News, Urge They Seek Peace," *New York Times*, Aug. 10, 1945, p. 1.

298 *The pressure intensified:* "Red Army Strikes," *New York Times*, Aug. 9, 1945, p. 1; "New 93-Mile Gain Made by Russians," *New York Times*, Aug. 15, 1945, p. 8; "The War," *Time*, Aug. 20, 1945, p. 26.

298 *On the Thursday:* Tibbets, *Return of the Enola Gay*, pp. 421–24; USSBS, *The Effects of the Atomic Bombs on Health and Medical Services in Hiroshima and Nagasaki*, p. 57; USSBS, *The Effects of the Atomic Bombs on Hiroshima and Nagasaki*, pp. 3–5.

298 *A radio announcer:* The Pacific War Research Society, *Japan's Longest Day* (Tokyo: Kodansha International, 2002), pp. 308–9.

299 *Only hours earlier:* Ibid., pp. 209–12.

299 *Even Hirohito:* Ibid., pp. 321, 327–28.

299 *Captives watched:* J. J. Woodward, "Report of Service from December 1941 to September 1945 of Capt. J. J. Woodward IMS/IAMC," 1946.

299 *O'Kane and other prisoners:* O'Kane, *Clear the Bridge!*, p. 466.

299 *The announcer asked:* The Pacific War Research Society, *Japan's Longest Day*, pp. 326–28.

299 *"To our good and loyal subjects":* Ibid., pp. 209–11.

300 *Fleet Admiral Chester Nimitz:* Potter, *Nimitz*, pp. 471–72.

300 *"The long awaited day":* COMSUBPAC msg. Aug. 15, 1945, Box 18, Charles Lockwood Papers, LOC.

300 *guards ordered O'Kane:* O'Kane, *Clear the Bridge!*, p. 466.

300 *Other work parties:* Boyington, *Baa Baa Black Sheep*, p. 337.

300 *Some of the Japanese:* O'Kane, *Clear the Bridge!*, p. 466.

300 *"The war is over":* Boyington, *Baa Baa Black Sheep*, p. 337.

300 *"Hey, fellows":* Ibid.

300 *The guards burned:* Lawrence Savadkin oral history interview with the Navy, Jan. 30, 1946.

301 *Boyington, O'Kane:* Boyington, *Baa Baa Black Sheep*, p. 338–40; William Leibold interview with author, July 13, 2009.

301 *Medics began sick call:* Lawrence Savadkin oral history interview with the Navy, Jan. 30, 1946.

301 *"It seems as if":* Ernest Norquist diary, Aug. 16, 1945, in Norquist, *Our Paradise*, p. 345.

301 *"We all stood out":* Harry Berry diary, August 25, 1945, in Harry Berry, *My Darling Wife: The True Wartime Letters of Harry Berry to Gwen, 1940–1945* (Hertford, England: Authors OnLine, 2004), p. 328.

301 *"Hang on!":* Fujita, *Foo*, pp. 310–11.

302 *The B-29s that had for months:* Headquarters Twentieth Air Force, APO 234, Report of Prisoners of War Supply Missions from 27 August to 20 September 1945.

302 *Prisoners climbed atop:* Boyington, *Baa Baa Black Sheep*, p. 342; "Captives to Take Charge of Prisons," *New York Times*, Sept. 5, 1945, p. 3.

302 *Supplies soon rained down:* Lawrence Savadkin oral history interview with the Navy, Jan. 30, 1946; Fujita, *Foo*, pp. 311–12; Harry Berry diary, August 26, 1945, in Berry, *My Darling Wife*, p. 328.

302 *"This is better":* Harry Berry diary, Aug. 27, 1945, in Berry, *My Darling Wife*, pp. 328–29.

302 *Some of the drums:* Ibid.

302 *"Everyone ran for cover":* Fujita, *Foo*, pp. 311–12.

302 *"Why don't you stay":* Boyington, *Baa Baa Black Sheep*, p. 341.

Chapter 22. *Tang*

PAGE

303 *"I have been dead":* Carl Quarterman letter to family, September 15, 1945.

303 *Commodore Joel Boone:* Joel T. Boone undated report, "Initial Release of Prisoners of War in Japan," NBMS.

303 *A former physician:* Joel T. Boone Navy Bio, April 1, 1966, ibid.

303 *American forces:* Report of Surrender and Occupation of Japan, Feb. 11, 1946.

303 *Supreme Commander:* Halsey, *Admiral Halsey's Story*, pp. 277–78.

304 *He fired off:* COM3RDFLT to SCAP info CINCPAC ADVANCE msg. 281101(GCT), August 1945, in "Nimitz Gray Book," vol. 7.

304 *Most of Halsey's Third Fleet:* Halsey, *Admiral Halsey's Story*, pp. 277–78; Joel T. Boone undated report, "Initial Release of Prisoners of War in Japan."

304 *The colorful admiral:* "Reno Makes Fine Saddle for Halsey's Tokyo Ride," *New York Times*, June 23, 1945, p. 3.

304 *the cruiser* San Juan: Report of Surrender and Occupation of Japan, Feb. 11, 1946.

304 *"Go ahead":* Halsey, *Admiral Halsey's Story*, p. 278.

304 *The landing craft:* Joel T. Boone undated report, "Initial Release of Prisoners of War in Japan"; Julius Ochs Adler, "Horrors in Japanese Prisons like Those of Nazi Camps," *New York Times*, Aug. 31, 1945, p. 1.

305 *The reduced rations:* Jesse DaSilva oral history interview with Douglas E. Clanin, Sept. 4, 1992; William Leibold interview with author, July 13, 2009; William Leibold e-mails to author, July 22, 2011; Clay Decker undated video oral history interview with Clark M. Brandt; O'Kane, *Clear the Bridge!*, p. 466; Charles Lockwood undated Navy Day Speech in Cleveland, Ohio, Box 17, RG 38, Records of the Office of the Chief of Naval Operations, World War II Oral Histories, 1942–1946, NARA.

305 *"What's that?":* Harry Berry diary, Aug. 30, 1945, in Berry, *My Darling Wife*, p. 331.

305 *"Nobody doubted"*: Ibid.

305 *"All these months"*: Boyington, *Baa Baa Black Sheep*, p. 342.

306 *"I had ended"*: Fujita, *Foo*, pp. 312–15.

306 *A few feet:* Gerald Landrum interview with author, Aug. 18, 2010.

306 *"The excitement"*: Joel T. Boone undated report, "Initial Release of Prisoners of War in Japan."

307 *"I have no authority"*: Halsey, *Admiral Halsey's Story*, p. 278.

307 *Rescuers pushed:* Joel T. Boone undated report, "Initial Release of Prisoners of War in Japan."

307 *a total of eighteen:* Report of Surrender and Occupation of Japan, Feb. 11, 1946.

307 *The 15,400-ton ship:* Details on *Benevolence* are drawn from the following sources: Emory A. Massman, *Hospital Ships of World War II: An Illustrated Reference to 39 United States Military Vessels* (Jefferson, N.C.: McFarland, 1999), pp. 411–14, 424–40; Madge Crouch Gibson oral history interview with Jan K. Herman, Nov. 22, 1995, NBMS; Alice Bruning oral history interview with Patricia A. Connor, Oct. 16, 1998, ibid.; V. J. Johnston oral history interview with Patricia A. Connor, Dec. 11, 1998, ibid.

307 *"It was just"*: Alice Bruning oral history interview with Patricia A. Connor, Oct. 16, 1998, NBMS.

307 *Clerks interviewed:* Joel T. Boone undated report, "Initial Release of Prisoners of War in Japan."

308 *"All were to a fair degree"*: Ibid.

308 *"These men were"*: Madge Crouch Gibson oral history interview with Jan K. Herman, Nov. 22, 1995, NBMS.

308 *Much to the frustration:* Ibid.

308 *"mechanical cow"*: V. J. Johnston oral history interview with Patricia A. Connor, Dec. 11, 1998; Massman, *Hospital Ships of World War II*, p. 429.

308 *"Boy, what a meal"*: Harry Berry diary, Aug. 30, 1945, in Berry, *My Darling Wife*, p. 331.

309 *"I personally accounted"*: Lawrence Savadkin oral history interview with the Navy, Jan. 30, 1946.

309 *"My God"*: Boyington, *Baa Baa Black Sheep*, p. 344.

309 *"I got some food"*: William Leibold interview with author, July 13, 2009.

309 *"The men would go through stages"*: Madge Crouch Gibson oral history interview with Jan K. Herman, Nov. 22, 1995, NBMS.

309 *"We were the first women"*: Ibid.

309 *"I was in no condition"*: Jesse B. DaSilva, "Survivor of the Mighty Tang," *American Submariner*, July–September 2001, p. 18.

309 Tang *skipper Dick O'Kane:* O'Kane, *Clear the Bridge!*, p. 466; William Leibold interview with author, July 13, 2009.

309   *seventeen submarine officers:* Stephen L. Moore, *Presumed Lost: The Incredible Or-deal of America's Submarine POWs During the Pacific War* (Annapolis, Md.: Naval Institute Press, 2009), p. 290.

310   *"He was just skin and bones":* Lockwood, *Sink 'Em All*, p. 364.

310   *"His eyes were yellow":* Charles Lockwood undated Navy Day Speech in Cleveland, Ohio, Box 17, RG 38, Records of the Office of the Chief of Naval Operations, World War II Oral Histories, 1942–1946, NARA.

310   *The Navy had learned:* Murray Frazee, Jr., "We Never Looked Back," *Naval History,* July–August 1994, pp. 47–51.

310   *"The saga of the submarine* Tang*":* Julius Ochs Adler, "Survivors' Battle Adds to *Tang's* Epic," *New York Times,* Sept. 1, 1945, p. 4.

310   *"Words are inadequate":* Ernestine O'Kane letter to *Tang* families, Sept. 2, 1945.

310   *One of the corpsman:* William Leibold interview with author, July 13, 2009.

310   *Savadkin in a trip:* Lawrence Savadkin oral history interview with the Navy, Jan. 30, 1946.

310   *Jesse DaSilva took a different:* Jesse B. DaSilva, "Survivor of the Mighty Tang," *American Submariner,* July–September 2001, pp. 16–18.

310   *"What about the old man here?":* William Leibold interview with author, July 13, 2009.

Epilogue

PAGE

313   *"Please take care":* Ira Dye letter to Evelyn Dye, Jan. 15, 1943.

313   *Dick O'Kane stood:* Harry S. Truman Appointment Calendar, March 27, 1946, Harry S. Truman Library and Museum, Independence, Missouri.

313   *O'Kane had earned:* "Richard O'Kane, 83, U.S. Submarine Hero," *New York Times,* Feb. 23, 1994, p. A16.

313   *Bill Leibold had come home:* William Leibold interview with author, July 13, 2009.

313   *Clay Decker had returned:* Clay Decker video oral history interview with Dan Clayton, March 2002.

313   *Fearful that his gaunt frame:* Lockwood, *Sink 'Em All*, p. 364.

314   *a grief so strong:* James O'Kane interview with author, Jan. 22, 2010; Ernestine O'Kane letter to Douglas Morton, March 23, 1994, Dudley Morton Family Papers, BSMP.

314   *He would return:* Richard O'Kane Navy Bio, March 15, 1967, NDL; William Leibold interview with author, July 8, 2009.

314   *The tribunal:* R. T. Brunckhorst to Alva C. Carpenter, Aug. 13, 1948, Box 1644, RG 331, Supreme Commander for the Allied Powers, Legal Section, Prosecution Division, USA Versus Japanese War Criminals, Case File, 1945–49, NARA.

314 *"It was the opinion":* Ibid.

314 *The tribunal sentenced:* Ibid.; Petitions of Koto Kitamura, Masanobu Kitamura, Tsuruko Arakawa, Takako Kitamura, and Kiyoji Kitamura, ibid.

314 *Kitamura's file:* Petitions of Kazue Kitamura, Koto Kitamura, Tamekichi Tojo, Yoko Ota, Yoshihiro Ota, Masanobu Kitamura, Hisaichi Arakawa, Tsuruko Arakawa, Takako Kitamura, Kiyoji Kitamura, Taki Ota, and Manjiro Hatakenaka, ibid.; Koto Kitamura letter to Mrs. Douglas MacArthur, July 24, 1948, ibid.

314 *Sixteen months after:* Action of Douglas MacArthur, July, 3, 1949, ibid.

314 *Commutations and clemencies:* Gavan Daws, *Prisoners of the Japanese: POWs of World War II in the Pacific* (New York: William Morrow, 1994), p. 373; E. Bartlett Kerr, *Surrender and Survival: The Experience of American POWs in the Pacific, 1941–1945* (New York: William Morrow, 1985), p. 296.

314 *Postwar records:* JANAC, p. 49 of the appendix; Blair, *Silent Victory,* p. 984.

314 *Only the submarine* Tautog: Blair, *Silent Victory,* p. 989; JANAC, pp. 49–50 of the appendix; History of USS *Tautog* (SS 199), October 1950, Office of Naval Records and History, Ships' Histories Section, Navy Department.

314 Silversides *sank:* JANAC, p. 43 of the appendix; Blair, *Silent Victory,* p. 989.

314 Drum *destroyed:* JANAC, p. 12 of the appendix.

315 *would count 182 on duty:* Facts and Figures for the Admiral, Size and Growth of Submarine Force, Oct. 20, 1945, Box 18, Charles Lockwood Papers, LOC.

315 *All told some 288 submarines:* Roscoe, *United States Submarine Operations in World War II,* p. 493; Blair, *Silent Victory,* p. 883.

315 *the 1,570 war patrols:* Facts and Figures for the Admiral, Size and Growth of Submarine Force, Oct. 20, 1945; Charles A. Lockwood and Percy Finch, "We Gave the Japs a Licking Underseas," part 1, *Saturday Evening Post,* July 16, 1949, p. 116.

315 *American submarines over the course of the war:* USSBS, *The War Against Japanese Transportation, 1941–1945,* p. 134.

315 *A postwar comparison:* JANAC, pp. vii, x.

315 *Japan had counted:* USSBS, *The War Against Japanese Transportation, 1941–1945,* p. 52.

315 *America lost fifty-two:* Roscoe, *United States Submarine Operations in World War II,* p. 493.

315 *The Japanese plucked:* Moore, *Presumed Lost,* pp. vii, 290.

315 *Of the 16,000 sailors:* Lockwood, *Sink 'Em All,* pp. 350–51; Naval History Division, Office of the Chief of Naval Operations, *United States Submarine Losses,* p. 1.

316 *The casualty rate:* Blair, *Silent Victory,* p. 877; Roscoe, *United States Submarine Operations in World War II,* pp. 493–94.

316 *In comparison to the enemy:* Roscoe, *United States Submarine Operations in World War II*, p. 494.

316 *rotted loads of cereals:* Parillo, *The Japanese Merchant Marine in World War II*, pp. 219–21.

316 *"The war against shipping":* USSBS, *The War Against Japanese Transportation, 1941–1945*, p. 6.

316 *Japanese military leaders:* Ibid., pp. 6–7.

316 *"It must be stated":* Interrogation of Vice Admiral Shigeru Fukudome, Dec. 9–12, 1945, in USSBS, *Interrogations of Japanese Officials*, vol. 2, p. 530.

317 *"The torpedo scandal":* Blair, *Silent Victory*, p. 879.

317 *O'Kane saluted:* Felix Belair, Jr., "World Leadership Ours, Says Truman," *New York Times*, March 28, 1946, p. 12; Medal of Honor Citation, included in Richard O'Kane Navy Bio, March 15, 1967.

317 *"The Medal of Honor":* Richard O'Kane letter to Paul Crozier, Nov. 2, 1990.

317 *"This, in my opinion":* Remarks on Presenting the Congressional Medal of Honor to Commander Richard H. O'Kane, USN, and Master Sergeant Charles L. McGaha, USA, March 27, 1946, Harry S. Truman Library and Museum, Independence, Missouri.

INDEX

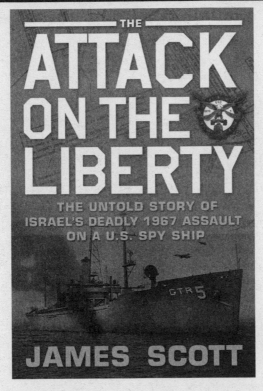